Zimbabwe
and Botswana

THE ROUGH GUIDE

There are more than eighty Rough Guide titles covering
destinations from Amsterdam to Zimbabwe

Forthcoming titles include
China • Corfu • Jamaica • New Zealand • South Africa
Southwest USA • Vienna • Washington DC

Rough Guide Reference Series
Classical Music • The Internet • Jazz • World Music

Rough Guide Phrasebooks
Czech • French • German • Greek • Italian • Mexican Spanish
Polish • Portuguese • Spanish • Thai • Turkish • Vietnamese

Rough Guides on the Internet
http://www.roughguides.com/
http://www.hotwired.com/rough

Rough Guide credits

Editor:	Paul Gray
Series editor:	Mark Ellingham
Editorial:	Martin Dunford, Jonathan Buckley, Samantha Cook, Jo Mead, Alison Cowan, Amanda Tomlin, Annie Shaw, Lemisse Al-Hafidh, Catherine McHale, Vivienne Heller
Online editors:	Alan Spicer (UK), Andrew Rosenberg (US)
Production:	Susanne Hillen, Andy Hilliard, Judy Pang, Link Hall, Nicola Williamson, Helen Ostick
Cartography:	Melissa Flack, David Callier
Marketing & Publicity:	Richard Trillo, Simon Carloss (UK), Jean-Marie Kelly, Jeff Kaye (US)
Finance:	John Fisher, Celia Crowley, Catherine Gillespie
Administration:	Tania Hummel, Margo Daly

Our thanks to the following people for accommodating us while writing: Jan Hulin in Harare, Larry Strelitz and Lynette Steenkamp, Lilly and Issy Pinchuck in Grahamstown, Pat McCrea in Port Alfred, Silke Ziehl, David Babsky and Anja Dashwood in London. Our thanks in Bulawayo to: Mike and Anna Scott, Denis and Sandy Paul, Richard and Bookey Peek, Anne Rorke. And also to: Annie Holmes, Michael Philips, Judy Kendall, Peta Jones, Rick Goncalves, Mags Varley at Safari Par Excellence, Dave Glynn, Fausto Carbone, staff at Ruckomechi Camp, Geoffrey Carew, Jane Hunt, Stewart Cranswick and staff at Landela camps, Kenneth Mukuwa, Bob at Delta Camp, Peter Sandenberg, Clive at Kandahar, Chipembere Safaris, Rita Harvey, Mr and Mrs Clarke, Davidson on the Zambezi, Kit Hustler, staff at Wild Horizons, Dave Wiley and all at Island Safari Lodge. Thanks to our meticulous editor, Paul Gray, for putting in long hours, to editors David Abram and Sarah McAlister, and to Martin Dunford for stepping in on chapters 3, 6 and 9, to David Callier for cartography, to Narrell Leffman and Carol Pucci for Basics research, to typesetter Helen Ostick, to indexer Margo Daly, to Henry Iles for designing the wildlife insert, and everyone else at the Rough Guides who has made a contribution to this guide. Thanks, too, to all the many unmentioned people in Zimbabwe and Botswana, who helped make this book.

The publishers and authors have done their best to ensure the accuracy and currency of all the information in *The Rough Guide to Zimbabwe and Botswana*; however, they can accept no responsibility for any loss, injury, or inconvenience sustained by any traveller as a result of information or advice contained in the guide.

This third edition published September 1996 by Rough Guides Ltd, 1 Mercer Street, London WC2H 9QJ. Distributed by The Penguin Group:

Penguin Books Ltd, 27 Wrights Lane, London W8 5TZ
Penguin Books USA Inc., 375 Hudson Street, New York 10014, USA
Penguin Books Australia Ltd, 487 Maroondah Highway, PO Box 257, Ringwood, Victoria 3134, Australia
Penguin Books Canada Ltd, 10 Alcorn Avenue, Toronto, Ontario, Canada M4V 1E4
Penguin Books (NZ) Ltd, 182–190 Wairau Road, Auckland 10, New Zealand

Typeset in Linotron Univers and Century Old Style to an original design by Andrew Oliver.
Printed in the UK by The Bath Press.

Illustrations in Part One and Part Four by Edward Briant; Ilustrations on p.351 and p.352 by Tony Pinchuck.

448pp. includes index

A catalogue record for this book is available from the British Library.
ISBN 1-85828-186-5

Zimbabwe
and Botswana

THE ROUGH GUIDE

Written and researched by
Barbara McCrea and Tony Pinchuck

THE ROUGH GUIDES

LIST OF MAPS

MAP SYMBOLS

Symbol	Meaning	Symbol	Meaning
▭▬▭	Railway	♦	Ruin/monument
═══	Main road	⌃⌃	Mountain range
───	Minor road	▲	Mountain peak
- - - -	Path	⌂	Cave
───────	River	◉	Swimming pool
─ ─ ─	Chapter division boundary	◉	Hotel
■─■─■	International boundary	⊠	Post office
⌐⌐⌐⌐⌐	Cliff face	■	Building
✈	Airport/airfield	▦	Park
△	Campsite	▦	National park
⌂	Lodge	⌐ ⌐	Delta
⌄	Viewpoint	⌐ ⌐	Salt pan

CONTENTS

Introduction viii

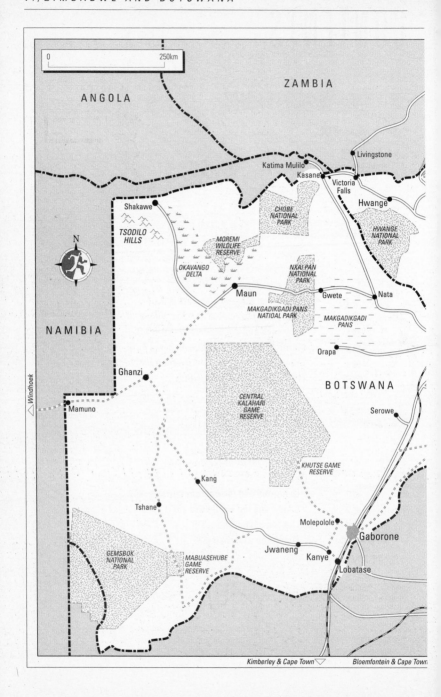

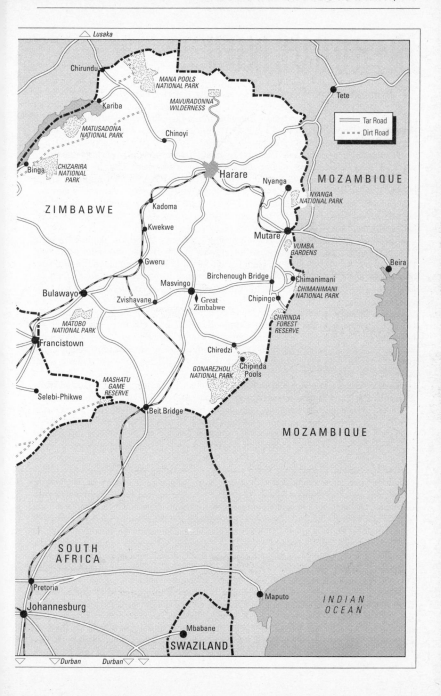

INTRODUCTION

Zimbabwe and **Botswana** are easygoing, safe and straightforward places to visit, yet they are still thoroughly African. Between them the two countries provide the most accessible introduction to the continent south of the Sahara, and visitors accustomed to desperate images of Third World chaos and decay are struck by their order and stability.

Zimbabwe is a warm and friendly destination – surprisingly, perhaps, given its recent history. Now in its second decade of independence it has, in the last two decades, weathered a **civil war** and more recently the worst **drought** in living memory. Both are thankfully now over – the war ended nearly twenty years ago and the drought broke at the beginning of 1993. Despite growing economic problems, the country has maintained its infrastructure of roads, transport, and communication links; and its people have, remarkably, maintained their good humour.

Botswana boasts Africa's fastest-growing economy, based on diamond wealth discovered, with majestic timing, within a year of the British surrendering power. Furthermore, it bears a unique distinction in Africa of having remained a multi-party democracy since its independence in 1966. Although it may lack the good transport links found in Zimbabwe, it nevertheless offers exciting opportunities to get off the beaten track.

Neither country is yet overrun by tourists, but the number of independent travellers coming is certainly on the increase – with good reason. Both countries share a range of beautiful landscapes, and are unquestionably among Africa's top five **game-viewing** destinations. Each has utterly unique habitats, outstanding conservation policies, and restrictions on numbers entering game parks – making them first-class safari countries.

While elsewhere in Africa **elephants** are seriously threatened, in Botswana's **Chobe National Park** and Zimbabwe's **Hwange** they are present in a superabundance of tens of thousands. You'll also find the rest of the **big five** – lions, leopards, buffalo and rhinos – in respectable numbers (though black rhinos persist only in intensively protected areas), and the two countries possess virtually all of Southern Africa's 291 recorded mammal species. Birdwatchers will find six hundred species to get to grips with.

Activity pursuits – kayaking, bush walking, horse riding and canoeing – are a fast-expanding area, often combined with opportunities to see game at very close quarters. For anyone keen on outdoor action, there are few experiences to beat **whitewater rafting** below the Victoria Falls, **canoeing** for two or more days down the Zambezi from Mana Falls, or travelling by dug-out *mokoro* among the islands and lilied waterways of the **Okavango Delta**. On land, there is a vast range of things to do, including tracking big game on foot with an armed guide in the national parks, and some superb mountain hiking, with possibilities for real wilderness at Chimanimani in eastern Zimbabwe. If you really want to let go, there's the option of bungee jumping and other adrenalin-charged pursuits at Victoria Falls, the region's adventure capital.

The huge **landscapes** of Zimbabwe and Botswana fulfil with ease all those African clichés of endless blue skies, wide-open space, and vermillion sunsets. Botswana, with the great **Kalahari desert** at its heart, is virtually flat, although peppered with rocky outcrops and the amazing **Tsodilo Hills**. Zimbabwe is more varied, with its **Eastern Highland** of peaks, mountain pools and well-watered valleys. The country is punctuated, too, by beautiful and distinctive granite hills and "rock-gardens" of vast boulders.

Both countries make up for their lack of coastline with some of Africa's great **water-ways**: the Zambezi River, Okavango Delta and Lake Kariba.

Although their present national boundaries are recent colonial inventions, human culture in Zimbabwe and Botswana goes back tens of thousands of years. Early inhabitants have left their marks in caves and on rock faces all over the subcontinent. The **rock paintings** at Botswana's Tsodilo Hills moved Laurens van der Post to talk of a "Louvre in the desert", while Zimbabwe has the highest concentration of rock art in the world. Finely realized paintings of animals and people in everyday life, ritual and myth, are scattered about the various granite rock formations, at their best at Matopos Hills. Zimbabwe also has an extensive sequence of stone ruins to explore, from the ancient states that once held domain on this great plateau. The awesome **Great Zimbabwe** is just the best known of several hundred complexes.

But, beyond any doubt, the art in which Zimbabwe most excels today is **music** – a major cultural export in recent years as Western ears have tuned into the high energy guitar pop of bands like the Bhundu Boys, the Real Sounds of Africa and Thomas Mapfumo's Blacks Unlimited. For each of these international stars, there are dozens of talents waiting to be discovered, playing every night in nightclubs, hotels, beer gardens and outdoor venues in Harare, Bulawayo and across the country. Explore and enjoy!

Climate: when to go

Though technically a tropical country, **Zimbabwe** refuses to conform to hot, sticky stereotypes. The highveld climate (Harare and Bulawayo) is as close as possible to perfection, with dry season temperatures similar to those of the Mediterranean, but without the humidity. Few people realize that Harare's highest recorded temperature peak of 35°C (95°F) is below that of London. Altitude is the most important determinant. The low-lying areas off the plateau – Kariba, the Zambezi river valley and Victoria Falls – get considerably hotter than the higher towns, and can be uncomfortably humid in the steaming rainy season.

Botswana weather follows a roughly similar pattern, although much of the country experiences extremes from the semi-desert that sweeps across its surface. Wet season temperatures in the southern Kalahari have exceeded 40°C (104°F), while in the cool months they can drop at night to -5°C (23°F). The climate around the Okavango Delta and Eastern Corridor tends to be less severe, though even here wet season temperatures can soar uncomfortably, and in some years the rains flood the roads.

Deciding **when to come** is really a question of what you're after:

• For **game-viewing**, the **dry season** (roughly May–Oct) is recommended, as wildlife concentrates around scarce water; it's very cold at night and in the early morning, but warm enough for T-shirts in the middle of the day. Temperatures climb towards September – an optimum "spring" month which combines good wildlife with vegetation coming into flower amidst the dust and browns. October, the hottest month, is the prime time for wildlife when animals are restricted to a few waterholes.

• The arrival of the **rainy season** in November does much to dampen temperatures. The rains, which last till March, are a time of lush new growth – a scenically beautiful period. Rain usually comes in the form of afternoon thunderstorms, leaving most of the day clear. There can be several days, or even weeks between falls. The Eastern Highlands receive the highest rainfall, where you may experience a series of cool, wet days.

• **April and May**, the "autumn" months, are perhaps ideal for overall travels – warm and dry with the land still fresh from the rains, though long grass may make game-viewing more difficult.

A detailed chart of mean temperatures and rainfall can be found over the page.

SEASONS

- **November to mid-March**. Rainy "summer" season: thunderstorms; hot.
- **Mid-March to mid-May**. Post-rainy "autumn" season: limited rainfall; cooling off.
- **Mid-May to mid-August**. Cool dry "winter" season: virtually no rainfall; cool to moderate but very sunny and clear.
- **Mid-August to November**. Warm dry "spring" season: virtually no rainfall; temperatures rise to peak.

MEAN TEMPERATURES (°C) AND RAINFALL (mm)

The first figure is the mean **maximum** temperature; the second the mean **minimum**; and the third the average rainfall per month.

	Jan	Feb	Mar	Apr	May	Jun	Jul	Aug	Sep	Oct	Nov	Dec
Harare	26	26	26	26	24	22	22	24	27	29	27	26
(Highveld: 1478m)	16	16	16	13	9	7	7	9	12	15	14	16
	188	169	80	43	11	5	0	3	8	32	93	189
Beit Bridge	33	33	32	30	28	25	25	28	30	32	32	33
(Lowveld: 457m)	22	21	20	17	12	8	8	11	15	19	20	21
	70	50	36	24	5	4	1	1	8	21	39	66
Nyanga	21	21	21	20	18	16	16	18	21	23	22	21
(Eastern Highlands:	13	13	12	10	8	6	6	7	9	11	12	13
1878m)	257	219	135	51	17	16	14	15	13	43	125	215
Francistown	30	30	29	27	25	24	24	26	30	33	32	31
(Eastern Botswana:	17	17	16	13	9	5	5	7	12	16	18	18
1100m)	106	79	72	19	6	4	0	0	0	23	55	85
Shakawe	30	30	30	30	27	25	27	29	32	34	32	31
(Okavango Delta:	20	20	19	16	15	6	5	8	12	16	17	18
1000m)	150	160	80	30	2	0	0	0	2	6	50	100

THANKS TO OUR READERS

A big thank you to the many readers of previous editions of this guide who took the trouble to write in with their comments and suggestions: Adrian Allan, Kaye Baker, David Bartell, Heather Beagley, M. Birt, Isobel Bonnell, Dorothy Brewer, Jelmer Buys, Anne Callan, Diana Clement, Daniel Ford, W. D. Galloway, W. G. Gleboska, Sharon Harris, J. L. Hayhurst, Jane High, Michael Holdgate, Clive Jenkins, Harriet and Mike Kendrick, Michael Kent, Ki Jinn Chinn (for an excellent and detailed update), A. Lane, Jonathan Lord, Jennifer Lount, A. Luebeschuetz, Roger Mason, James Murdoch, T. C. Odling, Siân Richetts, Vivienne Roberts, Erika van Robbroeck, Daniela Rose, Emily Sheeran, Jason Smith, Clare Stafford, Anne Strydom, Jeff Taylor, Margo Thomas, Anne and Anthony Tobin, Phil Vaughan, Thomas Walker, Bessie White, Rob Wilson, Kate Worster, Deborah Wright. Thanks especially to Will Bee, for an outstanding contribution on disabled travel.

PART ONE

THE
BASICS

GETTING THERE FROM THE UK

you the sights run on a number of routes, some starting in Britain.

NON-STOP FLIGHTS FROM BRITAIN

Air Zimbabwe (four times a week) and *British Airways* (three times a week) fly from Gatwick to **Harare**, a journey taking ten hours – the fastest currently available. Few people purchase tickets directly from the airlines at the officially quoted prices (£960/750 high/low season), booking instead through agents who offer discounts. However, look out for special offers on the officially quoted fares, which sometimes run as low as £550.

The only direct flight to **Gaborone** from anywhere outside Africa is on *British Airways* from Heathrow (twice a week), officially quoted at £660 (low season) and £1130 (high season).

FLIGHTS VIA EUROPE

The growing popularity of Zimbabwe means there's a choice of easy flights from London via Europe. Convenient transfers, relatively short journey times and discounted prices make these definitely worth considering.

London–Harare tickets on *Air France* (twice a week via Paris), *Lufthansa* (twice a week via Frankfurt), *KLM* (twice a week via Amsterdam) and *Air Portugal* (once a week via Lisbon) can often be had for as little as £500. Other European airlines which fly to Harare are *Aeroflot* (twice a month via Moscow) and *Balkan Bulgarian Airlines* (via Sofia), which is cheapest of all (frequently under £450) but takes 24 hours over the journey.

FLIGHTS VIA AFRICA

Johannesburg is set to become the most popular gateway into the whole of Southern Africa. *South African Airways* and *British Airways* fly daily **from London Heathrow** to Johannesburg with convenient connections on to Harare. Officially quoted economy fares are £660/750/850/1000 (basic/low/shoulder/high season), but it is possible to save up to £100 on these prices through bucket shops. For information on getting to Zimbabwe or Botswana from Johannesburg, and cheap deals on regional flights see "Travel in Southern Africa" (p.10).

A growing number of airlines fly **from Europe** to Harare via Johannesburg – a long journey

Most people travel to Zimbabwe or Botswana by air. There are direct flights to Harare from Britain and several other European countries, while direct flights to Gaborone operate only from London. The opening up of South Africa, though, has turned Johannesburg into the major gateway to the region, and a growing number of the scores of European airlines flying to Johannesburg now continue on to Harare.

Fares from London to Harare, Gaborone and Johannesburg depend on which **season** you're flying. For Harare, April and May are low season, while July, August, September, December and January are the high season. The rest of the year (June, October, November, February and March) is the medium-priced shoulder season. Expect small variations on these dates from one airline to the next. *British Airways*, the only airline flying direct to Botswana from outside Africa, operates no less than four seasons on the London–Gaborone route: April 11–May 31 is low season, December 10–January 14 is high season, and the rest of the year is shared between two medium-priced seasons. For Johannesburg, there are at present four seasons, with a fifth (a second shoulder season) planned. Cheapest is basic (mid-April to May), followed by low (June to November), shoulder (mid-January to mid-April), and, most expensive, high (December to mid-January).

Overland options include journeys via North or East Africa, either driving or travelling by rail or on economy buses. Organized trips that show

which entails backtracking but usually has the pay-off of cheaper fares on reliable airlines. Both *Air France* and *KLM* take this routing to Harare, which offers the option of getting off in Johannesburg, travelling overland to Harare and flying out from there. Competitive fares from London (starting at around £500 in low season) are sometimes available on these airlines.

AIRLINES IN THE UK

Aeroflot, 70 Piccadilly, London W1V 9HH (☎0171/355 2233).

Air Botswana, 177 Tottenham Court Rd, London W1P 0HN (☎0171/757 2737).

Air France, 177 Piccadilly, London W1Z 0LX (☎0181/742 6600).

Air Namibia, Beaumont House, Lambton Rd, West Wimbledon, London SW20 0LW (☎0181/543 2122).

Air Zimbabwe, Colette House, 52–55 Piccadilly, London W1V SAA (☎0171/491 0009).

Balkan Bulgarian Airlines, 322 Regent St, London W1R 5AB (0171/637 7637).

British Airways, 156 Regent St, London W1R 6LB; 146 New St, Birmingham B2 4HN; 19–21 St Mary's Gate, Market St, Manchester M1 1PU; 64 Gordon St, Glasgow G1 3RS; 32 Frederick St, Edinburgh EH2 2JR (all enquiries ☎0345/222111).

Egyptair, 296 Regent St, London W1R 6PH (☎0171/734 2395).

Ethiopian Airlines, 4th Floor, 166 Piccadilly, London W1 (☎0171/491 9119).

KLM, reservations ☎0181/750 9000; ticket office at Terminal 4, Heathrow.

Lufthansa, 10 Old Bond St, London W1 4EN (☎0171/408 0442).

Sabena, 10 Putney Hill, London SW15 6AA (☎0181/780 1444).

South African Airways, 6 Conduit St, London W1R 7FD (☎0171/312 5000).

Swissair, Swiss Centre, 1 Swiss Court, London W1V 4BJ (☎0171/434/7300).

TAP Air Portugal, 19 Regent St, London SW1 (☎0171/839 1031).

FLIGHT AGENTS IN THE UK

Campus Travel, 52 Grosvenor Gardens, London SW1W 0AG (☎0171/730 8111); 541 Bristol Rd, Selly Oak, Birmingham B29 6AU (☎0121/414 1848); 61 Ditchling Rd, Brighton BN1 4SD (☎01273/570226); 39 Queen's Rd, Clifton, Bristol BS8 1QE (☎0117/929 2494); 5 Emmanuel St, Cambridge CB1 1NE (☎01223/324283); 53 Forest Rd, Edinburgh EH1 2QP (☎0131/668 3303); 166 Deansgate, Manchester M3 3FE (☎0161/833 2046); 105–106 St Aldates, Oxford OX1 1DD (☎01865/242067). Student/youth travel specialists, with branches also in YHA shops and on university campuses all over Britain.

Comet Travel, 21 Newman St, London W1P 4DD (☎0171/580 500). Agents for *Air Namibia*.

Council Travel, 28a Poland St, London W1V 3DB (☎0171/437 7767). Flights and student discounts.

North South Travel, Moulsham Mill Centre, Parkway, Chelmsford, Essex CM2 7PX (☎01245/492882). Friendly, competitive travel agency, offering discounted fares worldwide – profits are used to support projects in the developing world, especially the promotion of sustainable tourism.

Nouvelles Frontières, 11 Blenheim St, London W1Y 9LE (☎0171/629 7772).

STA Travel, 86 Old Brompton Rd, London SW7 3LH, 117 Euston Rd, London NW1 2SX, 38 Store St London WC1 (☎0171/ 361 6262); 25 Queens Rd, Bristol BS8 1QE (☎0117/929 4399); 38 Sidney St, Cambridge CB2 3HX (☎01223/366966); 75 Deansgate, Manchester M3 2BW (☎0161/834 0668); 88 Vicar Lane, Leeds LS1 7JH (☎0113/244 9212); 36 George St, Oxford OX1 2OJ (☎01865/ 792800); and branches in Birmingham, Canterbury, Cardiff, Coventry, Durham, Glasgow, Loughborough, Nottingham, Warwick and Sheffield. Worldwide specialists in low-cost flights and tours for students and under-26s.

Trailfinders, 42–50 Earls Court Rd, London W8 6FT (☎0171/938 3366); 194 Kensington High St, London, W8 7RG (☎0171/938 3939); 58 Deansgate, Manchester M3 2FF (☎0161/839 6969); 254–284 Sauchiehall St, Glasgow G2 3EH (☎0141/353 2224); 22–24 The Priory, Queensway, Birmingham B4 6BS (☎0121/236 1234); 48 Corn St, Bristol BS1 1HQ (☎0117/929 9000). One of the best-informed and most efficient agents.

Travel Bug, 597 Cheetham Hill Rd, Manchester M8 5EJ (☎0161/721 4000). Large range of discounted tickets.

Union Travel, 93 Piccadilly, London W1 (☎0171/ 493 4343). Competitive air fares.

Other African routings to Harare include *Egyptair* (once a week via Cairo), *Ethiopian Airlines* (twice a week via Addis), *Air Namibia* (once a week via Windhoek) and *Air France* (once a week via Paris and Nairobi).

INCLUSIVE HOLIDAYS

There are quite a number of tour operators and travel agents that specialize in travel to Southern Africa. You can buy off-the-peg packages or ask them to organize a tailor-made one for you. It's not always cheaper to make arrangements on arrival, especially if you're planning to stay in safari lodges or hotels – which have to charge sales tax inside Zimbabwe, but not if you pay outside the country. Packages start at around £2000 for Zimbabwe only, £2600 for Zimbabwe and Botswana, for two weeks all in (flights, accommodation, tours). Alternatively, you might consider making reservations for only some parts of your holiday, particularly the more popular activities and places that may get overbooked. Canoeing trips, whitewater rafting and such frequently visited destinations as the Mana Pools and the Okavango Delta fall into this category. Most of the agents below can offer partial prebooking.

OVERLAND OPTIONS

Road conditions in Africa are best described as inconsistent. Major tarred routes are frequently good, although in some countries, where mainte-nance tends to be poor, they can get badly potholed. Some roads – usually those leading off the main arteries – are seasonal and will be out of commission during heavy rains. There's also a reputation for erratic opening and closing of borders which is hard to shift. It's wise to keep up with the news, as conflicts and coups occasionally erupt.

There are some interesting possibilities if you want to work your way down gradually through the continent. The longer routes start in **north-west Africa**, from where you make your way over the Sahara, loop around the west of the continent and cross to the east **via Zaire**. A less ambitious option would be to start in **Kenya** and then to head through **Tanzania**, **Malawi** and **Zambia**, to eventually arrive in Zimbabwe or Botswana. The once popular **Nile route**, through Egypt and Sudan, and into Uganda and Kenya, is currently off limits; the Sudanese civil war has effectively barred the route since 1984.

ORGANIZED OVERLAND TRIPS

Several overland operators run **trans-Africa routes** starting in Britain, working down through West Africa, across to Nairobi and down to Harare or even beyond (see box overleaf). A 23-week trip from London to Harare via West Africa costs in the region of £3300 (land arrangements only). A more modest nine-week trip from Nairobi to Cape Town via Harare will set you back £1900, and a five-weeker from Nairobi to Harare around £1100.

SOUTHERN AFRICA SPECIALISTS IN THE UK

Abercrombie and Kent Ltd, Sloane Square House, Holbein Place, London SW1W 8NS (☎0171/730 9600). Large upmarket operator with comprehensive and professional programmes in both Zimbabwe and Botswana.

Africa Travel Shop, 21 Leigh St, London WC1H 9QX (☎0171/387 1211). Experienced and knowledgeable Africa specialists with a wide range of interesting options.

Art of Travel, Bakery Place, 119 Altenberg Gardens, London SW11 (☎0171/738 2038). Highly flexible specialist agent, who book trips to suit any budget – and for all or just part of a trip – through tried and tested local operators.

Grenadier Safaris, 11–12 West Stockwell St, Colchester CO1 1HN (☎01206/549585). Small but expert; genuine knowledge of the countries with an affection for the region based on several years'

residence. Highly personalized with great attention to detail.

Okavango Tours and Safaris, Gadd House, Arcadia Ave, London N3 2TJ (☎0181/343 3283). Based in Botswana, this company can meet most of your requirements for both countries.

Wild Africa Safaris, Castlebrook House, Oak Road, Leatherhead KT22 7PG (☎01372/362288, fax 360147). Mix-and-match tailor-made safaris taking in all of Zimbabwe's major sights and activities.

Worldwide Journeys and Expeditions, 8 Comeragh Rd, London W14 9HP (☎0171/381 8638). Tailor-made travel programmes by a company with an excellent track record and outstanding first-hand knowledge of both Zimbabwe and Botswana.

GETTING THERE FROM NORTH AMERICA

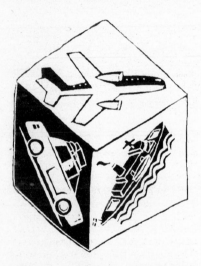

There are no direct flights into Zimbabwe or Botswana from North America, but there are direct services to Johannesburg from New York and Miami. From there, it's easy to catch a connecting flight into Zimbabwe or Botswana.

Fares from North America to Southern Africa depend on which **season** you're flying. Low season is January to May and September to November; high season is June, July, August and December. Expect small variations on these dates from one airline to the next.

From the US, *South African Airways* flies non-stop three to four times a week **out of Miami** to Cape Town with a direct service on to Johannesburg. **From New York**, *SAA* flies a non-stop service two to three times a week to Johannesburg. The round-trip Apex fare out of both cities to Johannesburg is US$1334 low season and US$1566 high season. **From Johannesburg**, *SAA* offers discounted fares to Zimbabwe and Botswana – fares range from US$46 to US$87 one-way.

Although less convenient, it might be cheaper to consider a route from the US into **London** or **Frankfurt** with onward connections to Johannesburg or Harare. Round-trip fares as low as US$1000 (East Coast) and US$1500 (West Coast) are often available from discounters on these routings. Check the ads in the Sunday travel sections of major newspapers.

From Canada, there are non-stop and direct flights on *Canadian Airlines* **from Toronto** into New York, Miami, London and Frankfurt connecting with **South African Airways** flights to Harare or Johannesburg. Round-trip fares range from C$1850 (low season) to C$2050 (high season).

Air Canada offers a daily non-stop service **from Vancouver** to Frankfurt or London with onward connections into Africa on *South African Airways*. Round-trip fares range from C$1859 (low season) to C$2089 (high season). Prices for flights from Vancouver via Miami or New York tend to be slightly higher. *KLM* flies non-stop four times a week from Vancouver to Amsterdam with onward connections on *South African Airways*. Round-trip fares range from C$2660 (low season) to C$2900 (high season).

AIRLINES IN THE US AND CANADA

Air Zimbabwe (☎1-800/742-3006). No flights from the US but will arrange travel to London or Frankfurt on other airlines with connections on *Air Zimbabwe* to Harare.

American Airlines (☎1-800/433-7300). Daily flights from major US and Canadian cities to New York and Miami connecting on *South African Airways* to Johannesburg.

British Airways (☎1-800/247-9297 or 1-800/668-1069) Daily non-stop service to London from major US cities.

Canadian Airlines (☎1-800/665-1177 in Canada; ☎1-800/426-7000 in the US). Daily non-stops from Vancouver to London or Frankfurt (9hr) connecting with flights to Harare and Johannesburg.

Cathay Pacific (☎1-800/233-2742 in the US; ☎1-800/555-1212 in Canada). Daily flights to Hong Kong from Vancouver BC and Los Angeles (10hr) connecting 3 times a week to Johannesburg (12hr).

Delta Airlines (☎1-800/241-4141 in Canada; ☎1-800/555-1212 in the US). Daily flights from major US and Canadian cities to New York and Miami

connecting on *South African Airways* to Johannesburg.

KLM (☎1-800/374-7747 in the US; ☎1-800/361-5073 in Canada). Four non-stops per week from Vancouver to Amsterdam (9hr) with connections 2–4 times a week to Harare and Johannesburg (10hr).

Singapore Airlines (☎1-800/742-3333). Mon and Sat from Vancouver to Singapore (16hr) and Tues and Fri from Singapore to Johannesburg (10hr).

South African Airways (☎1-800/722-9675). Direct flights 3–4 times a week from Miami via Cape Town to Johannesburg (16hr). Non-stop service 2–3 times a week from New York to Johannesburg (14hr).

Swissair (☎1-800/221-4750 in the US; ☎1-800/267-9477 in Canada). Four times a week from Los Angeles to Zurich (11hr) with connections to Johannesburg (10hr).

Virgin Atlantic Airways (☎1-800/862-8621). Daily non-stop service to London from major US cities.

It's also possible to reach Johannesburg from Vancouver via non-stop flights to Hong Kong and Singapore with onward connections to Johannesburg.

PACKAGES

Most North Americans coming to Zimbabwe and Botswana do so on **packages** which emphasize safaris. Many take in these countries as part of a larger African trip, often including both East and Southern Africa, although the notable game areas of Botswana and Zimbabwe are enough to warrant a trip on their own. The most desirable wildlife regions of both countries are concentrated to their northern borders making them a coherent and manageable region for travel. Obvious highlights include the Okavango Delta and Chobe National Park in Botswana, and Victoria Falls and Hwange National Park – all within a couple of hours of each other by air.

For more generalized packages, the demise of apartheid has opened the whole of Southern Africa into an integrated region. For first-time visitors, highlights are likely to include Cape

Town, the Winelands and the Garden Route in South Africa, the Okavango Delta in Botswana, Victoria Falls in Zimbabwe and a major game reserve in one of the three countries.

The more adventurous and those with a bit of time to kill can opt for several weeks travelling **overland** from North Africa to Harare or beyond. A number of operators have well-organized group trips of varying length on the continent. One of the most common routes takes you from Nairobi to Harare over five or six weeks.

Sample Round-the-World fares via Johannesburg

Los Angeles, **San Francisco** or **Seattle**—London—Paris—Frankfurt or Amsterdam—Zurich—Johannesburg—overland to Nairobi—Bombay—Bangkok—Hong Kong or Taipei—Los Angeles, San Francisco or Seattle $2105

New York—London—Athens—Johannesburg—Hong Kong—Los Angeles—New York $1886

NORTH AMERICAN DISCOUNT AGENTS

Air Brokers International, 323 Geary St, San Francisco, California 94102 (☎1-800/883-3273).

Air Courier Association, 191 University Blvd, Suite 300, Denver, Colorado 80206 (☎303/279-3600). Low-cost courier fares to Johannesburg.

Council Travel, 205 E 42nd St, New York, NY 10017 (☎212/822-2700), and branches in many other US cities. Discount travel agent, with student discount offers.

Flight Centre, S Granville St, Vancouver (☎604/739-9539). Discount air fares to Africa from Canadian cities.

High Adventure Travel Inc, 253 Sacramento St, San Francisco, CA 94111 (☎1-800/428-8735; WWW site: http://www.highadv.com; e-mail: airtreks@highadv.com).

Last Minute Travel, 132 Brookline Ave, Boston, MA 02215 (☎1-800/LAST-MIN). Discount air fares, plus hotel packages.

Overseas Tours, 475 El Camino Real, Room 206, Millbrae, California 94030 (☎1-800/323-8777).

STA Travel, 48 E 11th St, New York, NY 10013 (☎1-800/777-0112). Discount travel agent, with student discount offers.

Travel CUTS, 187 College St, Toronto, ON M5T 1P7 (416/979-2406), and other branches all over Canada. Student travel organization.

Travel Studio (☎1-800/810-8198; e-mail: Tsyyz@baxter.net). Discount air fares, plus flight-hotel and flydrive-hotel packages.

UniTravel, Box 12485, St Louis, MO 63132 (☎1-800/325-2222).

NORTH AMERICAN TOUR OPERATORS

A detailed list of tour operators in Zimbabwe can be located on the **World Wide Web** at http://super.sonic.net/spectrav/zimbab.html.

Abercrombie & Kent Ltd, 1520 Kensington Rd, Oak Brook, ILL 60521 (☎1-800/323-7308 or 1708/954-2944). Upscale tours in Zimbabwe and Botswana; a 15-day air safari in Zimbabwe and Botswana costs US$4000 plus air fare.

Adventure Center, 1311 63rd St, Suite 200, Emeryville, CA 97608 (☎1-800/227-8747; e-mail: adventctr@aol.com). Tours in all parts of Africa. A 22-day Zimbabwe-Botswana explorer tour, including a Zambezi river cruise and visits to several national parks, is US$1260–1500 not including air fare.

Africa Adventure Co, 1600 South Federal Highway, Suite 900, Pompano Beach, FL 33062 (☎1-800/882-943; e-mail: noltingaac@aol.com). Well-regarded agency with more than 100 Africa programs and optional extensions. President Mark Nolting has 20 years' experience researching and writing about Africa. An 18-day wildlife safari in Botswana or Zimbabwe costs US$2900 plus air fare.

Himalayan Travel, 112 Prospect St, Stamford, CT 06901 (☎203/359-3711). Camping/self-drive packages and short, specialized tours – 6 days in Zimbabwe, including Hwange National Park and Victoria Falls, costs $795 including transport by safari vehicle, camping and cooking equipment, and all game park fees. US agent for *Kumuka Expeditions*, a London-based tour operator.

Journeys, 4011 Jackson Rd, Ann Arbor, Michigan 48103 (☎1-800/255-8735). Budget camping and

luxury-style safaris in Zimbabwe and Botswana. A 10-day Okavango Delta camping safari in Botswana is US$1825 plus air fare.

Mountain Travel Sobek (in US, ☎1-800/227-2384; in Canada, ☎1-800/282-8747; e-mail: Info@MTSobek.com; WWW site: http://www.MTSobek.com). Safaris, cultural adventures, hiking and river rafting. An 18-day game tracking safari in Zimbabwe costs US$3290–3590, not including air fare; the tour includes hiking, canoeing and accommodation in luxury camps, hotels and lodges.

Nature Expeditions International (☎1-800/869-0639; e-mail: NaturExp@aol.com). Botswana wildlife safaris, Zambia and Zimbabwe walking safaris. US$4000 not including air fare for a 15-day safari led by a team of experienced naturalists and natural history experts.

Nordic Tours, 13 Hazelton Ave, Toronto, Ontario M5R 2E1 (☎416/964-2569). 14-day Southern Africa explorer tours, with a two-night safari, from C$4995–5295, including air fare from Toronto, Montréal or Vancouver on *British Airways* via London.

Safariplan International, 673 E California Blvd, Pasadena, CA 91106 (☎1-800/358-8530). A Johannesburg-based company which books accommodation for independent travellers in camps, lodges, hotels and cruise boats in all price ranges; plus customized safaris, escorted tours and self-drive itineraries.

GETTING THERE FROM AUSTRALASIA

The only direct flights from Australasia to Zimbabwe are the twice-weekly services on *Qantas* from Sydney via Perth to Harare, one of which touches down in Johannesburg before the last leg to Harare; fares vary from A$1910 in the low season to A$2630 in the high season. There are no direct flights to Botswana from Australasia but there are good connections from Johannesburg and Harare to Gaborone or Maun.

South African Airways fly **to Johannesburg** twice a week from Sydney via Perth and offer a free side-trip to Harare or Bulawayo in the fare – around A$2400/1700 (high/low season) from Perth and A$2700/2000 (high/low season) from Sydney.

Cheaper (saving up to A$500 over the more direct flights), but far more tortuous, are **flights via Asia or the Middle East**, which involve a substantial triangular detour. *Egypt Air* flies three times a week from Sydney to Harare (via Singapore and Cairo), while *Malaysia Airlines* (via Kuala Lumpur) goes twice a week. *Gulf Air* flies several times a week from east coast cities via Bahrain.

From Auckland, you can go via Australia and connect with one of the flights to Harare mentioned above for around NZ$3500/2600 (high/low season). There are also routings **to Johannesburg**, on *Air New Zealand* (via Sydney) twice a week (NZ$3350/2450 high/low season). The cheapest fares to Johannesburg are on *Malaysia Airlines*' twice-weekly service via Kuala Lumpur (NZ$2850/2375 high/low season).

The best value **round-the-world ticket** from both Australia and New Zealand is the *South African Airways/Air New Zealand* "Global", which allows unlimited stopovers and free side trips to destinations in Zimbabwe and Botswana (A$2600 in high season, 2400 in low season; NZ$2900 in high season, 2660 in low season).

AIRLINES IN AUSTRALIA AND NEW ZEALAND

Air Botswana, Level 6, 75 Miller St, North Sydney (☎02/9956 6620).

Air New Zealand, 5 Elizabeth St, Sydney (☎02/9223 4666); Quay St, Auckland (☎09/357 3000).

Air Zimbabwe, 456 Kent St, Sydney (☎02/9267 3944).

British Airways, 64 Castlereagh St, Sydney (☎02/9258 3300); 154 Queen St, Auckland (☎09/356 8690).

Egypt Air, 630 George St, Sydney (☎02/9267 6979).

Gulf Air, 403 George St, Sydney (☎02/9321 9199).

MAS Malaysian Airlines, 16 Spring St, Sydney (☎02/364 3500; local-call rate ☎13 2627); Floor 12, Swanson Centre, 12–26 Swanson St, Auckland (☎09/373 2741).

Qantas, Chifley Square, Hunter/Phillip St, Sydney (☎02/957 0111); Qantas House, 154 Queen St, Auckland (☎09/357 8900).

South African Airways, 5 Elizabeth St, Sydney (☎02/9223 4402).

TRAVEL AGENTS IN AUSTRALIA AND NEW ZEALAND

Accent on Travel, 545 Queen St, Brisbane (☎07/3832 1777).

Anywhere Travel, 345 Anzac Parade, Kingsford, Sydney (☎02/663 0411).

Brisbane Discount Travel, 360 Queen St, Brisbane (☎07/3229 9211).

Budget Travel, 16 Fort St, Auckland; other branches around the city (☎09/309 4313; toll-free ☎0800/808 040).

Destinations Unlimited, 3 Milford Rd, Milford, Auckland (☎09/486 1303).

Flight Centres, Australia: Circular Quay, Sydney (☎02/9241 2422); Bourke St, Melbourne (☎03/650 2899); plus other branches nationwide.

New Zealand: National Bank Towers, 205–225 Queen St, Auckland (☎09/309 6171); Shop 1M, National Mutual Arcade, 152 Hereford St, Christchurch (☎03/379 7145); 50–52 Willis St, Wellington (☎04/472 8101); other branches countrywide.

Harvey World Travel, Princess Highway, Kogarah, Sydney (☎02/567 099); plus branches nationwide.

Northern Gateway, 22 Cavenagh St, Darwin (☎08/8941 1394).

Passport Travel, 320b Glenferrie Rd, Malvern, Melbourne (☎03/9824 7183).

STA Travel, Australia: 732 Harris St, Ultimo, Sydney (☎02/9212 1255; toll-free ☎1800/637

TRAVEL IN SOUTHERN AFRICA

The huge region of Southern Africa is fast becoming integrated as a tourist destination. Namibian independence, democracy in South Africa, reforms in Zambia, and peace in Mozambique, and the well-oiled transport connections are facilitating the whole process.

In Southern Africa all roads, rail links and air routes lead to **Johannesburg**, the economic powerhouse and transport hub of the entire region. Zimbabwe's two principal cities, Harare and Bulawayo, are well connected to Johannesburg by direct air, road and rail links, and there are good, if skeletal, links to Gaborone by road and air. Good connections also exist to a number of other important springboard destinations, including Maun and Kasane in Botswana, and Hwange and Victoria Falls in Zimbabwe.

Flights from South Africa to Zimbabwe or Botswana are quick and convenient but tend to be expensive. Standard single **fares** from Johannesburg on *South African Airways* are around US$300 to Harare and Victoria Falls, and US$200 to Bulawayo; *Air Botswana* fares from Johannesburg are around US$160 to Gaborone and US$300 to Maun, the main centre for the Okavango Delta. Return fares cost 20–30 percent more than singles.

If you are travelling around the region, taking in a number of destinations in South Africa, Zimbabwe or Namibia, you should definitely consider the *SAA* **Africa Explorer** scheme,

444); 256 Flinders St, Melbourne (☎03/9347 4711); other offices in Townsville, state capitals and major universities. **New Zealand**: Travellers' Centre, 10 High St, Auckland (☎09/366 6673); 233 Cuba St, Wellington (☎04/385 0561); 223 High St, Christchurch (☎03/379 9098); other offices in Dunedin, Palmerston North, Hamilton and major universities.

Thomas Cook, 96 Anzac Ave, Auckland (☎09/379 3920); plus branches throughout NZ.
Topdeck Travel, 45 Glenfell St, Adelaide (☎08/8232 7222).
Tymtro Travel, 428 George St, Sydney (☎02/9223 2211).
UTAG Travel, 122 Walker St, North Sydney (☎02/956 8399); plus branches throughout Australia.

SOUTHERN AFRICAN SPECIALISTS IN AUSTRALIA AND NEW ZEALAND

The Adventure Specialists, 69 Liverpool St, Sydney (☎02/9261 2927). Agents who can put together a wide range of packages from the adventure tour wholesalers.

Adventure World (wholesaler), 73 Walker St, North Sydney (☎02/956 7766; toll-free ☎1800/221 931); 8 Victoria Ave, Perth (☎09/221 2300); 101 Great South Rd, Remuera, Auckland (☎09/524 5118). International air travel arrangements, car rental, rail, and a wide range of overland safaris and expeditions in Zimbabwe and Botswana to suit most interests and budgets. Their Auckland branch is the New Zealand agent for *Exodus* (see below).

Africa Travel, 21 Remuera Rd, Newmarket, Auckland (☎09/520 2000). Specialists in all aspects of travel in Africa.

African Wildlife Safaris, 1st Floor, 259 Coventry St, Melbourne (☎03/9696 2899). Specialists in upmarket camping and lodge-based safaris.

Destinations Adventure, 2nd Floor, Premier Building, Queen/Durham St, East Auckland (☎09/309 0464). Agents for *Peregrine* (see below).

Exodus Expeditions (wholesaler), Suite 5, Level 5, 1 York St, Sydney (☎02/9251 5430; toll-free ☎1800/800 724). Explore the Okavango Delta by punt, walk through the remote Chizarira National Park, then canoe along the Zambezi River on a 16-day safari.

Peregrine Adventures (wholesaler), 258 Lonsdale St, Melbourne (☎03/9663 8611); offices in Brisbane, Sydney, Adelaide, Perth and Hobart. A host of wildlife safaris for the adventurous.

Top Deck Travel (wholesaler), 8th Floor, 358 Kent St, Sydney (☎02/9255 0899). Overland specialists.

which can save up to 60 per cent on *SAA* regional and domestic fares. The Africa Explorer must be booked in conjunction with an international ticket to South Africa (you don't have to be flying *SAA*), must include between four and eight sectors, and is valid for a month with a minimum stay of three days in any one place. You can fly to all South African domestic destinations and also from Johannesburg to Bulawayo (US$100), Harare (US$150) and Victoria Falls (US$150); and between Windhoek and Harare (US$200), Victoria Falls (US$160) or Livingstone (US$160). A number of other African cities can also be reached on the scheme.

There are no bucket shops or cheap deals in Southern Africa other than those offered by the airlines themselves, so there's no point shopping around. You can buy tickets through *SAA* at Johannesburg airport (☎011/773 9381) for their own flights or those of any of the other regional

airlines. Any travel agent can provide a similar service.

Luxury coaches are much cheaper and far slower than air travel, but, if you have the time, they offer the added attraction of taking in some of the countryside en route. There are good connections from Johannesburg to Harare (18hr; US$55), Bulawayo (13hr; US$45), Victoria Falls (20hr; US$60) and Gaborone (5hr; US$30). The Victoria Falls coach also pulls in at *Hwange Safari Lodge*, which is handy for getting into Hwange National Park. The two main operators plying regional routes, *Greyhound* (☎011/434 3500) and *Translux* (☎011/774 3333), both have desks which can issue tickets at the Rotunda (see box overleaf).

Spoornet, South Africa's rail operator, runs one **train** a week from Johannesburg to Bulawayo (24hr; US$90 first class) and another to Harare (26hr; US$120 first class). Bulawayo is useful if

CONNECTIONS WITH JOHANNESBURG			
From	**Flights**	**Trains**	**Luxury coaches**
Bulawayo	5 weekly	1 weekly	5 weekly
Gaborone	1 daily	—	4 weekly
Harare	1–2 daily	1 weekly	6 weekly
Kasane	4 weekly	—	—
Livingstone	3 weekly	—	—
Maun	1 daily	—	—
Victoria Falls	2 weekly	—	3 weekly

you want to continue by rail all the way to Victoria Falls, as you can change trains there for the *Zimbabwe National Railways* daily service to the Falls. All three trains have first- and second-class accommodation with sleepers. Tickets are obtainable from the *Spoornet* reservations office (☎011/773 5878–9) at the station (see box below).

Although **hitching** in Zimbabwe and Botswana is an option, it certainly can't be recommended in South Africa, both because of levels of crime and the suicidal style of driving.

In addition to the scheduled transport services, there are a number of companies operating Southern Africa **overland trips** and **mobile safaris**, which can be a convenient and organized way of reaching less accessible parts. South African mobile safari companies covering Zimbabwe and Botswana are given in the box; many of those which operate in restricted localized areas are listed in the relevant section of the guide.

OVERLAND THROUGH AFRICA

For overland travellers coming down Africa there are several trodden paths to the south. **From Malawi**, the quickest route through Mozambique brings you into Zimbabwe's northeastern corner, a few hours from Harare. The other option from

Malawi is much longer, going through Zambia to Livingstone and into Zimbabwe at Victoria Falls, or into Botswana at Kazungula.

From **Mozambique** you can fly from Maputo (twice weekly) or Beira (three times weekly) to Harare. The road between Mutare and Beira is now safe, and minibuses go between the border post on the Mozambique side and the coast.

From **Zambia**, it's straightforward enough to hitch to the Victoria Falls or take a daily coach from Lusaka to Harare. A train connects Dar-es-Salaam in **Tanzania** to Kapiri Mposhi in central Zambia, where it's necessary to change. Another service from a nearby, but separate, station goes via Lusaka to Livingstone, from where buses and taxis ply the route to the Zimbabwe border. Victoria Falls town is a short walk across the bridge. There's also a regular coach service between Lusaka and Francistown in Botswana.

Zimbabwe and Botswana are both also directly connected by air to the independent enclave kingdoms of **Lesotho** and **Swaziland** – both effectively within South Africa.

OTHER AFRICAN AIR CONNECTIONS

Harare is well connected to a number of destinations in Africa, making multi-stop travel easy. *Air*

JOHANNESBURG ARRIVAL AND DEPARTURE POINTS

All Johannesburg **flights** leave from Johannnesburg International Airport (information ☎011/975 9963), still frequently referred to by its former name, Jan Smuts. Shuttle buses leave for the airport from Braamfontein, close to the city centre, every half hour (5am–10pm) from the **Rotunda Terminal**, Rissik St/Wolmarans St. The journey takes about 45 minutes. The Rotunda is also the central terminal for **luxury coaches** to destinations across the region including those going to Zimbabwe and Botswana. **Trains** leave from the central railway station, Wolmarans St (☎011/773 5878), adjacent to the Rotunda.

Warning: the Rotunda has a notorious reputation as a choice spot for muggers, preying on dazed and confused newly arrived tourists. Keep alert. Don't try walking anywhere from it, no matter how close it seems – take a metered taxi.

SOUTH AFRICAN MOBILE SAFARIS
COVERING ZIMBABWE AND BOTSWANA

Afroventures Safaris, PO Box 2339, Randburg (☎011/807 3720). Overland safaris in Botswana, Zimbabwe and South Africa graded according to difficulty. Can be joined in Victoria Falls, Maun or Johannesburg.

Karibu Safari, PO Box 35196, Northway 4065, Durban; 50 Acutt Ave, Rosehill, Durban (☎031/

839 774). Truckback overland camping trips through Zimbabwe, Botswana, Malawi, Namibia and South Africa with an upmarket alternative of lodge-based safaris.

Wilderness Safaris, PO Box 651171, Benmore 2010 (☎011/884 1458 or 884 4633); also at 180 Helen Rd, Strathaven, Sandton.

Zimbabwe flies between Harare and the following cities: Gaborone, Lilongwe, Lusaka, Nairobi, Dar-es-Salaam, Maputo, Mauritius and Windhoek.

If you plan to head on to further African travels, Nairobi is probably the most useful hub to

head for. You can also fly Harare to Addis Ababa non-stop for *Ethiopian Airlines'* excellent connections across the continent. Alternatively, for West Africa, you can fly direct to Lagos (*Balkan Bulgarian Airlines*) and Accra (*Ghana Airways*).

SAFARIS

Everyone wants to see big game on their African trip. Prepare to put away your watch and your preconceptions and relax. Even if you don't encounter the lioness with cubs that someone else saw half an hour ago, you're bound to be repeatedly rewarded with the unexpected: a bat-eared fox resting in the grass, a dung beetle determinedly rolling a ball of elephant droppings or a large grey mongoose stalking through the grass.

Spotting game takes skill and experience. It's easier than you'd think to mistake a rhino for a large boulder, or to miss Leo in the tall lion-coloured grass – African game is after all designed with camouflage in mind. Having someone knowledgeable to point things out makes it that much easier to have a good time.

Zimbabwe scores high as a wildlife destination precisely because it is eminently well endowed with first-class **game guides**. Although it's a pity not to take advantage of this resource, it's still possible to do it yourself more cheaply.

Safari operators are listed under their area in the guide. The main safari regions in Zimbabwe are **Kariba**, the **Middle** and **Lower Zambezi** and **Mana Pools** (Chapter Two), **Hwange** and **Victoria Falls** (Chapter Four) and **Gonarezhou** (Chapter Five). In Botswana the chief areas are **Chobe** (Chapter Eight) and the **Okavango Delta** (Chapter Nine).

DOING IT YOURSELF

The most basic way to see game is to hitch or drive into the parks and stay in National Parks accommodation – or to camp. For anyone on a tight budget it may be the only chance of getting into a national park and you won't be tied down by a fixed itinerary. In Zimbabwe, National Parks accommodation – geared mainly for locals – is extremely cheap. And if you're carrying a tent, you can take advantage of the excellent campsites for next to nothing.

Hitching cuts down your options of viable destinations and unless you're steel-nerved, intrepid and have endless time, it really isn't worth attempting anywhere more ambitious than **Hwange National Park**'s Main Camp. You could do a lot worse. Main Camp is one of the best places to catch sight of a wide spectrum of game in a small area. From here you can catch minibuses or more personalized game drives into the park.

The minibuses are unquestionably a second-rate option. Drivers on such trips are essentially there to get you around the park, and can't be relied on to be as well informed as a qualified guide.

ORGANIZED SAFARIS

MOBILE SAFARIS
The least expensive of the package deals, **mobile safaris** offer the chance to get off the

beaten track with a professional. You'll camp rather than stay in luxury lodges or fixed bush camps, but that doesn't mean you'll be excessively uncomfortable. While some mobile safaris do expect clients to share chores, many others are fully serviced. In the top-of-the-range versions, you'll sleep under canvas on camp beds, be woken in the morning with tea and you'll arrive back at camp to cooked meals.

Most mobile safaris set out from one of the main centres and set up tents in the National Parks campsites. **Prices** start at US$120 per person per day.

BUSH CAMPS AND SAFARI LODGES

Traditional-style safaris based in **bush camps or safari lodges** are still immensely popular. Zimbabwe's best camps and lodges are located either in national parks or in adjacent game-rich concessions.

Guests at the more exclusive places usually number between twelve and sixteen, giving an intimate atmosphere with the chance to talk to guides during meals. Some of the larger lodges resemble hotels and lack this personal feel.

Animals are often free to wander through the grounds, and you'll get a very direct experience of the wild. It's not uncommon for guests to peer through a window at a bush camp to see antelope grazing a few feet away or even a languid lion padding by. Many safari lodges have their own waterholes, where you can watch animals drinking from the safety of your room or the bar.

Accommodation is under canvas or in more permanent thatched structures. Chalets frequently have en-suite toilets and bush showers (a hoisted bucket of hot water with a shower nozzle attached) behind reed screens but open to the sky – one of the great thrills of the bush is taking a shower under the southern sky as an elephant strolls by.

Food is usually good and plentiful. On a typical day at a camp or lodge you're woken at dawn for tea or coffee followed by guided game viewing: a drive, walk or trip on the water depending on where you are. Outings are restricted to no more than seven people, which means personalized attention. Mid-morning you return for breakfast. After that there's the chance to spend until lunch on a viewing platform or in a hide (blind) just quietly watching the passing scene. Late-afternoon game viewing is a repeat of early morning but culminating with sundowners as the light fades.

Prices, from US$180 per person per day, are fully inclusive of accommodation, food and game activities.

ACTIVITY AND SPECIALIST SAFARIS

Safaris – in Zimbabwe at least – aren't just about sitting in Land Rovers and looking at animals. If you're moderately fit and active and game drives sound too sedentary, there are walking, canoeing, horse-riding and even elephant-back safaris. **Walking safaris** take groups of up to six people headed by a tracker and a licensed guide. Trips are supported by a backup vehicle which carries all supplies as well as your personal effects. All you carry is your own camera, binoculars and anything else you may feel you need for half a day's walking.

Supported trips are based at a tented camp where you eat and from which you take morning and afternoon walks. You will see fewer animals than you would from a vehicle but what you do see is more intensely experienced.

Part of the excitement of this kind of trip is in the actual tracking of the animal you're trying to see. There's a real sense of achievement when you finally catch sight of that rhino after a three-hour trek. But no less important is the insight you gain into the bush from your guide who will point out the minutiae of insect, bird and plant life, which seems part of the backdrop until you realize how integral it is to the whole system.

Canoeing safaris vary from those where participants muck in and help cater to those where it's all laid on. All go down either the **Upper Zambezi** above Victoria Falls or the **Lower Zambezi** beyond Lake Kariba, and some include sections of walking. **Whitewater kayaking** on the Upper Zambezi above the Victoria Falls has the added frisson of negotiating rapids at intervals between paddling down the river through the Zambezi National Park.

Horse safaris from Victoria Falls are open to experienced riders who can go on excursions of several days or novices who are restricted to shorter stints. There's nothing like riding close to a herd of buffalo, who allow horses far closer than they ever would lone humans. More exciting still are outward-bound horse safaris in the Mavuradonna Mountains, heading out into the wilderness and spending nights in bush camps.

With 640 recorded **bird** species Zimbabwe has a lot to offer birdwatchers. All licensed guides know a lot about the subject but a particularly good bet would be a specialist **bird safari**, as run by *Peter Ginn Birding Safaris* (PO Box 44, Marondera; ☎179/4543, fax 3340).

Trains are the focus of another type of safari. Chugging up from Bulawayo to Victoria Falls, **steam safaris** re-create the romance of rail travel in the days of empire (see pp.42 & 163). Part of the trip takes you through the Hwange National Park and there's a stop on the way with the option of spending the night at *Hwange Safari Lodge*.

And for something completely different you can even go riding **elephants**, at *Elephant Camp* near Victoria Falls or *Abu's Camp* in the Okavango Delta. Since starting in the early 1990s it has become an incredibly popular pursuit and gets booked out. The elephants aren't wild African beasts, having all been born in captivity, and are used to human company.

RED TAPE AND VISAS

Neither Zimbabwe nor Botswana requires that citizens of EU or Commonwealth countries (including South Africa), Scandinavia or the US obtain visas for stays of up to 90 days.

For both countries, all travellers need a passport valid for at least six months, an air ticket home (one flying to your place of origin from another African country will usually do) or enough money to get a ticket home, and sufficient funds to cover your costs in the country. These requirements are taken seriously, though there is no statutory daily minimum you are expected to spend.

BORDER FORMALITIES

For stays of up to 90 days, most passport holders can enter **Zimbabwe** with few formalities. **Botswana** issues one-month entry permits initially, and visitors are strictly allowed to stay no longer than three months in any year.

Don't overstay in Botswana, even by one day, without **renewing** your visa. Extending your permission to stay can quite easily be done through one of the local Department of Immigration offices; be warned that if you fail to do so they get very heavy about it. When dealing with Botswana officials, your best tactic is to keep your cool even if it all seems intolerably

DIPLOMATIC MISSIONS ABROAD

ZIMBABWE

Australia, 11 Culgoa Circuit, O' Malley, ACT (☎06/6286 2700).

Botswana, 1st Floor, IGI Building, PO Box 1232, Gaborone (☎4495 or 4497).

Canada, 332 Summerset West, Ottawa, K2P 0J9 (☎613/237 4388).

France, 5 rue de Tilsitt, Paris 75008 (☎1/763 48 31).

Germany, Victoriastrasse 28, 5300 Bonn 2 (☎0228/35 6071).

Kenya, 6th Floor, ICDC Building, PO Box 30806, Nairobi (☎721071).

Malawi, 7th Floor, Gemini House, PO Box 30187, Lilongwe 3 (☎784988).

Mozambique, Avenue Kenneth Kaunda, Caiza Postal 743, Maputo (☎499404).

South Africa, Bank of Lisbon Building, 37 Sauer St, Johannesburg (☎011/838 2156).

UK, 429 The Strand, London WC2 (☎0171/836 7755).

USA, 1608 New Hampshire, NW, Washington DC 20009 (☎202/332-7100).

Zambia, 4th Floor, Ulenda House, PO Box 33491, Lusaka (☎219025–6).

BOTSWANA

Australia, Parkes Place, Parkes, Canberra (☎06/6261 3305).

UK, 6 Stratford Place, London W1 (☎0171/499 0031).

USA, Suite 7M, 3400 International Drive, NW, Washington DC 20008 (☎202/244-4990).

Zimbabwe, Southern Life Building, Jason Moyo Ave, Harare (☎729551).

BOTSWANA BORDER OPENINGS

The following border crossings are open every day unless otherwise noted.

Zimbabwe	South Africa	
Kazungula Rd 6am–6pm	Baines Drift 8am–4pm	Ramatlhabama 7am–8pm
Kasane/Victoria Falls 6am–6pm	Bokspits* 8am–4pm	Ramotswa 8am–4pm
Mpandamatenga Mon–Fri 6am–6pm	Bray* 8am–4pm	Saambou 8am–4pm
	Martin's Drift 8am –4pm	Sikwane 8am–4pm
Ramokwebana 6am–6pm	McCarthysrus* 8am–4pm	Tlokweng 7am–10pm
	Parr's Halt 8am–4pm	Werda* 8am–4pm
Namibia	Pioneer Gate 7am–8pm	Zanzibar 8am–4pm
Mamuno 8am–4pm	Pitsane* 8am–4.30pm	**Zambia**
Ngoma Bridge 8am–4pm	Platjanbridge 8am–4pm	Kazungula Ferry 6am–6pm
Shakawe 8am–4pm	Pont Drift 8am to 4pm	

* Borders closed when Molopo River in flood makes crossing impassable.

bureaucratic. If you lose your temper they're almost certain to make life even more difficult for you.

If you're a **journalist** coming to Zimbabwe – particularly if you're just going on holiday – consider stating an alternative occupation on your entry form. Anyone even vaguely connected with the media is generally given a 24-hour visa, and must then get accreditation at the Ministry of Home Affairs. However, if you are on a press assignment, it's probably best to say so, otherwise you could get into a tight corner if found out later.

ARRIVING OVERLAND

If travelling overland, make sure things are timed so you don't end up stranded at a closed border post. Most of **Zimbabwe**'s border posts with Zambia, Botswana and South Africa open from 6am to 6pm, seven days a week, apart from Beit Bridge, which opens until 8pm. **Botswana**'s borders have more erratic opening hours, as detailed above.

WHAT TO TAKE

You can get most necessary items in Zimbabwe and Botswana, although in the remote rural areas you shouldn't expect more than the barest of essentials. The recent liberalization of import controls in Zimbabwe has brought it more in line with Botswana – you can buy most things you'd want now, but don't expect the variety or sophistication you might get at home. Locally manufactured products, however, such as shoes and clothes, are easy to come by and usually quite cheap. As far as food is concerned, unless you're on a macrobiotic diet, you'll have no problem finding a good selection, particularly in the major towns.

CLOTHES

You can generally get away with a few **light clothes** in Zimbabwe and Botswana. But don't be fooled by average temperature figures. The weather is capricious and even in mid-summer night temperatures can plummet in some places.

From the end of August to October, take light cotton clothes, a long-sleeved T-shirt and a sweater or jacket. The same goes for the period from November to March, though in this **rainy season** it's just as well to include a light plastic mac or hooded jacket. A light woollen jumper is a good idea, even in summer, if you're visiting the cooler Eastern Highlands, or planning on early-morning game drives. Modest-looking tracksuits are good game-viewing gear too, allowing you to peel off as the day warms, and practical for camping all year round.

From August to May, shorts or a light skirt are well worth having. **Sunglasses** are recommended all year round. **Hats** or caps are indispensable if you're spending a lot of time outdoors, for example canoeing or walking. A length of light cotton cloth, available from fabric shops in Zimbabwe, is extremely useful as a wrap to ward off the fierce summer sun, and it doubles as a makeshift towel.

Lightweight, quick-drying **walking boots** or shoes are a must if you're planning any energetic activities. Leave behind waterproof, heavy-duty leather hiking boots: while they may be excellent for European hikes, they weigh far too much and you'll just sweat in them. For less ambitious walks and scrambles, tennis or running shoes are ideal.

For **game viewing** you'll need dark or neutral-coloured clothes. Plain green or khaki gear available from army surplus shops is perfect. White might look stylish but it's not a good idea; in white clothes you stand out like a beacon to the animals you're discreetly trying to watch. And don't take camouflage clothes of any kind; they're illegal for civilians.

Finally, it's worth being forewarned about the Southern African idiosyncrasy of "**smart-casual wear**", demanded by many Western-style hotels after 6pm – cocktail time in other words. Exactly what they mean by it is somewhat ad hoc and most of it applies to men. Shorts are out, as are jeans. Trainer shoes are usually acceptable but sandals aren't. If you take a pair of slacks, closed shoes and a smartish shirt with a collar (short sleeves are okay) you should pass. Smart-casual doesn't appear to apply to women, unless you're looking really scruffy.

HEALTH

You can put aside most of the health fears that may be justified in some parts of Africa. Bad hospitals and even worse "tropical" diseases aren't typical of Botswana and Zimbabwe. As in the rest of Africa, HIV is rampant, but there's little chance of catching it other than through unprotected sex.

The sunny, dry climate and unpolluted air suits most people, and Zimbabwe's temperate central plateau – where Harare and most other major towns are situated – is exceptionally healthy, with a complete absence of malaria. There are generally high standards of hygiene and safe **drinking water** in all tourist areas.

INOCULATIONS

Although no **inoculations** are compulsory if you arrive from the West, it's wise to make sure that your **polio** and **tetanus** jabs are up to date. **Yellow fever** vaccination certificates are necessary if you've come from a country where the disease is endemic, such as Kenya or Tanzania. **Cholera** vaccination is unpleasant, pretty ineffective and not recommended unless you are going to be working for a period in terribly deprived areas. Some authorities recommend a course of **typhoid** shots, which for similar reasons is something to think twice about. Despite their terrible reputation, typhoid fever and cholera are both eminently curable and few, if any, visitors to Southern Africa ever catch them.

A Havrix shot protects against **hepatitis A**, which is caught from contaminated water or food, for a year in the first instance; a booster injection a year later gives protection for a further ten years. Hepatitis B vaccine is only essential for anyone involved in health work. It's spread by the transfer of blood products, usually dirty needles, so most travellers need not worry about it.

If you decide to have an armful of jabs, start organizing them six weeks before departure. If you're going to another African country first and need the yellow fever jab, remember that a yellow fever certificate only becomes valid ten days after you've had the shot.

STAYING HEALTHY

The best way to stay healthy is to keep your resistance up by eating a **healthy regular diet** and by avoiding **stress** – sometimes more easily said than done. The following tips should help you to stay well on your travels and help you over the illness if you succumb.

WATER – AND STOMACH UPSETS

Only in extremely remote places do you need to **boil** your water or use **water purification** tablets. **Stomach upsets** from food are equally rare. You'll only find salad and ice – the danger items in some other countries – in hotels and smarter restaurants. Both are perfectly safe and not to be missed. As anywhere, though, **wash**

MEDICAL RESOURCES FOR TRAVELLERS

For a comprehensive, and sobering, account of the health problems which travellers encounter worldwide, consult the regularly updated *Traveller's Health*, edited by Dr Richard Dawood (OUP/ Viking Penguin).

0127 685 040

BRITAIN

British Airways Medical Department, 156 Regent St, London W1 (☎0171/439 9584; for advice on other *BA* clinics around the country ☎0171/831 5333). 0891 224 100

Hospital for Tropical Diseases: Clinic, 1st Floor, Queen's House, 180–182 Tottenham Court Rd, London (☎0171/637 9899). Advice as well as all the jabs you need. The clinic can also provide the items you may need to stay healthy on your travels, including malaria prevention tablets and mosquito nets. **Healthline** (☎0839/337733). Up-to-the-minute advice on how to stay healthy in the tropics. Personal advice won't be given but the computer-operated system dishes out detailed health information about Zimbabwe (code 61) and Botswana (code 73). Calls are charged at 48p per minute peak rate. **Health-Fax** (☎0991/991992). A computer-generated report with the latest infor-

mation from the hospital tailored to your journey to a fax number you specify. This works out cheaper than the spoken Healthline service. You will need a touch-tone phone to key in the country codes for Zimbabwe (269) and Botswana (118), and to respond to the questions asked.

MASTA (*Medical Advisory Services for Travellers Abroad*), Bureau of Hygiene and Tropical Diseases, Keppel St, London WC1E 7HT. A commercial service providing detailed "health briefs" for all countries, and a Travellers' Healthline (☎0891/224100) providing written information tailored to your journey by return of post.

Trailfinders Immunization Centre, 194 Kensington High St, London W8 7RG (☎0171/938 3999). Inoculation service operated by the respected and knowledgeable travel agency.

USA AND CANADA

International Association for Medical Assistance to Travellers (IAMAT), 417 Center St, Lewiston, NY 14092 (☎716/754-4883); 40 Regal Rd, Guelph, ON N1K 1B5 (☎519/836-0102). A non-profit organization supported by donations, which can provide climate charts and leaflets on various diseases and inoculations.

Travelers Medical Center, 31 Washington Square, New York, NY 10011 (☎212/982-1600). Consultation service on immunizations and treatment of diseases for people travelling to developing countries.

Travel Medicine, 351 Pleasant St, Suite 312, Northampton, MA 01060 (☎1-800/872-8633). Sells first-aid kits, mosquito netting, water filters and other health-related travel products.

AUSTRALIA AND NEW ZEALAND

Auckland Hospital, Park Rd, Grafton (☎09/797 440).

Travel-Bug Medical and Vaccination Centre, 161 Ward St, North Adelaide (☎08/8267 3544).

Travel Health and Vaccination Clinic, 114 Williams St, Melbourne (☎03/9670 2020).

Travellers' Medical and Vaccination Centre, 428 George St, Sydney (☎02/9221 7133); 393 Little Bourke St, Melbourne (☎03/9602 5788); 29 Gilbert Place, Adelaide (☎08/8267 3544); 247 Adelaide St, Brisbane (☎07/3221 9066); 1 Mill St, Perth (☎09/321 1977).

Travellers Immunization Service, 303 Pacific Hwy, Sydney (☎02/416 1348).

fruit and vegetables as thoroughly as possible; and don't overindulge on fruit – no matter how tempting – when you first arrive.

If you do get a stomach bug, the best cure is lots of water and rest. Papayas, the flesh as well as the pips, are a good tonic to offset the runs.

Avoid jumping for **antibiotics** at the first sign of illness; keep them as a last resort – they don't

work on viruses and annihilate your "gut flora" (most of which you want to keep), making you more susceptible next time round. Most upsets will resolve themselves by adopting a sensible fat-free diet for a couple of days, but if they do persist unabated or are accompanied by other unusual symptoms then see a doctor as soon as possible.

MEDICAL AIR RESCUE SERVICE

Even if your worst nightmare comes true and you catch malaria in Zimbabwe's bush or you fall victim to some other medical misfortune, don't panic. Zimbabwe's **Medical Air Rescue Service**, 3 Elcombe Ave, Belgravia, Harare (☎734 513–5, fax 735 517), can rapidly fly you from anywhere in the country to a hospital. Most safari operators subscribe to the service, which is available to all their clients. Make sure your operator is part of the scheme. If not, or if you're an independent traveller, you can still be covered.

AIDS AND SEXUALLY TRANSMITTED DISEASES

Horror stories of rusty syringes and HIV-infected blood transfusions are not relevant to Zimbabwe or Botswana. Disposable needles are routinely used and the Zimbabwean health authorities have screened all donated blood for AIDS for several years. Zimbabwe was the third country in the world to do so – after the United States and Germany, and some months ahead of Britain.

So there's no special risk from medical treatment in Zimbabwe. If travelling overland, though, and you want to play safe, take your own needle and transfusion kit.

Your biggest chance of getting AIDS is through unprotected sex. AIDS, as well as various venereal diseases, is widespread in Southern Africa. Some estimates put HIV incidence at a staggering twenty percent of Zimbabwe's population. The chance of catching the virus through sexual contact is very real. Follow the usual precautions regarding safer sex: abstain – or use a condom.

BILHARZIA

One ailment which you need to take seriously in both countries is **bilharzia**, carried in all Zimbabwe's waterways outside the Eastern Highlands. Bilharzia (schistosomiasis) is spread by a tiny, water-borne parasite. These worm-like flukes leave their water snail hosts and burrow into human skin to multiply in the bloodstream. They work their way to the walls of the intestine or bladder where they begin to lay eggs.

Avoid swimming in dams and rivers where possible. If you're canoeing or can't avoid the water, have a test when you return home. White water is no guarantee of safety; although the snails favour sheltered areas, the flukes can be swept downstream. The chances are you'll have avoided bilharzia even if you swam in the Zambezi, but it's best to be sure.

Symptoms may be no more than a feeling of lassitude and ill health. Once infection is established, abdominal pain and blood in the urine and stool are common. Fortunately it's easily and effectively treated these days with praziquantel, although the drug can make you feel ill for a few days. No vaccine is available and none foreseen.

HEAT AND DUST

The **sun** could be the most dangerous thing you encounter. Sunglasses and a broad-brimmed hat are recommended, especially for children. Ordinary sun screens and lotions can be bought in pharmacies in Zimbabwe and Botswana, though you should buy the **total block** or **high-protection** variety before you leave. Tanning should be a very gradual process.

If you're not used to dealing with continuous heat over long periods of time, take care to avoid heat exhaustion. Be aware that you may be overheating, and if you start feeling ill – headaches or nausea – get to a cool shady place. Make sure you're getting enough water and that your salt levels aren't depleting.

MEDICAL KIT

Don't let your fears run away with you and lumber yourself with a heavy kit. You can buy medicines over the counter in pharmacies in both countries. If you need specialized drugs bring your own supply, but any first-aid items can be easily replaced. A very basic kit should include scissors, fine tweezers for removing thorns or glass, sticking plasters, one wide and one narrow bandage, lint, cotton wool, pins, aspirins and an antiseptic cream such as *Bacitracin. Nelson's* natural calendar ointment is invaluable as a healing agent for any stings, rashes, cuts, sores or cracked skin. A bottle of eyedrops is wonderfully soothing if you're travelling on dusty roads in Botswana. Some people also like to include a course of broad-spectrum antibiotics.

Botswana is particularly **dusty** – take this on board if you're asthmatic or allergic to dust. If you're just flying in to the Delta and staying near the water, you shouldn't have any problems.

TEETH AND EYES

Have a thorough **dental check-up** before leaving home. You'll find dentists in the main towns in Zimbabwe and Botswana, although they're few and far between in Botswana. In Zimbabwe, dentists are listed after doctors at the beginning of each town in the telephone directory. In Botswana, they're in the pink pages right at the front of the phone book.

If you wear **glasses** or **contact lenses** bring a spare pair with you, along with all the cleaning gear you need.

SNAKES, INSECTS AND OTHER UNDESIRABLES

Zimbabwe and Botswana both feature all sorts of potential bites, stings and rashes – which rarely, if ever, materialize.

Snakes are common, but hardly ever seen as they get out of the way quickly. Puff adders are the most dangerous because they lie in paths and don't move, but they're not commonly seen by travellers. The best advice if you get bitten is to remember what the snake looked like (kill it if you can, for identification) and get to a clinic or hospital. Most bites are not fatal and the worst thing is to panic: desperate measures with razor blades and tourniquets risk doing more harm than good.

Tick-bite fever is occasionally contracted from walking in the bush, particularly in March

MALARIA

Malaria, caused by a parasite carried in the saliva of Anopheles **mosquitos**, is endemic in tropical Africa: many Africans have it in their bloodstream and get occasional bouts of fever. It has a variable **incubation period** of a few days to several weeks, so you can become ill long after being bitten. If you go down with it, you'll know: the fever, shivering and headaches are like severe flu and come in waves, usually beginning in the early evening. Malaria is not infectious but it can be dangerous and even fatal if not treated quickly.

Protection against malaria is absolutely essential. Although much of Zimbabwe and Botswana, including most of the main towns, is free of malarial mosquitos, you have to keep taking the tablets to maintain your resistance for when you're bitten by a carrier mosquito, in a low-lying game park for example. However, remember that no anti-malarial drug is totally effective – the only reliable protection is to avoid getting bitten.

TABLETS

Doctors can advise on which kind of **preventive tablets** to take – generally the latest anti-resistant creation – and you can buy most without a prescription at a pharmacy before you leave. It's important to keep a routine and cover the period before and after your trip with doses. Take enough pills with you to cover your entire stay, as the types of tablet sold in Botswana and Zimbabwe are different.

NETS, OILS AND COILS

Female Anopheles mosquitos – the aggressors – are active between dusk and dawn. Sleep under a **mosquito net** when possible, making sure to tuck it under the mattress, and burn **mosquito coils** (which you can buy everywhere) for a peaceful, if noxious, night. Whenever the mosquitos are particularly bad – and that's not often – cover your exposed parts with something strong. Insect repellents containing diethyltoluamide work well. Other locally produced repellents such as *Peaceful Sleep* are widely available. Citronella oil is a help too, but hardly smells better.

Electric mosquito-destroyers which you fit with a pad every night are less pungent than mosquito coils, but you need electricity. Mosquito "buzzers" are useless.

IF YOU FALL ILL

If you contract malaria, you'll need to take a **cure**. Don't compare yourself with local people who may have considerable immunity. The priority, if you think you might be getting a fever, is treatment. Delay is potentially risky.

Warning signs include flu-like symptoms, fever, diarrhoea and joint pains. If you come down with any of these, from one week after arriving in a malaria zone to three months after leaving, you should immediately see a doctor and have a blood test.

and April when the grass is long and wet. The offending ticks are minute and you're unlikely to spot them. Symptoms appear a week later – swollen glands and severe aching of the bones, backache and fever. Since it is a self-limiting disease, it will run its course in three or four days. Ticks you may find on yourself are not dangerous, just repulsive at first. Make sure you pull out the head as well as the body (it's not painful). A good way of removing small ones is to smear vaseline or grease over them, making them release their hold.

Scorpions and **spiders** abound but are hardly ever seen unless you turn over logs and stones. If you're collecting wood for a camp fire, knock or shake it before picking it up. Contrary to popular myth, scorpion stings and spider bites are painful but almost never fatal. Most are harmless and should be left alone. A simple precaution when camping is to shake out your shoes and clothes in the morning before you get dressed.

Rabies exists in both countries. Be wary of strange animals and go to a clinic if bitten. It can be treated effectively with a course of injections.

HOSPITALS

Hospitals in Zimbabwe are fairly well equipped and attempt to maintain high standards. In remoter parts, the clinics are usually adequate although there are shortages of some drugs. Botswana has a few prestigious new hospitals.

Private clinics are often a better option for visitors and you're likely to get more personal treatment. Costs are nowhere as prohibitive as in the US and if you're insured they should certainly pose no problem.

In emergencies, or for extremely serious conditions, patients from both countries are sometimes flown to Johannesburg where the full range of up-to-date treatment is available.

TRAVEL INSURANCE

Most people will find it essential to take out a good travel insurance policy. This can be quite comprehensive, anticipating anything from lost or stolen baggage and missed connections to charter companies going bankrupt; however, certain policies (notably in North America) only cover medical costs. Bank and credit cards (particularly *American Express*) often have certain levels of medical or other insurance included, especially if you use them to pay for your trip.

If you plan to participate in adventure activities, watersports, or do some hiking, you'll probably have to pay an extra premium; check carefully that any insurance policy you are considering will cover you in case of an accident. Note also that very few insurers will arrange on-the-spot payments in the event of a major expense or loss; you will usually be reimbursed only after going home. In all cases of loss or theft of goods, you will have to contact the local police to have a report made out so that your insurer can process the claim.

BRITAIN

Most travel agents and tour operators will offer you insurance when you book your flight or holiday, and some will insist you take it. These policies are usually reasonable value, though as ever, you should check the small print. If you feel the cover is inadequate, or you want to compare prices, travel agents, insurance brokers and banks should be able to help. Basic cover for Zimbabwe and Botswana starts at £26 for 17 days, £33 for a month, and £85 for three months; rates are a little higher if South Africa is included in your itinerary. If you have a good "all risks" **home insurance policy** it may well cover your possessions against loss or theft even when overseas, and many **private medical schemes** also cover you when abroad – make sure you know the procedure and the helpline number.

As well as the companies listed in the box, try *Campus Travel* or *STA* (see p.4 for addresses) for competitive travel insurance schemes. Note that *Columbus* also does one of the best annual multi-trip policies, as well as long-term cover for periods up to a year.

THE US AND CANADA

US travellers should check their current insurance policies: you may find you are already covered for medical expenses or other losses while abroad. In Canada, provincial health plans typically provide some overseas medical coverage, although they are unlikely to pick up the full tab in the event of a mishap.

Holders of official **student/teacher/youth cards** are entitled to accident coverage and hospital in-patient benefits – the annual membership is far less than the cost of comparable insurance. **Students** may also find that their student health coverage extends during the vacations and for one term beyond the date of last enrolment. **Homeowners' or renters'** insurance often

covers theft or loss of documents, money and valuables while overseas.

After exhausting the possibilities above, you might want to contact a specialist travel insurance company; your travel agent can usually recommend one, or see the box below. Travel insurance policies vary: some are comprehensive while others cover only certain risks. Most North American travel policies apply only to items lost, stolen or damaged while in the custody of an identifiable, responsible third party, such as a hotel porter, airline or luggage consignment. Basic insurance packages start at around $65 for a two-week trip and $85 for three weeks to a month.

AUSTRALIA AND NEW ZEALAND

Travel insurance is put together by the airlines and travel agent groups in conjunction with insurance companies (see the box). They're all comparable in premium and coverage. Adventure sports are covered, except mountaineering with ropes, bungy jumping (some policies), unassisted diving without an Open Water licence; check your policy first. A typical insurance policy covering Zimbabwe and Botswana costs around A$180/NZ$210 for one month and A$330/NZ$380 for three.

TRAVEL INSURANCE COMPANIES

BRITAIN

Columbus Travel Insurance, 17 Devonshire Square, London EC2M 4SQ (☎0171/375 0011).

Endsleigh Insurance, 97–107 Southampton Row, London WC1B 4AG (☎0171/436 4451).

Frizzell Insurance, Frizzell House, County Gates, Bournemouth, Dorset BH1 2NF (☎01202/292333)

NORTH AMERICA

Access America, PO Box 90310, Richmond, VA 23230 (☎1-800/284-8300).

Carefree Travel Insurance, The Berkeley Group, 120 Mineola Blvd, PO Box 310, Mineola, NY 1150 (☎1-800/645-2424).

HealthCare Abroad/Health Care Global, Wallach & Company, 243 Church St NW, Suite 100-D, Vienna, VA 22180 (☎1-800/237-6615).

International SOS Assistance, 8 Neshaminy Interplex, Suite 207, Trevose, PA 19053 (☎1-800/523-8930).

Tele-Trip Mutual of Omaha, PO Box 31762, Omaha, NE 68131 (☎1-800/228-9792).

AUSTRALASIA

AFTA (Australian Federation of Travel Agents), 144 Pacific Hwy, North Sydney (☎02/956 4800).

Cover More, Level 9, 32 Walker St, North Sydney (☎02/9202 8000; toll-free 1800/251 881).

Ready Plan, 141–147 Walker St, Dandenong, Victoria (toll-free ☎1800/337 462); 10th Floor, 63 Albert St, Auckland (☎09/379 3208).

UTAG (United Travel Agents Group), 347 Kent St, Sydney (☎02/9819 6855; toll-free 1800/809 462).

MAPS, BOOKS AND INFORMATION

The Zimbabwe Tourist Organization (ZTO) is well organized and you can sometimes pick up basic maps and information on hotels and organized tours. If there's an office in your country, it's worth paying a visit just to browse around and whet your appetite. Elsewhere, contact the nearest Zimbabwe diplomatic mission (see "Red Tape and Visas") or office of Air Zimbabwe. Information about Botswana is more difficult to find but the High Commissions are worth a try.

ZIMBABWE

Really good **maps of Zimbabwe** are rare outside the country and it's probably most useful to go for a map of the whole Southern Africa region. The classic travellers' maps for Africa are produced by *Michelin*: #955 *Africa Central and Southern* is a good general map, though now a little dated. A better map, concentrating on

Zimbabwe, is produced by the Automobile Association of Zimbabwe and available at its branches in Harare, Bulawayo and Mutare, or through some newsagents and bookshops in Zimbabwe. The *Globetrotter* map of Zimbabwe, although the prettiest available, has some unfortunate inaccuracies. The Zimbabwe Tourist Office has produced quite a good free map which covers Zimbabwe only, accurate on main routes but weak on minor roads.

Zimbabwe is well covered by detailed ordnance survey (OS) maps, which are indispensible for walking in any of the national parks. They're available from the Surveyor General's Office, Electra House, Samora Machel Avenue, Harare. The office also has a wealth of maps covering everything that can be mapped, from rainfall patterns to geology and land use; it's fascinating just to browse around.

The **Parks Department** provides useful fact sheets, available in Harare, which cover facilities and attractions in most of the national parks. And finally, local information is available from town publicity associations. These are often very helpful, with up-to-date hotel and camping information, brochures and some usefully detailed (if often very old) regional maps.

BOTSWANA

The *Michelin #955* (see Zimbabwe) is again a reasonable general map. Botswana itself isn't as well documented as Zimbabwe, although there are several adequate maps. The best is the *Botswana Minimap* produced by *Okavango Tours and Safaris* (Gadd House, Arcadia Ave, London N3 2TJ; ☎0181/343 3283), which has a map of the whole country and up-to-date detailed plans of all the major tourist areas.

ZIMBABWE TOURIST OFFICES

Head Office, Tourism House, Fourth St/Jason Moyo Ave, PO Box 8052, Causeway, Harare (☎14/793666–9 or 763765).

Germany, Am Hauptbahnhof 10, Frankfurt am Main 1 (☎069/294042).

South Africa, Tower Mall, Upper Carlton Centre, Commissioner St, PO Box 9398, Johannesburg

2000, and 2 President Place, Jan Smuts Ave, Rosebank, Johannesburg (☎011/788 1748).

UK, 429 Strand, London WC2R 05A (☎0171/836 7755).

US, Rockefeller Centre, Suite 1905, 1270 Avenue of the Americas, Sixth Ave, New York, NY 10020 (☎212/332-1090).

In Botswana, *B&T Directories* (PO Box 1549, Gaborone; ☎37 1444) has produced a set of two maps – containing one of the whole country and plans of the main towns. It costs a few pula and is most easily available from Gaborone bookshops. The most detailed map of Botswana as a whole is a 1:1,000,000 sheet, which comes in two parts, available from the Director, Department of Surveys and Lands, Private Bag 0037, Gaborone. For identifying landmarks in a more confined area, the Department of Surveys and Lands has excellent OS maps at 1:50,000 – write off for their detailed catalogue. Aerial photographs are available if you're working in a small, featureless area of Botswana. There are also offices in Francistown and Selebi with 1:50,000 sheets of their immediate area.

For well-produced pamphlets about attractions in Botswana, get in touch with one of the country's diplomatic missions (see "Red Tape and Visas").

MAP OUTLETS

BRITAIN

Glasgow *John Smith and Sons*, 57–61 St Vincent St, G2 5TB (☎0141/221 7472).
London *Daunt Books*, 83 Marylebone High St, W1 (☎0171/224 2295); *National Map Centre*, 22–24 Caxton St, SW1 (☎0171/222 4945); *Stanfords*, 12–14 Long Acre, WC2 (☎0171/836 1321 for enquiries and **mail order**), 52 Grosvenor Gardens, London SW1W 0AG and 156 Regent St, London W1R 5TA; *The Travel Bookshop*, 13–15 Blenheim Crescent, London W11 2EE (☎0171/229 5260).

USA

California *The Complete Traveler Bookstore*, 3207 Fillmore St, San Francisco, CA 92123 (☎415/923-1511); *Map Link Inc*, 25 E Mason St, Santa Barbara, CA 93101 (☎805/965-4402); *Phileas Fogg's Books & Maps*, 87 Stanford Shopping Center, Palo Alto, CA 94304 (☎1-800/233-FOGG in California; ☎1-800/533-FOGG elsewhere in US); *Rand McNally*, 595 Market St, San Francisco, CA 94105 (☎415/777-3131); *Sierra Club Bookstore*, 730 Polk St, San Francisco, CA 94109 (☎415/923-5500).

Chicago *Rand McNally*, 444 N Michigan Ave, IL 60611 (☎312/321-1751).
New York *The Complete Traveler Bookstore*, 199 Madison Ave, NY 10016 (☎212/685-9007); *Rand McNally*, 150 E 52nd St, NY 10022 (☎212/758-7488); *Traveler's Bookstore*, 22 W 52nd St, NY 10019 (☎212/664-0995).
Washington DC *Rand McNally*, 1201 Connecticut Ave NW, Washington DC 20003 (☎202/223-6751).

Mail order *Rand McNally*, ☎1800/333-0136 (ext 2111).

CANADA

Montréal *Ulysses Travel Bookshop*, 4176 St-Denis (☎514/289-0993).
Toronto *Open Air Books and Maps*, 25 Toronto St, ON M5R 2C1 (☎416/363-0719).

Vancouver *World Wide Books and Maps*, 1247 Granville St, BC V6Z 1E4 (☎604/687-3320).

AUSTRALIA AND NEW ZEALAND

Adelaide *The Map Shop*, 16a Peel St (☎08/8231 2033).
Auckland *Specialty Maps*, 58 Albert St (☎09/307 2217).
Melbourne *Bowyangs*, 372 Little Burke St (☎03/9670 4383).

Perth *Perth Map Centre*, 891 Hay St (☎09/322 5733).
Sydney *Travel Bookshop*, 20 Bridge St (☎02/9241 3554).

FOOD AND DRINK

Food in Zimbabwe and Botswana is an unfortunate mishmash of traditional staples and English colonial diet – a very bland combination indeed. Standard dishes are either downmarket maize porridge and stew or more upmarket meat and two veg. Fortunately the meat is very good and cheap – steaks are not to be missed – and you'll find a range of international food in all the larger towns, which breaks the monotony of ubiquitous burgers, chips, pizzas and fried chicken takeaways, or more expensive sit-down cuisine. And there are those main-stays of white Southern Africa: *braaivleis* (barbecue) and *biltong* (dried meat).

You'll find all the usual drinks, but beer in various guises is the commonest. Zimbabwe produces its own drinkable wines and also spirits, and like Botswana imports a wide range of foreign liquor.

EATING IN ZIMBABWE

The traditional diet in Zimbabwe tends to be a variation on local produce: maize and beef. The local staple is **sadza** and relish, *sadza* being a stiff maize porridge slowly cooked for some time. Relish can be any kind of stew, sometimes based on vegetables but most commonly **nyama** (meat). The meat is unspecified – it can be goat, mutton, beef or chicken – but usually unpalatably plain.

If you stay at hotels and stick to the city centre, you're unlikely to sample any of this. You'll need to go to one of the many cheap eating houses around the bus or train stations which, besides *sadza*, serve deep-fried doughy concoctions, chips, filling buns and an unending supply of Coca-Cola. *Sadza* is usually steaming and freshly cooked. One **vegetarian** option at these places, which often sell a few groceries as well, is to buy a tin of baked beans and have that with *sadza*, instead of meat.

Bread, both brown and white, has become so expensive that it's now a luxury for many black families. Brown bread is available only in the big centres and not always in hotels. The national preference is definitely for white loaves, which are also somewhat cheaper.

STREET FOOD AND BREAKFAST

Street food, sold around bus stations, varies according to season, but you'll find boiled or roasted corn on the cob (*chibage*), peanuts, some varieties of beans, hard-boiled eggs and lots of fruit. Out of working class areas and into the middle class-dominated city centres, there's a noticeable absence of street food. Instead, you find western-style cafés, restaurants and burger joints.

Food in hotels, restaurants and snack bars is solidly British-based – old familiars such as tomato sauce, pickles, baked beans, peanut butter, marmalade, cornflakes and a marmitey spread called *Vegex*. Terrific-value English **breakfasts** are always on offer at the large hotels, suitable for vegetarians too. You can stuff yourself with fruit and fruit juice, cereal, eggs, bacon, sausages (and even steak sometimes), cheese, toast, scones and jam.

BUFFETS AND BARBECUES

If you skip breakfast and want a big lunch, the larger hotels do **buffets** of equally good value, with huge spreads of salad, cold cuts and puddings. Although they may appear at first sight to be expensive, you'll probably eat enough to last you the rest of the day. Among all this, you'll still find enough to eat if you're a vegetarian, and some places will give you a discount if you're not eating meat.

Barbecues – *braaivleis* – are an integral part of the social scene in Southern Africa. The centre of attraction is a slab of steak to gorge on and *boerewors*, a delicious spicy sausage of Afrikaans origin. A pot of *sadza* may well be on offer as an accompaniment at these occasions.

Every camping site in the country will have a place to cook outdoors and "**braai**" your meat.

The other meat speciality to try is **biltong** – sun-dried, salted meat cut into strips. It can be made from beef or, much tastier, from game, and is available from most butchers, or from supermarkets. *Biltong* is an invaluable camping food, but you can't always get it during the summer months when the sun is too hot for proper curing of the meat. **Game** meat – including crocodile tail, shoulder of impala, and warthog – is on offer at some of the expensive hotels.

FISH

Fish and **seafood** is generally an imported luxury in Zimbabwe, but in the Eastern Highlands there's excellent fresh trout and at Lake Kariba, bream. You won't find tinned fish or much fresh fish in supermarkets, but instead large packets of **kapenta** – tiny dried fish from Kariba. *Kapenta* has a strong taste and is eaten mainly by low-income families, but it's also served as a tasty snack at the Kariba hotels.

FRUIT AND VEGETABLES

Although Zimbabwe has no distinctive cuisine, the range of **fruit** and **vegetables** is special. Interesting vegetables to try include members of the marrow variety – gem squash, butternut and pumpkin. Avocados are plentiful, cheap and delicious.

Recommended fruits include guavas, paw-paws (papaya), lady-finger bananas and mangos. At markets you'll also see unfamiliar wild fruit, often delicious – but ask to sample before buying.

EATING IN BOTSWANA

Botswana, like its neighbour, has no great national dishes. Meat is cheap and plentiful and the range of foodstuffs – all imported from South Africa – is superior to that in Zimbabwe.

Botswana lacks good fruit and vegetables as it's too dry and sandy for most things to grow. In the big towns you'll find adequate imported fruit and vegetables in supermarkets, but nothing in rural areas. Rural desert-dwellers get their vitamins and minerals from a vast array of **wild food**. Some drought-resistant crops are cultivated too. Sadly, fewer and fewer people have the kind of knowledge necessary to gather wild food and the combination of overgrazing and

drought has decimated the vegetation. Moreover, there's a social stigma attached to eating roots – considered food for only the poorest of the poor.

Sorghum porridge, **mabele**, eaten with some kind of relish, has always been the staple food in Botswana, but it has now been largely replaced by white maize meal. Made into a stiff porridge, maize porridge is often called by the Afrikaans name *mielie-pap* (similar to *sadza* in Zimbabwe). Maize doesn't grow well in much of Botswana, but packets of meal are available cheaply in shops throughout the country. In dry areas people grow drought-resistant melons and beans, millet, gourds and groundnuts (peanuts). What you will find by the tubfull at markets is **madila**, a thickened form of sour milk drunk on its own or as a relish.

DRINKING

Alcohol – mainly **beer** – is cheap and consumed in large quantities in both Zimbabwe and Botswana. Beer comes as lager, pilsener or *chibuku*. In Zimbabwe, all that distinguishes the locally brewed lagers is brand name: *Castle, Lion, Black Label,* or the more expensive *Zambezi* and *Bohlinger.* Beer is always ordered by name brand, as loyalty is strong. Lager is served ice-cold; you won't find warm British bitter.

It takes a bit of courage to drink **chibuku** – a thick mixture more like porridge than lager, served in large containers. It's not available in hotels or bars, but only in working-class beer halls and beer gardens. Finely atmospheric focal points of social life as they are, the beer halls are not, however, recommended for women alone.

The ceremonial brewing and drinking of beer is an integral part of African life, for occasions ranging from marking a rite of passage to getting a new job. Even beer drunk at urban gardens is drunk ritualistically as the bucket-sized mugs are passed from one person to the next, or momentarily set down while people talk or exchange greetings. Night-time drinking happens in small shebeens in the high-density areas. You'd need to be invited to one of these, firstly to find it, and secondly to feel at all comfortable once you're in.

WINE

Zimbabwe produces its own **wine**, a product that is improving all the time. Even up to the early 1990s Zimbabweans were quick to joke about the local product, describing it variously as paint stripper or rat poison. Those days are gone and Zimbabweans will now proudly tell you that the country's wines consistently win bronze and silver medals – although no gold to date – at international competitions. The most serious competition, however, comes from South Africa. The easing of import restrictions has brought good Cape wines onto Zimbabwe's supermarket and bottle store shelves – and in large quantities. You may even find there's nothing else available in some restaurants, which is a great pity.

Among Zimbabwean **whites**, look out for Mukuyu Bin 16 and Meadows Estate Chenin Blanc. Awardwinning **reds** include bottles with the Meadows Estate label and those from Private Cellar, whose Cordon Rouge wins medals year after year. Other reds worth sampling include Private Cellar Cabernet Merlot and Cabernet Sauvignon as well as Mukuyu Renaissance. Of course the best way to find out about Zimbabwean wines is to try them – and at local prices, you can afford to.

SOFT DRINKS

Extremely cheap non-alcoholic drinks include Coca-Cola and also one of Zimbabwe's best products, Mazoe orange and lime squashes, which retain the gorgeous flavour of the fruit – not sickly sweet or chemical ridden. Zimbabwe has several varieties of bottled water – both still and sparkling – mostly from springs in the Eastern Highlands.

One iced soft drink speciality in both countries is the **rock shandy**, a mix of lemonade, soda water and Angostura bitters with ice and a slice of lemon. In Zimbabwe, Malawi shandies are a slightly sweeter alternative which replaces the lemonade with ginger beer. If you're offered a "Zambezi cocktail", refuse politely unless you

want water – a little local joke. In Botswana, a traditional non-alcoholic drink available in shops is *mageu*, made from both grain and fruit.

CAMPING FOODS

Zimbabwe has a limited range of **lightweight food**. If you're doing some serious hiking you'll probably manage on local goods, but it's worth considering bringing the odd packet with you. Locally, maize meal is extremely cheap and you can make either a thin porridge in the morning, or clods of *sadza* as part of a main meal. Other lightweight food includes dried milk, *Pronutro* breakfast food (a nutritionally balanced, and not unpalatable, concoction developed in South Africa), crispbread, *biltong*, packeted soup, groundnuts and dried slices of mango. Cheese is always available, as are tinned meat and beans, suitable fruit and vegetables, brown rice and pretty awful pasta.

Botswana has lots of (South African) imports on offer. Soya mince in various guises, on sale under the name of *Toppers*, makes an excellent fall-back, and there's always a good choice of tins, snacks and processed cheese triangles, all of which keep well. With rye bread, good crisp bread, tomato purée, pickled fish or tuna, dried fruit and just about anything else you could conceivably need, you're in no danger of facing starvation.

If you're four-wheel-driving and camping, fresh produce which keeps includes potatoes, cabbages, onions, carrots, oranges and lemons. Buy oil and vinegar in screw-top containers, rather than tops which can pop off from the pressure and bumping around. Dust gets in everywhere, so packet food such as dried milk or sugar should be decanted into screw-top containers. Keep a day or two's worth of food at hand in a separate, easy-to-reach box, and leave the rest in a food trunk.

PHOTOGRAPHY

Zimbabwe and Botswana are immensely photogenic and with any kind of camera, you can get beautiful pictures. What kind of camera you take depends on how much weight you're prepared to carry, how much like a tourist you want to look, and whether you want to photograph animals.

Small, compact cameras are great because you can keep them unobtrusively in your pocket and whip them out for a quick shot. But they're hopeless for wildlife – a nearby lion will end up a furry speck in savannah. Compacts can also be potentially dangerous – tales abound of tourists with little cameras sneaking up too close for comfort to big game and ending up in very sticky predicaments.

If you take your photography seriously, you'll probably want a single-lens reflex camera (SLR) and two or three lenses – a heavy and cumbersome option. For decent wildlife photography you definitely need a **telephoto lens**. A 300-mm lens is a good all-rounder; any bigger and you'll need a tripod. The smallest you could get away with for animals is 200mm, while 400mm is the best for birds. All long lenses need fast film, or you'll find you're restricted to the largest apertures, and hence the narrowest depth of focus. If you simply want good snaps from your SLR, think about one well-chosen zoom lens.

PROTECTION

The biggest problem in Botswana is **dust**, which will penetrate straight into a normal camera case or cloth bag. Cameras need to be inside sealed plastic bags, or in some dustproof container, and got out only for the business of taking pictures. You'll need to carry a blower-brush to blow dust off lenses.

Another problem – in both countries – is the heat. Never leave your camera or films lying in the sun. The film in a camera left exposed on a car seat, for instance, will be completely ruined. Keep rolls of film cool in the middle of your clothes or sleeping bag.

LIGHT READINGS

You really have to rely on a judicious combination of the camera's light readings and your own common sense. The contrast between light and shade can be huge, so expose for the subject and not the general scene. This can mean setting your camera to manual, approaching the subject to get a reading and then using that. With a zoom you can zoom in for a reading and then return. Some of the new multi-mode cameras will do much of this for you.

If you're photographing black people, especially in strong light, use more exposure than usual, otherwise they'll be underexposed; the light and your eyes (which are more sophisticated than any camera) can deceive you.

Early morning and late afternoon are the best times for photography. At midday, with the sun overhead, the light is flat and everything is lost in glare.

FILM

Film is readily available in both countries. Don't let anyone tell you it's unnecessary to have fast film because the sun is so bright in Africa. Even if you opt for a compact with a fast lens (ie one that's very light-sensitive) you'll need at least some 400 ASA film if you want to take pictures at dawn and dusk and in heavy cloud or forest. With long lenses on an SLR, fast film is essential. Also bring spare batteries as these can be impossible to replace.

SUBJECTS AND PEOPLE

As for subjects, **animal photography** is a question of patience and resisting taking endless pictures of nothing happening. If you can't get close enough, don't waste your film. While taking photos, try keeping both eyes open and, in a vehicle, always turn off your engine.

You should always ask before taking **photographs of people** or, for example, of a dwelling decorated with colourful paintings. Some kind of interaction and exchange is customarily implied; people often ask for a copy of the photograph and you'll end up with several names and addresses and a list of promises. In Botswana, desert-dwellers and Herero women appreciate and indeed expect a couple of pula; it's no good trying to bargain them down.

On the issue of **sensitivity**, don't take photographs of anything that could be construed as strategic. This includes any kind of military or police building, prisons, airports, bridges, dignitaries and anyone in uniform, as well as in refugee camps such as Dukwe.

TRAVELLING IN DEEPLY RURAL AREAS

Out in the wilds, you will need to tune into local sensitivities – and avoid some obvious pitfalls. You'll undoubtedly commit some unwitting faux pas but people are tolerant if they can see you're making an effort and are commonly too polite anyway to point out the error of your ways. Always remember that you are the stranger.

BEHAVIOUR

You should always ask before helping yourself to borehole or tap-water in rural areas – travellers are never refused. And if you come across a breakdown on a remote road, the form is to stop and offer assistance – yours may be the first vehicle in a week.

Women are expected to be modest, so wearing shorts, or short skirts, away from tourist areas is not a good idea. Nor is the display of affection in public. Gobbling your food and/or failing to share it with others present is not acceptable.

If you're travelling alone, people may find it very odd that you do so by choice, as being alone is regarded as a great affliction by many rural people. There's also common surprise and deep regret and condolences if you're the right age but haven't had any children.

GETTING INFORMATION

If you want reliable information, the way you frame questions is vitally important. People generally dislike disappointing a visitor, so when you ask "Is it far?" you will invariably hear "Oh no, not far at all." So, if you don't wan't to go astray, don't ask leading questions. It's better to ask "How long does it take you on foot/by bicycle?" By the same token, don't ask distances. The need to know specific numbers of kilometres or miles is rarely uppermost in people's minds in Africa.

Lastly, when asking about road conditions in remote parts of Botswana or Zimbabwe ask "How long ago has a car/bicycle passed here?", and not "Is this road passable?" It may be passable for cattle and people but not for cars.

CAMPING IN THE BUSH

Camping in the bush throughout **Botswana**, you'll find that people won't be suspicious and will be easy about you setting up camp in the middle of nowhere, although it is always polite to ask permission from the local chief if you're near a settlement.

In **Zimbabwe**, the situation is somewhat different. Land distribution patterns haven't yet changed significantly from colonial days. Generally the best land is fenced off in the hands of private farmers and the rest is called "communal land" (formerly "tribal trust lands"), with large numbers of peasant farmers.

Little more than a decade ago, rural people in the communal lands were in the midst of bitter and bloody conflict. The only whites in these areas at the time were those connected with the army, the government or missions. Today, while there are aid workers about, you still don't find people holidaying in the communal lands and there's certainly nothing in the way of camping sites or tourist facilities.

This is not to say that Zimbabwe's communal lands are off limits: you could have a fascinating and rewarding time in rural areas, where you'll find people terrifically friendly. You could ask for lodgings in a village hut, or stay in former district commissioner's or government official's accommodation in some of the bigger settlements. But do make yourself known to the district administrator so as to avoid arousing any concern or suspicion at your unusual behaviour.

WILDLIFE AND NATIONAL PARKS

With its progressive conservation policy and a budget to match – the biggest on the continent outside South Africa – Zimbabwe is rich in wildlife. You'll see herds of animals here that are heading for extinction elsewhere on the continent, and Zimbabwe's parks are literally trampled by elephants – a great conservation success. All the other herbivores you could want are also there: giraffes, zebras, buffaloes, hippos and many species of antelope (buck). Also represented is the whole range of African predators.

Conservation in Botswana is more *laissez-faire*, but it seems to have worked effectively thus far and you'll see many of the same animals as in Zimbabwe, including Africa's largest elephant herds – 67,000 strong – and several species not found across the border.

Photos and information for identification of the commonest larger mammals can be found in our colour wildlife section, with more detailed background in *Contexts*. For specific advice on safaris in Zimbabwe and Botswana, see p.13.

WILDLIFE

Between them, Zimbabwe and Botswana have among the world's finest and most diverse surviving cross-sections of **mammals**. If they exist in Southern Africa, these two countries are the likeliest places you'll see them. Of the 291 species recorded south of the Zambezi, most occur in Zimbabwe. Botswana, with its predominantly Kalahari sands habitat, contains a smaller and more specialized population – though a still impressive 140 species.

Large parts of the region remain untamed and you'll still find wildlife wandering beyond the unfenced confines of the national parks, though mostly only in rural areas. At Kariba, however, the **elephants** sometimes come into town to make a meal of trees growing in gardens, and around smaller towns, especially in the Zambezi and southern lowvelds, it's not uncommon to spot game – usually the odd antelope.

Antelope are the commonest species and the prolific impala are likely to become a very familiar sight. Other common herbivores that you're bound to come across if you spend any time at all in the national parks include zebra, giraffe, hippo and buffalo. Species mostly restricted to Botswana include gemsbok, sitatunga and red lechwe.

Wherever you find grazers and browsers, **predators** aren't far behind. The big cats are there as well as smaller and lesser-known felines such as the caracal and black-footed cat, but are only found far from human habitation. Night brings out a different cast and any operator taking game drives will have a spotlight to reveal hyenas, spring hares and – if you're lucky – porcupines, pangolins and leopards.

SMALLER CREATURES

In the smaller range, **spiders** and **scorpions** will do their best to get away from you, while the butterflies are all you could hope for. **Lizards** are common, often beautifully coloured and completely harmless, as are the prehistoric-looking chameleons, which are found absolutely everywhere, even in suburban gardens. And don't be disturbed if you see small gravity-defying reptiles running across the ceiling: they're insect-eating geckos (whose adhesive toes allow the acrobatics) and should be encouraged.

BIRDLIFE

With their diverse habitats, Botswana and Zimbabwe are home to a marvellous range of **birds** – a great attraction to ornithologists from all over. From exquisite, hovering sunbirds to huge land-bound ostriches, there are over 600 species in Zimbabwe alone, many of which are detailed in their relevant habitats throughout this book.

ZIMBABWE'S PARKS

Zimbabwe's national parks, administered by the Department of National Parks and Wildlife Management, are sanctuaries free of human settlement, except of course for tourist lodges and campsites. Of the eleven national parks, seven are primarily game reserves, the remainder being areas of outstanding natural beauty.

The game parks are: **Gonarezhou**, **Chizarira**, **Kazuma Pan**, **Mana Pools**, **Matusadona**, **Hwange** and **Zambezi**. Other areas have been designated as of unique cultural or scenic importance: **Chimanimani** (montane vegetation), **Matobo** (granite rock formations and rock art), **Nyanga** (scenery and grasslands) and **Victoria Falls** (the Falls themselves).

Game reserves are unfenced and animals are free to come and go, but they rarely venture into areas of human habitation. Reserves frequently abut on hunting areas, which tend to prevent animals wandering into rural farmland. In any case, animals tend to shy away from land occupied by people and domestic stock.

If you're **camping out** in a national park, there's little to fear from animals so long as you take a common-sense attitude. Safety hints are given on p.118. Rogue elephants and man-eating lions aren't serious dangers you need to worry about. Wildlife shies away from people and accidents invariably result from reckless human behaviour that threatens animals – rather than vice versa.

Entrance fees for the game reserves, paid at the reception office when you arrive, are standardized (and payable in local currency) at about US$2 per day for adults and half that for under-sixteens; one-week unlimited entrance is approximately US$5 for adults. For long stays, the Department of National Parks will quote an annual rate giving unlimited entrance for each park. Unless you've prebooked **accommodation**, that too can be arranged, if available, at reception on arrival, as can camping (US$2 per tent per night).

The parks and reserves are all open to private visits. With one or two notable and very exclusive exceptions, there is virtually no private accommodation within the national parks, but accommodation and facilities provided by the Department of National Parks are excellent by any standard – and very cheap.

Apart from Hwange – the most accessible of the game parks and serviced by reasonably priced game-viewing minibuses – the reserves are negotiable only in private cars or by going on organized safaris or game drives. Transport options for each park are outlined in the relevant chapters.

BOTSWANA'S PARKS

Botswana's national parks are far wilder than Zimbabwe's – and far less well maintained. There are few facilities laid on for self-caterers – a handful of campsites with makeshift showers and cold running water – but most of these are in a poor state. These public campsites, however, are not to be confused with what are called camps, or sometimes lodges. These camps, the only organized accommodation in the parks, are expensive and very comfortable with laid-on game drives and activities – all very much in line with Botswana's policy of "low-density high-cost" tourism.

This upmarket approach led the government to impose **hefty park entrance fees** in 1989 to discourage self-catering travellers (South Africans in particular), who bring their own supplies from outside the country and spend little or nothing during their visit. The wisdom of the policy is hotly debated in Botswana, but as long as it stands it means daily entrance fees of P50 per person in most parks, or P30 if you're staying in one of the lodges or on a licensed safari. There are additional fees for vehicles (foreign reg P10 per day, Botswana reg P2 per day) and for camping (self-catering P20 per person per night, through a licensed operator P10). Entrance and camping fees for children are half-price, and all charges for Botswana residents and citizens are a fraction of the cost.

This means that if you want to make your own way, camping in the national parks, it will cost a minimum of P70 per day per person. On the upside, because Botswana's small population (just over a million) is concentrated along its eastern flank, most of the country is very wild. A massive 35 percent of the country is unfenced wilderness, roamed by game. Outside the national parks, therefore, you'll still see wildlife, and while you won't get into the heart of Botswana's two prime game areas – **Moremi Wildlife Reserve** in the Okavango Delta and **Chobe Game Reserve** – without paying, you can still have a terrific time around the edges. With a 4WD vehicle and good supplies of food and water you could camp rough and have an unparalleled wilderness adventure. How and where to do this is covered in Chapters Eight, Nine and Ten.

PART TWO

ZIMBABWE

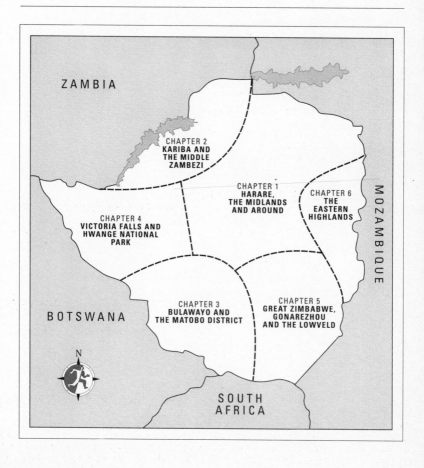

Introduction

In its second decade of independence, Zimbabwe is waking to the potential of tourism. Its natural assets – abundant wildlife and beautiful scenery – are now supplemented by a growing tourism infrastructure. Whether you're after a classic African safari or something more piquant – whitewater rafting, canoeing or tracking African wildlife with a professional guide – you won't find a better choice anywhere on the continent. Which is not to say the country is overrun by visitors – it's still possible to find solitude and wild places.

Despite post-Independence economic problems, Zimbabwe continues to develop its infrastructure, with well-maintained roads and a reliable, inexpensive transport network of buses, trains, coaches and planes. If you're travelling independently, you'll find Zimbabwe an easy and rewarding country, providing one of the friendliest African experiences.

Nevertheless, the country does not necessarily key with images of "unchanging Africa". For while Zimbabwe's beautiful wilderness and game areas feel thoroughly African, in other respects the marks of **colonialism** are deeply etched. Even in remote rural areas traditional costume has all but disappeared and the city suburbs retain those British niceties of milk, postal and newspaper deliveries. Things are changing, though, and in the towns most hotels have replaced tinkling pianos with the energetic guitars of Zimbabwe pop.

For a small nation, Zimbabwe has a generous share of **traditional cultural sights**, from the **rock art** of long-gone hunter-gatherers to the ruined stone palaces of past Shona rulers – most notably **Great Zimbabwe** itself. And on a contemporary level, if you look beyond the airport art of the curio shops, you'll find one of the most vibrant movements in modern African **sculpture**.

■ Physical geography

Physically, Zimbabwe is divided by the central **highveld** plateau, which is covered by massive granite outcrops called **kopjes** (pronounced like "copies"). Because of its malaria-free, moderate climate and prime lands, the highveld became the white-dominated political and economic hub of Rhodesia. Rising from the plateau for 350km

along the Mozambique border are the **Eastern Highlands**, peaking at 2400m in the narrow belt of the **Nyanga and Chimanimani Mountains**. The colonial carve-up of Rhodesia has left the country's richest farms and all the large towns and cities above 1200m, on the highveld.

To the north and south, the plateau falls away through the intermediate **middleveld plateaus**, lying between 900m and 1200m, to the **lowveld** regions. A further 600m below the northern lowveld is a narrow strip in the **Zambezi Valley** and a broader tract to the south, between the **Limpopo and Save rivers**. These two sections share a similar climate and vegetation, quite distinct from that of the highveld – lower rainfall and hotter. On Zimbabwe's dry western flank, the tree **savannah** of the **Hwange area** drifts across the border to merge with the Kalahari sands of Botswana.

■ Where to go

Obviously, your own personal interests – and time – will dictate where you travel. If you just have a couple of weeks to spare, then the major attractions must include **Lake Kariba**, with its boating and game viewing; **Hwange National Park**, the country's largest game reserve; the **Victoria Falls**; and the stone ruins at **Great Zimbabwe**. All are easily accessible on local transport, or you can make life easy with cheap flight packages or air tours that drop you down at hotels and take you to the sights.

Away from these brochure highlights, Zimbabwe has miles of untramelled country to offer, some easily reached and some remote. For **hikers**, the 350-kilometre strip of the **Eastern Highlands** provides dramatic and varied countryside in the shadow of Zimbabwe's highest peak, 2592-metre **Mount Nyangani**. The **Matobo Hills**, near Bulawayo, in the south, combine limitless walks through beautiful **granite hills** with one of the world's highest concentrations of ancient **rock paintings**. The finest national parks for face-to-face **game viewing** are **Mana Pools** and **Chizarira** in the north.

In the cities, lively sounds blasting out from street corners and small shops immediately confirm Zimbabwe's reputation for **music**. At nightclubs you'll certainly have a chance to hear some of the big names that form the country's number one cultural export. Music aside, the **cities** are enjoyable simply to stroll about, taking in markets, parks, beer gardens, street life and local style.

Languages and religion

Nearly seventy percent of Zimbabweans are mother-tongue Shona-speakers, spread across most of the country and beyond its borders, while Ndebele is the first language of fifteen percent, living around Bulawayo and the Matabeleland area of the southwest. Both are official languages, as is English – the most widely used language in Zimbabwe.

English is the language of the media, shop and street signs. You will need nothing else to book a room, eat out, make travel arrangements or ask directions – there's hardly anywhere in the country where you won't find someone who speaks it and particularly in the cities people speak it fluently.

Even between blacks, you'll hear English spoken – sometimes simply as a lingua franca, but also as a status symbol, especially among the middle class. In the city streets you may also hear a style of banter that lurches back and forth between English and Shona or Ndebele.

Although attempts to speak Ndebele or Shona as a means of communication may be more or less redundant, don't be put off trying – a symbolic attempt to greet people in their mother tongue is much appreciated, although also an invitation for you to be jokingly tested to the limits of your ability. Just mastering the greetings will open up channels of communication and assure friendly responses.

Ndebele

As a young language derived from Zulu within the last 170 years, **Ndebele** is fairly homogenous and closely related to its ancestral roots. When Mzilikazi (founder of the Ndebele) fled north from Zululand in the 1820s he forged a new state from his core of followers and Sotho, Pedi, Tswana and other elements that he collected on his way. Ndebele and Zulu, one of South Africa's most widely spoken languages, are mutually understandable – about 95 percent of the languages remains common.

Shona

Shona is a relatively ancient language which has had many centuries on the plateau to diversify into six main dialects, which are divided into over thirty minor ones. Of the major dialects, **Zezuru**, spoken in central Zimbabwe, has assumed the status of a prestige form because it's spoken in Harare and on the radio.

As a magnet for people from all over the country, Harare has become a linguistic melting pot, where a new Shona form, known as "Town Shona" or "ChiHarare", has begun to develop. Characteristics include borrowings from English and an informality, particularly in the disappearance of pronoun forms to denote respect.

Chilapalapa

Finally, it's worth mentioning **Chilapalapa**, a pidgin English/Ndebele that evolved so whites could give orders to their black workers. It has no proper grammar – all verbs exist only in the imperative form – and has now become a very unfashionable symbol of exploitation. It is nevertheless still used by some white households, and on farms.

■ Religion

Despite unfounded pre-Independence fears that "Marxist ZANU" would ban religion and abolish Christmas, Zimbabwe remains a predominantly Christian country – with a strong undercurrent of traditional religion. Spirit mediums are consulted to make contact with the ancestors, who are still important. Probably because it incorporated indigenous beliefs, **Catholicism** is the biggest church with nearly a million adherents. There's also a plethora of **African churches**, like the 300,000-strong **Zimbabwe Assemblies of God** denomination, which became independent in 1960 and now spreads throughout central Africa. Others, like the **Vapostori** sects, arose spontaneously in Zimbabwe and have their own practices and martyrs. The Mazowe Vapostori believe that their founder, Shoniwa, died and was resurrected as John of the Wilderness. You could well come across the characteristic services of these sects, held outdoors in remote places. There are also small **Hindu**, **Muslim** and **Jewish** communities, based almost exclusively in the urban centres.

SHONA AND NDEBELE WORDS AND PHRASES

GREETINGS AND RESPONSES

Greetings are very important in both Shona and Ndebele society. They can also get quite complicated. The following greetings will be appropriate for most situations you'll encounter, and are the ones to use when you first meet someone or pass them on the road. Other greetings exist for use between people who know each other. When you approach someone's homestead or yard it's polite to wait outside until you're invited in.

	SHONA	NDEBELE
A: Hello (sing.)	*Mhoro*	*Sawubona*
Hello (pl.)	*Mhoroi*	*Salibonani*
B: Hello (reply)	*Ehoi*	*Yebo*
A: How are you?	*Makadii/Makadini?*	*Unjani (sing.)/Linjani (pl.)?*
B: Fine, and you?	*Tiripo makadiiwo?*	*Sikhona, unjani wena?*
A: Fine	*Tiripo*	*Sikhona*
Good morning	*Mangwanani*	*Livuke njani*
Good afternoon	*Masikati*	*Litshonile*
Good evening	*Manheru*	*Litshone njani*
Thank you	*Ndatenda/Masvita*	*Siyabonga kakulu*
Come in/forward	*Tiswikevo*	*Ekuhle!*

AFTER GREETING

What's your name?	*Munonzi ani?*	*Ubani ibizo lakho?*
I am Tony	*Ndini Tony*	*Elami igama ngingu (pronounced "nyingu") Tony*
Pleased to meet you	*Ndinofara ku-ku-ziva-i*	*Ngiya thaba ukukwazi*
Where are you from?	*Munobva kupi?*	*Uvelaphi?*
I'm from Britain/ US/Germany	*Ndinobva kuBritain/ kuAmerica/kuGermany*	*Ngivela e Bilithani/ Melika/Jelimana*

SAYING GOODBYE

Stay well (Person leaving)	*Chisarai*	*U/Lisale kuhle*
Go well (Person staying)	*Fambai zvakanaka*	*Uhambe kuhle (sing.)/ Nihambe kuhle (pl.)*
See you	*Tichaonana*	*Sizalibona njalo*

TRAVEL

Where is the bus stop?	*Chiteshi chiri kupi?*	*Singaphi isiteshi samabhasi?*
When does the bus leave?	*Bhazi richaenda rihni?*	*Izawuhamba nini ibhasi?*
Is there a bus to Bulawayo today?	*Nhasi pane bhazi ririkuenda kuBulawayo here?*	*Kunebhasi leya KaBulawayo lamuhla?*
Does this bus go to Harare?	*Bhazi iri rinoenda kuHarare here?*	*Lebhasi iyaya yini e-Harare?*
Where's the road to Binga?	*Mugwagwa unoenda kuBinga uri kupi?*	*Uphi umgwaco loya e-Binga?*
Road	*Mugwagwa*	*Mugwaco*
Car	*Motokari*	*Imoto*
Train	*Chitima*	*Isitimela*
Station/bus stop	*Chiteshi*	*Isiteshi*
Go on foot	*Ku-enda netsoka*	*Hamba ngonya wo*

SHOPPING

Where's the market?	*Musika uri kupi?*	*Ikuphi imakethe?*
Have you got . . .?	*Mune . . . here?*	*Une . . . yini?*
I'd like . . . please	*Ndipei/Wo*	*Ngicela*
How much is it?	*Imarii?*	*Yimalini?*

BASICS AND SIGNS

	SHONA	NDEBELE		SHONA	NDEBELE
Yes	Ehe	Yebo	When?	... rihni?	... nini?
No	Aiwa	Hayi	Where?	... kupi?	... ngaphi?
Thank you	Tatenda/ masviita	Siyabonga	Now	Zvino	Khathesi
			Today	Nhasi	Lamuhla
Thank you (after a meal)	Taguta		Tomorrow	Mangwana	Kusasa
			Yesterday	Nezuro	Izolo
Please	Ndapota	Uxolo	DANGER	NGOZI	INGOZI
Good/nice!	Zvakanaka!	Kuhle	MEN	VARUME	AMADODA
Sorry	Ndine urombo	Ncesi	WOMEN	VAKADZI	ABAFAZI

FOOD

Fruit	Michero	Izithelo	Vegetables		
			Potatoes	Mbatatisi	Amagwili
Orange	Ranjisi	Ama-orintshi	Tomatoes	Matomasi	Utamatisi
Peanuts	Nzungu	Ama-zambane	Leaves/greens	Muriwo	Umbhido
Guava	Gwavha	Ama-gwava			
			Meat	Nyama	Inyama
			Meat of ...	Nyama ye ...	Inyama ye ...
Grains			chicken	huku	nkukhu
Stiff porridge	Sadza	Sadza	beef	mombe	nkomo
			goat	mbudzi	mbuzi
Maize	Chibage	Umbila	pork	nguruve	ngulube

Drinks			Miscellaneous		
Tea	Tii	Itiye	Bread	Chingwa	Sinkhwa
Coffee	Kofi	Ikofi	Salt	Munyu	Uswayi
Water	Mvura	Amanzi	Sugar	Shuga	Ushukela
Milk	Mukaka	Uchago	Honey	Uchi	Uju
Beer	Doro/hwahwa	Utshwala	Butter	Bhata	Ibatha
Fruit squash	Mazoe	Mazoe	Fish	Hove	Inhlanzi
			Eggs	Mazai	Amaqanda

In the UK, **classes in Shona and Zulu** (very close to Ndebele) are run regularly at the Centre for African Language Learning, Africa Centre, 38 King St, London WC2 (☎0171/240 1099).

Harald Vieth's **Shona phrasebook**, *Have a nice trip in Zimbabwe: a colloquial guide to Shona*, published by Mambo Press in Zimbabwe, is a useful start. Unfortunately no similar book exists for Ndebele.

PLACE NAMES

After Independence, many place names were changed. Some changes like Salisbury to Harare were substantial. Others were more subtle – orthographic adjustments and corrections of colonial mispronunciation. This can be confusing as some die-hards still insist on using the old names. These are the important ones you're likely to encounter:

NEW NAME	OLD NAME	NEW NAME	OLD NAME	NEW NAME	OLD NAME
Chimanimani	Melsetter	Harare	Salisbury	Mazowe	Mazoe
Chinoyi	Sinoia	Hwange	Wankie	Mutare	Umtali
Chipinge	Chipinga	Kadoma	Gatooma	Mvurwi	Umvukwees
Chivu	Enkeldoorn	Kwe Kwe	Que Que	Nyanga	Inyanga
Dete	Dett	Marondera	Marandellas	Shurugwi	Selukwe
Guruve	Sipolilo	Masvingo	Fort Victoria	Somabhula	Somabula
Gweru	Gwelo	Matobo	Matopos	Zvishavane	Shabani

Many **street names**, too, have been changed. The most important are detailed where relevant in the text.

Money and costs

Zimbabwe's currency is **Zimbabwe dollars (Z$ or ZWD)**, often styled *bucks*. Notes come in 2-, 5-, 10- and 20-dollar denominations and there are coins of 1, 5, 10, 20 and 50 cents and Z$1. At the time of writing the rate is around Z$8 to US$1, and Z$13 to £1.

■ Banks and exchange

Usual **bank opening hours** are Monday, Tuesday, Thursday and Friday 8am–3pm, Wednesday 8am–1pm, and Saturday 8–11am. The ongoing liberalization of the economy has led to the emergence of private **foreign exchange bureaux** at airports and in all the larger towns and resorts. These are usually quick and efficient and offer competitive rates. Out of hours, you can sometimes change money at hotel cashier's desks, particularly in larger establishments – but don't count on it if you're not staying there.

The days of strictly scrutinized currency declaration forms in Zimbabwe are thankfully over. You will, however, be asked on your arrival form to declare how much money you are bringing into the country to ascertain whether you can sustain yourself throughout your stay. Be sure to use up all your Z$ while in the country as it's virtually impossible to change them outside the country.

Judging by the number of hustlers around, the currency **black market** in Zimbabwe is flourishing, although it's difficult to see why. Black market trading is a serious offence, and the rates offered on the streets rarely make the risk worth it. In any case, the odds are that the dealer is running a scam, and you may find that the wad of notes offered in exchange for your hard currency is padded out with strips of newspaper.

■ Credit cards

Because sales tax (see box overleaf) is not levied on transactions settled in foreign currency, using a credit card for certain payments, such as car rental and making safari bookings, can save you money. The most useful credit cards are *Visa* and *Mastercard*, which can also be used to draw cash at Automatic Teller Machines (ATMs), found in the cities. *American Express*, however, is not all that widely accepted in Zimbabwe.

■ Costs

For visitors there are basically two economies in Zimbabwe: a tourist one linked to US dollars, which can be moderately to very expensive; and the local Zimbabwe dollar economy, which is relatively cheap for anyone with foreign currency (although not for Zimbabweans). What you spend will depend largely on how you navigate between the two. Staying in backpackers' lodges, self-catering or eating cheap snacks, you could scrape by on a basic US$10–15 a day. If you move up a notch and stay in medium-priced hotels, eating hotel breakfasts and, say, a pizza for lunch and a restaurant supper, expect to pay a basic US$30–45. At the top end, staying in exclusive game lodges where everything is included – from drinks and meals down to having your socks washed – will set you back upwards of US$150.

Transport is inexpensive. If you use economy buses rather than tourist-oriented alternatives you can cover large distances for a few dollars. Luxury coaches and train travel are more expensive but still quite reasonable. Car rental is a relatively expensive option but the only way of reaching some places. Travelling from Bulawayo to Victoria Falls, for example, expect to pay US$5 by economy bus, under US$10 by train (first or

---

A NOTE ON CURRENCY AND PRICES

Zimbabwe's currency has fluctuated wildly over the past five years. Meanwhile, Z$ prices have rocketed, making any attempt to give prices in local currency pointless. This has not, however, made the country much more expensive for foreign visitors. Despite the instability of the Z$, most prices, when translated into hard currency, have remained surprisingly constant. Many tourist facilities such as hotels and safaris now officially quote prices in US$, although other services such as car rental and transport are still officially quoted in Z$. In this book, for the sake of consistency, all Zimbabwean prices are quoted in a US dollar equivalent. (See also "Hotel and Safari Rates", p.40, for an explanation of Zimbabwe's three-tier pricing structure for hotels.)

Note also that, just before this book went to press, the government imposed a **two-percent levy on all overnight stays** in Zimbabwe, which will be reflected in increased accommodation and safari costs.

HOTEL AND SAFARI RATES

All Zimbabwe's hotels and safari lodges – though not backpacker lodges – are obliged to demand payment from foreign visitors in hard currency. You can pay either with travellers' cheques, foreign bank notes or by credit card.

To further complicate matters, most hotels and safari operators also charge a higher rate (usually quoted in US$) to visitors than to Zimbabwean nationals. They are not obliged by law to do so and there are signs the system will gradually be phased out. Even if you pay no more than a Zimbabwean, you do still have to pay it in forex.

Zimbabwe charges **sales tax** of around fifteen percent on many goods and services, including most tourist activities. The levy is already included in prices so you won't be aware of it most of the time. However, you can save the tax by booking before you leave home if you know you're going on safari. The same benefit can also be gained by paying in forex – foreign bank notes, travellers' cheques or with a credit card.

second class), US$20 by luxury coach, and twice that by air. By car it would total roughly US$55 (including fuel and assuming one-day rental) to cover the distance.

Accommodation is generally cheaper for two or more sharing, except in backpacker lodges where you can expect to pay US$3.50 per person in a dorm (about a dollar more if you share a double room). In larger towns, cheap doubles in hotels start at US$10, rising to a mid-range average of US$25, and peaking just short of US$100 for five-star luxury.

On safari, there's a huge gulf in cost between doing it yourself in National Parks accommodation or going for an all-in safari deal. Parks accommodation is excellent value but consequently often over-subscribed, starting at around US$5 per person sharing a self-catering chalet. Private hotels at national parks, such as *Hwange Safari Lodge*, charge around US$70 per person (B&B) – a premium for their proximity to the action not for their facilities. A typical bush camp or safari lodge in the thick of wildlife country will charge around US$200 per person, fully inclusive of meals, game activities (drives, walks or boat trips) and the on-hand expertise of one or more licensed game guides.

Food is cheap if you eat where the locals do and combine it with self-catering. You can easily eat a filling meal of *sadza* and chicken or meat for a couple of US dollars. Moving up a notch need not break the bank either. Breakfast at a Harare café can come out as low as US$2, or you can splash out for the works at one of the hotel breakfast buffets for little more than US$5. Light lunches like sandwiches and pizzas typically go for under US$3, while a main course such as fillet steak at a decent city restaurant shouldn't come to more than US$7.

Getting around

As elsewhere in Africa, patience is critical for getting around on public transport. Leave yourself plenty of time for journeys and be prepared for long waits if you take local buses or hitch. Trains are a bit erratic, sometimes arriving spot on time, sometimes hours late. Luxury coaches and air travel, on the other hand, are usually pretty reliable.

■ Buses and coaches

In the absence of a national bus system, the country is covered by a complex network of private, local bus companies, which are cheap and crowded. These **economy buses** run short routes as well as long hauls and while they're sometimes dilapidated, and irregular, they're also fun to travel in, even when they occasionally break down. Passengers are friendly and display remarkable stoicism on wearing journeys. There are also some new-style "articulated" buses, which are faster and less congested. If you've more money to spare, you can pay for more comfort on the **luxury coaches**, which operate along a few major routes.

Long-distance economy buses

Catching **economy buses** (still referred to by whites as "African buses") can be confusing. They're not geared to tourism, so clear information is thin on the ground. Several companies often ply the same route with no central coordination, and often you'll receive conflicting information about bus times. Ask around to build up a plausible picture of departure times.

The safest rule, however – certainly in smaller towns – is to **arrive early** at the bus station. Buses often leave at 6am and, although the 6am bus may be delayed for want of passengers until after 7am, it may also leave before schedule if there's heavy demand. Between the main cities an early start is less crucial as buses depart throughout the day.

Most centres have a **main bus station** – invariably adjoining the market. Cities have several: one for town services, one for the surrounding area, and another for long-distance routes. In most areas, the long-distance bus station is referred to as the **musika**, which means market (or in Bulawayo the *renkini*). The one for town or the immediate region is usually called the **terminus**. In rural areas the **bus stop** may be under a prominent tree with a hand-painted sign tacked onto the trunk.

Long-distance buses stop along the way. You can buy boiled eggs, cooked maize and beans, roasted peanuts, buns or local fruit through the window. Carry plenty of Z$2 and Z$5 notes, as change can be a problem. You can also get off to buy minerals, but it's advisable to carry an empty bottle to exchange against the deposit or the shopkeeper may be reluctant to let you take your drink away. Take a full water bottle – you'll need the liquid. Several hours' consumption of syrupy, tooth-stripping drinks can get a bit much.

A lot of travelling goes on at the **weekend**, especially towards the end of a month and around public holidays, most notably Christmas. Buses get jam-packed, so try to plan your journeys to avoid these times.

On all buses, most people are scrupulously honest, but it pays to watch your **baggage**. Especially during busy periods, **tsotsis** (crooks) prey on travellers, either picking pockets or stealing baggage from the roof-rack. Wherever possible travel light and take your luggage onto the bus, where you can keep an eye on it. Hefty packs are a distinct disadvantage in any case. There are no luggage racks inside and you may end up with your luggage on your lap if the bus is full, besides having to struggle past dozens of people.

Luxury Coaches

Luxury coaches run between main centres, stopping at important towns along the way. They are the most comfortable, reliable and fastest form of public transport, but cost twice as much as first-class rail travel.

Luxury coaches have a totally different ambience to the economy services. Efficiently run, they keep to an accurate timetable, have on-board refreshments and toilets, and make sched-uled stops for hotel teas; many pick up from one of the tourist hotels – easier to get to than local bus stations which are always some way from the centre. Between them, **Ajay**, **Translux**, and **Blue Arrow** run services Harare–Mutare, Harare–Bulawayo, Bulawayo–Victoria Falls, Harare–Victoria Falls and farther afield to Francistown in Botswana. There are also regular services from Harare to Blantyre in Malawi and to Johannesburg and Durban. It's usually possible to get a seat, though booking ahead is advisable (especially for an international run).

Town buses and commuter omnibuses

Municipal bus services operate in both high- and low-density suburbs in the larger towns: Harare, Bulawayo, Mutare and Masvingo. In the first two, though, buses are often full and infrequent, so expect to queue for a long time for a bus during rush hours. The problems of public transport in the cities have been considerably alleviated in recent years by privately run **commuter omnibuses** – commonly referred to as "commuters". These run up and down fixed routes at breakneck speed, providing a fast and relatively frequent alternative to municipal buses. On commuters there's an assistant who'll collect your fare during the journey; on ordinary buses you pay the driver when you board.

■ Trains

You'd have to be a jaded old cynic to pass up the opportunity to take the **train to Victoria Falls**, one of the world's great railway journeys. The two other routes, **Harare–Bulawayo** and **Harare–Mutare**, though by no means in the top league, also have a lot going for them.

Rail travel is a comfortable and laid-back way of getting around, particularly for couples cornering a *coupe* (small private compartment). As a couple, you need to go under the same name to fulfil notions of married respectability. On your own, you share a four- or six-berth (depending on which class you travel) single-sex compartment.

There's a **night service** on each of the three routes above, plus a day train between Harare and Bulawayo, which isn't recommended. Travelling overnight, your seat becomes a bunk, hence throwing in a night's accommodation for the fare. If you're keeping costs down, the berths are comfortable enough in a sleeping bag, but the inexpensive **bedding** offered on the train is well worth it for a night of freshly ironed sheets with plump feather

STEAM TRAINS

It's hard not to regard as eccentric a package that lists as attractions: supper in a dining car stabled at a steam depot, sleeping in a coach in the grounds of a railway museum, and travelling along the world's third longest stretch of straight track.

If, however, old locos steam you up, **Rail Safaris** offer the option of two weeks railing along Zimbabwe's tracks, passing nights among rolling stock in shunting yards and days making your acquaintance with Garratt locomotives. They also operate the more conventional six-day "Zambezi

Special" steam safari, aimed more at romantics than steamheads, and an overnight trip from Bulawayo to Victoria Falls, for which prices start at US$440, including lunch on the first day, a three-hour game drive in Hwange National Park followed by dinner, and breakfast on the second day.

In Zimbabwe you can book through *Rail Safaris*, 2c Prospect Ave, Raylton, Bulawayo (☎/fax 19/75575). **In Britain** contact *Leisurail*, PO Box 113, Peterborough PE3 8HY (☎01733/335599, fax 505451).

---

pillows and thick woollen blankets. Someone comes round once the train is moving to make up your bed. **Dinner** – meat and three veg style – and **drinks** are served on the Victoria Falls train. Don't expect linen tablecloths and silver service. It's all a bit cursory, but can be fun if you're not expecting too much. Take some snacks in case you're delayed in arriving as they don't do breakfast.

Reservations

To ensure a *coupe* you need to **book in advance**. The Bulawayo–Victoria Falls service costs around US$10 first class, US$8 second. Names and compartment numbers are posted up at the station an hour or two beforehand so you know where to board the train. First class has bigger compartments with wider and fewer beds and is much quieter. Second class is thoroughly acceptable, but can get a bit raucous, either from the level of partying, or the number of babies. Economy (third) class is best avoided; you sit upright all night with nowhere to stretch out.

If you want bedding on the train, buy your bedding voucher when you purchase your ticket at the station – it's a little cheaper and saves you the hassle of finding elusive ticket inspectors on the train.

■ Flights

Air Zimbabwe has efficient, regular and cheap flights between the main towns and to the big four tourist centres – Victoria Falls, Hwange, Kariba and Great Zimbabwe. The regular single fare between Harare and Bulawayo is roughly US$30. For US$130 you can get a return ticket from **Harare to Victoria Falls** which allows you to stop off at Hwange and Kariba at no extra cost

and for however long you like. If you travel on **stand-by** on some routes at the weekend, there are substantial reductions.

Flights are **bookable in advance** through *Air Zimbabwe*'s offices in the UK (☎0171/491 3783), in North America (☎1-800/742-3006), and in Australia (☎02/9267 3944). The main office in Harare is at Third St/Speke Ave (☎14/794481).

■ Taxis and ETs

Taxis and ETs (emergency taxis) run in most towns. **Taxis** are usually (but not exclusively) Renault 4s and will pick up any number of people for a single metered fare. They're moderately priced and are certainly worth using to get to nightspots outside city centres.

All official taxis are metered and there's little point in asking for an estimate before you leave – the drivers tend to make up a random underestimate. Few rides, however, should cost more than US$8 and most short trips in town will be closer to US$3. Illegal unlicensed taxis operate openly in spite of frequent fines, which they afford through higher fares. Licensed taxis are cheaper, but aren't always easy to find. The confusion is increased by the unlicensed taxis' practice of operating under remarkably similar names and logos to their legal counterparts. Amongst others in Harare you'll find *Rixi Taxis* (licensed) and *Trixi Taxis* (unlicensed).

ETs are larger, usually Peugeot 404s, and charge a fixed fare for a fixed route, usually leaving from a bus station. They set out only when they're bursting with passengers, which can mean an uncomfortable wait while people are gathered to shoehorn inside. They are quite difficult to use, because they're usually full and their routes require prior knowledge – but they

CAR RENTAL AGENCIES

BRITAIN
Hertz ☎0345/555888.
Avis ☎0181/848 8733.
Europcar ☎0345/222525.

USA AND CANADA
Hertz in the US ☎1-800/654-3001; in Canada ☎1-800/263-0600.
Avis ☎1-800/331-1084.

AUSTRALIA
Hertz, 10 Dorcas St, South Melbourne (local-call rate ☎13 1918).
Avis, Level 2, 15 Bourke Rd, Mascot, NSW (toll-free ☎1800/225533).

NEW ZEALAND
Hertz, 154 Victoria St West, Auckland (☎09/309 0989).
Avis, Building 4, 666 Great South Rd, Penrose, Auckland (☎09/525 1982).

are worth figuring out if you're staying in Harare or any of the big towns for a while.

■ Driving and car rental

Zimbabwe has comparatively little traffic and a well-maintained **tarred road network** covering most of the country. This combination makes for very pleasant driving. In a week – albeit a rather full one – you could hit most of the highlights, and in a fortnight you could do a full circuit of the country. Distances between towns aren't great: the 440km from Harare to Bulawayo takes four to five hours, for example, and it's three or four hours from the capital to the Eastern Highlands.

Car rental is expensive, with *Hertz*, *Avis* and *Europcar* the only operators with national networks. In Harare, however, you'll also find a substantial number of smaller companies offering competitive prices. In addition, other centres such as Victoria Falls and Bulawayo have their own cheaper independent firms. But be warned:

because their base is narrower, you may not get the same backup as with the big three.

If you know exactly when you'll want a car, it's also worth thinking about organizing rental in your home country before you leave – it can work out cheaper. Booking ahead, either from abroad or in Zimbabwe, is wise too at times of heavy demand.

Wherever you book, look through the **small print** before taking a vehicle. The collision damage waiver is usually invalid if you drive on unsurfaced roads. People do take the cars off track, but if anything goes wrong, the responsibility and expense are usually yours – check before you drive off.

Driving

Driving in this British ex-colony is on the left. Foreign driving **licences** are valid for up to 90 days, indefinitely if they're from the following countries: Botswana, Malawi, Namibia, South Africa, Swaziland or Zambia.

CAR RENTAL NETWORKS IN ZIMBABWE

(see listings for each town for addresses)

	Hertz	Avis	Europcar	Elite
Harare	✔	✔	✔	✔
Bulawayo	✔	✔	✔	✔
Victoria Falls	✔	✔		
Mutare	✔		✔	
Kariba	✔	✔		
Masvingo	✔			
Hwange	✔			
Chiredzi	✔			

Zimbabwe Distance Chart

Distances shown are in kilometres

	Beit Bridge	Bindura	Bulawayo	Chimanimani	Chinhoyi	Chipinga	Chiredzi	Chirundu	Chivhu	Gwanda	Gweru	Harare	Hwange	Kadoma	Kariba	Kwekwe	Marondera	Masvingo	Mhangura	Mutare	Mvuma	Mvurwi	Nyamapanda	Nyanga	Plumtree	Rusape
Bindura	670																									
Bulawayo	320	525																								
Chimanimani	545	500	565																							
Chinhoyi	695	205	430	530																						
Chipinga	505	530	520	555	70																					
Chiredzi	300	580	485	605	255	210																				
Chirundu	930	440	660	235	765	790	840																			
Chivhu	440	230	300	255	430	385	350	490																		
Gwanda	195	660	125	580	760	515	365	815	430																	
Gweru	470	360	165	460	260	860	135	500	480	320																
Harare	580	90	440	415	115	440	490	350	140	570	275															
Hwange	655	860	335	900	760	855	820	995	630	460	500	770														
Kadoma	605	230	300	555	130	550	515	365	265	450	135	140	630													
Kariba	950	460	780	300	255	810	860	135	510	835	515	370	1015	380												
Kwekwe	535	300	150	520	200	480	440	315	195	380	60	210	560	70	355											
Marondera	655	165	510	340	190	365	505	425	215	645	350	75	845	215	445	290										
Masvingo	290	380	280	405	405	235	200	640	150	280	180	290	620	315	660	245	365									
Mhangura	765	220	500	625	70	675	260	325	335	650	335	185	830	200	275	270	260	480								
Mutare	585	350	580	175	315	615	400	575	245	480	265	915	405	630	475	190	295	450	100							
Mvuma	390	245	380	310	335	235	545	50	375	280	80	190	580	145	560	145	265	100	455	395						
Mvurwi	680	110	525	540	100	590	385	240	150	670	375	100	875	245	350	315	175	390	110	365	295					
Nyamapanda	825	335	680	725	360	735	815	385	325	815	520	245	1015	385	615	460	320	535	430	510	430	435				
Nyanga	690	360	685	280	385	420	680	410	410	680	540	270	1020	410	640	480	195	400	455	100	455	500	370			
Plumtree	420	625	100	525	585	620	760	395	395	225	265	540	435	400	780	325	610	385	600	680	345	625	625	780		
Rusape	680	260	610	285	270	410	520	310	310	670	445	170	1000	310	540	385	95	390	360	95	390	270	435	350	705	
Victoria Falls	760	965	440	1000	865	960	920	1100	735	565	600	875	105	735	1120	665	950	725	935	1020	685	685	965	1145	1045	540

Petrol is easily available in all the towns, but because of the long distances between them, be sure to fill up whenever you can. **Strip roads** – narrow tarred tracks wide enough for only one vehicle – can take some getting used to. They tend to be found only in more remote areas, although you occasionally encounter them near towns. Approaching on-coming traffic, you're supposed to pull off the road with only your right-hand tyres on the tar and your left on the dirt hard shoulder, which feels decidedly hair-raising at first.

A few **words of warning**: because cars are often in poor condition, lights and brakes don't always work well. People tend also to drink and drive as a matter of course. So, always drive defensively and never rely on the good sense of other motorists.

■ Hitching

Hitching is easy and generally safe. People aren't afraid to pick up hitchers and they will often go out of their way to be helpful.

There are two types of hitching: either with middle-class people, where payment is not in question, or with people who pick up hitchers to help pay for the journey. "**Paying rides**" may well be obvious, because you'll be with fellow passengers in the back of a pick-up for instance, or not so obvious if it's just you in an ordinary car. In the latter case enquire if you can make a contribution. Payments never exceed the equivalent of local bus fares, so it's always affordable.

Leaving Bulawayo and Harare, it's easiest to catch a bus or taxi to the outskirts and wait on the main road.

■ Cycling

Zimbabwe is great for **cycling** if you have the stamina. Roads are generally in good shape and tarred, and in cities bikes are ideal as there are cycle tracks everywhere alongside the streets. The distances between towns are long, but there are small settlements en route where you can stop at rural stores for a rest and a drink. Zimbabwe's stable inland climate means strong wind isn't a problem, but cycling is nicest during the dry, cool months. Bicycles can easily be transported on top of local buses or on trains if you need a break.

The big drawback however is that a whole range of bicycle **spares** are not readily available. If you've brought a **mountain bike** with you, pack any spares you think you might need. **Bike**

rental is possible at Victoria Falls, in Bulawayo and Harare.

Accommodation

Finding places to stay in Zimbabwe should rarely pose problems. There's a wide variety of good accommodation across a broad price range – from under US$5 for a bed in a backpackers' lodge to US$100 per person and more for sheer luxury in Harare's international hotels and safari lodges. And if you're on the lowest of budgets you can rely on campsites throughout the country.

■ Hotels

There are few very cheap **hotels** in Zimbabwe but, considering the generally high (and frequently luxurious) standards, most are quite reasonably priced.

The cheapest hotels are to be found in the large towns. In Harare, Bulawayo and Mutare you'll find basic doubles from US$10. Smaller centres usually have a single hotel with doubles from US$30. In tourist areas like Victoria Falls, Kariba and Nyanga expect to pay US$35 upwards. All the main tourist centres also have hotels of international standard – which can be fun now and then, but are obviously far removed from the daily reality of Zimbabwe.

All but the cheapest hotels are invariably clean, with freshly ironed linen. The worst are noisy watering holes doubling up as brothels; warnings are given where relevant in the guide.

■ National Parks accommodation

The **National Parks accommodation** lodges, cottages and chalets are some of Zimbabwe's real bargains. Set in the loveliest spots in the parks, they offer outstanding self-catering deals, in one- or two-bedroomed units, at very low rates. All come with basic furniture, fridges, pots and pans, blankets, linen and towels, and are serviced daily.

Most basic are the **chalets**, starting at US$9 for one double bedroom and providing outside cooking and communal washing facilities. Self-contained **cottages** with kitchen and bathroom start from under US$12. The **lodges**, from US$14, have everything, including crocks and cutlery.

Across the country during school holidays (see p.55) and at weekends near the cities, National

ACCOMMODATION PRICE CODES FOR ZIMBABWE

Most accommodation options in our account of Zimbabwe have been given **price codes** to indicate the cost of a single night's lodging. The price on which each code is based is the non-resident rate, **per person sharing**; there is usually a supplement for a single person in a room. Prices for establishments that only offer all-inclusive rates (comprising meals, and perhaps guided tours and other services) have not been coded and are given in US$ (per person per night). Campsite prices, which are minimal and fairly standard across the country (generally under US$3 per person), have also been excluded.

Although some establishments still quote prices in Z$ and on odd occasions even in sterling, for consistency all Zimbabwe prices in this book are given in US$ (see box p.39).

① under US$8	④ US$25–35	⑦ US$65–80
② US$8–15	⑤ US$35–50	⑧ US$80–95
③ US$15–25	⑥ US$50–65	⑨ over US$95

Parks places get pretty full and advance **booking** is essential. It's not a bad idea to reserve at other times too, especially for more popular places like Hwange and Mana Pools. You can book up to six months ahead – not as excessive as it sounds as some places are in such demand that accommodation is allocated by ballot. Don't be put off, however, if you haven't reserved. You may be lucky if you just turn up, and you can always phone to check on the position if you're in the vicinity.

■ Private self-catering

Cottages, along similar lines to National Parks lodges, are rented out privately in several areas from around upwards of US$20 per night, depending on the number of beds.

BOOKING FOR NATIONAL PARKS ACCOMMODATION

IN PERSON

Harare: Department of National Parks and Wildlife Management, National Botanical Gardens (☎14/706077), open Mon–Fri 7.45am–4.15pm. To get there take Borrowdale Rd out of central Harare, turn left into Sandringham Ave, then take the first left into the gardens.
Bulawayo: Department of National Parks and Wildlife Management, 140a Fife St (☎19/63646).

BY POST

Department of National Parks and Wildlife Management, Central Booking Office, PO Box 8151, Causeway, Harare; or PO Box 2283, Bulawayo.

■ Bush camps and safari lodges

The ultimate place to stay in Zimbabwe is in a **bush camp**, set in a remote part of the country, with wildlife roaming through. You pay (from US$150 to several times that) not for conventional luxury but for the privilege of being in one of the world's great wilderness areas – and for the personal expertise of a professional guide constantly on hand. Accommodation is very variable as is location. You'll find stilted "tree-houses", walk-in tents, thatched chalets, old farmhouses, stone lodges and houseboats.

■ Safari farms and country lodges

Since the beginning of the 1990s a large number of farms have restyled themselves as **country lodges**. The emphasis is on intimacy and personalized service. You're made to feel a guest in someone's home (which indeed most of them are). They're all over the country, some near towns and others near game-viewing areas.

Those near towns provide a rural alternative to staying in the impersonal upmarket city hotels. The remoter ones are run as **safari farms**, set in their own game estates. The animals you'll see may include predators and antelope, but will usually represent only a small selection of Zimbabwean game. Most safari farms are no replacement for the real thing, but do provide a less demanding way of retreating to the country. Prices range from US$30 to US$200. See "Safaris" on p.13 for booking details.

■ Bed and Breakfasts

Another new departure for Zimbabwe is the **Bed and Breakfast**. There aren't many at the moment, but it's worth enquiring if you want decent accommodation that bridges the gap between backpackers' lodges and hotels. B&Bs in Zimbabwe are closer to the British model than the American, with accommodation normally consisting of a room in someone's home. Breakfast is included in the price, which is usually about US$20 for a double.

■ Youth hostels and backpackers' lodges

Harare and Bulawayo each has a **youth hostel** geared to budget travellers. **Backpackers' lodges**, of varying standards, but run along roughly similar lines, are a more viable option as the youth hostels fill up fast. New lodges are constantly springing up, mainly in the urban centres, with a particularly high concentration in Harare. Prices in dorms start at US$3.50 per person. The worst ones are fleapits, but some of the better ones offer an outstanding service to budget travellers, laying on meals and transport. Double rooms, where available, go for around US$10.

■ Camping

If you don't want to rely on hotels as a fallback then **camping** is a recommended option, with prices generally under US$3 per person per night. The white Rhodesian passion for outdoor life has left campsites in all but the remotest parts. In towns, too, a tent will prove a big money-saver.

On the whole, **campsites** are outstandingly well maintained. They provide good cooking and washing facilities, and there's usually an attendant, which greatly reduces the chances of theft. On the minus side, summer heat can make sleeping under nylon a bit of a sweat and in the national parks it's hardly any dearer to stay in a chalet. Taking a tent means you'll never be stuck for somewhere to stay, but it's worth trying to anticipate how much you'll actually use it. As for camping supplies, a **portable stove** is useful, though there are usually plentiful stocks of firewood and fireplaces.

Communications: post and phone services

Zimbabwe is pretty good for communications, both by phone – which now features direct dial – and by an albeit rather sluggish mail service.

■ Post

The **postal service** retains a British colonial flavour, with familiar-looking signs in post offices instructing you how to use services and pack parcels. On the whole, mail services are reliable, if slow – though letters do sometimes fail to arrive. If you are sending anything of value, it's wise to register it.

Post offices generally open at 8.30am, and close at 4pm Monday to Friday and at 11.30am

---

INTERNATIONAL PHONE CODES

Phoning Zimbabwe from outside the country

Country code: **263**

Zimbabwe's internal trunk codes begin with 1. Drop this digit (just after the country code) when phoning from abroad.

International calls from Zimbabwe

International access code: **110**

Country codes

Australia 61 (+6 to +8hr)	Ireland 353 (-1 to -2hr)
Britain 44 (-1 to -2hr)	New Zealand 64 (+10hr)
Canada 1 (-6 to -10hr)	US 1 (-6 to -10hr)

The following Southern African countries share the **same time zone** as Zimbabwe:

Country codes

Botswana 267	Namibia 264
Malawi 265	South Africa 27
Mozambique 258	Zambia 260

on Saturdays. **Airmail** letters to Europe don't cost much and take about a week to arrive on average. Aerogrammes are available and are even cheaper, and save the hassle of carrying a pad. All post offices (their addresses are given in the listings for the main towns and cities) offer **poste restante** facilities.

■ Phone

Zimbabwe's ever-improving **phone system** does sometimes get a little overloaded, but it'll usually work given enough persistence. International connections are much quicker and easier than local calls, with clearer lines overseas than to places close by. Internal lines worsen during the **rainy season**.

By far the easiest ways to make calls is to dial 0 (this will be changed to 967 at an as-yet-unspecified date) to use the **free operator service** to connect you, though you will have to wait. It is possible, however, to **direct dial** most places within Zimbabwe and outside. There are plenty of **public call boxes** and a growing number of **cardphones** in the cities – most of them modern, user-friendly Scandinavian instruments – though you can expect to queue for public phones, especially in Harare and Bulawayo.

PHONE NUMBER CHANGES AND DIRECTORY ENQUIRIES

Zimbabwe is currently in the process of upgrading to a digital telephone network – though when the project will be completed is anyone's guess. At the time of writing, work had been finished in Harare, but as areas outside the capital become affected, you'll find that some of the phone numbers quoted in this book have changed. Telephone **directory enquiries** if you experience problems: local ☎92 (962), trunk ☎91 (968) – the numbers in brackets will come into operation at an as-yet-unspecified date, along with a new number for international directory enquiries (☎965).

The Media: press, books, radio and TV

Considering Zimbabwe's economic climate, the country has a healthy range of papers, magazines and books available. And with
Africa's best music scene, the local radio can be a major attraction.

■ The press

You'll see a fair quantity of **magazines and newspapers** on sale at bookshops and on city-centre street corners. Most are in English, although you'll also encounter Shona and Ndebele publications.

There are two **national dailies**: **The Herald** based in Harare and **The Chronicle** in Bulawayo. Along with several other publications, they fall under the Zimbabwe Mass Media Trust, an organization formed in 1981 to foster a press more sympathetic to government policies, but not under direct government control. Both tend towards dull worthiness, but they have occasional sparks of independence. *The Chronicle* had its hour of glory during the "Willowgate" car corruption scandal of 1988: the editor stood up to the Minister of Defence, and pursued some valiant investigative reporting, causing the minister's eventual resignation. The editor was later "promoted".

On **Sundays** you can pick up **The Sunday Mail** in Harare and **The Sunday News** in Bulawayo. On Fridays the **Financial Gazette** comes out, providing a staunch capitalist alternative to the mainstream press.

For the best news coverage in Southern Africa pick up the South African liberal *Mail & Guardian*, which comes out on Fridays. In addition to good regional coverage you get the bonus of stories from Britain's *Guardian*, which owns a share in the paper.

Outside Harare and Bulawayo you might also check out the **local weeklies**. These tend to be quaintly parochial: reading the letters pages feels almost voyeuristic. In the Eastern Highlands look for **The Manica Post** and in Kwe Kwe the **Midlands Observer**.

Of the **monthly magazines**, the popular **Parade** achieves a delicate mix of feature articles, sport, politics and gossip, while the resilient **Moto** is definitely worth a read. A critical and very readable journal of analysis and opinion, *Moto* was founded in 1959 by *Mambo Press* (a Catholic publishing house), and reflected African views through the 1960s until its 1974 banning. It resumed publication in 1980, failed due to lack of money in 1981 and bounced back in 1982, fighting on contemporary issues like land reform.

■ Book publishing and bookshops

Zimbabwe's flourishing **publishing industry** produces fiction, poetry, drama, folk tales and children's literature. **Zimbabwe Publishing House** and **Baobab** concentrate on high-quality literature, while **Pacesetters** and **Drumbeat** produce fast-paced light reading.

There's also a wealth of well-produced and very readable school texts for all levels that provide excellent introductory material on history, geography and other aspects of Zimbabwe and a comprehensive array of reference material on flora, fauna, culture and geography. (See the *Contexts* pieces on "Writing from Zimbabwe" and "Books".)

Bookshops can be found all over the country, the largest chain being *Kingstons*. A modest selection of the latest British novels is available, but at higher prices than in the UK. Bring novels with you to swap or give away, and take the opportunity to sample the excellent and reasonably priced locally published books. The *Grass Roots Book Shops* and *Mambo Press* in Harare are worth visiting for wide selections of African literature.

■ Radio and TV

Zimbabwe has four radio stations and a TV channel, plus TV2 in Harare. **Radio 1** is the "English Service", a mixture of classical music and talk. **Radio 2** – "the music lovers' station" – broadcasts in Shona and Ndebele and plays local and South African jive. **Radio 3** is the charts-oriented "English Music Station", serving a mixed menu of local jive, "Europop", funk, rap, reggae, soul and so on. **Radio 4** is largely educational. Radios 1 and 3 are in stereo.

Although there are some locally produced **television** programmes, it's cheaper for ZBC (Zimbabwe Broadcasting Corporation) to import, hence the large quantity of American and British padding. Broadcasts are in colour though most TVs are still black and white.

Music and drama

For live music listings, scan the entertainments pages of the press (see "Media" above) and look for roughly printed posters wrapped around lamp-posts and on walls – every weekend brings a choice of bands competing for punters. Details on specific venues are included through the guide, and a personal selection of names to look out for is given in the *Contexts* piece on Zimbabwean music.

There's no awe of megastars in Zimbabwe. Musicians work hard for a living, and have to play often. **Harare** is the best place to see and hear them. The biggest events come at month-ends, when the names, like Thomas Mapfumo, hold *pungwes* – a word derived from all-night rallies held by guerrillas during the war – till the early hours.

Music and performance from Zimbabwe's **oral tradition** is less well known outside the country. A few collections of **folk tales and praise poetry** have been published in translation, but the tradition lives on and develops most effectively through **drama**. Find out about productions by affiliates of the Association of Community Theatres as well as those by the

---

BBC WORLD SERVICE AND VOA

If you want to keep in touch with world news, tune in to the **BBC World Service**, which gives wider coverage than local broadcasts, as well as some excellent programmes in its Africa Service. There can be considerable variation in reception, so it's worth surfing the airwaves to find the sharpest frequency. As a rule of thumb, the lower ones (below 7000KHz) tend to provide better reception from late afternoon and throughout the evening, while the higher ones are usually better during the early morning till about midday.

Frequencies for the BBC's principal English-language broadcasts on **short wave** are as follows (given in KHz; times are local): 3255 (5–

8am & 6pm–midnight), 6005 (5–6pm & 11pm–midnight), 6190 (5–10.15am & noon–midnight), 9600 (5–10am), 11835 (7.30–9pm), 11940 (8–10.15am & noon–6pm), 15400 (9.30am–noon & 7–9.15pm) and 21660 (1–4.30pm & 5.30–7pm). The BBC also relays these broadcasts on **medium wave** 1197KHz (midnight–9.15am, 3–4.30pm & 5.30pm–midnight). The BBC's Harare address is PO Box 3655.

Voice of America English-language broadcasts to Africa can be picked up on the following short wave frequencies: 6035 (8–9am & 6.30pm–midnight), 6080 (5–9am), 7375 (7pm–midnight), 7415 (7pm–midnight).

University theatre group in Harare and independent groups such as Amakhosi in Bulawayo. Most publishers have a drama list, which includes play scripts from Zimbabwe.

■ Records

Records (vinyl) are far cheaper than the equivalent outside the country and are usually good quality due to small pressing runs. Pre-recorded cassettes are another story and best avoided if possible, while blank cassettes are prohibitively expensive (when they're available). CDs are easy to come by, but pricy.

There are two record companies, **Gramma Records** and the **Zimbabwe Music Corporation** (**ZMC**). The fact that they pay no advances and low royalties to their groups enables them to take chances with recordings, which ensures that a large number of groups get onto vinyl, only to disappear if they show no instant profit. Several of the records recommended in the *Contexts* section on music may well prove to be unavailable – the negative flip side of small runs – and reissues are sporadic. Combing the smaller **record shops** often produces a rare gem, so don't give up on finding that original 7" single of "Take Cover" – try downtown.

Downtown, in fact, is always the place for 7" singles, old and new. The big record stores have binloads of LPs and 12" singles, but usually only the current top 20 hits. The best places for records, not surprisingly, are Harare and Bulawayo – the top shops are listed under these cities in the "Shopping" sections.

Sports and outdoor activities

White Rhodesians had a formidable taste for sports and the great outdoors. Although many left after Independence, the tradition has continued and even expanded. Outstanding public sports facilities exist all over the country and other more exciting activities, taking in the wild, are now becoming more common. On the spectator front, soccer is a national obsession, as are cricket and horse-racing.

■ Participatory sports

Every town of any size has at least one public **swimming pool** – wonderful outdoor Olympic-sized places. If you usually use goggles ·or earplugs, bring them along because you can't buy them inside the country. Bathing is also an option in **mountain pools**, particularly in the Eastern Highlands, which are bilharzia-free.

Tennis courts are plentiful too; if you're a keen player planning on a long stay, be sure to bring a racket. For the odd casual game, you'll find little-used courts at many of the national parks – and equipment for rental.

Many of the national parks also have small artificial lakes, where **fishing** is permitted with a licence obtainable from the park's reception – they'll also rent rowing boats where available. There's more exciting fishing at parks and resorts along the Zambezi and at Lake Kariba. The most sought-after catches include trout and bream, but the ultimate fishy adversary has to be the fighting tiger fish. You can buy tackle in the big cities or rent at resorts, but if you need anything fancy, again, bring it along.

Finally, if **golf** is your game, bring along your clubs – every town in Zimbabwe has at least one golf course.

■ Spectator sports

Like most African countries, Zimbabwe's national sport is **soccer**, which draws crowds of between 30,000 and 45,000 for big matches. The game is played in both rural and urban areas, but the competitive league structure is confined to the towns and cities. The **season** runs from February to November.

From provincial level, amateur teams seek promotion to the first-division **Super League** involving fourteen or so teams. Apart from the league there are four major club **competitions**: the Chibuku Trophy, the BAT Rosebowl, the Natbrew Cup and the Rothmans Shield. For most of the past decade Dynamos have dominated Zimbabwe's club soccer; among other **teams** worth looking out for are Highlanders, Zimbabwe Saints, CAPS United and Black Rhinos (the army team).

Horse-racing ranks as one of Zimbabwe's most popular spectator sports. Cutting across all race and class divisions the annual tote turnover tops Z$36 million – a huge figure for a small developing country. A number of events take place at the country's two main venues: Ascot in Bulawayo and Borrowdale Park in Harare. The principal racing **season** is May to July.

As far as international competition goes, **cricket** is Zimbabwe's most successful sport.

Every year two international sides come for month-long tours. Most have been beaten by the home team in limited-overs matches, although Zimbabwe has only won about half of its first-class competitions. At **national level** the premier events are the Rothmans National League and the Logan Cup. Matches are played on a limited-overs basis on Sundays. Because of the longer daylight hours, cricket in Zimbabwe is a summer game.

■ Outdoor activities

The post-Independence revival of Zimbabwean tourism has brought some exciting outdoor options that combine adventure activities with Zimbabwe's natural attractions; full details are given in the relevant chapters throughout this book.

Two Zambezi adventures must share the top spot as the most thrilling experiences available. For the ultimate one-day adrenaline surge **white-water rafting** on the rapids below the Victoria Falls can't be beaten (see p.173), and it's become a big attraction of the Falls in its own right. The other involves three or more days **canoeing** down the Zambezi through some of Zimbabwe's wildest and best game country (see pp.112–114).

Another exciting way to see **wildlife** is from horseback, and a couple of operators offer the option of **riding** into big game country, in the Mavuradonna Mountains and from Victoria Falls. For some less demanding riding, you can rent horses very cheaply in some of the national parks, although – obviously enough – only at ones with no big cats.

Hiking safaris too are an exciting way to experience the wild in a way that just isn't possible from the confines of a vehicle. There's a choice of going out with a licensed guide with everything laid on, which doesn't come cheap but is always good value, or self-catering outings with National Park game scouts, which is far cheaper.

And for less organized activities like **hiking** and **climbing** you'll find miles and miles of eminently walkable wilderness all over Zimbabwe, where you can do it yourself.

Crafts

In spite of the shortages of certain high-tech goods, there's a lot worth buying in Zimbabwe – and not just tourist souvenirs.

Zimbabwe produces its own fine **cotton** and you can get a good range of commercially made clothes and fabrics. Local prints, with vibrant designs and bold colours, are well worth looking at; they make useful multi-purpose wraps and easily transported souvenirs. A number of local artists also work with cottons to produce a distinctive and refined Zimbabwean school of **batik**, that appears on sale both as lengths of fabric or made up into garments – surprisingly cheap for handmade goods. Look for this type of stuff at the craft shops in Harare or visit the artists at home.

Much of the **carving** you'll come across, both in wood and stone, is of the repetitive "laughing hippo" school – not really worth buying when there's so much more creative work about. There are some real artists working in softwoods, and **Zimbabwe's stone carvers** represent a significant international art movement. In 1983 the London *Sunday Telegraph*'s art critic wrote that "it is extraordinary to think that of the ten leading sculptor-carvers in the world, perhaps five come from one single African tribe [ie the Shona]". His **top three** were Sylvester Mubayi, Joseph Ndandarika and Nicholas Mukomberanwa. You can see and possibly buy their work, as well as stunning sculpture by other big names, from Harare's commercial **galleries**. If you have an eye for it, you can also pick up cheap (but potentially valuable) work by unknowns at the **National Gallery shops** in Harare and Bulawayo, or from the sculptors' community at **Tengenenge** (see p.91).

In addition, good-quality **crafts** are available all over the country, at curio shops, at some of the markets in larger centres or from roadside stalls. Items to look for include distinctive **baskets**, which vary from region to region.

In Bulawayo and around Victoria Falls, look out for **Batonga crafts**, often antique family heirlooms that won't be around for much longer, and pipes and hardwood stools. Many of the repetitive items – walking sticks, grass hats, and full-colour wooden chickens and guinea fowls from Zambia – retain considerable vibrancy and are worth sorting through for the one that stands out from the crowd.

Easy-to-carry souvenirs include a range of Zimbabwe **T-shirts** decorated with above-average designs and beautiful polished, egg-shaped **stones**. And of course there's a host of rigorously commercial and tacky tourist bits and pieces, from ghastly stuffed animals to that copper clock in the shape of Zimbabwe that you always wanted in your front room.

Trouble

Violent crime is thankfully rare in Zimbabwe. However, in a country of great extremes of wealth and poverty, it would be a miracle if there wasn't some theft. Visitors are therefore advised to take all the usual precautions.

■ Crime

If you're robbed in Zimbabwe you're unlikely to be aware of it while it's happening. **Pickpockets** are quite common, though by taking a few simple precautions and being aware you can minimize the risk.

Be particularly mindful when in and around bus stations and markets – places where there are large numbers of people milling around. Keep tabs on what's going on around you. And carry your valuables where you can keep an eye on them – in crowded places, keep your bag or rucksack in front of you, rather than on your back, at least where nimble fingers can't dip into your goods without you noticing. You also should avoid leaving valuables in **vehicles** – another major target for thieves.

■ Drugs

Drug consumption in Zimbabwe has not reached the baroque proportions of the West, and all you're likely to come across is *dagga* or *mbanje* (cannabis in dried leaf form), which grows quite happily in Zimbabwe and can occasionally be seen alongside footpaths or at bus stops. Growing it is a criminal offence and seldom a week passes without press coverage of yet another *mbanje* queen going to jail. Nevertheless marijuana-smoking is widespread and if you're reasonably discreet you should encounter no problems.

■ Sexual attitudes and harassment

Despite a liberation struggle that saw **women** fighting and dying alongside men, gender distinctions still run deep in Zimbabwe. Even in urban areas African women are still expected to show due respect to men, though more extreme practices seem likely to dwindle as more women take up paid employment. Attitudes to black women are quite restrictive and there have been clamp-downs on single women out at night in Harare, including mass arrests and trumped-up accusations of prostitution. Tourists are unlikely to experience any of this, although women on their own are considered fair game by men.

Context is important, however, and if you want to avoid **harassment** you'll have to avoid certain places: cheaper hotels, bars and jive joints. Even if you're obviously with a male companion, many **drunks** at nightspots will fail to be put off. The alternative is to go out anyway but to let the suggestions pass – if you're a white woman the danger of sexual assault is minimal. There have been reports of single women being hassled on trains by drunks, but fortunately there are separate compartments for males and females and they can be locked from the inside. Away from drunks women can walk quite freely without fear of catcalls or being pestered.

■ The police

Most Zimbabwean **police** are friendly and polite and you're unlikely to have much contact with them unless you're robbed. If you do have any dealings then a respectful response is likely to pay off. Police resources are limited – they don't even have vehicles in some places – so don't place too much hope on seeing your goods again. It's worth weighing up the value and likelihood of getting your stuff back against the hassle of filling in forms and answering questions, which is often done with great thoroughness by policemen genuinely keen to help. For **insurance** purposes or replacement of **travellers' cheques** and **passports** you'll have no choice. Be sure to get a copy of the police report stating what you've lost or had stolen, to give to embassies, insurers or travellers' cheque companies.

Travellers with disabilities

Perhaps because Zimbabweans fought a war within living memory, they show little more curiosity about disability than you would normally encounter in the UK or US. On the whole, you can expect the usual Zimbabwean friendliness and consideration.

Getting to Zimbabwe need pose no problem, as both *Air Zimbabwe* and *British Airways* are sympathetic to disabled travellers, although you should give them advance warning that you may need assistance.

In general, **buildings** outside Harare are low-rise, with one or two storeys, and are often quite spacious, so access is easy as a rule. Hotels and hostels are also usually low-rise, with ground-floor accommodation. However, because of the tendency for rain to fall in heavy bursts, most buildings have an entrance step; and take care of the **floors**, which are often highly polished. If your balance isn't good or your gait stiff, brace yourself for regular slips (and crash landings).

Kerbs in main town centres tend to be one foot or more from street level (also because of the heavy rain showers). They are therefore difficult to climb and quite impossible to negotiate in a self-propelled wheelchair. In **Harare**, dropped kerbs are reasonably common and you should have little problem getting around the centre in a wheelchair. However, they're quite steep; once you've committed yourself, there's no going back. Dropped kerbs are rarer in **Bulawayo** (despite the fact the city has an internationally famous disabled mayor) and never appear on opposite sides of the road, but at least the roads are wide so it's not too severe a hardship to remain in the gutter for a while.

In **suburban areas** of Zimbabwean towns and cities, kerbs are often lower, but the surfaces of both the roads and pavements are correspondingly poor, which can make it just as difficult to get around. **Outside the main cities**, pavements are more of a rarity, and indeed almost all roads and paths bar the main highways are rough tracks. Sandy and stony, they are difficult surfaces for a wheelchair to negotiate and walking can be a problem if you have trouble with uneven surfaces. Any tarmac is regarded as being for vehicles, and pedestrians, cyclists and wheelchair users are expected to move to the verge. Failure to comply with this convention can have drastic consequences.

It's worth bearing in mind that even the most basic Western wheelchair is likely to be considerably more sophisticated than anything available in Zimbabwe, so if you are able, and decide, to walk around, find someone to look after it and be prepared to tip them for their efforts.

■ **Specific sites**
What follows is a disabled traveller's rundown of some of Zimbabwe's main tourist spots, highlighting the kind of problems and pitfalls you're likely to encounter at specific sites. The list is by no means exhaustive, but, used in conjunction with the accounts featured in the guide, it should help you to plan your trip.

Mbare Market
With its narrow walkways, Harare's bustling **Mbare Market** is far from ideal wheelchair territory. Nevertheless, if you can cope with the restricted views – mainly of bottoms – the whole place is quite an experience.

The main hall for crafts and gifts stands at the top of two very high steps. If you decide to leave your chair, make sure someone keeps an eye on it. Some of the outer areas of the market don't have established stalls and the paths through them are effectively off limits to wheelchair users.

Dombashawa and Ngomakurira rock paintings
Dombashawa cave, famous for its San rock art, lies about half a mile from the car park, and although the early stages might be travelled in a wheelchair, there is a steep scramble at the end – only worth the effort if you are really into cave painting. Unless you have unlimited energy, forget the cave at **Ngomakurira**, which requires the climbing technique of a mountain goat to reach.

Tengenenge
The sculpture park at **Tengenenge** is not well set out for disabled visitors. Its loose sand and gravel paths are difficult to negotiate in a wheelchair (at least without the help of a strong pusher), and the way the pieces of sculptures are packed together can make the site tricky to walk round if you are unsteady on your feet in confined spaces. However, the site is well worth the effort, and Shona sculpture enthusiasts with mobility problems should not be deterred.

Hippo Pools
Hippo Pools is flat and grassy, and easy to get around. The paths in the immediate vicinity are generally firm and can be negotiated in a wheelchair with the assistance of a strong pusher, although they tend to peter out the farther from camp you venture.

Matobo National Park
Much of the **Matobo National Park**'s stunning scenery is visible from a car, but the bare rocks

can make walking quite difficult. The cave paintings that are such a feature of the area are usually quite a scramble from the roadside, and tend to be only worth the effort if you are a real rock art fan.

A steady climb over bare rock for about half a mile from the car park, Rhodes' Grave is not reachable by wheelchair, but the view from the top makes it worth the effort. The chalets at Maleme Dam are single-storey. However, not all are situated near the toilet block, so when you check in ask for one that is.

Victoria Falls

As with many of Zimbabwe's main tourist sites, **Victoria Falls** is relatively uncongested, so movement around the site is fairly easy. Moreover, the main viewing points can be reached without difficulty, thanks to generally level and well-surfaced access paths.

Hwange National Park

Access to the **Hwange National Park** is only possible by car, unless, that is, you get there on one of the guided walks, which put the disabled in the same position as everyone else.

The chalets and lodges at Main Camp are single-storey, but most of the site as a whole is covered by a fine layer of sand that has drifted in places, making life difficult for wheelchair users. The main viewing platforms have good strong handrails. At Nyamandlovu platform, however, it is possible (although strictly speaking against the rules), to sit at the base if the climb presents a problem.

Great Zimbabwe

The sprawling archeological site of **Great Zimbabwe** encompasses a large area crossed by sand and gravel paths. It is too spread out to explore on foot, and the nature of the paths means that a good strong pusher is recommended.

The site's principal highlight, the Great Enclosure, can be reached by wheelchair, but you'll need to be prepared to get out if you want to explore a bit. The older structures are up a steep hill and accessible only to the very fit and determined.

Nyanga National Park

Ideal walking country, **Nyanga National Park** is not well geared to disabled people. However, some magnificent scenery can be seen from, or within easy distance of, the roadsides.

World's View is easily accessible by car, and can be comfortably explored on foot. For **accommodation**, the single-storey *Troutbeck Inn* is recommended rather than the *Rhodes Nyanga Hotel*, which occupies a hilly site with a number of steps. The National Park lodges are fully accessible.

Will Bee

Directory

AIRPORT TAX of US$20 is payable on leaving Zimbabwe. It can be paid in Zimbabwe dollars to the equivalent value – a good way to use up notes you can't export. You can buy the necessary stamp, which you should stick to your plane ticket, at banks or the airport bureau de change just before checking in.

CONTRACEPTIVES Condoms are available from pharmacies, as are contraceptive pills – on prescription – but to ensure the continued use of your particular type bring your own supplies.

ELECTRICITY is 220 volts; both round- and square-pin sockets are used.

EMERGENCIES Police, fire and ambulance ☎99. As part of the upgrading of Zimbabwe's phone network, there are plans to change the emergency services' numbers, at a date yet to be announced, as follows: general ☎999; police ☎995; fire ☎993; ambulance ☎994. Doctors are listed in the two telephone directories at the front of each town or city section.

GAY AND LESBIAN LIFE Homosexuality is illegal in Zimbabwe, and official statements deny that it exists among blacks, while white society remains largely macho and homophobic. In 1995 the whole issue made international headlines when the government put pressure on the organizers of the prestigious Zimbabwe International Book Fair to stop gays being represented at the event. Despite pressure from the US and neighbouring South Africa, President Mugabe made a personal intervention, asserting that in his opinion "gays have no rights"– sadly, a sentiment with considerable popular support in Zimbabwe. In the end, gays were barred from the fair, in spite of the ironic fact that its theme for the year was "Human Rights and Justice". Gay men and women nevertheless continue to campaign through GALZ (Gays and Lesbians of Zimbabwe), Private Bag A1631, Avondale, Harare.

SHOP OPENING HOURS Most things start early in Zimbabwe, and shops are no exception, opening at 8am, and closing at 5pm on weekdays and at noon or 1pm on Saturdays. You can usually expect shops to close between 1 and 2pm for lunch during the week in small places, although this isn't cast in stone. A few large city-centre supermarkets have late opening hours, while

HOLIDAYS
Public holidays
January 1 New Year's Day
Easter Good Friday to Easter Monday
April 18 Independence Day
May 1 Worker's Day
May 25 Africa Day
August 11 Heroes Day
August 12 Armed Forces Day
December 25 & 26 Xmas & Boxing Day

School holidays (approximate)
Early December to Mid-January
Mid-April to Mid-May
Early August to Mid-September

small suburban grocers and cafés selling basics also stay open after 5pm.

TAMPONS are available from supermarkets and general stores. If you do get caught out in a small village that's run out you'll always be able to get panty pads.

TIME is GMT +2hr, US Eastern Standard Time +7hr, Australian Eastern Standard Time -8hr. Daylight is roughly 6am to 6pm, slightly extended in mid-summer.

TIPS are rarely added to bills and are obviously appreciated. About ten percent or loose change, depending on the bill, should do.

TOILETS Public ones aren't that common, although you will find some in the big cities, rarely with any paper. Those around the tea-rooms and restaurants of department stores are always quite salubrious and do have toilet rolls. In rural areas you'll come across long-drop toilets – holes you squat over – and the ingenious Blair toilets invented in Zimbabwe.

TOPLESS BATHING is completely unacceptable in Zimbabwe – in fact it's an arrestable offence.

WORK Unless you line up a job or voluntary work before leaving for Zimbabwe, you have very little chance of getting employment. Particular skills are sometimes in demand, but you're unlikely to be granted a work permit while hundreds of thousands of Zimbabweans remain unemployed.

CHAPTER ONE

HARARE, THE MIDLANDS AND AROUND

ike most African capitals, after only a century of existence, Harare lacks an identifiable soul that might give it personality. That doesn't mean the city is devoid of charm. It's an unthreatening centre to spend time in and can be a great place to simply stroll around, bask in the languid warmth and enjoy the contradictions of a post-colonial city. British sobriety is collaged with the louder glass towers of the past decade and a very un-English tropical feel. It is the unrivalled metropolitan centre of Zimbabwe, at the same time exuding the parochial respectability of an English provincial capital. If you're passing through from wilder parts, you should draw some pleasure from its quiet, easy-going cityscape of flowering trees and tracts of red earth running between streets and exuberant gardens.

In the absence of compelling sights demanding your attention, there are a number of small but entertaining ways to pass a few easy hours – or even days. Harare has several **museums**, including a first-class collection of local **sculpture**, good **craft shops** and some pleasant outdoor cafés. If you're an enthusiast of Zimbabwean **music**, you'll find a scene of encouraging vitality here.

Sights in the **suburbs**, or a little way beyond, include the **rock paintings** at Dombashawa, set in typical Zimbabwean granite country, **Lake Chivero (Lake McIlwaine)**, the **Ewanrigg Botanical Gardens**, and **Mukuvisi Woodlands**; all these provide space when you want to get out of the city for a few hours. Given half a day's travelling you can plunge further afield into the wild country of the **Mavuradonna range** in the north, or push into the mellower provincial **Midlands**.

Harare is also an easy, secure, respectable place in which to make **travel arrangements** for more exciting parts. As a base or springboard for countrywide travels, the capital is, as you'd expect, very well connected, with excellent tarred roads radiating out to most places you're likely to want to go. Kariba and Bulawayo are five hours away in opposite directions **by road**, while Nyanga in the Eastern Highlands and Great Zimbabwe to the south are a mere three hours distant. Although there is no direct link by road to Victoria Falls and Hwange (you have to go via Bulawayo), you can reach

---

ACCOMMODATION PRICE CODES

Hotels and other accommodation options in Zimbabwe have been categorized according to the **price codes** given below, which indicate the cost, per person sharing, of a night's lodging.

For a full explanation, see p.46.

① under US$8	④ US$25–35	⑦ US$65–80
② US$8–15	⑤ US$35–50	⑧ US$80–95
③ US$15–25	⑥ US$50–65	⑨ over US$95

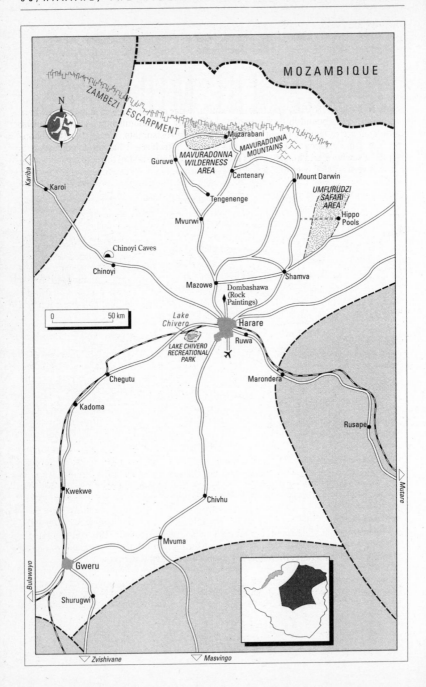

them from Kariba, taking the ferry westwards along the lake. **By train**, you can head east to Mutare, or south to Bulawayo (and thence to Victoria Falls). Inevitably, too, Harare is also the centre of all domestic and international **flights**.

HARARE

If you arrive in **HARARE** expecting the exotica, decay and vibrancy so familiar elsewhere in Africa, you're bound to be disappointed. The city is predominantly sedate and clean with its share of familiar urban symbols – fast-food restaurants, Western clothes shops and the same old petrol stations. As the nation's showpiece it has attracted resources denied elsewhere, and in many ways stands apart from the rest of the country. Gleaming glass towers erected over the last two decades proclaim post-Independence prosperity in striking contrast with the lacklustre, 1960s slabs that give the place its provincial feel. The pace is unhurried, and the centre pleasant and undemanding to stroll around.

There is an unquestionably African city alongside, however, and colonial planning still divides rich and poor. The influx of white immigrants over the last ninety years and the presence of a ready black workforce provided a development blueprint for Harare as an affluent town with elegant suburbs and hidden **working-class districts**. Walk through the downmarket, downtown **Kopje** and **Robert Mugabe Road** quarters and you'll discover a bustling area of ageing buildings and shops selling bric-a-brac and essentials. Mingling with the street clamour, the beat of local music thumps out from a hundred shop counter record players. A couple of kilometres further on you hit **Mbare** – a "high-density suburb", with its huge market spreading out, and also the country's biggest bus station, hub of the public transport network.

Some history

Many whites were outraged when Zimbabwe's capital was renamed **Harare** after Independence in 1980. But history was just completing a cycle. Long before Rhodes' pioneers pitched up, armed with intent to rename the area **Fort Salisbury** (after the British prime minister), the region was the domain of **Chief Neharawa** of Seki. The white government called one of the African areas Harare – from Harawa – but to generations of blacks through the colonial years Harare was the name of the capital itself. In **September 1890**, the Union Jack was hoisted on the site of present African Unity Square, and the British South Africa Company (BSAC) marched in and took over.

Salisbury was intended as a base for working the **goldfields** of the Zambezi Valley, which speculators believed matched the ore-rich veins of South Africa. This was wishful thinking, yet the unlikely marshland became the country's main urban centre as settlers were enticed by the promise of large farms and substantial mining claims. The town took its earliest shape from the traders who haphazardly set up shop at the foot of the Kopje; in 1891 Captain Thomas Ross was brought in by the Company to impose some town planning on this dangerously organic tendency. The result was the collision of two street grids: Ross incorporated the existing plots below the Kopje and created a rectangular grid parallel to Pioneer Street, ensuring that future development would be constrained by a second grid of martial regularity, aligned due north.

Important note: the stretch of **Chancellor Avenue**, leading north off North Avenue, past the **President's Residence**, is off limits from 6pm to 6am. A barrier operated by armed troops is usually lowered between these hours. This restriction is to be taken very seriously – several motorists have been shot dead for venturing down this no-go street during prohibited hours, even on occasion with the boom raised. If the **President's cavalcade** is passing anywhere in town, you're required by law to stop and pull over.

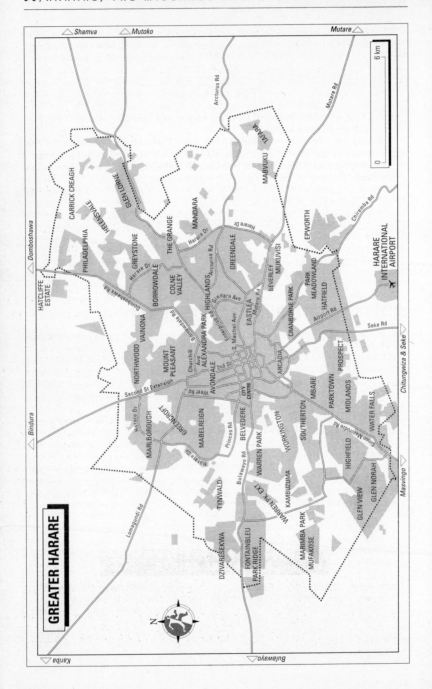

GREATER HARARE

During the 1890s Salisbury's commercial centre shifted east from the Kopje to the district around present-day **African Unity Square**. At the same time **racial segregation** crept in. The first "location" for black workers was a dismal affair, a kilometre south of Kopje, with a white superintendent and a nine o'clock curfew. Not surprisingly, few blacks were enticed to settle. It was only after the suppression of the First Chimurenga (liberation war) in 1896, and the imposition of **taxes** to force blacks to work in town, that the workers' housing shortage became serious. In 1907, a new location was built across the Mukuvisi River in a choice spot near the town cemetery, abattoir and sewage disposal works.

Salisbury was officially recognized as a city in 1923, when it became the seat of colonial government. But the real boost came after World War II, when it was made **capital** of the newly formed **Federation of Southern Rhodesia, Northern Rhodesia and Nyasaland**. The city expanded with new enterprises and industry. By the time the Federation broke up in 1963, the industrial base was firmly established. Following **UDI** in 1965, construction slowed down, and reached a standstill by the time the Smith regime capitulated. The pace picked up dramatically after **Independence** – especially during the 1980s – with an energy to make up for the stagnant years of sanctions. New buildings shot up around the centre with Yugoslav, Korean and Chinese construction agencies all involved in prestige projects in Zimbabwe's first decade of independence. Despite growing debt problems, prestige buildings have continued to go up in the 1990s.

Arrival, information and transport

By air you arrive at **Harare Airport**, 15km southeast of the city, which has a **bureau de change** open for all international flights. From the airport, when planes are arriving, there's supposed to be an hourly bus, which takes about twenty minutes and drops off in central Harare at the terminus opposite *Meikles Hotel* in Third Street, but it doesn't always come – ask around when you arrive at the airport. Metered taxis (the meters do work!) are thick on the ground and worth it if there are at least two of you. *Hertz*, *Avis* and *Elite* have car rental offices at the airport.

Trains pull into the station at the southern end of the city centre. Most central places are within walking distance, but if you need a taxi head for the rank outside the station in Kenneth Kaunda Avenue. Failing that try the one at *Meikles Hotel* four blocks up in Third Street.

Buses and coaches are more complicated. There is no central terminal for luxury coaches; instead, each company has its own departure and arrival point (see box). All are central and close to taxis or within walking distance of hotels in the Avenues. Long-distance economy buses terminate at Mbare bus station, although many pass through the centre on the way; from Mbare, catch an urban bus or taxi.

LUXURY COACH ARRIVAL AND DEPARTURE POINTS

Blue Arrow/Greyhound (for Bulawayo, Johannesburg and Mutare): Speke Ave (east of *Meikles Hotel*); ☎729514
DSB Coachline (for Nyanga, Lusaka and Chiredzi): *Sheraton Hotel*; ☎734837
Silverbird (for Johannesburg): *Sheraton Hotel*; ☎794777

Stagecoach (for Blantyre): *Blue Arrow/Greyhound* terminal (see above)
Translux (for Johannesburg): *Holiday Inn*; ☎725132
Zimi-Bus (for Johannesburg and Durban): *Holiday Inn*; ☎6782308

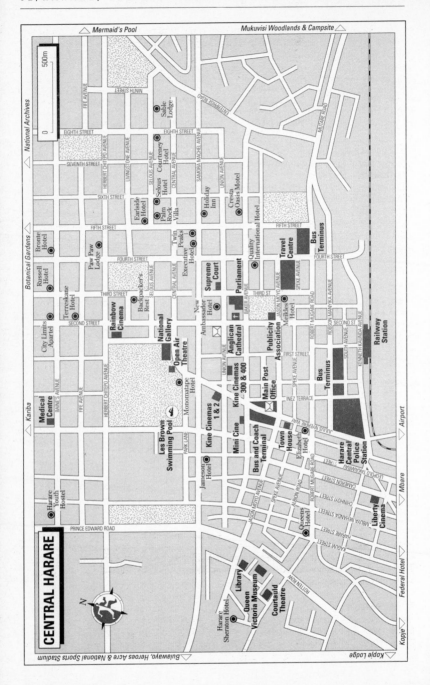

CENTRAL HARARE

△ Mermaid's Pool

△ Mukuvisi Woodlands & Campsite △

500m

0

National Archives ◁

FIFE AVENUE

NINTH STREET

ENTERPRISE ROAD

MUTARE ROAD

Sable Lodge

EIGHTH STREET

EIGHTH STREET

Courteney Hotel

SEVENTH STREET

HERBERT CHITEPO AVENUE

LIVINGSTONE AVENUE

SELOUS AVENUE

CENTRAL AVENUE

SAMORA MACHEL AVENUE

UNION AVENUE

Botanical Gardens ◁

SIXTH STREET

Earlside Hotel

Selous Hotel

Palm Rock Villa

Holiday Inn

Cresta Oasis Motel

Bronte Hotel

FIFTH STREET

FIFTH STREET

Bus Terminus

Russell Hotel

Paw Paw Lodge

Twin Peaks Hotel

Quality International Hotel

Travel Centre

FOURTH STREET

FOURTH STREET

City Limits Apartel

Terreskane Hotel

Executive Hotel

Supreme Court

Parliament

BAKER AVENUE

JASON MOYO AVENUE

SPEKE AVENUE

THIRD STREET

Backpacker's Rest

THIRD ST

Meikles Hotel

ROBSON MANYIKA AVENUE

SECOND STREET

Rainbow Cinema

New Ambassador Hotel

ROBERT MUGABE ROAD

SECOND ST

Railway Station

City Limits Apartel

National Gallery

Anglican Cathedral

Publicity Association

KENNETH KAUNDA AVENUE

BAINES AVENUE

HERBERT CHITEPO AVENUE

FIFE AVENUE

Open Air Theatre

UNION AVENUE

FIRST STREET

SPEKE AVENUE

SOUTH AVENUE

Kariba ◁

Monomatape Hotel

Kine Cinemas 300 & 400

Main Post Office

Bus Terminus

PARK LANE

Les Brown Swimming Pool

Kine Cinemas 1 & 2

Mini Cine

INEZ TERRACE

Harare Youth Hostel

Jameson Hotel

Bus and Coach Terminal

Town House

Elizabeth Hotel

Harare Central Police Station

JULIUS NYERERE WAY

ALBION ROAD

ROBERT MUGABE ROAD

CAMERON STREET

CHINHOYI STREET

LEOPOLD TAKAWIRA STREET

Airport ▷

PRINCE EDWARD ROAD

JASON MOYO AVENUE

SPEKE AVENUE

Queens Hotel

MBUYA NEHANDA STREET

HARARE STREET

KAGVI STREET

Liberty Cinema

Mbare ▷

ROTTEN ROW

Library

Queen Victoria Museum

Courtauld Theatre

Harare Sheraton Hotel

N

Kopje ▷

Federal Hotel ▷

Kopje Lodge ▷

STREET NAME CHANGES

The following Harare streets were renamed in 1990, although you may still come across the old names from time to time. The names in italics are the former names.

Beatrice Rd/Watt Rd/	Simon Mazorodze	*Mtoko Rd*	Mutoko Rd
Chandler Way	Way	*North Ave*	Josiah Tongogara Ave
Forbes Ave	Robson Manyika Ave	*Pioneer St*	Kaguvi St
Gaul Ave	Bishop Gaul Ave	*Queensway North/*	Airport Rd
Gordon Ave	George Silundika Ave	*Queensway Rd*	
Harare/Beatrice Rd	Masvingo Rd	*Rhodes Ave*	Herbert Chitepo Ave
Harare Rd North	Harare Rd	*Salisbury Drive*	Harare Drive
Hatfield Rd/Prince	Seke Rd	*Salisbury St*	Harare St
Edward Dam Rd		*Salisbury Way*	Harare Way
Kings Crescent	Julius Nyerere Ave	*Sinoia St*	Chinhoyi St
Manica Rd West/	Robert Mugabe Rd	*Sir James*	Rekayi Tangwena Ave
Manica Rd		*McDonald Rd*	
Mazoe Rd	Mazowe Rd	*Stanley Ave*	Jason Moyo Ave
Mazoe St	Mazowe St	*Umtali Rd*	Mutare Rd
Moffat St	Leopold Takawira St	*Victoria St*	Mbuya Nehanda St
Montagu Ave	Josiah Chinamano Rd	*Widdecombe Rd*	Chiremba Rd

Information

General **information** in Harare is thin on the ground and pretty poorly co-ordinated. Your best starting point is the *Publicity Association* on the Second Street side of African Unity Square, where staff usually appear reluctant to part with information, although you can sometimes get answers to specific questions. They do, however, have a heavily subscribed and chaotic noticeboard, which you can trawl through to find information about tours, car rental, places to stay and so on; they also sell a colour city map and publish a moderately useful monthly *What's On In Harare*, which lists coming events. For specific information about **concerts and movies**, your best bet is the otherwise dull *Herald*, which is sold on street corners in the centre as well as at all the bookshops and newsagents.

Probably the best source of information for backpackers is through the informal channel of lodges. Many of the better ones have good **noticeboards** and some even keep files of useful literature about other lodges around the country, tours, adventure activities and transport. If you're staying a while and venturing into the sprawling suburbs, one of the **street atlases**, available from bookshops such as *Kingstons* (see "Listings" for addresses), is essential.

For tourist-oriented **long-distance transport** – flights, luxury coaches and trains – you can usually get information from any of the decent travel agents in town (see "Listings"), or go directly to the relevant operators (see the box on p.61 for details of luxury coach companies). **Flight information** is available from Harare airport (☎737011); to find out about the availability of domestic flights and to make reservations, contact *Air Zimbabwe* (see "Listings" for addresses). **Train information** and timetables are available from the railway station at Second St/Kenneth Kaunda Ave. For long-distance economy buses, you'll need to turn up at the bus station and glean what information you can by asking people.

City transport

Most places of interest can be reached on **foot**, and Harare's wide streets and established cycle tracks make it an ideal city for **cycling** (see "Listings", p.80, for details of bike rental). For access to the suburbs, there are taxis, buses, commuter omnibuses (aka "commuters") and emergency taxis ("ETs", usually old Peugeot estate cars). **Taxis**

SECURITY

Although muggings are on the increase, Harare is no more dangerous than most cities, even at night. Theft is a major problem, however, and vigilance pays. Watch out particularly for **pickpockets** in crowded places: the bus stations and the market are favourite hunting grounds for nimble-fingered criminals. If you have a car, always lock it, and don't leave valuables inside – car break-ins are common. Beware particularly of the gardens and the area around the National Gallery at night. This vicinity is also favoured by kids with bogus sponsorship forms seeking donations. Check out their credentials.

are by far the easiest option in a city with crowded and poor public transport; around the centre fares, which are metered, are affordable, but expect to pay from US$5 upwards for a ride into the suburbs (see "Listings" for details of ranks and phone numbers). **Buses** are the least viable way of getting around, as they are infrequent and usually full. Like buses, **ETs** and **commuters** follow fixed routes and take a number of passengers. They charge a cheap flat rate for any distance, but it takes a while to work out routes – worthwhile only if you're planning a long stay. **Hitching** is also possible – you'll see many people thumbing to and from work, usually paying for a lift in privately owned cars.

Tours of sights in the city, in the suburbs and out of town, such as Mbare market, Mukuvisi Woodlands and Chapungu, cost around $US15 per person for half a day and are well worth considering given the poor state of Harare's public transport. They're run by a growing number of operators, including *Bushbeat Trails*, 6th Floor, Memorial House, 35 Samora Machel Ave (☎461172), and *UTC*, United House, 4 Park St (☎793701), who also have desks at some of the larger hotels including *Meikles* and the *Holiday Inn*.

Accommodation

Finding a bed in Harare is no longer easy. The four- and five-star **international hotels** are expensive, while the **mid-range** places tend to fill up fast. Middle-bracket rooms, however, are generally good value. Most are clean, well serviced, with swimming pools, and within easy walking distance of the centre. Options at the bottom of the range can be slightly seedy, as some **inexpensive hotels** double up as brothels. Better than these, if you're on a tight budget, are the **backpackers' lodges** that have mushroomed in recent years to cater for the influx of shoestring travellers. Most are old houses near the centre, with bedrooms converted into small dorms. Cooking facilities are provided, and some lodges even have gardens and pools.

A good area to start looking for somewhere inexpensive or mid-range to stay is **the Avenues** – the chunk northeast of the Harare Gardens (usually referred to simply as "the gardens") between Second Street and Enterprise Road. Lined with jacaranda and other flamboyant trees, these quiet streets are where you'll find the oldest colonial-style town houses, with their colonnaded verandahs and shady gardens. At the top end of the scale, well-heeled tourists can opt to avoid staying at the plush city centre hotels, and head out instead to the **game farms** and **country lodges** just outside the capital.

Camping and backpacker lodges

Backpackers and Overlanders Lodge, 932 Delport Rd, Airport (☎5074115). One of the city's best backpackers' lodges, with double rooms, a women-only dorm and camping facilities, plus a swimming pool and garden. It's near the airport and offers free and regular transport in and out of

The **area telephone code** for Harare is ☎14.

town (pick-up point *Lido Café*, Union Ave), as well as to the airport and railway station. You can self-cater or eat their reasonably priced evening meal. ①.

Backpackers Rest, Livingstone Ave/Third St (☎738593). En-suite double rooms with neither linen nor cooking facilities. Dorm space available. ①.

Coronation Park Campsite, 6km east of the centre on the Mutare Road (☎46282). An inexpensive and pleasant enough site, with good washrooms, a public phone and easy access to shops, but it's well out of town (hitch or take the Greendale bus from Rezende Street; the taxi fare will eat up any money saved by camping).

Daily Planet, 99 Josiah Chinamano Ave (☎730353). Colonial house turned budget hostel in the Avenues. Outside showers and indifferent rooms do little to justify rates at the upper end of its range. ①.

The Guest House, 164 Harare St (☎728512). The most expensive and efficiently packed dorms in Harare are only worth considering if you enjoy the challenge of climbing over several people to get into bed. Their doubles are also pricy. ①–②.

Harare Youth Hostel, 6 Josiah Chinamano Ave (☎796436). An unenthralling hostel which is often full. Bunks are in dorms and you can cook. Doors open only 5–10pm (you're thrown out in the morning). ①.

Kopje Lodge, 33 Fort Rd, parallel to Rotten Row (☎790637). Just outside the central shopping district, and among the most popular and best-run lodges in the capital. A victim of its own success when full, but very congenial at other times, with well-priced doubles, dorms and camping, as well as a bar, homemade pizzas and good food. There's also a free airport pick-up service. ①.

Modbella Lodge, 63 Kilwinning Rd, Hatfield (☎572206). Devoid of character, out of the centre and overpriced. ①.

Palm Rock Villa, 39 Selous Ave (☎724550). Arguably the best – and cheapest – of the lodges in the Avenues. Clean and well-maintained, with a generously equipped kitchen, plenty of showers and loos, and excellent facilities for budget travellers, including laundry, secure off-street parking, lockups for left luggage and a phone for incoming calls. ①.

Paw Paw Lodge, 262 Herbert Chitepo Ave (☎724337). A bit tatty, but offering the usual backpacker facilities in a central location. ①.

Peterborough Lodge, 11 Peterborough Ave, off Samora Machel Ave opposite *Water Whirld* (☎796735). Spotless lodge in the suburbs bordering the centre that's geared more for volunteers on postings to Zimbabwe than backpackers. Their dorms and doubles are among the best deals in the city, but fill up fast – especially over weekends. Facilities include a TV and pleasant garden. Self-catering only. ①.

The Rocks, 18 Seke Rd (city centre end). Essentially the terminus for a score of Africa overland companies. Clean and well run, with camping, cheap doubles and dorms, and a relaxing bar/dining room under thatch, but all the trucks around can make it feel like a huge car park. No phone or pick-up service, although Seke Rd is a major thoroughfare and buses and ETs are frequent. ①.

Sable Lodge, 95a Selous Ave (☎726017). The most popular of the city centre lodges, in a colonial-style house, with a swimming pool, kitchen, shared rooms and plenty of overlanders. Some double rooms also available. ①–②.

Twin Peaks, 130 Samora Machel Ave (☎730537). Opposite the *Holiday Inn* (in more ways than one), this dorms-only outfit is not the cleanest in town. ①.

Wayfarer Lodge, 47 Jesmond Rd, Logan Park, Hatfield (☎/fax 572125). If backpacker lodges were star-rated this would get five. In the suburbs near the airport, it offers camping – in your own tent or theirs – as well as very reasonable dorms and doubles; meals are also provided or you can self-cater, and there's a free pick-up service and cheap taxi into town. Traditional-style thatched rondavels in the garden and good organization make it a thoroughly pleasant place to hang out. ①.

Inexpensive hotels

Earlside Hotel, Fifth St/Selous Ave (☎721101). The elegant colonial facade with a swimming pool hides a tatty interior with shared facilities, though it is good value nevertheless. There is also a backpackers' dorm in the hotel, but valuables are not safe. Good, cheap dinners. ②.

Elizabeth Hotel, Julius Nyerere Way/Robert Mugabe Rd (☎753437–9). A regular venue for live music and haunt of pickpockets, though the rooms are clean. Not recommended for women travellers. ②.

Executive Hotel, Fourth St/Samora Machel Ave (☎792803). This central converted block of flats has large rooms, all en suite, and is good value. ②.

Feathers Hotel, Sherwood Drive, Mabelreign (☎228472–3). Out in the suburbs, but clean enough. ③.

Federal Hotel, 9 Harare St (☎752406). Close to Mbare and gives a good taste of African Harare. ②.

George Hotel, King George Road, Avondale (☎336677). Nicest of the suburban hotels, close to town and in a very good area, near shops. ③.

Mushandira Pamwe Hotel, Nyandoro Rd, Highfield (☎664355–7). Cheap rooms are offset by the taxi fare into central Harare from this former African township. But if you want music, you're on the doorstep of one of the capital's main music venues, with nightly gigs. ②.

Quality International Hotel, Baker Ave/Fourth St (☎729439 or 700333, fax 706560). Central and newly refurbished, but somewhat anonymous. ③.

Queens Hotel, Robert Mugabe Rd/Kaguvi St (☎738977). Live music here every weekend, and pretty frenetic. Watch out for pickpockets. Not recommended for women travellers, though rooms are clean with a cup of hot tea and two sugars provided first thing. ②.

Red Fox Hotel, Stewart Rd opposite Honey Dew Farm (☎495466). Pretty clean and decent hotel, a long way out of town, in an incongruous mock-Tudor style. ③.

Russell Hotel, 116 Baines Ave (☎791896). Plenty of acceptable rooms, but tends to get full, especially during polytechnic exams in October and November. ③.

Selous Hotel, Selous Ave/Sixth St (☎727940, 727948 or 727949). Decent rooms, all with bathroom. ③.

Terreskane Hotel, Fife Ave/Second St (☎707031–4, fax 790231). A bit of a drinking spot – lively, but not the place for a quiet night. ③.

Mid-range hotels and lodges

There are several mid-range places along the Avenues, many quieter than the cheap central city hotels. This range also includes some low-key hotels further out in the suburbs which are only worth considering if you have your own transport, or if the central hotels are full. Most have restaurants and bars attached.

Astor Jabulani Hotel, 190 Herbert Chitepo Ave (☎720122, fax 796179). Standing on the opposite side of the gardens to the *Monomotapa* (see below), this is definitely the less prestigious of the two. Perfectly adequate, if characterless, rooms. ④.

Bronte Hotel, 132 Baines Ave (☎796631 or 796635). Most rooms with bathroom, in a gracious colonial building with big gardens – highly recommended. ④.

Courteney Hotel, Selous Ave/Eighth St (☎706411). All rooms en suite, located in the quiet Avenues; pool, morning papers, free local phone calls and TV. ④.

Cresta Lodge, Samora Machel Ave/Robert Mugabe Rd, Coronation Park (☎487006 or 487008, fax 487009). Six kilometres from the city, offering international standards at a cheaper rate. All rooms are en suite, with colour TV, videos etc. Free transport can be provided to and from the city centre and airport. ④.

Cresta Oasis Motel, 124 Baker Ave (☎704217, fax 790865). Smart and comfortable place – all rooms with bathroom and TV, morning newspaper delivered, and a swimming pool. ④.

Kentucky Airport Hotel, 27 St Patrick's Rd, Hatfield (☎570109). Convenient for the airport, with free transport, but a fair distance from the centre. ④.

New Ambassador Hotel, Union Ave, PO Box 872 (☎708121). Central and smart, with radio, TV and phone in each room. ⑤.

International hotels

Harare's multi-star outfits match their counterparts throughout the world, and considering this, are relatively low-priced, though still firmly in the expense-account bracket.

Harare Sheraton, Pennefather Ave (☎729771 or 728728, fax 794308). Part of the flash international chain – inside, you could be anywhere. ⑨.

Holiday Inn, Samora Machel Ave/Fifth St (☎795611, fax 735695). Most casual of the hotels in this bracket, with a nice pool. ⑥.

Jameson Hotel, Samora Machel Ave/Park St (☎794641). Conveniently central and excellent value for this price. ⑤.

Meikles Hotel, Third St/Jason Moyo Ave (☎707721 or 795655, fax 707753). The best of the city's international hotels, overlooking African Unity Square; you can't get more central than this. ⑨.

Monomatapa, 54 Park Lane (☎704501 or 704511, fax 791920). On the edge of the Harare Gardens, with the best views in town; ask for the top floors. ⑥.

Out of town

None of the places listed below are more than an hour's drive from town, many being game farms that also offer day trips if you want to get out and see African wildlife. These mini-safaris are a far cry from Hwange's though, with the landscapes tamed and pretty, and the elephants, zebras, giraffes and lions enclosed behind electrified fences to guarantee brilliant photos. Other places are more modest guest houses, offering solid country-style luxury for weekends away or first and last nights in Zimbabwe, while a couple of the cheaper options are conveniently situated near the airport in a pleasant farming district. None, except a few at the cheaper end of the range, accept walk-ins; all offer free or inexpensive transfers to and from town/the airport. The luxury places do an all-inclusive rate, which covers all meals, drinks, walks and drives.

Duck Farm, PO Box 15, Ruwa (☎173/2494). Great for overlanders, with a resident mechanic on site. Turn right at the Ruwa supermarket on the main Mutare road, into Chiremba Road. The farm, 1km further on, has modest cottages, *braai* places and camping. Meals available. ①.

Imba Matombo, 3 Albert Glen Close, Glenlorne (☎499013–4, fax 499071). Luxurious modern house, 18km from the centre, with posh meals around the dinner table. From US$130 per person for dinner, bed and breakfast.

Landela Lodge, PO Box 66293, Kopje, Harare (☎734043–6, fax 750785). Wonderful farmhouse near Ruwa, 35min from the airport, with lush gardens and superb food, for the safari set. Highly recommended and a great option if international hotels pall. Sightseeing trips into town can be arranged, as well as trips to a nearby game farm where you can also ride. US$140 per person all in.

Mwanga Lodge, Bally Vaughan Game Park, PO Box HG886, Highlands (☎174431, fax 174430). Luxury lodge for 12 people, 44km north of Harare, on a game farm with enclosed lions, leopards and small cats (no drop-ins, but day trips can be arranged from Harare for US$25, which includes an elephant ride, canoeing, and a visit to a bird sanctuary and animal orphanage). Children under 12 welcome, others by arrangement. US$135 per person all in.

Mwena Lodge, PO Box 35, Selous (☎162/8270). The cheapest game lodge in Zimbabwe – and certainly better value than its pretentious neighbour, *Pamuzinda* – with a lively bar and earthy owner. The lodge lies an hour's drive south of Harare, and transport will be arranged when you book. Horse riding is a big attraction and there are game drives in an ersatz Model-T Ford retrieved from the film set of *King Solomon's Mines*. Around US$45 per person all in.

Pamuzinda Safari Lodge, PO Box 2833, Harare (☎751183). A lodge on a game farm in flat Msasa country, about 80km (one hour's drive) from Harare on the Bulawayo road. Their peaceful rooms have verandahs and are tastefully decorated with ethnic furnishings, though pricy. Ideal for jetsetters with no time for Hwange, or a recommended treat for your first or last night in Zimbabwe. US$140 per person all in.

Setanga Lodge, Setonleigh turning, off the Ruwa road, next to the *Ruwa Country Club* (PO Box 175, Ruwa; ☎173/2381). Exceptionally friendly guest house on a smallholding, close to the airport. The perfect place to spend your first or last few days in Zimbabwe: double rooms inside the house or thatched en-suite cottages, with access to facilities at the adjacent country club. Birdlife is good, too, and there are plans to introduce game onto the property. ④.

Thetford House, PO Box CY4, Causeway, Harare (☎393021, fax 724728). A large, English-style country mansion in the Mazowe Valley. The area is pretty with hills, farms and good walks. From US$95 per person all in.

The city centre

Harare's **city centre** splits up quite neatly into functional districts. The **main commercial area**, with smart shops, banks and restaurants, is largely confined to the section west of Fourth Street, around **African Unity Square** and up to the **Harare Gardens**. **First Street** is an attractive pedestrian mall where you can sit at outdoor cafés and survey the passing scene. The0 distinctively curving *Monomatapa Hotel*, scraping more sky than most, makes an effective landmark. **Jason Moyo Avenue**, between Second and Fourth streets, is a tourist strip, with the Publicity Association information offices, *Sun Hotels*, national parks booking office and travel agents, and the *Air Zimbabwe* terminal around the corner in Third Street. On the southwest side of the centre, in the **Kopje area**, the roads suddenly skew off-centre and you're in a different city. From here zip over the Kopje itself, and you'll find yourself in Harare's high-density suburbs, hidden from view – and conscience – by the hill.

The main attraction of the city centre is the **National Gallery**, with its superb array of modern sculpture and traditional African art. The capital's museums are less rewarding, though the **National Archives** feature some interesting historical material.

Historic buildings

You can read Harare's history in its skyline. Post-Independence confidence is reflected in individualistic 1980s towers, clad in coats of many colours, looking down on the post-World War II buff-coloured boxes. The liberation struggle years are on record, too, in the absence of buildings from the 1970s, when guns came before bricks.

One notable exception to the lack of 1970s buildings is the **Monomatapa Hotel** (frequently referred to as "Monos"), on the edge of the Harare Gardens, one of the few modern buildings to make reference to the meandering walls of Great Zimbabwe – and thus the country's ancient architectural tradition.

The **National Gallery of Zimbabwe** (see below for a description of its collections) is within spitting distance of the *Monomatapa* in Park Lane. Completed in 1957, the gallery is an example of the International Style developed by twentieth-century European and American architects and so named because they thought it was universally appropriate – a symbol of international modernity.

The **Judges' Chambers** of the **Supreme Court of Zimbabwe** occupy the corner of Third Street and Union Avenue. The 1927 building was originally conceived as the headquarters of Rhodes' British South Africa Company (BSAC), which governed the country in its infancy. When construction began in 1895 on the nearby **Parliament Buildings**, on the corner of Baker Avenue and Third Street, it was going to be a hotel. However, the First Chimurenga brought building to a standstill as troops putting down the rebellion were billeted in the unfinished shell. When the developers went bust in 1898 the BSAC took it over to use as a post office, but soon after the newly formed Legislative Assembly was installed. As the first session sat in 1899, the builders were still at work. For **guided tours** or seats in the **visitors gallery** during debates, apply to The Chief Information Officer, Parliament of Zimbabwe, PO Box 8055, Causeway, Harare.

Harare's **Anglican Cathedral**, on Baker Avenue and Second Street, took a mere fifty years to complete after inception in 1913. The designer, Sir Herbert Baker, was South Africa's leading architect; he was responsible for the Union Buildings in Pretoria and worked on the design of New Delhi with Lutyens, the master of imperial architecture. Baker wanted the Harare cathedral to have a cylindrical bell tower as a reference to the conical tower at Great Zimbabwe – a rare acknowledgement of indigenous forms – but this eccentric idea was, sadly, overruled. The sombreness of the interior, with its starkly impressive solid granite columns, is relieved by the cartoon-like murals of the stations of the cross. If you're lucky you may hear Shona women at choir practice, using traditional percussion, and for some beautiful vernacular hymns, try to look in on a Shona Eucharist (times are posted outside the cathedral).

The Town House in Julius Nyerere Way (between Speke and Jason Moyo Ave) is the seat of Harare's municipal government. It was built in 1933 in an eclectic classical style with somewhat incompatible Florentine and Art Deco features.

Stroll down **Robert Mugabe Road** for some of Harare's less studiedly monumental – and more rewarding – historic buildings. Most of these are found towards Fourth Street, but there are also a handful further west on the way to the Queen Victoria Museum, along Rotten Row. Among these are the 1902 **Vasan's Footwear**, originally an outfitters, with a typical turn-of-the-century pavement canopy supported on slender columns, and **Queen's Hotel**, dating from 1900 but largely refurbished in 1930. Nearby, bunched together in **Rotten Row**, are the **Courtauld Theatre**, the **Central Library** and the **Queen Victoria Museum**, with giant concrete snail, pangolin, praying mantis and chameleon standing guard outside (see below for a description of the museum collection).

A short walk away is the country's most controversial post-Independence building. The **Sheraton Hotel** and **Harare International Conference Centre** is a shimmering gilt glass slab of monumental proportions. Going inside is to step off the streets of Third World Harare and to enter a brassy Midas-world where everything that can be is gold, from the gold-tinted windows, gold light fittings and gold-finished furniture down to the guests' gold watches and medallions. The building is the work of the Yugoslavian *Energoprojekt* company, who brought in their own building teams and materials to produce this futuristic zone of theatrical totalitarianism. Rumour has it that the government wanted Zimbabweans to work on the project and, when they persisted in this demand in mid-construction, *Energoprojekt* deserted, taking their drawings with them and leaving local architects to work it all out. They must have succeeded.

The National Gallery of Zimbabwe

Julius Nyerere Way/Park Lane. Tues–Sun 9am–5pm. Nominal entrance fee (free Sun).
Opened in 1957, Zimbabwe's National Gallery houses a major collection of African art, drawn from throughout the continent, though from the outset it has also promoted local talent and has served as an institution for all races. An initial interest in painting was soon surpassed when the curators became aware of **stone sculptures** by Joram Mariga. In the 1960s a workshop was founded, with stone being brought in from Nyanga and given to the employees, and Zimbabwe's formidable movement in sculpture was thus established. Initially, under the directorship of Frank McEwan, it produced works geared towards European expectations, but in recent years the emphasis has become truly national, while the movement has gained world recognition.

Modern stone sculpture gets a good showing in the **ground-floor galleries** of the permanent collection and in a well-populated **sculpture garden**, inhabited by mythological creatures and beast-humans frozen in mid-transformation. **Bernard Matemera**, master of this species conversion, has a number of distinctively distorted works scattered about. Amongst other big names, the **Takawira brothers** drag exquisitely refined busts from rough-hewn stone that remains part of the work.

The interior walls, hung with mostly unexceptional **paintings** and **drawings**, pale against the boldly confident stone works that hold the floor. From time to time, however, the gallery holds **special exhibitions** of more interesting international works, while the annual **Nedlaw competition**, which draws entries from up and down the country, is always worth taking in.

The real treasure house of the museum is formed by the permanent collection of African art in the **upstairs galleries**. Oddly, the east and west of the continent dominate, though richly patterned domestic objects from Zimbabwe feature at the end of the collection. The works from Côte d'Ivoire, Mali, Ghana and the Central African Republic are more representational and less utilitarian than the Zimbabwean offerings of headrests, stools, beadwork and weapons. Throughout Africa there's no traditional concept of art for its own sake. These artefacts were social and religious objects in everyday use and carry their creators' belief in a universally present life force in all things. The carver was frequently a highly respected and feared figure who channelled the power of the spirits into works which seem to contain pent-up energy.

Among numerous highlights, look out for the large wooden carving of the mythical **porgaga** bird from Burkina Faso. With huge bill and distended belly symbolizing fertility, it adorns shrines where girls are taught womanly matters and go through the ritual passage of genital mutilation. The spherical face of the **akua'ba** doll from Ghana represents the Ashanti ideal of beauty; these dolls were carried by the pregnant women for perfect children. The Malian **chi wara** eland headress is used in ceremonial re-enactments of the birth of agriculture; Bambara legend has it that the antelope taught humans grain cultivation. It's worn to portray the animal's magical relationship to fertility.

The gallery shop

More than just a heritage display case, the National Gallery is also a market-place for arts and crafts, with the **gallery shop** extending the hands-on approach of the collections. In addition to the expected books and publications, you can buy a range of local arts and crafts. While much of it is mediocre, there's more **sculpture** in the shop than the gallery's own collection and you can pick up something good by an unknown name very reasonably – or pay thousands for works by the well-established figures.

There's also a good selection of **local crafts** at affordable prices (in spite of the often hefty mark-up): baskets from the Binga district, *gudza* dolls made from bark, gourds, jewellery and hand-dyed and printed fabrics and garments.

The National Archives

Borrowdale Rd/Churchill Ave. Mon–Fri 7.45am–4.30pm, Sat 8am–noon. Free.

The **National Archives**, 3km north of the city centre, are an important resource for researchers and, although the staff are strict about access to the closed shelves, much of the collection remains open to the public and is well worth a browse.

The **Beit Gallery**, on the first floor, is perhaps the best and most accessible collection – a rich reserve of historic books, documents, newspapers, stamps and paintings relating to Zimbabwe's history. Books dating back to the mid-sixteenth century include original African travelogues by Portuguese adventurers, with scientific and ethnographic coverage that reads like science fiction; one antique colour plate shows a fantastic hippo baring jagged carnivorous fangs. The **newspaper display**, on the same floor, traces Zimbabwe's history in press reports, through federation, UDI and post-Independence – interesting not just for the history, but the way events were reported at different times. Climb the spiral stairs from here and you'll reach the **stamp collection**, including some from turn-of-the-century Cape Colony, overprinted with the British South Africa Company's initials. True to British form, a postal service was one of the first things organized in the new territory.

The **reading room** and **illustrations room**, on the ground floor, are very browsable, and the former's glass wall, revealing an ornamental pond, must make it one of the most pleasant anywhere. You can ask for material to be dredged up from the archives if you're researching, or you can just immerse yourself in the large ready reference section. Dress warmly in winter – there's no heating and it gets surprisingly cold.

The Queen Victoria Museum

Rotten Row opposite the Sheraton Hotel. Mon–Sat 9am–5pm. US$2.
Knocked into a cocked hat by the excellent National Museum in Bulawayo, the capital's more modest historical museum nevertheless gives a digestible chance to whizz through Zimbabwe's basics before heading out – but if it's Bulawayo you're heading out to, don't waste your time here.

Amidst the motley collection of didactic bric-a-brac – freshwater aquaria, a history of life, the world and everything – just one exceptionally well-displayed gallery stands out. This is the **habitat exhibition** in the **natural sciences gallery**, a sure draw for any wildlife enthusiast en route to the game parks. More than just museum pieces, this series of displays re-creates Zimbabwe's variety of landscapes so realistically that you're left wondering how they got the granite kopje inside (adorned with appropriate flora and fauna). The other habitat displays are equally good – and more informative than a dozen books.

From far earlier times, there's a reconstruction of a fast-moving **dinosaur** – half bird, half lizard and warm blooded. In one place in the Zambezi Valley over twenty of these small predators were found in a group. The **oldest fossils** discovered were found near Bulawayo – primitive plants some 2700 million years old.

Parks and gardens

In central Harare, with its generous climate and heritage of British parks, you're never more than ten minutes from green space. **African Unity Square**, between Parliament and *Meikles Hotel*, is a pleasant, fountain-decked piazza frequented by relaxed *Herald* readers and jazzed up by flower sellers. Its former name, Cecil Square, was changed in 1988 to celebrate unification of Zimbabwe's two main parties.

Largest and loveliest of the city's public spaces, the **Harare Gardens** are well manicured and well used. On afternoons schoolkids loll about doing homework and on weekends wedding parties parade around, the women in white chiffons and shiny red fancy dress, the men charcoal-suited. People stroll the thoroughfare which cuts through it from Park Lane to Herbert Chitepo Avenue and it's a good place to take a break and watch Harare. In the park behind the *Monomatapa* is the Olympic-sized Les Brown public **swimming pool**, open throughout the year and with lawns for sunbathing. On Sundays, around late morning and lunchtime, a big market brings a bit of bustle to the gardens, and makes a pleasant place to go craft hunting.

The main attraction of **Greenwood Park**, between Seventh and Eighth streets and Herbert Chitepo and Josiah Chinamano avenues, is the children's playground with miniature railway and boating pool (Sat 2–5.30pm, Sun 10am–1pm & 2–5pm).

Fronting up to the northern suburbs, the **National Botanic Gardens** are Zimbabwe's answer to Britain's Kew, a place where you can immerse yourself in fantasy African vegetation, neatly divided into ecological zones (open sunrise to sunset). There's a fine collection of the continent's **trees**, including most of Zimbabwe's 750 species, while large areas are closely cropped **parkland** ideal for picnicking or lazy afternoons. The gardens are about thirty minutes on foot from the centre: go north up Fifth Street, which becomes Sandringham Drive, and the main entrance is on the right. Otherwise, catch any bus down Second Street and get off at Downie Avenue, where there's another entrance.

Mbare

If Harare has a heart, **Mbare** must be it: a quarter that should on no account be missed. Once away from the orderly centre, you plunge into a distinctly African city of which vibrant Mbare is the liveliest part – still close to the centre (3km), and with streams of people walking down the road and hanging about the run-down blocks of flats. Poverty is all around, though you're unlikely to see anything desperate. Begging is, however, on the increase, as are muggings, and only a foolhardy visitor would wander around here alone after dark; women on their own are especially vulnerable.

Called Harare Township during the colonial days, Mbare's new name comes from a chief who once held court on the kopje. The quarter is the decades-old trading area for Africans bringing their produce in from the country, and it remains so today, hosting the country's biggest **market** – known as the *musika* – at the nexus of all road transport. Leave by bus from here for the rural areas or the provincial towns and you'll be part of a vast crowd of travellers, especially at weekends and holidays.

Getting to Mbare from central Harare is easy. Regular **buses** leave from the city terminus on Angwa Street/South Avenue. You can also pick up **emergency taxis** or **commuters** just opposite, although regular **taxis** are a lot less hassle. If you're **walking**, head out along Rotten Row or Cameron Street and ask for the *musika*.

The market

In 1981, following Independence, the City Council developed Mbare's trading area by adopting the idea of "communal markets" being successfully propagated at the time in China, and laid on washing facilities and covered stalls for traders. The enormous complex of the **musika** nowadays has endless different sections, selling produce, clothes, crafts, live poultry, traditional medicines and the unrecognizable. This is also your chance to try *chibuku* at one of the **beer halls** or some **street food**. The **fresh produce** area is a banquet of primary-coloured fruits and vegetables – mounds of the stuff for bulk buyers or smaller carefully arranged piles if you just want a salad's worth. Expect to be approached by a market porter who will trail after you, usually with a wheelbarrow, carrying your purchases for a tip.

In another part of the *musika*, **second-hand gear** ranges from piles of clothes on the pavement, to old plastic bottles and bags. In this litter-free country nothing is thrown away, everything is recyclable and almost anything broken can be cobbled together again. Invention is boundless – one stall sells buckled spectacle frames and broken sunshades. Look out, too, for the sandals made from worn-down tyres with cross-over straps. It's a standing joke in Harare that if you get something ripped off, the second-hand market at Mbare is the first place to look.

Herbal medicines are sold at several stalls and you can track down traditional healers (*n'angas*) who work in the area. The stalls are a mishmash of skins and seed pods, things in bottles, bunches of dried plants, and prized items like cowrie shells and gemsbok tails. The government has passed a bill strengthening the position of *n'angas*. An association was formed in 1981 and there's now some co-operation between modern and traditional practices. Some spirit medium *n'angas* are concerned only with the cause of the illness, while others just treat the physical symptoms.

Mbare is also one of the best places around for **souvenirs** and all kinds of odd and easy-to-carry gifts, although the stuff on offer is not necessarily cheaper than in the craft shops downtown. **Baskets** and **carved work** are common. Look out for hand-lathed objects such as snuffboxes wrought from exotic woods, which are very popular with African women for whom smoking is traditionally prohibited. Hand-beaten copper and brass **bracelets** are good buys. The women, particularly, are open to bargaining, but they're tough dealers.

Not far from the market is the **Canon Paterson Art Centre**, where you can watch **stone sculptors** working. Their stuff is sold at a small shop crammed full of elephants, Zimbabwe birds and the like. The stone itself is much more beautiful than most of the pieces, but small sculptures are inexpensive and easy enough to transport.

The suburbs

The once exclusively white areas of the capital are worth visiting if only as a monument to the British – or perhaps more truly American – suburban dream. But most travellers only pass through these elegant garden suburbs when en route to a handful of other sights.

Heroes' Acre

Heroes' Acre should top any list of out-of-the-centre attractions. Although you may not share the aesthetic, this shrine to the liberation struggle is undeniably imposing. It's a mixture of abstract monumental architecture, sculptures and friezes in an Afro-Korean version of socialist realism. From the un-African result it's easy to see that the Koreans dominated the design team.

One of the soldiers guarding the place will guide you up the monumental black staircase, give you a run-down on the entombed heroes and provide a commentary on the two friezes. The hefty granite slabs scale to a crescendo at the **eternal flame**, echoed in the flag raised by the triumphant figures of the foreground **monument to the unknown soldier**. (The eternal flame is actually an electric light switched on nightly.) On the lower first tier, burnished slabs bear down on the **graves of heroes** of the revolution while another series of unmarked stones waits eerily for tomorrow's luminaries.

Back on the ground, two didactic **friezes** in bronze relief flank the monument. The first traces **oppression**: vicious BSAP cops (the Rhodesian police force continued to bear the name of the British South Africa Police right up until Independence) and dogs savage youngsters and a mother and child, while the outraged parents organize opposition, eventually sending their children across the border for military training. The second frieze depicts the **armed struggle**, with large dashes of heroism culminating in a triumphant, Leninesque, Robert Mugabe declaiming to the masses.

Permits for Heroes' Acre, issued while you wait, are required from the Ministry of Information's Enquiries and Public Relations Office at Linquenda House, Baker Street. The site is 5km west of the centre, just off the Bulawayo road: catch any Bulawayo **bus**, or the Warren Park bus from a block past the *Jameson Hotel* on Samora Machel Avenue for the fifteen-minute ride. Alternatively, jump in a taxi.

On the way, near Heroes' Acre, you'll see an impressive new **stadium**, Chinese-built to Olympic proportions. There's a story, hopefully apocryphal, that the running track falls short by one metre. Huge political rallies and celebrations are held here, with mega-screens projecting images of the president for all to see.

Mukuvisi Woodlands

Tucked away, 3km from the centre, in Harare's southern suburbs, the msasa-wooded **nature reserve of Mukuvisi** is stocked with antelope, zebra, wildebeest, elephants and rhino (daily 6am–6pm; US$3). Even before the enclosure was erected in 1980 there were resident populations of duiker, steenbok, hares and guinea fowl. Luckily for the wildlife, City Council attempts to put up a housing estate here were quashed when concerned residents appealed to the High Court.

The antelope roam free; fiercer denizens are penned off. Orphaned elephant calves, hand-reared at the woodlands, are a popular attraction, and easily seen at the 3.30pm feeding time. For intrepid urban adventuring, join one of the two-hour **foot safaris** that leave on Saturdays at 2.30pm and Sundays at 8.30am (US$3 per person). You can get refreshments from the kiosk, open on weekends. Most of the 168-hectare woodlands is open to all for walking and is thoroughly pleasant (though there have been odd reports of muggings). Over 230 **bird species** have been recorded: lucky ornithologists may spot the ground-nesting nightjars or some of the wildfowl. Most of the region's trees grow here in the last patch of indigenous woodland inside the city limits.

Chapungu

Despite the promise of an "insight into the cultural and traditional life of Zimbabwe", you'd be lucky to feel the pulse of Africa at **Chapungu Village** ("Doon Estate", 1 Harrow Road; daily 8am–6pm; small entrance fee), 8km east of town off the Mutare road, near *Coronation Park* campsite. Nevertheless, the attached **Chapungu Sculpture Park** is one of the nicest places in Harare to see sculpture, with carvings spread around the extensive grounds and some select works indoors, including plenty of quality, affordable pieces by unknown artists. There's a tea garden, traditional dancing at the weekend (Sat 3pm, Sun 11am & 3pm), and you can stroll around and watch the resident sculptors at work. Various tour operators run trips out here (see p.64).

Borrowdale Park

There is **horse racing** at **Borrowdale Park**, 7km northeast of the centre, most week-ends. Cutting across social classes, a day at the races is an enjoyable way of getting under the skin of local life, and one with food, drink and gambling on hand. If you just want to bet, try one of the off-course totes in town. The Borrowdale **bus** picks up in Second Street on its way to the track.

Epworth Balancing Rocks

The **balancing rocks** at **Epworth**, just outside the eastern city limits and about 12km from the centre, don't hold huge attraction if you're planning to visit the Matopos district (where such phenomena abound). The main appeal of the place is the sheer concentra-tion of rock formations in a small area. There's nothing unusual about the stones them-selves – you'll see similar along roadsides all over Zimbabwe – but en masse it feels they are there as if by design. Young boys from the nearby settlement are persistent with offers to guide you and demands for cash, but you are free to clamber about the rocks.

The local community here grew up on mission land as a squatter camp for **war refu-gees**. You'll notice how dissimilar it is from the rest of the country's planned suburbs, with its shanty-town look and some of Zimbabwe's worst living conditions. In the early 1980s a cholera epidemic was hushed up, but the government has since worked hard to improve the people's lot, with a successful programme of Blair toilet building and the installation of protected wells. Nevertheless, the area has acquired something of an unsavoury reputa-tion over the past few years, so take care if you decide to venture out here alone.

Frequent **buses** to Epworth leave from the Fourth Street/Jason Moyo Avenue termi-nus. By **car**, take the Mutare Road turning right into Chiremba Road just outside the centre.

Eating and drinking

There's no shortage of places to eat in central Harare, but don't expect anything too imaginative or beautifully presented. You can have *sadza* (maize porridge) and *nyama* (meat stew), the staple diet in Zimbabwe, for next to nothing, or for something more familiar use the transatlantic-style snack bars. Alternatively, pay a bit more and you can choose from steak houses, Italian, Indian or Greek restaurants; standards are reasonable, but don't expect anything out of the ordinary.

Vegetarian restaurants are a concept yet to hit Harare. However, a growing number of establishments offer meat-free dishes. Try the Italian or Indian restaurants listed below, or starters at the Greek restaurants, which can make filling vegetarian meals in themselves. Failing that, most chefs will, in typically Zimbabwean style, "make a plan" if you ask.

Breakfast

Full **English breakfasts** to set you up for the day are the rule at most hotels; they're usually also available to non-residents, which can make a useful start to the day if you're backpacking. The *Monomatapa,* the *Sheraton,* the *Holiday Inn,* and the *Cresta Jameson* do buffet breakfasts which give the opportunity to binge for a fixed fee.

Sadza and street food

Around the station and Kopje endless joints sell cheap and filling **sadza meals**. More centrally you'll get similar fare at *Toff's Take-aways* in Rezende Street or *Baker's Inn,* First Street (next to *Chicken Inn*). Street food is noticeably absent in the centre, but at Mbare Market you'll find roasted *chibage* (corn on the cob), boiled eggs and stalls for *sadza* and relish.

Coffee, snacks and light meals

The **coffee bars** serve reasonably priced sandwiches and snacks. With outdoor seating, for your contemplation of the passing scene, the best are the *Brazita* and *Le Paris* in the Parkade Shopping Centre, First Street, and the *Wise Donkey* in the First Street mall, open from breakfast till shop closing time. Harare's closest imitation of a continental coffee bar is the *Europa,* near the *Monomatapa Hotel,* in Samora Machel Avenue, open at night as well as for breakfast. Another trendy venue is the *Sandrock Café,* near the cinemas on Julius Nyerere Way, which has foreign newspapers and pavement seating. For reasonably priced breakfasts, lunches and teas, *Strachans Tea Terrace* at 66 Baker Ave is a popular spot, as is the highly recommended coffee shop at the *Alliance Française* at 328 Herbert Chitepo Ave. The best place for cappuccino, pastries and pizza is in the suburb of Avondale at the *Italian Bakery,* Avondale Shopping Centre, 144 King George Rd (6am–11.30pm). *Scoop,* in the same centre, does great Italian **ice cream**.

A good option for lunch is the outdoor restaurant on the ground floor of *Meikles Hotel,* as is *Barbour's Terrace Restaurant* on First Street; of the two parts to *Barbour's,* the outside is cheaper and less formal. If you want to pig out at lunchtime, the *Holiday Inn* and the *Monomatapa* do substantial poolside buffets with a great selection of salads – a good choice for vegetarians.

African restaurants

National Handicraft Centre, Chinhoyi St/Grant St (☎721815). More a café than a restaurant, open during the day and erratically in the evenings, this is a good place to try Zimbabwean staple food.

Ramambo Lodge, 1st floor, BB House, Samora Machel Ave/Leopold Takawira St (☎792029). This "safari camp restaurant" is the place to try game dishes you'll never taste elsewhere. The menu includes Zimbabwean fish as well as vegetarian specialities. There is marimba music at lunchtimes and traditional dancing in the evening.

Roots of Africa, Livingstone Ave/Seventh St (☎721494). The only bona fide African restaurant in Harare. Reasonably priced dishes with a meat and chicken bias give a real flavour of Zimbabwe, as does the easy-going ambience. Traditional dancing some evenings.

European restaurants

Alexander's, 7 Livingstone Ave (☎700340). The most expensive, and perhaps most over-rated, restaurant in town, with a French flavour.

Aphrodite Taverna, Strathaven Shopping Centre (☎355000). Harare's best Greek restaurant, but well out of the centre. Casual, quiet and very reasonably priced.

Coimbra, 61 Selous Ave (☎725467). Their speciality – spicy piri-piri chicken – is one good reason to eat at this Portuguese restaurant.

Demis, Speke Ave/Leopold Takawira St (☎723308). Greek restaurant, a favourite with locals, where starters can make a full meal.

Guidos, Montagu Shopping Centre, Josiah Chinamano Ave (☎723349). Popular and inexpensive pizzeria near *Harare Youth Hostel*. Expect to wait for a table, even though it's not brilliant.

L'Escargot, *Courteney Hotel* (☎706411). Excellent à la carte menu with lots of fish, in a formal atmosphere.

Pino's, 73 Union St (☎792303). Italian restaurant in the city centre specializing in seafood.

Sherrol's in the Park, Harare Gardens (☎725535). Nice location with shady trees, more especially during the day when the patio is open; various vegetarian options and freshly squeezed orange juice.

Spagos Restaurant, *Russell Hotel* (☎790565). Recommended for good Italian pasta, as well as other, non-Italian dishes. It's worth booking as it gets full.

Asian restaurants

Bamboo Inn, 81–83 Robert Mugabe Rd (☎705457). The best Chinese restaurant in town.

Bombay Duck, 7 Central Ave (☎721487). Big tasty helpings of rather un-Indian curries.

Manchurian, Second St Extension, Avondale (☎36166). Excellent and inexpensive eat-as-much-as-you-want Mongolian barbecue; the chef cooks your choice of vegetables and meat on a large central grill.

Mandarin, 1st floor, Ivory House, Robert Mugabe Rd (☎726227). Good Chinese food, reasonably priced.

Sitar Restaurant, 39a Newlands Shopping Centre, Enterprise Rd (☎729132). Inconveniently located in the suburbs, but the only Indian restaurant in Harare with an authentic feel.

Bars

Bars are usually attached to hotels. At the cheaper ones things tend to be more raucous, particularly as the evening wears on – but this is where you're likely to find music (see below) and company if you want it. The *Terreskane* in the Avenues is a recommended outdoor place as is the garden at the *Earlside*. For more sedate – and often a little sedative – imbibing, the upmarket hotels with their "smart-casual" after-dark dress code are the obvious choice.

Music, film and theatre

Music vies with drinking to be Zimbabwe's unofficial national sport – and there's no shortage of jive joints in Harare. You'll find **live gigs** virtually every night, but while the pop-jaded West looks to Africa for inspiration, many Zimbabweans prefer American funk. Night clubs and discos spinning British and American discs cater to different social cliques all over town. Nevertheless local rock music is easy to find.

Besides rock, there are one or two venues for **classical music**. Watch the press for visiting international orchestras and performing groups. Countries eager to make a cultural mark on the developing world often lay on performances and there's sometimes the chance to take in exceptional stuff. There's also a nascent **drama** scene and you can sometimes see interesting performances. And if all else fails, there's always the **cinema**.

Rock venues and nightclubs

Every weekend brings a choice of bands competing for punters. Zimbabwean musicians (see the *Contexts* piece for background and recommendations) work hard for a living, play frequently and often don't even own their instruments.

The biggest events are at the end of each month – right after payday. This is the time when you'll catch the big names well known in Britain, such as **Thomas Mapfumo**. Till the early hours they hold *pungwes* – a word derived from the all-night rallies organized by guerrillas during the war. The best way to find a gig is to look at the posters wrapped around poles or tree trunks, or pasted up around town. The *Herald* also advertises major gigs and has a listing of nightclubs. These include some decidedly un-African night spots frequented by young whites, or First-World-oriented blacks.

Daytime concerts, staged occasionally in one of the stadiums or gardens, tend to be fun, family-oriented affairs. On Sundays and national holidays (such as Independence Day) concerts with imported stars or local big names take place in the National or Rufaro stadiums. Look out, too, for daytime events at all the out-of-town venues.

Central

Archipelago, Linquenda House, Baker Ave. A cocktail bar and dancing place, mostly white.

Harpers, *Cresta Oasis*, 124 Baker Ave. The city's best jazz joint is open one night each week (check the *Herald*'s entertainment section to find out which).

Job's Nite Spot, 15 Wonder Shopping Centre, Julius Nyerere Way. Separate drinking and dancing.

Marilyn's, 99 Robert Mugabe Rd. You'll see the shortest skirts in town here, predominately a club for whites of all ages, with pop and jazz on different nights, and plenty of picking up.

Queens, Federal and Elizabeth hotels (see "Accommodation" for addresses). Hectic weekend venues, all very similar, but reliable spots for local bands. As big names often play at *Queens* or the *Liz*, these should be your first port of call if Zimbabwean pop is what you're after. Be on your guard for pickpockets. Muggings also occur frequently.

Sandro's, 50 Union Ave, corner Julius Nyerere Way. Pretentious haunt of government officials and journalists, with cabaret shows and restaurants.

Solos, corner Jason Moyo/Harare St. The city's swankiest club, in a converted synagogue with mirrored dance floor and waiter service. A wide variety of sounds, no sexual harassment and easy atmosphere.

Turtles, 66 Jason Moyo Ave. A popular bar and nightclub that occasionally hosts major crowd-pullers such as "Chimurenga King", Thomas Mapfumo.

Out of town

Most of the following venues are outdoor places where people go drinking and dancing on Saturday and Sunday afternoons and evenings.

Club Hideout 99, 36 Cedrella Ave, Lochinvar, Southerton. A major outdoor venue for big-name bands, with three bars and a big tent covering the whole place during the rainy season.

Seven Miles Motel, Masvingo Rd. Bands strike up every Saturday from 4pm till late.

The Skyline Motel, 19km peg, Masvingo Rd. You'll need your own transport to get here, or splash out on a taxi – worth it if someone good is playing. Reckoned by some to be the best music venue in Southern Africa, it's a favourite of the Real Sounds, and you'll find consistently excellent bands playing in the garden at weekends. Go in the evening and bop to the setting sun, while your steak sizzles. No need to take your own meat, buy it there and *braai* it yourself.

Spillway Restaurant, Lake Chivero (Lake McIlwaine). A good weekend venue with lakeside jams in the afternoons.

The high-density suburbs

You're in for a different experience in the **high-density suburbs**, where admission is less exclusive than in the centre or in the out-of-reach outer areas – though you may also feel a bit more of an outsider. For the undeterred, though not recommended for single women, there's often live music at *Club Saratoga*, Jabavu Drive, Highfield; *Machipisa Nightclub*, Nyandoro Road; and *Mushandira Pamwe Hotel*, Nyandoro Road – all within 100 metres of each other, and all a rave.

Film and theatre

Action-packed American **movies** are favoured by Zimbabwean cinema audiences, but only a limited selection of these and other popular films make the circuit. Check the *Herald* for what's on. The **central cinemas** are the *Rainbow* on Park Lane, the *Mini Cine* in Baker Avenue, the four *Kine* cinemas on Union Avenue, and the *Liberty Theatre* on Cameron Street, which specializes in kung-fu, violence and mayhem.

The most regular **theatre** consists of eminently missable musicals and sitting room dramas at the large *Reps Theatre* auditorium, down Second Street Extension; the theatre's small auditorium has more interesting productions from time to time. More adventurous productions of **African plays** like Soyinka's *Opera Wonyosi* have been staged in the courtyard at *Delta Gallery*. **Booking** for many events may be arranged through the *Spotlight Theatre Booking Office*, at the *Reps Theatre* (☎308159).

Shopping

There's little exotic about the actual experience of shopping in central Harare: malls, department stores and supermarkets give the place a humdrum feel. Nevertheless it's an excellent place to buy crafts and a few distinctly Zimbabwean items. **Crafts** worth buying include wall hangings and fabrics, inventive handmade wire toys and African printed fabrics. A growing network of informal African commercial links has meant the influx of traders from around the continent bringing West African **carvings** and Ethiopian silver **jewellery**. You can pick up wonderful items of **clothing** such as locally printed T-shirts with designs by leading Zimbabwean artists, extremely cheap and lively canvas shoes, and desert boots.

Stone sculptures by internationally acclaimed Shona carvers make more expensive and more substantial souvenirs – or investments. Locally produced **records** and **cassette tapes** cost far less than British pressings of Zimbabwean pop.

The centre of the city is good for curios, crafts and records, and the more colourful Kopje area for African fabrics. The most interesting place to buy souvenirs and food, however, is Mbare Market (see p.72), while, if you're keen on sculpture crafts, see pp.69–70.

Food

Grocers are liberally distributed throughout Harare and **food shopping** is easy. Try the big **supermarkets**, *OK* or *TM*, or one of the **delicatessens** in the Avenues selling slightly more exciting foods. The Fife Avenue shopping centre is recommended, as is the **greengrocer** in the central Parkade Shopping Centre – comparatively expensive but dependable for good fruit and vegetables.

All over the city, you'll find modest markets where women sell fruit and vegetables by the handful-sized pile, wrapped in newspaper. If you're mobile, try *Honeydew* farm shop just off Mutare Road (turn off at the *Red Fox Hotel* sign); the shop has a wide selection of produce, including bean sprouts, honey, jams and other home-made goodies.

Crafts and clothing

Harare has a surfeit of **souvenir shops** but as the quality of **curios** varies very greatly, it's worth looking around. There are several curio shops around First Street if you aren't too particular and just want to take something back. You're also likely to be pestered by people in the street selling small stone carvings – a laughing hippo or elephant – cheaper than the official curio outlets. Shops selling better-quality **arts and crafts** are thinner on the ground and listed below (for the National Gallery shop, see p.70).

For colourful **printed cottons**, walk along South Street near the station; check out *Dayal's* or *Adam Brothers*, cave-like and packed with prints from Zimbabwe, Zambia and Malawi. *Adam Brothers* also have a more spacious shop on Kenneth Kaunda Avenue. *Plaza Oriental*, Robert Mugabe Road (toward *Queens Hotel*), is the best shop for Java prints with a terrific selection, well displayed on the walls. If you're in Zimbabwe for a while, consider using one of the African **tailors** who could make up whatever you wanted from local fabrics for a modest fee – find one through the fabric shops or enquire from one of the men you'll see sewing at old treadle machines on the street. Bright pumps (*tackies*), sneakers and desert boots are available very cheaply throughout Zimbabwe at any of the *Bata* chain of **shoe stores**.

Danhiko Project, 123 Mutare Rd. The colourful and distinctive Danhiko products (prints, dyed cloths, bags, clothes and wooden carvings) sold at the better craft shops can be bought well below shop prices, directly from the project on the eastern side of town opposite *Jaggers* hypermarket, though you'll need your own transport or a taxi to get there.

Dendera Gallery, 65 Speke Ave (between First and Second St). The most upmarket of the craft shops with a superb collection of domestic and ritual artefacts, musical intruments, textiles and baskets. It's not cheap, but is the place to go if you are looking for something old. It also sells exceptional amber and Ethiopian silver jewellery, and beautiful necklaces and bracelets fashioned from clear-glass trading beads.

Jairos Jiri, Park Lane Building, Julius Nyerere Way. One of the countrywide chain selling crafts by disabled craft workers, close to the *Monomatapa Hotel* and National Gallery. Worth browsing, though the Bulawayo shop is better stocked.

Limited Edition, Africa House, 100 Jason Moyo Ave. Good-quality clothing, jewellery, prints and traditional arts and crafts. It's conveniently close to the *Meikles Hotel*, and next door to *Grass Roots* bookshop between Third and Fourth streets.

National Handicraft Centre, Grant/Chinoyi St. Spacious and modern craft outlet in the Kopje district where you're left to browse. A little out of the centre, but worth it for the great collection of reasonably priced basketware, drawn from various regions and the best of its kind in Harare.

Trading Company, First St between Samora Machel and Union Ave. Top of the list if you're after ethnic cushion covers and interior fabrics; their high-quality batik clothes, bolsters and tableware are particularly good value.

Ndoro Trading, First St between Samora Machel and Union Ave. Zimbabwe's most stylish contemporary craft outlet, with a carefully selected and unusual range.

Music and traditional instruments

Harare is second to Bulawayo for **record stores**, though there are some promising places nonetheless. Also worth a look are some of the record bars in the big department stores, plus the many small record shops and pavement vendors in the Charter Road area. Some sell **traditional instruments** too, as do most of the craft shops listed above.

Music, 86 Rezende St. Mostly second-hand LPs.

Pop Shop, First St. The selection here is pretty much up with Bulawayo standards. A good last stop to stock up on discs before leaving.

Spinalong, Hungwe House, George Silundika Ave. Great selection of West African sounds, as well as Zimbabwean.

EMBASSIES AND HIGH COMMISSIONS

Angola Doncaster House, Speke Ave/ Angwa St; ☎790675.

Australia Karigamombe Centre, 4th Floor, 53 Samora Machel Ave; ☎757774–7.

Austria Room 216, New Shell House, 30 Samora Machel Ave; ☎702921.

Belgium Tanganyika House, 23 Third St/ Union Ave; ☎793306.

Botswana 22 Phillips Ave, Belgravia; ☎729551.

Bulgaria 15 Maasdorp Ave, Alexandra Park ☎730509 or 730504.

Canada 45 Baines Ave; ☎733881.

Denmark UDC Centre, Union Ave/First St; ☎758185–6.

Ethiopia 14 Lanark Rd, Belgravia; ☎725822–3.

France Ranelagh Rd, Highlands; ☎498096 or 498098.

Germany 14 Samora Machel Ave; ☎731955–8.

Greece 8 Deary Ave, Belgravia ☎793208.

Italy 7 Bartholomew Close, Greendale; ☎479279.

Japan Karigamombe House, Samora Machel Ave; ☎757868.

Kenya 95 Park Lane; ☎792901.

Malawi Malawi House, 42 Harare St; ☎705611.

Mozambique 152 Herbert Chitepo Ave; ☎790837.

Namibia 31A Lincoln Rd, Avondale; ☎47930.

Netherlands 47 Enterprise Rd, Highlands; ☎731428.

New Zealand Batanai Gardens, 57 Jason Moyo Ave; ☎728681.

Portugal 10 Samora Machel Ave ☎725107 or 722291.

Russia 70 Fife Ave ☎720358.

South Africa High Commission, Temple Bar House, Baker Ave; ☎753147–9.

Spain 16 Phillips Ave, Belgravia; ☎738681.

Sweden Pegasus House, Samora Machel Ave; ☎790651.

Switzerland 9 Lanark Rd, Belgravia; ☎703997.

Tanzania 23 Baines Ave; ☎721870.

United Kingdom 7th Floor, Corner House, Leopold Takawira Ave/Samora Machel Ave ☎793781 or 793789.

USA 172 Herbert Chitepo Ave; ☎794521.

Zambia, Zambia Hse, Union Ave; ☎790851.

Listings

Airlines *Air India*, Batanai Gardens, 57 Jason Moyo Ave/First St (☎750275); *Air Malawi*, Throgmorton House, Samora Machel Ave/Julius Nyerere Way (☎752563); *Air Namibia*, Cecil House, 95 Jason Moyo Ave (☎794919); *Air Tanzania*, Lintas House, Union Ave (☎706444); *Air Zimbabwe*, City Air Terminal, Third St/Speke Ave, and at the airport (head office ☎575111, reservations ☎575021); *American Airlines*, 95 Jason Moyo Ave (☎794910); *Balkan Airlines*, Trustee House, 55 Samora Machel Ave (☎759271); *British Airways*, First Floor, Batanai Gardens, First St/Jason Moyo Ave (☎759173 or 759177); *Ethiopian Airlines*, CABS Centre, Jason Moyo Ave (☎790705); *Kenya Airways*, 1st Floor, Stanley House, Jason Moyo Ave (☎792181); *KLM Royal Dutch Airlines*, 1st Floor, Finsure House, Union Ave/Second St (☎731042); *Lufthansa German Airlines*, 2nd Floor, East Wing, 99 Jason Moyo Ave (☎793861); *Qantas*, 5th Floor Karigamombe Centre, 53 Samora Machel Ave (☎751228); *South African Airways*, 2nd Floor, Takura House, 69–71 Union Ave (☎738922 or 738928); *TAP Air Portugal*, 2nd Floor, Takura House, Union Ave (☎706231).

American Express is represented by *Manica Travel Services*, 2nd Floor, Travel Centre, Jason Moyo Ave (☎703421).

Automobile Association, Fanum House, Samora Machel Ave, between First and Angwa streets (Mon–Fri 8.30am–4pm; ☎752779, fax 752522).

Banks Branches are scattered all over town, with head offices as follows: *Zimbank*, First St/Speke Ave; *Barclays*, First St/Jason Moyo Ave; *Standard Chartered*, Second St/Baker Ave; *Grindlays*, Baker Ave (between First and Second St).

Bike rental Mountain bikes for day rent around Harare, or for extended trips around Zimbabwe from *Bushtrackers*, *Bronte Hotel*, Fourth St/Baines Ave (☎303025).

Book exchange *Treasure Trove*, 26 Second St, opposite the Publicity Association; *Booklovers Paradise*, 48 Angwa St, between Union Ave and Julius Nyerere Way.

Bookshops *Grassroots*, Jason Moyo Ave (between Third and Fourth St), has a selection of books covering social and political issues. The *Mambo Press Bookshop*, Mutual House, Speke Ave, is also good on history and politics, though with more emphasis on religious books. *Kingstons'* two book-shops, on Jason Moyo Ave/Second St and in the Parkade Shopping Centre, are the biggest in Harare and have a wide selection of periodicals. Finally, the *Book Centre* in the arcade on First St (behind *Meikles Hotel*) stocks a fair selection of titles on natural history as well as literature.

Camping equipment A selection of basic stuff including locally made gas canisters to fit Camping Gaz equipment can usually be found at *Fereday and Sons*, 72 Robert Mugabe Rd. Equipment hire at *Rooney's Hire Service*, Shop 1, St Barbara House, Baker Ave/Leopold Takawira St.

Car rental The big three international companies have the broadest network throughout Zimbabwe, with offices in major towns and resorts – especially useful if you want to drive only one way and drop off in another centre. They are: *Avis*, 5 Samora Machel Ave (☎720351); *Europcar*, 19 Samora Machel Ave (☎752559); and *Hertz*, Beverley Court, 100 Baker Ave (☎792791), or Harare Airport (☎575206). The growing number of smaller local companies are invariably cheaper, but make sure they offer some backup in the event of a breakdown. Of these the longest established are: *Elite*, 95 Belvedere Rd (☎738325) or Harare Airport (☎575411), with branches in Bulawayo; and *Impexo*, 9 Charter Rd (☎705763). For 4WD rental, *Vintage Motors*, 31 Lobengula Rd (☎465269), has extremely competitive rates on rather old vehicles, supplied with a tool kit, in case of breakdown.

Doctors are listed in the front of the Harare telephone directory.

Emergencies Police, fire and ambulance ☎99. As part of the upgrading of Zimbabwe's phone network, there are plans to change the emergency services' numbers, at a date yet to be announced, as follows: general ☎999; police ☎995; fire ☎993; ambulance ☎994.

Galleries Harare has a crop of good commercial galleries dealing mainly in sculpture, where the enthusiast can browse works by Zimbabwe's established names. *Gallery Delta*, "Robert Paul's Old House", 110 Livingstone Ave/Ninth St (daily 8.30am–5pm), has worthwhile exhibitions of graphics, textiles and ceramics. *Matombo Gallery*, 114 Leopold Takawira St (Mon–Fri 8am–6pm, Sat 8am–1pm), displays works by big and lesser-known names. Founded by the renowned sculptor David Mutasa, *Nyati Gallery*, Spitzkop Rd (17.5km out of town on the Bulawayo road), is a sculpture garden where you can watch sculptors at work; it's worth visiting particularly if you're out Lake Chivero (Lake McIlwaine) way. *Stone Dynamics Sculpture Gallery*, 56 Samora Machel Ave (Mon–Fri 8am–5.30pm, Sat 8.30am–1pm), emphasizes work by the so-called "second-generation artists" – newcomers developing on the work of 1960s veterans. *Vukutiwa Gallery*, a twenty-minute walk from the centre at Blakiston St/Harvey Brown Ave (daily 9am–6pm), has a crowded sculpture garden, arranged around the swimming pool of a once-grand house.

Hospitals and private clinics *Parirenyatwa Hospital*, Mazowe St/Josiah Tongogara Ave (☎794411). There's a fever ward at *Wilkens Hospital*, Drummond Chaplin St (entrance in Josiah Tongogara Ave). For a private consultation there are several doctors at the *Avenues Clinic*, Baines Ave/Mazowe St (☎732055), or *Medical Chambers*, Leopold Takawira St/Burns Ave.

Immigration Linquenda House (between First and Second streets) for visa extensions.

Laundrette Fife Ave/Sixth St (Mon–Sat 7.30am–6pm, Sun 9am–3pm; ☎720179).

Left luggage at the station "cloak room" costs a few cents per day per item. The one at the airport (daily 6am–10pm) charges US$3 per 24hr.

Libraries The *Harare City Library* in the Civic Centre, off Rotten Row (Mon–Fri 9am–5.30pm, Sat 9am–1pm) has a reasonable reference section with a lot on Zimbabwe. The *British Council Library*, Jason Moyo Ave/Park St (Tues–Fri 9am–5.30pm, Sat 9am–1pm) is also free, with a dazzling array of British periodicals and week-old (or more) newspapers in its reading room.

Maps The Surveyor General's Office, Electra House, Samora Machel Ave (near the *Jameson Hotel*), PO Box 8099, Causeway; for the best maps available of Zimbabwe, covering more or less anything you're likely to need including hiking maps.

Pharmacies are open during normal shopping hours, apart from *QV Day and Night Pharmacy* on Union Ave/Angwa St (daily 8am–8pm; ☎751422).

Post office The main one is on Inez Terrace/Jason Moyo Ave; another is in Union Ave, opposite the Parkade (both Mon–Fri 8.30am–4pm, Sat 8–11.30am).

Samaritans ☎722000 (24hr).

Shippers and packers *Airlink*, Boshoff Rd/Conald Rd, Graniteside (☎736783), can collect, pack, airfreight and ship even awkward-shaped goods.

Swimming pool The Les Brown Pool is an Olympic-sized affair off Park Lane, opposite *Monomatapa Hotel* (mid-May to mid-Aug daily 11am–4pm; rest of the year daily 10am–6.25pm).

Taxis can be called by phone: *Rixi* (generally recommended as the best; ☎753080–2); *Creamline* (☎703333); *A1* (☎703334); *Avondale* (☎335883); *Harare Minicabs* (☎572585); *Pfumo Minicabs* (☎662008). There are also a number of ranks: outside the station in Kenneth Kaunda Ave; the east side of Cecil Square; near the Civic Centre in Kaguvi St; and others peppered around the centre, especially at the big hotels.

Telephone booths are scattered about the centre, usually functional and well used – expect a very long wait. The nicest place to queue is outside the four booths in the First St mall; there are also phones outside the *Monomotapa Hotel*. The only viable way to make international calls from a call box is to use a cardphone and a Z$100 card. You'll find cardphones at the main post offices and a growing number scattered about elsewhere.

Telephone directory enquiries Local ☎92 (962); trunk ☎91 (968); ☎0 (967) for the operator to make trunk calls. The numbers in brackets will come into operation at an as-yet-unspecified date, along with a new number for international directory enquiries (☎965).

Thomas Cook Jason Moyo Ave/Fourth St (☎728961).

Travel agents are all over the place. Among the most reliable are *Safari Par Excellence*, 3rd Floor, Travel Centre, Jason Moyo Ave (☎720527), and *Run Wild*, 8th Floor, East Wing, Southampton Life Centre, Jason Moyo Ave/Second St (☎795841).

AROUND HARARE

If you're spending some time in Harare a number of nearby destinations make pleasant breaks, although they aren't really worth a special excursion if you only plan a brief stay in the capital. **Lake Chivero** is a popular weekend outing for Hararians and there's a string of low-key wildlife distractions along the way. **Ewanrigg Botanical Gardens**, too, are a pleasant place to spend a few hours. If the Matopos Hills (see p.143), with their typically Zimbabwean rock kopjes, aren't on your itinerary, then it's worth making a trip to **Dombashawa** north of Harare to see the inspiring granite formations and rock paintings. **Accommodation** at Lake Chivero is detailed below; other places to stay within easy reach of Harare are listed on p.67.

Lake Chivero

The damming of the Hunyani River in 1952, to provide year-round water for Salisbury's growing population, opened up an accessible "Recreation Park" around the artificial lake. Though very much a resort for Harare weekend trippers, **Lake Chivero**, 32km southwest of Harare (and known until the early 1990s as **Lake McIlwaine**), is pretty enough – *msasa*-clad hills encircling wide stretches of water – and has the lure of game-viewing in the national park on the southern side.

The northern side, which is generally a place for just a day out, is more developed and commercialized, but to the south there are national parks **chalets** for a cheap and restful weekend.

On the way: birds, snakes and lions

Tourist blurbs always promote the Lion and Cheetah Park, Larvon Bird Gardens and the Snake Park – all on the way to Chivero – as essential Harare excursions. Of the three, **Larvon Bird Gardens** (Mon–Fri 10am–5pm, Sat & Sun 9am–5pm) is the one with most allure. Housing around 400 species in reasonably spacious conditions, it provides a good opportunity to watch birds at close quarters. The large open-air aviary currently under construction will make the site even more worthwhile. If you're travelling there by car, turn right at the signpost, 17km out of Harare on the Bulawayo road. A few kilometres beyond the bird gardens is the **Snake Park** (Mon–Fri 10am–5pm, Sat & Sun 9am–5pm) which harbours a representative sample of Zimbabwe's snakes coiled behind glass-fronted cages; you're also allowed to handle some of the safer ones. A left turn further down the main road, at the 23km peg, takes you to the **Lion and Cheetah Park** (same hours as the Snake Park), little more than a zoo, but affording real close-ups of the big cats that lounge around the entrance waiting to be fed. A recent shock-horror press story featured someone who crept into the enclosure at night; all that was found the next day was a driving licence and car keys. A follow-up report revealed the victim was a fundamentalist Christian who committed suicide trying to emulate the Roman martyrs.

Northern Chivero

The north–south divide is strongly pronounced at Chivero. Southern shore wilderness purists curl up their lips at the thought of the developed north side, while north coast enthusiasts descend en masse for *braais* and boating.

Two roads branch off the Harare–Bulawayo highway towards the **northern side**. The first turn-off, 16km from the city, leads after 10km to the peaceful upper reaches of the lake, good for picnics. The second, 13km further on at *Turnpike Garage*, takes you to *Admiral's Cabin*, the *Hunyani Hills Hotel* and the sailing club. You can hire **canoes** at *Admiral's Cabin* (and at the *Ancient Mariner*) but there's little else to recommend it. Weekends draw hordes of radio-blasting picnickers who come here simply for a booze-up.

The *Hunyani Hills Hotel* (☎162-2236; ③) is much nicer; you can have **tea** in the garden, survey the lake and stroll along the shore to get a view of the dam wall. For this, go to the gate of the sailing club, and ignoring the No Entry sign, walk on past the club house to follow the path along the wooded lake shore until you see the wall; it's about 45 minutes there and back.

The **lake water** is always beautiful in the sunlight but bilharzia and the odd crocodile make it off limits for swimming. If the urge to cool off becomes irresistible, however, there's a **swimming pool** at *Admiral's Cabin*.

Getting there

Getting to the northern shore of Lake Chivero from Harare is easy enough. From the *Jameson Hotel* on Samora Machel Ave, **buses** to several destinations on the Bulawayo road can drop you at the second turn-off, just 2km from the lake, or at a point out of town you could hitch from. A daily bus also leaves Mbare at about 9am bound for fishing spots on the northern side; it takes an hour and then returns to the terminus, but may be difficult to track down. Alternatively, hitching should be pretty straightforward, especially at the weekend.

Lake Chivero National Park

With the rather wonderful exception of rhino, there's no big game in the **national park** lining the **southern shore** of Lake Chivero (daily dawn–dusk). There are, however, plenty of antelope, giraffe, zebra and smaller mammals to compensate, and a wide variety of water birds – as well as bird species favouring the *msasa* woodland. The lake provides a good opportunity to spot smaller denizens, too, like reptiles, amphibians, butterflies and other insects; look out for the tiny white and pink tree frogs clinging onto branches. The prettiest time for a visit is September, when the *msasas* confoundingly unfurl their autumn-coloured spring leaves in preparation for the rains.

The park is fairly small and covered well by a network of game drives. You'll invariably see zebra and antelope in open grassy areas, and giraffe browsing in more wooded spaces. Accompanied **horse riding** is an excellent way to get around the park if you don't have a car, and it can get you really close to the rhinos. Book at the parks office for a ride, either first thing in the morning or at 3pm.

Bushman's Point

Bushman's Point in the east is the only area where **walking** is permitted but you need a car to get there. This thickly wooded waterside area is alive with foraging *dassies* (rock rabbits). On a rock face overlooking the shoreline path are some faded **rock paintings**. Look for the line of thirteen identical kneeling figures at the bottom of the face – thought to be a dance chorus. Also low down are three figures with sticks, standing, sitting and recumbent, which overlie some striped forms.

Crocodile Rock

The other rock painting sites in the park are to be found at **Crocodile Rock**, for which you'll need transport and to take a parks guide with you. They are well worth seeing, though – two large crocs, one painted belly up, make a unique panel with nine hunters to the left of them executed in great detail – and the rock is the most attractive of the park's several designated **picnic sites**. It is the haunt of herons and pied kingfishers, rather than crocodiles, and has a marvellous view over the lake.

Practicalities

There's no public transport to the national park, but **hitching** or **bussing** to the turn-off is much the same as for the northern side; get off at the signpost after crossing the Hunyani River, from where it's 6km to the park entrance and office. The best bet is to wait at the signpost for a lift right into the park. Alternatively, various Harare-based companies, such as *UTC* and *Bushbeat Trails* (see p.64), run tours to the national park, combined with a visit to the Lion and Cheetah Park; if you want to stay, it may be possible to arrange to be picked up a couple of days later.

Chivero is incredibly popular and **accommodation** fills up quickly at weekends and school holidays, but at other times you'll usually find a place. Book through the National Parks Central Booking Office for the chalets (☎706077–8, fax 726089; ①–②); of these, *Kingfisher Lodge* has the best view of the lake.

Ewanrigg Botanical Gardens

Set in commercial farmlands, **Ewanrigg Botanical Gardens** are just half an hour's drive northeast of the city – and a lovely place to spend the day. They are most famous for **cycads** and **aloes** – red-hot-poker-like succulents whose flowers span the spectrum from yellow to a brilliant red – but there's also a herbarium and a water garden. During the week you can have a walk in solitude. At weekends the place fills up with trippers out for a lunchtime *braai* using the fireplaces and picnic spots provided. The most impressive time to visit is mid-winter, when the aloes are in flower. It's rather dusty and dried out in August and September before the pre-rains flowering.

For the traditional-style **herb garden**, head through the aloes and up steep steps colonnaded by thickly planted young trees. Down on the other side you'll find the **water garden**. Bear left through an open grassy area, planted with trees and massive bamboos, to get back to the entrance gate.

To get there by public transport, take the Shamva **bus** from Mbare and ask to be put down at the Ewanrigg turn-off; the gate is about 1km down the dirt road. **By car**, drive out on the Enterprise Road, taking the Shamva fork about 15km from the city centre; Ewanrigg is signposted.

Chinamora rock paintings

There's a multitude of painted caves in the communal lands around Harare. The two best-known sites are at **Dombashawa** and **Ngomakurira**, in the Chinamora Communal Lands north of the city limits. Dombashawa is well visited and you're unlikely to be alone. Ngomakurira, 10km further on, is a lonelier and altogether more arresting spot.

Transport to either site is straightforward. For both you should take the Bindura **bus** that goes via Dombashawa from Mbare bus station. For Dombashawa get off at its turn-off and for Ngomakurira continue on to the Sasa Road stop. Buses are frequent and leave central Harare along Chancellor Avenue and past Borrowdale race track. You could try catching one en route, or hitch from Chancellor; the route out of town is interesting in itself, passing by the mansions, pools and flourishing gardens of Harare's plushest suburbs.

By **car** or **hitching**, take the Borrowdale/Dombashawa road. For Dombashawa, turn right at the sign 30km from Harare. The car park for the main cave is just under a kilometre further on, and the cave is a twenty-minute walk along a clear path up the hillside.

Dombashawa

The attraction of **Dombashawa** lies in the enormous whaleback rocks of the site (admission fee US$2), which you can clamber over to gain vantage points – each allowing you to slip back in time as you survey the valleys. The paintings themselves are, by comparison, disappointing, having fallen victim to fire, smoke, vandalism, graffiti and cleaning. Don't base your judgement of the form on what you see here.

The largest collection of paintings spreads out on the inner walls of the **main cave**. Buffaloes, zebras, elephants, kudus and rhinos keep human figures company. One of the most interesting groups, in a cleft 20m left of the main cave, has an indistinct elephant harassed by hunters. Slightly further on, but off to the right, are some human and semi-human figures, believed to be associated with rain-making ceremonies. Around the area, several other clefts and small areas of rock are also daubed with the (now pale and delicate) pictures of animals and people.

A small **interpretation centre**, next to the parking lot at the foot of the hill, gives an interesting overview of the art, with astonishing facts about the age of some of these ancient works.

Ngomakurira

To reach **Ngomakurira**, carry on along the main road for just under 12km past the Dombashawa turn-off. Turn right at the signposted Sasa Road, and there's parking about 1km from the main road. For the half-hour walk up to the site, it's worth considering any offers from local kids to guide you as it's not that easy to find the way. From the large isolated tree on the left at the foot of Ngomakurira's massive dome, walk along a path between maize fields to the base of the hill, then take one of the paths which lead up to a wooded valley watered by a clear stream and rock pools. The stream leads to the bottom of a sheer cliff on which are the numerous faint but beautiful paintings.

The site

Some say that Ngomakurira, literally "the place where the spirits beat the drums", takes its name from the echoes one hears in this perfect amphitheatre. It's a powerful and otherworldly place, abundant with elegant paintings which decorate the bottom of the Day-Glo-orange-stained cliff. In such an enclosed space its sweep and height are enormously magnified. When you sit on the back of the granite hump opposite, you can hear your own words perfectly, and mockingly, reproduced by the ancestors.

The **paintings** here include four huge **elephants**, rated amongst the best of their type by Peter Garlake, Zimbabwe's leading rock art expert. There is no shortage of other fine renderings, either, with some fascinating scenes of **human groups**. One shows a man, arms raised in terror, being clubbed by another. It was scenes like these that led some anthropologists to impose an interpretation of ritual regicide (king-killing) on examples of Southern African stone age art. One conclusion was that such motifs could not have been produced by hunter-gatherers like the **San** (see p.346). Current theories disagree, pointing out that the lifestyles depicted in the paintings are very similar to those of San groups like the !Kung. And the regicide theory sounds, in any case, somewhat sensational. There is no evidence of such acts having been carried out anywhere in the country.

THE MIDLANDS

For its tourist image, the **Midlands** proclaims itself *the heart of Zimbabwe* – and each of its towns claims to distil the country's essence. **Gweru**, the only place that can make any real claims as an urban centre, declares itself *the big heart of Zimbabwe*, while diminutive **Kwekwe** asserts it's *the industrial heart of Zimbabwe*. In all fairness, there's some truth in these claims. The Midlands are rich in gold, asbestos, nickel and chrome, and the region is the base for the country's important textile and steel industries.

For visitors, much of the Midlands is eminently missable, but its towns aren't totally devoid of charm. To really get to know Zimbabwe, it's worth spending a night in at least one Midlands town – all are pretty, very quiet and, if you're in no hurry, they make likely stopovers for a north–south journey. (The real tourist highlights of the Midlands – the wonderful stone ruins at Danangombe and Naletale – are covered in Chapter Four with Khami, as they are sited midway between Gweru and Bulawayo.)

Two main arteries cut through this heartland, each splaying out from Harare. The **road and railway line to Bulawayo** takes in the larger towns of Gweru, Kwekwe and Kadoma, while the **Masvingo route** whips through the Chivu and the old mining town of Mvuma.

The Bulawayo road: Chegutu to Kwekwe

The towns on the Harare–Bulawayo road see few, if any tourists, but were well visited by **elephant hunters** in the past. The Portuguese set up an ivory-trading post in the eighteenth century near Chegutu. They soon went, but the hunters stayed; in fact, so many people came up to Chegutu from Bulawayo in the second half of the last century that the route became known as Hunters' Road.

Chegutu and Kadoma

First stop down the line towards Bulawayo is the tiny farming settlement of **CHEGUTU**, 105km southwest of Harare. The local hotel burnt down in 1989, leaving a village quiet even by Midlands standards. These days, its only noteworthy features are the two *Viscount* aircraft shells parked on the southern outskirts of town, which have been imaginatively converted into a restaurant.

KADOMA, 140km southwest of the capital, is larger, with its very smart *Ranch Motel*, Bulawayo Road (☎168/2321–4; ⑤), where the inter-city coaches break for tea or a meal. Beyond that, it's a typical colonial railway town, bypassed by the main road, with well-preserved buildings a short hop from the station. What bustle there is happens around the nearby **Cameron Square**, planted with palms, gum trees and jacarandas. Fronting the square is the Grand Hotel, its elegant facade recalling the gold-rush days when it hosted dancing girls, hunters and prospectors. Little more than a knocking-shop these days, it's best admired from the outside. The place to survey the passing scene is the *Blue Jay Café* also on the square.

If you're tempted to **stay** in Kadoma, splash out at the *Ranch Motel,* or head to the colonial-styled *Speck's Hotel,* Union Street (☎168/3302; ③).

Kwekwe

The Harare–Bulawayo road passes the scarred, mine-dumped outskirts of **KWEKWE**, where a colossal rifle aimed at the dumps announces "Kwekwe Shooting Club". Kwekwe represents the Midlands of hunched office blocks, with its downtown district an aspiring city centre lacking the means. Walk a hundred metres and you're in the suburbs among downmarket shops. Older, more photogenic buildings are concentrated a block up, in Second Street.

The National Museum of Goldmining

Kwekwe was built on **gold**, growing up as a mining settlement for the rich surrounding reefs, and its one tourist attraction is the **National Museum of Goldmining** (daily 8am–5pm). This is a treat if you enjoy antique machinery – suction pumps, engines and rock crushers – but otherwise it's not over-inspiring, except for the amazing **paper house**. This, almost a century old and made of wire-reinforced papier-mâché, was Zimbabwe's first prefabricated building. It has stood since 1894, when it was shipped out from England as a residence for the general manager of Kwekwe's *Globe and Phoenix Mine.*

Like most of Zimbabwe's mines, the *Globe and Phoenix* operated on **ancient diggings**, which had been run using manual implements, or fires lit against rocks to make them crack. Gold already had a thousand-year history here and trade in the precious metal was one of the ways the ruling classes consolidated their power. In the sixteenth century it had brought the first **European interference** in the region, with the arrival of Portuguese; their attempts at conquest and control flopped, but not before they'd brought in Spanish experts to develop the ancient workings.

In the late nineteenth century, after the defeat of Lobengula, **British** El Dorado-seekers flooded into the district. The gold rush never came to much but, by the 1930s, one in every thirty whites was a small-scale prospector. Today, a few big mines pull in the bucks, and there are still some determined prospectors. In the northeast, Shona women continue to pan the Mazowe and Luenha rivers with homemade wooden trays and transport their finds in porcupine quills.

Practicalities

In so small a place, it's a surprise to find no less than four **hotels**. Of the cheaper options, the *Sebakwe Machipisa Hotel* (☎155/2198; ③), with en-suite rooms just off the main road beyond Fifth Street, is a little more salubrious than the *Phoenix Hotel* (☎155/3748; ②), a run-down jive dive. More comfortable and reasonably priced, the smart *Shamwari Hotel,* First Street (☎155/2387; ③), is the best central place to stay. Prices are only slightly higher at the *Golden Mile Motel* (☎155/3711; ③), 2km out on the Bulawayo road, where *Ajay* and *Express* **coaches** set down and pick up. It has the added advantage of a swimming pool.

The cheap **campsite** has a macabre position next to the cemetery; look for the signs in First Street. Finally, just outside Kwekwe is an excellent **backpackers' lodge**, one of Zimbabwe's best. In addition to its attractive rural setting, the *Mopani Park Farm* offers competitive tariffs (dinner, bed and breakfast for US$10 per person; ☎247822) and the chance of a hack through the bush on horseback for US$3 per hour (or US$5 per hour for lessons), with the added attraction of game viewing.

Gweru and around

GWERU was established in the 1890s as a staging post between Bulawayo and Harare. Today it is mainly a goods marshalling centre, linked by rail to South Africa, Mozambique and Zimbabwe's major towns. As a stop-off between Bulawayo and Harare, it's no tourist magnet but an agreeable place nonetheless. With wide streets and some lovely colonial architecture blooming among the ubiquitous 1960s stubs, the town seems to bask in a permanent Sunday afternoon feel: the Midlands capital living like a suburb in search of a city.

Of the "tourist attractions" the town struggles hard to find, the unfortunately named **Boggie's Clock Tower** deserves some kind of booby prize. "Erected by Mrs Jeannie Boggie in memory of her husband Major Boggie", it stands at the junction of Main Street and Robert Mugabe Way (formerly Livingstone Avenue), the town's two major axes.

The 1898 **Stock Exchange Building**, a little further along Main Street, warrants at least a quick look. It's a splendid example of colonial architecture, the oldest building of consequence in the city, constructed after the defeat of the First Chimurenga – a reflection of business confidence.

The **Midlands Museum** on Lobengula Avenue (daily 9am–5pm; US$2) is another possible place to while away some time, with its impressive display of firepower from both

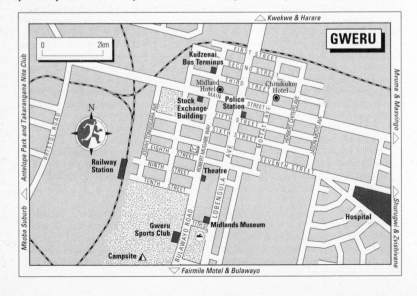

world wars: guns, aircraft, grenades, you name it. But there's little of note from the liberation struggle and the displays aren't very informative. The attached aircraft museum houses over sixty planes, one of the finest displays in southern Africa. The location is appropriate, as Gweru's Thornhill air base is the country's largest. The town is also the home of the Zimbabwe Military Academy, which trains officer cadets and junior officers.

Although well away from the main game parks, Gweru does have its **Antelope Park** (small entry fee), some 8km out of town on the road going past the industrial estate. It's pretty quiet, but you will see antelope, zebras, giraffes and other herbivores as well as a dozen or so (caged) lions in the centre.

Practicalities

Luxury **coaches** stop at the *Fairmile Motel*, and economy **buses** at the Kudzenai terminus by the town market (behind the *Midlands Hotel*). The **railway station**, with connections to Harare, Bulawayo and Johannesburg, is located at the end of Tenth Street. **Taxis** line up both at the *Midlands Hotel* and the bus terminus.

Of the six **hotels** that graced the town by 1895 only three remain, catering for travelling salesmen during the week and empty on weekends. Cheapest is the *Chitukuko Hotel*, Third St/Moffat Ave (☎154/2861; ③). Right in the centre, the *Midlands Hotel*, Main St (☎154/708121; ④), an impressive colonial building with an arcaded facade that conceals a smart if characterless interior, is definitely more upmarket. Slightly less expensive is the *Fairmile Motel*, 1.6km south of the city on the Bulawayo Road (☎154/4144; ④), an airy place with a swimming pool and a **car rental** company in the lobby (see "Listings" below). The **campsite** is at the Gweru Sports Club, along Robert Mugabe Way (which becomes the Bulawayo road). Conveniently adjacent is the public **swimming pool**.

After dark, the *Dandaro Bar* at the *Midlands Hotel* is the centre's hottest **nightspot**, playing disco and reggae, and second-rate live music on weekends; what the place lacks in glitter and sophistication, it makes up for with sheer energy. Away from the centre, taxi down to the *Takarangana Nite Club* in Mkoba High Density Suburb, where there's a better resident band and nightly disco. The council **beer hall**, in the same shopping centre, is where Harare bands play. Back in the centre, the *Embassy Cinema* in Fifth Street (off Robert Mugabe Way) shows mainly popular American **films**, but you might be lucky and coincide with one of the occasional performances at the *Gweru Theatre*.

For **food**, you've a choice between a slap-up meal at a hotel restaurant, or something less substantial in one of the **snack bars** strung down Main Street. Try the *Chicken Hut*, open late, for good, cheap chicken curry and rice, or the *Polar Milk Bar*, a little further on. In Fifth Street you can get sit-down pancakes, doughnuts and omelettes at the mainly white-patronized *Dutch Oven* or the similar place next door with a predominantly black clientele. Nearest the campsite, in Robert Mugabe Way, *Granny's Restaurant* serves reasonably priced snacks and larger meals.

Listings

American Express c/o *Manica Travel Services*, Zesa House, Sixth St (☎154/3316).

Automobile Association Fanum House, Lobengula Ave/Sixth St (☎154/4251).

Car rental *Europcar*, *Fairmile Motel*, 1.6km south of town on the Bulawayo Road (☎154/4144, fax 154/3189).

Doctors and dentists are listed at the beginning of the Gweru section of volume one of the telephone directory.

Emergencies Police, fire and ambulance ☎99.

Hospital General Hospital, Shurugwi Rd (☎154/51301).

Swimming pool The pool at Robert Mugabe Way/Eleventh St is the best thing in town (Tues–Fri 10am–2pm & 3–6pm, Sat & Sun 10am–12.30pm & 2.30–6pm; closed May–Sept).

Shurugwi

SHURUGWI, about 20km southeast of Gweru, nestles in a hollow in the Sebakwe Range. The name – from the Shona *Churugwe*, "pig pen" – refers to the surrounding topography. Shurugwi is actually the handsomest of the Midlands towns, a neglected and forgotten place somehow out of time. Its aptly named Grand Hotel has closed down; there are no eating places and not a single bar in town – a unique distinction in Zimbabwe. Shurugwi's gentle decay offers great photo opportunities: streets lined with fading pastel buildings and red corrugated iron roofs against a luminous sky.

For the nearest **hotel**, turn off just before town and continue 2km downhill; as its name suggests, the *Chitukuko Pleasure Garden* (☎152/6548; ③) is primarily a boozing establishment, but you can get hefty meals and cheap, seldom used double rooms. For ordinary **supplies**, there is no shortage of shops in the tiny centre, and a branch of the *Standard Chartered Bank* is open at the usual hours. Shurugwi is sometimes called "the highlands of the Midlands". In reality it's hardly higher than Gweru, but it is hilly and there are lovely **walks** through woods and waterfalls just south of town on the road to Zvishivane. As for entertainment, the store opposite the train station (goods only) has some antique pinball machines.

The Harare–Masvingo road

On the three-hour stretch from Harare to Masvingo in the lowveld, the only reason to stop is for drinks at the two main towns. **CHIVHU** used to be known by the Afrikaans name *Enkeldoorn* (lone thorn), after the particularly fine *acacia robusta* found growing at the site. It was first settled by **Afrikaners** in 1896 who were attracted by its similarity to the Boer heartland of the former Orange Free State (now simply Free State Province) in South Africa. Cecil Rhodes actively encouraged Afrikaners to settle in Zimbabwe and it's not uncommon to this day to hear Afrikaans spoken throughout the Midlands. Right up to the UDI years, the town was jokingly referred to as the "Independent Republic of Enkeldoorn", and became legendary for its bar in which anti-Smith comment was punished with incarceration in the bar's jail.

One popular stop for drinks or a meal is *Denise's Kitchen*, 16km after Chivhu at the 156km peg, on a ranch with zebra and kudu which come for morsels from your table. This place also offers upmarket **accommodation** (dinner, bed and breakfast for US$55 per person), as does its neighbouring sister farm, the *Tanghenamo Ranch*. The latter is more expensive (US$60 per person), but its rates include meals, horse riding and game viewing, with the chance to see elephant, lions and antelope.

Through the grasslands a further 51km from *Denise's Kitchen*, the mining town of **MVUMA**, like Shurugwi, has photogenic qualities, though on a considerably less grand scale. It enjoyed a gold boom from 1914 until 1925 when the local Falcon Mine closed, and nothing has changed since then. It's worth a quick stopover to check out the old-style stores in the two main streets but, regrettably, there's nowhere to stay. The name *Mvuma* comes from the local river – "place of the magical singing" – believed in legend to be the site of a pool from which drumming, singing and the lowing of cattle could be heard.

NORTH OF HARARE

Four roads radiate **north from Harare**, terminating at small towns on the edge of the Zambezi escarpment where it drops away to the remote, arid areas on the Mozambique border. The towns here have always been outposts, vulnerable to guerrilla attack and suffering severely during the bush war which had its origins in the region. Long before the Independence struggle, the spiritual inspiration for the **First Chimurenga** was conjured here and two famous early liberation heroes, Mbuya Nehanda and Mapondera (see box on p.101), operated locally.

The most travelled road in this region leads west to Kariba; apart from farmers and peasants, few people travel the others. One you might want to follow heads off through the citrus farms of Mazowe to Mvurwi and Guruve, nearest town to the marvellous **sculpture community** at **Tengenenge**. Further attractions lie north beyond Mvurwi, on the edge of the Zambezi lowlands, where the middleveld plateau rises in the upward swoop of the **Mavuradonna mountains**. This is one of the wildest regions of Zimbabwe, and home to the country's most adventurous – and best – horse-riding safari centres. The broken hilly country on the eastern side of this district was recently designated as a hiking area, most easily approached from the village of Centenary. For this and **Hippo Pools Camp**, off the road to Mount Darwin in the **Umfurudzi Safari Area** further east, you'll need your own transport.

Tengenenge

If Harare has awakened your interest in Zimbabwean sculpture, don't miss **TENGENENGE**, two hours north of Harare by car. This artists' community just south of the Zambezi escarpment in the rolling grassy hills of the Great Dyke requires some motivation to reach, but it's an extraordinary place and well worth the effort. Part of the final section of road is on gravel, but you'll know you're nearly there when you come across sentinel sculptures lining the way.

The sculpture community

So prolific is the output of Africa's largest artists' community that acres of land around Tengenenge seem to have been planted with sculptural works – primitive, crude, representational or grotesque, and in overwhelming quantities. Sculptures perch on walls, window sills and above the doors of derelict buildings; others stand on wooden plinths driven into the ground or lie tossed aside in the grass. You can walk around the village looking at the carvings and chat to sculptors chipping away at new works. Almost everything is for sale and if you're looking for a quality bargain by an unknown, this is definitely the place.

Tengenenge is one of the great formative influences in Zimbabwe's sculpture revolution. When **Tom Blomefield** took over the farm here after World War II, he began by ploughing with oxen until he discovered **chrome** on his lands, which earned him enough money in two years to make bricks to build drying sheds and to employ someone to manage his tobacco production. Then came UDI, sanctions and the collapse of the tobacco industry. Blomefield decided to chuck it all in and become an artist. But with an entire black workforce to consider, he thought of absorbing their labour in arts and crafts groups.

Miraculously, around this time, huge deposits of **serpentine** (the beautifully mottled stone in yellowish to almost black shades of green) were discovered on the farm. Blomefield was joined by **Lemani Moses**, a Malawian sculptor, and gradually the place began to attract people from all over. This was one of the hottest areas during the bush war, but Tengenenge was left alone. Blomefield believes this was because he always showed due respect to the local chief and respected the **ancestral spirits**, frequently arousing the ire of the local church, which was doing its best to suppress them.

Workers at Tengenenge come from Angola, Malawi, Zambia and as far away as Tanzania, and each brings a distinctive tradition which has breathed diversity into the Zimbabwe sculpture movement. Each culture has its own cosmology of **gods, ances-**

tors and spirits that influence humans in different ways and make all sorts of demands. The Shona supergod **Mwari** is a disinterested figure approached through the ancestors, while **Kalunga**, god of the Angolan Mbunda people, is very personal. The Malawian **Chewa** and **Yao** cultures express religion through very formal ritual dances using masks, and highly stylized mask-like sculptures are one hallmark of their work. Local **Shona** sculptors, too, frequently draw on folklore; cautionary tales and transformations of people into beasts are common subjects.

There are now over a hundred artists associated with the farm, some of them affiliates producing at home and using Tengenenge's distribution channels, but many resident and stipended if their talent is insufficiently recognized by the commercial art world to make ends meet. Several of Zimbabwe's big names are products of this community, and artists like **Bernard Matemera** still live here. Matemera was the winner of the 1986 Delhi sculpture triennial, produced a ten-ton stone sculpture for the non-aligned conference in Titograd and has several pieces in the National Gallery in Harare. Others, like **Henry Munyaradzi**, have exhibited in Europe, America and Australia.

If you come on Tengenenge's birthday (Feb 22) or Independence Day (April 18), you can expect to be treated to wild, inebriated celebrations in which secret dance societies compete publicly with ghoulish, satirical and bawdy displays.

Practicalities

Travelling to Tengenenge **by car**, turn on to Gurungwe Road 12km before Guruve at the 35.5km peg, and follow the signs for Tengenenge. The first 10km or so of this road are tarred, followed by about 5km of poor gravel track.

Getting there by **public transport** is a far more difficult proposition, only for the very determined: take a bus from Mbare to Mvurwi and change there for **Guruve**, getting off at the Gurungwe Road turn-off mentioned above; from here, walking is the only way to do the remaining 18km to Tengenenge; if you get stuck overnight, Guruve's one **hotel** has cheap doubles. Otherwise the best **accommodation** is at Tengenenge itself, where there are simple huts for rent and plenty of space for camping. Food is also available, and visitors are welcome to try their hand at some sculpture, but be prepared to fit into African village life if you choose to stay. The nearest upmarket alternative is *Kopje Tops Camp* in the Mavuradonna (see p.94).

Companies running organized **tours** out to Tengenenge from Harare include *Stonegate Safaris* (book through *UTC*), who charge around US$110, and *Bushbeat Trails*, who do the trip for half that price (see p.64 for addresses and phone numbers).

The Mavuradonna Wilderness

Relatively unknown, even by many Zimbabweans, the **Mavuradonna Wilderness Area**, around 190km from Harare, is one of the country's wildest conservation regions, an uncultivated and mountainous tract that was a no-go area for many years during the bush war. Largely hunted out, this beautiful and unpopulated part of the country is now being restocked and boasts growing populations of plains game and some small elephant herds.

Surprisingly, the hidden wilderness lies just two hours' easy drive (mostly on metalled roads) from Harare. Elephants have, over many years, worn paths into deep valleys tangled with bamboo thickets and streams that support palms and waterberries. Their routes, negotiable only on horseback or on foot, provide the only tracks here, threading through open countryside and rocky outcrops. The views across the Great Dyke, a massive fault looming out of the landscape, are always beautiful.

San hunter-gatherers (see p.346) have left their mark on scattered rock faces – often quite literally, in the form of small terracotta-coloured hand prints. Depicting animals,

---

MUTOTA: THE MAVURADONNA SPIRIT MEDIUM

The spirit medium **Mutota**, a renowned local religious figure, wields enormous influence in the Mavuradonna area: from time to time, even white farmers send him the customary offering of bolts of black-and-white cloth to ensure good rains, or to bring harm to poachers. This usually has to be done through a Shona intermediary as he finds the odour of whites offensive. Whether the farmers offer their tribute through genuine belief or for political reasons is a moot point.

The story goes that the current Mutota – a young Mozambican in his early thirties who doesn't speak the local language – was called in a dream after the old incumbent died. Guided only by this visitation, he walked hundreds of kilometres through difficult terrain to take over the mediumship here in neighbouring Zimbabwe. During trances, he takes on the persona of the **mhondoro** – the lion spirit of an ancestor – conveying his message in leonine growls and roars that are then translated by an interpreter.

---

humans and geometric forms, many of the paintings have yet to be scientifically investigated, leaving much to interpretation.

Accommodation and getting there

There are only two **places to stay** – one budget, the other upmarket and geared mainly to riding safaris (see below) – in the Mavuradonna Wilderness, which is a controlled area managed on behalf of the local council under the *Campfire* scheme (see p.122 for details). For budget travellers, the **Community Headquarters Camp**, east of the Muzarabani road, offers simple accommodation in 22 thatched A-frame shelters, with basic washing and toilet facilities. You have to bring everything you need, including food and drinking water, although built-in *braai* places mean you won't need a cooker. A network of waymarked trails of various lengths lead from the camp, but approach the nearby waterfall with care, as it can be treacherous. **Booking** for the camp, which costs under US$5 per two-person shelter, must be made in Harare through the *Wildlife Society Shop*, PO Box GD 800, Greendale (☎14/731596 or ☎/fax 700451) at Mukuvisi Woodlands (see p.73).

To get to Mavuradonna **by car**, take Second St Extension out of Harare to Mazowe. Turn left here and continue past Centenary, keeping to the tar on the Muzarabani road. The *Community Headquarters Camp* is a short walk off the main road some distance before the village. Two to three **buses** leave Mbare terminus for Mazurabani each day; ask to be dropped at the turning for the *Community Headquarters Camp*.

Riding safaris

The ultimate way to penetrate the valleys, peaks and hidden corners of the Mavuradonna is on horseback. For experienced equestrians, *Carew Safaris* operates adventurous **riding safaris** deep into the wilderness area. Other less ambitious trips, offering some of the best-run and most exciting riding in Zimbabwe, start from *Kopje Tops Camp*, where non-riders can also stay in stone and adobe en-suite lodges, each carefully positioned for maximum privacy. Led by one of Zimbabwe's handful of woman professional hunter-guides – formidably competent and thoroughly knowledgable about the local flora and fauna – rides head for Bat Caves tented camp, which can be used as a base for exploring the Tingwa Valley and surrounding area. All supplies are portered in, so you carry very little. On more intrepid excursions you can leave behind the security of the fixed camp – sleeping in caves and carrying whatever you need – to reach the remotest tracts, exploring precipitous paths or following elephant herds.

Trips last from two to six days and **cost** US$180 per person per day. Transfers by road or air can be arranged on request. Bookings can be made through Geoffrey

MAPONDERA – ZIMBABWE'S ROBIN HOOD

An inspirational outlaw-hero, **Mapondera** was an early **freedom fighter**, whose stamping ground was the Zambezi Valley, near the Mavuradonnas. In the late nineteenth century, he would slip eel-like across the river, between British and Portuguese territory, avoiding the armies of both.

An independent warrior-ruler, descended from a Rozvi royal family, he put up a firm **resistance to colonial rule** and rejected the hut tax. In 1894 Mapondera and a band of followers fled from a settler force sent to arrest them. They emerged from their refuge to raid administrative offices, ambush tax collectors and burn shops they felt were exploiting the peasants.

To the government he was nothing more than a bloody murderer, but the Zimbabwean and Mozambican peasants who fed and sheltered him passed a different judgement. For several years he and his army held out against the white invaders. In 1901, with an army numbering nearly a thousand he attacked their settlement at **Mount Darwin**, notorious as a place of fighting during the Second Chimurenga, and nearly wiped it out. But in the end, it was a stalemate.

Mapondera continued his campaign for several more years under increasing pressure from the multiplying tentacles of colonial control. As white influence on both sides of the Zambezi closed in, his operational zone became restricted. Hunted by Portuguese and British, unable to get food or grow crops, and exhausted by nearly a decade on the run, he returned to his home at Mount Nyota, resigned to defeat. He sent a final message to his people saying that the old order was now finished and offering words for the new: "I leave my children here. They must look after themselves."

Soon afterwards he was arrested, tried and sentenced to a hefty seven years. He found confinement unbearable, went on hunger strike, and starved himself to death. The Mugabe government has honoured him as a folk hero by naming a building in Harare after him.

Carew, Private Bag 295A, Harare (☎58/404); in the UK, contact *Campfire Adventure Sports* (☎ 01980/620839).

The Palm Reserve

Guests at *Kopje Tops Camp* also have the option of visiting the **Palm Reserve**, a small concentration of **raffia palms**. These incredible trees, which sport the longest leaves in the world, live only twenty or thirty years, producing exquisite waxy amber cones. Growing on the confluence of crystal-clear streams, no-one is quite sure how these isolated pockets of palms came to be where they are. One theory is that they were brought with trading Portuguese, and have clearly found an environment very much to their liking.

Umfurudzi Safari Area

Of the few established attractions in the north, the **Hippo Pools and Sunungukai camps**, in the **UMFURUDZI SAFARI AREA**, are the two most worthy of mention, offering hutted accommodation, river walks, game viewing, and plenty of peace and quiet. Situated on the banks of the Mazowe River in beautiful broken granite country, they are both highly recommended as weekend retreats from Harare, or as stop-offs if you're touring the northern circuit around Mount Darwin and Centenary.

The Hippo Pools Camp

The **Hippo Pools Camp**, consisting of **chalets** and a **campsite**, is a commercial operation administered by National Parks. Thankfully, hunting is forbidden, but you can fish, canoe, and walk along the Mazowe River, and there's a fair amount of game in the area, with the big five making rare appearances. **Getting there** requires your own transport. The camp is 160km from Harare, past Shamva on the Mount Darwin Road; turn off at Madziwa Mine and from there follow the road due east for 25km. The road is poor and ideally you need a high-wheel-based vehicle, though saloon cars can make it. There are only three chalets, so book ahead (Hippo Pools Camp, PO Box 90 Shamva; ☎3302; ②). Fridge and utensils are provided at the camp, but take your own food, linen, crockery and a sharp knife; the nearest **store** is at Madziwa Mine. It's also possible, and cheaper, to take your own tent and camp.

Sunungukai Camp

Sunungukai Camp (book through *Campfire*, 15 Phillips Ave, Belgravia, Harare; ☎14/790570) has the double advantage of being both far cheaper than Hippo Pools and accessible by bus. It also offers the chance of experiencing African village life at first hand. The camp was developed as part of the *Campfire* programme, which enables local villagers to channel revenue from tourism into projects that benefit the whole community, such as building schools and clinics. It's a pretty basic setup, with a campsite, four bucket showers, water from a borehole and a communal kitchen. Local guides can take you to San rock paintings and a sacred mountain – the "Breathing Mountain" of Mushambanhaka – or show you around villagers' homes.

Sunungukai is two hours by (mostly metalled) road north of Harare; full directions are given when you book. Two economy **buses** leave daily from Mbare bus terminus (1pm & 4pm); the bus is routed "Nyava via Shamva, Mazoe Bridge" or "Nhakiwa via Bindura, Glendale" and the stop to ask for is Nyagande, a small village 1500m from the camp. The journey takes around three hours, with frequent stops; departure times, as everywhere else in Zimbabwe, are approximate.

travel details

Harare is unsurprisingly the nexus of travel, with excellent, and lightly trafficked tarred **roads** to Mutare, Masvingo, Bulawayo and Kariba. Hwange and Victoria Falls, though, are reached by road from Bulawayo, not Harare. There are overnight **rail** services to Bulawayo and Mutare with comfortable sleepers. Harare has one international rail connection per week, a 26-hour journey to Johannesburg. Bulawayo and the Midlands are well served by **luxury coach** at least once per day, with one of the Sunday services continuing through to Victoria Falls. Coaches run to Mutare five times each week, and to Masvingo at the weekend only. **Local buses** from Mbare will take you almost anywhere, starting at undefined times early each day. They are slow and crowded. **Domestic flights** are excellent value with countrywide connections daily, though none to Mutare which only has a military airport. They are sometimes prone to delays, but international flights leave punctually.

Trains

Harare to: Bulawayo via Kwekwe, Gweru and Shangani, for Danangombe and Naletale ruins

(daily at 9pm; 10hr); Johannesburg via Beit Bridge (*Trans Limpopo Express;* Sun at 7am; 26hr); Mutare (daily 9.30pm; 8hr 30min).

Luxury coaches

Details of departure points for coach services from Harare are listed on p.61.

Harare to:

Blantyre (Tues & Fri; 10hr) – *Stagecoach Malawi.*

Bulawayo via Chivhu (1 daily, 3 on Fri; 6hr); via Kwekwe and Gweru (Thurs & Sun; 6hr) – *Blue Arrow.*

Chiredzi via Masvingo (Thurs & Sun; 4hr 15min) – *DSB Coachline.*

Johannesburg (Mon–Sat; 16–18hr) – *Blue Arrow, Translux, Zimi-Bus, Silverbird.*

Lusaka via Chirundu (Tues; 7hr 30min) – *DSB Coachline.*

Masvingo for Great Zimbabwe (daily; 4hr 15min) – *Blue Arrow, Translux, DSB Coachline, Silverbird.*

Mutare via Rusape (Fri & Sun; 4hr 15min) – *Blue Arrow.*

Nyanga via Rusape and Juliasdale (Fri; 4hr) – *DSB Coachline*.

Victoria Falls via Bulawayo (Sun; 13hr) – *Blue Arrow*.

Economy buses

In addition to long-distance routes, scores of commuter omnibuses run medium-distance services along the main roads.

Harare to: Bulawayo (at least 5 daily from 5am; 7hr); Chirundu/Lusaka (*Zupco Buses*; daily at 6.45 am; 7/12 hr); Kariba (daily; 7hr); Karoi/Siabuwa (daily); Masvingo for Great Zimbabwe (daily; 4hr); Mutare (daily; 3hr); Nyanga (daily; 5hr).

Flights
Harare to:

Bulawayo (2–4 daily; 50min).

Durban (Sun direct; 2hr).

Gaborone (2 weekly; 1hr 30min).

Johannesburg (1–2 daily; 1hr 30min). A one-month excursion fare is the best value on return tickets (minimum stay 10 days). Fares are the same on either *SAA* or *Air Zimbabwe*, with interchangeable flights. A number of independent airlines offering discounted tickets on this route have made brief appearances on the scene; among the better established is *Comair*, which operates twice-weekly afternoon flights.

Kariba, Hwange National Park, Victoria Falls (daily, to connect with international arrivals; plus 1 direct flight per day to Victoria Falls, without stops at Kariba and Hwange).

Masvingo (4 daily; 1hr 35min).

Air Zimbabwe has direct connections, at least once a week, to several African destinations – Maputo, Lilongwe, Addis Ababa, Mauritius, Manzini, Dar-es-Salaam, Windhoek and Nairobi. Other African airlines with flights to Harare include *Air Ghana*, *Zambia Airways*, *Air Botswana*, *Kenya Airways*, *Ethopian Airlines*, *Air Tanzania* and *Air Malawi* (see *Basics*, p.10).

CHAPTER TWO

KARIBA AND THE MIDDLE ZAMBEZI VALLEY

Z imbabwe's northern border is formed by the **Zambezi River**, which is dammed at Kariba to form the vast artificial **Lake Kariba**. The river traverses some of the wildest and hottest parts of the country, with **Mana Pools National Park**, below the dam, the **wildlife** centrepiece: a place where you'll see animals without the slightest effort, and where walking in a group – the big attraction – is permitted, provided you are used to the bush and observe safety procedures.

The **lake** itself has a strange quality – hardly surprising given that a whole valley was drowned to create it, and a people, the Batonga, moved out. From the shallows, dead treetops poke out, while camel-hump formations dominate the lakeshore, sprouting grotesque baobabs and dessicated mopane woodland. Amid the creeks and islands, however, lies the rewarding **Matusadona National Park**, and on the escarpment is **Chizarira National Park**, the best nature reserve in Zimbabwe for walking.

Independent access to these wildlife areas is, unfortunately, neither easy nor cheap, and this is a part of the country where it is generally worth joining an organized expedition. Many of these tours (see p126 for details of operators) are adventurous and fairly intrepid options. If you want a taste of African expedition life, with the reassurance of an experienced guide or leader, it's hard to beat the excitement of a **canoeing trip** down the Zambezi, taking in Mana Pools en route, or a **backpacking safari** in one of the three national parks, ensuring equally close encounters with big game.

Kariba Town, five hours by road from Harare and well connected by air, is the hub of Zambezi tourism, promoted as a fabulous riviera but perhaps a little defeated by its own hype. While the blues of mountain and lake are very beautiful, there's nothing much to do here without a boat and fishing gear. Kariba is often the first stop for visitors doing the "milk run" – Kariba, Hwange National Park and Victoria Falls. If you're **circuiting the country**, the **Kariba ferry** conveniently connects the northeast of Zimbabwe to its west.

ACCOMMODATION PRICE CODES

Hotels and other accommodation options in Zimbabwe have been categorized according to the **price codes** given below, which indicate the cost, per person sharing, of a night's lodging.

For a full explanation, see p.46.

① under US$8	④ US$25–35	⑦ US$65–80
② US$8–15	⑤ US$35–50	⑧ US$80–95
③ US$15–25	⑥ US$50–65	⑨ over US$95

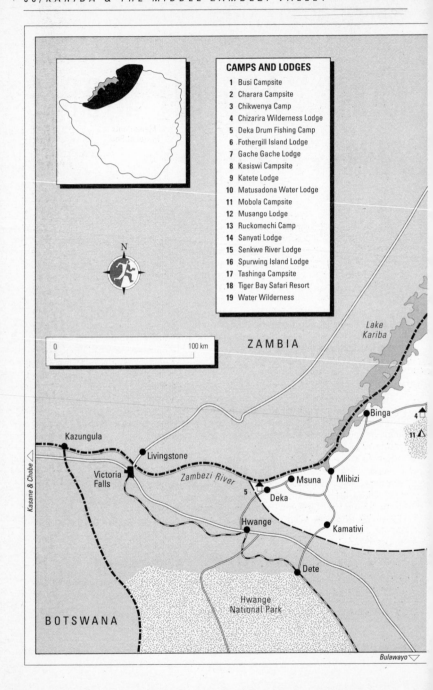

CAMPS AND LODGES

1 Busi Campsite
2 Charara Campsite
3 Chikwenya Camp
4 Chizarira Wilderness Lodge
5 Deka Drum Fishing Camp
6 Fothergill Island Lodge
7 Gache Gache Lodge
8 Kasiswi Campsite
9 Katete Lodge
10 Matusadona Water Lodge
11 Mobola Campsite
12 Musango Lodge
13 Ruckomechi Camp
14 Sanyati Lodge
15 Senkwe River Lodge
16 Spurwing Island Lodge
17 Tashinga Campsite
18 Tiger Bay Safari Resort
19 Water Wilderness

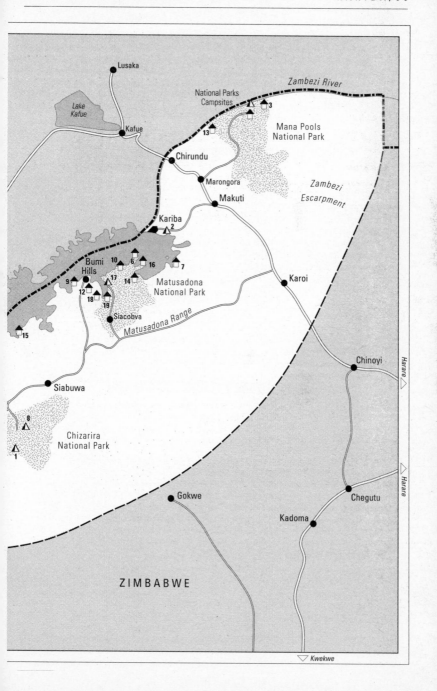

Travelling on overland, one of Zimbabwe's longest hauls by road runs through the dusty and remote **back routes south of the lake**. Starting at Harare, the road veers west at **Karoi** into some of the country's least developed communal lands, scattered with stilt-perched lookout huts, maize fields and sandy villages. A full day's drive, or two days on an economy bus, brings you to **Binga**, the thoroughly untouristed centre of Lake Kariba's west. It was to this harsh and infertile territory that the **Batonga** people – today perhaps the poorest group in the country – were moved after they were uprooted by the construction of the Kariba dam.

THE ROAD FROM HARARE

The towns diminish steadily in size as you head northwest from Harare towards Kariba. None particularly merits a night's stop, though all have at least one hotel should the need arise. Tobacco and maize farms line the route to the escarpment, with a scenic highlight as you cross the **Great Dyke**, a massive topographic spine which bisects the highveld plateau, and is the source of many springs and streams.

The road is an easy one to hitch on Saturday mornings and daily economy **buses** to each of the towns or right to Kariba leave Mbare bus station in Harare. If you're wondering what's in the small sacks people wave at you from the roadside, they contain worms for bream fishing at Kariba.

Chinoyi

CHINOYI, 115km from Harare, is a farming and mining centre and still a white stronghold. The petrol stations are all most people see of the town, though it has

ZAMBEZI VALLEY HISTORY

The Zambezi Valley has been inhabited since the first **hunter-gatherers** lived there, and Bantu-speaking **Iron Age farmers** have navigated the river for centuries. Numerous Iron Age sites are scattered along the Zambezi, including the **Ingombe Ilede** burial site near Chirundu which showed that external trade had reached this far up the Zambezi by the sixth century AD.

Later, **Muslim merchants** traded up the river for gold and ivory: romantic notions persisted of the Zambezi being one of the gateways to the biblical Ophir. At the Zambezi's Indian Ocean delta, in 1497, the Portuguese adventurer, Vasco da Gama, supposedly found Arab dhows laden with gold dust. Hot on his heels other **Portuguese** fortune-seekers arrived in large numbers, spending four centuries on the lower Zambezi in search of riches. Although the Portuguese didn't penetrate much further than Chirundu, below the lake, in the sixteenth century, this was considerably further inland than any European had previously advanced in Africa and, from their reports, we know something about the Mutapa State of the Zambezi Escarpment.

The Mutapas
The **Mutapas** were originally Shona-speakers, who had drifted north from Great Zimbabwe sometime during its disintegration (final collapse came around 1450), and had conquered the Tavara – another Shona group. The Mutapa state is only the most famous of several small Shona kingdoms around the northeast at this time. For the Portuguese, however, the Mutapa king, whom they knew as the Monomatapa, was a magnificent figure of untold wealth who ruled over an enormous empire. The empire was a myth, but the Mutapas did control the important Zambezi trade route.

claims to fame, with its much vaunted **caves**, and a place in history as the spot where the Second Chimurenga began, on April 28, 1966, with the killing of seven ZANLA guerrillas in a confrontation with Rhodesian forces. The date is celebrated as the annual Chimurenga Day, and a memorial to the "Gallant Chinoyi Seven" has been erected in the town.

The Chinoyi Caves

The **Chinoyi Caves** make an interesting break on an otherwise dull journey to Kariba. Enclosed by a recreational park 8km north of the town, they're open dawn to dusk.

The labyrinth of the caves centres on the legendary **Sleeping Pool**, whose waters appear strikingly deep and vivid blue as you approach via the passage. However, the none-too-fragrant odour does its best to deflate the dreamy atmosphere promised by the name. The best time to see the pool is at noon, when light pours from a natural skylight onto the still surface. If you don't find caves claustrophobic, descend into **Dark Cave**, nearby, which has steps and electric lighting until you get to the viewing platform at the end of the tunnel. There's a good view from here of the Sleeping Pool, overhung by stalactites in shades of blue that vary with the time of day. Numerous passages and galleries lead off from the Dark Cave for more serious exploration.

Archeologists have found ancient traces of troglodyte occupation in these subterranean dolomite caves. In the 1830s the Nguni are supposed to have used them as a place of execution, and later in the century Chief Chinoyi used them as a refuge from Ndebele raiders.

If you want to stay at Chinoyi Caves, there's a **campsite** within the recreational park and the comfortable *Caves Motel* (☎164/22340; ③) at the turn-off to it. The other (slightly more expensive) option is the *Orange Grove Motel* on Independence Way (☎164/22785; ③), which also has a caravan park.

According to tradition, the Mutapas had their own Adam and Eve: **Nebedza** and his sister **Nehanda**. Nehanda is Zimbabwe's archetypal mother-earth heroine, closely associated with the land, which is the fundamental element of religious, social and material life, the source of food, and the home of the ancestors.

The Chimurengas

Portuguese incursion into the interior marked the beginnings of colonial brutality and bloodletting in the north. Perhaps for this reason the **spiritual inspiration** behind both of the past century's **Chimurengas** came from here. In both liberation struggles, Nehanda rematerialized as a powerful figure, urging the people to liberate the country from the white invaders. On both occasions she spoke through mediums, who themselves took on her persona and became known by the respectful title Mbuya (grandmother) Nehanda.

In the First Chimurenga, a Nehanda medium from Mazowe, **Charwe**, encouraged people to avoid all dealings with whites. As far as the authorities were concerned, Charwe was a witch and rabble-rouser and she was arrested. Photographs taken just before her execution in Salisbury, in 1898, show her dignified and self-possessed. She's said to have gone to her death singing and dancing, confident that her spirit would return for final victory.

The spirit of Nehanda re-emerged in the **Second Chimurenga** winning the people's support for the guerrillas. When mediums of important spirits such as Nehanda gave their approval to efforts to win back the land, many peasants were persuaded to join the struggle. In 1972 ZANLA guerrillas secretly took the medium over the border to their base at Chifombo in Mozambique to rally the fighters.

Karoi, Makuti and Chirundu

Under a Rhodesian government land settlement scheme, many white farmers moved into the area around **KAROI** between 1945 and 1950. Tobacco-curing sheds and tall brick chimneys stand on each of these farms. The two **hotels** in town reflect the racial divide – white farmers assemble at the newer, smarter *Karoi Hotel* (☎164/6317; ③) a couple of kilometres from the centre, while blacks gather at the original hotel downtown, now primarily a bar and pretty run-down. If you're stuck in Karoi, there's a pleasant **campsite** overlooking the dam, though security there is minimal. Karoi marks the start of the bizarrely named **Nicolle Hostes Highway** – 400km of gruelling dirt to Matusadona, Chizarira and Binga.

Makuti

En route to Kariba or Mana, everyone stops for drinks at *Cloud's End Hotel* (☎163/526; ③) in **MAKUTI**, the high point with stupendous views before the road begins to tumble down into the Zambezi Valley. The *Cloud's End* bar is a real hunter's grotto, with buffalo leering from the walls; the hotel also organizes safaris. The village consists of little more than the hotel, and it is the last place for petrol and supplies before Mana Pools.

Chirundu

CHIRUNDU, 63km further on, is equally small, despite its border status as the point where you cross the Zambezi River into Zambia. There are daily economy **buses** from Mbare bus station in Harare, and the twice-weekly *Giraffe* bus runs right through to Lusaka. You can get **rooms** at the inexpensive, colonial-style *Chirundu Valley Hotel* (Chirundu ☎1637/618; ②) or **camp** along the river. They also have some family rooms for four to seven people which are even cheaper. Don't be put off by the hotel's array of parked trucks and trailers lining up for the border crossing – through reception are lawns, and a swimming pool which hosts thirsty elephants and buffalo from time to time. The steaks here are also excellent. A one-kilometre walk from the hotel to the top of the hill gives magnificent views of the Zambezi with game on the banks, but keep a wary lookout for elephants en route, especially in the late afternoon. Since the hotel is primarily run for fishermen, it's possible to hire boats and get onto the water, though you should look out for hippos and elephants.

LAKE KARIBA NORTH AND EAST

Kariba offers a remarkable choice of activities. For those who want a few day's lazing by the pool, the **town-resort** has all the facilities: a boon, since the lake (except for its deepest, central reaches) is frustratingly out of bounds for swimming due to crocodiles and bilharzia. With more adventurous pursuits in mind, there are a host of **wildlife safari** options, including the **Matusadona National Park**, with its massive dry-season herds of buffalo and elephant, and dazzling array of lakeshore animals and birds. And there's the chance of gliding down the **Zambezi by canoe**, headed for Mana (four days) or beyond.

The Zambezi, downstream from Kariba, creates a hunting enclave which spreads across 10,000 square kilometres to the Mozambique border, consisting of Charara, Sapi, Chewore, Dande and Doma Safari areas. In the centre of all this is **Mana Pools**, a unique wildlife sanctuary, where, because of the open terrain, the National Park authorities allow walking without guides, and weapons are prohibited.

The **area telephone code** for Kariba is ☎161.

ONWARDS TO VICTORIA FALLS

The quickest overland route between Kariba and Victoria Falls is to cross into Zambia, rather than travel around the south side of the Lake via Siabuwa. An economy bus leaves every morning from **Kafue** (across the Zambezi from Chirundu) and arrives at Livingstone in the afternoon. Heading in the opposite direction (from Victoria Falls), you can take the same bus, leaving Livingstone in the morning. The road on the Zambian side of the border is in much better condition.

Kariba Town

Engineers faced with the problem of building a road from the escarpment down the hill-ridden way to **KARIBA**, turned to the ancient paths worn by **elephants** who knew the easiest descent. The road built on that elephant track twists around massive bush-clad hills to the lakeside. As you near the water look out for elephants crossing the road or tugging at trees.

Orientation, arrival and getting around

The precise location of Kariba Town is perplexing, as there's nothing much on the main road besides a *Shell* garage. Every few kilometres, however, a small turn-off disappears through the trees to one of the lakeside resorts. Stretched over twelve kilometres, each of the **hotels** and **campsites** has its own hill-cupped bay, cut off from the next by the rising and falling landscape.

There are two commercial and residential centres – **Kariba Heights**, perched 600m above the lake, and **Mahombekombe** township on the shore. Before Independence, the Heights was the white residential area, with its palpably cooler temperatures and lofty views. Set slightly back from the commercial fishing harbour and creeping up Sugar Loaf hill, Mahombekombe was built to house construction workers and continues to be the main residential area for fishermen and people working in the tourist industry. It has the nearest shops and post office to the resorts and it's where the **buses** pull in. Some distance away, near the airport, **Nyamhunga** was built in the 1970s to increase housing for Africans.

Arrival

If you arrive **by air**, the *UTC* minibus which meets all flights will drop you off at any hotel, or at the harbour if you're connecting to Fothergill Island or one of the resorts further afield. For two people, taking a taxi is cheaper than the bus. There is no *Air Zimbabwe* bus as at the bigger airports.

Economy buses from Harare stop at Mahombekombe bus terminus, from where it's a three-kilometre walk to the *MOTH* campsite and chalets or *Tamarind Lodges* (see below). However, some buses go on as far as the *Swift Depot*, which is much closer.

Getting around

Without a car, you can reckon on doing a lot of walking around Kariba. A **bus** from the *Swift Depot* goes to Mahombekombe, Heights and Nyamhunga about every half-hour, and **hitching** along the main road is easy, but the myriad branches usually mean a walk at least part of the way. **On foot**, rather than climbing up to the main road, you can cut distances drastically by following any of the well-worn paths directly along the shorefront. During the dry season, keep an eye open for elephants, which sometimes wander about Kariba's hills and shoreline.

Taxis (☎2453 or 2454) are based at *Caribbea Bay*; *UTC* also runs between resorts. **Car rental** is another way of traversing the distances. *Hertz* (☎2662) has offices at the

Cutty Sark, *Caribbea Bay* and *Lake View Inn*, while *Europcar* (☎2321–2) has an office at Andora Harbour.

Accommodation

Kariba **hotels** are popular weekend destinations for people from Harare, especially during the winter when the town is much warmer than the capital. All have pools, shady gardens and are mostly air-conditioned to beat the humidity. There is also camping for the budget-minded.

Camping and self-catering

Caribbea Bay Resort, PO Box 120, Kariba (☎2454). This has campsites close to its hotel and casino complex, over on the other side of Mahombekombe.

Mopani Bay Campsite, Kariba Town Council, Box 130, Kariba (☎2485). Far from the action, Mopani's only advantages are its small store and swimming pool.

MOTH Holiday Resort, c/o The Warden, PO Box 67, Kariba (☎2809). The *MOTH* comprises a series of pleasant, shady campsites, as well as cheap self-catering rooms and chalets, but don't count on getting a room if you haven't booked. You can camp at *Lions Club*, next door, for the same

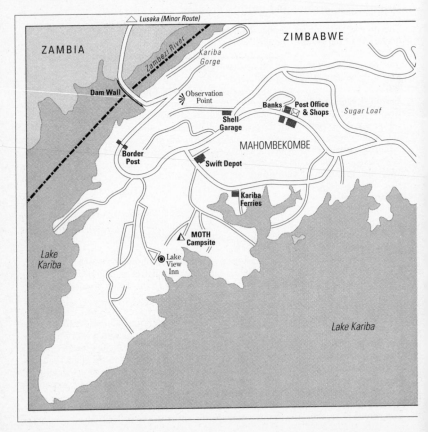

price, picking up the key at *MOTH*, which also rents out tents. Both complexes share the *Lions Club* swimming pool. From either resort, a 15-min short cut up the hill to your right (facing the lake) takes you to *Lakeview Inn* for food and drink. The Mahombekombe shops are some 3km away, and drinks and meat for braai are available at *MOTH*. ①.

Nyanyana Camp. If you're self-sufficient and want to be in the wild, this National Parks' camp, 28km from Kariba in Charara Safari Area, is perfect; campsites are next to the lake and there are elephants around. Located 5km off the Makuti road; nearest supplies at Kariba.

Tamarind Lodges, PO Box 1, Kariba (☎2697). The nicest of the self-catering options, these newish stone and thatch lodges are between the *Cutty Sark Hotel* and *Kariba Breezes Marina*. Although there is no pool, lodgers can use the one at the *Cutty Sark*, and also eat there if you're not into using the braai facilities at *Tamarind*. Lodges sleep either 4 or 6 people, and you're required to pay a fairly substantial deposit when you book in. ②–③.

Hotels

Although the hotels around Kariba do not have street addresses, each is clearly sign-posted off the main road.

Caribbea Bay Resort (see above). The most expensive of the resorts, and a big hit with Harare's golden youth, not least for its casino. ⑦.

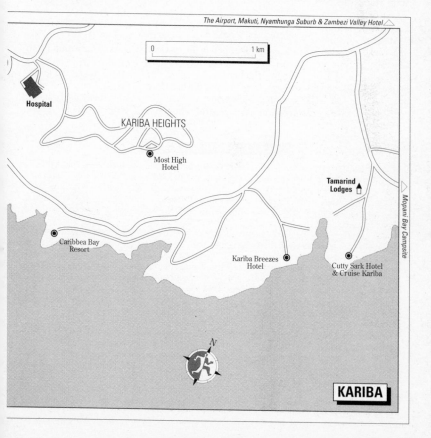

Cutty Sark (☎2321–2). Second choice after *Kariba Breezes* (below), with a nice pool and palm trees. ③.
Kariba Breezes Hotel, (☎2433). Relaxed and especially recommended. Boat rental from the hotel with a driver available. ④.
Lakeview Inn (☎2411 or 2413). Peaceful and elegant, offering great vistas. The most expensive after *Caribbea Bay*. ⑥.
Most High Hotel, Kariba Heights (☎2964–5). The cheapest of the central resorts but a long way from the water. Christian-run, complete with piped religious music. No smoking or drinking, and couples sharing a room must be married. ③.
Zambezi Valley Hotel, Nyamhunga near the airport (☎2926). A good place for live music – in the beer garden at weekends – and for meeting black Zimbabweans. ③.

Around the town

Nobody really comes to Kariba for the town. It's often too hot to do anything other than lie around, have an iced something or other, and maybe rouse yourself to go on a cruise. If you can beat the torpor, then take in the **Santa Barbara church**, built in memory of the workers who died during the construction of the dam, and have a look at the **dam wall** itself.

Observation Point

A couple of kilometres' walk from the *Lakeview Inn* or *MOTH Campsite* takes you to the dam wall, from where it's a long uphill trudge to the elevated **Observation Point**. From this vantage point, you can see the wall in its entirety – 128m high and 579m wide at its base, with the pent-up Zambezi, when in flood, leaping through the gates to the gorge below. To **walk on the wall**, you have to cross the border into Zambia. For a quick visit, however, you just report in with your passport; no long forms or currency declarations are involved. There are **refreshments** and a **craft shop** at the Observation Point, where

---

LAKE KARIBA DAM

Many animals, and not a few people, died in the **creation of Lake Kariba**, so that hydro-electric power could be harnessed to feed industry in Zambia and Zimbabwe. The dam was, at the time, the largest in the world, and its size and strength remains awesome. Its arching form is like a vast, Roman load-bearing arch turned on its side; the convex shape absorbs the pressure and the base, straining to spring apart, is solidly checked by the ancient gorge walls.

The Batonga, who suffered most of all, by being shoved off their ancestral riverside lands into the harsh interior, were convinced that the wrathful river god **Nyaminyami** would destroy the dam project. In July 1957, the first confirmation of their belief was delivered, as a once-in-10,000-years storm saw the Zambezi burst through the coffer dam to destroy months of work. Later, the angry god whipped up a tempest, which swept away the Zimbabwe–Zambia road bridge, and soon afterwards turned his attention to the suspension footbridge, which went the same way. When the rains stopped, Nyaminyami sent unusually murderous temperatures: workers died from heatstroke and the tools had to be carried in buckets of water. Eighteen men also perished when they fell into wet concrete during construction. The wall was, of course, eventually completed, but to some Batonga the battle isn't over – and, well, there are nervous reports of cracks.

The lake's biggest crisis to date has been the drought of the 1980s and early 1990s, which saw water levels sink below the level necessary to supply the country's hydro-electricity needs. Zimbabwe experienced frequent power cuts and in the end was obliged to buy in electricity from South Africa. Nor has the situation improved much since then. By the mid-1990s, the reservoir was still only a quarter full; a string of good rainy seasons will be needed to replenish it.

the best buys are intricately carved Nyaminyami (the fish-headed god with snake's tail) walking sticks, and the small wooden latticed **lampshades** that cast an attractive stripey light. The Kariba **publicity bureau** is here too.

Santa Barbara

The dam's main construction contracts went to an Italian company, and hence the chapel in Kariba Heights commemorating those who died is dedicated to an Italian saint. The chapel is a poignant place, built in a circular form to represent the coffer dam, with a trellised front open to the elements. The church's adaptation to the climate is perhaps the most interesting thing about the building, but it's not honestly worth much effort to get to, except on Sunday mornings, when traditional singing, of mostly black congregations, floats out. Evening services are at 6pm.

Cruises

Sundowner cruises are a Kariba institution. This is, after all, primarily a drinking person's retreat. On a launch, you can enjoy gorgeous sunsets, beer in hand, after the day's heat has subsided. *UTC* and *Cruise Kariba* (☎2697) both offer 4.30pm departures. You can book and get driven to the harbour from the *Cutty Sark*, *Lake View Inn* or *Caribbea Bay* hotels. *Cruise Kariba* also does a **siesta cruise** at 2pm which returns to shore in time to catch the Harare flight. The siesta cruise includes time for a **swim in the lake** – stopping in a croc-and-bilharzia-free area.

If you fancy spending more than a couple of hours on the water, **full-day cruises** to Fothergill Island are available from *Cruise Kariba* and *Lake Safaris* (☎2474). The advantage of a full-day cruise, which includes a stop for lunch, is that you go far enough afield to spot big game.

If money's no object, rent a **luxury cruiser** or **houseboat** for a few days; you can sleep on the roof, and meander down creeks for fishing or game viewing. Boats go with drivers and six to twelve passengers on board, and provide all cutlery, crockery and linen. Cruisers are restricted to the Kariba basin, which includes the game-rich area around Spurwing and Fothergill islands. Enquire at *Kariba Breezes Marina*, PO Box 15, Kariba (☎2475); or *Anchorage Marina*, PO Box 61, Kariba (☎2254).

The *DDF* (District Development Fund; PO Box 2694, Kariba; ☎2694), has boats for **rent by the hour** or longer and ships local people and cargo over the whole lake. In Harare, *Run Wild* (☎14/795841–5) is the best place to organize houseboat rental in advance. For groups of up to twelve people, cruises cost as little as US$37 per person per day, which works out much cheaper than staying at one of the Matusadona bush camps.

Eating, drinking and nightlife

For campers, self-catering is the cheap option, with **basic supplies** of fruit, vegetables and groceries available from the market and shops in Mahombekombe. A similar selection is available from *Emerald Butchery and Supermarket* in the Heights, while a small shop at *Caribbea Bay* provides essentials.

Around the Mahombekombe market you'll also find the usual cheap fare of *sadza* and relish. For snacks, refreshments and à la carte meals, try the **hotels**. Boasting the best views across the lake to the Matusadona Range, the *Lakeview Inn* terrace is worth visiting for a drink or for their gargantuan breakfasts. If you fancy a quick snack, try a plate of the local speciality, crunchy fried *kapenta* (tiny fish). The other, more expensive, regional dish is crocodile tail; it's a surprisingly light and delicate meat.

Drinking takes place at the hotels or the **beer hall** in Mahombekombe. The *Zambezi Valley Hotel* has its own band, and towards the end of each month, Zimbabwe's musical crowd-pullers occasionally appear at Mahombekombe town council stadium.

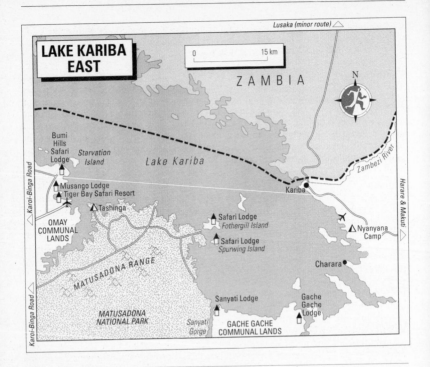

Matusadona National Park

Open all year. Entry US$2.

It is the **Matusadona Mountains** that form a backdrop to all those picturesque shots of Kariba sunsets, with drowned treetops in the foreground. The National Park, which harbours all the big game, borders the southern lakeshore and rolls over the Zambezi Escarpment into wild, largely inaccessible hills and valleys. The lakeshore with its inlets, gorges, bays and islands is the most easily reached area of the park, and certainly where the fauna congregates during the dry season.

Most visitors, largely white Zimbabweans with their own fishing or houseboats, camp at the **National Parks campsites** at **Tashinga** or **Sanyati**. Tashinga is the very appealing main park campsite and headquarters, bigger than Sanyati and with an airstrip. Both camps have tents for hire, though Tashinga is better stocked. Neither have shops or fuel supplies, so bring all you need.

In addition, three fabulous National Parks camps line the shore at **Ume**, **Muuyu** and **Mbalabala**, designed for the exclusive use of one party each (up to 12 people), for a minimum of a week's stay. For reservations, write to the Central Booking Office, Department of National Parks, PO Box 8151, Causeway, Harare (☎14/706077), or better still, go to their office at the Botanical Gardens in the capital.

If you're **driving**, only the dry season is recommended to attempt the 468-kilometre gut-shaking journey from Harare, and you'll need 4WD or a high-clearance vehicle. Access to the park is via the gravel road from Karoi to Binga. Approximately 150km west of Karoi, a signposted turn-off leads into the park through the Chifudze gate. With your own vehicle, you could easily and rewardingly combine a trip to Matusadona with Chizarira.

Without a Land Rover or boat, the only really practicable way to experience Matusadona is to splurge on one of the excellent **safari camps** bordering the National Park, from where you can see the massive dry season herds of buffalo and elephant and a dazzling array of other lakeshore animals and birds. A couple of safari companies based at Kariba organize **camping, walking, canoeing** and **photographic safaris** in Matusadona and around the Eastern Basin. The attraction of walking through Matusadona lies in following the rivers, which run into Lake Kariba and attract a greater diversity of game inland than along the shoreline. Antelope such as the magnificent black sable with their exquisitely masked faces and extremely long and gently curving horns, as well as bushbuck and duiker, prefer wooded inland areas.

There's an arduous way for backpackers to make it to Matusadona by catching the weekly *DDF* **ferry** (☎2694) running from Kariba's Andora Harbour to Bumi Hills via Tashinga. Leaving Kariba on Monday, this exposed and crowded journey takes around five hours. One-way tickets cost from US$2, and the ferry returns the following day. Unless you're doing it just to be on the water, it's not really worth going for just one night, so take adequate supplies for a week's stay, and book as far in advance as possible through the National Parks office in Kariba (☎2577). Without transport or a fishing rod your activities will be restricted to lazing around the camp, watching birds and beasts wandering through. If you're easily bored this isn't the place for you. A National Parks scout may be available to take you walking, but they are often out dealing with poachers or shooting crop-destroying "problem animals" in adjacent communal lands. **Canoes** are also available for hire.

Wildlife and fishing

You'll certainly see **elephants** drinking and frolicking in the water, and, if you're lucky, swimming. Most animals, including surprisingly enough lions, can swim well. Elephants swim using their trunks as snorkels. One remarkable – and photographed – story records an epic thirty-hour swim by two young bull elephants who crossed the lake from Matusadona, and passed Spurwing to land on a beach between two hotels at Kariba. Altruistic, even when exhausted, the one in front inflated his lungs for buoyancy while the other placed his front feet on the leader's back and did the paddling. Every hour or so they swapped over and finally made it, trunks and legs white from long immersion. The conclusion was that they were following ancient migration routes long since cut off, but still patterned into their memories.

Many people come to Matusadona to **fish**, particularly for the fierce **tigerfish** you'll undoubtedly see mounted in hotel bars – glassy-eyed and open-mouthed to display their razor teeth. Prime fishing months are September and October when Kariba hosts an international tiger contest. The big thing about tigerfish is their fighting ability; they make determined rushes, followed by an impressive leap from the water to shake the hook. **Sanyati Gorge**, a narrow tear in the map on the eastern boundary of the park, is a creek navigable for about 12km and has a reputation for having plenty of tigerfish just waiting for combat.

Birdlife

You'll see **fish eagles** sitting sentinel in riverine forest all over the Zambezi, and guarding their territory from Kariba's half-submerged trees. They're definitely among the most spectacular water birds, and always a thrill to see – especially swooping from the heights on an underwater fish. But according to recent reports they're facing extinction as the result of DDT, which is still not banned in Zimbabwe and is used extensively both in tsetse and malarial control and as a crop spray.

THE LAKE ECOLOGY

Matusadona and **Chete Safari Area** received some of the five thousand animals saved, in 1959, from the flooding Zambezi Valley. There are pitiful stories of animals moving to higher and higher ground as the waters rose and being besieged on shrinking islands with diminishing food supplies. Starvation Island had one of the biggest concentrations of stranded animals. Many thousands died and much of the money for the project (one of the earliest wildlife mass appeals) arrived too late. But **Operation Noah**, mounted by conservationist Rupert Fothergill, fought hard against the inevitable. Not only big game, but also the less obvious snakes and tortoises were bundled off to the mainland. Charles Nicholls' book *Operation Noah* recounts the story.

Nearly 5200 square kilometres of wilderness died with the valley. Desolate trees, still with branches poking from the water thirty years on, bear vivid testimony to the destruction. But all is not gloom and doom: a **new ecology** has replaced the old in a turn of events that shows the resilience of the natural world. Fish eagles and darter colonies nest in the branches and the decaying wood feeds underwater life. Buffalo and elephants graze on green swards of lakeside **torpedo grass** (*Panicum repens*), which miraculously saved the day for the young lake slowly being choked by notorious Kariba weed. In this crisis, weed-eating grasshoppers were introduced and arsenic-based poisons considered to clear the floating strangler which blocked all navigation in the west. Mysteriously, it began to die off on its own, piling up on newly barren shores and creating a mulch in which torpedo grass rapidly seeded.

Torpedo grass is able to survive long periods underwater, yet it also thrives when water levels sink during the dry season or droughts. The grass is gradually exposed to provide

Other birds in danger are the peregrine falcon, herons and cormorant, the black sparrowhawk and the rare fishing owl. All of these are at the top of their food chains, so DDT accumulates heavily in their bodies and is passed to their offspring in increasingly intolerable concentrations.

Bush camps

The most comfortable way to see Lake Kariba and the Matusadona wildlife is in one of the **bush camps** on the fringes of the park. These are stylish, thatched places with swimming pools that, unlike the Kariba resorts, are able to offer superb game-watching, walking and cruising or canoeing. There is daily **transport** to all camps, by air or boat. Two of the major resorts, *Spurwing* and *Fothergill*, are still usually mapped as adjacent islands, although they have in fact become peninsulas joined to the Matusadona mainland since the level of the lake dropped during the persistent droughts of the 1980s and early 1990s.

Luxury lodges and camps

All the lodges below operate full-board tariffs, and are pricy. The rates given are per person per day, but you pay extra for transfers to and from Kariba town (approximately US$80 return). Game activities, comprising drives, powerboat outings, canoe hire and conducted walks, are generally included.

Bumi Hills Safari Lodge, *Zimbabwe Sun Hotels*, Central Reservations, Travel Centre, Jason Moyo Ave, Harare (☎14/737944, fax 750133). *Bumi*, 50km up the lake from Kariba, is a beautiful place with excellent guides, and more like a chic (40-bed) hotel than a bush camp. Its open layout with narrow arched entrances prevents buffalo strolling into the bedroom wing, although they do occasionally come up at night and munch the lawn outside, around the swimming pool. Prices from US$275 per person per day. Linked to *Bumi* is **Water Wilderness**, where guests can safari for a night or two on a houseboat amid abundant and varied game and vegetation (US$366); this is also arguably the best-situated lodge for walking.

lush grazing for wildlife forced down to the lake when inland grazing and water becomes exhausted. Once the rains begin the animals disperse into the interior and the grass is covered again by the rising water. This movement to the water echoes an old pre-lake pattern, when game came down to the Zambezi riverine forest as it still does at Mana.

Aquatic life is rich. Apart from tiger fish, people catch bream, pink lady, chessa, barbel, mudsucker, eel, bottle nose and huge vundu. Freshwater sponges and tiny jellyfish are some of the less familiar species. The Zambezi was habitat to the same fish as are now found in Kariba, with the exception of the tiny sardine-like **kapenta**, introduced for **commercial fishing** from Lake Tanganyika in the 1960s. At night you'll see myriad lights on the lake from *kapenta* rigs attracting the fish into deep water nets. You can walk around and see the *kapenta* drying on racks in Mahombekombe; it's cheap and sold in big plastic bags throughout the country as an accompaniment to *sadza*.

Trawling is a tough job – contract-based, wet, uncomfortable and dangerous. Fishermen working for commercial companies have a more reliable income, though it's still low. The **gill-net fishermen**, however, freelancers after the big fish, live along the shoreline and are plagued by completely unpredictable catches. Some waters are fished out and the strict allocation of fishing territory prevents them moving elsewhere, with poaching in richer waters an unfortunate consequence. The **fishing villages** are rather deserted, despondent places; wives and families generally live inland, coaxing crops out of barren soil. The catch is dried and salted, and sold in communal areas surrounding the lake, or else sold fresh to commercial boats that do the rounds of the camps, usually for a pittance. To address the problems of distribution, low prices and fishing rights, a number of **fishing co-operatives** have been formed, some successfully increasing profits for their members.

Elephant's Point, c/o *Run Wild*, PO Box 6485, Harare (☎14/795841–5, fax 795846). New luxury camp overlooking the Sibolilo Lagoon. US$180 per person.

Fothergill Island Safari Lodge, book through *Zimbabwe Sun Hotels* (details above). Among the largest luxury places at Kariba, with facilities for 40 guests, and several guides on hand for game drives and cruises. Fothergill was where Operation Noah began, and is today one of the few places in Zimbabwe where lion sightings are virtually guranteed. US$160 per person.

Gache Gache Lodge, *Landela Safaris*, PO Box 66293, Kopje, Harare (☎14/734043 or 734046, fax 750785). A very pleasant lodge, overlooking the Gache Gache River on the shores of Kariba, with walks, game drives, canoeing and excursions by motorboat, but not on the best part of the lake for wildlife or scenery.

Katete Lodge, *Suns Hotels*, Travel Centre, Jason Moyo Ave, Harare (☎14/737944, fax 750133). Winning the prize for the most expensive and luxurious of the Kariba camps, though not necessarily the best, Katete has 16 lodges and is near Bumi Hills, on the border of Matusadona. From US$376 per person.

Matusadona Water Lodge, *Wilderness Safaris* (☎Johannesburg 884 1458, fax 883 6255). Guests sleep on a small boat moored around a sister ship, ensuring a close-to-the-water experience, with birds and animals all around. US$250 per person.

Musango Lodge, PO Box UA 306, Union Ave, Harare (☎14/796821). Situated on a small island near the Ume River between Bumi Hills and Tashinga in the Matusadona National Park, accommodation at this highly reputed lodge is in six luxury tents under thatch. Run by two young professional guides who can lead game walks and drives in the park. Transfers to the camp are by light aircraft to Bumi Hills and then a 15-min boat trip to the camp. Canoeing and boating are on offer in the all-inclusive rate of US$220.

Sanyati Lodge, *Landela Safaris* (details above). One of Zimbabwe's top lodges, at the mouth of the Sanyati Gorge. Thoroughly luxurious and relaxing with excellent food. Guests (max. 12) sit en famille under cool thatch, on a stony hillside overlooking the lake. The lodge has hosted the likes of Prince Philip and doesn't allow kids. US$250 per person.

Senkwe River Lodge, *Top of the Range*, 16 Fortunes Gate, Bulawayo (☎19/45684). Up the Senkwe River, this highly recommended lodge is run by top guide Chris Worden (who stood in for Clint Eastwood during the elephant-charging sequences in the film *White Hunter Black Heart*, which was filmed in Kariba and Hwange). US$230 per person.

Spurwing Island, Private Bag 101, Kariba (☎2466). A casual and friendly place 40 minutes by boat from Kariba. It's one of the least expensive, with strong local loyalty – many white Zimbabweans take advantage of the good fishing and come by boat with their families. Accommodation is in chalets, cabins or tents and it has great views of the Matusadona mountains. The activities include game viewing by boat and canoeing, and there is a swimming pool next to the thatched bar for lazing about. US$170 per person.

Tiger Bay Safari Resort, PO Box 102, Kariba (☎2569). Primarily a fishing resort up the Ume River with 12 comfortable thatched chalets and game viewing by boat or land rover. It's the cheapest of the bunch, but has gone downhill in recent years and is no longer especially commendable. From US$60; activities cost extra.

Canoeing and walking safaris

There are few roads in the Matusadona, making it a superb place for **hiking** and **canoeing**, with an excellent chance of encountering wildlife.

Buffalo Safaris Zambezi Canoeing and Lake Wilderness Safaris, PO Box 113, Kariba (☎2645 or 2827). Hans van der Heiden, an ex-game ranger and hunter who is now a professional guide, organizes very good canoeing safaris from Kariba to Chirundu, Mana Pools or Kanyemba. He also has houseboats along the Matusadona national park's shoreline, used as safari bases for walking trips, fishing and lakeside game viewing by canoe.

Craig McCrae, c/o *Run Wild*, 8th Floor, Southampton Life Centre, Jason Moyo Ave/Second St, Harare (☎14/795841–5, fax 795846). A reputable guide who leads walks both in Matusadona and Mana Pools. Safaris are for a minimum of three nights, and cost from US$180 per day.

Matusadona Walking and Canoeing, Graham Lemon, c/o *Kariba Cruises*, Box 186, Kariba (☎2839, fax 2885). One of Zimbabwe's top professional hunter-guides, who runs walking safaris in the national park for a minimum of three nights, and canoe trips to order. US$200 per day.

Kariba to Kanyemba: canoeing the Zambezi

Gliding for a few days down the Zambezi through stunning wilderness areas is one of Zimbabwe's great travel experiences: spend the money and steel your nerves. Depending on the depth of your pocket and your adrenalin reserves, you can take on the whole course from **Kariba to Kanyemba** in nine days or do a portion of the river in three or four. Once on a trip, you won't come across other canoes – only one small party per day is allowed on each stretch of water – so you feel it's all just for you. In two-person canoes, moving with the current, paddling isn't too strenuous, although it can be very hot from November to February, and in August and September strong winds can make it tough going.

Being in a silent vessel is a great way to approach game. You can get right up to watering elephants and skim past grazing buffalo, heads raising quizzically as you pass by. Herds of antelope splash through the shallows from one sandbank to the next and, if you're lucky, you'll see lions on the bank shading under an acacia or mahogany. The water itself is exquisite, changing colour and texture during the day. And of course there are those sunsets.

You don't need to have had previous canoeing experience, but obviously it helps; you may feel rather vulnerable setting off on this massive river having just signed an indemnity form. Take a hat, sunglasses, loads of sunscreen and a *kikoi* for your legs – the sun reflected off the water is fierce. The **pace** is leisurely, with frequent stops for campfire meals, walks on the banks and swimming in shallow places safe from crocodiles. **Camping** is usually on sandy islands where there is less game, although you're still sure to be regaled with the sounds of the African night as you lie under your mosquito net close to the fire: lions and hyenas calling, something being chased in the grass, baboons shrieking in alarm and hippos stomping around. In a very rare incident

ZAMBEZI CANOE OPERATORS

The operators listed below use experienced and licensed (but unarmed) **canoe guides**; they are allowed to take you on the water, although only 50m inland, which can be a bit frustrating on days when you don't have to paddle more than 25km, and have quite long rest periods on the river bank. However, most have a good knowledge of birdlife, flora and fauna and carry reference books. The Chirundu–Mana trip takes place year-round, but longer safaris, such as Chirundu–Kanyemba, only from March to December. If you do want to **walk**, *Shearwater* (see below) does a luxury trip with a professional hunter-guide along the national park river frontage, as does *Natureways* (PO Box 5826, Harare; ☎14/756600, fax 756602).

In the listing below, we've generally given rates for Chirundu–Mana, the most popular trip, for the sake of comparison. The variation in prices between different companies is usually to do with the level of participation in setting up camp, the quality of food and service, and amount of alcohol provided. It's also worth noting that many companies drop their prices in low season (Nov–June), and that residents of Zimbabwe and the rest of Southern Africa pay less than the non-resident prices quoted below. Whoever you go with, though, **book in advance**, as the trips fill up.

Buffalo Safaris, PO Box 113, Kariba (☎2645). Good year-round trips along the Zambezi, and less expensive than *Shearwater*. Prices range from US$515 per person for the Chirundu–Mana section, with low-season discounts between Nov and April.

Chipembere Safaris, PO Box 9, Kariba (☎/fax 2946). Throughout the year, their Chirundu–Mana run departs every Sun, returning Wed. The cheapest deal in this section, from US$460 per person. This company also organizes walking safaris in Mana Pools (see p.115).

Goliath Safaris, *Bronte Hotel*, Baines Ave/Fourth St, Harare (☎/fax 14/708843). Three nights Chirundu–Mana from US$460; year-round. Their higher prices ensure some luxury in the bush.

Safari par Excellence, PO Box 5920, Harare (☎14/720527, fax 722872). Three- to five-day luxury canoe safaris from Chirundu to Mupata Gorge on the

Zambian side, as well as four-day trips from Chirundu to Chongwe Falls.

Shearwater, PO Box 3961, Harare (☎14/735712, fax 735716). Three departure days per week on the Chirundu–Mana trip, from US$600 in high season, US$420 off-peak. One has the enticing option of two nights at *Ruckomechi Luxury Camp*; another takes in the wild stretch of river between Ruckomechi and Chikwenya (April–Nov), with walks.

Sobek, c/o *Run Wild*, 8th Floor, Southampton Life Centre, Jason Moyo Ave/Second St, Harare (☎14/795841–5, fax 795846). *Sobek* runs the Chirundu–Mana equivalent on the Zambian side of the border; US$627 in high season, or US$440 off-peak.

Tsoro River Safaris, PO Box 161, Kariba (☎2426). This company departs on the Chirundu–Mana run every Wed, and charges US$450 per person.

in 1992, a tourist was attacked by a lion which had crossed from the mainland, with Zambezi water levels exceptionally low from the drought.

You'll certainly see all the **hippos and crocodiles** you ever wanted to. Crocodiles are obviously very shy creatures, slithering off the bank as you approach, while hippos tend to duck under the water. To avoid hippos you should steer very close to the bank and shallows when passing – they always make for the deep water. One or two territorial old bulls can make fearsome displays on occasion, but the canoe leaders know the channels where they lurk and warn you beforehand that Mad Max or Harry has to be negotiated. Despite the potential dangers, these canoeing trips have an excellent safety record.

Itineraries

Safaris begin at Kariba, Chirundu or Mana. **From Kariba**, you paddle through the steep gorge below the dam wall into the wide country of the Middle Valley flood plains. It takes three days **to Chirundu** and five or six **to Mana**, an obvious goal. The Kariba–Chirundu section is perhaps the least interesting part of the river – you can expect little game and it's a pity to get so close to the real wilderness of Mana without touching it. Nevertheless, this stretch can be convenient if you're already at Kariba, and the Kariba gorge is spectacular. The longest trip, nine days from Kariba **to Kanyemba**, passes mostly through completely wild country.

The **Chirundu to Mana** trip (four days and three nights) is the most popular, costing around US$500. A great deal of the trips on this section runs through channels, past sandbanks and islands, with the Zambian escarpment mountains flanking the river all the way.

Mana to Kanyemba (US$800) is even more exciting, with the added thrill of coping with whirlpools in the precipitous **Mpata Gorge**. Ironstone cliffs with baobabs growing from them replace savannah, creating a magnificent entrance to the chasm. You exit by way of "the gate", a triangular-shaped granite outcrop where the river widens again. Towards Kanyemba, as the hills disappear, huts and farmlands claim the river banks, a transition from a magical, elemental realm to the more worldly. Many of the people here are **VaDema** – the only hunter-gatherers left in Zimbabwe – removed from their land in the Chewore Safari Area, and now tilling instead of hunting. A genetic defect giving a small percentage of the VaDema the appearance of having a couple of toes missing gave rise to the incorrect nickname, the "Three-toed People".

Transfers are arranged from **Kariba or Harare** to starting points at **Chirundu** and **Mana** and back out again at the end of the trip, but this isn't included in the cost of the safari. The best option of all is to arrange your own party of at least six friends to do the trip, but choose your paddling partner carefully: it helps to go with someone you don't have full freedom to shout at!

Mana Pools National Park

Open May–Oct; closed during the rainy season (Nov–April). Entry US$2.

At **MANA POOLS** the Zambezi meanders through a wide valley, repeatedly splaying out into islands, channels and sandbanks, and with escarpments rising dramatically on either side. Looking across to Zambia, the land appears as an alluring quilt of blue mountains descending into another tract of wilderness – the Luangwa Valley. On the Zimbabwe side, alluvial river terraces, reaching inland for several kilometres, flank the 50km river frontage of the **National Park**.

Along these banks are the pools which give Mana its name – depressions filled with water in abandoned river channels. **Chine** and **Long Pool** hold water throughout the year, and attract large animal concentrations in the dry season. Magnificent trees grow on the fertile terraces. The enduring image of Mana is of thorn trees, *Acacia albida*, which create park-like expanses on the river bank, before giving way to dense stands of dark green mahogany, figs, sausage trees, rain trees, tamarinds and tawny *vetivaria* grass. Away from the water, the valley floor is a harsh environment, especially in the dry season. Spikey *jesse* bush deters any thoughts of walking; mopanes are stark and lifeless, while baobabs punctuate the greys and browns. Several baobabs, in fact, remain tenaciously in the middle of the park's main road, which splits to accommodate them.

The great attraction of Mana, though, is the **wildlife** – and, specifically, the possibilities of close contact, because due to its open terrain, you're allowed to **explore on foot**, as long as you are not alone. This doesn't however mean there's nothing to worry about.

Lions roar nightly around the river bank campsite and elephants, stepping carefully over guy ropes, think nothing of investigating tents and cars if they smell fresh fruit, or fancy the seed pods beneath the tree you've chosen. After dark, hyenas and honey badgers prowl about, and anything edible, even shoes, will be chewed up. There are still a few black rhino away from the river, in thick bush, with heavily armed poachers after them.

Many in the safari business believe that it is irresponsible to allow tourists to walk in the vicinity of dangerous game. There have been some fatalities and heart-stopping incidents over the years because of tourists' lack of bush experience – mainly through people wanting to get too close to animals for the sake of a good photograph. If you want to stay alive, you must follow certain fundamental bush rules (see p.118); if you do so, the whole place is enormously thrilling and rewarding. Unless you've walked in the bush before, it's much safer to explore the Mana area on an organized walk.

Mana Pools has been declared a **world heritage site** by UNESCO, and the number of visitors to the park is strictly controlled. There are no striped combis here to wheel the dust, nor other ugly products of tourism – a situation that, ironically, makes it impossible to reach without a car (or canoe). Without your own vehicle, there are only two ways to see the park, either on a canoe or walking safari that takes in Mana, or to fly into one of the two luxury bush camps – *Chikwenya* or *Ruckomechi*. There is no cheap way to do it; intrepid **hitchers** have succeeded, but local supplies are non-existent, it is illegal to hitch, and you've no guarantee of getting a lift out again. Nor do many **car rental** companies allow their vehicles to go to Mana because of the rough roads, although a few Harare-based firms offer 4WD vehicles – ring around to find the best deals, as fleets and companies change all the time.

If you have your own car, you'll probably be **camping**. National Parks have several campsites, but the two lodges are so popular that they're allocated on a lottery system.

Getting there

By car, the 400km from Harare to Mana takes six hours on the Chirundu–Lusaka road. This is tarred to the park turn-off at the foot of the escarpment. You need to get an **entry permit** by 3.30pm from **Marongora**, a National Parks outpost on top of the escarpment, before winding 80km into the valley and across the dry-riverbed country to **Nyamepi Camp**. This road, which takes around three hours to drive, is exceedingly rough but you don't need 4WD.

Accommodation and walking safaris

Mana's campsites and lodges are all on the river, where you'll be serenaded by hippos and other sounds of the night. There are just two **lodges**, which are allocated on a draw system. Booking for them at the main parks office in Harare opens six months before the time you want to go – a fair indication of their popularity. Lodges sleep eight and go for the usual modest National Parks cost.

Most people stay at the **campsites**, which also need prior booking, though you can usually get in at **Nyamepi** by the park headquarters. This is a large site and gets a bit crowded at peak times; buffalo graze around the office, and elephant amble through. Secluded and 8km west of Nyamepi, **Mucheni** has four campsites; **Nkupe**, a few kilometres east of Nyamepi, and **Old Tree Lodge**, between Mucheni and Nyamepi, have one each, while **Vundu**, 13km upstream, has some basic huts for one party plus hot and cold water, which the other exclusive sites lack.

Walking safaris

One reasonably priced option, and certainly an adventurous one, is to explore Mana with *Chipembere Safaris* (PO Box 9, Kariba; ☎/fax 2946). For the all-in charge of

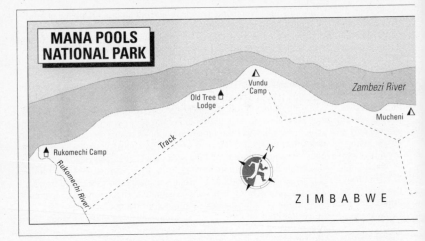

US$600 per person, a fully licensed professional guide leads a four-day **back-packing trail** on the Zambezi flood plain in the wilderness area east of the main camp sites, where game viewing is maximized by camping in the vicinity of the places where animals come to drink. Their similarly priced "Chitake Spring Wilderness Safari", run over four days at full moon between May and October, which ventures 50km from the Zambezi to the Chitake Spring, at the foothills of the escarpment on the edge of the National Park. As the only source of water for a vast area, the spring attracts large herds of animals and lots of predators. *Chipembere* now has a tent camp at the base of the escarpment, close to the Chitake Spring; it's affiliated to the Campfire scheme (see p.122), which ensures that revenue from tourists directly benefits the local community. Craig McCrae also runs recommended walking safaris at Mana Pools – see p.112.

Luxury camps

The two **luxury camps** in the area – *Chikwenya* and *Ruckomechi* – fly their guests in from Kariba in very small planes, though some clients reach *Ruckomechi* by road and boat. They provide the ultimate in safari experience in Zimbabwe, set upon the river, and have professional guides to show you the abundance of birds and animals – with prices to match.

Situated in its own small concession on the eastern boundary of Mana, *Chikwenya* is the smaller of the two luxury camps, having capacity for a maximum of twelve guests (closed Nov–April; book through *Suns Hotels*, Travel Centre, Jason Moyo Ave, Harare; ☎14/736644, fax 736646). Guests are picked up from their thatched chalets after dusk and have an armed escort – elephant and lion regularly walk right through camp. Meals are under a marvellous canopy of riverine trees and you can look at the stars from the en-suite shower and toilet which are open to the sky. Activities include game drives, river cruising on a pontoon, early-morning escorted walks and late-morning sitting in game hides perusing the changing wildlife displays. This is undoubtedly one of Zimbabwe's top five bush camps, with rates from US$338 per day (transfer US$280 return).

If you stay at only one safari camp in Zimbabwe, it should be *Ruckomechi Camp* (closed Nov–April; book through *Shearwater Adventures*, PO Box 3961, Harare; ☎14/735712, fax 735716). Located in an enormous stand of acacia and mahogany on

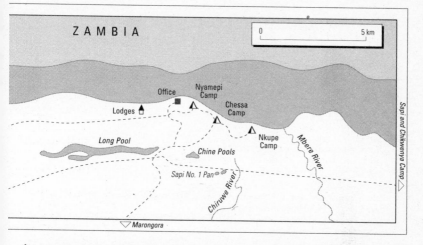

the western reaches of the Mana Pools flood plain, *Ruckomechi* is a bigger and more stylish camp than *Chikwenya*, able to welcome a maximum of twenty guests. Its advantages include a wider choice of game viewing activities, canoeing, a more extensive area for game spotting and a greater number of guides. Lions are also plentiful in the area, and you'd be unlucky not to see one over a three-day stay. Besides en-suite chalets, the camp boasts a marvellous roofless bathroom on the high river bank, with one side completely open to the water. Daily all-inclusive rates start at US$240 per person in high season (July–Oct), and US$130 at other times; transfer by speedboat from Chirundu costs US$100 per person, US$200 by light aircraft from Kariba.

Wildlife viewing

Mana experiences similar **seasonal game movements** to Kariba. Soon after the rains, when food and water in the deep bush begins to dry out, the animals move to the Zambezi to find enough food to carry them through the dry season. By October, Mana's abundant wildlife is concentrated around the pools and river.

Elephant are so common you become quite blasé about seeing them, while **buffalo** congregate in herds up to two thousand strong. **Impala**, **waterbuck** and **zebra** are everywhere and numerous predators stalk in their wake. Nearly everyone sees **lions**; **cheetahs** are rare, but around in small numbers, as are packs of **wild dogs** and secretive **leopards**. Animals you won't see include giraffe, wildebeest and white rhino. **Nyala antelope**, found only at Mana and Gonarezhou, are a special sight not to be confused with **kudu** or hefty **eland** browsing off the mahoganies.

Dawn is the best chance for seeing **hippos** on land, before they move into the water. Creatures of habit, they use well-worn paths up the bank where they graze at night, crunching up long grey sausage tree pods. They also have similar underwater paths on the riverbed.

The crescent-shaped seed pods of the *Acacia albida* are gourmet delicacies for elephant and buffalo; each tree bears several hundred pounds of them, which elephants shake to get down or vacuum clean from the ground underneath. The trees have a reverse foliage cycle, their leaves developing during the dry season to nourish

SAFETY CONSIDERATIONS

In order to enjoy the **walking** at Mana without feeling paralysed by fear, you need to know some basics. Meeting a lion on foot feels very different from staring at one from a safari vehicle. Most animals, though, aren't out to get you and will only cause problems if surprised, scared or threatened, any of which you *can* do unwittingly. To forestall disaster (accidents are exceptionally rare), follow this eight-point survivor's guide to tramping the bush.

1. **Keep a safe distance**, especially from large animals like buffalo and elephant, and when taking photographs.
2. **Don't run if you come across a lion**: stand still, keep quiet, then back off slowly. Running triggers their impulse to chase. Remember too, as you fill your viewfinder, both lions and hyenas may defend their kills if you come near them.
3. **Stay well clear of cow elephant herds** with calves. Get downwind and detour or let them pass.
4. **Don't cut off an animal's retreat.** Hippos on land usually make for the river, land mammals for dense bush or woodland.
5. **Keep a keen lookout** at all times and don't enter thick bush or grass where your visibility is severely reduced.
6. **Leave** white clothes at home, they're a loud announcement of your presence to the animals you're trying to see.
7. **Bilharzia** isn't common on this stretch of the river but **crocodiles** are. Watch out when you draw water.
8. **Fresh fruit** (particularly oranges) courts disaster: elephants possess a remarkable sense of smell and have been known to totally trash cars to get at it. And if any succeed, they may be shot as a consequence.

You're sure to be regaled with some **horror stories** about Mana. Often it's the same bush myth recycled: the man who had his face ripped off by a hyena, or the hunter who retreated from a buffalo up a tree and had the soles of his dangling feet licked away (through shoes and all!) by the vindictive beast's abrasive tongue, or the person who got trapped all night in the campsite loo by a herd of elephants. A few people have been injured or lost their lives at Mana over the years, but when the orchestra of the night begins, remember you're safe in your tent, but not if you sleep out in the open. **Hyenas** come to the campsites nightly, finding even such unlikely items as shoes, tin trunks of food and unwashed pots and pans very attractive.

and shade animals on the river bank, and falling once the rains begin and the animals move to fresher grazing.

The **birdlife** at Mana will leave you gasping, with over 350 species recorded. Brilliant **scarlet carmine bee-eaters** nest in colonies on the river bank, keen-eyed **fish eagles** watch from treetops, while solitary **goliath herons** wade through the shallows searching for fish and frogs. You'll see the brilliant flashes of **kingfishers** and numerous **geese** and **storks**. Away from the river, look for **hornbills, eagles, kites** and Zambezi chickens – a long-standing local name for **guineafowl** – especially the less common crested ones.

What's most appealing of all, perhaps, is not having to go on long game drives to see animals. Besides campsite action you can go to the permanent **Long Pool** near Nyamepi or the rarely dry **Chine Pool** – both good places to spend a couple of hours watching creatures coming to drink. Hippo and croc spotting at Long Pool is always fun even when nothing much else turns up. Chine Pool, 1km south of Mana River Drive, straddles the river terraces and valley hinterland, attracting animals such as sable and nyala antelope, which don't come to terrace woodlands very often.

LAKE KARIBA
SOUTH AND WEST

The **south and west sides** of **Lake Kariba** are much less developed than the east, and all that most people experience of them is a view from the cross-lake ferry. However, doing Kariba **overland** – on the faint road to the south of the lake marked "uninhabited" on some maps – is worthwhile if you can organize a sturdy vehicle or take your chances on local buses veering off the main Harare–Chirundu road at Karoi. Beware that the road is sandy, skiddy and impassable during heavy rains.

In fact, the area is not uninhabited, but to the west of Karoi the commercial, largely white-owned farms fade out into an area of desert, where the post-Kariba **Batonga** were dumped. Their communal lands stretch out to **Binga**, the regional administrative centre. Long stretches are just bush with the odd tree thrown across the track by elephants; schools form the nuclei of dotted settlements announced by homemade bus stop signs tacked onto baobab trees.

You won't find tourists in the villages (there's nowhere to stay anyway), except for the odd person foraging for Batonga crafts or perhaps hoping to photograph the old women, bones through noses and minus front teeth, smoking long *mbanje* (marijuana) pipes.

Those few who bother to take this road do so to see **Chizarira National Park**, the least visited but arguably most beautiful and isolated of all Zimbabwe's game reserves. Until very recently, this was also a major sanctuary for black rhinoceros. Sadly, the few rhinos that survived the poaching were translocated to a safer park in 1995. The best way to see the park is to walk it with a safari company such as *Backpacker's Africa* or *Khangela Safaris*, who organize walking safaris with excellent professional hunter-guides. It is not the most rewarding park to see game if you're in your own vehicle as the thick bush hides the animals. If camping and walking doesn't appeal, a spell in a new luxury lodge, perched on a hill just outside the national park, might. The only other tourist development hinges on small **fishing resorts** like Binga, and, on a slightly larger scale, **Mlibizi** – the Kariba ferry terminus.

The Kariba ferry

The **Kariba ferry** between Kariba town and Mlibizi is by far the easiest way to journey the length of the lake, saving the circuitous 1250-kilometre route you have to follow to drive to Victoria Falls via Bulawayo on tarred roads. But while the voyage has an *African Queen* romance to it, through wild country all the way, the experience rather depends on who you're sitting next to and how active the boozers are: people often rave it up for the entire 22-hour journey.

Tickets for the trip cost $US70 for a reclining seat, with meals, tea and coffee all included; cars cost $US45 to load up (Zimbabwe residents pay less). The ferry is often booked up months in advance and you need to pay half the cost to secure your reservation two weeks before the sailing date. After this time, seats are sold off, so keep on enquiring if you're told it's full. Without a car, your chances of getting on are better. On board, there's an outside sun deck and a shaded lounge, but you're unlikely to spot many animals en route, as the ferry sails in the centre of the lake. Nevertheless, it's still worth bringing your binoculars.

Departure dates vary. During peak months and school holidays (Jan, April, May, July, Aug, Sept & Dec) ferries sail four days each week, although only once per week in February and March; sailings are also less frequent in June, October and November.

THE BATONGA

The **Batonga** are some of Zimbabwe's poorest rural people, still living mostly outside the influences of the modern nation. Cut off for centuries in the Gwembe section of the Zambezi Valley, upriver from Portuguese trading stations, they maintained a subsistence lifestyle until the building of the **Kariba dam**. In 1959, when the last lorry – piled high with evicted villagers and their belongings – was on the point of departure from the doomed valley, a small green bush was tied to the vehicle's tailboard to trail along behind. Villagers explained this was to allow their ancestral guardian spirit to ride until they reached their new home: it was essential that this spirit remained on the ground during the journey for it to settle comfortably into its new surroundings and maintain a relationship with the ancestors.

The **removal of the Batonga** created considerable anguish abroad (not to mention among the people themselves). Anthropologists rushed to amass details of Batonga society before everything changed. Some interesting theories about their **origins** still question whether they ever migrated to their present area in Southern Africa, as other Bantu people are supposed to have done. Unique among Bantu-speakers, the Batonga have no migration myth, so the puzzle arises: have they forgotten their history, or have they been in the Gwembe valley since much more ancient times? Anthropologists have suggested that they were indigenous hunter-gatherers who adopted the language stock and farming methods of Bantu immigrants, but not enough research has been done to be sure. Certainly, **Tonga** is a very old language, apparently a proto-form of Shona, though they may both derive from an earlier Bantu tongue, Shona having undergone more profound changes over the last millennium.

Little of this heritage seems to have found its way back to enrich **the Batonga today**. The people no longer engage in beadwork because they can't afford to buy the imported beads. Indeed, many have sold off their beaded family heirlooms, as well as some very beautiful stools and carved hut doors, in order to raise money for the next meal. There's no evidence of traditional dress either, and the cosmetic practice of knocking out women's front teeth has (perhaps mercifully) died out. You may see the occasional old woman with a bone through her nose, but it's just as likely to be a stalk of grass. **Baskets** are certainly still being made either for domestic use or for co-operatives which distribute them through the mainstream curio centres.

For further details, timetables and bookings, contact *Kariba Ferries (Pvt) Ltd*, PO Box 578, Harare; the local office in Kariba on ☎161/2475; or Johannesburg ☎789 2440.

If you're **hitching**, once across the lake you should be able to line up a lift with a driver while on the ferry. Alternatively, there are organized but pricey **transfers**. *Kalai Safaris*, Zambezi Service Station, corner of Clarke and Livingstone roads, Victoria Falls (☎113/2168, fax 5855) will pick up four or more passengers from the ferry terminal for a trip to Hwange, or Victoria Falls; they also collect at these places for the return to Mlibizi. Book ahead.

Siabuwa

The land **south of Lake Kariba** is among Zimbabwe's poorest and most remote. Travelling around the region, unless on an organized tour or with your own vehicle, you are dependent on a very few local buses – somewhat erratically scheduled and none too comfortable. **Hitching** would be very chancy – traffic is very sparse and about your only hope would be to find an aid vehicle prepared to take you. Carry food and plenty of water, and expect long delays.

It's best not to get off except at villages as wild animals abound in this region. A familiar sight along the roadsides are aid-built pumps where locals fill buckets, and

After this checklist of loss, at least the layout of villages and **architectural techniques** remain much as they've always been. The thatching is an untidy affair, not groomed into flawless sections like Ndebele huts. The small huts on stilts are for chickens or children, with ladders removed at night to keep the precious charges safe from attack by wild animals. Huts on stilts in the fields are baboon watchtowers, occupied all day long before the harvest. These days, high-status building materials like cement and corrugated iron are used if someone has the money.

The Batonga live over the border in Zambia, too, both in the Zambezi Valley and on the plateau (before the existence of political frontiers, valley people crossed the river in dug-outs). But studies of the language and culture have concentrated on the plateau Batonga, who have always been broadly integrated with the rest of the country. In contrast, the isolation of the Gwembe valley inhabitants has earned them the label "backward" among urban Zimbabweans. An obvious target for **aid money**, they attract attention from organizations like the Save the Children Fund, who have concentrated on improving **sanitation and water supplies** to communities with some of the worst child mortality rates in the country. Land Rovers shuttle between villages transporting pipes and machinery for other projects like collective grain winnowing. And the government's desire to see universal primary **education** has seeded schools in many settlements. People no longer have to walk for days to get to a secondary school. One worker at Bumi Hills, remembering his schooling, recounted walking three days at the start and end of each term, accompanied by his older brother armed with axe and spear to fend off wild animals.

However, nothing can compensate the Batonga for the forced substitution of a viable – even flourishing – farming and fishing economy on the Zambezi, for the poor soils and uncertain rainfall of the interior. Evicted overnight from familiar, well-watered ancient lands, the Batonga have floundered ever since in their new and alien home.

An ironic postscipt to the story of the Batonga is the **trendiness** they've accumulated. Perhaps it's their *mbanje* smoking (women from long calabash pipes, men from shorter clay ones) that's created a special niche for these people in colonial cosmology. You come across tales of young middle-class whites who became strange and went to live among the "Tonkies". Often this seems to be a symbolic fall from grace into liberalism or socialism: usually the person who "went native" is alive and well and living in a city somewhere.

Blair toilets, built behind huts in every settlement. These are an ingenious Zimbabwean design, solving the problem of flies and smell that plague the traditional long-drops; painted black inside and spiral-shaped with a chimney air vent, they trap flies escaping to the only source of light – the gauze-covered air vent, which also allows air to circulate.

SIABUWA is the halfway staging post on the 400-kilometre trip from Karoi to Binga, the largest settlement en route and the place where buses begin and terminate. Eaten out by goats, it's a sizeable agglomeration of huts, schools, a garage and a basic store or two. A daily **bus** sets off in the early hours of the morning for Bulawayo via Binga on what must be the longest haul in the country; people sleep at the stop to ensure catching it, as the drivers leave when they get up. Getting here from Karoi involves catching a couple of buses, so be prepared for waits at stops along the way.

Binga

The Kariba ferry sails past **BINGA** without stopping, so if you are planning to visit this village, with its Chizarira Mountain view, you will have to come overland or take the *DDF* ferry (see below). Which is all the better, if you're prepared for the isolation, for this is both an interesting and scenic settlement, as yet undeveloped, and spreading

PARKS VERSUS PEOPLE

As elsewhere in Zimbabwe, there's extreme tension between villagers and the National Parks over **wildlife** – a conflict which has deep roots.

Game parks were set up from the 1930s to maintain game populations that had been decimated by hunting and habitat removal for commercial farming. White rhinos had been completely exterminated and diaries of early settlers reveal obscene hunting excesses – twenty-five giraffe in an afternoon was nothing. To create the parks, however, people were moved out and banned from subsistence hunting. Long-established balances had enabled people to coexist with wild animals for thousands of years, yet, suddenly, wildlife had become a luxury for the rich. Colonial legislation stated that wildlife in communal (black) areas was state property, while on private (white) farms, it was not.

Shortly after Independence a host of new conservation measures were introduced, but the problem of human versus animal interests remains unresolved and **poaching** is still heavy in all the national parks. One major way forward is the **Campfire Project** (Communal Areas Management for Indigenous Resources) which has a philosophy of sustainable rural development to enable rural communities to manage, and benefit directly from indigenous wildlife and other resources. Getting a community interested in the Campfire programme rests on changing the belief that the State owns the wildlife, to the belief that the wildlife is owned by the community who lives with it.

The first Campfire Project to be set up was the **Nyaminyami Wildlife Trust** in the Omay Communal Lands, adjoining Matusadona National Park. Wild animals tend to be viewed either as food or as a crop menace by peasant farmers, who resent wildlife getting so much land, while they're forced to keep livestock numbers low to prevent encroachment on game areas. As hunting is forbidden, National Parks and the District Council are frequently called out to shoot "problem animals" that are endangering either lives or crops in the fields. From this arrangement, the people get the meat, while National Parks sells the tusks or hides on behalf of the council (elephants are frequently the culprits and victims). One difficulty is that the number of claims for crop compensation, paid in cash, tends to exceed the budget and may be open to abuse. Another is that people spend compensation money on other necessities and then lack the funds to buy the equivalent in grain.

The Campfire Project is also trying to make people aware that although they want to acquire cattle, it's in their interests to limit numbers as wildlife is potentially more lucrative. In the Omay Communal Lands, the number of goats is roughly equal to the number of impala, even though the meat value alone of the latter far exceeds that of the former, and the hunting of impala brings in considerable revenue.

On the hunting front, to provide local people with the incentive not to poach, and to foster the perception of wild animals as having a high commercial value, Campfire channels revenue from game back to the communal lands. The council receives in the order of fifteen percent of the proceeds from hunting – money that can then be deployed to erect solar electric fences to protect crops, or to build clinics and schools. Privately run safari camps recently established on communal lands also pay a percentage of their income to the local council to fund projects, or for distribution to individual families. At present, 53 percent of the Zambezi Valley participates in the Campfire programme.

over a couple of hills and along the lakeshore. Like Kariba, it has no real centre, so without a car you'll find yourself doing long, sandy trudges to get around.

The Town

Binga was created as an **administrative centre** for Batonga resettlement, though, ironically, despite the dam's creation for hydroelectric power, electricity has only recently arrived, and the water supplies, piped uphill, don't always work.

GETTING AROUND SOUTH OF KARIBA

Public transport is minimal, with wildly erratic bus timetables, so keep asking around to get a reasonable idea of what's going on. However, **buses** can get you to Bulawayo, Hwange National Park and Victoria Falls without too much difficulty. Services connect Bulawayo and Siabuwa via Binga – once daily in each direction. For Victoria Falls (all-day trip) change at Dete Cross; for Hwange National Park (4hr) get off at Safari Cross. For Harare, sleep at the Siabuwa bus stop and catch the next morning's bus (or a series of buses) via Karoi. There are no buses between Binga and lakeside Mlibizi (see below), as the Mlibizi ferry terminus is 15km off the main road; once on the main road however, you could pick up a bus. With your own **car**, Binga is more accessible thanks to a recently completed tarred road all the way from Hwange (188km). **Hitching** is not easy as traffic is sparse; start out early in the morning and take the bus if nothing else has materialized.

Missionaries, however, are well ensconced, and a **hospital** and foreign aid worker village, secondary school and surprisingly well-stocked **supermarket**, near the main **bus stop**, form an ensemble of public buildings. The **school** is interesting, with an impressive library open to the community, and innovative experiments in farming are under way. On the river bank, the Batonga used to cultivate millet, which doesn't thrive inland, so agriculturalists are trying poor soil crops like **manioc**, with the hard work done by schoolchildren in exchange for remission of their school fees.

Pupils come from both Batonga and Ndebele communities. Teachers notice big differences in the children's responses to authority. The Ndebele, who come from a highly organized culture, accept what they are told, without demur, whereas the Batonga, whose social system of virtually autonomous homesteads is much looser, question everything.

Batonga craft

The Binga area is the source of the much sought-after **Batonga handicrafts** sold at Victoria Falls. A major cooperative at Kariangwe, about 60km south of Binga, collects baskets from all over the region for resale and they're available from the craft shop in Binga. There are also several roadside sellers dotted along the road from Hwange towards Chizarira. Prices are so low that bargaining is not on.

The best items are the wide-mouthed **winnowing baskets** with plaited square bottoms, tricoloured V-patterned **beadwork** and the **carved stools** you see people sitting under on the trees. The Batonga are people who really know about travelling and roadside waits, and they make wonderful, portable stools with carrying handles. You won't be able to stash one of the free-standing Batonga **drums** in your baggage, but they're worth seeing (or even playing) all the same. Traditionally decorated with beautiful, archetypal zigzag motifs, they are now, sadly, a disappearing art.

Village visits

One of the most rewarding ways to experience traditional rural Zimbabwe is to take a day trip to one of the remote **Tonga homesteads** with Dr Peta Jones, an archeologist and anthropologist living in Binga. You'll walk along paths (for a maximum of two hours) with pack donkeys to a homestead for a meal which would normally be served to the family's own friends or visitors. Secondary school graduates from Tonga villages in the area are on hand to act as interpreters. The organizers stress that people should dress modestly, so as not to make their hosts feel disadvantaged, and if you feel philanthropic not to hand out money directly to people, but make a donation instead to an educational fund. The day includes a visit to the **community craft centre** where you can buy baskets and the like. Charges for a day out are very reasonable, and bookings should be made well in advance through Dr Peta Jones, Chilangililo Co-operative Society Ltd, Private Bag 5713, Binga (☎115/2407).

Practicalities

Binga has a few lakeside villas – holiday homes for the affluent from Bulawayo – which the locals refer to as "The Palaces", and a couple of dozen houseboats for the fishing and drinking crowd are moored here and available for charter hire. **Boats** are fully equipped and come with a skipper who knows the lake; for details contact Enzo Rossi (☎155/2405).

As for **accommodation**, the former District Commissioner's residence down at the lakeside (5km downhill from the administrative centre and bus terminus) is now the *Binga Rest Camp* (☎155/244; ③), which has the only camping facilities and restaurant in the area. Its swimming pool, filled by a nearby hot spring is distinctly reviving and the hotel gardens with their exotic trees provide a wonderful respite from the dust. More comfortable are the luxury cottages opposite the *Rest Camp* at *Kulizwe Lodge* (☎155/286; ④), where you'll also find Binga's only filling station.

Ten kilometres from Binga, off the Kamativi–Binga road are two more places to stay, both on the lakeshore. *Chilila Lodge* (☎155/2201; ③) is the smarter of the two, though less luxurious than *Kulizwe Lodge*. For self-sufficient backpackers there's a great opportunity at *Chilangililo Co-operative* (☎155/2407; ①) to stay in a traditional Tonga hut built on stilts, where you can enjoy the lake as well as meet locals in the nearby family compound. Not much more is on offer so you'll need to be self-sufficient and ready to adapt to African life, but it's a rare opportunity to get under the skin of a local community. Safe boiled water is available and two basic rural shops near *Chilangililo* can provide necessities.

Getting there

Across the lake, the **DDF ferry** runs from Kariba to Binga twice a month (☎161/2694 to find out when the next one leaves) and takes two and a half days to complete the journey, stopping at fishing villages along the way, so take food and water. If you're planning on staying at *Chilangililo Co-operative*, ask to be dropped off at the fishing co-operatives near Chilila, from where it's a short walk.

The easiest way to get to Binga by **economy bus** is from Bulawayo, which runs daily on tarred road all the way. There are also daily buses from Mbare in Harare, but the journey is longer and more tortuous, taking in 100km of dirt track. From Victoria Falls an awkward change at Dete Cross or Hwange means you'll have to leave at 6am at the latest.

For *Chilangililo* and *Chilila Lodge*, get off the bus at the stop after Chilila Gate, 6km before Binga. Head straight through the gate and up the gravel road for *Chilila*; for *Chilangililo*, take instead the parallel road nearer the bus stop and follow the arrows on yellow signs.

The western fishing resorts: Mlibizi and Deka

Since game has been shot out at this southwest end of the lake, fishing is the main reason to come here. To catch the Kariba ferry (see p.119) you'll have to overnight at **MLIBIZI** to catch the 9am departure. The *Mlibizi Zambezi Resort* (PO Box 2335, Bulawayo; ☎78060 or 78064; ④) here has Spanish-styled self-contained **chalets** as well as camping.

On the confluence of the Zambezi and Deka rivers, 50km from Hwange, the **Deka Drum Fishing Resort** (PO Box 2, Hwange; ☎50524; ③) is a more modest and a wonderfully old-fashioned place – cheap, with camping and **chalets,** a swimming pool and bar. It's not worth a special trip unless you're fishing, but definitely warrants a stop if you're in the region. It is also one of the few places selling petrol in the area and you can call in for a drink or lunch on the verandah. A rural store nearby sells basic foods if you're camping.

Chizarira National Park

Open year-round. US$2 entrance fee.

Very few travellers make it to **CHIZARIRA**, Zimbabwe's most remote National Park. Isolated and undeveloped, it is a spectacular region, a kingdom on top of the steep Zambezi Escarpment well watered by rivers cutting sheer gorges through the mountains and full of natural springs. The usual Zambezi Valley game is to be seen, including elephant, buffalo, zebra, kudu, reedbuck, waterbuck, bushbuck, eland, grysbok, impala and tsessebe. It's not a great place for lions, though you will hear them and are more likely to see them in the south. There have been some exceptional daytime sightings of leopard, less shy here than in other parks because tourists are few and far between. But when people talk about the park, it's invariably the beautiful **scenery** that makes them wax lyrical.

RHINO POACHING

Until recently, Chizarira offered your best chance of seeing the virtually extinct **black or hook-lipped rhinos,** which used to browse freely around thick bush and wooded gulleys in the northern part of the park. In 1995, however, following decades of ruthless **poaching,** the last few remaining animals were translocated to more intensively protected zones (IPZs) in other parts of the country, where they are guarded day and night.

Zimbabwe has the world's last viable breeding herd of black rhinos, yet nothing seems able to halt their steady extermination. Twenty years ago there were 40,000 in Africa. In early 1992, it was estimated that fewer than 3000 individuals survived on the continent, of which 2000 were in Zimbabwe. However, in November 1992, a count throughout Zimbabwe found only 250 black rhinos living in the wild. Experts predict that Zimbabwe's last rhino will be finished off in the next few years. Despite the international ban on the trade in rhino horn, it is, even today, widely available in markets in Hong Kong and Taiwan at sky-high prices. The market for knife handles in the Yemen and apothecarial ingredients in the Far East continues to propel their unrelenting slaughter.

In 1985, the Zimbabwean government began shooting poachers on sight and capturing and translocating rhinos to safer parks, but this strategy hasn't worked. Poachers move quickly on foot, cutting out only the horn before ferrying back to their camps in Zambia. In an area of dense bush, they often escape undetected. The poachers themselves are not the ones to cream off vast amounts of money, but are offered enough by middlemen to make it worth risking their lives. Many are unemployed Zambians. Zimbabwe's next step in the early 1990s was a massive **dehorning programme.** Since then, sadly, dehorned rhinos have been killed simply for their stumps.

Zimbabwe has longed blamed Zambian poachers, backed by international rings, for killing rhino, but there is evidence of **high-level government involvement** in the trade. An MP was jailed in early 1993 for five years for possession of two horns. The deaths in suspicious circumstances of two army officers who were looking into top-level military involvement in rhino, as well as elephant poaching, have led to calls from Amnesty International for a government investigation. Some people are even campaigning for **legalization of the rhino horn trade;** rhinos would be legally farmed and their horns humanely removed, thereby undercutting the black market to ensure the survival of one of Africa's most beautiful creatures – albeit in enclosures.

This becomes understandable as soon as you approach the reserve. From a long way off the jagged mountains of Chizarira are visible, dominated by **Tundazi** – home, local legend has it, to an immense and powerful serpent. Once you've arrived, the views across to Lake Kariba, 40km north, are equally magnificent. The **Chizarira mountains** give you a clue to the nature of the place. Their name derives from a Tonga word meaning "to close off" or "create a barrier", defining the craggy edge of their baobab-wooded world, the **Gwembe valley**. The escarpment's roof is another world altogether, of slender trees spaced out across grasslands and well-watered scrub savannah. The **river gorges**, such as Mucheni and Lwizilukulu, are really exciting, with their thick vegetation cascading down places too steep for any vehicle. This doesn't stop the **elephants**, however; you'll notice their paths, less than a metre wide, cutting into slopes held together by the determined roots of stunted trees. On the escarpment in the north are plateaux of typical highveld Brachystegia woodland and mopane scrub and woodland as you move southwards. The southern boundary is marked by the Busi River which is flanked by plains of characteristic *Acacia albida* trees.

Chizarira also offers superb prospects for ornithologists, with no less than 406 of Zimbabwe's 580 species of **birds** recorded here, among them the rare and beautiful Angola pitta, the Livingstone flycatcher, African broadbill, Taita falcon and elusive black stork.

Getting there

You won't have much company at Chizarira: it's just too far for most people, when other parks are far more accessible and better stocked. Most of those visitors who do come drive from Victoria Falls or Hwange, an eight-hour journey mostly on dirt roads. While 4WD isn't essential for the north, except during the rains, it is necessary for the south where you have to cross sandy rivers to reach Busi camp. The nearest **petrol and supplies** are 90km away at Binga so bring all you need. From Harare, Chizarira is reached via 300km of dirt road, once you turn off at Karoi, with Siabuwa the only place en route for petrol.

Accommodation and walking safaris

Guests fly in to *Chizarira Wilderness Lodge*, the only tourist place. The lodge has eight thatched stone **chalets** shaded by a grove of mountain acacia dramatically overlooking the Zambezi Valley. It's just outside the park, half an hour's drive from the park headquarters, and is managed by a fully licensed professional guide who can take walks into the reserve, and do game drives and birdwatching. The lodge itself now has a **tent camp** (Taita), slap in the centre of the park itself and an ideal base for hikes. Costs are US$190 all in, with an additional US$200 for transfers from anywhere in Zimbabwe. Book through *Run Wild*, PO Box 6485, Harare (☎14/795841 or 795845, fax 795846).

If you want to do more hiking and tracking, contact *Backpacker's Africa* or *Khangela Safaris* (see below) who camp right in the park and unlike most other operators venture into the south. Their walking safaris in Chizarira offer guaranteed solitude and some of the most inspiring hiking in Zimbabwe. Most of *Backpacker's* safaris are fully backed up – a 4WD carries two camp attendants who put up the tents, make the fires, prepare all the food and heat the water for your portable washbasins and bush showers. You don't have to carry anything besides your binoculars and camera. Nor is the walking uncomfortable – you're not pushed excessively and you rest up during the heat in the middle of the day. Bookings for *Backpacker's Africa* can be made through *Safari Par Excellence*, Phumula Centre, Parkway, Victoria Falls (☎113/2051 or 2054); expect to pay US$195 all in. If this sounds too cushy, *Khangela* does safaris where you carry everything yourself and are free to walk into areas far from any roads or designated campsites. Their professional guide is excellent and the food good. Prices range from US$120 per day all in, and trips normally last four days. Bookings can be made direct through *Khangela*, PO Box FM 296, Famona, Bulawayo (☎19/49733, fax 68259).

With either company, an African tracker walks with the armed guide and you spend a good deal of time identifying and following game tracks. It's a fascinating experience, estimating how far ahead the elephants are by feeling the warmth of their dung (it's mainly grass after all), or how old the remains of a lion kill are, and noticing the insects and birds you miss when driving. While you can do a walking trip just to Chizarira, *Backpacker's* offers a twelve-day "Tundazi Trail" once a month which takes in the Zambezi National Park, Hwange, Kazuma Pan as well as Chizarira. *Khangela Safaris* offers a similar eight-day multi-park trip that takes in Hwange, the southeast of the country, Gonarezhou, Great Zimbabwe and Matobo Hills. Prices range from US$120 per day if you carry your own gear, to US$140 for the softer option of a trip with a back-up vehicle.

If you're visiting the park under your own steam, you can ask an armed **National Parks game scout** to take you walking. They will take groups out for a small fee. Unlike Mana Pools, however, you can't wander off on your own.

The overland safari company *Afroventures* (PO Box 261, Victoria Falls; ☎113/4588), spends a night or two at Chizarira en route to Kariba from Victoria Falls, but they only go to the northern section. *Afroventures* sometimes hires a professional guide to take walks in Chizarira, or uses a Parks game scout to accompany a group.

National Parks camps

The national park headquarters are at **Manzituba**, 22km up the escarpment from the Binga–Siabuwa road. There are no chalets or lodges here but there are three **camping sites** nearby, the most developed of which is at **Kasiswi** on the Lusilukulu River, 6km from the park HQ, which has thatched shelters on stilts. Two spectacular sites overlooking the Mucheni Gorge have no facilities. Only one party at a time is allowed in each; booking is through National Parks' Central Reservations office in Harare and the costs are reasonable as usual for the Parks.

Mabolo Bush Camp on the Mucheni River, below the Manzituba spring, 6km from the camp HQ, has running water, a flush toilet and shower. If you prefer flood plains and lowveld vegetation, go 35km over very rough roads to **Busi Bush Camp**, which has thatched sleeping shelters, but no running water (you have to dig water from the riverbed and boil it). It's a marvellous site under *Acacia albidas* with herds of impala wandering around and a night chorus of hyenas and lions.

travel details

Economy buses

The length of these routes, and Zambezi Valley road conditions, compound the usual vagueness of local bus times. On the Karoi–Binga road buses break down more than is usual elsewhere and the drivers often set off when they wake up. Many of the buses start somewhere else and what's happened en route is a mystery. Ask around. The best advice is to be there as early as the locals.

Binga to: Bulawayo (2 daily from 5am; 8hr); Harare via Siabuwa (1 daily around 2am; all day).

Chirundu to: Harare (1 daily at noon; 8hr); Lusaka (1 daily at 2pm; 7hr).

Kariba to: Harare (2 daily first thing; 8hr).

Siabuwa to: Binga (daily between 2.30pm and 5.30pm; 3hr); Harare (daily between 1am and 2am; all day).

Luxury coaches

Various coach companies take on the Harare–Kariba route from time to time, then stop because of unprofitability. Check with local hotels in Kariba or the Publicity Association in Harare for the latest.

Chirundu to: Harare (Wed; 5hr 30min; *DSB Coachline* ☎14/734837); Lusaka (Tues; 3hr 30min; *DSB Coachline*).

Ferries

The timetable of the private *Kariba Ferries* varies seasonally; ring Harare ☎14/65476 or Kariba ☎161/2475. The government ferries, run by the *District Development Fund* (*DDF*), also run to a flexible timetable; enquiries on Kariba ☎161/2349. The following details are a rough outline:

Kariba to: Binga (2 monthly; 2–3 days; enquire *DDF*); Matusadona (weekly; all day; enquire *DDF*); Mlibizi (Mon, Tues, Thurs & Fri at 9am; 22hr; enquire *Kariba Ferries*).

Mlibizi to: Kariba (Tues, Wed, Fri & Sat at 9am; 22hr; enquire *Kariba Ferries*).

Flights

Kariba to: Bulawayo (2 weekly; 1hr 35min); Harare (2 daily; 55min); Hwange (2 daily; 55min); Johannesburg (2 weekly via Harare; 5hr 50min); Victoria Falls (1 daily; 1hr 50min).

CHAPTER THREE

BULAWAYO AND THE MATOBO DISTRICT

Set apart by language and history from the rest of the country, **Bulawayo** is often bypassed by travellers. This is a pity, for Zimbabwe's second city is unquestionably more interesting than its capital. Whereas Harare uses Western symbolism to make its mark as an international capital, Bulawayo's character comes from a history of going its own way and developing its own style. Although Bulawayo's citizens have long considered their city to have suffered unjust neglect at the expense of Harare, the upside is that there has been little demolition or hasty redevelopment, and the wide, regularly gridded streets remain studded with gracious colonial-era buildings. Overall, in fact, the city has something of a sepia-toned feel, compounded by rather conservative dress and ageing cars, and a slow, laid-back ambience that makes it a thoroughly pleasant place to stroll about and explore.

Perhaps the best reason to visit the city is for the nearby **Matopos Hills** and **Matobo National Park**. Although such granite outcrops can be found all over the country, the Dali-esque compositions of lichen-streaked balancing rocks and grassy valleys are at their best at Matopos. The world's highest concentration of prehistoric **rock paintings** is found here, too, and you can spend days climbing kopjes and discovering painted caves and rock shelters – human history in the area goes back over 100,000 years. Much later, the **Torwa** and **Rozwi** states had court centres in the Bulawayo region, the remains of which lie scattered in the countryside. None competes with Great Zimbabwe in size but the local style is exemplified by the beautifully laid walls at **Khami**, 22km from Bulawayo.

Since colonial times, Bulawayo has served as a **transport hub** between the African hinterland and the continent's southern tip. It is the jumping-off point for Hwange and Victoria Falls and onward journeys to Zambia, Botswana, and South Africa, as well as being well positioned for eastward travel to Great Zimbabwe and the Highlands.

BULAWAYO

The name **BULAWAYO** means, in Ndebele, "Place of Slaughter", a reference, it is thought, to the fierce succession of battles that took place in the late nineteenth century. These culminated in the accession of one of the key figures of pre-colonial Zimbabwean history, **King Lobengula** in 1870. His reign, peppered with heavy doses of heroism, lying, betrayal and murder, reads like mythology or grand opera. This era which came to a close in 1894, with Lobengula's death, and Ndebele collapse before the relentless northwards advance of the **British South Africa Company**. For a summary of these events, see "The Historical Framework", in *Contexts*.

Although Bulawayo kept its name, the new **colonial town** was re-sited along a classic British grid. Almost immediately it was at the centre of a mining rush: within

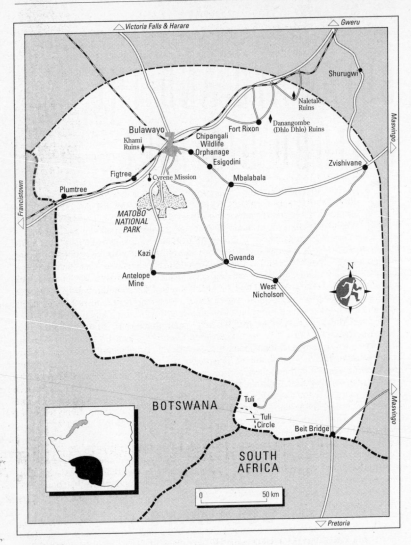

two months four hundred gold prospectors had acquired licences and within ten years the population had reached six thousand. Quick to see an opportunity, the *Standard Bank of South Africa* set up its first branch in a tent, guarded day and night by the Matabeleland Mounted Police. In 1898, as the proposed Cape to Cairo **railway** reached Bulawayo, the town developed into an important clearing house for goods from the colonies further north, and became the country's main communications centre.

Resistance to the white invasion, however, hadn't ended in 1894. While the first *Chimurenga* marked the last great survival struggle of the old societies, colonial rule brought new forms of protest. Bulawayo – because of its strong industrial base in

ACCOMMODATION PRICE CODES

Hotels and other accommodation options in Zimbabwe have been categorized according to the **price codes** given below, which indicate the cost, per person sharing, of a night's lodging.

For a full explanation, see p.46.

① under US$8	④ US$25–35	⑦ US$65–80
② US$8–15	⑤ US$35–50	⑧ US$80–95
③ US$15–25	⑥ US$50–65	⑨ over US$95

engineering, metal founding, manufacturing, garment making, printing, packaging and food production – was at the forefront of the development of worker organizations. The first African **trade union**, the Rhodesian Industrial and Commercial Workers Union, was formed here in 1927; African railway workers staged a successful strike in 1945; and the country's first general strike began here in 1948. **Joshua Nkomo**, general secretary of the railway workers' union and president of the TUC, later emerged in the 1950s as leader of the Bulawayo-based **African National Congress**.

Nkomo's strong regional following in Matabeleland led inevitably to much bad feeling when he was cold-shouldered by the government after **Independence**. The **dissident years** that followed – in which tens of thousands of people in Matabeleland were brutally murdered by government forces – posed a threat to stability, and fuelled white fears that tribal warfare might sound the death knell of the new Zimbabwe. The grievances of the early Eighties, however, turned out not to be beyond negotiated settlement.

With the May 1988 **Unity Accord**, dissidents left the bush and laid down their arms. Joshua Nkomo became vice-president and the formerly jailed Zipra lelader, Dumisa Dabengwa, became home affairs minister. A second national university has been built in Bulawayo to equalize some of the disparity between developments in the capital and neglected Bulawayo. Horrific evidence, though, of the extent of the killings, particularly by the notorious Fifth Brigade in the early 1980s, continues to emerge – the 1992 drought revealed skeletons down dried-out mineshafts – and there have been calls for the report of a full inquiry held into the atrocities to be published.

Arrival, information and city transport

However you **arrive** in Bulawayo, getting into the city centre should present few problems. An *Air Zimbabwe* bus meets all flights at the **airport** (☎26491–2), 22km north of town on Robert Mugabe Way, and deposits passengers at the central *Bulawayo Sun Hotel*. There are also metered taxis at the airport.

The *Sun Hotel* also serves as the depot for *Translux* and *Ajay Motorways* **bus services** to and from Harare, Hwange, Victoria Falls and Johannesburg, while *Blue Arrow* drops passengers at Unifreight House, 73a Fife St. There is no central bus station; most **economy buses** arrive at **Renkini terminus** in Sixth Avenue Extension, opposite the Mzilikazi Police Station and near the high-density areas. From there, assorted **local buses** head into town, although you may prefer to avoid the hassle and take a taxi. A few economy buses also arrive at the more central terminus on Lobengula Street/Sixth Avenue also near the high-density areas. Bulawayo's **train station**, at the end of Lobengula Street, is a short hop by taxi from the centre.

The **area telephone code** for Bulawayo is ☎19.

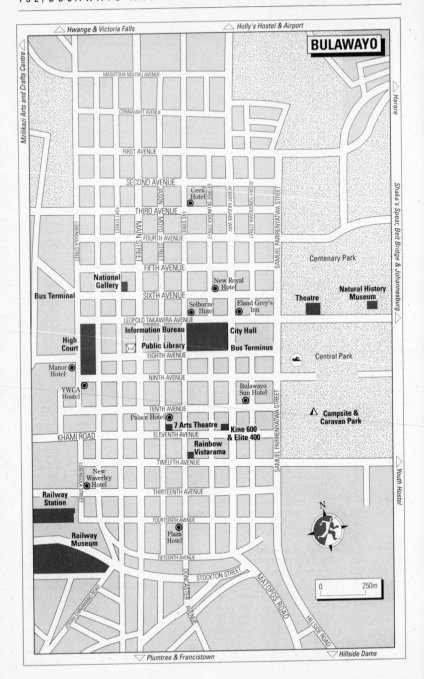

△ Hwange & Victoria Falls   △ Holly's Hostel & Airport

BULAWAYO

Mzilikazi Arts and Crafts Centre

Shaka's Spear, Beit Bridge & Johannesburg ▷

Harare

MASOTSHA NDLOVU AVENUE

CONNAUGHT AVENUE

FIRST AVENUE

SECOND AVENUE

Cecil Hotel

THIRD AVENUE

FOURTH AVENUE

FIFTH AVENUE

Centenary Park

National Gallery

New Royal Hotel

SIXTH AVENUE

Theatre

Natural History Museum

Bus Terminal

Selborne Hotel

Eland Grey's Inn

LEOPOLD TAKAWIRA AVENUE

Information Bureau

City Hall

High Court

Public Library

Bus Terminus

Central Park

EIGHTH AVENUE

Manor Hotel

NINTH AVENUE

YWCA Hostel

Bulawayo Sun Hotel

Campsite & Caravan Park

TENTH AVENUE

Palace Hotel

7 Arts Theatre

Kine 600 & Elite 400

KHAMI ROAD

ELEVENTH AVENUE

Rainbow Vistarama

Youth Hostel ▷

TWELFTH AVENUE

New Waverley Hotel

Railway Station

THIRTEENTH AVENUE

FOURTEENTH AVENUE

Railway Museum

Plaza Hotel

FIFTEENTH AVENUE

STOCKTON STREET

N

0   250m

▽ Plumtree & Francistown   ▽ Hillside Dams

Bulawayo has Zimbabwe's best **Publicity Association**, under the City Hall's clocktower in Fife Street (daily 8am–4.30pm; ☎60867), where you'll find maps, accommodation and touring information for Bulawayo and the rest of Zimbabwe. Booking for the Matopos and any of Zimbabwe's **national parks** can be done at 140a Fife St (☎63646–7); it's best to go in person, with plenty of time and patience.

City transport

Central Bulawayo is easy to **get around** on **foot**, and although the wide streets make the distance from one side of town to the other feel endless, most places around town can be reached in under half an hour.

Bulawayo's flatness, its wide and quiet streets, and cycle lanes make it ideal for cycling. For **bike rental**, try the *Youth for Christ Centre*, 117 George Silundika St/ Twelfth Ave (☎63656), *Transit Car & Truck Hire*, Robert Mugabe Way/Twelfth Ave (☎76495–6), or, better still, the delivery service of *Miles Ahead Cycle Hire* (☎41747).

Taxis are cheap for short trips, and can be booked by telephone (see "Listings"). Otherwise, the best places to catch them are outside the *Bulawayo Sun Hotel* on Tenth Avenue, or around the City Hall area. **Buses** are more practicable for destinations further afield such as the Townsend Road Youth Hostel, the Hillside Dams, or for reaching a spot out of town from which to hitch to the Matopos.

Bulawayo has two urban **bus stations**. The **City Hall terminus**, on Eighth Avenue between Fife Street and Robert Mugabe Way, serves all but the western suburbs. Services are fairly frequent and there's a patchily accurate timetable. Buses to the low-income western suburbs run from **Lobengula Street terminus**, at the west end of Sixth Avenue, but are invariably jam-packed.

Accommodation

Bulawayo's **hotels** accommodate all but the emptiest of pockets, and most are conveniently central and clean. Budget travellers, however, will do best at the city's recently opened **backpackers lodges** than its cheap hotels, which are invariably seedy. At the other end of the scale, small safari operators have blossomed, and it's certainly an option to stay **out of town** on a game farm at an all-inclusive rate, rather than a city hotel. Several alternatives have opened up in the Matopos if you plan to head straight there. Note, too, that the city centre hotels tend to fill up during the Trade Fair at the end of April, so book ahead at that time. The excellent Publicity Association in City Hall has the most up-to-date information on all types of accommodation.

Campsites and backpackers lodges

Berkeley Place, 71 Josiah Tongogara St, between Sixth Ave and Leopold Takawira Way (☎67701). Cheap and clean boarding house with shared bathrooms. The lack of a licence for alcohol ensures a quiet night. ②.

Holly's Hostel, 35 Robert Mugabe Way, North End (☎77602). A popular backpackers' place, 2km along the road towards the airport (not to be confused with another 35 Robert Mugabe Way, closer to town on the right-hand side); dorms, some doubles and cooking facilities. ①.

Municipal Campsite, off Jason Moyo Ave, opposite the museum. Adjoining the park, this immaculate site is shaded by jacarandas and palms and has the advantage of being a stone's throw from Josiah Tongogara St swimming pool. A few chalets are available (①), and although there's no kitchen, you can braai and picnic. The site also has 24-hour supervision, and you can leave your luggage in the guard's hut during the day. Take a taxi at night as muggings are on the increase.

Shaka's Spear, 44 Pauling Rd/Leopold Takawira (☎61385). Beyond the campsite, but not far from the museum, this once-grand suburban house has been converted into dorms and cheap doubles.

They also do tours to Matopos. Once again, take a taxi along Leopold Takawira at night, as it's none too safe. ①.

Youth Hostel, Townsend Rd/Third St (☎76488). An old colonial house, with two 8-bedded rooms and a kitchen for self-catering. Inconveniently located out in the suburbs, but close to shops. From the City Hall take either of two buses: the Waterford bus runs down 12th Ave and will drop you outside the hostel; alternatively, catch the hospital bus and get off at the *Holiday Inn* and walk from there. ①.

YWCA hostel, 35 Ninth Avenue/Lobengula St (☎60185). The YWCA caters for both sexes, though in term-time it is usually filled with scholars and students from out of town. Pricier than the cheap hotels for double and single rooms in male and female wings, but you can get a good deal on full board. ①.

Inexpensive hotels

Cecil Hotel, Fife St/Third Ave (☎60295). A bit more comfort than usual in this price bracket, with breakfast thrown in, and a TV and radio in each room. A private bath is a little extra. ③.

Manor Hotel, Lobengula St/Eighth Ave (☎61001). Backs conveniently onto the bus terminal, but has a poor reputation for safety. ②.

New Waverley Hotel, 133–134 Lobengula St/Thirteenth Ave (☎60033). The cheapest hotel you're likely to find in Zimbabwe, but with a good share of prostitution and drunkenness. Near to the station, it's an exuberant place, with a local band playing every evening. Definitely not recommended for women travelling alone. ①.

Palace Hotel, Jason Moyo St, between Tenth and Eleventh Ave (☎64294). A few bucks more and pretty noisy, but marginally more salubrious. The beer garden is a popular venue for visiting bands. Not recommended for women alone. ②.

Plaza Hotel, Fourteenth Ave, between Jason Moyo and Fife streets. Clean rooms in a slightly decaying building; ask for one with a balcony. The public bar is raucous, but it's okay for women travelling together. ③.

Mid-range hotels

Banff Lodge Hotel, Banff Rd/Leander Ave (☎43176). More a suburban guest house than a hotel, this quiet colonial house near Hillside Dams is good value at this price, and has a restaurant. ③.

Eland Grey's Inn, Robert Mugabe Way/Jason Moyo Ave (☎60121). Reliable, though unexciting mid-range place in a conveniently central location, with a small pool. ③.

Hilltop Motel, Gwanda Rd (☎72493). 6km out of town, and suitable only with your own car, but pleasant enough and recently revamped. ③.

Jamaica Inn Dark City, Johannesburg Rd, opposite Chipangali. A long way out of Bulawayo, 25km from the centre, but a convenient motel-style roadside stop if you're driving up from Johannesburg. ③.

New Royal, George Silundika St/Sixth Ave (☎ 65764). Similar to *Eland Grey's Inn*, with all rooms en-suite. ③.

Rio Hotel, Old Esigodini Rd (☎41384). Old hotel with pleasant gardens, 11km out of town, heading out east along Twelfth Ave – you'll need your own transport. The bar can be noisy at weekends, but the hotel is good for kids, with a playing area. ③.

Selborne Hotel, Leopold Takawira Ave (☎65741). Smack in the centre, opposite the City Hall, this is popular (and often full), but it has a fair bit of style and is as pleasant a place to stay as any of the more expensive hotels. ③.

Expensive hotels and lodges

Bulawayo Sun Hotel, Josiah Tongogara St/Tenth Ave (☎60101). Central Bulawayo's smartest hotel, though a rather airless, characterless option. ⑨.

Cresta Churchill, Matopos Rd/Moffat Ave (☎41016). Best and least expensive of the upmarket options, though further out. ④.

Holiday Inn, Ascot Centre/Milnerton Drive (☎72464). Part of the no-surprise chain of comfortable hotels, with the advantage of a swimming pool and is recommended for families. ⑨.

Induna Lodge, 16 Fortunes Gate Rd, Matseumhlope (☎45684). Comfortable suburban house for the safari set. Tours organized by the professional guide owner. US$90 for dinner, bed and breakfast.
Nesbitt Castle, 6 Percy Ave, Hillside (☎427726). Luxurious suites, mainly for businessmen, in a castle built by an eccentric former mayor of Bulawayo. The most expensive place in town, but certainly the most interesting, with excellent food. US$180 for dinner, bed and breakfast.
Southern Comfort Lodge, 22 Jaywick Rd, Matsheumhlope (☎/fax 41340). Four twin-bedded chalets set in a huge property overlooking a small dam, in one of Bulawayo's most beautiful suburbs, ten minutes' drive south of the centre. ⑤.

Out-of-town lodges and camps

The following list of places to stay **around Bulawayo** does not include accommodation for the Matopos area, which is reviewed on p.146.
Bembezi Safaris, 130a Josiah Tongagara (☎68910). Stone and thatch cottages overlooking a lake with good birdwatching, 80km north of Bulawayo. From US$100 per person all in, although cheaper self-catering rates are available.
Chief's Lodge, PO Box 7, Bulawayo (☎79563, fax 76658). Luxury lodge on large farm, 15km out of Bulawayo on the Harare road. Run by the very friendly Parsons family who organize tours to the Matopos and historical sites, including Naletale and Danangombe. US$182 per person per night all in; self-catering at a reduced rate available for Southern Africa residents.
Country Rest Camp, 19km peg on Falls Rd (☎73491 or 73236). Chalets, dorms and camping: convenient if you're heading to Victoria Falls in your own vehicle. ①.
Mimosa Lodge, Box 2348, Bulawayo (☎79494). A congenial old farmhouse whose land, crossed by riding and hiking trails, harbours some game. 35km out of town towards Victoria Falls, at Nyamandhlovu; US$10 for transfers from the airport. US$165 per person all in.
Springhaven Rest Resort, Umzingwane Rd (☎188/33515). Camping on a farm: good if you're en route from Johannesburg, or fancy a few days out of the city. Meals are available, and there's a small shop for basics. Free transport to *Springhaven* leaves the railway station at 8am, and City Hall at 9am daily. By car, take the Umzingwane road (left at the 18km peg off the Johannesburg road), and follow the Springhaven sign for 8km.

The City

Arriving in **BULAWAYO** is like jumping back fifty years. More like the set of an old movie than a modern African city, the town stood in for late-1950s Johannesburg in the shooting of *A World Apart*, the film about South African anti-apartheid activist, Ruth First. The South African connection actually goes deeper than film maker's licence. In the nineteenth century, Bulawayo was the capital of the **Ndebele state** and the majority language, Sindebele, is very close to the original Zulu, while the local *Smanje Manje* **music** has crossover elements of Shona and South African township pop.

Tourist **attractions** in town are limited, but what there is can fill a day or two. In Centenary Park, the **Museum of Natural History** is the finest in central Africa. The **art gallery** has some excellent Ndebele craft work and the **Mzilikazi Art and Craft Centre** is good for a few hours, set as it is in the oldest and most interesting high-density suburb. On the fringes of the city, the **Tshabalala Animal Sanctuary** – which is completely wild – offers walking or horse riding, plus the chance to see antelope, while, further out, **Chipangali Wildlife Orphanage** obliges with big cats and elephants.

The centre of Bulawayo is marked by **City Hall**, right outside which is **Eighth Avenue**, the town's principal axis. This leads on to the main public buildings and ends up at the **High Court** – a colossal building with a copper dome mounted high on a three-storey plinth. In earlier times a statue of Cecil Rhodes stood dead in the middle of Eighth Avenue and Main Street, framed by the powerfully symbolic high court; after Independence the statue was literally pulled from its pedestal, to be kicked and beaten by bystanders. It has now found a new home behind the Natural History Museum.

Along **Leopold Takawira Way**, which parallels Eighth Avenue, a long stretch of **parkland** shelters the campsite. On the opposite side of town, off Lobengula Street, is the **train station**. The stretch from here down Lobengula Street to the **bus terminus** is the centre's main **African quarter**, where bicycles weave through the traffic, small colonnaded shops sell cloth, blankets and cooking pots, and local music bellows from record bars. West of Lobengula Street lie the **industrial sites** and **high-density residential areas**.

Peaceful **suburbs** surround central Bulawayo. The wealthiest are in the hillier east, where granite outcrops grace the large gardens, and the poorest in the west, where maize and the odd stubby pawpaw and mango trees grow fitfully in the dusty backyards of one- or two-roomed dwellings. The oldest and most interesting houses lie just south of the city centre in what was the earliest white residential area – inventively called **Suburbs**. Here, colonial-style homes with wrap-around verandahs front onto jacaranda-lined streets.

Bulawayo's museums and galleries

After Harare, Bulawayo is the best place in the country to catch up with local high culture and get general background information on Zimbabwe as a whole. Between the **museums**, the **Public Library** and the **National Gallery** you can provide yourself with a one-day crash course in Zimbabwean Studies.

Museum of Natural History

Centenary Park, Leopold Takawira Ave. Daily 9am–5pm, except Christmas and Good Friday; US$2.

If you see nothing else, don't miss the **Museum of Natural History**, the highlight of the city's cultural offerings. Imaginative exhibits not only cover the usual natural history topics of wildlife and botany, but also extend into ethnography, geology and history. The strength of the collection is that it concentrates exclusively on Zimbabwe, without spreading itself too thinly by attempting to cover life, the universe and everything.

The **wildlife gallery** gives excellent background to Zimbabwe's fauna – superb preparation if you're planning to go off to Hwange. The extensive **ornithological collection**, with endless stuffed birds crammed like battery hens into boxes, is a little off-putting, but the dioramas of **indigenous mammals** are excellent and include the second largest mounted elephant in the world, which very nearly reaches the ceiling of its ground-floor home.

Surprisingly interesting displays of gold, emeralds and the other minerals found in Zimbabwe are on show in the **geological section**, which is partly designed to simulate a mine shaft. The adjoining outdoor display of mining antiques demonstrates how the industry operated in the nineteenth and early twentieth centuries.

The **ethnographic collection**, which includes some superb carved wooden stools and head-rests, gives some kind of yardstick for assessing modern curios. But for social and historical coverage, the **Hall of Man** is the best thing in the building. It gives amazingly comprehensive insights into all aspects of the region's **history**, from ancient prehistory to the twentieth century. Human activity is handled in terms of social practices – hunting, mining, art, healing, war and trade – before culminating in the **Hall of Chiefs**, devoted to Mzilikazi, Lobengula and stacks of Rhodes memorabilia.

Railway Museum

Prospect Ave, Raylton. Tues, Wed & Fri 9.30am–noon & 2–4pm. Sun 2–5pm; nominal entrance fee.

Although near the station, Bulawayo's **Railway Museum** is confusingly signposted and perhaps not worth the difficulty of finding. Created by and for railway enthusiasts, its collection of steam-age artefacts is badly let down by an absence of interpretive or background information. Tantalizing displays – the coach of some long-past railway chaplain; items from royal visits of several decades ago; turn-of-the-century letters from Secretary of State for the Colonies Joseph Chamberlain endorsing the extension of the Bechuanaland Railway to Lake Tanganyika – leave you frustrated and mystified.

If you're a steam fan, of course, you'll find the visit rewarding just for the chance to stroll around pristine engines. And, without doubt, **Rhodes' private coach** is a treat: a really lavish construction, used on many trips after 1895 including the one which carried his body 2500km from the Cape to Bulawayo after his death in 1902.

If you're keen on railway history, and are going to the Victoria Falls, you should also make time for the Zambian Railway Museum in Livingstone (see p.182), which is more informative than its counterpart in Bulawayo.

The National Gallery

Main St/Leopold Takawira Ave. Tues–Sun 9am–5pm; nominal entrance fee.

Housed in a splendidly restored Edwardian-colonial mansion in the centre of town, Bulawayo's **National Gallery** is well worth a visit, if only because unlike most exhibitions of Zimbabwean art, it is not dominated by stone sculpture. Instead, it showcases work in a variety of different mediums, among them numerous **cultural artefacts from Matabeleland**: baskets, sitting mats and other woven products. The work of **local painters** is displayed, too, and there's usually a **visiting exhibition**, while on Sundays you can watch artists at work in the specially provided studios lining the courtyard; most offer pieces for sale. The gallery also hosts life drawing classes and art sessions for kids that are worth checking out if you're in town for any length of time.

Bulawayo's open spaces

The urban planners have made a concerted effort to keep Bulawayo's commercial district separate from the rest of the city. In consequence a "moat" of **open space** – which comprises a golf course, race track, show grounds and school playing fields – surrounds the middle of town. The parks in the central zone form part of this cordon, while the **Hillside Dams**, out in the suburbs, are an appealing area of natural granite and indigenous trees. Best of all, though further out, is the **Tshabalala Sanctuary**.

The town parks

The shade of **Centenary Park**, ten minutes' walk down Leopold Takawira Avenue, is welcoming after traversing Bulawayo's wide streets. Although not the most inspiring park, it is especially good for kids. On the museum side of the park are a large **aviary** and pens with small **buck**, a **miniature railway** which goes round a lake, the usual swings-and-roundabout **playground**, and a place under the trees for tea and ice creams – all very Sunday afternoonish.

Central Park, almost a continuation of Centenary Park, is separated only by Leopold Takawira Avenue as it runs into Suburbs. For picnics or roaming it's much the nicer space, with more trees, flowers and lawns and a large illuminated fountain. Best of all, it includes the **Samuel Parirenyatwa Street Swimming Pool** (Sept–May 10am–2pm & 3–6pm), on the town side of the park, with its stylish 1930s changing booths, and lawns and palm trees for lazing about in the sun.

Hillside Dams

A small nature reserve surrounds **Hillside Dams**, located some 6km southeast of the centre. Drought has dried out the dams, but it's a peaceful place for a stroll nevertheless, the path between the upper and lower dams lined by indigenous trees and granite boulders. To get to Hillside Dams, you take the Hillside Road **bus** from the City Hall terminus as far as Cecil Avenue and walk the remaining (signposted) two kilometres.

Chipangali Wildlife Orphanage

Tues–Sun. Nominal entrance fee.

The **Chipangali Wildlife Orphanage** is a good place to see the big cats head-on, as well as other African animals you may not have spotted in game parks. The sick, abandoned or orphaned animals are penned up, which gives the place the feeling of a zoo, but they're relocated when possible to the wild after rehabilitation.

A favourite place for family weekend outings, Chipangali is a fairly easy 23-kilometre hitch out of town, leaving on Leopold Takawira Avenue, which becomes the Gwanda/Johannesburg road. It's also possible to spend the night (①), to hear the lions roar. Three companies, *UTC*, *Black Rhino Safari* and *Africa Dawn* run trips there – current prices can be obtained from the Bulawayo Publicity Association (☎60867).

Tshabalala Sanctuary

Daily 6am–6pm. Nominal entrance fee.

The main appeal of the small **Tshabalala Sanctuary** is that it offers an opportunity to walk or ride a horse to spot giraffe, kudu, zebra, impala, wildebeest, tsessebe and many species of birds, free from the fear of stumbling into dangerous game such as big cats, elephants or rhino. It's a modest place, set in flat thornbush country, 8km from the city centre on the way to the Matopos, where the animals are free to roam in a natural setting. Driving around the sanctuary is possible, but riding is the most rewarding way to see and get close up to the animals. Book for accompanied rides, which are fine for novices, at the park entrance. The best times to go are early morning and late afternoon.

If you don't have the energy to rent a bike (see p.133) and cycle to the sanctuary, take the roughly hourly Matopos Road **bus** from the City Hall terminus to **Retreat**, and walk or hitch the last couple of kilometres to the entrance.

Markets and shops

Most of the **shops** in Bulawayo that you might need lie within five minutes' walk of the City Hall. However, you can get a better view of local life if you make for **Mzilikazi** suburb and its lively beer halls, markets and the Mzilikazi and Home Industries Craft Workshops.

Groceries and Makokoba market

Probably the best places to pick up **fresh fruit and vegetables** in central Bulawayo are the shops along Eighth Avenue, between Robert Mugabe Way and George Silundika Street, opposite the bus terminus.

A few **bakeries** stand out, including *Downing's*, which sells bread and excellent pies opposite the City Hall in Leopold Takawira Ave. For cakes and biscuits *Haefeli's*, Fife St/Tenth Ave, has a long-standing reputation throughout the city's middle-class suburbs, and *Walter's*, Robert Mugabe Way/Twelfth Ave, is the only place you'll find rye bread.

If you just want to pick up **basic supplies**, try the *TM Supermarket* near the railway station, which has a wide selection of groceries and stays open till late, or *Haddon and Sly*, Fife St/Eighth Ave, an old-fashioned department store with a good supermarket on the ground floor.

Around the **Lobengula Street** bus terminal, several street vendors are cheap for fruit and vegetable shopping. For the city's main – and best – **market**, however, you'll need to take either a bus or emergency taxi out to the suburb of **Makokoba**. This is definitely worthwhile, with stalls selling local delicacies like **dried mopane worms** (sold by the cupful), plus **herbal medicines** and a good selection of **baskets and beads** not especially intended for tourists.

Record shops

There's no better place in Zimbabwe to buy and browse for **records** than Bulawayo. Exploring the small **downtown record bars** around Lobengula Street and Sixth Avenue makes for a more atmospheric outing. Otherwise the two best stores are both in Jason Moyo Street: **Clinton's**, Clinton House, 88c Jason Moyo St (☎60264), which has the finest stock of South African jive north of the Limpopo River; and **Music**, Jason Moyo St/Fort St (☎66895 or 71607), which offers the country's best selection of Zimbabwean pop.

Crafts shops

Art Gallery, Main St/Leopold Takawira Ave. Specialists in the art and crafts of Matabeleland, with some fine **baskets**, **sculptures** and **wood carvings**. Also a good selection of cards, books and cassettes on sale.

Chitrin Wholesalers, Jason Moyo St/Sixth Ave. Four-metre and upwards lengths of central African prints.

Designers' Collective, Pioneer House, Eighth Ave. A good collection of T-shirts, cards and contemporary crafts; the most stylish shop in Bulawayo.

Jairos Jiri, Robert Mugabe Way, behind the City Hall, is among the better branches of this chain, found in the main towns, selling products by disabled craft-workers, cards and a wide selection of local handmade goods. There's a large array of **Matabeleland baskets**, local **pottery**, the usual unexceptional soapstone carvings and some good **Ndebele beadwork**, notably dolls. You're under no pressure to buy, so browse as long as you like.

Mzilikazi Art and Craft Centre

Mon–Fri 8.30am–12.30pm & 2–4pm.

Mzilikazi is a thoroughly established township, with kids playing in the street, freshly swept yards and a strong sense of community. The **Art and Craft Centre** here, set up in the Sixties by the City Council, is near Mpilo Hospital. It is known for its **ceramics** and the sales are used to subsidize an art school and the training of others to work with clay. In the centre's shop, you can stand around and admire the effortless skill of the potters, laughing, chatting and listening to the radio while, without seeming even to watch what they're doing, pots emerge below their fingers. The stuff is pretty standardized and as close to mass-produced as hands can make it, but there are some nice, modern, ethnic designs. It's cheaper to buy works here than at any of the outlets in town, and in the seconds shop you can pick up stuff very cheaply.

Besides potters, you can watch sculptors working in stone; painting and drawing classes are held here and there's a small permanent collection of students' work. Across the way at the **Bulawayo Home Industries Centre** they sell **batiks** and **handspun angora pullovers** and **mats**. A new departure is **sisal basketry** – copied from Kenya's best-selling *vyondo*. Workers, drawn from social welfare lists, are paid a piece rate.

The easiest way to get to Mzilikazi is to **walk** down the Old Falls Road as it veers from the northwest corner of the city from Kings Avenue, though there's a more interesting short cut (which takes around 30min) through the township itself, along Third Avenue extension. The less energetic can take the **Mpilo bus** from the Lobengula Street terminus or the less frequent service from the terminus at the City Hall.

Eating and drinking

Without any regional cuisine to speak of, Bulawayo's food is acceptable but unexceptional. Places serving snacks and light meals tend to open only during the day in

Bulawayo, along with the sadza spots and greasy takeaways around the train station and bus terminals. Hotels such as the *Selbourne* do good buffet lunches with generous salad selections. Steak houses are another safe bet, serving great-value Zimbabwean meat for lunch or dinner. Some of the more old-fashioned restaurants cater for a predominantly white clientele, with formal dress codes and night-time dinner dancing.

Tearooms, takeaways and snacks

Bonne Journee, 105 Robert Mugabe Way. A cheap hangout out for western Europeans, with grills, excellent piri-piri chicken and good coffee. Open evenings until 9pm.

Courtyard Café, at the National Gallery, Main St/Leopold Takawira Ave. The most congenial spot in town for tea or lunch, with fresh flowers, stripped wooden floors, and tables inside or out, and good, cheap food.

Eskimo Hut, at the entrance to Showgrounds. Very popular for drive-in ice creams and takeaways.

The Grass Hut, 188 Fife St. Cheap for steak rolls and sandwiches, though you may find the darkness of the place more oppressive than atmospheric. It's also open early for egg breakfasts, and is a popular meeting place.

Mary's Corner, 88 Josiah Tongogara St/Eighth Ave. Great old-fashioned roast-and-three-veg set meals served at lunch time. Good value and handy for the campsite.

Himalaya, Josiah Tongogara St/Ninth Ave. Also close to the campsite, a great, cheap Indian restaurant, with vegetarian thalis, generous vegetarian and meat dishes, and delicious papaddums, roti and chutneys.

Oriental Takeaway, Eighth Ave. Vegetable burgers, curries and spring rolls.

Palace Hotel, Jason Moyo St/Tenth Ave. Essentially a beer garden with palm trees that serves meat-and-chips dishes at lunchtime. A good place to meet black Zimbabweans.

Pizzaghetti, Eleventh Ave between Robert Mugabe Way and George Silundika St. One of the few takeaways open evenings, for chicken and chips as well as good pizza.

Sister's, 2nd Floor, *Haddon & Sly*, Fife St/Eighth Ave. Imaginative, reasonably priced food like bagels and flower salads, rounded off with a selection of scrumptious cakes and desserts: try their strawberry and vanilla terrine with butterscotch sauce. Recommended for vegetarians. Daytime only.

YWCA, Ninth Ave/Lobengula St. The cheapest and cleanest place for sadza and traditional accompaniments, dishing up lunch (12.30–3pm), mainly for the resident students, but open to outsiders who don't mind the institutional ambience.

Restaurants

Buffalo Bill's, next to the *Selborne* in Leopold Takawira Ave. Mainly steak – though vegetarians can get baked potatoes, salad and (mediocre) pizzas.

Cape to Cairo, Robert Mugabe Way/Leopold Takawira Ave. Specializes in game dishes and Zimbabwean fish.

Cattleman Steakhouse, Josiah Tongogara St/Tenth Ave. Excellent charcoal-grilled steaks and a table of salads, opposite the *Sun Hotel*.

Golden Spur, Robert Mugabe Way (between Eighth and Ninth Ave). One of the most popular steakhouses in Bulawayo. Vegetarians steer clear.

Maison Nic, Main St/Fourth Ave. Wins the best restaurant prize year after year for its French cuisine and fish specialities, although it's really more English than French. Cheaper than *Les Saisons*.

The Peking, near the *Palace Hotel* in Jason Moyo St. Reasonable and recommended Chinese food.

Les Saisons, Josiah Tongogara St, between Sixth and Leopold Takawira Avenues. The best of Bulawayo's formal restaurants, serving an imaginative selection of great vegetarian dishes.

Beer gardens

Beer gardens are a must if you want to get to grips with how Zimbabweans live in the high-density areas. And they're fun – people will always chat to you, after they've stared a while. Essentially daytime places, serving *chibuku*, braaied meat and *sadza*, they're open from 10.30am to 8pm.

One of the easiest beer gardens to find in the city is the *Madlodlo*, situated on the Mzilikazi side of the Renkini bus station. It's a pretty typical example, with lots of wooden benches under trees and a predominantly male clientele queuing up to buy mega-sized pots of beer to be shared and passed around. Other good areas for hunting out beer gardens include Luveve Street and around Mzilikazi suburb (see previous page).

Entertainment and nightlife

Films and any other entertainments on offer in Bulawayo, including occasional classical music concerts in the City Hall, are listed in *The Chronicle*, and as elsewhere in Zimbabwe, look out for posters wrapped around trees advertising live local music.

Live music and nightclubs

You'd be really unlucky not to find **live music** in Bulawayo on any weekend, and there's invariably something good at the end of the month. Hotels are the most common venues, though big concerts do occasionally take place at the White City Stadium in the western townships. Here in Matebeleland you should look out for **Smanje Manje** music, which, with its strong South African influence caused a revolution in Zimbabwean pop in the late 1960s by displacing the previously dominant rhumba rhythms from Zaire. If you're lucky enough, your visit to Bulawayo may coincide with a performance by one of the city's accomplished **marimba groups** (see *Contexts*, p.395). The marimba, a type of xylophone that nearly died out following the forced migrations of the colonial era, was revived in the 1960s at Bulawayo's renowned **Kwanongoma College**, whose orchestra, the **Kwanangoma Marimba Ensemble**, ranks among the best in the country and is well worth keeping an eye out for.

Clubs tend to play American **disco** and **funk** and are not the places to find Zimbabwean music. If you do venture out on to the seamier side of the town, watch out for "the girls" at the end of the evening, who are great to dance with, but may insist on accompanying you home.

Venues

Bulawayo Sun Hotel, Josiah Tongogara St/Tenth Ave (☎601101). Live jazz every evening from sunset time on at the *Alabama*. Smart casual dress required.

Cecil Hotel, Fife St/Third Ave (☎60295). Nightly disco playing mid-Atlantic pop and some local stuff.

Silver Fox, Robert Mugabe Way/Tenth Ave. Local music and disco.

Talk of the Town, in the Monte Carlo Centre, Fife Street/Twelfth Ave. One of Zimbabwe's hottest clubs, with a mix of house, jive and reggae.

Township Square Cultural Centre, Old Falls Road (☎76673 or 79379). The best place to sample bona fide traditional Zimbabwean music and dance, this recently opened performing arts venue is a first for Bulawayo and is still finding its feet – although its history dates back to Mzilikazi's era of the last century, when national dance festivals were a regular feature of cultural life. In keeping with the traditional ethos, the buildings have been designed in Ndebele style, and the restaurant serves authentic African food. A pioneering drama company, the *Amakhosi Theatre*, is also based here, training people in acting and music.

Waverley Hotel, 133–134 Lobengula St/Thirteenth Ave (☎60033). Raucous venue opposite the train station, hosting end-of-month gigs in the beer garden and local bands most evenings. Entrance is free unless a visiting big name is playing.

Cinema and theatre

Bulawayo's few **cinemas** are cheap and comfortable, and show mainly middle-of-the-road British and American films. The two *Kines* on Robert Mugabe Way, the *7-Arts Theatre* on Jason Moyo Street and the *Rainbow Vistarama* on George Silundika Street, are central and near each other, while the *Nitestar Drive-In* off the Harare Road is excellent value. The *Alliance Francaise* (☎70245) shows subtitled French films.

As for drama, the **theatre** in Leopold Takawira Avenue occasionally hosts interesting visiting productions, while the large and small city halls are usual venues for concerts and shows. Check the *Chronicle* for entertainment listings.

Listings

Automobile Association Fanum House, Leopold Takawira Ave/Josiah Tongogara St (☎ 70063). Very friendly and helpful.

Air Zimbabwe office Trager House, Jason Moyo St (☎72051).

American Express agents *Manica Travel*, Fife St/Eleventh Ave (☎62521).

Banks The most central is the *Standard* in Fife St (Mon, Tues, Thurs & Fri 8.00am–3pm, Wed 8.30am–2pm, Sat 8.30–11.30am).

Ballooning *Wildfire Balloons*, 57 Josiah Tongogara St (☎65383), fly over the Matopos Hills, launching outside Bulawayo, at US$200 a go.

Bookshops *Philpott and Collins* on Jason Moyo St have a good selection of books published in Zimbabwe and a remaindered table with some decent paperbacks. *Kingstons* on Jason Moyo St are also recommended. Book exchange at *Basement Book Mart*, 81 Jason Moyo St.

Camping equipment *Eezee Kamping*, 99 George Silundika St/Tenth Ave. Good for fishing equipment, but nothing sophisticated.

Car rental *Avis*, Robert Mugabe Way/Tenth Ave (☎68571 or 61306); *Hertz*, George Silundika St/Fourteenth Ave (☎ 74701 or 61402); both also have offices at the airport. *Echo*, 9a Africa House, Fife St (☎67925 or 74157). *Transit Car Hire*, corner Twelfth/Robert Mugabe Ave (☎76394), and *Compass Car Hire*, Ninth Ave/Fifth St (☎78576), are the cheapest.

Doctors and dentists are listed in the front of the Bulawayo section of the telephone directory.

Hospital Central Hospital, St Lukes Way (☎72111) is the easiest to get to.

Immigration Department ☎ 72101.

Laundrette 109a Josiah Tongogara St, between Eleventh and Twelfth Ave; open daily.

Libraries Not many people seem aware of the marvellous resource at the Bulawayo Public Library in City Hall (Mon–Fri 9am–4pm). For background information on any aspect of Zimbabwe, there are few better places in the country than this historic book collection; until quite recently it was a legal deposit library, which meant that all books and newspapers published in the country were sent there. The librarians are exceptionally helpful, and will guide you to any obscure subject which may interest you. In addition, the National Free Library, on Leopold Takawira Ave just past the Museum of Natural History and Centenary Park, has reading rooms and a special section on local history.

Pharmacies 86 Robert Mugabe Way (Mon–Sat after the shops have closed till 8pm, Sun & hols 9am–8pm; ☎69781); *Dae-Nite Pharmacy*, Eighth Ave/Robert Mugabe Way (Mon–Fri 8am–6pm, Sat, Sun & hols 9am–noon & 5–7pm; ☎66242).

Photos Of the several one-hour processing places around town, *Photo Inn*, next to *Haddon's* on Fife St, is the largest.

Post office The principal office for telephones and telegrams etc is at Main St/Eighth Ave (Mon–Fri 8.30am–4pm, Sat 8.30–11.30am).

Shop hours These are generally Mon–Fri 8am–4 or 5pm, Sat 8am–12.30pm. Some cafés stay open after shop hours for the sale of bread and milk. Business is best conducted in the mornings.

Train enquiries ☎322411. Reservations ☎322310. It's usually best to ask in person.

Travel agents There's no shortage of travel agents, but if in doubt one of the biggest is *Sunshine Tours*, Old Mutual Arcade, Eighth/Jason Moyo Ave (☎67791). *Gemsbok Safaris*, also in the Mutual Arcade (☎63906), have an efficient manager who can do all your Zimbabwe bookings, while *Manica Travel*, Tenth Ave/Fort St (☎62521) is recommended for booking coach tickets.

Tour operators *UTC*, George Silundika St/Fourteenth Ave (☎61402), run tours to Matopos, Khami ruins and Chipangali. The highly recommended *Black Rhino Safaris* (☎41662) offer the same as well as camping safaris to the main national parks. *Africa Dawn* (☎70488) arrange recommended walks to Matobo cave paintings. Another option is *Mzingeli Tours* (☎79178) whose tours include visits to local markets and low-income districts.

Swimming pool Samuel Parirenyatwa St Baths (Sept–May, 10am–2pm & 3–6pm).
Taxis Call one of the following numbers: ☎60666, 61933, 72454, 60154 or 60704.

AROUND BULAWAYO

A place of incredible power and beauty, the **Matopos Range** is the most compelling reason to explore the **Bulawayo area**. Here, among the smooth granites of whale-backed hills and crenellated castle kopjes, the descendants of Zimbabwe's earliest **hunter-gatherer** inhabitants painted elegant images on the walls of overhangs and in weather-scooped caves. These paintings survive to be seen today in the **Matobo National Park**, which also offers some of the best hiking in the country. Although now officially known as the Matobo Hills, you'll invariably hear the colonial pronunciation "Matopos" used, and see both versions in print.

The hills themselves have the appearance of volcanic eruptions, though they are in fact geologically extremely ancient, having lain covered for thousands of millennia by softer material. This covering has been gradually worn down to the present-day ground level, exposing the previously buried hills – an impressive illustration of just how hard these rocks are.

Besides the Matopos, the area around Bulawayo takes in the beautiful and deserted stone ruins at **Khami**, a convenient half-day's outing from the city. Other stone ruin sites lie, far less accessibly, off the Harare road at **Naletale** and **Danangombe**, best visited on an overnight jaunt, staying at one of the guest farms nearby. Lastly, in the little-visited far southwest of the country, the **Tuli Circle** fauna and flora enclave is worthy of serious investigation by determined enthusiasts – or as a detour on the way **south to South Africa**.

Matobo National Park

Many people visit the Matobo National Park (entry US$2), some 50km south from Bulawayo, for a day's jaunt, but it's well worth spending a couple of days here, in the park itself or at one of the luxury lodges on the perimeter. The landscape itself is staggering, and there's miles of walking, as well as the world's highest concentration of ancient rock paintings, leopards and black eagles.

The park is punctuated with artificial, though very beautiful dams. The easiest to reach from Bulawayo is **Maleme Dam**, which has National Parks lodges, camping, horse riding, tennis and some short walks to nearby painted caves. Most day-trippers head here for a picnic, stopping off on the way at **World's View**, topped by the grave of Cecil Rhodes. The remote **Toghwe Wilderness Area**, with campsites at **Toghwana** and **Mtsheleli Dams,** and two of Zimbabwe's finest **painted caves**, is another day trip. Also, the **Game Park** in the **Whovi Wilderness area**, although modest compared to Zimbabwe's great game areas, and accessible only by car, provides a wonderful granite backdrop to views of its grazing and browsing herds and regular sightings of rhino.

White heritage and black nationalism

While giving the appearance of being one of old Africa's unchanging places, the **Matobo National Park** is really a colonial invention, the story of which is fraught with politics and competing black and white ideologies.

At a date to be advised, the **area telephone code** for the **Matopos** will be changed to ☎183-8 (the hyphen indicates a second dialling tone); at present most numbers are on the Bulawayo exchange (☎19).

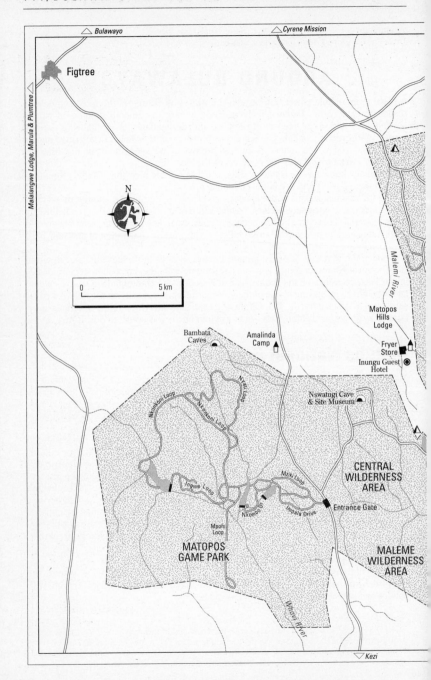

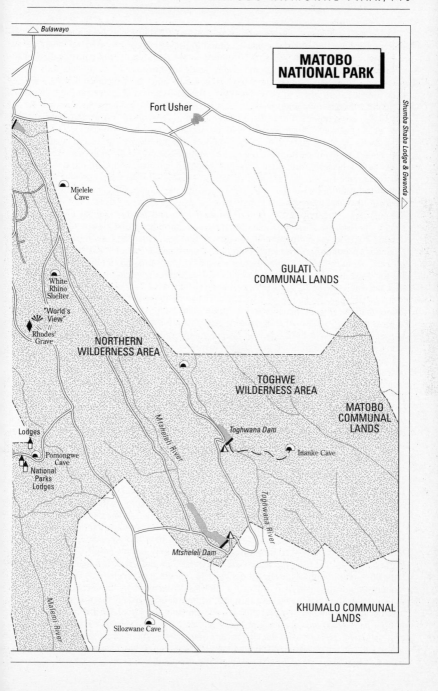

Bulawayo

MATOBO NATIONAL PARK

Fort Usher

Shumba Shaba Lodge & Gwanda

Mjelele Cave

White Rhino Shelter

"World's View"

Rhodes' Grave

GULATI COMMUNAL LANDS

NORTHERN WILDERNESS AREA

TOGHWE WILDERNESS AREA

MATOBO COMMUNAL LANDS

Mtsheleli River

Toghwana Dam

Inanke Cave

Lodges

Pomongwe Cave

National Parks Lodges

Toghwana River

Mtsheleli Dam

Maleni River

Silozwane Cave

KHUMALO COMMUNAL LANDS

From the early days after the defeat of the first Chimurenga, the white Matopos settlers were worried about a supposed threat to their heritage posed by the presence of blacks on the quasi-sacred site of Rhodes' grave. Later, with the consolidation of racial segregation, concerted attempts were made to shove the black peasant farmers elsewhere. However, even as the whites were developing their theories that Africans were hopeless farmers who were destroying the wild game and upsetting the balance of nature, African ideologies arose in parallel, mirroring white claims to the land. By the 1940s, when attempts to shift Africans hotted up, there was a growing conscious-ness of the hills as a holy place of Ndebele tradition (see box overpage), and white accusations of black land mismanagement were countered by the blacks' claims to have been effectively farming the region for centuries before white settlers arrived.

For over a decade, Africans successfully opposed removal, both through the courts and by passive resistance campaigns, but, by 1962, a scheme was approved to clear part of the Matopos to create a national park. Residents were deported south to the Khumalo and east to the Gulati Tribal Trust Lands. African resentment was manifest in the destruction of fences, the lighting of veld fires and petrol-bombing of the park office. The furore was closely linked with burgeoning **nationalist politics**: the young Robert Mugabe even threatened to dig up Rhodes' grave and send the body to England. Through the 1960s fence cutting and resistance continued. **ZIPRA guerillas**, who arrived in the 1970s, took refuge in the perfect hideouts offered by the hills, gain-ing the support of local people who believed that the park would be returned to them after the war.

It was perhaps the failure of this to materialize that prompted **dissidents** to return to the Matopos Hills in the early 1980s. Although it's still difficult to gauge, they appear to have had the support of frustrated peasants who felt betrayed by the government. The government sent in troops who brutally murdered and repressed people all over Matabeleland, although much was hushed up at the time.

Following the **Unity Accord** and amnesty in 1988, the Matopos was once again peaceful, although the government declined to give back the national park to its former residents – to deregulate an area nominated for world heritage status would damage its international reputation. The farmlands are now a wilderness and the cultural life that once thrived here is gone, while the **rain shrines** inside the park are deserted. Ironically, it's outside the confines of the heritage-preserving national park, in the adjoin-ing communal lands, that spiritual shrines like Njelele are still flourishing.

Accommodation

There is **National Park accommodation** available at Maleme Dam (see p.148). It gets pretty full in peak season, but during the week and outside school holidays a lodge is easy enough to come by. Although Maleme Dam rest camp is the only place with roofed accommodation, it is possible to camp at several different sites in the park.

There are no **hotels** in the park itself, but one cheap accommodation option lies just outside its boundaries. The *Inungu Guest House* (②), next to *Fryer's Store* 10km from Maleme Dam, can be booked through *Sunshine Tours* in Bulawayo (☎19/67791). It's not marked on the *Tourist Map of Rhodes Matopos National Park* (available from the Surveyor General's office in Harare) but you can locate it at grid reference 559331. From Maleme, follow the main road to World's View for 3.5km and take the second turning to the left (after the Pomongwe cave turn-off); where the road branches, after about 6km, bear left and the guest house and shop are on your right one kilometre further on.

The nearest garages are back at Bulawayo, and it's best to bring everything you'll need while you're here from the city. *Fryer's Store* itself is the nearest place to the park where you can top up supplies, though there is also a shop selling basics at Maleme Rest Camp.

Private lodges and camps

In the last few years, several **exclusive camps and lodges** have opened up in dramatic settings on the edge of the national park, all of them in the hills. Prices listed below are for all-in rates, and are much lower for Zimbabweans. Transfers from Bulawayo cost extra, but you can drive to all of the lodges in an ordinary car.

Amalinda Camp, *Londa Mela Safaris*, PO Box 130, Queens Park, Bulawayo (Turk Mine 0-00831). Safari tents under thatch nestle amongst boulders with the dining area under a granite overhang. Close to the game park where walks can be arranged to track rhino. US$170 per person per night.

Big Cave Camp, PO Box 88, Bulawayo (☎19/64104 or 245). Close to the caravan park, at the 46km peg. Small, reasonably priced camp with thatched A-frame cottages on top of a kopje. The cost includes walks, but game drives and drinks are extra. From US$90 per person.

Malalangwe, *Impi Safaris*, PO Box 1325, Bulawayo (☎74693). Luxurious, small camp on a magnificent game farm on the western edge of the Matopos range, one hour from Bulawayo at Marula, with a good share of animals, rock paintings, archeological remains and fine walks. Environmental awareness is high on the agenda and you'll have some of the best informed guides in Zimbabwe. US$195 per person per night.

Matopos Hills Lodge, *Touch the Wild*, P/Bag 6, Hillside, Bulawayo (☎19/41225). Close to Maleme and Rhodes' Grave and set high up in the hills, with great views and all the usual luxury of the *Touch the Wild* chain. But with up to 40 guests, it can lack the intimacy of other camps. US$187 per person per night.

Shumba Shaba Lodge, *Zindele Safaris*, PO Box 1744, Bulawayo (☎19/64128). Stylish chalets perch on a huge granite whaleback known as Red Lion, with truly spectacular views (you can watch the sunrise over the hills from your bed) and rock paintings nearby. Ideal for walking and highly recommended for a recuperative few days. Transfers from Bulawayo cost US$30. From US$195 per person per night.

Seeing the park

The best ways to see the park are **by car** or on one of the recommended **tours** offered by Bulawayo-based companies. There's no public transport to the Matopos, but if you're prepared to walk, there are fairly regular local **buses** from Bulawayo to Kezi, stopping at the edge of the park. Ask to be dropped off at the road leading to Maleme Dam; from here it's about a twelve-kilometre walk to Maleme, taking you past the Nswatugi cave rock painting and site museum. **Cycling** the 50km from Bulawayo is fine, but heavy-going in summer, and it's certainly not possible to cycle there and back in one day. One less strenuous option is to take your bike on the bus and save it for getting around the park. If you're **hitching**, get the Matopos Road bus from Lobengula Street terminus to Retreat (the last stop) before thumbing. Weekends are not difficult, but during the week the road is extremely quiet.

Tours

One of the best ways of seeing the hills, expecially if you do only have a day in hand, is to take a **tour** with *UTC*, *Black Rhino* or *Africa Dawn*, who do half- or full-day tours with knowledgeable guides. *Africa Dawn* do fantastic day-long walks to the remote Inanke Cave and three-day camping trips through the park. See Bulawayo "Listings" for details of these three companies. With one of the best guides in Zimbabwe, *Khangela Safaris* offer four-day walking and camping tours of the Matopos, which can be combined with a trip to Great Zimbabwe and Gonarezhou National Park (☎49733, fax 68259; from US$120 per person per day).

Maleme Dam (The Central Wilderness Area)

Maleme Dam, with its parks accommodation, is the usual first stop on a good tarred road from Bulawayo. The popular route by car to Maleme from Bulawayo takes you past

THE MWARI CULT IN MATOPOS

As the Great Zimbabwe state in the east of the country disintegrated, its Shona-speaking inhabitants dispersed, looking for new homes. Some, known as the **Torwa**, went west and eventually arrived in the **Matopos** region, establishing themselves around the fifteenth century as the ruling class of the district, with a headquarters at Khami. Imitating their predecessors at Great Zimbabwe, the Torwa built up a large centralized state, over which they ruled until the arrival in the 1680s of the **Rozvi**, another Shona-speaking group from the Mutapa state in the northeast. The Rozvi conquered and took control of the Torwa state, but without destroying it.

It was under the Rozvi that the **cult of Mwari**, the supreme creator, became dominant. Mwari wasn't the exclusive focus of all religious life, and wasn't a personal god: the ancestral spirits still held sway in the lives of ordinary people, while Mwari, as the deity of politics, dealt with matters of state. Most important of these was the bringing of rain – the basis of all economic life.

The Rozvi *mambo*, or king, had the power to intercede with Mwari, and when custom was broken, the god would administer punishments in the form of sickness or natural disasters. On these occasions the *mambo* would consult Mwari and become possessed by the *mhondoro*, the original ancestor, a cross between Adam and god, whose spirit had entered a lion. A Mwari priesthood mediated between the possessed king and the people, interpreting the leonine growls of the possessed ruler, passing judgement and punishments, and restoring the natural order.

At the turn of the nineteenth century the religious headquarters of the Rozvi state was in the Matopos and the political capital at Danangombe. The state was in the throes of a political revolution and a **power struggle** that had been developing between the Mwari priest-

White Rhino Shelter, with the best rock art in the rare outline style, and **World's View**, the colonial equivalent of the liberation struggle's Heroes' Acre in Harare. Maleme is good for walking, or just scrambling over boulders. One exciting short walk goes over vertiginous hills to the barely visible paintings in **Pomongwe cave**, though the outstanding prehistoric images of Nswatugi Cave 7km in the other direction are much better. The remote Toghwe Wilderness Area with campsites at Toghwana and Mtsheleli dams is a full day's walk from Maleme if you're exploring the park on foot.

Maleme Dam

Right at the centre of the park, **Maleme Dam** provides a good base for day trips into the other parts. It is also a good place to get your bearings – and an idea of the terrain – before heading off into the wilder east.

You can stay in **national parks accommodation** or **camp** – barely cheaper than the one-roomed chalets – along the dam, but if possible, it's worth forking out a little extra to stay in one of the two **luxury lodges**, *Fish Eagle* and *Black Eagle* if they're available, perched like their namesakes high among the rocks, and treating you to a superb panorama when you wake. Book ahead through the *Bulawayo National Parks Booking Agency*, 140a Fife St (☎63646–7), and keep your lodge door shut to prevent monkeys investigating your groceries.

Around the dam

There's enough of interest **around the dam** to keep you busy for a week, and the best ways to see the area are on foot or horseback. Book at the office the night before if you want to try **riding**. Most of the guides are sensitive to your riding ability – you won't be forced to walk if you can canter – and you'll go cross-country through veld and bush too high to negotiate on foot. If committed, you can organize to go for longer than the usual one and a half hours, to get further afield.

hood and the secular *mambo* came to a head. According to oral tradition the *mambo* became fed up with the god's interference. When the king heard Mwari's voice coming from the top of his favourite wife's hut, "using a flintlock gun acquired from the Portuguese", he fired at the roof, whereupon the voice moved into the hut and the *mambo* razed the building to the ground. The voice kept on speaking from trees, grass and rocks, and when the *mambo* continued to harass it, the voice finally in a "wrathful tone" told the *mambo* that because he had chased Mwari away, in his place would come "men wearing skins".

The skin-clad men came in the form of **Nguni raiders** – waves of them, wearing animal hides. These warriors were by-products of battles taking place in South Africa, where Zulu conquests of the early nineteenth century pushed northwards a series of ruthless refugee armies, which raged through the Rozvi state. When the first blood-thirsty forces under **Zwangendaba** swept through, the *mambo* fled to the Matopos and in despair threw himself off a kopje. Zwangendaba's invasion broke down what remained of the already divided Rozvi state; by the time Mzilikazi's **Ndebele** arrived, the softening-up process was complete and Rozvi country was quickly conquered. The Ndebele forged the tattered fragments into a new, well-controlled and centralized state, occupying present-day southwest Zimbabwe.

The **priesthood** of the Mwari cult retreated to the caves of the Matopos, where Mzilikazi, eager to be on good terms with the local god – a wise move considering the *mambo's* fate – sent regular offerings to the shrines. In more recent years, the cult survived even the colonialists. During the 1946 drought many white farmers paid for rain dances to be held in National Park caves; while, acknowledging the still-potent force of the cult, ZAPU leader **Joshua Nkomo** held regular rallies during the liberation struggle at **Njelele**, one of the biggest rain shrines in the Matopos. It is taboo for outsiders to visit these shrine caves.

You'll see animals, however, on most outings. Herds of **sable antelope**, **impala** and **zebra** graze in valleys outside the confines of the park; **kudu** and **bushbuck** are to be seen in the grass; and there's no shortage of **baboons and monkeys**. Around Maleme you'll also hear the whistling calls of **klipspringer** antelope which leap up rock faces. Dassies are everywhere and high on unreachable boulders you'll see the nests of one of the world's largest concentration of **black eagles**. **Leopards** also adore this rocky, cave-riddled terrain but, as usual, you'd be lucky to see one.

The dam area offers **walks** appropriate to all energy levels. A half-hour ramble takes you over the hill to **Pomongwe Cave** or, to avoid the climb, stroll the two-and-a-half kilometres along the road. The cross-kopje route is the more interesting but not for vertigo sufferers; its start is signposted and the route waymarked. Steep in parts, it takes you over the hilltop, with a magnificent view and a descent into a thickly wooded granite amphitheatre with a giant cave at one end.

The **cave** is impressive, though its paintings have been annihilated by a well-intentioned smearing of glycerine in the 1920s, supposed to preserve them; it seems unbelievable to have oiled the whole cave before experimenting on a small part. Yet this is an important archeological site and digs have uncovered tens of thousands of Stone Age implements and artefacts as well as Iron Age pottery. It's estimated that people lived here for at least 50,000 years. Many of the objects unearthed are displayed in the modest **site museum**.

Nswatugi Cave

Some of the best rock paintings of the area adorn the walls of nearby **Nswatugi Cave**. This is *the* place to visit if you've time for only one site. The animals are beautifully realized, full of life and movement, and will knock on the head any ideas about rock art being crude or primitive. You only need look at the superb giraffe series or the delicate kudu to realize these result from an intimate knowledge and years of keen observation of the subject. An informative **site interpretation display**, overseen by an attendant, provides useful background. Nswatugi was one of the shrines in which people used to dance for rain before they were removed from the area in 1962.

To get to the cave, **drive** or **walk** the 7km of road from the parks lodges past the dam. It's easy going on foot. **By horse**, you ride through grasslands surrounded by towering kopjes and through a shallow reedy swamp.

World's View

North from Maleme Dam lodges, it's a ten-kilometre walk to **World's View** – known to the Ndebele as *Malindidzimu*, "Place of Benevolent Spirits" – and **Rhodes' Grave**. With its 360-degree panorama this bald hill is an imposing burial site and a fine goal for a hike.

Rhodes' Grave and the Allan Wilson Memorial

As requested in his will, **Rhodes' Grave** has been cut into the rock and a simple brass plaque placed over it. Six years before his death, Rhodes had gone riding in these hills and found this grandiose spot. When he died in Cape Town in 1902, his body was taken by train to Bulawayo (presumably on ice). Nearly two weeks later, the cortege of

---

MATOPOS ROCK ART

The best of the **Matopos rock paintings** compare favourably with Stone Age art anywhere in the world. Yet the handful that are reproduced represent only a small fraction of the hundreds that exist in these hills – all of them within a relatively small radius and some reachable without a car.

Over the last century, anthropologists, archeologists and historians have speculated as to the meanings of the paintings. Many **theories** were simple projections of what they knew about sites elsewhere in the world – or the imposition of their own, private assumptions. One eminent archaeologist, basing his conclusions on art deep in caves in Spain, suggested that both arose from the symbolic use of sympathetic magic – the depiction of a dead animal would ensure a successful hunt. Others have concluded that the paintings depict aspects of daily life – menus of animals and plants in the area. Newer ideas reject such interpretations. Zimbabwean rock art is unlikely to be an expression of sympathetic magic, which is unknown in any African hunting society; nor is it simply a menu – the remains of animals found at sites don't correlate with the pictures. Researchers now believe the images were concerned with the way people thought about human existence and actions, depicted through animal icons or metaphors.

The problem with attempting to interpret the paintings by means of an understanding of the people who painted them, though, is that no one knows exactly who they were, beyond the idea that they were **Stone Age hunter-gatherer** predecessors of today's Zimbabweans – possibly San ("Bushmen"), hunter-gatherers who roamed all over Southern Africa until quite recently. It seems likely that the paintings were executed between twenty thousand and two thousand years ago.

Many of the paintings have **religious themes**, which share features with the San focus on the ritual dance. This is used to take people into a **trance state** in which a potency or vital force called *n/um* is released. During trance, the experience of feeling stretched out is often described and some trancers have visions of light or movement. These elongated figures appear in rock art and the visions described correlate with the paintings.

As the picture of **hunter-gatherer cosmology** is built up, it may become possible to develop a more sophisticated interpretation of the paintings. Some tentative connections suggest that kudu are a symbol of potency, elephants are associated with rain and baboons with legends in which they taught human beings to dance and sing.

For more information on the subject, the best books by far are Peter Garlake's *The Painted Caves* and *The Hunter's Vision* (see "Books" in *Contexts*).

coaches, carriages, carts, horses, bicycles and pedestrians left the city for Rhodes' hut on the Matopos farm, stopping overnight before continuing to the top. The old colonialist was then given a traditional salute by assembled Ndebele chiefs (making Rhodes the only commoner to be granted the honour), who asked for shots not to be let off by the firing party, because it would disturb the resident spirits. An **interpretation display** at the foot of the hill has a collection of old photographs covering Rhodes' life.

Contrasting with this quiet resting place and erected at Rhodes' request on the same hilltop, the **Allan Wilson Memorial** commemorates the so-called **Shangani Patrol**. This odd stone confection, penetrating the skyline, is visible for miles. That this colonial monument still stands after Independence is an interesting reflection on the government's regard for white opinion. The facts are these: after Bulawayo fell to the British South Africa Company in 1893, Wilson was part of a hot-pursuit team running to ground the fleeing Lobengula. His patrol went ahead of the main column but, just as they were approaching the king, the Shangani River flooded, separating them from reinforcements. On December 4, the entire party of 34 was wiped out by the Ndebele, who suffered over one hundred casualties in the day-long battle. The men were first buried where they fell, then transferred to Great Zimbabwe, and finally brought to the present position in 1904, when the memorial was erected. The heroic reliefs that wrap around the plinth depict the members of the party in a colonial equivalent of socialist realism.

Lizards and curios

The most intriguing and unusual spectacle on offer at World's View, though, is the **lizard-feeding**. Three times daily an elderly attendant repeats his self-appointed task. At first the idea seems hopeless, as he holds out a small ball of sadza and calls to the dumb rocks. But gradually a multi-coloured collection of lizards gathers, emerging in incredible numbers from beneath boulders, flying across Rhodes' tomb and clambering over their feeder to attack the meal in a wild scrum. Egging them on, he holds out the ball and shouts "jump" to the frenzied reptiles. He's pretty old now, so don't delay if you want to witness this – and take a camera.

Nearby, on the road to White Rhino Shelter, you will see the only **curio stall** authorized in the national park. Look for the **Matopos baskets**, typical of the area, and strange little carved baboons with furry tails and gleaming red eyes.

White Rhino Shelter

For some extremely fine **outline paintings**, continue 2km north past the World's View turn-off to **White Rhino Shelter**. The paintings are in a small overhang along a clearly marked footpath off the Circular Drive.

The series of wildebeest painted here in different postures has been used to refute the idea that rock art is often used to conjure up a successful hunt. Why would someone interested in the animal purely as meat take the trouble to make subtle distinctions in posture, goes the argument, when one position would be as good as another? Line paintings are quite rare in Zimbabwe and seem to have been executed for only a short experimental period. Some of the most beautiful of all Stone Age paintings were done in this style, in outline only, before being superceded by more elaborate, polychrome works. The outline rhinos of the shelter are to the right, and there's also a black rhino head. The polychrome figures of humans and animals, including a lion, date from a later period (probably executed within the last 1000 years).

Matopos game park (Whovi Wilderness Area)

The **Matopos game park** (aka the Whovi Wilderness Area), which is open daily from dawn to dusk and charges a reasonable admission fee, is one of the easiest places in

Zimbabwe to see **rhino**. Many of the animals in the park have been reintroduced, but it's National Parks' policy only to replace animals in areas which their species has previously inhabited. White rhinos were brought back after a lengthy absence on the strength of very accurate rock paintings at White Rhino Shelter, which show not some generalized animal but clearly distinguish it from its hook-lipped ("black") relative (see p.151). You can normally also see giraffe, zebra and a variety of antelope, though no elephants or lions. You'll need your own car to get into the park or you can take one of the many organized day tours which include it (see p.147).

Toghwe Wilderness Area

Completely undeveloped, bar a couple of campsites, the **Toghwe Wilderness Area**, in the east of the Matobo Park, offers adventurous hiking. With a single road brushing along its western flank, connecting **Mtsheleli** and **Toghwana Dams** to the main road, walking is the only way to penetrate it. The outstanding focus, **Inanke Cave**, with its excellent paintings, makes a challenging expedition from Toghwana Dam, while **Silozwane Cave**, just outside the park, but more accessible from **Mtsheleli Dam**, is also impressively decorated. Hitching from Maleme to the Toghwe dams is a long shot and you should be prepared to **hike**. About 18km to Mtsheleli or Toghwana Dam, it's a pleasant walk along a deserted road that twists around granite outcrops, descending and rising from valleys. There are **campsites** at both dams, where drinking water should be boiled.

Silozwane Cave
Of the two notable **rock art sites** in the area, **Silozwane**, 11km southwest of **Mtsheleli Dam** in the Khumalo Communal Land, is the easier to reach. From the Cave road, take a left fork just before you get to the school and continue for about 2km along a decrepit track which virtually collapses into the river in places. From the car park, the route heads through forest and up the side of a steep dwala (smooth granite hill).

There's a strange atmosphere as you climb the bald rock faces, escaping the workaday existence below. You hear village sounds, donkeys braying, people talking and cow bells tinkling distantly on the edge of the unearthly silence. **Silozwane Cave** is a surprise on this smooth rock-sea – a sudden scooped-out cavity. A few steps closer, and you make out a series of huge human figures emerging from the grey granulated wall.

At first these appear to be just a reddish blur smeared along the lower part of the wall, but closer approach reveals a richly detailed surface of image over image in a multitude of sizes and styles. Human figures are bold and clear, and noticeably plentiful. To the right of centre, some two-metre long serpent-like antelope-headed creatures look as if they are being ridden by humans, fish and animals, while to the left one especially comical giraffe with a cartoon head seems crude next to the better observed one nearby. The closer you get, the easier it is to pick out animals, humans and abstract shapes from the swirling jumble of figures – painted, faded, peeling and overpainted.

Inanke Cave
Surpassing Silozwane, the paintings at **Inanke Cave**, a seven-kilometre trek east of Toghwana Dam, mark the highest expression of local prehistoric art. The cave is teasingly tricky to find, but marked at regular intervals by painted arrows and small cairns. Should you lose your way, don't try short cuts. Do your best to retrace your steps – it's easy to become disoriented in the hills and after a while the endless valleys and ranges start to look alike. The walk itself is fabulous, along a wooded stream in a valley with an enormous granite cliff on one side, where black eagles nest, over hills and through open grassland dotted with kopjes. En route you'll pass two small overhangs with paintings, as well as a well-preserved iron-smelting furnace. The final ascent to the cave, up bare

rock, is very steep but the richness and complexity of the paintings is sufficient reward. Ten minutes' climb further takes you to the bald summit, with its tremendous views in all directions.

Cyrene Mission

CYRENE MISSION, 40km south of Bulawayo on the northern edge of Matobo National Park, is worth a visit for anyone interested in African art. Named after Simon of Cyrene, the African who helped carry Christ's cross, it was founded in 1939 by one **Canon Paterson**, a Scottish reformed atheist who'd studied art in England – and who later founded the Art Centre in Harare.

From the beginning, the aim of the mission was to teach self-sufficiency. Pupils were instructed in farming, building and carpentry in order to construct, furnish and decorate their own homes. Art was also compulsory and students were given the chance to experiment. Paterson was firmly against imposing the western artistic tradition on students and no reproductions were put up on walls. Instead, kids were given a sheet of paper and told to draw, and the buildings are now decorated with their work.

The simple, thatched **Chapel** is decorated with murals and carved furniture which blend African and Christian mythology in a number of scenes from Ndebele history. The paintings are in a naive style, African-influenced but not wholly African. Some of the more symbolic stutter towards lifelessness, but they are at their best when depicting stories using familiar local imagery. The *Good Samaritan* spread, for example, is inspired by local rural life, with its *daga* (dried mud) huts and the earthy colours of the Matabeleland countryside. Another success is the *Parable of the Talents*, which blends stylized huts, rocks, trees, plants and people into a whirling abstract composition.

To get to the mission **from Bulawayo**, hitch or take the Figtree or Plumtree **bus** from Renkini terminus and walk the remaining 2km from the main road. **From the Matopos**, it's 12km from the northern gate, past the arboretum and one of the camp-sites in the recreational park; the mission is on a minor detour back to the main Bulawayo road, so hitching is not recommended from this side.

The Torwa centres: Khami, and Naletale and Danangombe ruins

Some of Zimbabwe's best **stone ruins** stand within striking distance of Bulawayo. All of them are dwarfed in size by Great Zimbabwe (see Chapter Five), but, built later in the Torwa period, they are in many ways more sophisticated, and reflect a development of the state's masonry traditions.

The largest site – and the closest to Bulawayo – is the Torwa capital **Khami**, just outside the city limits. Further out, off the Gweru road in Midlands farming country, lie **Danangombe**, a subsequent Torwa headquarters, and the tiny **Naletale**, perhaps the finest expression of the style.

The Torwa state and architecture

From the tenth to mid-nineteenth centuries, southwestern Zimbabwe enjoyed a political continuity nearly without precedent in Africa. By the twelfth century, offshoot states of **Great Zimbabwe** had walled capitals in the area and were living alongside people of the local **"Leopard's Kopje"** culture, an urban society under a wealthy ruling class. Cattle and gold were the bedrock of Leopard's Kopje wealth, and the elite were often buried with objects covered in the precious metal. They were able to organize teams of labour to produce stone platforms on hillsides, on which their houses were built.

The relationship between the two cultures is unclear, but it is known that by the time Great Zimbabwe collapsed in the fifteenth century, the southwest had been pulled together into a single state. This **Torwa State** was a progressive development of its Great Zimbabwe predecessor in the southeast. Although less extensive, it was more efficient, introducing improvements in architecture, pottery and urban layout, and changes in the economy.

Combining Zimbabwe masonry skills with the Leopard's Kopje stone platform tradition, the Torwa produced beautifully decorated **court complexes**. The old hill platforms were enlarged and turned into huge stages by the accomplished use of retaining walls and the decorative possibilities of stone walling.

Khami

The largest concentration of stone wall terracing at **KHAMI**, or Kame as it is sometimes spelt (daily 8am–5pm; US$3), surrounds the ruler's personal hill complex above the Kame River. Like his Great Zimbabwe counterpart, the ruler (or *mambo*) lived in great privacy, with his hill-perched court surrounded by the zimbabwes of the ruling class. A secret passage went under the platforms to his palace, its top forming the pavement of the courtyard.

As you ascend the stairs to the **upper platform** you can see remains of the posts that held up the daga roof. Elephant tusks once lined the passage. On the lowest step, a secret room was uncovered during excavations in 1947. Royal regalia had been hidden there at some time, perhaps when Khami was set alight during the invasion around 1680, when the Rozvi ("destroyers") of the Changamire dynasty swooped down from the Zambezi and conquered the Torwa. The spears and axes of copper and iron, ivory carvings and drinking pots with the *mambo*'s traditional red and black pattern are housed in the Natural History Museum in Bulawayo.

Several stone platforms **south of the hill complex** probably belonged to acolytes – wives or courtiers – of the *mambo*. The walks around this part of the site can be steep, but worthwhile, revealing such details as a **tsoro game** carved in stone. The board, of which there are several examples at Khami, has four rows of holes, with usually about fourteen holes per row. Like a cross between backgammon, chess and chinese checkers, *tsoro* is still played today throughout central Africa, under a variety of names. The speed of play achieved by participants, involving remarkable mental arithmetic feats, can be quite bewildering.

On the **east side of the hill**, to the north and west of the stone structures, are the remains of **huts** belonging to the ordinary people who occupied most of the site. These commoners didn't build their homes on platforms, so the mud walls have by now all but collapsed and consequently there's a lot less to see.

Among the finds interpreted in the small **museum** – worth visiting before you explore the site – are some which date back 100,000 years, providing evidence of a human presence at the site long before Khami was built. A useful pamphlet, *A Trail Guide to the Khami National Monument*, is on sale at the museum.

Getting to Khami

Khami stands on a minor road 22km to the west of Bulawayo. The only buses along the route, impractical for visiting the ruins, are those serving nearby Khami Prison; Khami train station is no nearer the ruins than Bulawayo; and hitching would be very much hit or miss. Without a car, the best bet is to take one of the reasonably priced excursions run by *Africa Dawn* or *Black Rhino Safaris*. If you are going to drive, cycle or hitch, follow Eleventh Avenue (near Bulawayo train station) out of town through the industrial area. There's nowhere nearby to stay, but there are lovely picnic spots overlooking Khami dam.

Naletale and Danangombe

Naletale and **Danangombe**, both of them set in isolated ranching country roughly an hour and a half's drive from Bulawayo off the Harare Road, are equally rewarding sites, but harder to reach than Khami. The turn-offs to both ruins are about two-thirds of the way to Gweru (see p.88) and approached via two southbound dirt roads which converge just west of Shangani Station: the more westerly one heads to Danangombe, the other to Naletale. It is possible to drive from one to the other, although Naletale is about 45km east of Danangombe on a poorly signposted road that veers wildly north and south, making the trip considerably longer than the direct distance between the two sites.

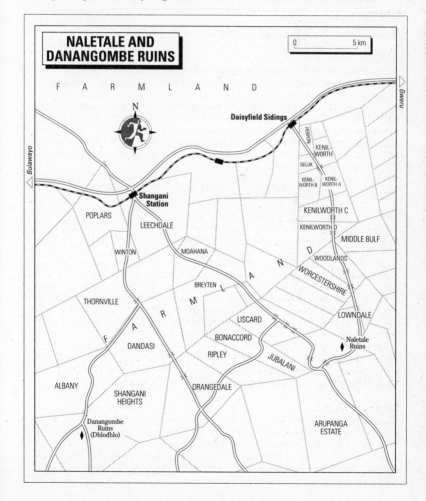

You'll need your own vehicle to get to either site, unless you take your bike on a train or bus and cycle the twenty-odd kilometres along dirt track to Danangombe from **Shangani**, a simple farming settlement with nowhere to stay; all Harare-bound buses and trains stop here.

If you don't have access to your own transport, and/or if you feel like spending a couple of days in the area, the best option is to contact *Jabulani Safaris* (☎150/248; ④) who arrange transfers from Shangani, Gweru and Harare. Their **game farm**, *Bon Accord*, abuts the ruins, and is a great place to spend a weekend, with plenty of walks and the opportunity to view game on foot; tariffs include breakfast and dinner. *Embukisweni Safari Lodge*, PO Box NE67, Northend, Bulawayo (☎150/2332), on a neighbouring farm, is in a similar mould, although much pricier, with rates from US$180 per person.

If you're visiting these ruins simply as a stop-off en route to Harare and want to sample just one of the sites, then Naletale is the more direct to reach. The southbound dirt track that branches off the main Harare Road, just east of Daisyfield siding is slightly quicker than the road from Shangani.

Naletale

The most interesting of all the zimbabwes, **NALETALE** stands at the top of a natural granite dome. As you gaze onto the wooded valley, it's difficult to imagine a better prospect, with trees growing between the long-deserted walls and *daga* hut fragments. The site is small in size – you could do a circuit of the whole place in fifteen minutes – but it's easy to while away half a day wandering about.

From close up the **walls** don't look terribly special but step back from the northwest section, the best preserved, and take in the patterning. Better still, lie down, prop your head on one of the pillow-sized rocks scattered about, and just gaze. The tapestried wall

MISSIONARIES IN ZIMBABWE

Missionary support was a major source of strength to **Rhodes** in his advance into central Africa. However, many missionaries believed that neither their teaching nor white settlement could be effective until the power of the Matabele was broken. **Lobengula**, in particular, scorned missionary teachings, which he felt consisted mainly of passing the buck for human misdeeds to Christ. He observed that the doctrine was what one might expect from whites because "whenever they did anything wrong they always wanted to throw the blame onto others".

The early missionary lessons literally fell on deaf ears. At the site of the **Jesuit Mission** next to Old Bulawayo you can see the graves of two missionaries murdered in the 1896 Chimurenga, along with their one and only convert who was deaf and dumb. **African converts** were particularly vulnerable to attack during the uprising and Bernard Mizeki, one of the first African proselytes, was killed. But once the uprising was defeated, the way was prepared for the full introduction of Christianity, which is now the predominant religion in Zimbabwe. Inside two years, the *American Brethren of Christ* had established one of the first fully fledged missions in the Matopos hills, while by 1909 there were more black than white Anglicans in Rhodesia.

Subsequently, the church began to concentrate on developing schools, clinics and hospitals – often attached to the old missions. Mission schools have educated many of Zimbabwe's leading figures, Robert Mugabe among them, and in the latter years of white rule they became increasingly involved in politics. During the 1950s a number of church leaders were outspoken against right-wing trends, and many guerilla fighters received mission support during the struggle for independence. At this time, gross atrocities were committed against missionaries, blamed by the Smith government on guerillas, but claimed by nationalists to be the work of government forces committing outrages for propaganda purposes.

is, without doubt, the pinnacle of the Zimbabwe-Khami masonry tradition, the only one standing that includes all five types of patterning: chevron, chequer, herringbone, cord and ironstone. The outer wall, originally topped by small towers with monoliths, enclosed a large raised platform which was surrounded by a number of courtyards and other smaller platforms. When Donald Randall McIver, the first professional archaeologist to investigate Great Zimbabwe, dug here, he found elephant tusks embedded in the remains of one of the huts.

A path leads up to the site itself from a picnic site and parking place at the bottom of the hill. It's possible to **camp** there, but you should ask for permission from the attendant, who lives in a house on the right of the car park turn-off (and will show you round if you want).

Danangombe (Dhlo Dhlo)

DANANGOMBE, better known by its old name **Dhlo Dhlo**, is equally enjoyable to explore, clambering about the ruins and sitting high up on rocks in the shade to look out over the rolling countryside.

The site became the capital of the Torwa state after Khami and was razed to the ground during a combined attack by a dissident Torwa leader and the Portuguese forces of Sismundo Dias Bayao. Later, in their eagerness to pilfer the riches of Danangombe, European treasure hunters managed to destroy many of the buildings by treating them as gold-mining stakes. Unworked gold and jewellery were systematically removed. Early digs found a silver chalice, a bell and medallions of sixteenth-century Portuguese origin. The walls that remain reveal beautiful decorative motifs similar to those at Khami.

As at Naletale, you may be able to camp at the site, but the resident attendant makes it clear that it is only as a favour at his discretion. There's no water or shop nearby.

Routes to South Africa

The usual way to Johannesburg from Bulawayo is through **Beit Bridge**, Zimbabwe's busiest border post, where you can expect long queues in the trying heat. An alternative route **west of Bulawayo** goes briefly into Botswana (at Plumtree) before heading south, and is now quicker than the Beit Bridge road, with far less traffic. The A7 is now tarred from Serule, on the main Plumtree to Gaborone road, to Selebi-Pikwe, and then onto Sherwood Ranch and the South African border crossing at Martin's Drift. Once in South Africa, the R35 takes you directly to Potgietersrus, where you join the N1 for Johannesburg.

South to Beit Bridge

Bulawayo to Beit Bridge is one of the major arteries to South Africa – a four-hour journey through remote and dry country. Nevertheless, the area holds several game farms, most notably the Bubiana wildlife conservancy, an hour's drive from the small town of West Nicholson, halfway to Beit Bridge, and the odd little trading post of Tuli Circle.

Gwanda, West Nicholson and the Bubiana conservancy

One of the best stopping-off places, if you're heading straight for the border, is **GWANDA**, where the recently refurbished *Hardy's Hotel* offers reasonably priced doubles and good meals. Closer to West Nicholson is *Tod's Guest House* (West Nicholson ☎5403), which makes a pleasant night's stop or tea place. Petrol and diesel are available and you camp and braai.

In 1991 some of the farmers in the West Nicholson area got together and pooled their ranches to create a wildlife zone, primarily in an attempt to save the local rhino population. The 160,000-hectare conservancy they founded, encompassing grassland, thorn trees and dry, rocky hills, harbours one of Matabeleland's top game lodges. Beautifully situated high amongst the granite boulders, *Barberton Lodge*, Box FM 444, Famona, Bulawayo (☎64638 or 79829, fax 72870), is a great place to clock up some of the 335 species of birds recorded in the conservancy, track black rhino and view elephants, cats and plains game. Most guests fly in from Bulawayo, but self-drive is possible; rates start at US$100 per person.

Tuli Circle

TULI CIRCLE, an odd little salient west of the Shashi River, off the main road to Beit Bridge, should by rights be in Botswana – the Shashi defines the border most of the way along here. This was, however, the first gateway into Rhodesia, and provided a fort, hospital and supply post for pioneers eyeing the interior. After the defeat of the Ndebele, it was eclipsed by Bulawayo and has since dwindled into a trading post serving the local communal lands.

The pioneer presence is marked by a cemetery, a memorial and a flag marking the site of the fort. There are three **botanical reserves** and a **safari area** in this small enclave. Few maps give any indication that it's worth visiting, but it's recommended if you have a 4WD and plenty of time in Zimbabwe; the palm-lined sandy Shashi is startling amid the unpromisingly parched southwest. **Elephants** favour the area, and you can expect periodic good game sightings, the circle biting into the best private game reserve in neighbouring Botswana. There are no fences and the animals migrate across the border freely, something visitors are strongly advised against.

To get to Tuli, avoid the road running parallel to the Limpopo, which is used by the military to patrol the border with South Africa. Take the turnoff near Gwanda instead. It's rugged 4WD country, so you should allow as much as ten hours for the drive from Bulawayo. A daily **bus** goes from Bulawayo via Tuli to Beit Bridge and vice versa but serves the communal areas, not the botanical reserves.

Beit Bridge

Though no one would willingly choose to spend the night in **BEIT BRIDGE** itself, a couple of perfectly reputable **hotels** line the main road leading to the border. *Peter's Motel* (☎186/309 or 321; ③) is the most pleasant of the bunch, with the *Beit Bridge Hotel* (☎186/214 or 413; ③) a good fall-back. There are no cheaper places to stay in the town, and neither is there a campsite, though you can ask to camp on the front lawn of *Peter's Motel*.

travel details

Trains

These are the details given in timetables. Don't expect trains to run on time, but travel is very inexpensive.

Bulawayo to: Gaborone (daily at 2.30pm; 16hr), via Francistown (7hr); Harare (daily at 9pm; 10hr), via Gweru, Kwekwe and Midlands towns; Johannesburg (Thurs; 24hr), via Beit Bridge; Victoria Falls (1 daily 7pm; 12hr 30min).

Luxury coaches

The most reliable form of surface transport: the drivers turn punctuality into an art form, beating the train. *Blue Arrow* coaches depart from Unifreight House, 73A Fife St, Bulawayo (☎65548); *Translux* work out of the *Bulawayo Sun*.

Bulawayo to:

Harare via Chivhu (daily; 6hr); via Kwekwe (Thurs & Sun; 6hr) – *Blue Arrow*.

Johannesburg (daily except Wed & Fri; 12–14hr) – *Blue Arrow* and *Translux.*

Victoria Falls (Mon, Wed, Fri & Sun; 6hr 15min), via *Hwange Safari Lodge* and Hwange town – *Ajay Motors* and *Blue Arrow.*

Economy buses

You'll find buses to most places you'll be going. This is an attempt to make some sense of the confusing information about the main places. Arrive early to get a place and pay on the bus.

Bulawayo Lobengula Street Terminus to:

Great Zimbabwe turn-off (Mon–Sat at 1.30pm; 5hr 30min) via Masvingo.

Bulawayo Renkini Terminus to:

Beit Bridge (daily; 6hr).

Binga via Kamativi and Hwange (daily; 8hr).

Harare (5 or more daily 5–11am; 7hr or longer).

Kezi for the Matopos (daily; 2hr).

Masvingo (2–3 daily 6–8.30am; 5hr); *Hwange Express* (Mon, Wed 1.30pm & Tues 11.30am; 3hr 30min–4hr 30min).

Plumtree (daily; 4hr).

Tuli (daily; 10hr).

Flights

Bulawayo to: Harare (3 daily; 50min); Johannesburg (daily except Tues & Sat; 1hr 30min); Victoria Falls (daily except Tues & Sat; 50min).

CHAPTER FOUR

VICTORIA FALLS AND HWANGE NATIONAL PARK

The **Victoria Falls** are one of Africa's most enduring images and one that has remained surprisingly untarnished despite its tourist boom. The town, which aptly takes its name from its fabulous attraction, developed principally to serve a relatively modest influx of visitors, but has recently exploded into the undisputed tourism capital of the country.

Vic Falls is now Africa's **adventure sport** hub, with a host of high-quality activities that might tempt an extended stay: the world's most adrenaline-charged one-day **whitewater rafting** trip surges through the gorge below the Falls, and the bungee jumping from the bridge overhead is the highest commercial leap anywhere. **Kayaking** for several days through rapids on the stretch above the Falls, and **game trails** in the nearby reserves – either on foot or on horseback – are equally inspiring options.

With the growing focus on adrenalin and adventure, its easy to forget that the town is also one of the best bases in the country to start a **safari**. Trips leave from Victoria Falls for remote and adventurous regions such as Chizarira National Park and Mana Pools (see Chapter Two), but closer to home, thousands of square miles west and south of Victoria Falls are a patchwork quilt of national parks, safari areas and private wildlife concessions. Here, **safari lodges and bush camps**, although far from cheap, promise truly exciting experiences of the bush; and the personalized expert attention you'll get make them worth saving up for.

Among the wildlife reserves, the impressive **Zambezi National Park**, which begins on the outskirts of Victoria Falls Town, is famed for its herds of beautiful sable antelope. From the town you can also take walking safaris (the only way in) to the game-rich grasslands of **Kazuma Pan**, south on the Botswana border. However, Zimbabwe's wildlife showpiece is the extensive **Hwange National Park**, just 100km south of Victoria Falls by road, and connected by daily flights. The most accessible of the country's wildlife parks, Hwange has easy game viewing and low-cost

---

ACCOMMODATION PRICE CODES

Hotels and other accommodation options in Zimbabwe – as well as those in Zambia covered in this chapter – have been categorized according to the **price codes** given below, which indicate the cost, per person sharing, of a night's lodging.

For a full explanation, see p.46.

① under US$8	④ US$25–35	⑦ US$65–80
② US$8–15	⑤ US$35–50	⑧ US$80–95
③ US$15–25	⑥ US$50–65	⑨ over US$95

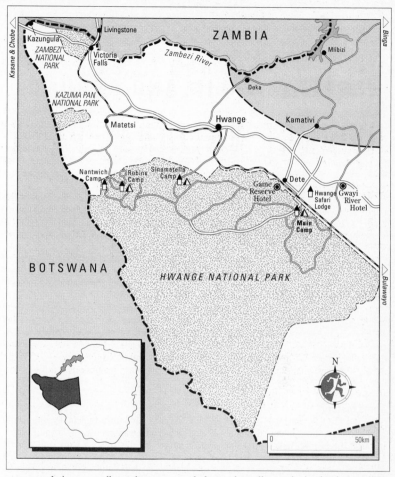

accommodation, as well as a luxury game lodge and smaller exclusive bush camps for real safari style.

The Falls are shared with Zambia – the Zambezi River defines the Zambia–Zimbabwe border – and lie a short distance from Botswana and Namibia. This makes Victoria Falls town a good base for **onwards travel**, as well as an obvious point of entry for overlanders working their way down from the north. From Zimbabwe you can make a hassle-free day sortie into **Zambia**, crossing the Victoria Falls Bridge to look at the gorge from a different angle, or venturing 10km further into the country to

---

TELEPHONE CODES

The area telephone code for **Victoria Falls** is ☎113.

The country code for **Zambia** is ☎260, and the area code for **Livingstone** ☎3.

visit the regional centre of **Livingstone**. Heading west into Botswana, it's possible to base yourself at Kasane on the Chobe River for a couple of days of game viewing in the fabulous elephant country of Chobe National Park. From here, it's a straightforward detour northwards into Namibia, provided you have your own transport.

VICTORIA FALLS AND AROUND

The energy and power of over a mile's width of the **Zambezi River** thundering 100 metres down a sheer chasm is a pretty compelling sight, and combined with the clouds of sunlit spray and rainbows, reason enough to spend a day or two gazing at **Victoria Falls**. But the banks of the river, before it takes the plunge, are enticing, too – a wonderful place to contemplate the **palm-dotted islands** and the water, which changes from sheeny pink at dawn to metallic blue at dusk. And, for closer views, you can get on the water with one of the **cruises**.

The **rainforest** fed by the spray of the Falls, with its ilala palms, white river sand, fiery sunsets and more or less constant humidity makes for a lush, "darkest Africa" landscape, found nowhere else in Zimbabwe. Immediately surrounding the Falls is the **Victoria Falls National Park** where you can see antelope, warthog and vervet monkeys amid the spray.

Beginning a few kilometres upstream, the **Zambezi National Park** extends for forty forested kilometres along the river, with dry bush and grassland further inland. Stalked by a wide range of Zimbabwe's wildlife, this is one of the many diversions that make it possible to spend days around the Victoria Falls.

At the centre of all this lies **Victoria Falls town**, unashamedly geared towards tourism, though surprisingly sleepy and undeveloped. It provides a springboard for the Falls themselves, but is now expanding into a host of diversions, especially **adventure activities**, to keep visitors here – and spending. Each of its scattered hotels exists as a self-contained resort, from which guests venture out to stroll down to the water, visit the curio shops and snake park, or to take part in the standard excursions – a flight or a cruise.

Some history

Set amid the flat, hot bush of Matabeleland, Victoria Falls town is actually one of the oldest in Zimbabwe, having become a centre for intrepid traders, travellers and hunters through the second half of the nineteenth century. By the 1890s a store and a hotel complete with roulette wheel had been built, though the town was temporarily abandoned following an outbreak of malaria and blackwater fever; the settlement moved to higher ground away from the river, at Livingstone, across the newly completed railway bridge. The town on the Zimbabwean side of the river only really came back into its own in the late 1960s, when hotels, banks and, most important, an airport were built.

The 1990s has seen Victoria Falls become the tourism capital of Zimbabwe. Backpackers have begun arriving in increasing numbers, putting some pressure on budget accommodation, and the growing number of activities on offer are attracting more and more visitors who want adventure as well as contemplation. At the end of 1991 the airport was upgraded to international standards – for the benefit of visiting leaders coming "on retreat" at the conclusion of the Commonwealth Heads of Government Meeting (known locally as CHOGM).

With the rapid influx of tourists the town continues to expand. New facilities have sprung up in the fertile entrepreneurial grounds around the Falls. Most controversial of these is the hefty *Elephant Hills Hotel*, which doubled the total bed capacity of the resort at a single stroke.

Getting there, orientation and information

The slowest, but arguably pleasantest, way to get to the Falls is on the **Bulawayo–Falls train**. It's a twelve-hour overnight affair, leaving Bulawayo daily at 7pm. There are sometimes inexplicably long delays and stops at the tiniest of junctions but the journey is worth the time to view some of Zimbabwe's best wildlife areas from the comfort of a self-contained compartment. At dawn on the following day of the trip, you travel through remote bush, and there are good chances of seeing such **game** as antelope, zebra, or perhaps even one of the big five watching the train as it chugs past. On its return leg from the Falls, the train passes through some of this area at dusk, an equally prime time for viewing game.

Victoria Falls station itself is delightful – an Edwardian concoction shaded by flame-flowered flamboyants, sweet-smelling frangipanis and syringas, and with a platform boasting pond and palm trees. From the ceremonial exit (High British Empire), you can stroll down a colonnade of trees to the *Victoria Falls Hotel*; for the town's main street, walk north along the platform.

By car, Vic Falls is 440km from Bulawayo, and 875km from Harare, all on tarred roads. The stretch between Bulawayo and the Falls is very isolated, and once you leave the city there are no filling stations, or any signs of human habitation for 160km.

Blue Arrow and *Translux* **coaches** from Bulawayo and Johannesburg arrive and depart from the *UTC* office in Livingstone Way, while the *Ajay* terminus is over the road at the *Makasa Sun Hotel*, just beyond the *Victoria Falls Hotel*. The *Makasa Sun* is also the end of the line for the **airbuses** that meet all *Air Zimbabwe* flights at the **airport** (20km out of town on the Bulawayo road). **Economy buses** drop off on Livingstone Way near the *Sprayview Hotel*, before going to the hidden **Chinotimba township** down Pioneer Road. All the shops you're likely to need are strung along Livingstone Way, which leads straight to the **Falls National Park** entrance. Almost everything closes for lunch and the town is dead by 4.30pm, so do your business in the morning.

Cycling is the most flexible way to get around, and several places offer bike rental. You can take them overnight to the Zambezi National Park lodges or pedal across to Zambia. **Car rental** can also be arranged (see "Listings" on p.177 for both services).

Information

The **Tourist Information Centre**, Parkway/Livingstone Way (☎4202), conveniently right in the centre next to the *Town Council Rest Camp*, has a slightly haphazard collection of brochures and other information, but it may be worth popping in to find out the latest information about accommodation options (although they don't arrange bookings). The private sector is streets ahead for anything to do with adventure activities, packages or safaris. Among a number of helpful **agencies** (see box p.172 for a full list), the biggest are the fiercely competing *Safari Par Excellence* and *Shearwater*, each of which will push their own products – be prepared to shop around. The **National Parks** office, at the Bulawayo end of Livingstone Way (☎4222), is the place to make bookings for the Zambezi National Park.

Accommodation

Accommodation in and around Victoria Falls ranges from upmarket hotels down to budget options like camping or chalets at the *Town Council Rest Camp*. However, the town has yet to experience the proliferation of backpackers' lodges that has occurred in most other Zimbabwean tourist centres. The growth area here is at the other end of the scale: luxury safari lodges, located beyond the Falls' immediate environs, which

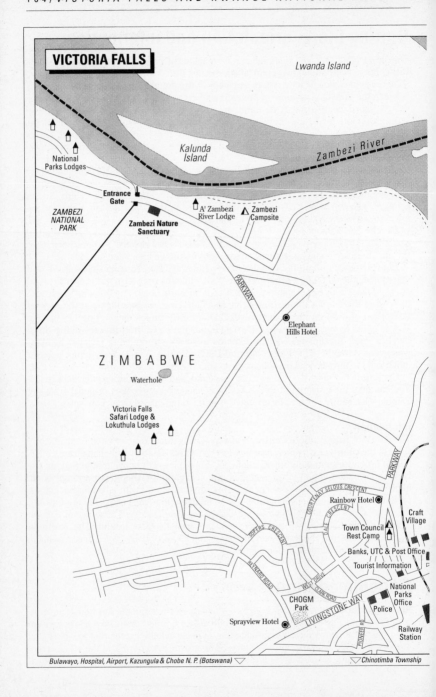

VICTORIA FALLS

Lwanda Island

Kalunda Island

Zambezi River

National Parks Lodges

Entrance Gate

A' Zambezi River Lodge

Zambezi Campsite

ZAMBEZI NATIONAL PARK

Zambezi Nature Sanctuary

PARKWAY

Elephant Hills Hotel

ZIMBABWE

Waterhole

Victoria Falls Safari Lodge & Lokuthula Lodges

PARKWAY

COURTENAY SELOUS CRESCENT

Rainbow Hotel

Craft Village

DALE CRESCENT

Town Council Rest Camp

SOPERS CRESCENT

Banks, UTC & Post Office

Tourist Information

REYNARD ROAD

WEST DRIVE

CLARK ROAD

National Parks Office

CHOGM Park

LIVINGSTONE WAY

Police

PIONEER RD

Sprayview Hotel

Railway Station

Bulawayo, Hospital, Airport, Kazungula & Chobe N. P. (Botswana) ▽

▽ *Chinotimba Township*

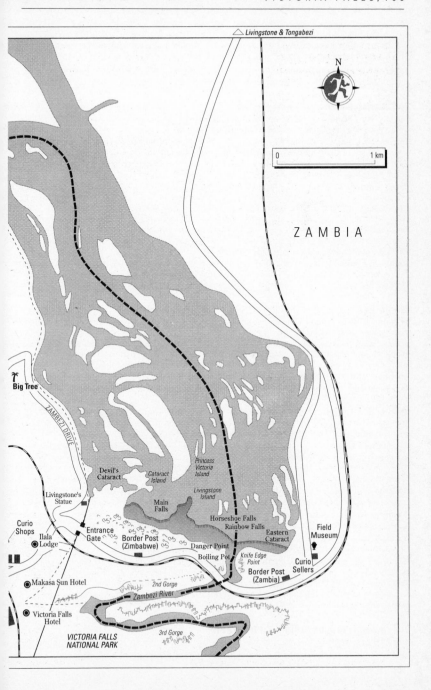

△ Livingstone & Tongabezi

N

0   1 km

ZAMBIA

Big Tree

ZAMBEZI DRIVE

Livingstone's
Statue

Curio
Shops

Ilala
Lodge

Entrance
Gate

Border Post
(Zimbabwe)

Devil's
Cataract

Cataract
Island

Princess
Victoria Island

Livingstone
Island

Main
Falls

Horseshoe Falls
Rainbow Falls

Danger Point

Boiling Pot

Eastern
Cataract

Knife Edge
Point

Field
Museum

Curio
Sellers

Border Post
(Zambia)

Makasa Sun Hotel

2nd Gorge

Zambezi River

Victoria Falls
Hotel

VICTORIA FALLS
NATIONAL PARK

3rd Gorge

provide a pricy but unquestionably interesting alternative to staying in town. National Parks also offer inexpensive (and thus hugely popular) self-catering accommodation in the bush, 6km outside of town along Parkway. Be warned, however, that the increasing numbers of visitors arriving in the country's premier resort mean a bed for the night is by no means guaranteed. Advance booking, especially for budget places, is essential.

Inexpensive

Inyati Valley Motel and Rest Camp, Parkway. Campsite, caravan park and chalets, 2km from the centre, in a new development that should provide some relief at the budget end of the scale. ②.

Sprayview Hotel, Livingstone Way/Renard Rd, PO Box 70 (☎4344, fax 4713). Cheapest of the Vic Falls hotels, but none the less pleasant for that, with en-suite bedrooms and a swimming pool. About 20min on foot from the centre, it has a pleasantly nostalgic atmosphere. For families it has the advantage of a daytime creche. ③.

Town Council Rest Camp, Livingstone Way/Parkway, PO Box 41, Victoria Falls (☎210). The cheapest accommodation with a roof over your head is in segregated men's and women's mini-hostels – cramped, but good for meeting other travellers. Moving up a bracket, the triple-bedded, and slightly run-down, chalets are still extremely cheap; all the basics are provided, including pots, pans, a small fridge and firewood for braaing outside. Washing facilities are in shared blocks, with hot showers and baths. There are also two-bedroomed en-suite cottages that won't break the bank, and a large, sandy campsite. ①.

Zambezi Campsite, alongside the river on Parkway, next to *A'Zambezi Lodge*. While not as convenient for the town centre, it is recommended as the nicer of the two campsites with splendid views of the water.

Upmarket

A'Zambezi River Lodge, 5km out of town along Parkway (☎4561, fax 4536). Located right next to the Zambezi National Park, this riverside lodge is a pleasant escape, built in a semicircle with rooms facing the river. It claims to have the largest thatched roof in the world, and warthogs, monkeys and occasionally other animals roam about the grounds. A courtesy bus service operates for residents without their own transport so it's easy to get to and from the centre. ⑧.

Elephant Hills, 3km out of town just off Parkway (book through PO Box 8221, Harare; or ☎4793, fax 4655). Hideously obtrusive, with piped muzak throughout, this is unquestionably the most controversial new development at the Falls. ⑨.

Ilala Lodge, Livingstone Way, PO Box 18 (☎4737, fax 4417). Highly recommended lodge where rooms look onto manicured lawns receding into indigenous forest, from which small game emerges in the mornings and late afternoons. Retains an intimate feel by limiting guest numbers. ⑦.

Lokhuthula Lodges, off Parkway, about 2.5km from town (see *Victoria Falls Safari Lodge* below for booking details). Beautifully designed self-catering lodges that are part of the *Victoria Falls Safari Lodge* development, and share many of the same facilities. The two-bedroom lodges sleep six, those with three bedrooms eight. Expensive for a couple, but excellent value for six or more sharing. ⑦.

Makasa Sun Hotel, Parkway/Mallet Drive, PO Box 4275 (☎4275, fax 4782). On the main drag, with a casino that belies this otherwise characterless slab. ⑧.

Rainbow Hotel, Parkway/Courtney Selous Crescent, PO Box 150 (☎4585, fax 4653). Reasonably central, built in a Spanish style with the attraction of a bar *in* the swimming pool. ⑧.

Victoria Falls Hotel, Mallet Drive (opposite the railway station), PO Box 10 (☎4203, fax 4586). The place to splurge, it positively oozes bygone elegance (see box below). ⑨.

Victoria Falls Safari Lodge, off Parkway, 2.5km from town (☎3202, fax 3205; book in London ☎0171/225 0164; Johannesburg ☎011/331 8911; or Victoria Falls ☎4728). The most imaginative hotel development at the Falls, impressively set on the brow of a hill overlooking a waterhole, and complete with wildlife (including lions and buffalo) roaming freely around. An hourly shuttle bus takes guests to and from town. ⑨.

All-in safari lodges around Victoria Falls

For visitors wanting to combine game viewing with a visit to the Falls, a number of distant lodges offer luxury in the bush, with game drives, walks or, in some cases,

THE VICTORIA FALLS HOTEL

The **Victoria Falls** is Zimbabwe's grandest hotel – and must be seen even if you can't afford (or can't find a room) to stay.

The first tourists to the Falls had to eat and sleep in the train at the station. In 1905, just after the railway arrived, work began on the construction of a wood and corrugated iron hotel, close to the terminus. That shack has come a long way, with the avenue of scented trees from the station creating merely a build-up to the hotel's colonial legacy of architectural style and impeccable service.

Guests, largely foreign tourists, enjoy rich-*bwana* fantasies here, waited on by discreet and highly efficient black staff in starched white uniforms and gloves. The terrace opens onto views of the low greeny-grey hills of Zambia rising behind the filter of spray. It's all part of the careful setting – the site was chosen for its view of the second gorge and the daring railway bridge.

The short walk from the hotel was too much for Edwardian tourists, so a trolley took them down to the Falls. A number of old snaps in Bulawayo's Railway Museum show well-dressed ladies and gents being pushed by black "trolley boys". The tracks were pulled up some time ago but the remaining path is still a thoroughfare, the trolleymen replaced by hustlers hawking curios at odd spots along the route.

cruises thrown into the all-inclusive price – expect to pay upwards of US$200 per person per night. Although some may seem far out of town, by Zimbabwean standards they aren't, and all are packaged as adjuncts to a Falls visit. Transfers to and from Victoria Falls or the airport are provided.

The Elephant Camp, 25km west of Victoria Falls, next to the Zambezi National Park. Book through *Wild Horizons*, Parkway, PO Box 159, Victoria Falls (☎4219, fax 4349). Accommodating no more than eight guests on a 35,000-acre private game reserve, the camp centres around four trained, tame young African elephants. Elephant-back safaris are a focal activity, but these aren't so much children's fun-fair rides as a serious part of fostering an understanding of the animals. You can also pet and swim with the elephants, or opt for conventional game viewing activities, including drives in the neighbouring national park, night excursions and guided walks.

Imbabala Safari Camp, 72km from town on the Kazungula road. Book through *Wild Horizons*, Parkway, PO Box 159, Victoria Falls (☎4219, fax 4349). On the Zambezi flood plain, near the Botswana border; you can see the meeting point of four countries (Zimbabwe, Botswana, Namibia and Zambia) from lawns which slope down to the water. Accommodation is in A-frame, en-suite chalets, catering to a maximum of 18 guests; lie on your bed and watch the reflected sun set on the river. Excellent guides, good game viewing and outstanding opportunities for birdwatching, with species present that don't occur elsewhere in Zimbabwe.

Masuwe Lodge, 7km from Victoria Falls to the Masuwe turn-off along the main airport road, and then several kilometres along a private dirt track. Book through *Landela Safaris*, PO Box 66293, Kopje, Harare (☎14/734043, fax 750785; or ☎Johannesburg 706 6468, fax 706 7627). Set in its own concession, with promising prospects for game viewing. A broad range of habitats means birdwatching is also good, with common sightings of birds of prey. Large walk-in tents (consciously re-creating an *Out of Africa* ambience) sit on stilted wooden decks providing panoramas of the surrounding valleys. The lounge/dining room jetties out over a valley, and also has dramatic views.

Sekuti's Drift, 25km out of town, next to the Zambezi National Park. Book through *Landela Safaris* (see *Masuwe Lodge* above for details). Hilltop re-creation of a nineteenth-century colonial homestead on private safari land, with green tin roof and polished verandahs, which outdoes even the *Victoria Falls Hotel*. Maximum of 20 guests.

Tongabezi, Zambia. Book through Private Bag 31, Livingstone, Zambia (Livingstone ☎323235 or 323296, fax 323224; e-mail: tonga@zamnet.zm). On the Zambian side and geared more to style than game viewing. Some rooms provide the thrill of sleeping in a four-poster bed on a deck overlooking the Zambezi; other accomodation is under canvas and there's also an island camp in the middle of the Zambezi.

The Falls

When Livingstone arrived at the **Victoria Falls**, and named them after his queen, they already had an apt designation, **Mosi oa Tunya**, "The Smoke That Thunders". This name had been given to the waters by the **Makololo**, who, like Livingstone, were newcomers to the region. Following the early eighteenth-century Zulu expansion (in what is today South Africa's KwaZulu Natal province), a refugee fragment had fled north, finally coming to rest around the Falls. They became the Makololo and held domain here briefly during the nineteenth century, ruling over the local tribes.

Stone Age tools uncovered in the area record that humans were living around the Falls for two million years before that. The Zambian side has a dig showing finds at different depths corresponding to different epochs, and the museum in Livingstone has a fine collection of stone tools found at the dig.

Victoria Falls National Park

Daily 6am–6pm. Admission fee US$2.

Few geological faults can evoke such anticipation as "The Smoke That Thunders": the moment you arrive in Victoria Falls Town, and hear the roar and see the smoky mist rising half a kilometre skywards, you'll be drawn down the main street to the **national park** entrance. A walk from here through the rainforest will take at least an hour. At full moon you can see the faint lunar rainbow.

The Falls are at their most impressive in **April** and **May**, when the river is in full spate, although the dense spray can sometimes obscure the views, which are clearest, if somewhat less spectacular, in **September** and **October**, at the end of the dry season. The **best times of day** to visit are around opening and closing times, when the light is at its best, and fellow tourists relatively sparse. Take waterproof protection (or pick it up at the entrance) for your camera and other susceptible possessions.

The Chasm and Devil's Cataract

You can walk all along the side of the **chasm** opposite the park entrance, through the woods with their sudden spray showers – although beware that some of the most vertiginous drops are unfenced, with just the occasional thorn bush as a barrier. In the dry season, when the Falls are lowest, you'll probably escape a soaking, but once the rains have swelled the Zambezi, you'll get the full force of the spray; wear a swimming costume or raincoat. The wettest viewpoints are those directly opposite the Main Falls, in the areas unprotected by trees.

The first view that you get, at the western end of the the chasm, is known as **Devil's Cataract**. Turning left from here takes you to a statue of **David Livingstone**, beyond which the river path leads off upstream. It's hard to avoid Livingstone in this neck of the woods. His commanding effigy, overlooking Devil's Cataract, portrays the qualities expected from famous explorers – will and determination. More critical accounts record that he was pig-headed, selfish and sanctimonious. Nevertheless, anti-slavery campaigning was part of his reason for exploring the Zambezi, his aim being to find a west–east route to end the human traffic in the region.

Livingstone's reverential account that "on sights as beautiful as this Angels in their flight must have gazed" has become one of the clichés of the Victoria Falls: a phrase that's even been deconstructed and reassembled to package the daily air tours – "The Flight of the Angels" – that flit above the chasm. To Livingstone, however, there was a real element of revelation in his vision of Mosi oa Tunya, and he backed his own religious emotion by writing about how local chieftains used two of the islands right on the lip of the Falls as "sacred spots for worshipping the deity".

Other falls and Danger Point

Wander through the rainforest beyond Devil's Cataract and you will see the **other falls** that roar down the mile-wide fissure: **Main, Horseshoe, Rainbow** and the **Eastern Cataract**. A highlight is **Danger Point**, at the east end, where your walk on the Zimbabwean side finishes with a dizzy promontory near the Victoria Falls Bridge. From the rocks here you can look down into the frightening depths of the abyss, and also get great views of the eastern half of the Falls and of the **Boiling Pot**, a seething whirlpool where two branches of the river collide. It can be wet and slippery at the viewpoint with deluges of spray; during the flood season you won't see much, but when the river is low it's mesmerizing.

Rainforest wildlife

The rainforest is eminently explorable and there's plenty of **wildlife** about. Baboons, monkeys, waterbuck, warthog and banded mongooses roam around, while the four hundred or so species of **birds** include: Livingstone's lourie with its bright leaf-green breast and crimson flight feathers; the comical trumpeter hornbill; the paradise flycatcher; the nectar-feeding sunbird; and more common bulbuls, warblers, barbets and shrikes.

Butterflies are numerous, too, blowing through the mist between rainbows and shiny grass. During the rainy season the undergrowth acquires a special luxuriance with large blood lilies, scarlet among the mosses and ferns. Wild yellow gladioli grow in patches of open grassland, while palms, ebonies, figs, mahoganies and waterberries thrive in the rich, moist soil.

Excursions and leisure activities

It's easy to while away a few hours around the Falls strolling, sightseeing and buying crafts. More institutionalized leisure activities include flights over the chasm, sunset booze cruises on the river, and game drives and birdwatching trips in the Zambezi National Park.

Crafts, crocs and curios

The curio shops around the **Falls Craft Village**, behind the post office and banks, are ganged together in a single conglomeration which spills over down Parkway. The first stall was opened in 1903 by the earliest white settler, Percy Clarke, and in 1910 one Jack Soper opened a shop next door with a crocodile pool to attract customers. *Soper's Curios* is still there and so is a pool (a new and larger one) with large **crocs** snoozing in the slimy water. The stuffed lion in the window with fierce teeth and glassy eyes is part of the range of great-white-hunter goods.

Some of the best **craft works** are available at the *Jairos Jiri* shop (closed Sun) in the Falls Craft complex; they include Batonga baskets from the Zambezi Valley, attractive

---

THE HIPPO'S TALE

A San folktale relates how the first hippo begged the Great Bureaucrat's permission to live in the water, which it loved more than the earth, the sun, the moon or the stars. However, the application was rejected: such a big mouth with such teeth would soon devour all the fish. The hippo begged again, promising to eat nothing in the water, and to emerge at night to graze on the grass and plants of the earth, but once again, permission was denied. Finally, it agreed to emerge daily and scatter its dung, so all creatures could examine them for fishbones.

spoons made from local wood, and carved giraffes with delicate long necks – the best of them eight or nine feet high. For an eclectic mix of antiques and airport art, *Studio Africana* is worth a look. Some things aren't actually for sale – like the carved, wooden **ape god** from Zaire, with a head made from a smoked gorilla skull – but if you want something old this is the place. In a sort of **indoor market** nearby, local women compete with each other to sell **crochet ware**, **baskets**, **carvings and bracelets** – cheaper and with considerably more buzz than the curio shops but not half as easy to browse.

The **Falls Craft Village** proper (Mon–Sat 8.30am–4.30pm, Sun 9am–1pm) is set to one side of the curio shops, and seems designed to prop up out-of-date touristic images of Africa – a mishmash collection of nineteenth-century huts from all over the country. More interesting, if a little startling, is bumping into one of the two **fortune-telling** *n'angas* huddled in the darkness of one of the exhibit huts. For a few dollars they'll lay it all out for you. Though they work out of context here, *n'angas* are widely used in Zimbabwe, by town and country dwellers, as healers and interpreters of the workings of the ever-present ancestors. They have a deep knowledge of illness and both herbal and ritualistic ways of dealing with it. Since Independence, the government has actively encouraged their profession.

The Snake Park

The **Snake Park**, close by the Crafts Village, can be diverting for the odd hour or two. The snake attendant has a great line in ghoulish information (where snakes like to hide; how likely they are to bite you; how long you'll live if they do), concluded with graphic descriptions of agonizing death. And if you've always wondered how those lifelike animals in museums are created, go to the **taxidermy workshop** where they have mounts on display in various stages of completion and people who'll happily tell you some of the secrets of their morbidly fascinating work. Their shop explores the depths of bad taste for all pockets: a copper ashtray plinthed on an impala leg goes for a few pounds, while there's a lion-skin rug (with snarling head) for those with more money than subtlety.

River walks for free

If you can't afford any of the organized trips, go on your own up the river towards the Zambezi National Park. A ten-kilometre **walk** starts outside the Victoria Falls National Park fence just beyond Livingstone's statue along a four-kilometre riverside path to the *A'Zambezi River Lodge*, then 6km back along the road. You'll probably be alone – most people don't venture upstream beyond the first rapids. This excursion can be conveniently combined with a visit to the Zambezi Nature Sanctuary and the *A'Zambezi*.

Be wary of **hippos** leaving the river at dusk for their bankside browse. They return to the water first thing next day. Watch out then too, and avoid blocking their route to the water. During the day they emerge occasionally to scatter their dung on land with a vigorous tail movement, but all you're likely to see of them are noses and ears above water far upriver from people. Be alert as well to the fact that other species of **wildlife** sometimes venture onto the path.

Walk upriver to see the riverine forest and the changes in current as it gets smoother and quieter. If it's blistering, just walk a kilometre or so to the **Big Tree** and come back along Zambezi Drive and Parkway, which brings you to the doorstep of the campsite. The Big Tree, a large baobab, is no crowd-puller, but it has historical interest. Early pioneers camped here and it became a traditional gathering place for crossing the river to the Old Drift Settlement and later to Livingstone.

The Zambezi Nature Sanctuary

The **Zambezi Nature Sanctuary** (8am–12.30pm & 2–4.30pm), 7km up Parkway just past the *A'Zambezi*, is *the* place to see loads of **crocodiles**. The sanctuary serves the dual purpose of restocking the badly depleted river and rearing the much-maligned reptiles for their skin; every year they collect about 2500 eggs, a proportion of which are hatched, reared and returned (some as healthy three-year-olds). The crocodile has an important **ecological role** in balancing the fish population, eating the predators which prey on the marketable fish such as bream. You can also see leopards, servals and caracals, as well as birds, trees and an aquarium.

Without a car, the easiest ways to **get to the sanctuary** are to cycle down Parkway, or to take a taxi. *Touch the Wild* also run excursions, leaving town at 10am and costing US$10. There's a pleasant tea kiosk at the sanctuary, and an interesting little museum.

Cruises

The most famous of local leisure activities are the "**booze cruises**". Drinks used to be free – with riotous results. Now you buy your own and there's a stiff fine for jumping in or attempting to swim home. The last (early evening) departure is the best time to be on the river, with the darkening forest backlit by a molten sky. Though the launch doesn't berth en route, it does pause for photographs, and you're bound to see hippos and perhaps elephants on the banks and islands. The morning and afternoon cruises stop at Kandahar Island for tea where monkeys try to take your biscuits off you.

Boats **depart** from the jetty next to the *A'Zambezi River Lodge* at 10.15am, 2.15pm and 5pm in winter (10.15am, 2.15pm and 5.15pm in summer). **Tickets** are sold by *UTC*, who pick up from the central hotels thirty minutes before departure. Drinks are still included for a supplement on the more exclusive *Ilala*, which carries no more than ten passengers.

Flights

To conservationists on the ground, the proliferation of flying machines buzzing over the Falls is a major irritant that has eroded the calm of this previously tranquil environment. It's undeniable, though, that from the air things look different; soaring above the spray, the sheer immensity of the gorge and Falls is dramatically revealed. Formerly, the only airborne joyrides on offer here were in a five-seater light aeroplane; now you can also choose a seaplane, helicopter, microlight or ultralight aircraft. "The Flight of the Angels", the oldest-established of the aerial excusions, lasts fifteen minutes, and the price covers transport to the airport; longer, 75-minute options include a game flight. Prices for short sorties in a **light aeroplane** or **seaplane** start at US$45 for a basic flight; expect to pay more for **helicopters**.

Microlights and **ultralights** bear a strong resemblance to airborne 50cc motorbikes – it's just you and the pilot. Flights lasting around 35 minutes take in views of local villages, the gorge, the rainforest, Zambezi National Park and, of course, the Falls themselves. According to the aficionados, the main difference between the two is safety. Ultralights, bookable only through *Safari Par Excellence*, are rated the less risky of the two, partly because of their design, and partly because pilots hold commercial licences. Prices for these flights start at US$65.

Game drives

Touch the Wild's excellent **game drives** in the nearby game reserve are a more down-to-earth way of enjoying the area's natural splendours. The Zambezi National Park (see section following for a full treatment) runs along the southern bank of the Zambezi towards Botswana. During the three-hour trips, you can expect to see elephant, buffalo, lion, zebra and many different species of antelope – worth it for whistle-stoppers, but not if Hwange's on your itinerary. *Touch the Wild* pick up from central hotels at 6.00am and 3.30pm daily in summer (8am and 3pm in winter); book through them.

Victoria Falls also makes an excellent starting point for one-day – and longer – safaris into northern Hwange and Chobe in neighbouring Botswana. The two-hour drive to **Hwange National Park** (see p.182) takes you through State Forest and the Matetsi safari area, so the game viewing starts almost straight away. Trips leave at around 6am and you get back to town by 7pm. *Ulinda Safaris,* led by one of Zimbabwe's few women professional hunter-guides, and *Touch the Wild,* among the longest-established operators in the Hwange area, both go to Hwange for the day. Prices are around US$100, including meals; *Ulinda* also does a two-day/two-night camping excursion to Hwange for around US$350.

Even if you don't plan to include Botswana in your itinerary, it would be a pity to miss out on **Chobe National Park** (see p.300), one of Africa's great elephant sanctuaries, and an easy drive from Victoria Falls. Inconveniently, none of the Zimbabwean car rental companies let you cross the border in their vehicles, but you can still get there with a minimum of hassle – as long as you're prepared to pay for the privilege. For a stiff US$150, *Ultimate Africa Safaris* will get you there and back the same day, feed you, and take you on an expertly guided game drive in the reserve, and a river cruise on the exceptionally photogenic Chobe River. They also run three-day trips to Chobe from around US$500.

Birdwatching

You don't have to be a twitcher to enjoy a **birdwatching** trip with Dr Kit Hustler, one of Zimbabwe's top ornithologists. The former curator at the Natural History Museum leads full-day trips to the Zambezi flood plain, looking for slaty egrets and greater

---

ADVENTURE AND SAFARI BOOKINGS

VICTORIA FALLS

Afroventures
Elephant Hills Hotel (☎/fax 113/4588).

Backpacker's Africa
PO Box 44 (☎113/4424 or 4570, fax 113/4683); or book through *Safari Par Excellence.*

Dabula Safaris
309 Parkway, PO Box 210 (☎/fax 113/4453).

Frontiers Rafting
Victoria Falls Centre, Parkway (next to *Wimpy*), PO Box 35 (☎113/4772).

Kalambeza Safaris
PO Box 121 (☎113/4644, telex 51668 ZW).

Kandahar Safaris
Shop 9, Sopers Arcade, Parkway, PO Box 223 (☎/fax 113/2014).

Safari Par Excellence
Pamula Centre, Parkway, PO Box 108 (☎113/2051–4, fax 113/4510).

Shearwater Adventures
Parkway, PO Box 125 (☎113/4471, fax 113/4341).

Touch the Wild
Elephant Hills Hotel and *Victoria Falls Hotel* (☎113/46222 ext 1867, fax 113/4676).

Ultimate Africa Safaris
PO Box 180 (☎/fax 113/2051); or book through *Safari Par Excellence.*

UTC
Zimbank Building, Livingstone Way (☎113/4267).

Wild Horizons
Off Parkway (Hertz Corner), PO Box 159 (☎113/4219, fax 113/4349).

LIVINGSTONE

Sobek Expeditions
Katombara Rd, PO Box 60957, Livingstone, Zambia (☎321432, fax 323542).

HARARE

Frontiers Rafting
Cecil House, 95 Jason Moyo Ave, PO Box 4876 (☎14/732911 or 732948, fax 14/704759).

Safari Par Excellence
3rd Floor, Travel Centre, Jason Moyo Ave, PO Box 5920 (☎14/720527, 700911 or 700912, fax 14/722872).

Shearwater Adventures
Safari Booking Office, First St/Baker Ave (☎14/757831–4, fax 14/757836).

swamp warblers, as well as half-day excursions around the Falls to look for bat hawks and rarities such as the taita falcon. The trips, run by *Wild Horizons*, start at US$40.

Activities for children

One of the drawbacks of most activities at Victoria Falls, including many game drives, is that children aren't allowed to participate. *Safari Par Excellence* turns the tables with their **Kids Stuff day out**, pitched at three- to fifteen-year-olds, which bars adults. For US$40 they promise that "well-trained and patient guides and couriers" will take your offspring off your hands from dawn to dusk. The day includes a game drive, and a child-centred tour of the Falls area; and there's breakfast at the Zambezi Nature Sanctuary plus a picnic lunch.

Village visits

The majority of Zimbweans still live rural subsistence lives, yet most visitors leave the country without having set foot in a typical village outside some artificial romanticized reconstructions. *Baobab Safaris* offer the chance to correct the stereotypes, to find out how people really live and to meet them. The tour, established with a village development committee (a proportion of the fee goes to the village), takes you to **Monde**, 14km from Victoria Falls. Here you'll learn about traditional building methods, sample indigenous foods, meet a healer, visit the fields and talk to crafts people. The tours, which run from 8am to 1pm by arrangement, cost US$35 per person and can be booked directly through *Baobab Safaris* (☎/fax 4283) or any agent at Victoria Falls.

Outward bound and adventure activities

Victoria Falls has become a major centre for **outward bound and adventure activities**. Whitewater rafting established itself in the 1980s as an attraction to rival the Falls themselves. It has since been joined by kayaking, horseback game-viewing, foot safaris, bungee-jumping, mountain biking, walking safaris and even skydiving.

Whitewater rafting

Riding the rapids has become one of Zimbabwe's biggest attractions, rivalling even the Falls themselves in popularity. The section starting in the gorge is reckoned to be the most exciting one-day commercial trip in the world, and despite the well-publicized deaths – averaging about two a year since 1992 – punters keep coming in increasing numbers. In fact, the run is reckoned to be relatively safe for its level of difficulty, almost as if it has been designed especially for rafting. The eighteen **rapids**, including several grade fives (the most difficult commercially runnable category) are immediately followed by stretches of calm in which "long swimmers" (people who have fallen overboard and gone adrift) can be quickly retrieved. This combines the maximum adrenaline surge with a relative degree of safety. And, if at times you feel like the ball in a massive pinball machine, the names given to the rapids – Devil's Toilet Bowl, Gnashing Jaws of Death, Overland Truck Eater, Terminator and Oblivion – do nothing to dispel the sensation.

Most people go down in a **highsider**, an inflatable steered by a trained oarsman who does all the work while you do little more than cling on, shift your weight when instructed, and occasionally fall out. If this all sounds too passive, you could opt for a **paddle raft**, in which the passengers help to steer using paddles. Given a well co-ordinated team, this is a more precise way to navigate the rapids, which means the raft is less likely to flip over than a highsider. But because you have to perch on the edge of the craft, leaning out to paddle, you're much more likely to get thrown out. Whichever way you do the trip, though, the most strenuous part is the steep 230-metre climb out the gorge at the end of the day.

The **Zimbabwe** stretch starts at rapid 4, and has the advantage of avoiding the bureaucracy of the border crossing. But if you're set on doing the full run, opt for a trip starting in **Zambia**; most operators can arrange to get you there. Zimbabwe-based rafting outfits *Frontiers, Safari Par Excellence* and *Shearwater* have trips on both sides of the river, while *Sobek* operates only on the Zambian side; only *Safari Par Excellence* and *Sobek* offer both paddle rafts and highsiders. One-day trips cost around US$90. Book well in advance to ensure getting on; weekends are invariably fully reserved by Zimbabweans. The "high-water" trips go from mid-January to March and during June and July, and the "low-water" runs (when, naturally, the rapids are at their fiercest) from August to sometime in December or January, depending on river levels. No rafting takes place in April or May.

Besides scrambling down to it and walking, rafting is the only way you'll get into the hundred-metre deep **Batoka Gorge**, which had never been navigated until *Sobek* achieved it in 1981. Apart from day trips, there are two-day and week-long **marathon excursions** right the way through the gorge to the mouth of the **Matetsi River**, near Deka – special but expensive trips that only operate in August, September and October. A third of the way through, you come to the **Moemba Falls**, which are exceptionally beautiful even if they're nothing on the scale of the big ones. They're also very rarely visited; few people even know of their existence and there are no marked roads in the vicinity, just 4WD tracks.

Kayaking

One of the most interesting of Vic Falls' aquatic attractions is **kayaking** on the white water of the Upper Zambezi. Run under the supervision of licensed guides, the sport's emphasis on seeing and feeling the wild distinguishes it from the more immediate buzz offered by rafting.

Trips include walking on islands, and looking at flora and fauna as well as paddling. And, of course, there's the intermittent frisson of riding those churning rapids. Craft on one-day trips are stable two-person inflatables, and on longer excursions are solid and well-balanced klepper canoes – so don't worry about the constant duckings novices might experience in faster but less stable eskimo-style kayaks. And should you end up in the Zambezi, you'll be soaked but safe – guides and assistants are on hand to haul you out if you capsize. Under the guidance of these trained professionals you can be assured that safety is primary and also that you'll get first-class commentary on local natural history.

One popular trip takes two-and-a-half days. The first afternoon offers a long game drive through the Zambezi National Park to get to the first night's camp. Each night is spent under canvas in two-person tents; camps are prepared ahead with meals cooked by camp staff. During the day, your belongings are carried by vehicle to the next evening's stop while you travel light on the river. You'll paddle along extensive stretches between rapids with the chance of seeing the national park's wildlife from the water. Elephants are plentiful along this stretch, and birdwatchers will particularly relish the chance of floating close to the local waterfowl.

Kandahar Safaris runs both **whitewater canoeing** and **canoe adventure** safaris between April and October inclusive. Whitewater trips last anything from half a day (too rushed) up to three days, with prices from US$60. The three-day Kazungula to Victoria Falls trip runs only from April to the end of June and costs about US$400. *Kandahar's* adventure safaris are equally divided between walking and canoeing, with prices starting at just under US$120 for one day and US$600 for four. Similar trips are operated by *Frontiers*.

Foot safaris

Foot safaris are a lot more interesting than driving around in search of game. Though you'll actually see fewer animals than on a drive, because you cover less ground, what you do see is more intensely witnessed. There's nothing like hearing branches cracking next to you and glimpsing the horns of a buffalo as it turns tail and crashes into the thicket.

Guides are reassuringly armed and the stringent standards necessary to obtain a licence in Zimbabwe ensure they're able not only to halt a charging elephant, but also know everything you ever wanted to know about the bush. Before you set out, there's an interesting safety talk about what to do if you meet a lion or encounter enraged buffalo, elephant or rhino. In reality you probably won't have such encounters, but the thought certainly keeps you on your toes. All walks include meals or refreshments in beautiful spots on the river bank.

Backpacker's Africa (book through *Safari Par Excellence*) have some of the most exciting foot safaris anywhere in Zimbabwe, including trips and activities offered by no one else. Apart from their standard backed-up safaris, where a vehicle carries the luggage while you walk unencumbered, they run intrepid excursions (by prior arrangement) for outward-bound types who want to carry all their own stuff. The advantage of this, of course, is that you can go deep into places vehicles can't reach. They take substantial foot safaris (backed-up) into the dramatic broken country of rarely visited **Chizarira National Park** (see p.125) – great fun and highly recommended. Most ambitious is their twelve-day **Tundazi Trail**, which takes in Chizarira, Kazuma Pan and Zambezi National Park as well as Hwange. They, along with *Khangela Safaris*, are virtually the only operators allowed to walk in an undeveloped region of water seeps, which are the only year-round source of natural water in the vast game reserve, and consequently a great attraction to Hwange's wildlife.

Kalambeza Safaris have standard packages, from morning walks in the Zambezi National Park to three-day safaris in Kazuma Pan (see p.179). They'll usually take a minimum of two people and pick you up wherever you're staying. **Prices** start at around US$75 for a half-day walk, rising to US$200 per day for longer fully inclusive safaris.

Horse safaris

Another prime way to see game is on **horseback**. The *Zambezi Horse Trails* outings give a rare chance to see the bush, accompanied by informed commentary. Two-hour rides start at the outskirts of town and follow the river to end up at the national park boundary.

Full-day rides last from 9.30am until 4pm and include lunch, and for experienced riders an overnight outing is also available. Prices start at around US$35 for two-and-a-half-hour rides, which are open to novices. For the experienced, the choice ranges from half-day rides to four-night fully backed-up safaris, with prices from US$50. Bookings can be made through *Safari Par Excellence*.

Mountain bike trails

With horseback safaris becoming almost commonplace, seeing a lion from the saddle of a bike would be a yarn worth relating. *Safari Par Excellence* runs half-day mountain-bike trips along the river and into the bush. Led by a trainee professional guide, they are a novel way to see wildlife and learn something about the local flora and fauna. And if you do ride into that big cat, remember, out here they have right of way.

Bungee jumping

In keeping with the town's gung-ho image is *African Extreme*'s 111-metre plunge from the Victoria Falls Bridge, the highest commercial bungee jump in the world. If voluntarily hurtling into a gorge tethered to the end of an elastic band (albeit a thick one) sounds dangerous, rest assured that there have been no deaths so far. There have, however, been reports of spinal injuries, and even detached retinas. At US$90, it will probably be the most expensive ten seconds of your life.

Skydiving

More conventional than bungee jumping, and arguably more rewarding, are the two types of **sky dives** offered by *Zambezi Vultures Skydivers Club*. If you want the thrill of free falling from 3000 metres, but not the hassle of training, try the tandem jump, where you are harnessed to an instructor. After about 30 seconds, the parachute opens and you canopy ride for about five minutes before coming in for a piggyback landing, in which the instructor takes the full weight. Alternatively, opt for a one-day course that usually allows you to jump by mid-afternoon. You leave the plane at about 1000 metres, attached by a static line that opens the chute automatically. Tandem jumps cost US$150; the day training and jump is US$105, with the option of additional dives for US$20.

Eating and drinking in Victoria Falls

The hotel dining rooms and terraces pose stiff competition to the growing number of restaurants springing up in town. All of the hotels offer à la carte menus with something affordable for lunch, as well as midday and evening braais; of those in the centre, *Ilala* has the best reputation for food. Most of the restaurants, cafés and takeaways are concentrated around the arcades in Parkway.

The Boma, *Victoria Falls Safari Lodge* complex, 2.5 km from the centre. Popular and frequently full: good-value outdoor breakfast, lunch and dinner menus, including excellent eat-as-much-as-you-like evening braais that come with a huge choice of meats, salads and first-class desserts for under US$10. A cheaper vegetarian alternative is also available. Without a car you can hop on the hourly *Victoria Falls Safari Lodge* shuttle bus or take an inexpensive taxi.

The Cattleman Steakhouse, Pumula Centre, Clark Rd. The ultimate place to eat any cut of beef you can think of, served in a variety of sauces; moderately priced.

Naran's, Sopers Arcade in Parkway. Not a place to linger, but one of the town's cheapest places to eat, serving vegetable curries and good *sadza*.

The Pink Baobab, Parkway. Vic Falls' only attempt at a café serves breakfasts, snacks, light meals, teas and coffees throughout the day, and is a congenial venue for postcard writing.

Pizza Bistro, Sopers Arcade in Parkway. The best pizzas in town – although there's not exactly stiff competition – with an entrepreneurial delivery service: they'll even take pizzas to your tent door in the municipal campsite.

Wimpy, Parkway and Livingstone Way. Better beef burgers than you might expect, but otherwise the usual bland stuff from this worldwide franchise.

Zambezi Nature Sanctuary, Parkway, just before Zambezi National Park. Green and pleasant lunchtime snack venue that provides a countryside alternative to the town joints.

Victoria Falls nightlife

At Victoria Falls, **nightlife** is generally synonymous with drinking, but there are a few alternatives. High rollers should check out the **casinos** at the *Elephant Hills* and *Makasa Sun* hotels, where you'll be relieved of your remaining cash even faster than usual for the Falls. More educational is a potentially fascinating **night game drive** onto a private reserve, though after five hours beetling about in the bush trying to make out animals in the spotlight, the trip can become something of an ordeal. Most drives include a stop at a bush enclosure, where you're served a dinner of hot dogs with a choice of umpteen sauces in the dark. Sightings of hyenas and other nocturnals rarely encountered during the day are almost guaranteed.

Tribal dancing, by contrast, is short and sweet, with performances nightly from 7pm to 8pm at the *Falls Craft Village* and the *Victoria Falls Hotel*. The masks are impressive and the stilt dancing particularly worth seeing; a brief explanation precedes each performance, putting the dances in some kind of context. If you prefer taking part rather than observing, the very un-African *Down Time* **disco** at *Ilala Lodge* is the place to go.

Bars

Bona fide bars are a rarity at the Falls, but the phenomenon is now beginning to catch on. This doesn't mean it's a dry place – quite the opposite. Every one of the hotels has at least one drinking hole, while some have several. Surprisingly, though, few seem to make anything of the superb views on their doorsteps. If you want to enjoy the river with your drink, your best bet is one of the many booze cruises that float along the Upper Zambezi every evening (see p.171 for details).

Explorers, Sopers Arcade, Parkway. Loud and lively joint, with whitewater videos and pounding music, where the rafters hang out after a hard day on the river. Midday and evening meals served.

Makasa Sun Hotel. Noted for its top-floor bar, with the best views across the gorge and into Zambia.

Victoria Falls Hotel. The antithesis of *Explorers*, offering sedate terrace drinks with views of the bridge and the spray rising into the reddening sky. The quietest place to drink in town.

Victoria Falls Safari Lodge. The bar on the impressive timber deck overlooks the hotel's floodlit private waterhole, where in the dry season you stand a chance of seeing major African wildlife.

Listings

Air Zimbabwe (☎4136) has offices in the main administrative block, Livingstone Way, opposite the *Makasa Sun*.

Airport ☎4250.

Banks In the same block as *Air Zimbabwe* in Livingstone Way. Open Mon, Tues, Thurs & Fri 8am–3pm, Wed 8am–1pm & Sat 8–11.30am. There are also bureaux de change in Parkway.

Bicycle rental At *Avis* garage, Livingstone Way adjacent to the *Makasa Sun Hotel*; outside the campsite at *Michael's* in Parkway; outside the *Victoria Falls Hotel*; at the *Sprayview Hotel* or at *Randdik Enterprises*, 309 Parkway.

Car rental *Avis*, Livingstone Way, adjacent to the *Makasa Sun Hotel* (☎4532), and *Hertz* on Parkway (☎4267–8).

Doctor Victoria Falls Surgery, West Drive, off Parkway (☎4319; Mon–Fri 7.30am–4pm).

Emergencies ☎99.

Hospital Pioneer Rd (☎4692–3).

Laundrette Opposite the Publicity Association on Hertz corner.

Police Livingstone Way, open Mon–Fri 8am–4pm, Sat 8–11.30am (☎4206 or 4401).

Taxi rank Sopers Arcade, behind *Spar* supermarket (☎4529).

Telephones Cardphones are to be found outside the post office and at the campsite.

Zambezi National Park

Daily 6am–6.30pm. Admission fee US$2.

Six kilometres upstream from the Falls begins the **ZAMBEZI NATIONAL PARK**, the most accessible area of the Upper Zambezi, with the possibility of getting in on your own, so long as you have transport. You can ride rented bikes to lodges at the park's edge, but not into the park itself. Take Parkway, which becomes a narrow strip road with bush all around; pass the *Elephant Hills Hotel* and, at the point when the *A'Zambezi* appears on your right, you're nearly there.

The park is best known for its large herds of **sable antelope**. Elephants and rhinos are gratifyingly common and kudu, impala, waterbuck, zebra, lion, leopard and hyena are all about for the conscientious spotter. **With a car**, there are lovely riverside **picnic sites** where you can recline in palmy shade and contemplate the flow, although increasing numbers of boats and planes are spoiling the peace. The odd fruits under the palm trees that look like cricket balls or exotic animal droppings are the remains of **mulala fruits**, much prized by elephants. They eat them whole, digesting the succulent outer fruit and depositing the inner seed in a ready-made grow-bag. Remarkably, the old seasonal elephant migration routes are marked by effectively dispersed cross-country lines of ilala palms. In the riverine woods you'll also find ebony trees, figs and *Acacia albida*.

There are two main **roads** through the park, the most popular being the Zambezi Drive which continues past the lodges along the river. The other option is to take the turn-off 6km south of town on the Bulawayo road to join the Chamabonda Drive, which follows the course of the Masuwe River. Provided you've prebooked with National Parks in Victoria Falls (see p.163), you can spend the night on the Chamabanda viewing platform, overlooking a waterhole; full moon is the best time.

The National Parks lodges

Facing the Zambezi, National Parks' wonderful self-catering **lodges** (②) are laid out for maximum isolation – with riverine forest separating each – so you really do feel alone. In the swathes cleared between lodge and river you'll spot buck, monkeys, warthogs and plenty of birds. Occasionally, **elephants** stray into the lodge gardens and in the dry season they sometimes swim across from the mainland to the islands of Lwanda and Kalunda opposite the lodges, midway between Zimbabwe and Zambia.

The lodges (book ahead, as usual, through the Harare office) are almost always full, but it might be worth going there in the afternoon to check for vacancies if you're feeling lucky. Close by, and relieving a little of the pressure for places to stay, are the Zimbabwe National Army's **chalets** (☎113/4273; ②). These are considerably newer and have two bedrooms, but are not always available, as army officials sometimes use the camp. Bring all your food from the Falls or eat at the *A'Zambezi*.

There are **walks** along the river in front of the lodges. Keep your eyes peeled for smaller animals: **turtles** bask on the banks and splash waterwards for safety and you can even see baby **crocodiles** on tree branches that stroke the water's surface. Beware any bigger specimens, and the occasional elephant that wanders through.

Birds are also prolific: cormorants, darters and kingfishers perch on half-submerged dead trees waiting for the right fish to swim by. Hadedas wander about on the grassy margins; the name of these large grey birds is inspired by their raucous call, a familiar Zambezi sound.

Fishing camps

The National Parks **fishing camps**, further up the river off the Zambezi Drive, are in wilder locations than the lodges. You don't have to go fishing to enjoy the magnificence of the undisturbed bush and river, but tough nerves and excellent bush knowledge are required to enjoy sleeping virtually in the open. It's a thoroughly recommended experience, but you'll need your own transport to get there.

Of the camps, **Kandahar** (a few kilometres upstream from *A'Zambezi Lodge*) is open throughout the year. Further upstream, **Mpala Jena** (17km) and **Sansimba** (30km) are open during the dry season only (May–Oct). Facilities are basic: concrete shelters, cold showers, flush toilet and drinking taps. There are braai places, and you can buy limited firewood at reception, but take your own cooking gear. They all need to be booked in advance at the Central Booking Office in Victoria Falls (see p.163).

Kazuma Pan National Park

KAZUMA PAN, south of the Falls on the Botswana border, was first opened to the public in 1987 and you can still only visit with a licensed guide. There's no accommodation here – it remains strictly a wilderness area. The landscape in the 315-square-kilometre park is unique in Zimbabwe but similar to the great pans in Botswana – miles of treeless, open grassland rich in game. The depression is surrounded by dense teak forests and well watered with streams and rock pools.

Backpacker's Africa (book through *Safari par Excellence*; ☎113/2051–4, fax 4510) will pick you up at the Falls for three-day **expeditions** to the Pan. You may see rare species such as roan antelope, gemsbok, tsessebe, cheetah, black rhino, bat-eared fox and wild dogs as well as lions, elephants and buffalos. About the only animals you won't see here are hippopotamuses. The "Tundazi Trail" expeditions operated by *Backpacker's* tack Kazuma onto Hwange, Chizarira and the Zambezi National Park if you want a longer trip. Another way to see the park is to join *Wild Horizon's* camping trail (PO Box 159, Victoria Falls; ☎113/4219), which goes between their two camps, Jijima, near Hwange, and Imbalala, near the Falls, taking in Kazuma en route. The trip costs US$200 per person per day all in.

When the **pans fill** – as they do every few years – you'll see an extraordinary variety of **waterbirds**. Montagu's harriers are frequent visitors and the rare wattled crane actually breeds in the park. One of Kazuma's curiosities is a small variety of **fish** – as yet unidentified – which remains dormant during dry years and becomes active when it's wet. How this species survives prolonged drought is a mystery.

OVER THE BORDER

Victoria Falls is the closest town to the junction of Zimbabwe and three of its neighbours. **Botswana**'s main cross-border attraction is Chobe National Park, easily reached by road at Kasane – which is also the gateway to the Caprivi Strip, the onward corridor to **Namibia** and Botswana's **Western Okavango Delta**. And **Zambia**, just a few hundred metres across the Zambezi, is easy to visit for the day or even a couple of hours.

Into Zambia

Most visitors can get a special one-day pass without undue formality to cross to the **Zambian side of the Falls**; non-Commonwealth passport holders, however, need a visa, issued at the border for US$10. The border is open from 6am to 6pm, and the distance easily walkable, but allow plenty of time to clear both sets of Customs and Immigration. For travellers on tight budgets, crossing to the Zambian side may be the only option if the campsite and chalets at Victoria Falls are full.

Zambia, formerly Northern Rhodesia, had a special place in the demonology of the last generation of Rhodesians and continued into the 1990s to exert a morbid fascination in some circles south of the border. The supposed breakdown of civilization after Independence in 1964 was considered living proof of the need for eternal white rule. Kenneth Kaunda, president until 1991, was branded by many Rhodesians and South Africans as a Marxist bent on destroying Christian values.

While, in retrospect, Kaunda led his country down the dead-end road of one-party corruption and mismanagement, he appears to have retained more personal integrity than most other African leaders. Kaunda was a devout Christian, if a misguided one, who tried to synthesize Christianity and Socialism into an authentically African philosophy that he dubbed "Humanism".

That Kaunda left Zambia in a shambles is indisputable. But some credit is due to him for the gracious – and for Africa virtually unprecedented – way in which he peacefully accepted the people's judgement and stood down after being defeated in democratic elections by Frederick Chiluba.

The Zambian Falls

Dawn to dusk. Admission fee US$2.
Once in Zambia, head for **Knife Edge Point** which is, without doubt, the most awesome view of the Falls. You reach it on a path that winds down to a slippery, spray-dashed footbridge and onto an island of high ground where the water roars deafeningly around you. You can also descend to the very bottom of the **Boiling Pot** gorge and watch from a safe distance as the powerful river surges into a terrific whirlpool.

These oblique views from Zambia are very different from the head-on aspect from the Zimbabwean side, and the gorges are displayed with much more clarity. The "tourist show" on this side of the Falls, however, is more tattered: no well-kept national park to grace the scene here, just a half-broken, sad memorial plinth to the Northern Rhodesian war dead. The **Field Museum**, built around a small archeological dig, has prehistoric hand tools and elementary wall displays of information about local finds.

Next door, the **Craft Village** – its stall holders desperate to sell – offers much run-of-the-mill stuff, but also some items that are quite different from Zimbabwean craftwork. There's excellent **basketry** and colourfully decorated **wooden guinea fowls**. And if you're into bartering, take along any spare clothes, particularly T-shirts, as they are much sought after.

Near the boat club, departure point for the Zambian sundowner cruises, lies the **Mosi oa Tunya National Park**. As parks go, this is rather pitiful and really doesn't merit a visit unless you're not planning to visit any of the far better reserves nearby. *Makora Quest Safaris* in Livingstone (☎321679) do day trips to the park, museums and historical parts of the town.

Livingstone

For a peek at Zambia proper, make a sortie into **LIVINGSTONE**, 11km on from the Zambian side of the Falls. Now run down, this former Falls capital remains a more convincing urban centre than its upstart successor in Zimbabwe. Its main attraction is the **National Museum**, which displays a host of beautiful artefacts from all over Africa.

Mosi oa Tunya Road runs all the way from the border, slicing through Livingstone's centre. About halfway, you pass the **Maramba Cultural Centre**. The weekend **traditional dancing** here, from 3pm until 5pm, draws tourists and locals. There are also performances on Fridays between June and October, and it works out cheaper than the "Africa Spectacular" at the *Victoria Falls Hotel*.

Once across the Maramba River, you meet Livingstone's industrial suburbs trailing into the countryside. You'll know you're close to the **centre** of town when you can hear shouts from the sidewalks offering packets of Zambian *kwacha* for dollars. People openly play the black market here, and you'll often be approached.

Getting there

Getting to Livingstone is easiest with a rented **bike**, but if this sounds too much like hard work, get one of the frequent Livingstone **buses**, or catch a **taxi** from the craft market on the Zambian side. Another way, slow but direct, is to take the thirty-minute

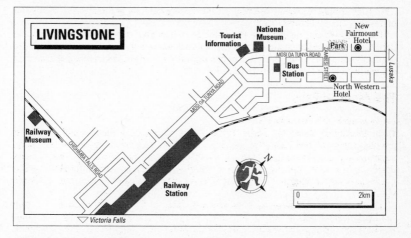

train ride across the bridge from Victoria Falls station to Livingstone. A twice-daily passenger coach is tagged to the back of a goods train and immigration formalities are done en route, cutting out the border delays.

Accommodation

If Victoria Falls is booked out, you may have no option but to cross the border and stay in Livingstone, which fortunately has some cheap **hotels** and a **campsite**, as well as a wide choice of transport links back to the Falls. See p.161 for the Zambia and Livingstone telephone codes.

Maramba River Campsite and Caravan Park (Livingstone ☎324189, or contact *Kalai Safaris* at Vic Falls on ☎113/2168). Situated 5km from the border in the Mosi oa Tunya National Park (the turn-off is at the Maramba Cultural Centre). Braai packs are available, or else take your own food. ①.

New Fairmount Hotel, Mosi oa Tunya Rd, beyond the park (☎730726). One of Livingstone's more salubrious hotels. ③.

North Eastern Mansions Hotel, Zambezi St (diagonally opposite the *Northwestern*). Cheapest place to stay in town; clean enough, but nothing special. ②.

North Western Hotel, bottom of Zambezi St (☎320711). A recently renovated Edwardian building. ③.

Triangle Hotel, near the bus station. Inexpensive, and convenient if you're travelling overland to Kafue and Chirundu. ①.

The National Museum

Daily 9am–4.30pm. Admission fee US$5.

The **National Museum** is a peculiar place, containing some of the most interesting ethnological items in the region, yet with little explanation – stimulating and mystifying by turn. Helpful Zambian visitors, however, might offer illumination – this is the country's main museum and highly popular. Among its many and various collections are displays of weaponry, hunting equipment, reconstructed villages and the cape, trunk, thermometer and surgical instruments of David Livingstone.

The collection of **religious fetishes** is fascinating and ghoulish. There's also a very fine range of **Tonga artefacts** from the Gwembe Valley, collected before it was flooded to create Kariba, including head rests, stools and a finely decorated waist-high drum used to send long-distance messages at night.

On the ground floor, one of the most interesting exhibits is the **Broken Hill Man of Kabwe**, a copy of the 110,000-year-old Neanderthal skull found in 1921. The original was stolen by the British and the Zambians are still trying to get it back. In return, the British want David Livingstone's case and instruments – negotiations continue.

In the same part of the museum as the Livingstone memorabilia are some revealing old **photographs**. Don't miss the picture of four Arab traders examining an African slave. The hopeless look on the manacled man's face is tangibly painful, while the arrogance of those around has to be seen to be believed. Nearer the present, the story of Zambia's **path to Independence** is told through press cuttings and photos.

The Railway Museum

Daily 10am–5.30pm. Nominal admission fee.

The turning to the **Railway Museum** is clearly signposted on your left as you approach the centre of town. Opened in 1987, it aims to educate Zambians about the importance of the railways. A yard full of decrepit coaches and engines lets everyone indulge childhood fantasies; clamber up and fiddle with the knobs or walk down the corridors of decaying carriages.

Inside, rooms full of antique rail souvenirs evoke the old days: wood and brass morse code machines and gleaming brass signal lamps. Exhibits also give accounts of the development of railways in Europe and Africa along with loads of photos.

Into Botswana: Chobe

Botswana's **Chobe National Park** is Africa's top **elephant sanctuary**, with a population estimated at as many as 50,000 (for further details, see Chapter Eight). Touching Botswana's river-bounded northern frontier, the parts near Zimbabwe consist of beautiful flood plain with abundant birds and the continent's southernmost population of **red lechwe** antelope.

Afroventures and *UTC* are among the operators in Victoria Falls that offers transfers to Botswana; they'll drop you off at any of the hotels or lodges in **Kasane**, just outside the game reserve. *UTC* also offers an expensive one-day excursion to Chobe – or two days for the well-heeled, with an overnight at the exclusive *Chobe Game Lodge*. A better option perhaps is to go with a trained guide, on one of *Ultimate Africa Safaris'* one-day Chobe trips. The big hotels at Vic Falls also offer transfers for clients to the Chobe lodges and hotels; drivers are sometimes prepared to carry passengers on an informal basis for a small fee.

HWANGE NATIONAL PARK

Once regarded as a vast wasteland, useless for farming, **HWANGE NATIONAL PARK** is now Zimbabwe's premier wildlife showcase. During August, September and October, the **game watching** can be truly spectacular: the park has a shifting population of around 40,000 elephants, and a huge variety of animals and birds. And the great advantage of Hwange is that it is accessible, whether on a tour or doing it your own way – using National Park's budget accommodation or staying in one of the many privately run safari camps. Hwange's thornbush, savannah, mopane and teak forests aren't as spectacular as the landscapes of the great East African parks – there are no huge mountains, craters or vast plains – but the bush savannah has its own striking beauty, the tracks are considerably less worn and you'll be able to see much the same game without thousands of tourists dogging your heels.

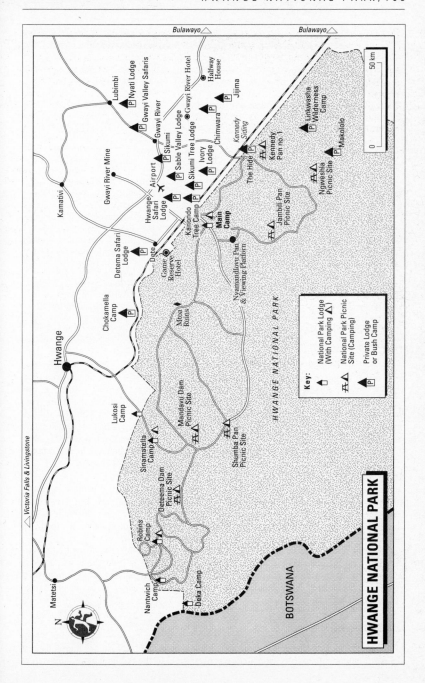

HWANGE NATIONAL PARK

Bulawayo △

Bulawayo △

50 km

0

Lubimbi
Nyati Lodge
Gwayi Valley Safaris
Gwayi River
Halfway House
Jijima
Gwayi River Hotel
Linkwasha Wilderness Camp
Sikumi
Makololo
Sable Valley Lodge
Ivory Lodge
Sikumi Tree Lodge
Chimwara
Kennedy Siding
Kennedy Pan no. 1
The Hide
Gwayi River Mine
Kamativi
Hwange Safari Lodge
Ngweshla Picnic Site
Kanondo Tree Camp
Jambili Pan Picnic Site
Detema Safari Lodge
Dete
Main Camp
Game Reserve Hotel
Nyamandlovu Pan & Viewing Platform
Hwange
Chokamella Camp
HWANGE NATIONAL PARK
Mtoa Ruins
Lukosi Camp
Sinamatella Camp
Mandavu Dam Picnic Site
Shumba Pan Picnic Site
Deteema Dam Picnic Site
Robins Camp
Nantwich Camp
Deka Camp
Matetsi
BOTSWANA

Victoria Falls & Livingstone △

Key:

National Park Lodge (With Camping △)

National Park Picnic Site (Camping)

Private Lodge or Bush Camp

TIPS FOR GAME VIEWING AT HWANGE

Hwange's highest concentrations of game occur during the **dry season** (May–Oct) when animals congregate around the pans. Once the rains come and there's surface water they disperse all over the park, while long grass after the start of the rains tends to screen the animals from view.

If you plan to do some serious game viewing, it is well worth getting hold of some **field guides** (see "Books", p.402, for recommendations).

• **Binoculars** are a must for scanning the horizon when you're out viewing. Don't try consciously to spot animals – many are well disguised. Instead, watch for any movement or something that strikes you as a bit out of place. Driving really slowly also pays off, particularly if you stop often. You can sometimes see more in a stationary hour alongside a pan than in a day's frantic driving.

• **Viewing platforms** at the major pans frequently provide the best chance to see something. High off the ground they give good, unobscured panoramas of the surroundings. All animals have to drink at some time.

• Early morning is the best **time of day** for animal watching, when you'll see some of the nocturnals slinking off and others feeding before they hide away in the shade. Dusk is almost as good and certainly the best time to see elephants drinking. The usual pattern for safari operators is two game drives a day: dawn and dusk. An appetite-whetting chart at Main Camp reception shows exactly what you'll see when and each beast's cycle: lions, for example, usually drink early, rest in the heat and hunt in the late afternoon.

• Because it's on the edge of the Kalahari, **temperatures** in Hwange are extreme, particularly just before the rains and during the summer dry season when it can soar to the high thirties (°C) during the day. Nights, however, are always cool and in the dry season can drop below freezing. Whatever the season, always take a sweater on game drives, especially in the early morning, and in the dry season an anorak won't come amiss.

It's only fair to point out, however, that you need to have luck on your side if you're dead set on seeing the big cats, or action as exciting as a lion kill. Frustratingly, you may repeatedly hear about the wonderful things seen by others the day before, or the bounding cheetah and the lion cubs you just missed. If you visit during the **rains**, you may not even clock an elephant. There's the story of a foreign tourist who complained that he had spent a whole day in the park and seen nothing except a pair of tortoises; the game ranger replied that he was actually very lucky as they're not often seen in pairs. Don't be too big-game oriented – take your binoculars and a good field guide, and relax.

Some history

On the easternmost edge of the Kalahari, Hwange was formerly peopled by **San** hunter-gatherers able to survive with little water. The national park was created in 1929, largely because the land was hopeless for agriculture, and borehole water pumped into over sixty pans began attracting large numbers of animals. It's to these pans, several of which are around Main Camp, that visitors too are drawn.

Before adventurers and hunters arrived, parts of Hwange formed a royal **Ndebele hunting reserve**. Dete Vlei, where *Hwange Safari Lodge* is now sited, was later a favourite elephant-hunting ground for **Frederick Selous**, most famous of Zimbabwe's Victorian adventurers. Two hunting areas still adjoin the park, where the rich pay thousands to bag trophies.

Orientation

Although Hwange National Park spreads across a total of 14,620 square kilometres of dry bush country, only the eastern edge is accessible to the public. Here many waterholes have been created to attract animals, and roads built for game viewing – all sand surfaces apart from 10km of tar at Main Camp. The dams, or **pans** as they're more usually known, are pumped with water throughout the year and remain the best places to spot animals. Surrounding the park boundaries are buffer zones, massive tracts of land used for forestry, game ranching and safaris, as well as hunting. The park itself is not fenced, and animals wander freely between it and the buffer zones, mostly attracted by the availability of water. Almost all of the safari camps lie outside the park boundaries, some a few minutes from one of the park entry gates, others up to an hours' drive away. The three major National Parks camps – Main Camp, Sinamatella and Robins – act as the **main entry points** into the park (daily 6am–6.30pm; admission fee US$2).

Hwange National Park is served by three small towns, each with a hotel and petrol. Near the park's northeastern border, **Gwayi River** is the main halfway stop between Bulawayo and Victoria Falls, consisting of little more than the *Gwayi River Hotel*, at kilometre peg 247 (PO Box 9, Dete; ☎118/3400; ④), an old-style country lodge with a lingering colonial charm. It boasts a pool, pleasant walks and a pottery at the back that allows children to work with clay. A couple of safari companies run game drives from here into the park for around US$18; enquire at reception. In addition, coach operators make a stop here for tea before pulling into *Hwange Safari Lodge* and the final leg to Hwange town and Victoria Falls. Don't confuse the *Gwayi* with the *Halfway House Hotel* (③), closer to Bulawayo at kilometre peg 222, which has functional, small chalets and a 24-hour service station.

Hwange National Park should not be confused with **Hwange Town**, a stifling coal-mining town of absolutely no interest. Named after a local Rozvi chief, it had the undignified colonial misspelling of Wankie – which it shared with the game park. If you need to stay in Hwange Town, head for the *Baobab Hotel* (☎181/323; ③) on top of a hill on the Bulawayo side of town; it's very pleasant and good value.

The third settlement is **Dete**, 19km northwest of Main Camp, built around the railway station serving the park. Many of the park's and safari industry's workers live at Dete, which has a post office, shops selling basics, and the seedy *Game Reserve Hotel* near the station (PO Box 32, Dete; ☎118/331; ②). Although it's the cheapest hotel in the area, it's geared more for workers partying than for serving as a base to go game viewing in the park.

Getting there

Reasonably priced *Air Zimbabwe* **flights** connect Harare, Kariba and Victoria Falls to Hwange daily – if you buy a return ticket from Harare to Hwange, you can stop off at Kariba and Victoria Falls at no extra cost. **By road**, the park is two-and-a-half hours from Victoria Falls, and three from Bulawayo, on an excellent and lightly trafficked highway, which, however, has virtually no settlements en route – petrol and facilities are only available at Gwayi River and Hwange Town. The **coach** that runs almost every day between Victoria Falls and Bulawayo, stopping off at *Hwange Safari Lodge*, the park's unofficial arrival terminus, is preferable to the Bulawayo–Victoria Falls **train**, which arrives in the middle of the night at Dete, 19km from Main Camp.

By road

Of the three Hwange National Park camps, which serve as entry gates into the park itself, **Main Camp** in the northeast is the most popular and usual route in, straightforward to reach on tarred road, 31km from the Bulawayo–Victoria Falls road. Without a car, this is the only realistic camp to make for. The easiest way to get to Main Camp on public transport is to take one of the *Blue Arrow* or *Ajay* **luxury coaches** running between Bulawayo and Victoria Falls, which drop passengers at *Hwange Safari Lodge*. They make an additional stop at *Gwayi River Lodge*, useful if you're being collected by one of the safari operators in that area. To get to Main Camp from *Hwange Safari Lodge*, hop on the *UTC* game drive, or hitch. There is also a *Hertz* office at the lodge, where you can **rent a car**, mainly for use around Main Camp where the roads are good. **Economy buses** which run along the Bulawayo–Victoria Falls road do not deviate to *Hwange Safari Lodge*, so get off at the turn-off known locally as Safari Cross, and hitch south towards Main Camp. While you can thumb a lift to Main Camp, hitching into the park itself is not allowed, nor is walking or cycling. *Shamwari Safaris* (☎118/248) do reasonably priced transfers, for a group up to seven, from *Hwange Safari Lodge*, Safari Cross and Gwayi River to Main Camp, if arranged in advance; *Shamwari* can also be contacted to provide transfers from Dete station, Hwange airport and the Kariba ferry terminal at Mlibizi.

An alternative route into the park, but not recommended if you're trying to hitch, is to go via **Sinamatella Camp**. The turn-off, just south of Hwange Town, leads on to 45km of fairly good dirt road, with sparse traffic. Alternatively, you can drive from Main Camp through the park itself to Sinamatella, which will take the best part of the day with game viewing all the way. **Robins Camp** is nearer Victoria Falls, in the north-west section of the park – the turn-off is 48km north of Hwange Town, leaving 70km of variable dirt road to Robins.

By train

Taking the **train** to the park's nearest station at Dete is a poor idea. From Victoria Falls it's timetabled to arrive at Dete at 00.13am; coming from Bulawayo, it pulls in at the even more inconvenient time of 1.26am. In any case the precision suggested by these times can't be relied on. If you're intent on this approach, the *Game Reserve Hotel* (☎118/366; ③), 300m from the station, has cheap rooms, but you're advised by phone to tell them you're coming, otherwise you'll find it closed. Once the park's only hotel, it's now run-down and the favoured drinking spot for all the railway workers. With prior warning, *Hwange Safari Lodge* and other camps will meet guests at the station; *Wildside Backpackers Hostel* near Dete (☎118/395) meets every train and offers free transfers.

By air

Flights arrive at Hwange National Park Airport, a few kilometres north of *Hwange Safari Lodge*, and should be booked as far in advance as possible. **Minibuses** operated by *UTC* meet planes and convey passengers to the lodge or Main Camp; although not cheap, the service is well used, so it's a good idea to book ahead from any *UTC* office. The safari camps all meet clients arriving at the airport.

Park accommodation

Hwange provides budget accommodation in its **National Parks chalets** and **self-catering lodges**, built for the local market rather than for foreign tourists, and often full. Booking beforehand through Parks Central Office in Bulawayo or Harare is virtually essential (see box p.46 for addresses), although if you turn up on the off chance you may be lucky – any vacant lodges are let from 4pm onwards. Main Camp has a **campsite**, the only one you can get to without your own car; camping is also permitted at the fenced-in picnic sites inside the park, but needs to be prebooked, as the picnic sites are heavily in demand from mobile safari companies. Further details on each of the National Parks camps are given on pages 190–192. National Parks also have **exclusive camps** near Robins and Sinamatella – not luxurious as the name suggests, but remote camps, very popular with Zimbabweans, that are restricted to the use of one group at a time.

A growing number of **safari camps** operate in land concessions inside the park or in the bordering forest lands and safari areas – as far south as the Gwayi Valley – which all share Hwange's wildlife. All meet their clients at Hwange National Park Airport; you can also arrange to be picked up at *Hwange Safari Lodge*. Several are close to Main Camp and the more crowded part of the park; the camps that use alternative access points to the park, such as Kennedy Gate, promise their guests a more exclusive experience. The top three camps lie deep within the park itself – *Linkwasha*, *Makalolo* and *The Hide*.

Hotels in the service towns of Gwayi River, Hwange Town and Dete are detailed on p.185.

National Parks camps

Main Camp. Situated in the most visited eastern section of the game reserve it has lodges, chalets, cottages and camping. You can cater for yourself using communal electric cooking facilities. Lodges and chalets have electric lights and fridges in each living unit. A bar and restaurant add a touch of comfort and a store sells basic items. Good value if you can get a booking. ①–②.

Robins Camp. In the northwest section of the national park, Robins is most easily reached along a dirt track off the main Hwange–Victoria Falls road; it's 48km from Hwange to the turn-off and a further 70km to the camp itself. Lodges, chalets, camping and an exclusive camp, with a restaurant and bar, and a small grocery store. Game-viewing roads in the vicinity are closed Nov–April (inclusive). *Nantwich Camp*, 11km west and administered from *Robins*, has three two-bedroom lodges. ①–②.

Sinamatella Camp. Take the turning just south of Hwange Town off the main Bulawayo–Hwange road, which soon becomes a dirt track and passes *Mbala Lodge* before continuing the 45km to Sinamatella. The situation on a plateau gives wonderful vistas of the plains below. Similar facilities to Main Camp, including restaurant and bar. ①–②.

National Parks exclusive camps

Sited in the Robins-Sinamatella region, each of Hwange's exclusive camps is bookable by groups of up to twelve who have the entire camp to themselves. **Bumbusi Camp**, 24km northwest of Sinamatella, has four twin A-frame chalets and a cottage. Cooking and washing/toilet facilities are communal. Neighbouring **Lukosi Camp** has similar facilities but is only open November to April outside the hunting season. **Deka Camp**, near Robins, has two family units, a sitting room, a dining room and a kitchen.

National Parks picnic sites

Areas have been fenced off at the following pans: **Deteema**, **Jambili** (near Main Camp), **Kennedy 1**, **Mundavu** (Sinamatella-Robins vicinity), **Shumba** (midway between Main Camp and Sinamatella), and **Ngweshla**. They have outdoor braai facilities and toilets, hand basins and running water. You can **camp overnight**, provided you have a tent – wildlife can, and does on occasion, leap over the chicken wire fencing in the enclosure.

Budget safari camps

Budget safari camps are geared to backpackers and the local market. They come with none of the posh trimmings of the upmarket camps and, taken as a whole, offer a lower standard of guiding.

Nyati Lodge, *Gwayi Valley Safaris*, PO Box 17, Gwayi (☎118/3401). Full-board or self-catering rondavels on a family-run working farm in the Shangani River area, not far from the *Gwayi River Hotel*, with a swimming pool and tennis court. You can get picked up from the *Gwayi River Hotel*, Main Camp or Hwange airport, or drive yourself there (a 4WD is not necessary). Full-day excursions into Hwange Park cost from US$35 per day, less for half-day trips. If you're staying at the National Parks campsite at Main Camp, you can ring *Gwayi Valley Safaris* and join one of their afternoon game drives for US$18.

Kalambeza Lodge, 7km from the *Gwayi River Hotel* in the Gwayi Valley, or 45min from Hwange's Main Camp (*Kalambeza Safaris*, 306 Parkway, Victoria Falls; ☎113/4480, fax 4644). From US$95 per person all in; US$44 for dinner, bed and breakfast only, if you don't do any game activities.

Wildside Backpackers Hostel, Dete (☎/fax 118/395). Decent dorms, chalets and tree lodges conveniently located near the park; camping is also available. Budget game drives into the park, from US$15 for a three-hour trip. Free transfers from Dete station, and at reasonable rates from other locations. ①–③.

Upmarket safari camps

Upmarket safari camps offering all-inclusive packages to no more than twenty guests at a time are located either inside the park boundaries in private concessions, or on private land adjoining the national park. Often in exclusive regions, they have the added attraction of expert guidance once you're there: all employ professional guides and offer expertly directed game drives. Their all-inclusive rates typically include all meals, drinks, snacks, laundry and game-viewing activities, though transfer fees to and from Hwange airport are extra. You can be assured of plenty of pampering, excellent service, and a degree of formality. Closed to casual visitors, the camps should be booked in advance.

Chimwara Camp, *Run Wild*, 8th Floor, Southampton Life Centre, Jason Moyo Ave/Second St, Harare (☎14/795841, fax 795846). Comfortable tent camp on the seasonal Gwayi River, 15km from the *Gwayi River Hotel*, near the Kennedy entrance. Often guides take picnics and spend the day out watching game. Armed walks are done on the large Chimwara property itself, where you'll see mostly plains game, with glimpses of buffalos and lions. Closed during the rainy season. US$180 per person per day.

Chokamella Camp, *Landela Safaris*, PO Box 66293, Kopje, Harare (☎14/734043–6, fax 750785). 35km from Hwange airport, due west of Main Camp entrance. Accommodation for up to 20 people in thatched bungalows set on sand cliffs above the (usually dry) Nkamella River. Their rooms are beautiful and the food excellent, but the camp's best feature is its low ratio of guests to professional guides, who lead walks and drives. One excursion is to the Chakabika area, near Sinamatella, where you may sight some of the few black rhinos left in Hwange, intensively protected by game scouts. US$220 per person per day.

Detema Safari Lodge (book through *UTC*, PO Box 2914, Harare; ☎14/793 7015). Close to Dete, these luxury chalets and tree lodges are a good bet if you're self-driving and want somewhere smaller, with more of a bush feeling, than *Hwange Safari Lodge*. From US$155 per person.

The Hide, Box GD305, Greendale, Harare (☎14/498548 or 495650, fax 498265). One of Hwange's top three camps, *The Hide* boasts an enviable location, right next to the quieter Kennedy Gate park entrance, with plains full of giraffe, wildebeest and zebra. Once you've travelled the 90min from the airport, you don't need to go anywhere else. The safari-style tents accommodate 16 people and the camp has its own waterhole. US$250 per person.

Hwange Safari Lodge, PO Box 5792, Dete (☎118/331). Located outside the park boundaries with all the comfort you'd expect from a luxury three-star establishment with en-suite rooms and drinks by the swimming pool. Game drives are provided and you can watch elephants frolic in the lodge's own drinking hole – ultimately disappointing, though, if you're after a raw experience of the wild. Both the lodge itself and *UTC* run game drives that start here and pull in at Main Camp; the lodge also does game trails on foot when they have a guide available. Non-residents are charged an admission fee, but it could be worth having access to a poolside drink if you've arrived from a long, hot trek. There's also a viewing platform, which overlooks a pan where you'll usually see some game. ⑨.

Ivory Lodge, near Main Camp (booking details as for *Detema*, above). The closest of the lodges to Main Camp, *Ivory* is also one of the most imaginatively conceived. Dispensing with the usual style of tended lawns, it has instead left intact as much as possible of the indigenous bush. The disadvantage is that there are no long views across flattened countryside, but this is more than compensated for by the feeling of being in the wild. Accommodation is in 10 thatched tree houses, each with its own shower and toilet. US$200 per person.

Jijima, overlooking Jijima Vlei on a private estate bordering the national park. Book through *Wild Horizons*, PO Box 159, Victoria Falls (☎113/4219, fax 4349). *Jijima* is owned and operated by a family of two generations of professional guides. If you want to hear ripping yarns about close shaves with lions then this could be just the place. *Jijima* uses the Kennedy Pan – *the* place for lions and less crowded than the Main Camp area – for game viewing. Accommodation is in safari tents under thatched canopies and the number of guests is limited to 16. US$230 per person.

Kanondo Tree Camp, *Touch the Wild*, Private Bag 6, Hillside, Bulwayo (☎19/74589 or 41225, fax 60868). Most rustic of *Touch the Wild*'s camps, with no pools or lawns. Just 20min by vehicle from Hwange airport, it is set among a stand of camel thorn acacias on a private concession next to the game reserve. Six en-suite twin-bedded tree houses are grouped around a central area. Each has its own view of the waterhole which is regularly visited by a special herd of elephants, protected in perpetuity by a presidential decree. US$190 per person.

Katshana Camp, *Touch the Wild* (see *Kanondo* above). Close to the top of Dete Vlei, this camp has six tree houses overlooking a waterhole. Game drives take you into the park, or around the neighbouring estates. US$250 per person.

Linkwasha Wilderness Camp, *Nemba*, PO Box 4, Gwayi (☎118/189 or 271). This camp takes its name from the area in which it stands, four hours' drive through game country from the airport. It's one of the few private bush camps inside Hwange National Park itself. Apart from visiting *Linkwasha* or *Makololo*, there's no other way of seeing this astonishingly beautiful section of Hwange. Vast open plains punctuated with ilala palms and waterholes, which attract profuse game and birdlife, form a landscape that resembles the plains of East Africa more than any other area you're likely to see in Zimbabwe. Probably the most thrilling camp in Zimbabwe, it has played host

TOURS, GAME DRIVES AND WALKS

Getting into the park itself is pretty easy, and not too expensive. Hitching (and cycling) are prohibited in the park, but you may well meet people at Main Camp who have a car and are willing to take you along.

The hassle-free way to see game is to hop on the *UTC* **tourbus** as it calls in at Main Camp. This outing can be frustratingly uninformative and has little to recommend it, but their drivers are old hands at finding animals.

Game drives, operated by *Hwange Safari Lodge*, are more than twice as expensive, but you pay for the knowledge of eagle-eyed guides, who know their stuff. These tours are also more intimate than the *UTC* offerings – not more than eight people in an open Land Rover – and the scouts are in radio contact with each other and alert their colleagues to anything exciting. They're able to answer questions on any aspect of wildlife and local ecology and will often make detours off the tar into parts that are further afield. A list of people offering game drives and whole-day outings may be found at the payphone at Main Camp. Among these, *Shamwari Safaris*, PO Box 53, Dete (☎118/248) has a consistently good reptutation, with reasonably priced excursions in the park from US$35 per person.

National Parks **escorted walks** are great value, going out for an hour or two in a group of no more than six, accompanied by an armed game ranger. Because of their popularity, they are frequently rationed to one outing per person. The guides often do the two-kilometre walk to the hide at Sedina Pan, where you sit a while and watch; few cars ever come here, so it's wonderfully quiet. At the time of a full moon, the Parks also do unmissable **night game-viewing**, when you'll have the chance to see some of the more rarely viewed nocturnal species.

An exciting option is to join one of the **mobile safaris** which make use of National Parks campsites. The great thing is that you stay inside the park at night when most other visitors have returned to their hotels or lodges. Two of the best such operators are *Africa Dawn Safaris*, PO Box 128, Bulawayo (☎19/70488), whose professional guide has a special knowledge of Hwange stretching back two decades (he was based there as a warden and helped build the fence around the park); and *Zindele Safaris*, PO Box 1744, Bulawayo (☎19/64128), who offer a good personalized trip with a cheerful and knowledgeable guide. However, none of the mobile safaris or overland excursions are able to take you on foot into the park: game viewing is done only from vehicles or while sitting at waterholes. For **walking safaris** of two or three days, two companies with professional hunter-guides can be highly recommended: *Khangela Safaris*, PO Box FM 296, Famona, Bulawayo (☎19/49733, fax 68259) and *Backpacker's Africa*, c/o *Safari Par Excellence*, Phumula Centre, Parkway, Victoria Falls (☎113/2051, fax 4510). Both hike and track big game in remote areas of the park between Main Camp and Sinamatella, where you'll come across some hot springs and the occasional rhino.

to the likes of Gerald Durrell. There are no fences here and wildlife is free to roam through the camp at will. Accommodation for a maximum of 14 guests is provided in safari tents under thatch, with en-suite facilities. The dining area is in the shade of a massive leadwood tree. On full moon nights guests can spend the night viewing game from a hide next to a waterhole. US$300 per person.

Makololo Camp, book through *Touch the Wild* (see *Kanondo* above). Set under palm trees on the banks of Makololo Pan, this is one of the oldest of the Hwange safari lodges. In the same exquisite vicinity as *Linkwasha*, with a maximum capacity of 24 guests, it doesn't quite match the intimacy of its neighbour, but nevertheless offers a rare experience of a little-visited region. Accommodation is in large tents and there are showers and flush toilets. US$312 per person.

Sable Valley Lodge, book through *Touch the Wild* (see *Kanondo* above). Set in the teak woodlands of Sable Valley estate, a 250-square-kilometre private area adjacent to Hwange, the lodge is just 20 minutes' drive from the airport. Because the estate has seen no hunting or culling for over two decades, wildlife tends to be less skittish than elsewhere in the region. Manicured lawns add to the sense of luxury and the whole complex is surrounded by an electrified fence to keep animals out at night. Eleven en-suite thatched bungalows accommodate a maximum of 22 people. US$250 per person.

Sikumi Tree Lodge, book through *Touch the Wild* (see *Kanondo* above). In the Sikumi Forest, not far from *Hwange Safari Lodge* and a few minutes' drive from the airport. Guided walks in the forest are among the activities offered. One of the handful of lodges permitting children. Accommodation is in tree houses – huts on stilts built among the trees rather than attached to them – with facilities en suite. US$275 per person.

Main Camp and around

For most people, the gateway into Hwange is **MAIN CAMP**. Touring the park by car you'll start or finish here and without your own transport it may be as far as you'll get. But you don't need to venture much further to get an eyeful of game. The immediate surroundings of the camp have the park's highest concentrations: the **Ten-Mile Drive** between Main Camp and **Nyamandlovu Pan** regularly shows off all the animals one could hope for. Lions sometimes lie on the road in the evening – the fact that it's tarred doesn't seem to deter them – and elephants often water at Nyamandlovu Pan and nearby **Dom Pan**. Even if the lions evade you you're bound to see giraffe, zebra, wildebeest, waterbuck, sable, impala, kudu and buffalo.

CREATURES OF THE NIGHT

Night animals occupy special places in African mythology. One, which you'll hear at night from Main Camp and may well see on a night walk, is the **hyena** – said to be the consort of witches. Their special status is due to the female's false scrotum and erectile clitoris, giving rise to the belief that they're hermaphrodites.

Hyena's powerful jaws and teeth can crunch up the hardest of bones or hides. Even sharp-beaked vultures have to hold back until the hyenas arrive to tear open something with a tough hide like an elephant. Hyena's don't only scavenge, however; they're capable of hunting down animals as large as a wildebeest or zebra. The eerily drawn out *whoo-op* is their usual call, while the famous giggling laugh is usually heard only when they are burrowing into a kill. The commonest are spotted hyenas, but the rare and shy **brown hyena** – found only in southern Africa's arid terrain – are around too.

Pangolins, primitive scaly anteaters, are seldom seen, except stuffed in museums. Nevertheless, at Hwange you may observe them creeping around at night in their search for ants. Holding an important role in local tradition, they're often presented to chiefs or spirit mediums. When Mugabe came into office, scores of pangolins were brought into Harare for him. The intriguing thing about pangolins is their tongues – as long as the head and body combined, enabling them to lick up ants from deep holes. The heavy scales are a protective armour – especially useful when they curl into a fircone-like ball, which is all that most people, having alarmed them, ever see.

Main Camp is situated on Kalahari sand, shaded by aptly named *Acacia giraffae*, arching over the bar and restaurant. Walks, campsites and onward **bookings for other Hwange camps** can all be arranged through Main Camp.

The Main Camp **store** stocks supplies of fresh milk, bread, meat and various tinned food – but no fresh fruit or vegetables. The camp **restaurant** is open for breakfast and also serves steaks and one or two vegetarian dishes for lunch and dinner: despite its monopoly it's reasonably priced. Main Camp's **bar**, next door, is well known locally as a watering hole, and the barman, a great talker, is bent on consolidating his already formidable repertoire of cocktails.

Main Camp is surrounded by teak **forests** that gradually merge into Kalahari woodlands of thorn trees, mixed scrub and grassy clearings. Assuming you're up in the morning, go for a stroll around the clearings to look for antelope. There are certainly always hundreds of **impala** about. Come to Hwange in the rainy season and you're sure to see their young, just delivered and utterly appealing. Many animals give birth at the onset of the rains when the new grass springs up, but impala can prolong gestation by up to two months if the rains are late or inadequate. If you walk to the edge of the Main Camp offices, you may also spot **giraffe**, heads above the trees, and you're bound to see **zebra** and **wildebeest** on the plains; these two species always graze in company.

Sinamatella and around

SINAMATELLA is smaller than Main Camp and sited in hillier terrain, high up on a granite summit with views over a deep valley favoured by huge herds of buffalo. While it doesn't have the same concentration of game as Main Camp, the surroundings are prettier – it must be one of the most spectacular views anywhere – and there's a network of roads passing through tall mopane forests. A popular local viewing spot and campsite is **Mundavu Dam**, haunt of hippos and crocodiles. There are no *UTC* drives but you can go on **walks** with Parks' guides.

Most visitors with a car (there's no public transport) get to Sinamatella by driving through the park from Main Camp; day-tripping, you're required to leave by 2pm to make sure you have ample time to complete the journey back before dusk. A tough vehicle is advisable during the rains. Two National Parks exclusive camps, Lukosi and Bumbusi, are administered by Sinamatella, both heavily booked by Zimbabweans.

LIONS AND WILD DOGS

Lions are famed as fearsome hunters, but their ambushes are successful only one time in four, and most antelope can outrun them. You sometimes see pitifully thin lions unable to get it together, and much of the time they scavenge or resort to targets as unlikely as porcupines. A good kick from a fleeing zebra or giraffe is enough to break a jaw, which usually leads to starvation. Cattle are easy prey and lions frequently wander out of the national park onto adjoining farms where owners have the right to shoot them – one farmer on the Sikumi side of Hwange is a notorious lion-killer, taking dozens every year. **Robins Camp** is reputedly *the* place for lions.

The most successful hunters at Hwange are **wild dogs**, and you may be lucky enough to see a pack trotting along in the evening out on a hunt. Capable of sustained high speeds over long distances, wild dogs lunge at their prey *en masse*, tearing it to pieces – a gruesome finish, but perhaps no slower than the suffocating muzzle-bite of a lion. The whole pack participates in looking after the **pups**, bringing back food – and regurgitating it – for them. For many years dogs were shot on sight; they had gained an unfair reputation as wanton sheep- and cattle-killers and, up to 1975 nearly four thousand were destroyed in vermin control operations. They are now as much at risk of extinction as the black rhino.

Lukosi is only open from May to October, outside the hunting season. There are natural springs near Bumbusi that attract game, especially in the dry season. An underground hide has been constructed at one of them for close-up photography.

Robins, Nantwich and Deka

These three northwestern camps – the smallest and most secluded in Hwange – are out of reach unless you have a car, and closed from November to March. **ROBINS** and **NANTWICH** camps are within 11km of each other, in the northwest of the park – closer to Victoria Falls than Hwange. People either drive along slow, sandy roads from Main Camp during the dry season (you must set out by noon), or gain access along a gravel road 48km south of Victoria Falls on the Bulawayo road; from the turn-off it's 70km to Robins. En route you'll pass the track to Mpandamatenga, just over the border in Botswana. Robins has the reputation of being a good place to see **lions**, and guided walks with game scouts are available.

    DEKA exclusive camp, 25km west of Robins in the far western corner of the park, near the Botswana border, requires 4WD for access. The Deka and Gwayi rivers rise on the watershed here to flow north into the Zambezi, softening the landscape a little. The river courses on the southern side of the watershed once flowed into Botswana. All that remains of them today are long expanses of grassland where game can be spotted.

ELEPHANTS AT HWANGE

With the densest population in Africa, you'd be very unlucky not to see elephants in Hwange. During the rains, however, they can be elusive, disappearing to fresh vegetation in remote zones of the park.

Hwange's elephants are in fact a conservation over-success story. By the time the park was created, hunting had reduced the number of elephants to less than a thousand and their extermination was on the cards. But by the 1970s, the elephant count had bounced back dramatically to twenty thousand – an **over-population** which led to habitat destruction. **Culling programmes**, a euphemism for controlling elephants by wiping out whole families, targeting the breeding females and youngsters, were started and continue today, along with a controlled level of trophy-hunting. The park can only properly support around 12,000 elephants, although there are still far more than that even today.

The question of elephant management is more than merely a moral dilemma (shootings are arguably as traumatic for the animals as they would be for defenceless human families) but also leads into arcane **ecological puzzles** in which new factors are continually emerging. While animal over-populations are usually the result of old migration routes being cut off, forcing the creatures into new, unnatural reserves, the consequent foliage destruction caused by crowded herds also puts new life into the soil: experiments carried out at Hwange have shown that four times as many camel acacia seeds sprouted after being eaten and dunged by elephants than a control sample which was left on the ground. Dung beetles, of which Zimbabwe is blessed with a multitude of varieties, gratefully tackle the football-sized elephant droppings, breaking them into pellets and pulling them into their burrows where the seeds later germinate. Elephants also dig up dried-out waterholes, providing moisture for other animals.

More mysteriously, there's evidence of a new natural adaptation to unnatural pressures – **tuskless cow elephants** – which present less attractive targets for poachers. This may change feeding habits, and even breeding cycles, as an elephant uses its tusks (and is either right- or left-tusked) to dig for essential minerals and strip tree bark.

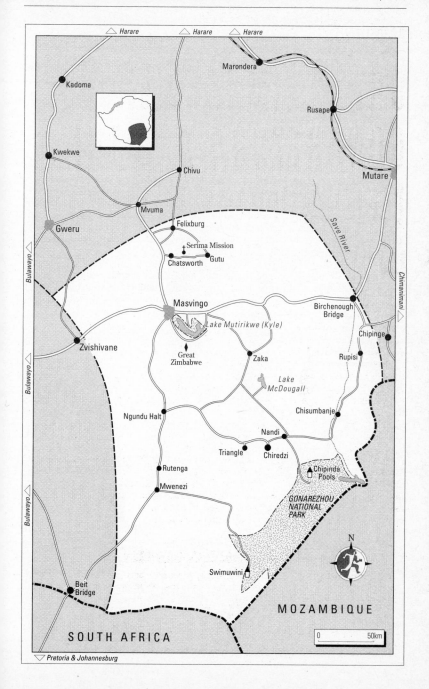

Masvingo

Most people just pass through **MASVINGO** – Rhodesia's first white settlement – on their way to the ruins and Lake Mutirikwe. There's not much to keep you in this humdrum town, three hours by car from either Harare or Bulawayo, unless you happen to arrive as nightfall approaches. But if you are travelling under your own steam, you'll find it a solid enough base, and a useful place to stock up with supplies before camping at the ruins or Lake Mutirikwe.

Some history

Masvingo was established in 1890 by pioneers trekking north, beyond the parched lowveld, to the cooler middleveld plateau. The settlers pitched and fortified their camp and named the spot **Fort Victoria** to link it with the global sisterhood of lakes, falls, towns, pubs and hotels named after the unamused queen. After some days of festivities – reportedly resembling an English village fair – the main force headed off, leaving the earthwork fort under heavily armed protection. When they realized there was little convenient water about, a new and stronger brick fort was built along the Mucheke River, a few kilometres away. One of its watchtowers, perforated with vertical gun-slits, still stands on Masvingo's main street, a reminder of frontier days.

Fort Victoria was the portal to Southern Rhodesia for northward trekking fortune-hunters, and Mashonaland's gold centre: the town's early inhabitants had ambitious hopes of a big strike. In an ironic twist, however, the **Matabele War** of 1893 crushed these local aspirations. After an Ndebele raiding party entered Fort Victoria and killed a

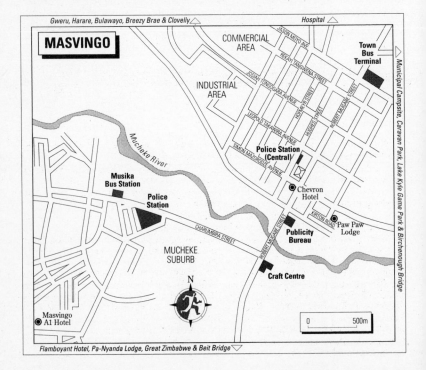

number of local Shona tributaries, a force was recruited to invade Bulawayo – a convenient excuse, as it turned out, to lay claim to the richer goldfields of Matabeleland. The destruction of Lobengula's kraal in Bulawayo subsequently served a great propaganda coup in recruiting immigrants from the south. Enticed by the gold – not to mention the spoils of Ndebele farms and cattle – the whites had few reasons to return to Fort Victoria, condemning it to the small-time provincial status that it has stuck to ever since.

Arrival, information and getting around

Masvingo enjoys the twin advantages of being both the best jumping-off point for Great Zimbabwe, and well serviced by **public transport**. *Blue Arrow* and *Translux* luxury **coaches** pass through ten times a week (in either direction) between Johannesburg and Harare, while *DSB Coachline* stops twice each week on its Harare–Chiredzi run. *Translux* and *DSB* pull into the *Chevron Hotel*, while *Blue Arrow* stops at *Riley's Truck Inn* (also known as "Shell City") – a filling station and mini shopping complex 5km south of town.

Long-distance **buses** from Harare and Bulawayo will drop you in the town centre, before terminating in Mucheke high-density suburb's *musika*, 2km west of the centre, where you can catch one of the regular buses to Great Zimbabwe.

Across the road from the *Chevron Hotel*, on the south side of the railway line, the **Publicity Association office** (☎62643) has a helpful attendant and a good collection of leaflets, as well as information on local accommodation.

If you want to drive to the monument and Lake Mutirikwe yourself, head for the *Hertz* office in town, at *Travelworld*, Founders House, Robert Mugabe St (☎62131); however, cars are often unavailable, so book ahead. You can also pick up **taxis** in town, on Simon Mazorodze Avenue behind *TM Supermarket*, or around Mucheke Bus Terminus.

> The **telephone code** for the Masvingo area, including Great Zimbabwe and Lake Mutirikwe, is ☎139.

Accommodation

Accommodation in Masvingo is a very mixed bag, but includes a number of backpacker lodges and old-fashioned hotels in the lower price ranges.

Backpackers' Rest, First Floor, Dauth Building, Josiah Tongogara St/Roberston St (☎63960 or 63282). A ropy, crowded former block of flats, converted into backpackers' accommodation. ①.

Breezy Brae, 6km from town on the Bulawayo road (☎64650). Sombre B&B accommodation in an unwelcoming house, geared principally for visitors with cars. ③.

Chevron Hotel, Robert Mugabe St (☎64751 or 62346). Opposite the publicity bureau, with a small pool: the most central and best value of Masvingo's three hotels. ③.

Clovelly, Glyntor Rd, 6km from town on the Bulawayo road (☎64751 or 62346). Unquestionably the best of the backpackers' lodges, with dorms and doubles on a shady, out-of-town plot. The friendly owners collect and drop off guests at the post office in town, and keep a useful file of up-to-date information for travellers. A swimming pool and horse riding are added attractions. ①.

The Cottage, 6 Citrus Rd (☎63340). Guests have exclusive use of a three-room, self-catering garden cottage, 1.5km from the centre in the suburbs. The owners go out of their way to make guests welcome and will collect from town. Ideal if you're a family, with under-11s half price. ②.

Flamboyant Hotel, 2km from the centre on the Beit Bridge road (☎53085 or 52898). Reasonably priced, decent hotel, but inconveniently far out of town unless you have your own car. ③.

Masvingo A1 Hotel, Dare St, just west of Jongwe St (☎62917). At a hilltop location in the high-density suburb, and with the best bar in town, but not recommended if you want a quiet night. ③.

Muncipal Campsite and Caravan Park, 2km out of town on the Mutare road. A vast, and incredibly clean, site that is convenient for getting a lift to Mutirikwe's north bank and the game park.

Pa-Nyanda Lodge, PO Box 199 Masvingo, 11km from town on the Beit Bridge road (☎67353 or 63412). Thatched chalets, set among hills overlooking a waterhole on a private game farm. The most congenial accommodation around Masvingo, but you'll need your own car. Lodges (for up to 5 people) cost US$80 if you self-cater, or there's a bed and breakfast rate (⑤).

Paw Paw Lodge, 18 Kirton St (☎65231). The only advantage of this impersonal and slightly dingy lodge is its proximity to the publicity bureau. ③.

The Town

In the typical style of colonial town planning, the railway line (goods only) slices Masvingo in two: the more salubrious avenues and commercial centre lie to the north, with Mucheke high-density suburb hidden on the wrong side of the tracks.

In the **commercial centre** the focus is provided by **Mucheke Market**. Though this doesn't stand out from its counterparts elsewhere in the country, it has lots of small stores, kiosks and the festive blare of local music. People lounge about waiting for long-distance buses on a grassy island between the shops and beer halls along Charumbira and Makuva streets.

Masvingo's only noteworthy sight is the **Chapel of St Francis**, known as the "Italian Chapel", 5km east of town off the main Mutare road. You can almost feel the homesickness of the Italian POWs who built it during the 1940s, in memory of 71 of their fellows who died in captivity in Rhodesia. The interior of the simple, corrugated-iron roofed building breathes Italy, every surface covered with **paintings**. One elaborately worked shrine has nostalgic scenes depicting St Francis in Italian fields and the Virgin in an arcaded Tuscan courtyard. But the real stars of the show are the meticulously painted **mock mosaics**, which you'd swear are real until you get closer. The chapel is an easy stopoff on the way to Kyle game park, just a short walk from the main road, next to an army base. Hitch, or catch any **bus** going beyond the Copota Mission turn-off on the Birchenough Bridge road.

Eating, drinking and nightlife

Whether you want a full-scale **meal** or a snack, you're best off picking one of the **hotels**. Among the alternatives are a sprinkling of grease parlours down Fitzgerald Avenue, while *What's Cooking* in Hofmeyr Street is a good sit-down option, popular with locals and dishing up **cheap eats** like *sadza* and relish, and toasted sandwiches. For a more sedate atmosphere, *Meikles* department store in Robert Mugabe Street has a tearoom. The *Rising Sun*, opposite *Richards Hardware*, is recommended for snacks, while the *Breadbasket* opposite *OK Bazaars* is good for bread and pies. Away from the centre in **Mucheke**, you'll find the usual street food around the bus terminus and a selection of cheap restaurants.

The main town **bar** and **nightlife** venue is the *Omar Khayyam* on Hellet Street: those bands that come to town play here. The *Mokorokoto Masvingo Bar* at the *A1 Hotel* in Mucheke is another possibility. You might also check what's on at the **theatre**, which hosts good visiting productions from time to time.

Shopping

For provisions, the grocers along Robert Mugabe Street have **fresh produce**, or, check out Mucheke Market, alongside the bus terminus, which offers greater choice. You could also stock up at one of the big supermarkets: *OK Bazaars*, Josiah Tongogara St or *TM*, Hughes St/Leopold Takawira Ave.

Other shopping tends to be equally functional. Locally made **handicrafts** are available at the stalls just past the publicity bureau, but there's nothing much to lumber yourself with unless you like crochet work or anonymous soapstone carving. There are better baskets – and lovely wooden aeroplanes – for sale on the roadside near the ruins. The only shop that makes any real concessions to the taste of passing tourists is the *Roselli Gallery*, 39 Hughes St (Mon–Fri 9.30am–4pm, Sat 9.30am–12.30pm), which stocks a mix of local paintings, sculpture and ceramics.

Listings

Banks *Barclays, Standard Chartered* and *Zimbank*, all down Robert Mugabe St, are open Mon, Tues, Thurs & Fri 8am–3pm, Wed 8am–1pm, Sat 8–11.30am.

Books and stationery are sold at several shops, but the national chain, *Kingstons*, has marginally the best selection, including copies of the South African newspapers, the *Mail & Guardian* and *New Nation*.

Doctor's surgery ☎62424 (after hours ☎62420).

Hospital Hay Robertson St (☎62112).

Pharmacies *Masvingo Pharmacy*, Kubatana Centre, 35 Hughes St (☎63884; after hours ☎64136); *Barry Nell Chemist*, Josiah Tongogara Ave (between Hughes and Hofmeyr St).

Police Hughes St (☎62221).

Post office Robert Mugabe St/Leopold Takawira Ave (Mon–Fri 8.30am–1pm & 2–4pm, Sat 8–11.30am).

Telephones are outside the courthouse in Leopold Takawira Ave (between Hughes and Hofmeyr streets). You'll also find cardphones at the post office and (less conveniently) at *Riley's Truck Inn*, 5km south of the centre, where *Blue Arrow* coaches stop.

Travel agents *UTC* trips may be booked through *Travelworld*, Founders House, Robert Mugabe St (☎62131). *Zimtours*, recommended for local tours as well as safari bookings countrywide, are at the Publicity Association Building, Robert Mugabe St (☎64054), opposite the *Chevron Hotel*.

Great Zimbabwe National Monument

Open daily 6am–6pm; US$5.

On a continent more used to impermanent buildings of mud, wood and grass, **GREAT ZIMBABWE** is almost miraculous. For nearly a thousand years, ever since it was built, this mysterious city has exercised the imaginations of those who held it, and right up until the nineteenth century it inspired hundreds of other Shona stone palaces, in a unitary sphere of influence from the desert lands of the west to the Indian Ocean in the east. The first Europeans who saw it took it both as evidence of the rumoured riches of the country and proof that tentacles of classical civilization – Phoenicians, Egyptians, Gulf Arabs, they weren't sure who – had been here before and built in stone. And for nearly a hundred years, from the time of Rhodes' incursion to the present day, the struggle for symbolic possession of this central monument has shadowed the struggle for liberation.

The word *zimbabwe* is derived from Shona phrases used freely to mean either "stone houses" or "venerated houses", which may have amounted to the same thing – buildings in stone being statements about permanence and power. The Great Zimbabwe is the best known of the country's several hundred zimbabwes. It was the stone heart of a city of as many as 10,000 people, and the home of its ruler, who lived surrounded by his family, court and tributary rulers.

Getting there

Buses run roughly every half-hour during the day from Masvingo to Morgenster Mission, dropping passengers at the turn-off, a kilometre from the monument. **By car**

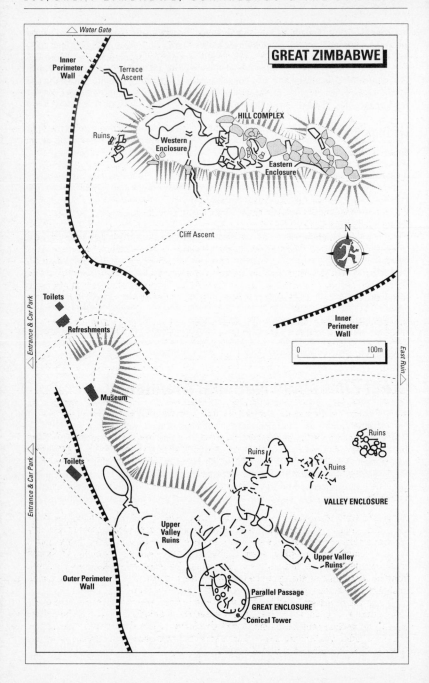

△ *Water Gate*

Inner Perimeter Wall

Terrace Ascent

HILL COMPLEX

Ruins

Western Enclosure

Eastern Enclosure

Cliff Ascent

N

Inner Perimeter Wall

0   100m

◁ *East Ruin* ▷

◁ *Entrance & Car Park*

Toilets

Refreshments

Museum

◁ *Entrance & Car Park*

Toilets

Ruins

Ruins

Ruins

VALLEY ENCLOSURE

Upper Valley Ruins

Upper Valley Ruins

Outer Perimeter Wall

Parallel Passage

GREAT ENCLOSURE

Conical Tower

GREAT ZIMBABWE

from Masvingo, take the well-signposted turn-off on your left, about 4km out of town, and just keep going. *Sunbird Safaris* in Masvingo (☎/fax 62718) offer transfers from town to Great Zimbabwe for US$10, and operate the best **guided tours** of the site. **Hitching** the 26km from Masvingo isn't difficult, either, though you may end up waiting for a while; stand opposite the craft sellers, past the Publicity Association office. **Taxis** from Masvingo – hail them behind the *TM Supermarket* on Simon Mazorodze Avenue, or around Mucheke Bus Terminus – cost around US$10 and will take up to four people.

From Harare, it's possible to take one of the *UTC* **air tours**, which combine a flight to Masvingo, bus trip to the ruins and Lake Mutirikwe, and comfortable lodging at the *Great Zimbabwe Hotel*.

Accommodation

Despite being one of Africa's most impressive ancient monuments and the inspiration behind the country's name, Great Zimbabwe has remained surprisingly undeveloped. That's starting to change with the once-lone *Great Zimbabwe Hotel* now joined by a broadening choice of lodges and self-catering accommodation, as well as a campsite – all adjacent to or actually within the bounds of the national monument (at the time of writing, a new upmarket development, *Karanga Lodge*, was planned, which will provide activities and tours focusing on the ruins – for further information contact *Sunbird Safaris* in Masvingo, ☎/fax 62718). There are also several places on the southern shores of Lake Mutirikwe (see p.207) that are very handy if you're in a car.

Great Zimbabwe Hotel, adjacent to the national monument (☎62274). The oldest hotel in the area provides comfortable en-suite rooms, but has a reputation for poor service which it will hopefully throw off once a planned refurbishment is completed. ⑦.

Lodge of the Lost City, book through *Touch the Wild*, Private Bag 6 Hillside, Bulawayo (☎19/74589). A new departure for a group with a long track record in running safari camps, the lodge is set among the granite kopjes so prolific in the Great Zimbabwe area. ⑨.

National Monument campsite, within the grounds of Great Zimbabwe. One of the best-sited places in the vicinity of the monument, with good ablutions and braai places. Although you pay normal campsite rates, you're also supposed to cough up for the US$5 entrance fee for the ruins for each day you stay.

National Monument lodges and rondavels, managed by the *Great Zimbabwe Hotel* (☎62274 or 62449). Like the campsite, the rondavels (shared ablutions) and the self-contained lodges are within the grounds of the national monument, which is the main factor in their favour. They're pleasant enough, though wildly overpriced. ⑦.

The site

The whole Great Zimbabwe area has a nonchalant setting and, surprisingly, the ruins don't attract hordes of visitors. For maximum impact, the **best visiting times** are early morning before the heat and most tourists arrive, or in the evening, after they've gone. Walking among the brooding, silent rubble, you may even see how the Victorians could have been led on their flights of fancy about lost classical civilizations. At dawn, from the highest point, the rising sun drenches the expanse of bush and lake in a pink wash. Later in the day, you can escape the heat in the **museum**.

Unless you're driven by more than mere enthusiasm, you won't need to see every detail of the ruins; half a day is sufficient to see the highlights. There's an incredible quantity of walling, but it's mostly based on simple repeated elements. After a few hours you'll find you acquire a sort of architectural "vocabulary" and everything begins to seem, if no less alien, then part of a coherent vision.

Orientation

On first approach you can hardly discern more than the castellate form of the ruins' hilltop section. This is one of three main complexes of **walls**, spread with abandon across the lifting and dipping contours, covering several square kilometres. If the bush has invaded over the centuries, it was never intended thus: Great Zimbabwe wasn't built to be hidden, nor for defence. It was a loud declaration of power and wealth by the rulers of the first state in this part of Africa.

THE "LANGUAGE" OF ROZVI PLANNING

The architecture of Great Zimbabwe is a unique innovation of this part of Africa. Under its spreading cultural influence hundreds of other zimbabwes were built across Central Africa from Botswana to Mozambique. **Khami**, near Bulawayo, took up the architectural principles and developed the style, which became the means for any self-respecting ruling class to gain recognition and publicize itself.

The **walls** meander with a disturbing licence, confounding all western architectural expectations. Their function was mainly symbolic; they twist and turn at will and were never intended to carry roofs. It was these walls that separated commoners from nobility, and you can still see the remains of monumental entrances that gave access to the ruling class homesteads.

One of the reasons it's assumed that Great Zimbabwe wasn't a fortification is that there's no evidence of any doors in the **entrances**. The north entrance of the Great Enclosure, in particular, warrants a good long look. The problem of finishing off a wall without an abrupt and jarring halt is brilliantly resolved, by curving the wall back in on itself. The **stairs** that take you up into the elevated world of the ruler are, meanwhile, fully incorporated as sensuously curving courses, incorporated into the wall's depth – all pure sculpture. Around and about – usually at entrances and particularly on the wall facing the cliff ascent of the hill complex – you'll notice **stone pillars**. It's likely they were topped by totems, which told you which family lived inside – a kind of street address. The zimbabwe birds were probably the totem of the royal family.

Although the walls are monumental in scale, the architectural **"language"** used is an adaptation of traditional Shona domestic themes: the circular pole and daga hut was the fundamental element of the Shona homestead, as it remains today in the rural areas. In the ruling class sector, stone walls adjoined daga huts to form an enclosed family living unit. The complexes are organized around the principle of **privacy**: important homes were located at the centre, and walls radiated out to provide secluded courtyards. As they do today, each of the **homesteads** consisted of several huts arranged in a swept, open courtyard – a useful firebreak, and clear space in which intruders, snakes and rodents could be spotted.

Each room had a function. At the heart of the home lay the **kitchen** building, with the hearth at its centre. Each group of huts had stepped platforms, still present in traditional Shona homes, to display a woman's **household pots**. The pots are highly valued vessels and the platforms celebrate the household, marriage and woman's centrality in the family. Close to the kitchen was the main **sleeping** unit, where married couples spent the night together, but in polygamous households the husband would rotate himself about the huts of his several wives. Adolescents slept in sexually segregated dormitories, where visitors would stay if there were no separate guest quarters.

The homestead also included places for **food storage and livestock**. The granary took the form of a hut, but had a metre-high raised floor as protection against damp, insects and rodents; all surfaces were thoroughly plastered to preserve the precious food supply. There was a chicken coop (often on stilts), and a kraal for cattle or goats, although prized animals were sometimes kept inside the main sleeping hut in a special partition.

One of the most important spaces was the **dare** (meeting place), where important family questions or community issues were discussed. Frequently beneath the shade of a tree, it was located near the homestead. During the Second Chimurenga the official title of the supreme military council and government-in-waiting, *Dare re-Chimurenga*, incorporated this ancient notion.

The **hill complex** is probably the earliest part of the city, and an extraordinary *tour de force* of organic architecture. Its builders, rather than try to force its shapes onto the landscape, melded their masonry with existing boulders, harmonizing nature and technology in the most beguiling way. The **Great Enclosure**, which you'll most likely come to first, down below to the south, has entered the record books as sub-Saharan Africa's greatest stone monument. It is also Zimbabwe's most photographed building: the massive tower and narrow, snaking parallel passage instantly recognizable from publicity pictures.

After the other areas, the **Valley Enclosure** offers variations, but little that's new. More dispersed structures repeat many features on a smaller scale. It's likely that the area between this and the hill was at one time a dense maze of *daga* and wooden buildings for the mass of the population, the enclosed stone constructions erected by wealthier citizens accessible via a series of grand entrances. Although a humbler area to look over now, it's still worth rambling about through the jumble of collapsed walls, set amid grassy, thorn- and aloe-dotted countryside.

The Great Enclosure

The pinnacle of Rozvi architecture (see box), the **Great Enclosure** sits at the foot of the hill. Originally a **royal palace** and a powerful symbol of the community, it provided privacy to the state's rulers; at the peak of their power, the enclosure is thought to have housed the king, his mother and his senior wives. Following Great Zimbawe's collapse, the building was occupied by the Mugabe dynasty, who headed a minor nineteenth-century tribal grouping. Like the other complexes, its walls are a mixture of fourteenth- to nineteenth-century traditional work, with some (at times inaccurate) modern reconstruction.

Whatever the **conical tower** signified to its builders, it provided ample scope for the imaginations of those who followed. Clearly, it can be seen as a phallic symbol, and some interpreters have suggested, further, that the **stairs** represent femininity, and the **chevron patterns** on some of the walls, fertility. But, whether symbolic male organ, hefty symbolic grain store, or prototype safe – all of which are theories that have been considered – the romantics were convinced that it contained hidden treasure, until archeologists delved beneath in the 1920s and found . . . nothing. It is in fact solid all the way up. The bulging cone, which in form is remarkably similar to the pillar tombs of the East African coast, marks the highest accomplishment of Rozvi masonry skills, and was one of their last constructions. The top of the pillar, now decapitated, was once decorated with three zigzagging lines. Look on the east side of the outer wall for the best remaining example of these.

Leading out of the tower enclosure, a **parallel passage** stretches 70m to the north entrance. It gives a good idea of the value of privacy to the Rozvi rulers, screening their domestic arrangements from even the privileged few invited inside. You can walk to the tower enclosure for example, or even to the central area, and still not see where the main huts were. Look, too, at the improvements in Rozvi masonry skills as they gained experience – the inner wall was built at least a century earlier than the smoother, more accurately laid, outer leaf.

The Hill Enclosure

The oldest inhabited part of Great Zimbabwe, the **Hill Enclosure**, was for some time known as the "acropolis", a kind of Hellenic compulsion having gripped some of the early observers. It's perhaps even more intriguing than the Great Enclosure, with its slender entrances and passages working their way around enormous balancing boulders. It's also harder work to get to, requiring a steep ascent of one of several stepped routes: this deters a fair proportion of the visitors who ramble about the tower below.

But the rewards – at the least, a peaceful view over the kopjes, *vleis* and beyond to Lake Mutirikwe – are well worth sweating over the climb.

This hill was the site of the earliest settlement of simple **daga and pole huts**, built sometime around the eleventh century. The increasing wealth of the growing state later made the building of stone walls possible. Like the Great Enclosure, the Hill

THE STRUGGLE FOR GREAT ZIMBABWE

For nearly four centuries, European knowledge of Great Zimbabwe was based entirely on hearsay. One of the earliest accounts came from the Portuguese, **Gaspar Veloso**, who wrote of "a fortress of the King of Monomotapa, which he is making of stone without mortar". Almost a hundred years later a fellow countryman, **Brother Joas dos Boas**, had elaborated this modest account into a fantasy of biblical dimensions. He wrote that "these houses were in olden times the trading depots of the Queen of Sheba, and that from these depots they used to bring her much gold".

It was the gold that brought a glint to the eyes of European adventurers in the nineteenth-century scramble for Africa. **Adam Render**, a German hunter, was the first white to set eyes on the ruins of Great Zimbabwe, in 1871, later showing them to **Carl Mauch**, a compatriot geologist, who, hungry for fame, took the credit for "discovering" them. Clearly no stranger to embroidering the truth, Mauch went on to explain that "the fortress on the hill was a copy of King Solomon's Temple".

But it was in the 1890s that these overblown musings took on a serious significance that ran parallel to the ruthless **colonization** that was beginning in Rhodesia. Great Zimbabwe stood like a beacon that couldn't be ignored. Adventurers were eager to believe that it was the remains of a long-gone and wealthy civilization centred in Mashonaland, and that there were precious relics and gold for the taking. At the same time none of the Victorian entrepreneurs or politicians who were poising themselves to exploit Mashonaland's wealth, wanted to believe that the black people they planned to subjugate were capable of a complex social system. To think otherwise would make nonsense of the supposed civilizing mission with which they wrapped the colonial ideology.

It was to resolve this glaring contradiction that the so-called **"Mystery of Zimbabwe"** evolved. The hard-headed Rhodes was the first to see the political importance of the issue, and in 1893 he employed an amateur antiquarian, **Theodore Bent**, to excavate the stones. After all his digging and delving, Bent was disgusted to find that "everything was native". This, however, didn't stop him concluding that an "ancient Mediterranean race" was responsible for the buildings. He nominated, as candidates, "the mythical Pelasgi who inhabited the shores of Greece", Britons, Phoenicians, Arabs, Romans, Persians, Egyptians or "Hebrews" – anyone, in fact, but Africans.

In 1905, **David Randall-McIver** became the first professional archeologist to investigate Great Zimbabwe. He concluded that the buildings were unmistakably African and of medieval date – and that there wasn't a shred of evidence for European or Oriental involvement. White outrage at this distasteful news was voiced by the journalist R. N. Hall who lambasted McIver's lack of first-hand knowledge of local Africans, asserting that no "authority" believed in "McIver's hazarded hypothesis of 'the natural and unaided evolution of the negroid'". The battle lines were clearly drawn – the professionals standing their ground and building on the findings of McIver, while the white community and white politicians searched more and more frantically for some scrap of ammunition to shoot down the indigenous origin hypothesis.

As the **liberation struggle** escalated, the battle to reclaim the ruins as African heritage intensified. By the time of UDI in 1965 there was scarcely any doubt at the National Historical Monuments Commission that Great Zimbabwe was the work of a powerful indigenous culture that once dominated the region. Responding to the discomforting onslaught of scientific findings, Colonel Hartley, MP for Victoria Province, rose in Parliament in 1969 to denounce the Commission, whose portrayal of the "ruins as only being of Bantu origin", he felt should be "corrected".

Complex was originally a **royal palace**. It seems likely, however, that it later became the seat of a Rozvi **spirit medium** – the religious counterpart to the secular king's court, some 80m below in the Great Enclosure.

The older hill site would naturally have had closer contact with the Rozvi **ancestors** who once dwelt there, than the newer and more temporal great enclosure. A flight of

The following year, **censorship** prevented official publications – guidebooks, museum displays, school textbooks, radio programmes, newspapers and films – from stating unequivocally that Great Zimbabwe was an African creation. Yet while explanations like the Queen of Sheba fantasy implied BC origins, **radiocarbon dating** revealed that the state flourished after 1000 AD. The curator at the ruins commented that not since Nazi Germany had archeology been so brazenly censored, and for most Rhodesian archeologists it was the last straw. **Peter Garlake**, the leading expert on Great Zimbabwe, left Rhodesia. Throughout the 1970s the Rhodesian Front regime and its white supporters were left free to wallow in dreamland theories, without fear of informed contradiction.

Current thinking

Garlake returned home in 1981, following Independence, to continue his work, and with censorship set aside, serious research into Great Zimbabwe resumed. Controversy certainly continues among researchers, but it's about detail rather than substance. It's generally agreed now that **Shona-speakers** conceived and built Great Zimbabwe themselves, in response to local conditions.

One theory asserts that the **Zimbabwe state** was transformed from an undistinguished village to a regional power by its pivotal position near the head of the Save River, which placed it perfectly to control the thirteenth-century **gold trade** between Matabeleland and Sofala on the coast. Taxes increased the economic and political power of its ruling class, enabling it to employ craftsmen like stone-carvers, goldsmiths and stonemasons. The rulers found themselves able to finance public works – the great walls – which enhanced their prestige and helped to cement the growing state that was evolving.

Peter Garlake, however, emphasizes the primacy of cattle in the growth of the Zimbabwe state, playing down trade as the kingpin of its economy. Garlake's scenario is less titillating than the idea of a trans-African gold trade focused on Great Zimbabwe, but it has a simple, compelling elegance. He points out that Great Zimbabwe, like a number of other similar centres, is positioned at the interface of the highveld and the lowveld, and he argues that the Great Zimbabwe state evolved to cope with a complex **herding system** that grazed huge areas of land. In the hot wet season cattle fed on the fresh grass of the highveld; in the winter they were herded to the better-watered lowveld when the risk of sleeping sickness was at its lowest. This method required a centralized state that was powerful enough to control a vast territory. The simplest way to co-ordinate cattle movement was as a single herd – the king's property, with animals granted to subjects for private use – moved en masse and protected by armies of men. Organized companies of men could also defend large territories and form a labour force to build walls.

The strength of Garlake's interpretation is that it corresponds to the way powerful cattle-owning states, like the Ndebele, were organized in recent times. Trade could simply have been a sideline, completely consistent with imported goods discovered at Great Zimbabwe. And in the end what made Zimbabwe great – **centralization** – was what destroyed it. Although Great Zimbabwe revolutionized the state, it failed to develop solutions to the problems of over-population that resulted. By the mid-fifteenth century, the lands around the capital had lost their fertility, game was hunted out, firewood was in short supply, and people began to drift away.

Although Great Zimbabwe collapsed, its culture continued. Some Rozvi migrants went west, and took their wall-building know-how with them, merging with the Leopard's Kopje platform-makers of the west at Khami, near Bulawayo (see p.153).

curved steps leads to a space sealed off with a huge rock, probably the domain of spirit mediums who communed with the ancestors here and participated in healing ceremonies. It feels a powerful place and it's wonderful to investigate the crevices, openings and warren of passages that sometimes bring you unnervingly close to sheer drops.

The museum

Like all great archeological sites, the ruins of Great Zimbabwe have been diligently pillaged over the years and bits and pieces from it have turned up all over the world. For this reason, the poorly assembled site **museum** (daily 8am–4.30pm; free), near the entrance to the Great Enclosure, houses disappointingly few of the truly exceptional artefacts that have been unearthed here over the years. Nevertheless, some worthwhile exhibits remain. Most notable among these are the seven and a half **soapstone birds** – the inspiration behind the ubiquitous Zimbabwean symbol, and much copied these days by modern airport artists. Mystery surrounds the significance of these strange, composite creatures, which have been identified as badly executed fish eagles by ornithologists, though archeologists doubt they signify real birds at all, suggesting, rather, that they are mythological.

Iron tools such as hoes may seem pretty ordinary items nowadays, but the ones on display here were extremely valuable possessions, and very expensive to make in terms of labour and organization. A hoe was like a car – a tribute item of conspicuous royal wealth – and just one was valuable enough to seal a marriage. Other metal tools like gongs, strikers and spears were also royal regalia, and the quantity discovered in the royal hoard shows the extent of the gulf between rich and poor at Great Zimbabwe. While the king had stacks of symbolic, but functionally useless, metal objects, an ordinary peasant would own just one or two utilitarian items.

A small collection of **Oriental goods** provides evidence of Great Zimbabwe's trading links. From the twelfth century onwards, the Rozvis were indirectly in contact with the coast, the Islamic world and even China. Finds include Indian beads, crockery from China and Persia, and odds and ends brought via Swahili traders.

Lake Mutirikwe (Kyle)

LAKE MUTIRIKWE (KYLE)* is an obvious destination to pair with Great Zimbabwe, just 6km away: a peaceful, undemanding place, with promising, if somewhat low-key wildlife. Coming from Masvingo, you have a choice of roads – going via Great Zimbabwe to the south bank, or heading direct to the game park on the northern shores.

Zimbabwe's second largest lake – artificial like almost all the rest – Mutirikwe has a varied shoreline of rocky beaches, wooded backdrops and sheer cliffs. Its small islands are secure refuge to a booming **bird** population and the compact game park on the north bank hosts the country's biggest cross-section of **antelope** species, as well as a thriving herd of **white rhinos** – all free from predators. However, the "lake" itself was sadly little more than a muddy pool in 1995 after several years of drought, and it will take plentiful rains to bring the water back to former levels.

The lake is not merely recreational – its *raison d'être* is to irrigate Hippo Valley and Triangle, the mammoth sugar estates to the south. When the lake first dried up after the failed rains of the early 1990s, the plantations withered, causing shortages of sugar, food riots and leaving Zimbabwe with no other choice than to import sugar, at great expense.

---

*Until the 1990s the lake as well as the recreation park were both called "Kyle". The waters themselves have now been renamed "Mutirikwe", but the two names are still used virtually interchangeably.

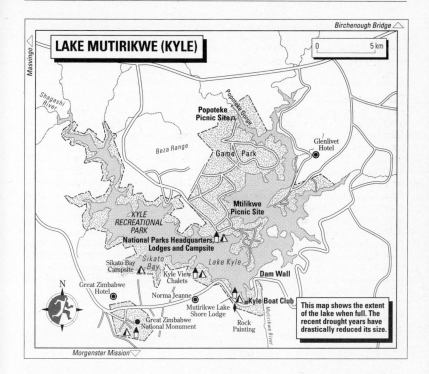

The south bank

Southern Lake Mutirikwe is a collection of **campsites** and **resorts**, where people used to come to boat, fish and water-ski before the drought. The advantage of the less attractive south bank is that it's near enough to walk, or hitch, to from Great Zimbabwe.

Chesvingo Lakeside Village, next to the *Kyle Boat Club*, is worth a visit for an opportunity to experience rural life in Zimbabwe. Being developed by local people at the time of writing, it will provide budget accommodation (see below) and visits to local villages and cultural sites. In contrast to most other tourist offerings around Great Zimbabwe and Kyle, it is run by Shona-speaking people. By public transport, take the Topora/Zano bus from Mucheke bus station and ask to be let off at the boat club; walk the remaining 200m to the signposted entrance.

If you're staying at *Kyle View* (see below) you can sometimes get a **boat ride** across to the game park on the north. *Mutirikwe Lake Shore Lodges* also have a cruiser, which may drop you off there. Otherwise it's a long haul around the lake by road – some 65km via Masvingo, slightly longer on the circular drive.

Accommodation

Chesvingo Lakeside Village, 12km east of Great Zimbabwe and 200m beyond the *Kyle Boat Club* entrance (PO Box 237, Masvingo; book through *Travelworld* in Masvingo, ☎62131, fax 64205). Clean and comfortable basic accommodation in traditional thatched huts, plus camping, in a development run by the local community. Meals available. ②.

Kyle View Lakeshore Lodges, Private Bag 9055, Masvingo (☎7202). Six kilometres east of the monument, these slightly scruffy self-catering chalets have showers, kitchens and linen. There's a camping and a caravan park and a store selling basics, as well as a bar and pool. ③.

Mutirikwe Lake Shore Lodges, PO Box 518, Masvingo (☎7151). Two kilometres beyond *Kyle View*, this outfit provides better value with similar facilities; camping allowed. ②.

Norma Jeanne's Lake View Chalets, 8km east of Great Zimbabwe on the lake road (PO Box 196; ☎7206). Self-catering, self-contained cottages set in lush gardens overlooking the lake. You'll need your own transport. ②.

Sikato Bay Campsite, 6km from Great Zimbabwe on a good dirt road. The most beautiful place to stay along the lake, and the closest to the ruins. Because the road to Sikato doesn't lead anywhere else, hitching could be tricky. There are washing facilities and each site has a braai stand, concrete table and water tap.

The north bank

Mutirikwe's north bank is much less developed. The **campsite and lodges** are set high above the water, with enchanting views – better than the resorts on the south bank. National Parks lodges go for the usual prices, booked in advance at Parks offices in Harare or Bulawayo, or last minute at Mutirikwe itself (☎2913); *Elephant Lodge*, at the summit of the hill, has the most commanding lake vista. Bring all your supplies from Masvingo and fill up with petrol, as there are no shops or garages nearby. Besides National Parks' accommodation, there is also one **hotel**, the pleasant, colonial-style *Glenlivet Hotel* (PO Box 146, Masvingo; ☎7611/62846; ④). Situated on Murray MacDougall Drive, it is only accessible if you're driving.

Kyle Game Park

Open 7am–6pm. Admission fee US$2.

Kyle Game Park has no big cats and few other predators, and most of its animals have been introduced. But while it's no Hwange or Mana Pools, nor is it tame. You'll get a full viewfinder of a whole range of herbivores – including buffalo, warthog, white rhino, giraffe, zebra and an astonishing variety of antelope – as well as numbers of hippos.

The terrain ranges from grassland to wooded clumps and rocky outcrops. Some of the kopjes in the southeast are adorned with **rock paintings**, though none is especially notable. The easiest to reach are the ones signposted above *Kyle Boat Club*, a couple of kilometres past the *Mutirikwe Lake Shore Lodges*.

For a real treat, take a ninety-minute **guided horse ride** through the park. No experience is required, but if you're proficient, you can get permission from the warden for serious riding. At any pace, though, you can get to within a whisker of the wildlife. Rides can be arranged at park headquarters near the campsite.

Part of Zimbabwe's very active **anti-poaching** campaign involves relocating **rhinos** to reserves in the country's heart, well away from the borders. It was once believed that poachers were all outsiders who sneaked over the border, chopped the horn and zipped back. Sadly, in 1989, two rhinos were killed in Kyle Game Park, probably by people posing as tourists. Don't be alarmed if the wardens ask to search your car.

With a **car** you can meander around the park's 64-kilometre network of dirt tracks. The most reliable source of information is the *Tourist Map of Lake Kyle and Great Zimbabwe*, but park headquarters often runs out of this; if possible, plan ahead and try to buy one from the Surveyor General's Office in Harare. The Masvingo Publicity Association blurb also has an adequate map.

There are two **picnic sites** with braai facilities and toilets (camping not permitted) – **Mtilikwe**, on the point, and the more remote **Popoteke** on the river. The approach to the latter is often sentinelled by zebra along the road, who relish its wooded surroundings.

Even without your own transport it is still possible to get around. The official **walking area** is **Mshagashe Arm**, a small peninsula around the lodges and campsite. The walks aren't in the game park proper, but you can get to the lakeside and see **hippos**. Stroll down to the water, sit quietly on the rocks and you may be lucky enough to get a close view through binoculars. Be cautious, though: it's easy to regard these amusing snorters as some kind of oversized aquatic pigs, but they kill more people than any other mammal in Africa. Generally they mind their own business but, if threatened, they can attack viciously. The real danger is getting between them and their element – water. Be vigilant during their landing period after sunset, and especially at dawn, when they're plodding sleepily back to the lake or river.

Serima Mission

Central Mashonaland is an unlikely place for a medieval church, but the **SERIMA MISSION**, north of Masvingo, 20km from the road to Mvuma, does a more than competent impersonation. One of the most striking buildings in Zimbabwe, it was constructed after the last war completely in the spirit of Europe's Middle Ages – both in concept and realization, the work involving members of the local community in a lengthy process (if you can't make it to Serima yourself, be sure to have a look at the photographic display at the National Gallery in Harare).

The mission was founded by Swiss priest-architect **Father John Groeber** in 1948. The carved doors, beams and altar were all produced by pupils at the mission school between 1956 and 1959, training that was intended to further Christian beliefs. West and Central African carved masks were used as models for the students, and among former pupils of the school is Zimbabwe's leading stone sculptor, Nicholas Mukomberanwa.

The church
You step inside the church into a pure space that feels sculpted from the solid shafts of light patterning the walls from clerestory windows. Gloriously carved totem-like, timber columns, worked into the forms of African angels, rise ten metres from floor to ceiling, and at the centre a crucifix is similarly sculpted. The materials are all pared back: simple concrete, furnished with benches, makes the superb carvings on every wall stand out.

Getting there
Serima is tricky to get to and poorly signposted. Without your own transport, the best bet is to get the **bus** that passes through Serima four times weekly on its way from Harare to Gutu. If you are **driving**, make for Chatsworth and keep going, turning left at the first dirt road after the river; the church is more or less straight down this road, but keep asking directions as you go. Or, much easier, take the Felixburg turn-off from the main Harare–Masvingo road; the mission is signposted from this dirt track. This turn-off is the best place to try **hitching** from, but expect to wait.

Triangle and Chiredzi

Neither **Triangle** nor **Chiredzi**, the main towns south of Masvingo, provide any incentive to venture deeper in the lowveld, but they do make diverting stops on the way to Gonarezhou, the ultimate destination in the southeast. Callow children of a 1960s sugar boom, with little evidence of rooted urban culture, both are useful places for refreshments or to stretch your legs, but have little more to offer.

MACDOUGALL SUGAR

Thomas Murray MacDougall first encountered sugar cane in Demarara, British Guyana, where he had arrived, aged fourteen, after running away to sea from Britain on an Argentine cattle boat. After World War I he fetched up in Rhodesia, where he was granted a vast tract of dry lowveld. Here he began by grazing cattle, under a registered brand – a triangle – bought from a bankrupt rancher, but his fortunes collapsed in 1924 and he turned to agriculture. Despite official scorn, he was determined to prove that, properly irrigated, the country's parched southeast could be productive.

He spent the next seven obsessive years boring 420 metres through granite to bring the waters of the Mutirikwe River onto his land, and in 1931, at last, managed to grow wheat, cotton, fruit and tobacco. However, large flocks of quelea birds and swarms of locusts feasted on his crops and, on the point of despair, MacDougall recalled his Demarara days. He applied to import sugar plants. The unhelpful government gave him permission to bring three pieces of cane from the Natal sugar estates in South Africa. MacDougall brought his three sticks, and a whole lot more, in bundles hidden beneath his car. The experiment was an unqualified success and the **Triangle Sugar Estates** company was formed in 1939 – just in time to profit from World War II.

Only then did the government take notice and begin work on the lowveld's comprehensive **irrigation scheme**. Although the land is dry much of the year, around a third of Zimbabwe's rainfall run-off flows through the Save and Runde River catchment areas. There was enough water; it just needed storing on its way to the Indian Ocean. Lake Mutirikwe was created from that need in 1961.

Triangle

TRIANGLE, 164km south of Masvingo, is without doubt the sugar capital of Zimbabwe, its surroundings full of memories of **Thomas Murray MacDougall**, an old-style pioneering Scotsman who wrestled with hostile conditions to green the lowveld with endless expanses of cane (see box). Now the archetypal company town, all Triangle's trimly arrayed facilities – schools, hospitals, housing and recreational facilities – are out of the same packet. The Triangle corporate logo (the company is now owned by Anglo-American Corporation) is everywhere, on vehicles, buildings and signs. Local workers from Triangle speak very proudly about corporate excellence, and of the beautiful greenness of the place in times of plenty.

You can hang about a bit, but there's nowhere to stay and not really very much to do except visit the **MacDougall Museum** in the pioneer's former house (daily 8.30–9.30am & 3.30–4.30pm; small entrance fee). His whole heroic life story is told with excellent old photographs and school-projectish stuff on how sugar is grown and refined.

Chiredzi

CHIREDZI, 20km east of Triangle, is a creation of the 1960s, established as a centre for the fast-growing lowveld region, and still expanding today. It's neatly laid out and pretty, with baobab-specked hills, but there's nothing to do and the town's only interest for travellers is as a stopoff for Gonarezhou. You'll find the basics in the centre – **banks**, **post office** and **shops** – but what life exists is in the black side of town around the bus station. Turn down Msasa Drive and left into Lion Drive, about a kilometre from the centre: here you'll find cheap **food**, and **taxis** and **buses** for Harare, Bulawayo, Masvingo and Mutare.

If you find yourself stranded and in need of a **hotel**, the business-oriented *Planter's Inn*, Marula Drive (☎133-8/2281 or 2230; ③), a couple of minutes' walk from the main street, is the only option in town. They also do toasted snacks, drinks and teas on a very pleasant shaded terrace. If you're mobile, make for the much nicer *Tambuti Lodge Hotel*

(☎133-8/2575; ③), 10km east of Chiredzi on the road to Nandi and the turn-off to Gonarezhou. It's set on the banks of the thickly wooded Chiredzi River, with the advantages of a beautiful setting, birds galore, and a pool beneath shady acacias.

Gonarezhou National Park

Designated a national park in 1967, remote and undeveloped **GONAREZHOU** is the second largest, yet least-known game reserve in Zimbabwe. Adjoining Mozambique, it was closed for several years during the Mozambican civil war and subsequent droughts. You're unlikely to see an enormous amount of game here, but the 5000-square-kilometre park encompasses an inspiring wilderness area with spectacular scenery, and attracts only the occasional tourist.

Gonarezhou (or Gona-Re-Zhou) derives from a Shona name meaning "place of the elephants", and has long been renowned as a source of highly marketable ivory, its tuskers being inordinately well endowed. In pre-colonial times, Arab ships are reputed to have navigated the Save River from the Indian Ocean to trade in ivory, gold and slaves. The area was also the stamping ground in the 1920s of the notorious poacher, **Cecil Barnard**, who felled the elephant Dhlulamithi ("Taller-than-the-Trees") here. As his name suggests, Dhlulamithi was huge; his tusks were reckoned to be the largest taken south of the Zambezi, with a combined weight of 110kg.

The park has been ravaged by **poaching** since then, perpetrated by commercial poachers, soldiers from Zimbabwe, Mozambique and South Africa and, to a lesser

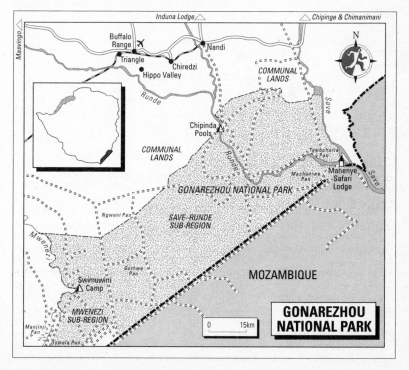

extent, the Shangaan, who formerly occupied the area. Combined with drastic culling for tsetse fly control and, in more recent years, horrific droughts, the illegal slaughter has seriously depleted game stocks. Indicative of the extent of the problem is the fact that Gonarezhou's **elephants** either charge or run away. According to National Parks, they "bear a grudge against man due to persecution and harassment over the years", and visitors are warned to be extremely cautious when encountering them. However, the good news is that animal numbers have been increasing annually over the past few years, due mainly to local conservation initiatives, such as the Mahenye Campfire Project, which have helped to curb poaching.

Birdlife, though, is undiminished, and an impressive four hundred species have been recorded in the park. Notable sightings include green coucal, Pel's fishing owl, brown-throated golden weaver, narina trogon and mottled spinetail.

The park

Gonarezhou is dominated by the **Save** and **Runde rivers** (more often than not mere sandy swathes dotted with pools) and the towering **Chilojo cliffs**. Two distinct regions have been developed for visitors: **Chipinda Pools** to the north, accessed via Chiredzi, and **Mabalauta** in the south, reached from the Masvingo–Beit Bridge road. As the park is so large and the road between these two regions virtually impossible to traverse, you basically have to choose between them.

Unless you are highly experienced, intrepid and equipped with a 4WD vehicle, Gonarezhou is not a place to attempt on your own. There are scant facilities and no shops, filling stations or even running water in most of the park. Apart from National Parks campsites and chalets, **accommodation** is restricted to fly-in safari camps. An alternative, but highly recommended, way to see the park is to take a **walking safari**. *Khangela Safaris* offer a southeast Zimbabwe safari that combines a hiking and camping trip in Gonarezhou with a stopover at Great Zimbabwe and a visit to the Matobo National Park. They are led by an outstanding professional guide who'll not only take you out to track dangerous game, but also cooks superb bush meals and will tell you everything you could want to know about local flora and fauna. Taking in the Chilojo Cliffs and beautiful riverine areas around the Runde and Save, prices start at US$140 per day per person, including game drives, or US$120 for straight backpacking. For information and booking, contact Mike or Anna Scott, PO Box FM 296, Famona, Bulawayo (☎19/49733, fax 68259).

Chipinda Pools

The campsite at **Chipinda Pools** is open throughout the year and accessible with an ordinary car, although anywhere beyond is 4WD territory that is only open from May 1 until October 31. The site lies equidistant from Harare and Bulawayo (550km), and 59km from Chiredzi: take the signposted dirt road 20km east of Chiredzi. As there are no stores or filling stations beyond Chiredzi, bring everything you need.

The **campsite** itself, set under trees overlooking pools that are alive with crocs and hippos, has the luxury of hot showers and flush loos, with gazebos and braai places. The only **lodge** close to this northern section of the park is the upmarket *Induna Lodge* (bookable through *Wilderness Safaris*, PO Box 651171, Benmore, 2910 South Africa; Johannesburg ☎884 1458), a tranquil place with spectacular views over a large dam. Outside the park boundary, north of Chipinda Pools, the lodge is accessible by road from Chiredzi via the signposted Malilangwe Trust road, though most guest fly in.

The Save-Runde river confluence

Passing through miles of dull mopane and combretum woodland, the difficult road from Chipinda Pools to the rudimentary campsites near the **Save-Runde river**

confluence takes around four hours to drive. En route, however, two hours from Chipinda Pools, are the much photographed **Chilojo Cliffs**. These towering red and ochre sandstone precipices are as impressive when viewed from the road below as from the viewing platform erected by Operation Raleigh on top of the escarpment. Once at the confluence, you're greeted by a wild and beautiful landscape of rich river-ine vegetation, huge nyala berry and fever trees, ancient baobabs and dense thickets of ilala palms.

Each campsite along the river accommodates one party only. Facilities are basic, with toilets of the long-drop variety, water has to be drawn from river pools, and all rubbish taken away with you. However, you're compensated by a much better than average chance of sighting big game, and the diverse habitat of the lower Runde harbours no less than six species of very pretty antelope not normally found together: duiker, steenbok, oribi, grysbok, klipspringer and suni, collectively known as "the small six". Rare nyala antelope are another prize of this park.

The only commercial **place to stay** in the area is the *Mahenye Safari Lodge* (book through *Suns Hotels*, Travel Centre, Jason Moyo Avenue, Harare; ☎14/736644, fax 736646). Situated close to the confluence, this is a luxurious lodge, set in riverine trees on the edge of a wide, though invariably dry river. Arguably the the most beautiful section of the park, the surrounding countryside is a birdwatcher's paradise, and ideal for the walks and game drives run for hotel guests. Tariffs at *Mahenye* start at US$206 per person; transfers from Buffalo Range airport (near Chiredzi) cost extra. Just upstream is the *Mahenye*'s sister hotel, which boasts electricity, faxes and phones, and is geared to a business getaway clientele.

Swimuwini and Mabalauta

The southern section of the park has a rest camp at **Swimuwini**, comprising separate chalets – each with its own baobab – that overlook the Mwenezi River. You can also camp 8km away at **Mabalauta**. Both places are open throughout the year, and booka-ble through the National Parks offices in Harare and Bulawayo.

The best way to reach the south of Gonarezhou is to turn off at Mwenezi police station, 20km south of Rutenga on the main Masvingo–Beit Bridge road; 105km of dirt track brings you to the warden's office at Mabalauta; Swimuwini Camp lies 8km further on. While sedan cars can make it, a high-clearance vehicle is recommended as it will allow you to see more of the park. Note, too, that the road running through Gonarezhou from the north is awful and visitors are not advised to use it.

Towards the Eastern Highlands

Masvingo is well connected by road to the Eastern Highlands, with Chimanimani 280km away via Birchenough Bridge. Leaving Masvingo, you gradually slide off the escarpment into the **lowveld**. Progress is marked by increasing numbers of baobab trees, donkeys and goats, and long views ahead of the silvery **Birchenough Bridge** arching across the wide **Save River**. In the brown water, sand shows through and crocodiles lurk, though people wash their clothes undeterred. The ribbed steel struc-ture of the bridge, incongruous in the flat, thorny landscape, provides a vital link.

The drab village of **BIRCHENOUGH BRIDGE**, hard by the southern tip of the Save Communal Lands, is another of those needy, out-of-the-way places designated by the government as Growth Points. From its *musika*, you can catch **buses** to Mutare, Chipinge and Chimanimani. A couple of hundred metres across the road from the bus terminus, the only **hotel** in town, the *Birchenough Bridge Hotel* (☎127/225819; ③), is used mostly as a call-in for drinks, though it has a few rooms with pleasant balconied prospects of the river and hills.

Just beyond Birchenough Bridge, the road forks, with the main branch heading 124km **north to Mutare**. The *Hot Springs Resort* (PO Box 190, Nyandyazi; ☎126/367–8, fax 328), 40km towards Mutare, is a relaxing place to pull over, where you can have lunch rounded off with a bath in their open-air hot mineral tubs (admission fee US$2). Stranded backpackers are welcome to camp out of sight of the main resort; hotel guests, on the other hand, enjoy the comfort of thatched chalets overlooking a dam, with good birdlife. The tariff of US$40 per person includes dinner and breakfast.

On the **Chipinge road**, some 7km southeast of Birchenough Bridge, stands a group of **crafts stalls**; their goods are of unusually high quality, particularly the rust-coloured baskets with plaited seamless bases joined onto decorated wooden rims. Other tempting buys are the woven vegetable-dyed, bark mats – available in other parts of the country but a lot cheaper here. In season, baskets of furry green baobab pods are also on sale; locals soak the cream of tartar seeds in milk to make a kind of yoghurt.

At **TANGANDA JUNCTION**, a stark red-earthed place on a bend, the road splits south down the Save Valley to Chisumbanje and Chiredzi and east to Chipinge and Chimanimani. The junction consists of a bus stop and a collection of plastered and peeling stores. Women, relying on the passing traffic, sell small piles of fruit laid on plastic on the ground. An early-morning **bus** from Chipinge goes via Chisumbanje to Chiredzi through the intensely cultivated and irrigated middle Save Valley.

travel details

Economy buses

Masvingo's historical role as a gateway to the hinterland has placed it in a pivotal transport position, from which you can get buses to almost any part of the country.

Masvingo (Mucheke bus terminus) to: Beit Bridge (throughout the day; 3–4hr); Bulawayo (4 daily; 3–4hr); Chimanimani (1 daily at 11am; 4–5hr); Harare (throughout the day; 4–5hr); Morgenster Mission for Great Zimbabwe (every 30min; 30min); Mutare (3 daily 8–10am; 4–5hr).

There are also buses to Chatsworth (for Serima Mission), Chipinge, Chiredzi, Gweru, Hwange and Shurugwi.

Luxury coaches

Masvingo to: Chiredzi (Sun at 4pm & Thurs at 11am; 2hr 15min) – *DSB*; Harare (1–2 daily; 4hr) – *Translux, Blue Arrow* and *DSB*; Johannesburg (1–2 daily; 13hr 30min–14hr) – *Blue Arrow* and *Translux*.

THE WILDLIFE
OF EAST AND
SOUTHERN AFRICA

A ROUGH GUIDE

This field guide provides a quick reference to help you identify the larger mammals likely to be encountered in East and Southern Africa. It includes most species that are found throughout these regions, as well as a limited number whose range is more restricted. Straightforward photos show easily identified markings and features. The notes give you clear pointers about the kinds of **habitat** in which you are most likely to see each mammal; its daily rhythm (usually either **nocturnal or diurnal**); the kind of **social groups** it usually forms; and general **tips about sighting** it on safari, its rarity and its relations with humans.

■ HABITAT ◩ DIURNAL/NOCTURNAL ◪ SOCIAL LIFE ☑ SIGHTING TIPS

Baboon *Papio cynocephalus*

⊠ open country with trees and cliffs; adaptable, but always near water

⊠ diurnal

⊠ troops led by a dominant male

☑ common; several subspecies, including Yellow and Olive in East Africa and Chacma in Southern Africa; easily becomes used to humans, frequently a nuisance and occasionally dangerous

Eastern Black and White Colobus
Colobus guereza

⊠ rainforest and well-watered savannah; almost entirely arboreal

⊠ diurnal

⊠ small troops

☑ troops maintain a limited home territory, so easily located, but can be hard to see at a great height; not found in Southern Africa

Patas Monkey *Erythrocebus patas*

⊠ savannah and forest margins; tolerates some aridity; terrestrial except for sleeping and lookouts

⊠ diurnal

⊠ small troops

☑ widespread but infrequently seen; can run at high speed and stand on hind feet supported by tail; not found in Southern Africa

Vervet Monkey *Cercopithecus aethiops*

⊠ most habitats except rainforest and arid lands; arboreal and terrestrial

⊠ diurnal

⊠ troops

☑ widespread and common; occasionally a nuisance where used to humans

PRIMATES

**White-throated or Sykes'
Monkey/Samango**
Cercopithecus mitis/albogularis
◨ forests; arboreal and occasionally
terrestrial
◨ diurnal
◨ families or small troops
☑ widespread; shyer and less easily
habituated to humans than the Vervet

Aardvark *Orycteropus afer*
◨ open or wooded termite country; softer
soil preferred
◨ nocturnal
◨ solitary
☑ rarely seen animal, the size of a small pig;
old burrows are common and often used
by warthogs

Spring Hare *Pedetes capensis*
◨ savannah; softer soil areas preferred
◨ nocturnal
◨ burrows, usually with a pair and their
young; often linked into a network,
almost like a colony
☑ fairly widespread rabbit-sized rodent;
impressive and unmistakable kangaroo-
like leaper

Crested Porcupine
Hystrix africae-australis
◨ adaptable to a wide range of habitats
◨ nocturnal and sometimes active at dusk
◨ family groups
☑ large rodent (up to 90cm in length),
rarely seen, but common away from
croplands, where it's hunted as a pest

PRIMATES - AARDVARK - RODENTS

Bat-eared Fox *Otocyon megalotis*
- ■ open country
- ■ mainly nocturnal; diurnal activity increases in cooler months
- ■ monogamous pairs
- ☑ distribution coincides with termites, their favoured diet; they spend many hours foraging using sensitive hearing to pinpoint their underground prey

Black-backed Jackal *Canis mesomelas*
- ■ broad range from moist mountain regions to desert, but drier areas preferred
- ■ normally nocturnal, but diurnal in the safety of game reserves
- ■ mostly monogamous pairs; sometimes family groups
- ☑ common; a bold scavenger, the size of a small dog, that steals even from lions; black saddle distinguishes it from the shyer Side-striped Jackal

Hunting Dog or Wild Dog
Lycaon pictus
- ■ open savannah in the vicinity of grazing herds
- ■ diurnal
- ■ nomadic packs
- ☑ extremely rare and rarely seen, but widely noted when in the area; the size of a large dog, with distinctively rounded ears

Honey Badger or Ratel
Mellivora capensis
- ■ very broad range of habitats
- ■ mainly nocturnal
- ■ usually solitary, but also found in pairs
- ☑ widespread, omnivorous, badger-sized animal; nowhere common; extremely aggressive

DOG RELATIVES · HONEY BADGER

African Civet *Civettictis civetta*

■ prefers woodland and dense vegetation

◨ mainly nocturnal

■ solitary

☑ omnivorous, medium-dog-sized, short-legged prowler; not to be confused with the smaller genet

Common Genet *Genetta genetta*

■ light bush country, even arid areas; partly arboreal

◨ nocturnal, but becomes active at dusk

■ solitary

☑ quite common, slender, cat-sized omnivore, often seen at game lodges, where it easily becomes habituated to humans

Banded Mongoose *Mungos mungo*

■ thick bush and dry forest

◨ diurnal

■ lives in burrow colonies of up to thirty animals

☑ widespread and quite common, the size of a small cat; often seen in a group, hurriedly foraging through the undergrowth

Spotted Hyena *Crocuta crocuta*

■ tolerates a wide variety of habitat, with the exception of dense forest

◨ nocturnal but also active at dusk; also diurnal in many parks

■ highly social, usually living in extended family groups

☑ the size of a large dog with a distinctive loping gait, quite common in parks; carnivorous scavenger and cooperative hunter; dangerous

WEASEL RELATIVES – SPOTTED HYENA

Caracal *Caracal caracal*
🔲 open bush and plains; occasionally arboreal
✖️ mostly nocturnal
🔲 solitary
✅ lynx-like wild cat; rather uncommon and rarely seen

Cheetah *Acionyx jubatus*
🔲 savannah, in the vicinity of plains grazers
✖️ diurnal
🔲 solitary or temporary nuclear family groups
✅ widespread but low population; much slighter build than the leopard, and distinguished from it by a small head, square snout and dark "tear mark" running from eye to jowl

Leopard *Panthera pardus*
🔲 highly adaptable; frequently arboreal
✖️ nocturnal; also cooler daylight hours
🔲 solitary
✅ the size of a very large dog; not uncommon, but shy and infrequently seen; rests in thick undergrowth or up trees; very dangerous

Lion *Panthera leo*
🔲 all habitats except desert and thick forest
✖️ nocturnal and diurnal
🔲 prides of three to forty; more usually six to twelve
✅ commonly seen resting in shade; dangerous

CATS

Serval *Felis serval*
■ reed beds or tall grassland near water
■ normally nocturnal but more diurnal than most cats
■ usually solitary
☑ some resemblance to, but far smaller than, the cheetah; most likely to be seen on roadsides or water margins at dawn or dusk

Rock Hyrax or Dassie *Procavia capensis*
■ rocky areas, from mountains to isolated outcrops
■ diurnal
■ colonies consisting of a territorial male with as many as thirty related females
☑ rabbit-sized; very common; often seen sunning themselves in the early morning on rocks

African Elephant *Loxodonta africana*
■ wide range of habitats, wherever there are trees and water
■ nocturnal and diurnal; sleeps as little as four hours a day
■ almost human in its complexity; cows and offspring in herds headed by a matriarch; bulls solitary or in bachelor herds
☑ look out for fresh dung (football-sized) and recently damaged trees; frequently seen at waterholes from late afternoon

CATS - HYRAX - ELEPHANT

Black Rhinoceros *Diceros bicornis*

■ usually thick bush, altitudes up to 3500m

■ active day and night, resting between periods of activity

■ solitary

✔ extremely rare and in critical danger of extinction; largely confined to parks where most individuals are known to rangers; distinctive hooked lip for browsing; small head usually held high; bad eyesight; very dangerous

White Rhinoceros *Ceratotherium simum*

■ savannah

■ active day and night, resting between periods of activity

■ mother/s and calves, or small, same-sex herds of immature animals; old males solitary

✔ rare, restricted to parks; distinctive wide mouth (hence "white" from Afrikaans *wijd*) for grazing; large head usually lowered; docile

Burchell's Zebra *Equus burchelli*

■ savannah, with or without trees, up to 4500m

■ active day and night, resting intermittently

■ harems of several mares and foals led by a dominant stallion are usually grouped together, in herds of up to several thousand

✔ widespread and common inside and outside the parks; regional subspecies include *granti* (Grant's, East Africa) and *chapmani* (Chapman's, Southern Africa, right)

Grevy's Zebra *Equus grevyi*

■ arid regions

■ largely diurnal

■ mares with foals and stallions generally keep to separate troops; stallions sometimes solitary and territorial

✔ easily distinguished from smaller Burchell's Zebra by narrow stripes and very large ears; rare and localized but easily seen; not found in Southern Africa

RHINOCEROSES – ZEBRAS

Warthog *Phacochoerus aethiopicus*

☒ savannah, up to an altitude of over 2000m

☒ diurnal

☒ family groups, usually of a female and her litter

☑ common; boars are distinguishable from sows by their prominent face "warts"

Hippopotamus *Hippopotamus amphibius*

☒ slow-flowing rivers, dams and lakes

☒ principally nocturnal, leaving the water to graze

☒ bulls are solitary, but other animals live in family groups headed by a matriarch

☑ usually seen by day in water, with top of head and ears breaking the surface; frequently aggressive and very dangerous when threatened or when retreat to water is blocked

Giraffe *Giraffa camelopardalis*

☒ wooded savannah and thorn country

☒ diurnal

☒ loose, non-territorial, leaderless herds

☑ common; many subspecies, of which Maasai (*G. c. tippelskirchi*, right), Reticulated (*G. c. reticulata*, bottom l.) and Rothschild's (*G. c. rothschildi*, bottom r.) are East African; markings of Southern African subspecies are intermediate between *tippelskirchi* and *rothschildi*

WARTHOG · HIPPOPOTAMUS · GIRAFFE

African or Cape Buffalo *Syncerus caffer*
- ◪ wide range of habitats, always near water, up to altitudes of 4000m
- ◪ nocturnal and diurnal, but inactive during the heat of the day
- ◪ gregarious, with cows and calves in huge herds; young bulls often form small bachelor herds; old bulls are usually solitary
- ☑ very common; scent much more acute than other senses; very dangerous, old bulls especially so

Hartebeest *Alcelaphus buselaphus*
- ◪ wide range of grassy habitats
- ◪ diurnal
- ◪ females and calves in small, wandering herds; territorial males solitary
- ☑ hard to confuse with any other antelope except the topi/tsessebe; many varieties, distinguishable by horn shape, including Coke's, Lichtenstein's, Jackson's (right), and Red or Cape; common, but much displaced by cattle grazing

Blue or White-bearded Wildebeest
Connochaetes taurinus
- ◪ grasslands
- ◪ diurnal, occasionally also nocturnal
- ◪ intensely gregarious; wide variety of associations within mega-herds which may number over 100,000 animals
- ☑ unmistakable, nomadic grazer; long tail, mane and beard

Topi or Tsessebe *Damaliscus lunatus*
- ◪ grasslands, showing a marked preference for moist savannah, near water
- ◪ diurnal
- ◪ females and young form herds with an old male
- ☑ widespread, very fast runners; male often stands sentry on an abandoned termite hill, actually marking the territory against rivals, rather than defending against predators

BUFFALO – HARTEBEEST RELATIVES

Gerenuk *Litocranius walleri*
- ◪ arid thorn country and semi-desert
- ◪ diurnal
- ◪ solitary or in small, territorial harems
- ☑ not uncommon; unmistakable giraffe-like neck; often browses standing upright on hind legs; the female is hornless; not found in Southern Africa

Grant's Gazelle *Gazella granti*
- ◪ wide grassy plains with good visibility, sometimes far from water
- ◪ diurnal
- ◪ small, territorial harems
- ☑ larger than the similar Thomson's Gazelle, distinguished from it by the white rump patch which extends onto the back; the female has smaller horns than the male; not found in Southern Africa

Springbok *Antidorcas marsupalis*
- ◪ arid plains
- ◪ seasonally variable, but usually cooler times of day
- ◪ highly gregarious, sometimes in thousands; various herding combinations of males, females and young
- ☑ medium-sized, delicately built gazelle; dark line through eye to mouth and lyre-shaped horns in both sexes; found only in Botswana, Namibia and South Africa

Thomson's Gazelle *Gazella thomsoni*
- ◪ flat, short-grass savannah, near water
- ◪ diurnal
- ◪ gregarious, in a wide variety of social structures, often massing in the hundreds with other grazing species
- ☑ smaller than the similar Grant's Gazelle, distinguished from it by the black band on flank; the female has tiny horns; not found in Southern Africa

G A Z E L L E S

Impala *Aepyceros melampus*
- ■ open savannah near light woodland cover
- ■ diurnal
- ■ large herds of females overlap with several male territories; males highly territorial during the rut when they separate out breeding harems of up to twenty females
- ☑ common, medium-sized, no close relatives; distinctive high leaps when fleeing; the only antelope with a black tuft above the hooves; males have long, lyre-shaped horns

Red Lechwe *Kobus leche*
- ■ floodplains and areas close to swampland
- ■ nocturnal and diurnal
- ■ herds of up to thirty females move through temporary ram territories; occasionally thousand-strong gatherings
- ☑ semi-aquatic antelope with distinctive angular rump; rams have large forward-pointing horns; not found in East Africa

Common Reedbuck *Redunca arundinum*
- ■ reedbeds and tall grass near water
- ■ nocturnal and diurnal
- ■ monogamous pairs or family groups in territory defended by the male
- ☑ medium-sized antelope, with a plant diet unpalatable to other herbivores; only males have horns

Common or Defassa Waterbuck
Kobus ellipsiprymnus
- ■ open woodland and savannah, near water
- ■ nocturnal and diurnal
- ■ territorial herds of females and young, led by dominant male, or territorial males visited by wandering female herds
- ☑ common, rather tame, large antelope; plant diet unpalatable to other herbivores; shaggy coat; only males have horns

IMPALA - REEDBUCKS - WATERBUCKS

Kirk's Dikdik *Rhincotragus kirki*
- ■ scrub and thornbush, often far from water
- ■ nocturnal and diurnal, with several sleeping periods
- ■ pairs for life, often accompanied by current and previous young
- ☑ tiny, hare-sized antelope, named after its alarm cry; only males have horns; not found in Southern Africa except Namibia

Common Duiker *Sylvicapra grimmia*
- ■ adaptable; prefers scrub and bush
- ■ nocturnal and diurnal
- ■ most commonly solitary; sometimes in pairs; occasionally monogamous
- ☑ widespread and common small antelope with a rounded back; seen close to cover; rams have short straight horns

Sitatunga *Tragelaphus spekei*
- ■ swamps
- ■ nocturnal and sometimes diurnal
- ■ territorial and mostly solitary or in pairs
- ☑ very localized and not likely to be mistaken for anything else; usually seen half submerged; females have no horns

Nyala *Tragelaphus angasi*
- ■ dense woodland near water
- ■ primarily nocturnal with some diurnal activity
- ■ flexible and non-territorial; the basic unit is a female and two offspring
- ☑ in size midway between the Kudu and Bushbuck, and easily mistaken for the latter; orange legs distinguish it; only males have horns; not found in East Africa

DWARF ANTELOPES – BUSHBUCK ANTELOPES

Bushbuck *Tragelaphus scriptus*
■ thick bush and woodland close to water
■ principally nocturnal, but also active during the day when cool
■ solitary, but casually sociable; sometimes grazes in small groups
☑ medium-sized antelope with white stripes and spots; often seen in thickets, or heard crashing through them; not to be confused with the far larger Nyala; the male has shortish straight horns

Eland *Taurotragus oryx*
■ highly adaptable; semi-desert to mountains, but prefers scrubby plains
■ nocturnal and diurnal
■ non-territorial herds of up to sixty with temporary gatherings of as many as a thousand
☑ common but shy; the largest and most powerful African antelope; both sexes have straight horns with a slight spiral

Greater Kudu *Tragelaphus strepsiceros*
■ semi-arid, hilly or undulating bush country; tolerant of drought
■ diurnal when secure; otherwise nocturnal
■ territorial; males usually solitary; females in small troops with young
☑ impressively big antelope (up to 1.5m at shoulder) with very long, spiral horns in the male; very localized; shy of humans and not often seen

Lesser Kudu *Tragelaphus imberbis*
■ semi-arid, hilly or undulating bush country; tolerant of drought
■ diurnal when secure; otherwise nocturnal
■ territorial; males usually solitary; females in small troops with young
☑ smaller than the Greater Kudu; only the male has horns; extremely shy and usually seen only as it disappears; not found in Southern Africa

BUSHBUCK ANTELOPES

Gemsbok *Oryx gazella gazella*

■ open grasslands; also waterless wastelands; tolerant of prolonged drought

■ nocturnal and diurnal

■ highly hierarchical mixed herds of up to fifteen, led by a dominant bull

☑ large antelope with unmistakable horns in both sexes; subspecies *gazella* is one of several similar forms, sometimes considered separate species; not found in East Africa

Fringe-eared Oryx *Oryx gazella callotis*

■ open grasslands; also waterless wastelands; tolerant of prolonged drought

■ nocturnal and diurnal

■ highly hierarchical mixed herds of up to fifteen, led by a dominant bull

☑ the *callotis* subspecies is one of two found in Kenya, the other, found in the northeast, being *Oryx g. beisa* (the Beisa Oryx); not found in Southern Africa

Roan Antelope *Hippotragus equinus*

■ tall grassland near water

■ nocturnal and diurnal; peak afternoon feeding

■ small herds led by a dominant bull; herds of immature males; sometimes pairs in season

☑ large antelope, distinguished from the Sable by lighter, greyish colour, shorter horns (both sexes) and narrow, tufted ears

Sable Antelope *Hippotragus niger*

■ open woodland with medium to tall grassland near water

■ nocturnal and diurnal

■ territorial; bulls divide into sub-territories, through which cows and young roam; herds of immature males; sometimes pairs in season

☑ large antelope; upper body dark brown to black; mask-like markings on the face; both sexes have huge curved horns

ORYXES – ROAN ANTELOPE – SABLE ANTELOPE

Grysbok *Raphicerus melanotis*

■ thicket adjacent to open grassland

■ nocturnal

■ rams territorial; loose pairings

✔ small, rarely seen antelope; two subspecies, Cape (*R. m. melanotis*, South Africa, right) and Sharpe's (*R. m. sharpei*, East Africa); distinguished from more slender Steenbok by light underparts; rams have short horns

Oribi *Ourebia ourebi*

■ open grassland

■ diurnal

■ territorial harems consisting of male and one to four females

✔ localized small antelope, but not hard to see where common; only males have horns; the Oribi is distinguished from the smaller Grysbok and Steenbok by a black tail and dark skin patch below the eye

Steenbok *Raphicerus campestris*

■ dry savannah

■ nocturnal and diurnal

■ solitary or (less often) in pairs

✔ widespread small antelope, particularly in Southern Africa, but shy; only males have horns

Klipspringer *Oreotragus oreotragus*

■ rocky country; cliffs and kopjes

■ diurnal

■ territorial ram with mate or small family group; often restricted to small long-term territories

✔ small antelope; horns normally only on male; extremely agile on rocky terrain; unusually high hooves, giving the impression of walking on tiptoe

CHAPTER SIX

THE EASTERN HIGHLANDS

Ranged along the Mozambique frontier, the **Eastern Highlands** of **Manicaland** rise from the plains to form a natural barrier. Peaking at almost 2600m in the Nyanga belt, these mountains reminded the original British settlers of the Scottish Highlands, and they set about creating dams and lakes and planting pines in the mist – features that induce a sense of familiarity for Europeans. However, the climate is thoroughly Zimbabwean; there are some real expanses of jungle; and the earth is an unmistakeably African red.

What the Highlands lack is big game (this was shot out early here), or indeed any very real tourist highlights. The appeal of the region lies more in exploring the superb hiking trails and indigenous forest, waterfall swimming pools and national parks, each quite different in character. The **Nyanga National Park**, closest to Harare, has long been a major holiday resort for Zimbabweans, with its forests and trout fishing, but hasn't yet been packaged much for foreign visitors. Adjoining its southern edge, the less easily accessible **Mtarazi National Park** is a much wilder zone, with undisturbed indigenous forest, Africa's highest waterfall, and the luxuriant **Honde Valley**. The region also offers numerous possibilities for outdoor pursuits, particularly whitewater rafting, kayaking and abseiling.

The southern reaches of these Highlands are a little out on a limb – several hours' drive from the capital and not on the road to anywhere else. They are, however, connected to Mutare by daily local buses and should on no account to be missed. The **Chimanimani National Park**, accessible only on foot, has the best **hiking** in Zimbabwe, with spectacular mountains, and waterfalls and rivers to bathe in. Still further south, **Chipinge**, a workaday town in the centre of tea and coffee estates, serves as a base for **Chirinda Forest**, a primeval woodland reserve with ancient red mahoganies.

As for more urban attractions, **Mutare**, Zimbabwe's third city and the capital of Manicaland, is beautifully sited in a broad, mountain-rimmed valley on the Mozambique border, with the wonderful **Bvumba Botanical Gardens** and little-visited **Bunga Forest Reserve** within easy day-trip reach.

The road from Harare

Getting to the Eastern Highlands from Harare is easy enough, with regular trains and buses covering the 263km to Mutare. On the way you can linger at strategically placed

ACCOMMODATION PRICE CODES

Hotels and other accommodation options in Zimbabwe have been categorized according to the **price codes** given below, which indicate the cost per person sharing of a night's lodging.

For a full explanation, see p.46.

① under US$8	④ US$25–35	⑦ US$65–80
② US$8–15	⑤ US$35–50	⑧ US$80–95
③ US$15–25	⑥ US$50–65	⑨ over US$95

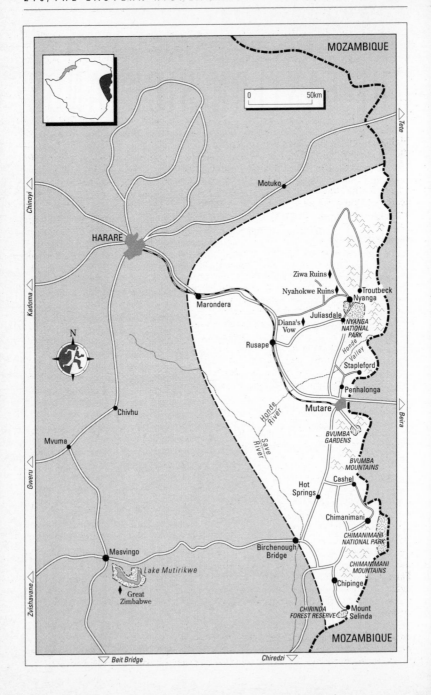

tea gardens and craft shops, and there are a few hotels should you get stranded. **Rusape**, midway, offers the opportunity of heading straight to Nyanga National Park, as well as a highly recommended detour to the controversial rock paintings at **Diana's Vow**.

Marondera

MARONDERA, 74km east of Harare, was set up as a staging post between Mutare (or Umtali as it was then known) and the capital, and for travellers to the Eastern Highlands this remains its main, and perhaps only, interest. The town, the highest sited in the country, stands at the centre of a prosperous farming region, amid a green and pleasant landscape of grazing sheep, orchards of pears and apples, and vineyards.

Marondera is one of Zimbabwe's **wine** regions, a product that's improving all the time and is now marketed abroad. Some of the country's finest wines originate at the nearby **Mukuyu Winery**, 30km south of town on the Wedza road, where the tours wind up with tasting sessions (☎179/24501 or 341625; phone in advance to find out times of tours). Also just outside town is the swanky British-style private school, **Peterhouse** – presumably located here for the cooler climate.

These sights apart, the main reasons for a stop in Marondera are to have lunch at the surreally titled *Ye Olde Tea Shoppe* in Fourth Street, the principal shopping street, off the main Mutare road, or to stay at the clean and comfortable *Marondera Hotel* (☎122/24005; ③), on the main road – a useful fall-back if you're taking the journey to Mutare slowly. In town, the *Burgundy Terrace* restaurant in the *Food Giant* supermarket on Fourth Street also offers reasonable British-style meals. Much the nicest stop, though, is the *Malwatte Farmhouse Restaurant* (☎122/23239, or 344112 after 5pm), beyond Marondera at the 82km peg on the main Harare–Mutare road, where you can take tea in the garden or browse around their good craft shop. They also have double en-suite rondavels (③) and camping facilities. Finally, exactly halfway between Harare and Mutare, just outside Rusape, the Dutch-gabled *Halfway House* is similar, offering outdoor meals, takeaways, excellent fresh produce, cakes, bread and crafts.

Rusape and Diana's Vow

At the next stop, **RUSAPE**, 170km from Harare, the road splits, heading northeast to Nyanga or southeast to Mutare. If you're here for the night, you could stay at the *Balfour Hotel* (☎125/2945; ③), a slightly run-down colonial-style hotel where many locals gather to booze. Another option, on the Harare side of Rusape, is the good-value *Crocodile Motel* (☎125/2404; ③).

However, the main reason for stopping off at this, now nondescript, town is to make a detour to the magnificent Diana's Vow – site of some of the finest, and certainly amongst the most unusual, rock paintings in the country.

Diana's Vow

You'll need a car to get to **Diana's Vow**. From Rusape, take the road to Juliasdale; on the edge of town, just past the church on the left, a sign points left to **Diana's Vow Farm**, a 28-kilometre drive, mostly on a tarred road of variable quality. The paintings are indicated by a very discreet sign at a farm gate on your right. Drive through the gate for half a kilometre until you reach a fenced enclosure around the painted overhang, set in a dramatic circle of granite boulders.

A large recumbent figure, evidently in ceremonial dress and a sable antelope mask, dominates the tableau. According to Peter Garlake (see "Books" in *Contexts*), it depicts a **ceremonial dance** in which the life force *n/um* is being activated. The stretched figure is shown in an advanced state of trance – elongation being a sensation commonly reported by modern-day San dancers on achieving altered consciousness. The oval attached to the bodies is believed to represent potency, and hence the spiritual culmination of the dance. A now discredited interpretation had the central figure as a dead king wrapped in bandages, and about to be buried.

Mutare

MUTARE lies in a majestic location but has a distinctly provincial feel, with no hint of high-rises on its main street, and the rest of the town centre a neatly organized grid of flower-bedecked avenues. It is at its best in September and October, when the hills around the town are a burnished red and yellow with spring msasa leaves. There is not much to see in the town itself, but there are some minor local attractions within easy reach, including **Murahwa's Hill** and **Penhalonga**, and, a little further away, the wonderful **Bvumba Botanical Gardens**.

Some history

Mutare's nineteenth-century history is bound up with **gold** and **railways**. The traditional head of the area was one **Chief Mutasa**, a man much courted by both Portuguese and British settlers wanting to prospect for gold in the **Penhalonga Valley**, north of modern Mutare. Two days after the British occupied Mashonaland in 1890, however, they took over the granting of prospecting rights and rapidly constructed a fort to "protect" the chief from the Portuguese.   A year later, as numbers began to swell, the fort was abandoned and a new township, **Old Umtali**, was established on the Mutare River. At the same time, the **rail** line begun in Beira was approaching the surrounding hills. These proved too big an obstacle, and everyone packed up and moved 14km south into the wide valley of Mutare's present position. The **American Methodist Church** took over Old Umtali, with a mission and school which are still going (on the left on the way to Penhalonga). In 1982 the name of the city was revised from *Umtali* to the more accurate *Mutare*, though many older people still use the pre-Independence name.

Chief Mutasa's descendants remain in the area today. In beautiful, granite country on the Nyanga–Mutare road, a hand-painted sign with an arrow points "To Chief Mutasa". The present chief's sphere of influence is said to be extensive, although rural areas are now under the official control of rural and district councils. As ex-officio members of the district councils, chiefs are still consulted and retain a certain amount of status and power, but the kingpins are government-appointed District Administrators, who have replaced the colonial Distict Commissioners. One of the main functions of chiefs is their right to settle out-of-court disputes.

Missions and chiefs aren't the only things to survive the last hundred years. **Traders** like the Meikles brothers set up shop and still have a department store in Mutare, where you can sit on the balcony for tea and scones from a silver service. Many lovely old verandahed houses remain too, while the elegant building taken over by the Mutare Club, in Main Street above the *Manica Hotel*, was the former Central Hotel built in 1898.

> The **telephone code** for the Mutare area is ☎120.

Arrival and information

Arriving in Mutare **by road** from Harare or Nyanga is a real event: as you hit the top of Christmas Pass, the whole panorama of the town lies below you in a wide valley, the Bvumba Mountains rising to the southeast. Like all Zimbabwean towns, Mutare

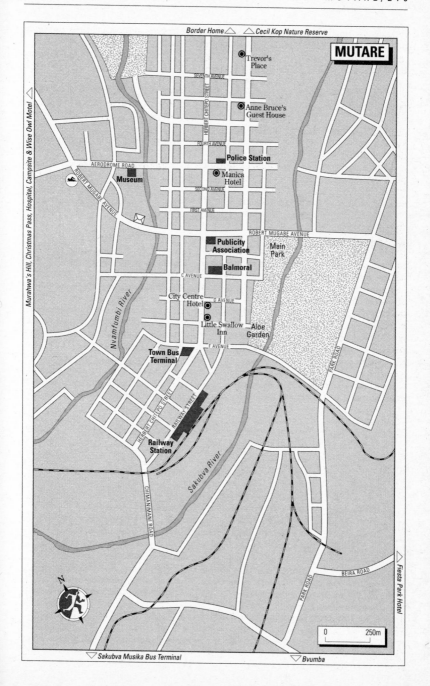

MUTARE

Border Home △ △ Cecil Kop Nature Reserve

Murahwa's Hill, Christmas Pass, Hospital, Campsite & Wise Owl Motel

SEVENTH AVENUE

● Trevor's Place

HERBERT CHITEPO STREET

● Anne Bruce's Guest House

FOURTH AVENUE

■ Police Station

AERODROME ROAD

■ Museum

● Manica Hotel

SECOND AVENUE

FIRST AVENUE

ROBERT MUGABE AVENUE

ROBERT MUGABE AVENUE

■ Publicity Association

Main Park

■ Balmoral

C AVENUE

City Centre Hotel

D AVENUE

● Little Swallow Inn

Aloe Garden

PARK ROAD

E AVENUE

■ Town Bus Terminal

Nyamtumbi River

HERBERT CHITEPO STREET

RAILWAY STREET

Railway Station

Sakubva River

CHIMANIMANI ROAD

BEIRA ROAD

PARK ROAD

Fiesta Park Hotel

N

0   250m

▽ Sakubva Musika Bus Terminal   ▽ Bvumba

remains informally segregated, with **Sakubva**, the factory and sawmill side, and high-density suburb, set apart from the more salubrious areas of the city centre.

Buses from the north come down Christmas Pass before pulling into the **town terminus**; hop off here, before the bus roars off to **Sakubva Musika** (4km out of the town – and with nowhere to stay). **From the south**, most buses continue to the centre *after* stopping at Sakubva; if yours doesn't, take any **urban bus** from outside the *musika* bus station gates, or one of the **taxis** that are always lined up. **Luxury coaches** from Harare pull in at the conveniently central *Manica Hotel*. The **train station**, arrival point for the overnight service from Harare, lies on the opposite, south side of town, a longish walk from most of Mutare's accommodation. Note that the majority of backpackers' lodges will collect guests for free.

Mutare has a good **tourist information office**, on Market Square, Herbert Chitepo St/Robert Mugabe Ave (☎64711; Mon–Fri 8.30am–12.45pm & 2–4pm, Sat 8.30–11am), with helpful and well-informed staff, who can supply information and maps on Mutare and the rest of the Eastern Highlands. They have a list of cottages to rent in Bvumba, Nyanga and Chimanimani, and details of organized tours.

Accommodation

Mutare has plenty of accommodation to suit all pockets, including two **campsites**. The nicest **hotels** are out of the centre in the hills, and tend to cater for commercial travellers and business people. As a bunch, Mutare's **backpacker lodges**, located in rambling old houses in the suburbs, are the best in the country. Most are a longish walk away from the centre, but their owners will pick you up if you arrange in advance.

For a more rural, inexpensive alternative, try one of the growing number of out-of-town places, most of which offer game viewing, walks, and trips to rock paintings.

Backpacker lodges

Anne Bruce's Guest House, 99 Fourth St/Sixth Ave (☎63569). Among the nicest of the budget options, this homely establishment has shared rooms and excellent food. The cheerful owner will fill you in on the latest developments in other places, as well as current information on the route to Beira and places to stay once you're there. ①.

Border Home, 3A Jason Moyo Drive, off Third St (☎63346). A wide array of options for budget travellers, including dorms, singles, doubles, a timber shed and a self-contained cottage. Somewhat overcrowded and drab, but the owner is helpful and friendly. ①–②.

Mr McIntyre, 5 Livingstone Rd (☎63968). The poshest of Mutare's backpackers' lodges – and the cheapest. Rooms in this well-maintained and comfortable double-storey house make you feel like a guest in someone's home. They'll cook breakfast, but other meals must be self-catered. ①.

Trevor's Place, 119 Fourth St (☎67762). A gently run-down house with double and triple rooms. Cheap and pleasant enough, and there's a kitchen for self catering. ①.

Hotels

Balmoral Hotel, C Ave (☎61435). A slightly seedy rooming house, near the station and park, with basic rooms. Those leading onto the sunny verandah are best. Used extensively by truck drivers, so you could be subjected to the sounds of revving engines and prostitution. ①.

City Centre Hotel, Herbert Chitepo St/D Ave (☎62441). In the same vicinity as the *Balmoral*, but more comfortable, a little pricier, and a major (though rough) nightlife venue, where pickpocketing is rife. The quietest rooms are those facing onto Third Avenue; all have private baths. ②.

Christmas Pass Hotel, (☎63818, fax 63875). On the brow of the hill at Christmas Pass, 5km from Mutare, with nice gardens and a swimming pool. ③.

Manica Hotel, Aerodrome Rd/Herbert Chitepo St (☎64431, fax 64466). The only central upmarket hotel, usually full of business travellers. They offer a great weekend (Fri–Sun) deal, with rooms at half price. ⑤.

Wise Owl Motel, near the campsite on Christmas Pass (☎64643). Best of the mid-range hotels, a friendly place, with good food, a pool and nice gardens. ③.

Camping

Mutare's **Caravan Park and Campsite** is halfway up Christmas Pass, 6km from the centre. If you're arriving by bus from Harare, get off at the *Christmas Pass Garage* and walk 2km downhill to the site, just off the main road. Alternatively, take a taxi back up again once you reach the central bus station. Unless you've brought supplies, you'll have to go to town to stock up anyway. The site is clean and wooded, but be prepared for lorries rumbling past all night with their headlights shadowplaying on your tent. The campsite is near Murahwa's Hill Nature Reserve, covered on p.222.

There's a quieter site at Tiger's Kloof Dam, 3km north of the centre at Cecil Kop Nature Reserve (see overleaf), where you'll be close to game and have a good chance of seeing samango monkeys.

Out of town

Drifters, PO Box 1646, Mutare (☎62964). Camping, spacious dorms and pleasant double rondavels in a thatched game farm development in the hills, 21km west of Mutare off the Harare road. Meals are provided, or you can self-cater. Activities include day trips to Bvumba and Nyanga, and walks up the adjacent mountain to look at rock paintings. Free transfers from town by arrangement. ①.

Mapor Estates, PO Box 98, Odzi (Odzi ☎03013). Budget farmhouse accommodation, 15km from Odzi village (or 48km from Mutare), with two en-suite twin bedrooms and camping. Breakfasts available, but other meals must be self-catered (equipment is provided). The environs offer good mountain walking and plentiful birdlife, as well as rock art and archeological sites. If you can get through on the phone, the owners will collect you. If you're driving yourself, the farm is a good, if remote, stopoff en route to the Highlands; the turn-off for Odzi is off the main Harare–Mutare road, 32km west of Mutare. ①.

The town and around

Mutare has no grand sights, but, with its parks and surrounding natural landscape, plus a surprisingly good museum, it's a thoroughly pleasant place to pass a leisurely day before moving on into the Highlands proper.

The park and aloe gardens

To call Mutare the "Garden City" is a slight exaggeration, perhaps, but its **park** and **aloe gardens** are a great place to picnic and while away hot afternoons. They are popular, too, and the park benches are invariably taken up by students.

The park is shaded by numerous exotic trees and has a palm-lined stream running down its centre. The heart of the botanic collections are some ten thousand **aloes** – large tropical succulents at their best when they flower in fiery tones in June and July. Besides aloes you'll find ancient and protected **cycads**, one of the slowest-growing and most primitive plants on earth.

Mutare Museum

The **Mutare Museum** (daily 9am–5pm; US$2), on Aerodrome Road, is worth a visit, if only to marvel at the goriness of its collection of stuffed animals. **Taxidermy** is quite an art, and each practitioner is apparently able to recognize the work of others. If you look at enough stuffed animals you'll notice that some taxidermists are good at putting expressions on the faces, others better at sculpting the forms on which the skins are mounted, or at painting and reproducing the exact hide and hair tones. The taxidermist in Mutare was clearly fascinated by the hunt, and the more dramatic and fearful the better: in his tableaux, eagles sink talons into quivering hares, owls pounce on terrified rodents and red-eyed serpents prey on petrified rats.

Echoing the violence in nature, the museum also has an enormous collection of **weaponry** – from inlaid silver pistols to crude trading rifles. And there is a hall packed with **vintage vehicles**, some of which look like the thirty-year-olds still going strong on Zimbabwean roads. The more serious **historical exhibits** are good, too, with explanations of the successive farming cultures in the region and examples of trade goods from the Arabs and Portuguese on the coast.

Lastly, don't leave without stepping into the **walk-in aviary**, a large and peaceful enclosure bursting with birdsong, where you'll spot one of the most striking birds of the Highlands – the vermilion and jade **purple-crested lourie**, whose appearance is so at odds with its harsh, grating croak of a call.

Cecil Kop Nature Reserve

An easily walkable 2.5km from the centre (up Herbert Chitepo Street past the *Manica*, then follow the "Tiger's Kloof" sign), the **Cecil Kop Nature Reserve** (open dawn–dusk; US$1) is a pleasant tea-time venue, and popular with locals over the weekend. It's a contrived place, perhaps, but very pretty: in the late afternoon, you can sit overlooking a **dam** where elephant, buffalo, giraffe, wildebeest, zebra and antelope are drawn to food laid out for them at 4pm each day. Alternatively, go earlier and have the place to yourself; you won't see the same number of animals, but with luck you may spot shy blue duiker, or samango monkeys, darker and with longer tails than the common vervet. These are species unique to the Eastern Highlands and you may well spot them in the wild.

Murahwa's Hill Reserve

If you've a few more hours to kill, and feel energetic, **Murahwa's Hill** – behind the most obvious kopje in the valley as you look from the town centre towards Christmas Pass – is a beautiful place to wander around. The drawback is the hour-long walk from town, though Murahwa is easy to get to from the campsite.

To walk around the kopje will take you quite some time: the path initially snakes through the thick draping forest at the base, but then it tracks fairly steeply up to the rocky summit where you find the **remains of a village** protected on three sides by immense granite boulders. This abandoned settlement is thought to be of about the same vintage as Great Zimbabwe; its few remaining artefacts are now in the museum. In a nearby cave there's a collection of unexceptional paintings – evidence of a much earlier settlement.

One way **to get there** is to bus or walk to the *Wise Owl Motel*, where a road on the valley side climbs to one of the park entrances. There's also a gentler incline from the rear of the showgrounds in Jan Smuts Drive. A **map** of sorts at the reserve entrance shows the locations of these archeological titbits but it's quite easy to get lost. Leave yourself plenty of time to get down while it's still light.

Mutare's markets and shops

Mutare's **markets** are worth exploring, even though they're on nothing like the scale of those in the Harare or Bulawayo. The **Sakubva Musika**, by the long-distance bus terminus, is entertaining when you're killing time waiting for transport. Handicrafts on sale are generally utilitarian, but you can rummage around for something interesting and try to guess a use for some of the unidentifiable objects.

Elsewhere, due to the abundant forests of the region, good **wooden crafts** are easy to find: *Jairos Jiri* (41 First St) and the Museum Shop (Aerodrome Rd) have ebony snuffboxes and vials, and the former wooden platters, bowls and spoons in ebony and other hard woods. Their stylish brown-and-white **woven hats** are also great – with narrow brims, white zigzags and pleated crowns.

For more mundane requirements, the **Green Market** – just past the railway bridge on the right before the Bvumba turn-off – is a good place to stock up on fruit and vegetables; macadamia nuts are a particularly nice regional speciality. Regular shops include the *TM Supermarket*, on the station side of town at Herbert Chitepo Street/B Avenue, and *Omar's Hyper*, near the *Manica Hotel* on Herbert Chitepo Street/Aerodrome Road. Mutare is also home to *Mitchells Bakery*, producers of the best **biscuits** in Zimbabwe.

Eating, drinking and nightlife

Though not the most lively of cities, Mutare has plenty of snack and cheap food joints open during the day, and a couple of good nightspots where, as well as drinking, you can pick up something to eat. The compact town centre means that most places are easy to get to.

Breakfast options range from basic eggs and toast on the terrace at *Meikles* to the expensive and overwhelming morning menu at the *Manica* and the similar *Wise Owl*, near the campsite. For a bottom-line tea-and-bun breakfast while you're waiting for a bus, try the *Povo Store* at the *musika*, or hard-boiled eggs, mealies and fruit from vendors there and at the bus terminus.

Restaurants

Dairy Den, Manica Arcade, Second Ave. Inexpensive hamburgers and sandwiches served until 7.30pm during the week, later at weekends.

Jenny's Cottage, Eighth Ave/Herbert Chitepo St. Recommended for light lunches and tea on the verandah.

Manica Hotel, Aerodrome Rd/Herbert Chitepo St. The best place in town for gargantuan – though not cheap – buffet breakfasts, which will fill you up for the day. It's also a comfortable place to have a drink or snack at other times, but a smart dress code is enforced in the evenings.

Meikles, Herbert Chitepo St. Old-established joint that really should be experienced at least once. Its terrace is the pleasantest place in town for a drink or light British-style meal, but is open only during the day.

Station Kiosk, Railway Street. Inexpensive *sadza nyama*, handy if you're waiting for the 9pm Harare train.

Stax Steak House, Norwich Union Centre, Herbert Chitepo St. Apart from the hotels, the sole restaurant open in the evenings, around the corner from the *Manica Hotel*. The steaks hang over the edge of the plate, and they do delicious veggie burgers. There's also a cheaper takeaway section.

Wimpy, Shopping Mall, Herbert Chitepo St/Third Ave. Familiar burgers and fast food from this worldwide franchise.

Wise Owl Motel, near the campsite on Christmas Pass. Famous for its moderately priced flambé steaks and Sunday braais.

Music and dance venues

Little Swallow Inn, next to the *City Centre Hotel*. Known locally as *Swallows*, this is the place to be if you feel like dancing and drinking heavily on weekends, when guest bands play live. Beware of pickpocketing and prostitution.

The Night Place, Robert Mugabe Ave, between Fourth and Fifth St. Worth a visit if someone good is playing, otherwise expect the usual mix of disco and drink.

Stirrup Cup. Through the car park behind the *Manica*, this smoky bar spins rock during the week, and a band performs transatlantic cover versions on Fridays and Saturdays.

Cinema and theatre

Both Mutare's **cinemas**, as well as its theatre, are to be found in Robert Mugabe Avenue. The two cinemas show a fairly meagre selection of action-packed popular stuff, but you might strike it lucky if there is a visiting (foreign) performance at the *Courtauld Theatre*.

Listings

American Express Handled by *Manica Travel Services*, Herbert Chitepo St/Second Ave (☎64112).

Automobile Association Fanum House, Robert Mugabe Ave (☎64422).

Banks *Barclays, Zimbank, Grindlays* all in Herbert Chitepo St (Mon, Tues, Thurs & Fri 8am–3pm, Wed 8am–1pm, Sat 8.30–11.30am).

Bookstores *Books*, 94 Herbert Chitepo St, next to *Manica Travel*, will trade in your paperbacks. *Book Centre*, Norwich Union Centre, Herbert Chitepo St/First Ave, sells a small selection of African and British novels.

Car rental *Hertz*, based at the tourist information office (☎64711), offer discounts at weekends, if cars are available, but only on a stand-by basis – you can't book ahead. Other firms include *Europcar*, at *Grant's Service Station*, 21 Robert Mugabe Ave (☎62367).

Chemists *Lancasters Pharmacy*, 95a Herbert Chitepo St (☎62579 after hours). *Central Pharmacy*, Cuthbert Building, Herbert Chitepo St (☎61211 after hours).

Hospital There is a casualty department at the hospital on Robert Mugabe Ave. If you don't want to have to wait, it's better to go to the private *Seventh Avenue Surgical Unit*, 123 Herbert Chitepo St (☎64635 or 64681).

Immigration Department Robert Mugabe Ave (☎62322).

Petrol *Grants Service Station*, on Robert Mugabe Ave, is open 24hr.

Police Aerodrome Rd, opposite *Manica Hotel* (☎64212).

Post office and public phones Robert Mugabe Ave (Mon–Fri 8.30am–4pm, Sat 8–11.30am).

Swimming pool off roundabout on Robert Mugabe Ave. Tues–Sun 6–7am & 10am–5pm. Closed May 15–Sept 1. Admission nominal.

Tours *Hertz*, based at the tourist information office (☎64711), do minibus tours of the Eastern Highlands, and *African Overland Expeditions*, 25 Selous Ave, Harare (☎14/790677), offer similar tours in their eight-seater Mercedes minibuses.

Taxis Ranks behind the Publicity Association, bus terminus and *musika* (☎63344).

Train station Ticket office (Mon–Fri 8am–12.50pm & 2–4pm; ☎62835). For 1st- and 2nd-class tickets on the day of travel, if the office has closed, queue up at the economy class ticket booth a couple of hours before departure.

Travel agents *Manica Travel Services*, Herbert Chitepo St/Second Ave (☎64112), is the place to buy tickets for the coach to Harare.

Visas for Mozambique These can be arranged in town, but passports must be sent to Harare, which can take up to two weeks. Enquire at *Manica Travel* (see above).

Around Mutare

When people in Mutare talk about "the mountains", they generally mean the **Bvumbas**, which lie south of Mutare. Bvumba – the name derives from a seventeenth-century Shona kingdom that spread well beyond the range into Mozambique – is often used simply to refer to the famous **botanical gardens** at the top of the mountains, though it's actually a large area encompassing tea and coffee plantations, commercial forestry stations and fruit farms. The botanical gardens, along with the nearby **Bunga Forest Reserve**, is the undoubted highlight, and worth any amount of hassle to get to. Accommodation is available to suit all pockets, with choices ranging from the famous *Leopard Rock Hotel* to camping at the most spectacularly sited of all Zimbabwean campsites. There are several self-catering cottages available for rent in the area as well as a backpackers' lodge.

The pretty gold-mining town of **Penhalonga** and the **La Rochelle Gardens** can be easily combined on a day's outing north of Mutare.

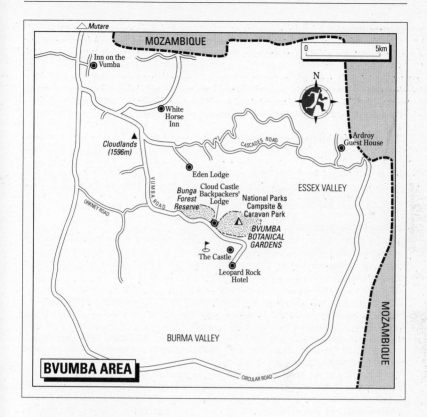

Bvumba Botanical Gardens

An annual rainfall higher than that of London has created lush cloud forest in the **Bvumba Mountains**, known in Manyika as "the mountains of the mist". Such dream-like connotations have inspired the **Bvumba Botanical Gardens** (open daily; US$2), which lie 32km south of Mutare, harmoniously landscaped in the best romantic tradition of English formal gardens. Surrounded by indigenous forest, they were the creation of a former Mutare mayor and his wife, who lived here from the 1920s to the late 1950s and called them – in true homesick fashion – the Manchester Gardens. Remarkably, throughout the mayhem of the bush war, the gardens were kept in immaculate condition; they are now run by National Parks.

Paths meander delightfully through flowering shrubs and trees gathered from all over the world. Waterlilies float on the central ornamental lake; scattered gazebos invite contemplative rests; and pristine lawns and flowerbeds give way on the fringes to a more African feel where giant tree ferns adorn streams – as they do all over the Eastern Highlands. The full range of Zimbabwe's upland flora is represented at Bvumba, including many varieties of orchid.

Summer downpours can flood everything in sight and it's a lot chillier up here than in Mutare. Weather permitting, a **teashop** is open every day from 10am until 4pm.

The rainforest

You can explore the **rainforest** that adjoins the gardens along a number of waymarked paths; maps are available at the main entrance. A **path** from the edge of the campsite takes you through the forest and back to the gardens – a two-hour circuit. It begins by leading down into jungly forest, where the indigenous trees rise about you – all darkness and silence until the monkeys catch sight of you and the birds screech in alarm. Further on you begin to hear the sound of chattering streams cascading over slippery rocks. For a shorter walk, several paths branch off the main trail.

Chinyakwaremba (Leopard's Rock)

Outside the gardens, it's possible to climb **Chinyakwaremba**, or **Leopard's Rock** hill. A path from a lay-by on the right of the main road, leads up one and a half kilometres from the turn-off to the botanical gardens. It's an easy twenty-minute walk up to the top, where there are lovely views into Burma Valley, across to Mozambique, and down to the chateau-like hotels below (see "Accommodation" below).

Getting to the gardens

Bvumba is not well served by public transport. The only **bus** to the gardens is a weekend service that departs from Mutare's E Street terminus, opposite the Customs House, on Fridays, Saturdays and Sundays at approximately 9am and 3pm, returning at 10am and 5pm.

Prospects for **hitching** are reasonable, especially over the weekends when the gardens are a popular tea-time trip; on weekdays, a number of people living on smallholdings and farms in the mountains also go into Mutare to work, so late afternoon would again be a good time. Wait at the *Bvumba Service Station* on the corner of Park and Bvumba roads, where you'll get cars from the centre bypassing the bottom end of town. Many of these lifts, however, don't go all the way to the gardens, so be prepared for a longish walk.

At Cloudlands, the road forks, uphill to the gardens and down to the Essex and Burma valleys, where there are commercial farms and communal lands. The **walk** from here to the gardens is a rewarding hike through smooth green hills, flower-specked pastures and thick stands of forest and pine trees. Modern-day Bvumba comprises indigenous woodland as well as commercial wattle forest, interspersed with farmhouses, cottages and workers' huts that have inviting English-style country gardens. As you slog on, the road curves higher to reveal even more vistas. These are best enjoyed from the lay-bys, with their off-the-road concrete tables and seats – created for family outings by a nation of picnickers. On the Bvumba road, before you reach the gardens, you'll pass through **Bunga Forest Reserve**, an extension of the rainforest preserved in the gardens and also waymarked.

Accommodation

Bvumba has **accommodation** to suit most pockets, ranging from the ultra-luxurious *Leopard's Rock Hotel*, which boasts its own casino, down to basic backpacker's lodges and campsites. Most of the places to stay are strung along the main road leading to the gardens. In addition, the tourist information office in Mutare has a full list of **cottages** to let in the Bvumba and Essex Valley. They're usually fully booked during the school holiday season and are not places you can expect rent on spec, but ring ahead from town and you may strike lucky. Two, reasonably close to the gardens, are sited on an ornithological station (PO Box 812, Mutare; ☎215125). The station isn't open to the general public, but the proprietor takes guests birdwatching. Another possibility is *Far Forest Cottage*, about 3km from the gardens near the summit of the Bvumba (PO Box 234, Mutare; ☎218524).

Ardroy Guest House, Blue Mountain Rd (☎217121). An atmospheric farmhouse, 34km from Mutare, that has views over the plains of Mozambique. It once belonged to novelist Doris Lessing's late son, and has been left much as it was when he died: minimally maintained, and with an air of gentle decay. In one of her short stories, Lessing describes its trellised verandah with "creepers weighing down the roof". Small dorms and doubles are available. There are no cooking facilities, but tasty, inexpensive meals are served. Getting there by car from Mutare takes about an hour, much of the route along winding dirt roads that can be tricky when wet. Best phone for directions. Without a car you can still get there on the 6am Mapofu bus or the 11am one headed for Burma Valley. ①.

The Castle, Private Bag V7401, Mutare (☎210320). Splendid Italian-POW-built accommodation, on a choice site just beyond the Botanical Gardens. Its owners only take one party at a time, cooking lavishly for them. A wonderfuly private, secluded place to stay, but you need to book well ahead. The prices are reasonable, with a two-night minimum at weekends. ③.

Cloud Castle Guest House, just before the entrance to the Botanical Gardens; postal bookings through PO Box 957, Mutare (☎21760). Relaxed atmosphere, and a prime location that makes this a good base for a day or two's walking in the area. Small dorms and doubles with bunks as well as camping, and a self-contained family flat. Cooking facilities are available. The owner picks people up from the Mutare Publicity Association three times a week. If you decide to make your own way to the guest house, look for a sign on your left just beyond the 28km peg on the main Bvumba Road, 20m before the dirt road that leads to the entrance of the Botanical Gardens. Bring fresh meat and vegetables from Mutare and get the rest at the nearby *Naro Moru Store*, which sells bread and milk, tinned food and drinks, and doubles up as a bar at weekends (closed Mon). ①.

Eden Lodge, Freshwater Rd, off the Essex Valley road; postal bookings through PO Box 881, Mutare (☎62000, fax 62001). Smart hotel, 21km from Mutare, set in a forest overlooking the Zohwi Valley, with comfortable en-suite timber chalets. Recommended for wildife enthusiasts (you can watch birds and monkeys from the rooms). ③.

Inn on the Bvumba, signposted off Bvumba Road 8km from Mutare (☎81025, fax 60722). A lovely old-fashioned hotel, with views across the valley and homely touches like fresh flowers on tables and biscuits served with tea. It's a fair way from the botanical gardens, but good value. Highly recommended and often fully booked, so reserve in advance. ④.

Leopard's Rock Hotel, top of the Bvumba road; postal bookings through PO Bvumba (☎14/733073). Zimbabwe's most romantic hotel is a mountain resort, complete with a casino, golf course and prices to match. ⑨.

National Parks Camping and Caravan Site, Bvumba Botanical Gardens. This attractive National Parks campsite is set amid thick, shaded lawns that are scented in the summer by magnolia blossom. The bathrooms are spotless, and there's no shortage of hot water from the wood boiler outside. In the evening, you have the whole estate to yourself and the views over Mozambique's Lake Chicamba Reial, a thousand metres below, are simply stupendous.

White Horse Inn, Laurenceville Rd, signposted off Bvumba Road (☎60325 or 216612). Splendidly sited in mountains near *Cloudlands*, with the best food in the area, though smart-casual attire is insisted upon. Cheaper and a lot nicer than the *Manica* in Mutare. ③.

Penhalonga and La Rochelle

A good day's excursion north from Mutare easily combines **Penhalonga** – an attractive village with run-down period buildings, trading stores and its own working gold mines – and the somewhat overgrown **La Rochelle Gardens**, with the option of overnighting (or even spending a few days) at one of the charming cottages at La Rochelle.

Penhalonga

Hidden in a valley on the old scenic route to Nyanga, 17km from Mutare, **PENHALONGA** feels like a neglected outpost of the 1940s. It was the first of the settlers' **gold prospecting** sites (gold is still mined here) and retains the appearance of a trading post. All the shops have dark interiors, with tailors on the pillared verandahs sewing with old treddle Singers, and, inside, lengths of cotton-print hanging from the ceiling. Two of the town buildings are particularly handsome – the corrugated-iron **church** built on pillars and the red-roofed **school**. Dating from the beginning of the century, the church is in a Victorian-Gothic style, a tin version of a medieval English country chapel.

Getting to Penhalonga is straightforward. **By car,** you take Robert Mugabe Avenue out of town and continue up Christmas Pass, following the clear signposts. Several **buses** a day also pass on the way to Stapleford and Honde Valley from Mutare's *musika*, while three buses (at 6am, 11am and 3pm) go to Penhalonga itself from the town terminus. Alternatively, catch any of the numerous buses up Christmas Pass from Robert Mugabe Avenue, get off at the Christmas Pass Service Station – where the road to Penhalonga begins – and **hitch**, or catch another bus, from there. The **campsite** and

MOVING ON TO MOZAMBIQUE: THE BEIRA CORRIDOR

The port of **Beira**, 300km east of Mutare on the coast of Mozambique, is the obvious outlet for landlocked Zimbabwe's trade, and was used extensively as such until 1974, as well as being the place where many Rhodesians took their seaside holidays. However, the overthrow of the Portuguese and the establishment of the Marxist **Frelimo** government obliged Rhodesia to export its goods via the long, expensive rail link with Durban in South Africa.

In response, Smith's intelligence agency set up a 500-strong destabilization force, the Mozambique National Resistance Movement (MNR) or **Renamo**. When majority rule emerged in Zimbabwe, Renamo was handed on to the South Africans, who built it into a monster of (according to some estimates) twenty thousand fighters. During the 1980s, South Africa used Renamo as an instrument of foreign policy, supplying it by means of parachute drops, its main function being to bring Mozambique to its knees. In this it was devastatingly successful: large parts of Mozambique were overrun by Renamo, whose grisly attacks helped to grind the country down into its status as one of the world's poorest nations, and one easily manipulated by its neighbour.

After Independence Zimbabwe began once again exporting goods by rail to Beira. But Renamo attacks on the line brought traffic to a standstill in 1984. The crisis led to pragmatic co-operation between Zimbabwe's socialist leadership and predominantly white, capitalist interests, who formed the **Beira Corridor Group** to oversee the rehabilitation of the coastal link. Hundreds of millions of US dollars were pumped into the programme in a concerted effort to break South Africa's stranglehold on the economies of both countries.

Up to seven thousand Zimbabwean troops were sent in to guard the route, costing around US$70 million annually. Meanwhile, Renamo carried out its own atrocities against Zimbabwean border villages, as well as continuing the civil war in Mozambique. The peace accord brokered in 1992 stipulated that Government soldiers and Renamo fighters be disarmed and formed into a unified army. Thankfully, a successful reconstruction is now underway and traffic along the Beira Corridor is once again on the increase.

Border practicalities

Forbes border post, ten minutes' from Mutare by car, is the gateway to the Beira Corridor and the obvious crossing point for overland travel into Mozambique. As recently as the early 1990s, the civil war made this road hazardous, but tourists are now passing through safely.

Minibuses leave from **Machipanda**, on the Mozambique side, 10km from Mutare, taking passengers to the palm trees and beaches of Beira. One or two backpackers' lodges have even sprouted along the route – a sure sign that it is opening up. Check out the current situation with the Mutare backpackers' lodges, or with the town's helpful Publicity Association.

Note that to enter Mozambique you must already have obtained a **visa**, either issued in Harare through one of many travel agents who can arrange things on your behalf (see "Listings" p.82) or a Mozambican embassy abroad; allow five days or more for it to be processed.

caravan park is sadly under threat of closure: despite its backwater charm few visit Penhalonga these days.

La Rochelle

LA ROCHELLE, 4km south of Penhalonga in the Imbeza Valley, is a pleasant walk from the main Mutare road (3km), past farms and smallholdings and some beautiful stands of *Acacia abyssinica* in the valley. Although not a patch on Bvumba, the gardens nevertheless make a pleasant and easy trip from Mutare if you have your own vehicle. A network of pathways, with scented plants and braille directions for the blind, is one of only two such garden trails in Africa (the other is at Cape Town's Kirstenbosch). The **teas** are good, too, and there are some inexpensive **cottages** for rent in the garden (PO Box 34, Penhalonga; ☎22250; ②), as well as a **caravan and camping site**.

An infrequent **bus** goes to the Imbeza Valley from Mutare's **town terminus**; otherwise take any Penhalonga-bound bus and walk from the signposted turn-off.

Nyanga National Park

One-and-a-half hours' drive north of Mutare (and just three hours from Harare), on good, tarred roads, the **NYANGA NATIONAL PARK** attracts Zimbabwean outdoor enthusiasts, who come for the mountains and forests, and for trout fishing. The park is devoid of big game, though most of the smaller animals and antelope are present in large numbers. But it provides some rewarding walking country, criss-crossed by hundreds of well-defined footpaths and by current or abandoned fishing roads. There are less energetic pursuits on offer, too, such as lazing around the pools and waterfalls at one of the national parks' three camps (see below).

In the southern sector of the park, there is more remote **wilderness territory**, where you could easily spend several days hiking, while, in the east, the looming, myth-bound mass of **Mount Nyangani** (2593m) is a simple enough summit to scale. The Nyanga region is also scattered with intriguing **ruins and forts**, mostly unrestored and hidden beneath shrouds of ferns and undergrowth. On the grandest scale, Van Niekerk's ruins, now known as **Ziwa ruins**, straggle across at least fifty square kilometres of open country northwest of the park borders, in a jumble of rubble-strewn stone terraces and levels. On the western edge of the park itself are the mountain resorts of **Juliasdale** and **Troutbeck**.

Practicalities

The best **seasons** to visit are either side of the school holidays, in April–May and August–September. The scenery then is especially lovely and the weather as warm and dry as it ever gets. Be prepared, however, for cold nights all year round, and – if you come during the rainy season – for wet weather that can sometimes last for days on end. It never snows, though.

Where you **base** yourself in the park is largely a matter of how pressed for time you are, and how well equipped. The most convenient concentrations of overnight options are at **Rhodes Dam** and **Udu Dam** – at the western edge of the park, within a few kilometres of the main entrance and headquarters – and at **Mare Dam**, further afield to the east. Admission to the park is US$2, and lodges go for the normal National Parks fees.

Apart from the single luxury hotel at Nyanga (situated in the north of the park), the only roofed **accommodation** consists of one- and two-bedroomed **lodges** (note that Udu has large lodges only). These can sleep up to eight people, and each is fully serviced, right down to there being loads of chopped wood and laid fires. During school holidays or long weekends, it's virtually impossible to get lodge accommodation

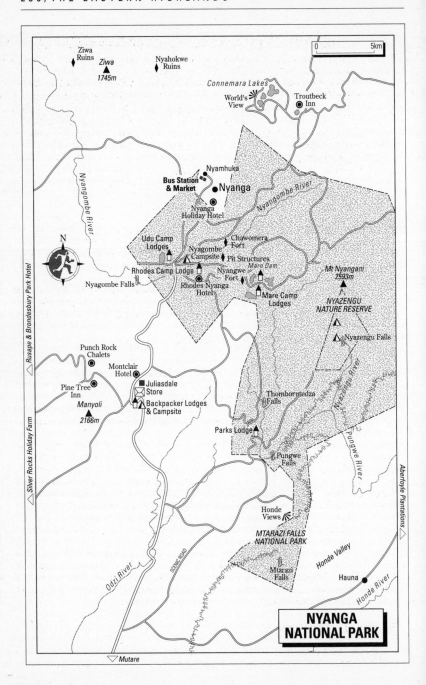

NYANGA
NATIONAL PARK

NYANGA REGION PRIVATE COTTAGES

Unless otherwise specified, the cottages below are fully equipped and are serviced. Prices per cottage are between US$15 and Z$40 per night, or around US$5 per person (a minimum stay of two nights is the rule), depending on what facilities are offered and the time of year; public holidays are usually more expensive. Book ahead.

Brackenridge Cottage, PO Box 27, Juliasdale (☎26321). On a fruit farm 3km from Pungwe Falls, the cottage sleeps ten. Bring towels, cutlery and toilet rolls.

Silver Rocks Holiday Farm, PO Box 27, Juliasdale (☎21719). Located 10km south from the Juliasdale–Rusape road. Has the added enticement of a swimming pool.

Ezulwini, PO Box 12, Troutbeck (129-8-61121). Two fully equipped and serviced cottages. Turn left at the 26.5km peg beyond *Troutbeck Hotel* and follow the signs.

The Follies, PO Box 101, Kopje, Harare (☎/fax 721696). Overlooking the Connemara lakes near World's View, this cottage can sleep up to ten people.

without having **booked** six months or more ahead (you can do this through the National Parks Booking Office in Harare; see p.46). In the off-season though, or during the week, you stand a fairly good chance of a place just turning up at the Parks' Office at Rhodes Camp. **Camping** is cheap and space is never a problem. The river water throughout Nyanga is bilharzia-free and drinkable.

You will need to bring most provisions with you. There is just one park **shop** (on the south side of Rhodes Dam, open daily 9am–2pm) which sells essential food supplies, but nothing fresh. The national park has no **moneychanging** facilities, but there are two banks in Nyanga Village.

Juliasdale

Straggling along the main road to Nyanga, **JULIASDALE** is the last settlement before the park, a regional centre consisting of little more than a couple of shops, a petrol station and post office. The area around is a popular retirement location for white Zimbabweans; Robert Mugabe, too, has a country retreat somewhere among the forests and fruit farms. Lower down, there are splendid granited valleys, msasa trees and tempting *gomos* to climb.

Accommodation in the district is restricted to a backpackers' lodge, three plush hotels and some **rented cottages** (for which advance booking is essential; see above). Of the **hotels**, the *Montclair Casino* (☎129/449, fax 447; ⑥) is seriously upmarket, with an evening dress code for the casino. However, you don't have to be a guest, or smartly dressed, to enjoy its valley-sided gardens for tea or drinks, or go one-armed banditing in its darkened gambling hall. The other hotels are the *Brondesbury Park*, on the Rusape side of Juliasdale, at the start of the Nyanga "vacationlands" (☎129/342, fax 343; ④), and the *Pine Tree Inn* (☎129/25916, fax 25388; ④), which lies between it and the town, hard by some accessible granite tops, and has a top reputation for its food. If you're on a tighter budget, head for the *Camp and Cabin* backpacker's lodge next to the Juliasdale post office (☎129/202; ③), which has tiny log cabins and a campsite. Adjacent to the bus stop, it is convenient for transport to and from Harare, Rusape and Nyanga, and is also close to the local shops, where you can pick up basic supplies. The lodge also has a bar and lounge, but you have to cook your own meals.

Rhodes Dam and around

RHODES DAM is the most convenient, though the least exciting, of the camps, close to the main road and near the shop and hotel, and site of the local Parks office (office open daily 7am–6pm; ☎129-8/274384). The **lodges** here, tucked between the pines, face onto a small lake, one of several recreational lakes in the park. The area is tame, but pleasing, and it provides easy access to some historical sites as well as walks around the rest of the park.

Nyangombe campsite and Brighton Beach

A couple of kilometres from the office, on the main Nyanga road, is **Nyangombe campsite**, reached via a short cut over the Nyangombe River. Along the river you'll see a natural pool known – by the local ex-pat community at least – as **Brighton Beach**, complete with changing rooms and gazebo. A small waterfall and rock slide culminate in a large pool of icy water surrounded by a river-sand beach – good for sunbathing, and not as crowded as the name might suggest.

Rhodes Nyanga Hotel and Museum

After visiting the Nyanga area in 1896, Cecil Rhodes wrote to his agent:

> *Dear McDonald*
>
> *Inyanga is much finer than you described. I find a good many farms are being occupied. Before it is all gone, buy me quickly up to 100,000 acres and be sure to take in the Pungwe Falls. I would like to try sheep and apple growing. Do not say you are buying for me.*
>
> *Yrs. C. J. Rhodes.*

The old colonialist was successful in acquiring a substantial slice of territory and, indeed, the park was known up until Independence as "Rhodes Inyanga".

Rhodes's former residence, a simple Georgian-style stone house set among English oaks and chestnuts, stands just across the lake from Rhodes Dam. It is now incorporated into the **Rhodes Nyanga Hotel** (☎129-8/377; ④), where the room rate includes dinner and breakfast (it's cheaper to stay in a rondavel than an en-suite room). Non-residents are allowed to drift in to laze in the rose garden and look round its **museum** in the old stables (Tues–Sat 9am–1pm & 2.30–5.30pm), where, alongside a fair amount of Rhodes memorabilia, an interesting photo exhibition gives the history of colonization in the area from the Portuguese and British up to recent resistance.

There's a comprehensive display in homage to **Chief Rekayi Tangwena**, one of Zimbabwe's nationalist stalwarts, buried at Heroes' Acre in Harare. Tangwena fought against the eviction of his people from their land in the Nyafara area beyond Troutbeck during the Smith era, gave considerable assistance to guerillas throughout the **bush war**, and provided a link with the spirit mediums who encouraged resistance. In 1975 he helped **Robert Mugabe** and **Edgar Tekere** escape into Mozambique. After Independence and his appointment as a senator, he participated in a programme here to resettle orphaned and homeless children.

The Rhodes Dam Pit Structure

A common sight throughout the Nyanga area are **pit structures**, or "slave pits" – roofless, two- to three-metre-deep enclosures that are something of a mystery. No archeological evidence has been found to support the notion that they were used to detain slaves – certainly no one seems to know who kept the slaves, who the slaves were and why they didn't escape. Other interpretative stabs have included fortified refuges for women and children, grain stores, gold-washing tanks, and symbolic representations of the Phoenician fertility goddess Astarte's womb. The most widely accepted theory is that the pits were livestock pens, some say for miniature cattle that Portuguese travellers were supposed to have seen. But in view of the reputation of the Portuguese explorers for tall stories, and in the absence of any supporting material, most people keep an open mind about this. It's more likely that ordinary goats, sheep and pigs were corralled in these sixteenth-century enclosures.

The restored pit structure which everyone visits is near Rhodes Dam on the road to Mare, but there are thousands more in Nyanga which you'll stumble across, sometimes literally, on walks. They occur singly or in groups of as many as twelve or more – look out for an isolated clump of trees or thick bush when you're walking in the region. If you're interested, it's as well to visit the developed site first so you know what you're looking for, and because the reconstruction spares you the difficulty of imagining what they might have been like in use.

At the **Rhodes Dam Pit Structure**, a dry stone wall pit on an earth platform is partially cut into the side of a hill and held back by a retaining wall on the lower slopes. This was the centre of the homestead, and from here you can creep into a pit, through a narrow, curved tunnel, roofed with flat stone slabs. You can't see the exit from the entrance, but halfway along the sky penetrates through a gap that used to open into the largest hut on the platform above. A nifty floor slot enabled the occupants to block and unblock the passage at will with a timber pole. According to one theory, the master of the house had his head-rest at the top of the pole and no one could tamper with the security system without waking him. Evidence of a drainage system in the pits reinforces the idea that animals rather than grain were kept in them.

Chawomera Fort

The other ruins at Nyanga, equally mysterious, are of fort-like hilltop structures, always commanding superb views across the valleys and plains. From the pit structure exhibit, there's an agreeable one-and-a-half-hour walk to **Chawomera Fort** and pits, one of the easiest hilltop fort ruins to reach.

The function of these so-called forts, which are invariably sited next to a few pits, is uncertain, as all sorts of things indicate that they weren't actually built for defence. While all the walls have small, square **loop holes**, reminiscent of gun slits, when you look through them the views are restricted and no weapon could effectively have been fired from them. Assailants, moreover, would have quite easily been able to fire through the wide inside openings. And although the forts are in easily defensible positions, none has a nearby water supply, so inhabitants couldn't have withstood a siege for long. One theory suggests they were a series of beacons or signal points, from where a kudu horn sounded messages carried across the valleys. It is in fact possible to see several forts from one site, once you can recognize the hills on which they're constructed.

As you head for Chawomera from the Rhodes Dam Pit Structure, you'll see a dirt road leading to workers' houses attached to the **Government Experimental Orchard**. Follow it for a few metres and, just before a fence, take a well-defined path next to a pine plantation on your left. This path continues down to the **Nyangombe River**, hugging the river bank and passing several bathing spots along the way. Cross the river at the second bridge and continue uphill along the path until it hits the gravel road from Rhodes Dam.

Mare Dam, Mount Nyangani and Nyazengu

MARE (pronounced *mah-ree*) is the camp closest to Mount Nyangani and the isolated areas between the "back" of Nyangani and the Pungwe Falls in the south. Despite its proximity to these remote parts, though, pine-forested Mare Dam itself has no hint of the back-of-beyond. In a rare flight of fantasy, National Parks have built the well-sheltered **lodges** like Swiss chalets, complete with pitched roofs, wooden finishings and laid log fires (bring your own matches). If you're into riding, Mare is a convenient camp, just 3km from the national park's stables.

FISHING, HORSE RIDING AND TENNIS

Boat rental is possible at any of the dams – though more for an afternoon drifting in the sun rather than any serious rowing (the lakes are pretty small). You need to claim a boat quickly though, as many are taken by trout fishermen. The **fishing** is good, too: rainbow, brook and brown trout can be hooked all year, though you need a licence from Rhodes Dam office, and your own rod.

Horse riding can be arranged at Rhodes, Udu or Mare camps; the stables are an hour's walk from Rhodes, on the Mare road. The horses come with a guide who'll take you on paths through the park for an hour and a half to the pit structures, Nyangwe Fort or the experimental orchard. Proficient riders can also book a horse for a full day's escorted ride. The terrain is ideal for brisk gallops and the Nyangombe river provides delightful picnic sites.

Tennis rackets can be rented at the rather under-used courts at Rhodes Camp.

Nyangwe Fort

Nyangwe Fort, half an hour's uphill trudge (or a rather easier ride) above Mare Dam, would be worth visiting for the view alone. It is also, however, the most complex of the forts here, five enclosures surrounding the original one on the summit. Within the structure – possibly dating back to the sixteenth century – are the remains of nineteen circular stone bases for huts or granaries.

From Nyangwe you look straight across to **Chawomera Fort** (see above), a good two hours' walk away. To reach it, head down the hill just before the pony trails office and stables on the main road, from where a well-defined path on your right skirts pine plantations and heads straight across the grassy valley, over the Nyangombe River to the fort's twin hills.

Climbing Mount Nyangani

Unlike Mount Ziwa in the north, which rises abruptly from the plain, **MOUNT NYANGANI**, long and flat-topped, seems scarcely higher than the mountains around it. Nevertheless, at 2592m it's a substantial mountain, Zimbabwe's highest, and often mist-wrapped and shadowy. According to local legend it has frightening people-eating tendencies, and one or two walkers have disappeared without a trace over the years; mostly, it seems, teenagers. The mountain holds considerable religious significance for Shona people. Locals from the Honde Valley say the mountain should be approached very respectfully – one should never shout or make a noise on it – and that they wouldn't dream of climbing it themselves.

Despite the taboos, Nyangani is frequently climbed as a morning's hike. The two-hour **ascent** is clearly marked from the car park, and there are white cairns along the way to guide you where the path becomes indistinct. The climb reveals spectacular panoramas into Mozambique, and around the summit you'll find lots of water; several rivers rise here. There are areas of quicksand up here too – it's certainly marshy towards the summit – and it's not difficult to see how the people-swallowing reputation might have arisen. Go up only in fine weather and take something warm in case the mist comes down. The very active **Mountain Club of Zimbabwe** does this climb regularly and has its own hut on Nyanga.

To **get to the trailhead** without a car you have to hitch the 10km from Mare. If you decide to walk, it means making camp at the base, which is in any case ideal if you intend to hike for a few days beyond Nyangani to Mtarazi National Park and into the Honde Valley. An ambitious and very beautiful three-day hike of 48km will take you from Nyangani to the Pungwe Falls, Mtarazi Falls and into the Honde Valley (see below), from where you can catch a bus back to Mutare.

Nyazengu Nature Reserve

Perhaps the most rewarding way to explore the Nyangani area and beyond is to camp and hike through the privately owned, and very remote, **Nyazengu Nature Reserve** in the national park. The reserve, at the base of Nyangani, has exceptionally beautiful views of the mountain and across the grasslands towards the Pungwe Gorge. There's a choice of several well-marked trails, some of which take you to waterfalls and clear pools of amber rocks. The **Nyazengu Falls**, deep in forest, are easily as dramatic as the better-known Mtarazi Falls. One trail takes you right to their valley base, or you can climb upwards to the top of Nyangani.

While it's possible to go for a day's hike in the reserve, for a modest fee per vehicle and per person, it makes an ideal base for a couple of days' walking. The main **campsite**, near the office, is spectacularly situated and completely undeveloped, apart from a long drop. Staff provide water for cooking – all the river water is safe to drink. It's also possible to camp at the Nyazengu Falls, in a sheltered forest site, though there are no facilities at all. If camping doesn't appeal, there is a lovely **bungalow** for rent, sleeping six people for a total rent of $US24 per night, perched on the side of the mountain. Book through Dr Trace, *Inyangani Farms*, 128 Upper East Road, Avondale, Harare (☎303518).

Unless you hike in on foot, which takes a full day from Mare Dam, you'll need a high-clearance 4WD vehicle to get to Nyazengu – you have to ford a river, but the rough road is passable all year round. Take the road marked *NO ENTRY*, on the right just before the road climbs to the Nyangani car park. From here it's 8km to the office where you obtain a permit to walk. There are no shops or supplies available in the reserve, but you can buy fresh trout at the office.

Udu Dam

Unlike Rhodes and Mare, **UDU CAMP**, in the far west corner of the park, provides the opportunity to get out of the pines and into granite and indigenous vegetation. The **lodges**, with long sloping roofs, based on traditional Nyika thatching, overlook the dam and ruin-capped hills, and *Acacia abyssinicas* grow in a smooth V-shaped stand, up the facing slopes. The **Udu River** flows through here, too, forming an exquisite, wide valley where waterbuck feed, before leading into the dam and out into a bathing pool, and eventually joining with the Nyangombe.

The **Udu Valley** preserves the gentle steps of ancient terracing, and remains dotted with pit structures, including one outside the back door of the Parks office. The chunky **Nyangombe Falls** with square-cut rocks are near Udu and make a nice walk. And it's easy to find your way around Udu: wandering in the encircling hills you can always spot the valley.

The two-kilometre **walk to the camp** from the main Nyanga road, opposite the Nyangombe **campsite** is pretty, heading first uphill, then opening out into a view of the camp in the valley; you'll invariably get a lift from a passing car, if you want it. Well-worn short cuts between the loops in the road take you straight to the nearest **shop** – at Rhodes Hall.

Nyangombe Falls

The **Nyangombe Falls** are an impressive cubist plunge, half an hour's walk if you take the dirt road, or one-and-a-half if you go over the saddle of the hills facing the lodges.

The Nyangombe tumbles dramatically over steep blocks before smoothing out into a densely wooded gorge below. Inviting as it looks, several people have been killed trying to climb down the walls of the gorge or edging too close to the waterfall, where the rocks are treacherously wet. You can see the waterfall quite clearly from dry rocks, a short downhill walk from the car park.

To reach the falls over the hills, take the path that starts at the back door of Udu Camp reception and keep bearing right to cross the river, then cut up to the saddle between two hills through woodland with dwarf bonsai-like msasas, wild fruit trees and the odd antelope. Follow your nose down until you turn right onto the dirt road to the falls. Instead of descending, you could carry on to the top of the highest hill to inspect a collapsed **fort** marked by a single big tree, clearly visible from the Udu Camp office. A path from the ruins leads back down through trees, across the dam wall (next to the pool) and to the lodges.

Nyanga Village

NYANGA VILLAGE nestles in a valley surrounded by mountains and extensive grass-lands, 23km north of Juliasdale on a good tarred road. A charming if unexciting place, it makes a good base, with fine walks nearby and easy hitching to the national park. It also services the nearby communal lands with shops and buses, and has the area's cheapest hotel.

The **Three Sisters** mountain, its slopes dotted with smart houses, dominates the village, with the huge rampart of the Troutbeck Massif beyond. The village itself straggles between two distinct characters: at the more upmarket end is the *Nyanga Holiday Hotel*, at the other the **Nyamhuka** township. **Buses** for Mutare, Harare and Troutbeck leave from Nyamhuka, which has a small **market**, street food and better stocked shops than in Nyanga centre.

Near Nyamhuka, your eyes will be drawn to a couple of brightly painted huts proclaiming a **craft village**. Quite a modest place, it sells mostly woven woollen mats and rugs made by local women in competition with the *Zuwa Weaving Co-op* in Nyanga centre. *Zuwa* has lovely handmade stuff in wool and cotton, subtly coloured with local plant dyes. You might consider posting home their chunky woollen rugs with bold and imaginative designs, or the handspun blankets.

The friendly and comfortable, if slightly barrack-like, *Country Inn* (☎129-8/336; ④) does a reasonable full-board deal. They also have a swimming pool, and you can pop in for a meal, or tea and excellent homemade biscuits. The obliging owner can arrange trips to Ziwa ruins and to the Nyanga township. A path leads up the Three Sisters mountain from the hotel; you could make a day of it from here to Nyangombe Falls or the stone forts, even on foot.

Troutbeck and World's View

Up in the mists beyond the northeast boundary of the national park, **TROUTBECK**, 17km from Nyanga Village, was the fantasy creation of one Major McIlwaine, an Irishman who established the very swish **Troutbeck Inn** (☎1298/305 or 306, fax 474; ⑥, half-board), planted acres of forest on the bare hills – in the early days of the inn he made each visitor plant a tree – and built several lakes. Almost in conspiracy with the artifice, the weather up here can be cool and drizzly when the rest of the country is sweltering.

They claim at *Troutbeck* that the log fire in the foyer has been kept burning since the place was built in 1950. It's very much a mountain resort, with all sorts of leisure-time activities from croquet to riding. The conspicuously rich take their holidays here, bringing the nanny along to look after the kids. Still, the *Troutbeck* offers the best **cream teas** and meals in the area and non-residents are able to hire **horses** to ride up through the bracken and ferns to **World's View** – a thrilling scarp-edge panorama.

Opposite the gates of *Troutbeck Inn*, you'll find a general store selling basics, a garage, bus stop and a very quaint post office.

NYANGA'S FLORA AND WILDLIFE

The vast grassy areas of Nyanga hold a fantastic range of **wild flowers**. Look out for Zimbabwe's national bloom, the delicate **flame lily** (here more often yellow than red), **gladioli**, **ground orchids** and different kinds of **heather**. **Aloes** of all sizes grow in the various ruins, forming beacons in June and July when they flower red and orange. After grass fires, the red **fire lily** springs up with extraordinary vigour in the blackened stubble. South Africa's floral emblem, the furry **protea**, grows well here too; eight species are native to Zimbabwe and three endemic to the Eastern Highlands. They are easily recognizable – small trees with white or pinkish-white flowers surrounded by rose, or deeper pink bracts covered with silvery hairs.

There's an amazing diversity of local **wildlife**, too. It's not as spectacular as in the big game parks, but kudu, reedbuck, klipspringer, leopard, hyena, and herds of wildebeest all inhabit the park, and Nyanga is well known for its populations of samango monkeys and blue duikers, which are found nowhere else in Zimbabwe. One of the former wardens compiled a checklist of mammals and birds – including rare sightings of buffalo, which occasionally penetrate into the Pungwe Gorge, and even lion passing secretively through. However, you're highly unlikely to meet any of these travellers.

World's View

World's View – not to be confused with the World's View where Cecil Rhodes is buried – is a seven-kilometre hike, or ride, from Troutbeck. At the summit of the steep neighbouring high ground, the remains of a **fort** are connected to the mountain by a narrow ridge. With precipices on three sides, this is definitely the wettest and windiest stonework site of all. In the wide-open treeless moorland of this lakes district, you can get an idea of what the country was like before the *Troutbeck* transformation. The lakes, disappointingly, aren't for public use.

Access

Getting to Troutbeck without your own car is not too difficult. Occasional **buses** run from Nyanga Village to Troutbeck and Nyamaropa Communal Lands, or it's a rather more reliable **hitch** from the Troutbeck turn-off, a couple of kilometres south of Nyanga on the main road. Buses back to Nyanga leave from outside the trading store opposite the hotel.

If you're just up for the day and get to **World's View** early enough, you can **walk** 10km directly back to Nyanga Village. Just below the World's View car park, a steep, narrow path leads down the mountain for 4km until it reaches a prominent dirt road, from where it's another 6km to Nyanga Village.

Ziwa and Nyahokwe

The remote (and tricky to reach) **ruins** at ZIWA spread for miles across the hillsides north of Nyanga. Their central reserve is forty square kilometres in extent but this vast complex rambles very much further than that. They are also, confusingly, known by their old colonial name, **Van Niekerk's Ruins** – after the Boer major of nearby Bideford Farm, who led the archeologist Randall McIver around the site in 1905.

The ruins

Exploring **the ruins** you meander on and on, drawn by yet another pathway or area of terracing to the next hill. Little restoration has taken place: stepping about the stone-littered bush you can feel what it must have been like for early archeologists. At first it all seems somewhat puzzling, but after a time patterns do begin to emerge, with Ziwa

Mountain a point of orientation back to the road. To help out, there's now a small **museum** on site, and guides to show you around.

The settlement's seventeenth- and eighteenth-century builders may have been influenced by Great Zimbabwe masonry techniques. But these are no monuments to a wealthy ruling class, rather the **homesteads** and **farms** of ordinary people. When the uplands over to the east lost fertility and crops began to fail, people shifted westwards into the valleys. They built **terraces** for crops and **enclosures** for huts and livestock; platforms for huts are less common than in the uplands as the abundance of stone meant that surrounding walls could be used for protection. Typically, entrances are lintelled and you may notice slots in the inner doorway for a wooden drawbar. **Grooves** are worn into some flat stones within enclosures where women ground grain.

You can walk down the networks of walled **lanes**, probably for driving livestock and still in good condition, but with candelabra trees and aloes growing out of the heavy stonework. And, if you've visited the Rhodes Dam reconstruction, you'll quickly be able to spot the tree-spouting **pit structures**.

Standing back and trying to grasp the extent the ruins, it's tempting to imagine an enormous community inhabiting the hills and valleys. However, it's more likely that these structures were the work of a relatively few agriculturalists, spread over two centuries, who had to move on every few years when the soil lost its fertility. Although scant excavations have been carried out, it is clear that the stonework was done by **Bantu people** and not by Portuguese or Arabs.

Getting to Ziwa

Visiting the ruins without your own car is pretty well impossible, as there is no public transport and apart from the odd visitor few vehicles, if any, pass this way. The ruins and museum are 29km from Rhodes Camp and signposted. The best route is to travel north out of Nyanga village for 14km, turning left to reach the Nyahokwe Village site (see below), 5km on; from here it's a further 8km to Ziwa.

Nyahokwe

The granite-built **NYAHOKWE VILLAGE SITE** lies crouched under the cliff face of the top of Nyahokwe Mountain and has similar characteristics to the other Nyanga ruins. One really interesting feature is a **dare**, or meeting place for elders – a large circular area with upright stones around it. Also, about 100m below the ruins (on a bare granite plateau just off the path), there are some eighty or so **grinding hollows** in groups. Probably several people would have sat around each group grinding down iron-bearing rock for smelting. The remains of **furnaces** have been found in the area and trade was certainly pursued with border-crossing Portuguese.

Some of the nearby granite outcrops – as at Ziwa – are **sacred mountains**, probably centres of the old **Mwari Cult** and not a good idea to climb. Two North Korean officers who were training Zimbabwean brigades in the 1980s took a disdainful attitude to local prohibitions about Ziwa, climbed it, and were never seen again.

Mtarazi National Park

Adjoining Nyanga Park's southern edge, the **Mtarazi National Park** is essentially considered part of the Nyanga region. It is, however, a much wilder zone, with undisturbed indigenous forest, and is somewhat difficult to reach without a car. But, if you've time, you can hike there: two recently rebuilt National Parks' cottages in the dramatic **Pungwe Gorge**, plus the unparalleled views into the luxuriant **Honde Valley** and Mozambique, provide strong incentive. It's magnificent country.

Most people tend to get only as far as the viewpoints along the **Scenic Road** which loops eastwards from the main Mutare–Nyanga Village road. These take in the much-photographed vistas of the **Pungwe Falls** and **Gorge**, the 762-metre drop of the **Mtarazi Falls** and the deep seat of the **Honde Valley**. If you're **hiking**, it's possible to penetrate these panoramas, either from the ridge of the Scenic Road itself or more adventurously walking the park from Rhodes Camp to Nyangani in the west, south to Pungwe and Mtarazi Falls, then dropping into the Honde Valley – approximately 60km in all.

Traffic is light along the Scenic Road and you'll end up walking much of it if you're car-less. Hikers have got stranded along this route – not an experience to be recommended, as it's very wild, entirely without facilities, and patrolled by leopards and even the odd lion.

Accommodation

Places to stay in the area are thin on the ground and it's advisable to make arrangements before you arrive. Above Mtarazi Falls, most accommodation, apart from the National Parks lodges, lies along the Scenic or Brackenridge Road. For the latest details on private cottages, contact the Publicity Association in Mutare. In the Honde Valley, below the Falls, the *Aberfoyle Country Club* is the only realistic possibility.

Aberfoyle Country Club, 90km from Juliasdale in the Honde Valley (☎14/708239). Situated on the Aberfoyle tea estate, this elegant club has lovely gardens, great views and a swimming pool, with accommodation open to non-members. ④.

Far and Wide, on the Mtarazi Falls road (☎129/26329). Set in the forest and based around an adventure centre, timber cabins provide dorm accommodation and cheap en-suite, self-catering lodges. There is also a campsite, and meals are available. If you don't have a car, you can arrange to be collected from Juliasdale. ①–②.

National Parks Campsite, above Mtarazi Falls, just past the national park entrance. Basic facilities, but a definite option if you're intepid, or in a car.

National Parks Lodges, Pungwe Falls, above the Pungwe Falls (book through National Parks Central Booking in Harare or Bulawayo). If you're after solitude, these are the best-located places to stay in the Nyanga-Mtarazi area. Limited to a pair of two-bedroom, fully equipped self-catering lodges (for max 5 persons) on either side of the river, they're in great demand at peak season. ②.

Pungwe Gorge and Falls

The first obvious stop on the Scenic Road is for the bird's-eye view of **PUNGWE GORGE** and the top of the falls before the Pungwe River, which rises at the foot of Mount Nyangani and flows southwards through the park before plummeting 240m into a dramatic tree-gridded gorge and eventually descending into the Honde Valley and Mozambique. Although you can't see the falls themselves, you'll certainly hear their roar.

Pungwe Drift and lodges

Getting down to the river from the scenic drive isn't as daunting as it looks from the top, and the National Park **lodges**, set idyllically next to the water at Pungwe Drift, must be the choicest places to stay anywhere in Nyanga (see above). They also make a wonderful base for hikes.

From the Scenic Road, follow the signposts to **Pungwe Drift** (40min on foot) then walk another twenty minutes along a riverside path to the top of the falls. There's a great swimming spot in the river above the falls; the current here won't tow you over the edge and you can float downstream and safely duck out before the flow gathers speed. The bush comes right to the water's edge amid smooth rocks and clean river sand.

MTARAZI ADVENTURE

If you thought Victoria Falls was the only place in Zimbabwe for **whitewater rafting and adventure**, then the Eastern Highlands will surprise you. *Far and Wide* runs a range of outward bound activities which are more challenging than those at the Falls. Whitewater rafting and kayaking are the most popular options. One-day trips start at the Pungwe Gorge in the Honde Valley and traverse a series of rapids – many of them with steep drops – including seven grade-fours. On the **rafts**, you're not rowed by a guide, as at the Falls, but navigate yourself in a two-person inflatable instead – more difficult, and consequently more rewarding. **Kayaks** along the same route are single-person crafts. Safety kayakers accompany the trips, which cost US$60 for a full day; a less difficult one-day "family" rafting trip through grade two and three rapids starts at US$35. Finally, if – and only if – you're an expert, you may want to try a specialist kayaking option along the Gairezi River, taking in grade-six rapids.

Other activities include half-day guided **mountain biking** trips through the Nyanga Wilderness, **abseiling** off the Honde Valley escarpment, **rock climbing** and **guided walks**. Guides on all activities are knowledgeable about the flora and fauna of the area, and fully inclusive prices start at US$35 per day. Book through travel agents or contact *Far and Wide*, Box 14, Juliasdale (☎129/26329).

Basing yourself here, or hiking around the park, you can continue northeast along the **Drift Road** as it follows the valley and climbs onto the escarpment: high mountains rear up on your right and fantastic views open into the gorge all the way to the car park at the base of Mount Nyangani (24km). From this track you can drop into some very wild montane forest down in the gorge.

If you've less time, a couple of disused fishing roads leading off the Scenic Road make good shorter walks. Some 4km north of the turn-off to Pungwe Drift, a no through road leads a kilometre down to **Thomborutedza Falls**. Here, the fast-flowing river rushes over sink holes, which create an effervescent, natural Jacuzzi. Two kilometres beyond, a similar dead-end track passes various pit structures and trails the Pungwe nearer to its source on Nyangani.

Mtarazi Falls and Honde View

MTARAZI FALLS – the highest in Zimbabwe – are at the end of the line for Scenic Road view-spotters and a fair walk from their signposted car park. They spout from the cleaved edge of the vertical green cliff to disappear in virgin forest half a mile below.

The **best time** to be here is late afternoon, when the sun behind the water makes the slender falls gauzy and golden. To **swim** nearby, make your way to the river above the falls, marked by beautiful tree ferns. Here, brown rocks, sloping into the river pools, warm the water a few more sufferable degrees. On the road to Mtarazi, don't miss the turn to the **Honde View**; the aerial view of the **Honde Valley**, where its contours relax to enter Mozambique, is stunning.

Into the forest

Several well-trodden **trails** lead down from the escarpment into the **Honde Valley**: two used by workers from the Valley connect the Pungwe and Honde viewpoints, but you'd really need a local person to show you. One of the overgrown paths is about half a kilometre from Mtarazi, heading east into the valley; without a guide, it's hard to know which fork to take when the path splits. The other, equally teasing trail drops right into the Pungwe Gorge and hugs the river bank into the Honde Valley below. If you find someone to show you the way, though, either walk makes a good, day-long hike to the valley floor and back, through awesome **montane forest** which opens into clearings with views of the valley. From Honde you can catch a bus to Mutare if you're moving on.

The mountainous regions of Nyanga have over one hundred species of **fern**, including four different kinds of the giant tree fern. Overhead, epiphytes – orchids of many varieties – dangle from the branches. This kind of forest, increasingly whittled away by tree clearance, once covered the whole of Nyanga. **Hardwoods species** include mlanje cedar and yellow wood. **Flowering trees** to look out for are cape chestnut, the forest fever tree with its giant leaves and sweet-scented flowers, the glossy-leaved wild holly and the tube-flowered notsung.

While you admire the canopy above, spare the odd glance for the forest floor, which has its own absorbing interest and occasional dangerous encounter. The **gaboon viper** spends its days half-buried in the leaves and litter of the forest floors of the Eastern Highlands. Although less aggressive than other vipers, it's the largest of the family and heavily built: up to a metre and a half long, gorgeous and deadly. Brightly patterned with white, buff, purple, pink and deep brown diamonds and triangles, it looks the epitome of the African zigzag pattern snake.

The Honde Valley

During the Zimbabwean liberation struggle some of the bloodiest fighting and atrocities took place in the **HONDE VALLEY**. That's all, however, that most people know of it. Lying at the foot of the Nyanga range, adjoining Mozambique, it is effectively cut off from the rest of Zimbabwe.

The possible trails into the valley are detailed above. By bus, the easiest approach is to take any Mutare-bound bus from Nyanga to the Honde turn-off, then pick up one of the buses from Mutare into the valley; there are no direct buses from Nyanga. The turn-off for the valley is 25km along the main Juliasdale to Mutare road.

Masimike and the Pungwe River

Dramatic landscape and temperature changes occur as you wind down the single tarred road from the main Mutare road into the valley's lush hothouse – a district of intensively worked communal lands and shiny green hills of tea. Dominating the centre of the valley are the **Masimike** – sentinel granite pinnacles up to 100m high, which make good orientation points. The **Pungwe River** flows through the valley, with rope footbridges crossing the clear water in a couple of places. The final section of the forested river gorge is well worth exploring if you're based in the valley.

Tea estates were established around Honde in the 1950s, when planters crossed Nyangani on foot into the roadless vale. In the populous **communal lands** people grow rice as well as maize, tea, and coffee; you can buy tropical produce from women who walk up the mountains to Juliasdale. While the land is very productive, villagers have a hard time deterring wild pigs and baboons which ravage their crops, while the absence of roads to some of the settlements, and thinly spread facilities, force people to trek up to 10km to the nearest shop or clinic. No strangers to foot-slogging, those who live closest to the mountains climb two to three hours to the top every day to work on commercial farms or private homesteads.

Mtarazi Falls – from below

To see the **Mtarazi Falls** again, but from below, take a path from Hauna, a village with a couple of main-road stores – to the base of the falls, camouflaged by cliff-base jungle. Lion-hearted hikers can push through to the secret **waterfall pool** which locals believe is inhabited by siren-like beings who'll lure you into its depths. If you decide to venture into the vegetable gloom, leave early: a night in the damp forest isn't recommended.

The Chimanimani Mountains

At the southern end of the Eastern Highlands the **Chimanimani Mountains** are completely different from the rest of the range and geologically unique in Zimbabwe. The apparently modest size of the peaks – Binga, the highest, is 2240m – gives no idea

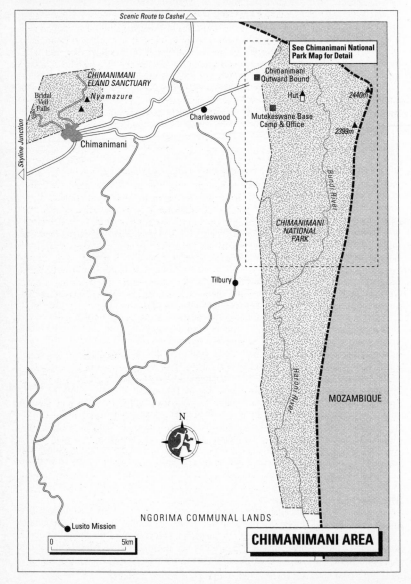

of their scale, the mountains rising in rugged ridges. Sheltering in this fortress, the **Chimanimani National Park** is an enthralling wilderness of rocks, caves, waterfalls and gentle valleys.

Chimanimani Village

The village of **CHIMANIMANI**, 148km south of Mutare, comprises a small collection of shops, a hotel, a post office and a group of houses gathered around a red-earthed "village green". The 1899 administration building is a handsome example of an early colonial type that seems all roof – dominated by ruddy corrugated iron. Basically a centre serving the farms and forestry estates in the vicinity, the village is surrounded by mountains, with the **Chimanimani Rampart** in the blue distance; on some evenings the mountains appear to catch fire with a pink glow as the rays hit the rose quartz embedded in the rock face. It is a wonderful place to idle away a few hours, or even several days: so pleasant, indeed, that visiting government officials reportedly ask to be put up here rather than in Chipinge, the region's real administrative centre.

White settlement in the region began after the pioneer **Dunbar Moodie** visited in 1890, and told his friend Marthinus Martin about the beauty and potential of the countryside south of Umtali. It sounded too good to pass up and, true to colonial form, Martin led a party from South Africa to take over the area in 1894. Sinking roots, they named the district **Melsetter**, after Moodie's family home in the Orkney Islands.

After Independence, Melsetter became **Chimanimani**, a name previously reserved for the nearby mountains. One version of the name's meaning has it that the main footpath between Zimbabwe and Mozambique runs in close parallel to the Msapa River and is so tight in places that you have to walk single file or even sideways: a *chimanimani*.

Chimanimani hold few full-blown tourist attractions, but the local **craft shop** across from the post office has a desultory collection of regional handiwork – *gudza* dolls, bags and mats and fun, articulated wooden snakes. *Gudza* products are woven from bark that's been chewed and dyed in browns, ochres and oatmeal. No trip to Chimanimani is complete, either, without sampling the village's delicious, homemade **cheese and jam**, available from *Frog and Fern B&B*, signposted of the Bridal Veil Falls road.

Arrival, information and transport
Buses arrive at the local **market**, where you can buy ridiculously cheap avocados, pineapples, bananas and vegetables. It's conveniently located next to the excellent **Publicity Bureau** (daily 10am–4pm), who can provide information about places to stay and transport to the park; there's also a **cardphone** outside.

Landrovers (with drivers) can be rented for excursions or transfers to Chimanimani base camp from *Nyati Travel* (☎126/2515). **Petrol** is available in town, but if you're planning to self-cater or are shopping for an expedition, buy **provisions** in one of the larger centres before you arrive – the local stores are poorly stocked. You should also aim to change **money** before arriving in Chimanimani: the bank is only open once a week, and the hotel will only change travellers' cheques for residents.

Finally, although it never snows you should bring warm clothes, especially in July and August when the mountains can be very chilly. During the rainy season, a waterproof is recommended for hiking and evenings are cool enough for jumpers.

Accommodation and eating
As well as the **accommodation** options listed below, there are a couple of self-catering cottages to rent in Chimanimani – enquire at the Publicity Bureau which arranges bookings. Most people eat where they stay, but there's also *The Beta*, a modest **restaurant** next to the post office, serving hamburgers, pies and omelettes.

Chimanimani Hotel, PO Box 5, Chimanimani (☎126/2511). This charmingly old-fashioned hotel has a 1950s lounge, complete with sleeping cats, polished floors, wicker chairs and log fires; they also serve inexpensive but dull meals, and have a pricy bar. The cheapest rooms are at the back, but consider spending a little extra for one with a glorious view of the mountains – and a bath. ③.

Frog and Fern, a short way from town off the Bridal Veil Falls road; PO Box 75, Chimanimani (☎126/294, fax 120/62995). Excellent-value, comfortable bed and breakfast accommodation, with friendly, knowledgable owners. ③.

Heaven Backpackers Lodge, just out of town on the national park road (☎126/2701). Mostly shared rooms, though there are a couple of single and double rooms, as well as timber A-frame chalets in the garden (best if you want to avoid the noise), where you can also camp. The food is cheap and good, and the lively bar has a log fire for cold weather.

Walks from Chimanimani

There are a couple of good **walks** out of Chimanimani Village that are worth considering if you're not in a rush to move on to the National Park. For these and other possibilities, it's a good idea to invest at the craft shop in the excellent local **map** produced by *Milkmaps* in aid of the rural hospital. Alternatively, *Heaven* provides its own local maps, which are slightly easier to follow.

The Eland Sanctuary

The **Eland Sanctuary**, a large area north of the village on the slopes of **Nyamzure** – or "Pork Pie" as it's also known – is a rugged terrain of cliffs, waterfalls and dense bush. It was created to provide a refuge for **elands**, Africa's largest antelopes, which are indigenous to the area, and were coming into conflict with the timber-growing industry. The elands are now successfully kept away from the bark and buds of pine saplings behind a fence in an eighteen-square-kilometre tract. You'll also see zebra, waterbuck, bushbuck, klipspringer and noisy troops of baboons. Antelope can be spotted, too, roaming wild in the surrounding farmlands, though in considerably smaller numbers than the vast herds locals remember.

There are two **roads to the Sanctuary**, but you can explore it further on foot along the ridge. Alternatively, scale Nyamzure, either from the village or from the car park halfway up if you're driving. To get onto the Nyamzure road turn left at the end of the road past the Chimanimani post office, then first right and keep on up. The Sanctuary (free admission) is open all hours.

Bridal Veil Falls

The showpiece of the sanctuary, the **Bridal Veil Falls** cascade down a sheer rock face into an inviting pool of beautifully clear water that looks as if it ought to be inhabited by water sprites draping themselves across the mossy rocks. The falls are at the bottom of a green, wooded valley where there is a neglected picnic site under the trees.

It's a two-hour **walk** to the falls on a seldom used dirt road which meanders through msasa-clad valleys full of birds. You need to take the road leading out of town with the *Beverley Building Society* on your left, and then just keep going. If you want a challenging and longer walk back, take the ridge route, which runs to the south of the Eland Sanctuary.

Chimanimani National Park

The only way to penetrate the **CHIMANIMANI NATIONAL PARK** (admission fee US$2 per day, or U$S4 per week) is by scaling the blue rampart you see from Chimanimani village. It's possible to do this route as a day's hike, if you have your own transport to get to the foothills and back to the village, but you'll enjoy the trip more if you spend some days exploring the mountains.

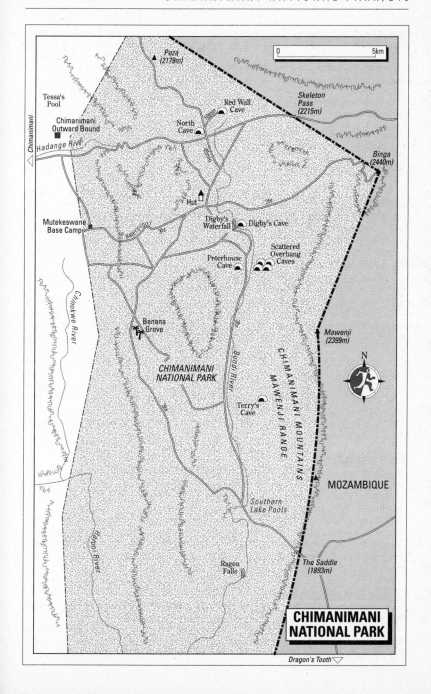

CHIMANIMANI NATIONAL PARK

Between the Parks mountain hut (at the centre of the park) and the soaring peaks shared with Mozambique, spreads the ample **Bundi Valley**. Spliced by the Bundi River, this is covered in grass which changes from wet-season green to maizy yellow and dried brown after the rains subside. Its downhill course is broken by a series of waterfalls splashing into icy cola-coloured pools, with smooth rocks to bask on. Giant **tree strelizias** (wild bananas), **tree ferns** and **cycads** fringe the banks, while the grass slopes are dotted with bright yellow helichrysm, grass aloes and small mauve gladioli.

But it's the **rocks** on the way up the valley which are most astonishing. Completely different from the granite formations peppering much of Zimbabwe, the folded and faulted silvery schist and quartz has been sculpted into fantastic stone forms. In the fine white soil, wild hibiscus, heather, aromatic tree shrubs and fiery pincushions grow.

Getting to the park

In the absence of any public transport, it's not easy to get to the National Park without a car, and prospective hitchers may end up walking the 19km on the Tilbury Road to **MUTEKESWANE** base camp from Chimanimani village; traffic is sparse on this rough road, though you may pick up the odd motorist heading for the Park or nearby Outward Bound School, or to wherever you're staying. *Nyati Travel* (see above) also offers transfers to the mountain, and the Publicity Association can tell you if anyone in the village is organizing pick-up truck trips to and from the national park, although this depends entirely on the availability of vehicles in good order.

If you do have to **walk**, the route is some compensation, taking you through pine, eucalyptus and wattle plantations as the mountains loom closer. When the mountains seem almost on top of you, the road swings steeply up and along the **First Range**, thick with msasa trees. It then forks, heading left to *Chimanimani Outward Bound* and **Tessa's Pool** (see below) and, continuing to the right another 3km uphill to the **base camp** where you report in. You will have to give details of your length of stay and agree to foot the bill if you get hopelessly lost and a search party comes looking for you. The **Ordnance Survey map** (1:50,000 Melsetter 1932 D4 and 1933 C1, C3, available from the Surveyor General's office in Harare) is invaluable, although the Publicity Bureau also supplies hiking maps. The Parks people provide a much less detailed version, if they haven't run out of copies.

Accommodation

Camping is permitted anywhere in the **National Park**. If you arrive too late in the day to go into the mountains you can **camp** at Mutekeswane, with the usual facilities but no roofed accommodation. However, you don't have to lug a tent around. The **mountain hut** overlooking the Bundi Valley, two hours up from the base camp, has wooden beds and thin mattresses plus two gas cookers and washing facilities. You can choose one of the two dorms to sleep in (they are not segregated) or use the verandah. This is the place to meet other walkers and line up a lift back to Chimanimani Village.

An **attendant** lives nearby, down a discreetly camouflaged path (to give the feeling that he's not really there). Don't break in if you find the hut shut up – there's always someone around to unlock the door. If you plan to do day trips from the hut, it's safe to leave all your gear, but if you want to be extra cautious bring a padlock – the benches in the central area double as lockers. Bring all your **food** with you – and a torch – as there's no shop in the Park.

There are also several well-used "**commercial caves**", so called because they are well known and often get "overbooked". Each has its own informal name, and one or two are floored with dried grass.

HIKING IN CHIMANIMANI: THE PRACTICAL LIMITS

Two-thirds of the Chimanimani range is actually in Mozambique. On the Zimbabwean side, **hiking** is confined to a long thin stretch from the peaks in the north, scaleable on day trips from the hut, down the Bundi Valley to **Dragon's Tooth** and beyond, in the south. In the north, local mountaineers often ignore the border, which is drawn through Skeleton Pass, and head off to Martin's Falls, Valley of the Wizards and endless deserted peaks. There's no way up from Mozambique to this northern side of the park but Mozambicans do cross over at the **Saddle** in the far south, on a well-worn track to the store at Tilbury. We even saw two women, each with a bed on their heads, making their way back over the mountains to Mozambique – an incredible feat given the distance and steepness. As you'd expect, the army also uses this path.

It's not a good idea to go beyond the **Saddle and Ragon Falls**; besides army presence, the path fizzles out on the Zimbabwean side and you have to cross into Mozambique to get further south.

Routes to the peaks – and Tessa's Pool

Three routes head up to the mountain hut and peaks. **Bailey's Folly** is the most direct, leading straight up behind the Parks Office. It takes about three hours to the hut, with several false tops on the way – whenever you think you're nearly there, another ridge appears. The route is waymarked with cairns which should be diligently followed; when the path braids, keep going left.

Banana Grove – the "bananas" are actually tree strelizias – is a much gentler approach, good if you're heading for the **caves** along the Bundi River on the way to the Southern Lakes. From Mutekeswane follow the fire break until you meet the path going up from Dead Cow, the former base camp.

Hadange River, the third way up, is a route people more often take down because it leads to Tessa's Pool (see below). When it's **wet**, the Hadange route is not advised, however, as the path cuts through a very slippery forested ravine and criss-crosses the river, which is impassable after a storm. If you are caught out by the river – or any other in Chimanimani – simply wait a couple of hours and the water will subside. If you're descending, the path gives out about a third of the way down and seems to fork: keep to the left on higher ground rather than right which takes you into a tangled gully. Otherwise the path is good.

En route you'll pass a massive rock face – the aptly named **Temple of Doom** – where the Outward Bound people practise rock climbing and abseiling. **Tessa's Pool** is to be found down a clearly marked path off the main driveway. Surrounded by luxuriant palm trees, lianas and ferns at the bottom of a waterfall, it is the perfect spot to cool your steaming heels after the descent. Either get permission at the Outward Bound before you swim, or check at the *Chimanimani Hotel* before you set out, to find out the latest position.

Peaks, caves and pools

Like all mountain climbs, once you've made it to the top there are still more tops. **Peza** and **Binga** (Kweza on some maps) are each a couple of strenuous hours' climb from the hut on good paths, with fantastic views. **Peza** is easier and you go along beautiful open stretches of the Bundi Valley to the waterfall at North and Red Wall caves before you start climbing. Both caves are big enough to sleep a troop of boy scouts. **North Cave** is located right above the waterfall while **Red Cave** is a bit higher up on the other side of the river and not quite as easy to find. A path leading straight down from the hut goes right across the valley and up formidable Binga. **Skeleton Pass** is an easy walk from here, but the views are not as exceptional as you might have expected.

If you want to **swim** and laze about, there's a waterfall, pool and a small overhang – **Digby's Cave**, a good night shelter – a steep half-hour down from the hut on the main path to Southern Lakes. A little further on is yet another waterfall and **Peterhouse Cave**.

For a **full-day trip**, you could continue on the path all the way to the **Southern Lakes**, where the swimming is exceptional. On your left, slate-blue **Mt Mawenje** (also called Turret Towers) dominates the horizon, while the river widens into a big oxbow creating reed-fringed, wine-dark pools – the "lakes".

Midway is **Terry's Cave**, set under a massive boulder, and with two compartments in the unlikely event of two parties arriving. No one seems to know who was responsible. One theory is that a priest spent some time here before leaving the country and this was his goodbye present. Terraces have been built to keep out the draughts, a fireplace made and the floor covered with masses of dried grass.

The snag is that the cave is difficult to find. If you want to spend the night here, locate it before going down to the lakes. It's in a very rocky area, quite a long way from the main north–south path; there's no direct route to get from it to the lakes, so you have to come back to the river. To get to the cave you must rock-jump the river. One path to it veers off opposite a small tributary, the other where a minor path back to Banana Grove joins the north–south one. Another, and possibly easier route is to take a path on the east side of Peterhouse Cave. From Southern Lakes it's a three-hours-plus hike back to Base Camp.

There are no caves at the lakes themselves.

Corner

The only part of the national park accessible by car is the northeast corner – known as **CORNER** – approached along an extremely rough, unsignposted road through commmunal lands. National Parks may build cottages here, which would open up the area, but at present few venture in.

South to Chipinge and Chirinda

CHIPINGE, 64km southeast of Chimanimani, is a working town that sees little tourism. Its small centre hides bottling plants, a brewery and storage depots down the backstreets, and two banks in the centre – hinting at the wealth produced from this industry and from the surrounding commercial tea and coffee plantations. Chipinge is also the nearest town for the sugar plantations of the extreme eastern low veld. However, its main attraction for visitors is its proximity to the **Chirinda Forest**.

Chipinge practicalities

The *Chipinge Hotel*, on the main street (☎127/2226), is clean, and gives surprisingly good value given its local monopoly. It's also the place for full-blown and reasonably priced **meals**, served with surprising panache. Half a kilometre from town, there's also a slightly derelict and little-used **campsite**. If you're driving, however, the best base for exploring the forests is the *Kiledo Lodge*, 8km outside Chipinge on the Eastern Border Road, which has timbered self-catering cottages set on tea and coffee estate. Linen and crockery are provided, and you have the option of a B&B rate (③) or full board. Bookings should be made through D Wenham, Box 11, Chipinge (☎127/2944, or 14/786521).

There's **cheap food** in abundance from takeaways in town, down Seventh Avenue toward the market/bus station, and in the high-density suburbs. In the evening, try the **late-night** *Tasty Foods* on Joubert Street, open until 8pm. Otherwise, most of Chipinge shuts shop at 5.30pm. After dark, the best scene is the Joubert Street takeaway, or the

Chipinge Hotel bar – you don't come here for the nightlife. An occasional **concert** brings the city beat to the high-density suburb's Gaza Hall or there may be **football** at the nearby Gaza Stadium.

Chirinda Forest Reserve

All that remains of a large primeval woodland is preserved in the tiny enclave of **CHIRINDA FOREST RESERVE**, 30km south of Chipinge. It is almost a fantasy African jungle, with thick, dark undergrowth, lofty trees reaching skywards, science fiction plants with outsized leaves, and loud bird calls.

Getting to Chirinda – and camping

The forest surrounds a hilltop mission, known as **Mount Selinda**. On the road to Mozambique, the mission, which provides education and basic health care to the local community, is passed by a fair amount of traffic, including a number of **buses** from Mutare, Bulawayo and Masvingo, all of which pass through Chipinge en route. Chipinge's bus stop is just outside *Ron's Motors* on the corner of Main Street and Seventh Avenue. By far the best idea, though, is to travel up in one of the many fare-charging **pick-ups** that can be taken from the corner of the main drag and the Mount Selinda road. Many of these rides terminate at Chako Township, but try to make your way 2km further on to the mission hospital, close to the (signposted) "**Big Tree Path**" that heads into the forest. If your lift ends at Chako, get off at the T-junction and walk uphill to the signposted forest entrance.

Chirinda has a **campsite** with cheap chalets (①). To book, write to Muguze Forest Research Station, Box 59, Chimanimani (☎126/24841 or 127/224116). There's also a small rural **store** at the Chako T-junction, but it makes more sense to pick up supplies from the better-stocked shops in Chipinge.

Mount Selinda

There's no mountain as such at **MOUNT SELINDA**, just a big forested hill visible from some distance. It's a steep climb from Chipinge's farmlands; maize fields, grazing cattle and neat rows of coffee bushes fill the passing scene.

The mission was founded by Americans in 1889, but its main claim to fame is as the point of arrival in 1919 of Africa's first *agricultural* missionary. One of his big successes was the Nyanadzi irrigation scheme on the Birchenough Bridge to Mutare road – long before Triangle and Hippo Valley estates undertook their complex water diversions. Peasant agriculture thrives at Nyanadzi today: good grain and fruit yields are achieved in an otherwise dry and unpromising environment.

Across the tarred road, and a little further toward the mission hospital, is the over-grown plinth of **Swynnerton's Memorial**, another evocation of good colonial works. Apparently forgotten, Swynnerton was an English entomologist who settled in Chimanimani in 1898. He researched tsetse flies and butterflies, and was appointed Tanzania's first game warden in 1919. His researches there led to an acclaimed paper on the reclamation of tsetse-afflicted districts, but he's best known in Zimbabwe for his work as a naturalist, and gave his name to a number of plants and birds.

Into the forest

A web of paths weaves through the forest. From the picnic site, marked trails lead to the **Big Tree** and the **Valley of the Giants** – both routes worth taking.

The **Big Tree**, 70m high and 16m round, is probably the oldest living thing in the forest. The wildest estimates claim it as a contemporary of Christ, a nice myth for a tree near a mission. More realistic stabs reckon it's a thousand years old – and in decline, judging by the large sections of dead wood. Like many Valley of the Giants goliaths, it's a red mahogany, *Khaya nyasica*, used by Africans to produce massage oil from the seeds and an anti-colds infusion from the quinine-bitter bark.

Another remarkable lumber-type at Chirinda is the orange, yellow and black timbered **zebra wood**, found nowhere else. And, on the wildlife front, you may encounter the **forest elephant shrew**, which is unique to a small part of the southeast. This rat-like creature has kangarooish back legs and a mini-trunk, and beneath each lower eyelid a fluorescent spot acts as a recognition signal for other shrews in the forest's evening gloom. The more common **samango monkeys** emerge from the treetops at dawn and, after catching some sun, head off to breakfast on Chirinda's leaves, fruits and berries.

travel details

Economy buses

Chimanimani to: Mutare (daily at 5.45am; 4hr).

Chipinge to: Bulawayo (2 daily; 9hr); Harare (2 daily; 8hr); Mount Selinda (5 daily until 11.30am; 1hr); Mutare (5 daily until 11.30am; 4hr).

Mutare to: Beit Bridge (daily at 6am; 9hr); Bulawayo (3 daily, 6am–noon; 8hr) via Masvingo (4hr); Bvumba (Fri, Sat & Sun at 9am & 3pm; 1hr); Chimanimani (4 daily, 6am–noon; 4hr or more); Chipinge (2 daily, 6–9am; 4hr or more); Harare (6 or more daily, most before noon; 5hr); Nyanga (3 daily, 6am–noon; 3hr 30min).

Nyanga to: Harare (3 or more daily; 7hr); Mutare (2 daily; 3hr 30min).

Luxury coaches

The only reliable service is run by *Blue Arrow*, departing from the *Manica Hotel*, **Mutare**, to Harare (daily except Tues & Thurs at 1pm; 4hr 30min), via Rusape (1hr) and Marondera (3hr). Book at *Manica Travel Services* (see Mutare "Listings").

Trains

Mutare to: Harare (daily at 9pm; 9hr).

PART THREE

BOTSWANA

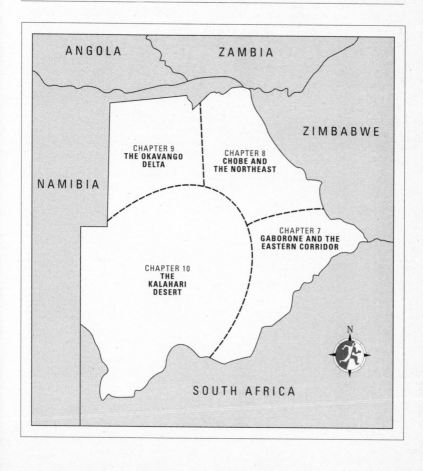

ANGOLA　　　　　ZAMBIA

ZIMBABWE

NAMIBIA

CHAPTER 9
**THE OKAVANGO
DELTA**

CHAPTER 8
**CHOBE AND
THE NORTHEAST**

CHAPTER 7
**GABORONE AND THE
EASTERN CORRIDOR**

CHAPTER 10
**THE
KALAHARI
DESERT**

N

SOUTH AFRICA

Introduction

Despite its natural bounty – magnificent landscapes trampled by some of Africa's finest wildlife herds – Botswana remains all but unvisited by independent travellers. Official policies designed to entice the well-heeled to luxury lodges, while neglecting other tourist facilities, are partly to blame. But away from the glamour zone, endless miles of untouched wilderness invite unparalleled – and safe – adventure.

In its fourth decade of independence, Botswana enjoys a rare distinction as a harmonious, peaceful and stable African country. While retaining a firm commitment to multi-party democracy, it has been transformed from one of the world's twenty poorest nations by the discovery of diamonds. It now boasts one of Africa's fastest-growing economies, and is at last able to develop health services and primary education, neglected under British colonial rule.

Nonetheless, Botswana has never fully slipped from the grasp of South Africa. Unlike Zimbabwe, it has no manufacturing sector of its own, and therefore imports almost all its manufactured goods from South Africa. During the apartheid years Botswana had to walk a precarious tightrope, being simultaneously a leading member of SADC – an economic union of front-line states committed to reducing dependence on white-ruled South Africa – and also a member of the Southern African Customs Union, which linked it to a system of tariff-free trade with South Africa. Though constrained by these pragmatic questions of survival, Botswana consistently refused to have truck with apartheid, and always offered asylum to political refugees from South Africa.

While cities such as the capital, Gaborone, have been replanned and modernized, and whole towns have appeared in the new mining areas, urban Botswana is still no place for the traveller seeking excitement. However, the wildlife tourist industry is burgeoning, especially around the Okavango Delta in the north, with facilities available to suit every budget. But if Botswana looks undeveloped now as you travel through, imagine what it was like twenty years ago. President Quett Masire recently remarked:

The other day I saw the floodlights turned on at the new stadium in Gaborone. I remembered that in 1967 I flew to Kinshasa and saw street lights and wondered if ever such lights would be seen in some towns in Botswana. We have come a long way since then.

■ Physical geography

Botswana, in contrast to varied Zimbabwe, is flat – basically a shallow sand-filled basin between 800 and 1300m above sea level. A plateau broken with small hills runs along the eastern corridor – bordering South Africa and Zimbabwe – to form a **watershed**. Eighty percent of the population lives in a small area along the central watershed and the lands to the east up to the Limpopo River. There's just enough rain here for growing hardy crops, but also easily tapped underground water and ample grass ideal for rearing cattle.

Westwards, conditions are less favourable, giving way to the **Kalahari Desert**, which covers the central and southern two-thirds of the country and extends north, south and west – well into Angola, South Africa and Namibia. Although in essence the desert forms itself into huge dune fields, these are now largely stabilized by scrub, bush, forest and grasslands. Only in the extreme southwest do you find archetypal desert dunes.

In stark relief, the northwest of the country is watered by the vast **Okavango Delta** – 15,000 square kilometres of channels, oxbow lakes, flood plains and islands. The entire north is splashed by periodically watered **lakes and salt pans**, which are more usually covered by a dried-out, greyish, salt-saturated clay hostile to any vegetation.

■ Where to go

Botswana's main appeal lies in its wild outdoors. For practical reasons most visitors concentrate on the accessible northern and eastern sections of the country. The top attractions, in the north, are the **Okavango Delta**, and its **Moremi Wildlife** and **Chobe Game reserves**. Also in the north, the **Makgadikgadi and Nxai pans** – each with a game reserve – are worth visiting for their plains and the vision of the endless salt pans.

Throughout the **Kalahari Desert** are huge game reserves, more or less inaccessible without 4WD. **Ghanzi** in Botswana's wild west is an unlikely community where Batswana farmers, San hunter-gatherers and Afrikaner ranchers somehow work things out together.

Most of the **large towns** lie along the eastern corridor, with Mochudi, near Gaborone, worth a visit as a traditional village with vividly patterned hut walls. Sandwiched between the tar and the border with Zimbabwe is the farmland of **Tuli Block** – an obvious destination for the budget-minded – with fine private game reserves among red sandstone hills and the riverine forest of the Limpopo River.

Languages and peoples

The official language of Botswana is English. Newspapers are in English, which is used in parliament and in schools, from the fifth year upwards. However, many other languages are spoken, and Setswana is understood by ninety percent of the population. Setswana is a Bantu language, part of the western section of the great Sotho-speaking group that includes the people of Lesotho, and the South African Venda. It's useful to grasp the implications of its prefixes. The language is *Se*tswana, one Tswana person is a *Mo*tswana, while several Tswana people are *Ba*tswana. *Ba* is prefixed to all ethnic group names, for example *Ba*kgatla, *Ba*sarwa, *Ba*ngwato.

■ Peoples

Botswana is one of the most integrated countries in Africa. Although only around half of the country's people are Batswana, there's a tradition of incorporation in Tswana history, which meant that members of other groups were gradually absorbed (admittedly sometimes as second-class citizens) to build up a Tswana community. In modern Botswana this custom has been adapted to forging a harmonious nation with scrupulous attempts by the government to promote equality.

One of the oddities resulting from the colonial carve-up of Africa is the existence of national borders that slice through ethnic and linguistic communities. Fewer than a quarter of **Setswana-speakers** live in Botswana, the vast majority being resident in South Africa. In Botswana there are several lineages, some of which you'll come across periodically in this book. Broadly speaking you'll find the **Batawana** in the north centring on Maun, the **Bangwato** along the east with their capital at Serowe, and in the southeast the **Bakwena** around Molepolole, the **Batlokwa** around Gaborone and Lobatse, the **Bakgatla** just south of the Bangwato, and the **Bangwaketse** in the southwest. Despite these divisions, however, most people regard themselves first and foremost as Batswana* – citizens of Botswana – and only members of a subgroup as an afterthought.

Because of its forthright opposition to apartheid the Botswana government has always declined to take a census of its people along tribal lines. Every citizen of the country regardless of origin or colour of skin is a Motswana. Nevertheless, here's a quick rundown of minorities mentioned in this book and elsewhere.

The oldest inhabitants of Southern Africa are the **San-speakers** (often called "bushmen" –

TRIBES

In Southern Africa – probably more than almost anywhere in the world – the idea of a "tribe" is pregnant with political connotations. In South Africa the concept was used to attempt to divide the country's black majority into "separate nations" and to sow ethnic division. The idea of "tribes" as concrete entities – with connotations of backwardness – is a controversial one. One fundamental problem is that cultures, linguistic groups and national boundaries frequently fail to coincide, making the absolute definition of a particular tribe hazardous. Secondly, the idea of "tribes" implies something fixed, whereas the history of the Batswana – who routinely oscillated between splitting up and incorporating other groups – shows that cultures are in a constant process of change.

Today the industrial and economic dominance of South Africa continues to change traditional patterns of life throughout the subcontinent. The large-scale flow of migrants across national boundaries to the great industrial magnet of South Africa means that, even where people continue to define their identity in ethnic terms, traditional ways fail to conform to banal stereotypes. Tribal definitions are at best rough categories denoting people from a particular region and linguistic group.

---

* Batswana/Motswana has two subtly different meanings. In the first place it refers to the roughly three million Setswana-speaking people of Botswana and South Africa. But it also means any citizen of Botswana, irrespective of ethnic origin.

LANGUAGE

SETSWANA GREETINGS AND RESPONSES

People customarily **greet** each other, whether strangers or not, with the older person greeting the younger one first. Greet people courteously in all situations – at roadblocks, when asking directions, or meeting people at the roadside, or when talking to the person servicing your room. The magic word is *dumela* with the stress in the middle, which means "hello" and can be said at any time. Onto *dumela* you tag *Mma* for women and *Rra* for men; thus *dumela Mma* and *dumela Rra*. Use *Mma* and *Rra* after questions (even when speaking English) like "Where is the station, Mma?", "How much is it, Rra?" The pronunciation of the "-a" is short, close to the "u" in "fun". The "Rr" is slightly rolled if you are up to that. To round off a conversation or to indicate everything's okay, say *Go siame*.

Hello (to one/many)	*Dumêla/dumêlang*	Goodbye (person leaving)	*Sala sentlê*
Hello (in response)	*Dumêla/dumêlang*		
How are you?	*A o sa tsogile sentlê?*	Goodbye (person remaining)	*Tsamaya sentlê*
Fine thanks	*Ee, ke sa tsogile*		

BASICS

Yes	*Ee*	What is your name?	*Leina la gago e mang?*
No	*Nnyaa*	My name is Peter	*Leina la me ke Peter.*
Thank you	*Kea itumêla*	Where do you come from?	*O tswa kae? (sing)*
Please	*Tsweetswee*		
Today	*Gompieno*	I come from England	*Ke kwa England*
Tomorrow	*Ka moso*	Do you speak English?	*A o bua Seenglish?*
Yesterday	*Maabane*	It is hot	*Go molelo*
Come in	*Tsena*	Rain	*Pula*

TRAVEL

What town is this?	*Motse o ke ofe?*	Is it far to town?	*A go kgakala kwa motseng?*
It is Molepolole	*Ke Molepolole*	Is there a hotel?	*A go ne le hotele?*
Where is the station?	*Seteisene se kae?*	Is the pan still far off?	*A mogobe o sa le kgakala?*
Where is the road to Maun?	*Tsela Maun e kae?*	Where are you going to?	*O ya kae?*

PHRASEBOOK

The *Setswana–English Phrasebook* by A. J. Wookey, sold in bookshops in the country, is old-fashioned, inadequate, and difficult to use. Many phrases are inappropriate and often in the imperative. The first entry under general expressions is *my sister's child is dead* and the section on travel concentrates on inspanning the oxen for the wagon. Nevertheless it has a mini-dictionary and grammar worth looking at.

covered in some detail on p.346), whose traditional hunter-gatherer lifestyle has all but died out, but who still exist as a linguistically and ethnically distinct group. Botswana's earliest Bantu-speakers were the **Bakgalakgadi**, members of the Sotho-Tswana group. Migrants from South Africa who arrived well before the Batswana, they settled in the Kalahari Desert – which owes its name to them – and intermarried freely with the San.

Around the Francistown area is a pocket of **Bakalanga**, descendants of Zimbabwe's Rozvi state, who speak a Shona dialect. After the collapse of the Rozvi state in the 1830s, the Bakalanga became tributaries of the Bangwato, but have otherwise continued to live autonomously. The **Bayei**, who live in shallow river areas, and the **Mbukushu**, living along deep waters of the Okavango Delta in the northwest, both originated in Angola. The **Herero** (see p.331) were turn-of-the-century refugees from German brutality in neighbouring Namibia, and finally there are the **English- and Afrikaans-speaking whites**, who came from South Africa in colonial times.

Christianity is now the official religion of Botswana, yet only one person in five can be regarded as a practising Christian – the remainder hold traditional beliefs. Most Christians belong to the United Congregational Church of Southern Africa.

Money and costs

Although Botswana remained tied to the South African rand until well after independence, it now has its own currency, the pula (P). That pula is the Setswana word for "rain" demonstrates the enormous value of water in a dry land. Pula come in notes of P5, 10, 20 and 50, and there are P1 and P2 coins. Each pula is divided into a hundred thebe (t), of which there are 1t, 5t, 10t, 25t and 50t coins. At the time of writing the exchange rate was £1 to P4.5 and US$1 to P3.

■ Banks and exchange

As the pula is effectively a hard currency, and residents are permitted to export considerable sums, there's no black market in Botswana. You can change travellers' cheques at banks or the larger hotels in big centres. However, there are no banks in the vast tracts of the rural countryside: change money when you're in towns and make sure you're carrying enough cash with you. The following towns offer **full banking facilities**: Francistown, Gaborone, Ghanzi, Jwaneng, Kanye, Kasane, Lobatse, Mahalapye, Maun, Mochudi, Molepolole, Palapye, Selebi-Phikwe and Serowe.

■ Costs

Unless you want simply to trek along the deserted backways of Botswana, it's going to be difficult to get around on a shoestring. The government's policy of low-density high-cost tourism, instituted in mid-1989 in an attempt to maximize revenue while minimizing the harmful impact of too many visitors, has made things more difficult than they were before. In all the major game reserves it costs over P70 a day just to be there and to use an ill-equipped campsite.

Outside the National Parks things are more affordable, and you can still have a good time. There is some good private game country in the Tuli area in particular, where you can stay in reasonably priced self-catering camps.

Long-distance **travel** is reasonably cheap in Botswana, with the *Greyhound* luxury coach travelling the 400km or so from Gaborone to Johannesburg for P80. A less salubrious, but more eventful journey by combi (minibus) or long-distance economy bus on the same route would work out at around P50. A second-class train fare along a similar distance from Gaborone to Francistown costs P80; and first-class would be about half that again on top. Perhaps the best way to see Botswana is in a four-wheel-drive vehicle, but **4WD rental** doesn't come cheap: around P220 a day plus P2 per kilometre travelled.

Prices for **accommodation** vary wildly, depending more on the location than the quality of the room. Around the fringes of the sought-after Okavango Delta you'll pay upwards of P150 for a double room, whereas it could easily be four times as much once inside the reserve. Elsewhere expect to pay around P80–150 for a modest double, and P240 or more for a posh one. **Camping** is a cheaper option, working out at P10–20 a head around Okavango. Free camping, on the other hand, is allowed anywhere outside urban areas.

There's more scope to get by cheaply when it comes to **eating**, either buying takeaways or self-catering from shops or supermarkets. Even though most food is imported from South Africa, prices are considerably cheaper than in the West. A sit-down snack will set you back P8 and a takeaway about half that. For P25–35 you can eat well at a hotel or restaurant.

Getting around

Distances in Botswana are huge and the roads can be surprisingly bad. Apart from a few main highways and one or two short tarred stretches elsewhere, roads are dirt track of variable standard and in very sandy areas it can take hours to cover 40 or 50km in a 4WD vehicle. Neither is public transport plentiful in Botswana, except up and down the one main highway (and railway line) in the east. An alternative to formal public transport is to get a paid lift in a passenger-carrying truck; these may well stop for you

---

AIRLINE OFFICES

AIR BOTSWANA

See "Getting there from the UK" and "Getting there from Australasia" for addresses in London and Sydney.

Francistown *Thapama Lodge*, Blue Jacket St (☎212393).

Gaborone IGI House, The Mall (☎351921).

Kasane Airport (☎650161).

Maun Airport turn-off (☎660391).

AIR CHARTER COMPANIES

Gaborone
Executive Air, Sir Seretse Khama Airport, Private Bag SK-6 (☎375257).
Kalahari Air Services, Sir Seretse Khama Airport, PO Box 41278, Broadhurst (☎351804).

Maun
Aer Kavango, Maun Airport, PO Box 169 (☎660393).
Delta Air, Maun Airport, PO Box 39 (☎660044).
Northern Air, Maun Airport, PO Box 40 (☎660385).

Kasane
Chobe Air, PO Box 280 (☎650532).

---

when you're hitching. **Generally hitching is safe enough, although there's a lot of drinking and driving.**

■ Buses, combis and minibuses

The few **buses** and **minibuses** that run in Botswana operate almost exclusively on the tarred highways.

It's quite easy to travel between the principal towns: Gaborone is connected with them all, although in the absence of fixed timetables you have to ask around the bus station for specific times; and there's a service from Francistown to Maun. In Gaborone and on short-haul trips from the capital you'll also find **combis** (small minibuses; see Chapter Seven for details). Elsewhere, however, services are meagre, if not non-existent. Public transport is simply not a viable option to get you around most of the country's vast west.

Perhaps the most useful of the buses are the **international economy services** that run to neighbouring Zimbabwe and Zambia. Both routes begin at Francistown and are covered under its transport details (see p.292). There's also a luxury service between Gaborone and Johannesburg.

■ Trains

Rail travel in Botswana is totally straightforward. A single main line runs from Gaborone to Bulawayo via Francistown, passing through the major towns along the eastern corridor. It's extremely slow and in mid-summer can be desperately hot. On the other hand if you find doing nothing easy, and have plenty to read, it's superbly relaxing. There's more space than on a bus and for a couple a **coupe** is luxury – your own (admittedly small) private compartment, with washing facilities and bunks if you want to siesta away the afternoon through the scrublands.

Daily overnight trains link Lobatse and Gaborone with Bulawayo. In addition, two trains a day run each way between Francistown and Gaborone with refreshments available. *Botswana Railways* boasts that these luxury daytime trains provide the only air-conditioned regular scheduled service in Africa.

■ Flights

Air Botswana operates services between Gaborone and a handful of main towns: Francistown, Kasane, Maun, Selebi-Phikwe and Ghanzi. **Charter companies**, based in Maun, Francistown and Gaborone, run flights to smaller destinations in the Okavango Delta, Tsodilo Hills and elsewhere in Botswana. It's often worth enquiring at their offices whether they have unoccupied seats on charters that they're prepared to sell. If the flight is leaving imminently some operators may even discount the fare.

■ Driving practicalities and routes

While foreign driver's licences are valid for six months, driving is less a matter of a licence than of being able to cope with difficult road conditions and knowing how to mend punctures (of which you'll have many) and to effect minor repairs. Above all, **four-wheel driving** requires a fair amount of expertise, and you should familiarize yourself with what's involved before undertaking any major expedition into the wilderness. Many places are trackless and if you get stranded you may not see another human being for some time. If in doubt take along someone who knows the scene, and make sure that someone knows where you're going. A useful source of detailed information to help plan a 4WD expedition down the back routes is the *Visitors' Guide to Botswana* by Mike Main, John and Sandra Fowkes (see "Books" in *Contexts*).

Botswana's main north–south artery is a very good, wide, tarred road, as are the roads to Maun and Shakawe. Several of the major dirt roads like the Tuli Block roads are passable in an ordinary, though necessarily tough vehicle. Many of the roads, however, require 4WD or at the very least a high-clearance vehicle. Some roads are seasonally passable – ask locally for up-to-date information. Each chapter gives details on the road situation.

Car rental

For **car rental** two companies have national networks: *Avis* with branches in Gaborone, Francistown and Maun (see p.43 for details of their offices abroad), and *Holiday Car Rentals* with offices in Gaborone and Kasane. **Rates** for a saloon car are from P150 per day plus P1.2 per km, and for 4WD you'll pay from P220 per day plus P2 per km; for both there's an extra collision damage waiver.

■ Hitching

Hitchers have succeeded in thumbing virtually everywhere in Botswana, and you'll certainly make it to any of the larger destinations. The amount of traffic in the more remote areas can be pretty limited, but that means drivers tend to be more sympathetic. The essence of hitching in Botswana is to be in no hurry and to carry enough supplies for roadside waits of a couple of days, depending on where you're waiting. Travel well-prepared; motorists have come across hitchers stranded in the middle of game areas, virtually starving after several days without food.

■ Dugout canoe

A leisurely exploration of the waterways by dugout canoe or **mokoro** (plural *mekoro*) is one of the most satisfying and adventurous modes of travel –

for short stretches. Most visitors aim to go out for at least a few days on the Okavango Delta. This can best be arranged from Maun; see Chapter Nine for details, including practical tips on how to get the best out of a *mokoro* expedition.

■ Mobile safaris

Mobile safaris are essentially mini-overland expeditions taking clients across Botswana in 4WD vehicles, and camping on the way. One typical route runs along a triangle from Maun through Chobe National Park and Moremi Wildlife Reserve and back to Maun. A longer one starts at the Victoria Falls in Zimbabwe and drives the full length of Chobe, through Moremi, to end at Maun. See "Through Chobe Overland", p.302, for further details. Some South African-based companies start their safaris in Johannesburg (see p.13 for booking details).

Accommodation

Accommodation outside Botswana's tourist areas is limited. Even the capital Gaborone makes few concessions to the needs of visitors not there on business. In the tourist areas there's a fair scattering of lodge-style accommodation, which doesn't come cheap unless you really hunt around. There's always the rock-bottom option of camping.

■ Hotels

Gaborone has a number of hotels, mostly upmarket and usually fully booked. All the main centres outside the capital – Francistown, Ghanzi, Lobatse, Mahalapye, Maun, Molepolole, Palapye, Selebi-Phikwe, Serowe – have at least one hotel, where you'll generally find a room. They're rarely something to write home about, but you can count on getting clean linen and reasonable facilities.

Prices tend to reflect demand – based on the hotel's location – rather than the standard. Outside the capital the rates go from P100 upwards for a double room.

■ Lodges

As you approach big-game country, the workaday business hotels begin to give way to **tourist lodges**. These are found in the region around the Okavango Swamps, north and west of Nata, and in the private game reserves of the Tuli Block, clustered around the Motloutse River. They aren't always prohibitively expensive, although you can

ACCOMMODATION PRICE CODES IN BOTSWANA

Most accommodation options in our account of Botswana have been given **price codes** to indicate the cost of a single night's lodging. The code for each establishment is based on the cost **per person sharing**; there is usually a supplement for a single person in a room. Prices for establishments that only offer all-inclusive rates (comprising meals, and perhaps guided tours and other services) have not been coded and are given in pula (per person per night).

① under P20	③ P40–60	⑤ P80–100	⑦ P120–140
② P20–40	④ P60–80	⑥ P100–120	⑧ P140–160

expect to pay a lot in the Okavango Delta and Chobe National Park.

The more reasonably priced lodges are mostly on the fringes of these select areas. Prices range from P135 to P165 for a double room. Inside the boundaries of the Delta and Chobe National Park you'll pay between P450 and P750 per person, but don't forget that the price includes all meals and game-viewing, activities, drives, water safaris or guided walks. Cheaper camping packages into the Delta start at P550 for five nights.

■ Camping

Camping, as always, is the cheapest way to spend the night, but in Botswana it has the added dimension of being a really adventurous and exciting way to see the country. Once you get well away from urban areas you can camp anywhere. Near settlements, however, you should make an effort to contact the local chief for permission. Most National Parks charge P20 camping fee. Facilities are frequently limited to cold running water, showers and flush toilets, and even these can't always be relied upon to work.

Many areas adjoining the reserves are just as wild, and you're allowed to camp free of charge – but be cautious of game (for advice on safety in the bush, see p.118). Take care not to add to Botswana's litter problem, which is particularly severe – and notorious – in the Okavango Delta.

INTERNATIONAL DIALLING CODES

To **phone Botswana from abroad**, the country code is **267**, to be followed simply by the destination number (there are no area codes).

Phoning out from Botswana, the international access code is **00**. This is followed by the country and area codes and finally the destination number.

Country codes are the same as those dialled from Zimbabwe (see p.47).

Communications: post and phone services

Keeping in touch with home poses no problem in Botswana. The postal service isn't bad and the phone system is modern, with up-to-date call boxes – including new cardphones – from which you can usually dial direct to the rest of the world.

■ Post

There are post offices in all towns and the larger villages, open Monday–Friday 8.15am–12.45pm and 2–4pm, and Saturday 8.30–11.30am. Services tend to be slow but are reliable and cheap. Telegrams are the quickest form of mail. There are no poste restante services in Botswana.

■ Phone

All international calls to or from Botswana used to be routed through South Africa; the decision to develop its own phone system is another example of the country's determination to break out of that degree of dependency. There's now direct dialling between most of the larger towns, which have their own automatic phone exchanges. Even the smaller towns have public call boxes, usually around the post office. There are no area dialling codes.

The Media: press, radio and TV

In theory the media in Botswana remain uncensored, although custom and tradition act as curbs on what is considered acceptable in this still-conservative society.

■ The press

The press consists of three independent weekly tabloid newspapers and the *Daily News*, a freesheet published by the Department of Information and Broadcasting and available from their offices. Because it's gratis, the *Daily News* is very popular, but it consists of little more than official press releases and statements by ministers.

The most popular of the independent papers is *The Botswana Guardian*, published on Friday, which has a lot of hard local news. From the same stable, the *Midweek Sun* comes out on Wednesday; this and *The Gazette*, which also comes out on Wednesday, tend toward unimaginative and safe coverage.

Of much greater interest is *Mmegi – the Reporter*, published every Saturday, with its vociferously independent and campaigning stance. It goes in for investigative coverage rather than hard news and has high journalistic standards. Politically, it supports a more equitable distribution of wealth in Botswana, with a policy toward the government of constructive criticism. Although it's undoubtedly the most exciting of Botswana's papers it has the lowest circulation and can be difficult to find in the smaller centres.

Of the **South African newspapers**, the daily Johannesburg-based *Star* and *Business Day* are available in Gaborone on the day of publication. Both give reasonable news coverage. For more lively coverage, look out for the weeklies *New Nation* and the *Mail & Guardian*.

International magazines like *Time* and *Newsweek*, and ones with an African emphasis like *New African* and *Africa*, are also available in the capital and larger centres.

■ Radio and TV

Radio Botswana has a talk station (RB1) broadcasting in both English and Setswana. Programmes are a mixed bag of religion, music, schools broadcasts and good news coverage, while RB2 broadcasts continuous music from 6am to 2pm. **Radio Mmabatho**, broadcasting from South Africa's Northwest Province, pumps out music which can be picked up in parts of Botswana; South African and Zimbabwean music are played as well as Western pop, but sadly little modern local music.

The frequencies and times of BBC World Service and Voice of America broadcasts are the same as for Zimbabwe; see the box on p.49.

Gaborone Broadcasting Corporation (GBC) transmits a couple of hours of TV exclusively to the capital every evening, but you'll be most unlikely to encounter it. Far more popular and widespread is **South African TV**, available in all areas adjacent to that country's border.

Music and entertainment

Botswana has little in the way of public entertainment, and most of what there is centres on the capital. The country's only "place of culture" is the Maitisong Centre at Maru-a-Pula School in Gaborone. Although the centre is run by the school, it's open to the public and there are varied events every week, from Kalahari Conservation Society films to theatre festivals. Look for press and radio announcements.

Other entertainment tends to be of a more familiar and mundane variety. Each of the larger towns has one or two cinemas showing unexceptional programmes, and the most popular pastime of all is drinking in bars and at nightclubs, which are concentrated in Gaborone. On most evenings there'll be live music in at least one of the clubs in the capital, and lively DJing at the others. A few local bands have emerged, but the **music scene** has yet to develop the vibrancy offered in Zimbabwe or the diversity of sounds in South Africa. The most popular bands, *Afro Sunshine* and the *Botswana Defence Force Bands*, can usually be relied upon to provide a couple of hours of snappy listening.

Crafts

Botswana is known for its very beautiful basketry. The best-known style was brought to the country with Mbukushu refugees in the nineteenth century, followed more recently by a second wave in 1969, fleeing the Angolan war of independence. Most weaving therefore comes from those areas closest to the northern border, in Ngamiland. The baskets are woven from the mokolane palm (*Hyphaene ventricosa*), and the root of the mothakola tree is used to dye it in various brown shades. You'll find an incredible variety of baskets on sale in town shops, or you can go direct to the weavers in rural areas.

There's a **language** to the design motifs of the baskets, which plays with the contrasting chocolates and oatmeals. A dazzling variety of patterns signify events or important aspects of life. The "urine trail of the bull" – like those swirling hypnosis wheels you can get in novelty shops – celebrates the centrality of cattle in traditional life. Other spiralled and petalled forms have names like "ribs of the giraffe" and "back of the python". Some have schematic animals and figures woven in.

The best range is in **Maun**, with a more expensive selection in **Gaborone**. If you travel up the **Panhandle**, you can buy them directly from the weavers. Tourist lodges usually keep a small collection and many in the Delta use the baskets for decorating the walls. Ngamiland baskets are not cheap, although in view of the fact that they're handmade and take many days of work, they can hardly be considered expensive. Cheaper baskets are also made in the **Shashe** area in the southeast, not as tightly or finely woven and using grass instead of palm. **Francistown** is the place to buy these.

Crafts created by the **San people** are unique and worth buying, not simply because Botswana is the only place you're likely to find them, but because they are traditional items which haven't yet moved into the realms of airport art or synthesized Western bric-a-brac. The handmade **ostrich egg beads and bracelets** look no different from anything you'll see in a museum case. You may well come across really old stuff amongst the newly produced **leather beaded aprons and bags**. Among objects which are made solely for tourists (but still look like the real thing) are skilfully crafted bow and arrow **hunting sets**. Ghanzi has by far the best and cheapest array, but you'll find San jewellery, bags and hunting kits dotted around the craft shops in Maun and Gaborone.

Trouble

Violent crime is rare in Botswana, but petty theft is as endemic as in any area where poverty and wealth exist side by side. Avoid having your goods lifted in the first place, because once they're gone you're unlikely to see them again. Take common-sense precautions and keep an eye on your valuables.

If you're ripped off consider carefully whether it's worth the hassle of reporting the loss to the police and going through all the paperwork and bureaucracy. Of course, if you're insured you'll need to do so. Police are conscientious about taking down details and they'll give you the copy of the police report required for your insurance claim.

■ Sexual attitudes and harassment

If you're a woman travelling on your own you are unlikely to be sexually harassed, although macho whites may well seriously chat you up in places like Maun. Topless swimming and sunbathing is not on, but otherwise there are no dress restrictions.

In general, **attitudes towards women** are conservative. There is no women's movement as such, but there is a group of intellectuals in Gaborone who are concerned with women's issues. Joyce Anderson at the *Women's Affairs Unit*, Ministry of Home Affairs, Private Bag 002, Gaborone, should be able to provide information about women's agricultural cooperatives and publications.

Directory

CONTRACEPTIVES Oral contraceptives, on prescription, and condoms are available from pharmacies in all the main towns.

EMERGENCIES Ambulance ☎997, Fire ☎998, Police ☎999.

PUBLIC HOLIDAYS

January 1 New Year's Day

January 2 Public Holiday

Easter Good Friday to Easter Monday

Ascension Day

3rd Monday (plus the day after) in July President's Day

September 30 (plus the day after) Botswana Day

December 25 & 26 Christmas & Boxing Day

SHOP OPENING HOURS in Botswana are generally 8am to 5pm, with some closing for lunch between 1 and 2pm. Bottle stores (off-licences) open and close two hours later. In larger centres you'll usually find a general store that stays open until 8 or 9pm. Many shops are closed on Saturday afternoon and all day Sunday.

TAMPONS Available in all the main centres. But if you're doing any adventurous travelling, bear in mind that you may be far from shops, so take your own supplies.

TIME Like Zimbabwe, Botswana is two hours ahead of GMT. Daylight is from 6am to 6pm, slightly extended either side in mid-summer.

Unlike Europe, darkness falls quite quickly, so you shouldn't expect to count on lingering evening twilight.

TOILETS Hotel toilets are generally fine. There are toilets at National Park campsites but few public ones elsewhere. On any journeys into the hinterland take a supply of toilet paper, particularly if you're camping rough. You'll have to get used to digging a hole in the ground. Remember to burn the paper fully.

WORK You shouldn't go to Botswana expecting to pick up casual work. Nonetheless, a skills shortage is developing as diamonds continue to fuel the fastest-growing economy in Africa, which means that there may be vacancies in some specialized sectors such as building design and construction. Your best bet is to write to private firms asking about work and including a CV – it's all a question of the right qualifications at the right time.

CHAPTER SEVEN

GABORONE AND THE EASTERN CORRIDOR

Most travellers see no more of Botswana's **eastern corridor**, where the bulk of the population lives, than a passing dusty landscape glimpsed through a train or car window. It's the **railway line**, with towns dotted along its length in a concentration found nowhere else in Botswana, that defines the eastern flank of the country; the road that runs parallel to it was only tarred after Independence. The railroad was always very much a through route, created by the British South Africa Company and used by Britain for the sole purpose of bringing raw materials such as copper and coal from its lucrative northern colonies to the South African ports. However, the riches carried by the train never spilt over into the vast undeveloped stretches of Bechuanaland, as it was then called.

Gaborone was just a dusty railway siding throughout the colonial years. Only after Independence did it take on its current status as national capital, and it feels as if it has yet to put down roots. Once you've checked out the handful of sights in town there's little reason not to make a hasty escape. However, the nearby weavers' village, **Odi**, and the historic Bakgatla capital of **Mochudi**, just to the north, are worth a visit, as is the **Mokolodi Nature Reserve** on the route south towards Lobatse.

The landscape to the northeast of Gaborone is flat and thorny. Apart from **Serowe**, royal seat of Sir Seretse Khama and adopted home of writer Bessie Head, and the **Khama Rhino Sanctuary**, there's nothing very much of interest until you come to that part of the country sandwiched between the tracks and Zimbabwe. Here, in the **Tuli Block** – one of the country's few freehold tracts (most of the country is still common land) – you'll find some of Botswana's most striking landscapes and fine private game country. Around **Mashatu Game Reserve** – Southern Africa's largest private wildlife park – there's ample opportunity to see animals at a much smaller cost than elsewhere in Botswana. There are no add-on game park fees here and the several camps and lodges offer a wide range of accommodation. Even though the cheaper options won't get you into Mashatu itself, they share the same pool of animals, which wander back and forth across the boundaries of the reserve.

ACCOMMODATION PRICE CODES IN BOTSWANA

Most accommodation options in our account of Botswana have been given **price codes** to indicate the cost of a single night's lodging. The code for each establishment is based on the cost **per person sharing**; there is usually a supplement for a single person in a room. Prices for establishments that only offer all-inclusive rates (comprising meals, and perhaps guided tours and other services) have not been coded and are given in pula (per person per night).

① under P20	③ P40–60	⑤ P80–100	⑦ P120–140
② P20–40	④ P60–80	⑥ P100–120	⑧ P140–160

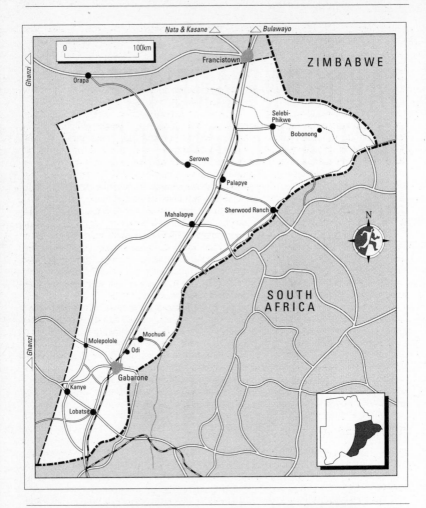

GABORONE AND AROUND

GABORONE is an amorphous sort of place – the kind of town where you drive around trying to find the centre only to escape as soon as you can, not precisely because it's unpleasant, but because it's incredibly vague and unsatisfying.

Part of the problem is that Gaborone is a new city and still growing. Although it was meticulously replanned to become the showpiece capital of an independent Botswana, the life of its inhabitants has effectively refused to fit in with the new layout. Beyond **The Mall** – the cohesive main shopping precinct and *de facto* centre – footpaths crisscross any open space and, independently of roads, make connections between one area and another. New buildings sprout seemingly at random, to create a mess of construction sites.

While the town is new, the settlement site certainly isn't – Stone Age tools are unearthed in almost every major building operation. Colonialists set up the village of

Gaberones around 1887 on the banks of the Ngotwane River where it functioned as a district headquarters. The name came from Gaborone, the king of the Batlokwa, whose capital perched on the opposite bank of the river. A couple of years later, when the railway arrived, another small colonial village was built 4km away at the station, known, reasonably enough, as **Gaberones Station**.

Gaborone's position on the **South African border** symbolizes the ambivalent links between the two countries. The British government regarded it as such a foregone conclusion that Bechuanaland would become part of South Africa, that throughout the colonial years the Protectorate's capital was in **Mafeking** (now Mafikeng) inside South Africa. Despite increased pressure to take over the territory following South Africa's Act of Union in 1910, skilful manoeuvring by Batswana leaders avoided the cession of the country. The city you see today, situated between the two earlier settlements, was built in the years immediately before Independence in 1966, when it became necessary to create a new capital in time to move the administration from Mafeking.

There's really very little reason to visit the functional and administrative city of Gaborone for any longer than a day, though it's nice enough to wander about The Mall and visit the excellent **museum** and art gallery. Most tourists pause only at the airport to change planes, and visitors are barely catered for in town. There's nowhere cheap to stay – the central hotels are frequently booked up by officials and business people, and there are no hostels open to travellers or public campsites, although there are a few reasonable options slightly out of town.

The city's main interest lies in what it's becoming. In a country with vast areas of wilderness, bad communications and two tarred roads, Gaborone is as urban and sophisticated as Botswana gets. The most independent-minded **newspaper** has its offices here and prestigious Maru-a-Pula School draw Botswana's middle class and intellectuals. **Television** broadcasts don't get further than the city outskirts, although in addition to local programming there's pirated South African TV (you can also pick it up in Francistown and Lobatse). A couple of South-African-influenced **pop groups** shuttle around at the sprinkling of nightclubs and discos, and there's a dawning sense of urban culture emerging. It is in Gaborone's expansion, too, that the country's diamond revenue is most clearly evident, not in the remote rural areas where, despite improvements, life mostly stays the same.

Arrival, getting around and information

If you arrive in Gaborone by **air**, the only transport from Seretse Khama Airport are **minibuses** or **combis** run by the three main hotels, which will carry you the 14km into town even if you don't intend to stay at any of these places. You're by no means certain of being able to find a taxi, and neither is there an airport bus.

In the town itself, the principal transport hub is the **railway station** – despite the fact that there are only a couple of trains per day in either direction. At least the trains are reliable, if slow. A **left-luggage** service is available at the railway station (Mon–Fri 8am–1pm & 2–4pm).

Most **long-distance buses** and **combis** arrive at the newly built bus station on the opposite side of the railway track, linked to the train station by a metal bridge. If you're departing from here, note that destinations are marked on blue signs at each rank but there is no timetable, and no bus offices or officials about – the only way to get information is from waiting passengers. If you're coming in on the *Greyhound* bus from Johannesburg you'll be deposited opposite the *Kudu* service station which, contrary to appearances, is in the centre of town. To get to The Mall, the main focus of the city, go down the alleyway beside the service station.

Although Gaborone is dispersed and you'll end up doing a fair amount of walking, it's easy enough to find your way around. From the railway station it's a fifteen-minute

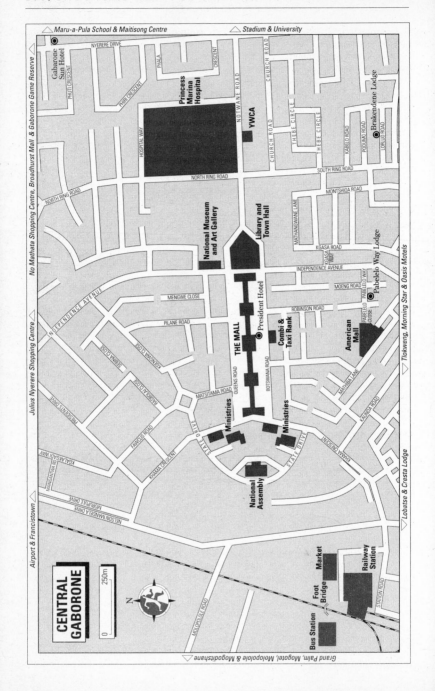

CENTRAL GABORONE

0   250m

walk to the bottom end of **The Mall**. Follow Station Road eastward and then north as it becomes Khama Crescent.

To travel **to the suburbs**, or one of the cheaper out-of-town hotels, take a **combi** from outside the station, or flag one down on the roadside (they run till 10pm around town, 8pm out of town). Each destination has up to four different routes so be sure to tell the driver exactly where you want to go. They stop virtually anywhere for passengers and cost very little; the idea is that you should just squeeze in, whether or not there appears to be any room. **Taxis** are reasonably priced, and you'll find ranks at the station and on Botswana Road, opposite the *President Hotel*; here, you can also pick up Broadhurst combis (routes 1–4). Once in the suburbs, you'll notice that unlike former British colonies with entrenched class-segregation, Gaborone has been planned deliberately to mix low- and high-cost housing.

The **tourist information office** in the lower Mall, opposite BIC House, is not desperately helpful but you can pick up a few useful leaflets.

Accommodation

Unless you have a wad of notes, accommodation in Gaborone is a nightmare. Even if you're prepared to fork out for one of the **luxury central hotels**, you'll probably find them all full of business travellers (though weekends are more promising). By ringing around, you may find a cheaper bed **away from the centre**. Some of the **lodges** which normally cater for long-stay guests will take people passing through if there are vacancies. However, they are not particularly cheap and often full – ring before you turn up.

Hotels

Gaborone Sun, Private Bag 0016, Nyerere Drive (☎351111). Pleasant surroundings and pool, not far from the centre of town. ⑧.

Gaborone Travel Inn, Private Bag 00127, Molepolole Rd (☎322777). Brand new and central (by the station), with a good bar and live music at the weekend. It's very popular so book in advance. ④.

Grand Palm, Molepolole Rd, between Gaborone West and Mogoditshane (☎304282). The prison-like exterior hides a glamorous international hotel (formerly the *Sheraton*), strictly expense accounts only. If you look confident, you can use their pool. ⑦.

Mogotel, PO Box 1352, Molepolole Rd, Mogoditshane (☎372228). Clean, cheap and relatively pleasant. Single women may feel uncomfortable as rooms are also rented by the hour. ②.

Morning Star Motel, Tlokweng Village (☎328301). Six kilometres out on the Zeerust Road, this rather seedy, medium-range hotel is particularly convenient for the South African border. ②.

Oasis Motel, Tlokweng Rd (☎328396). Out of the centre, airy and pleasant, with a nice patio restaurant and pool (open to non-residents for P7). Gardens and golf for residents. Rooms and chalets available. ③–④.

President, The Mall (☎353631). Smack in the centre, with a terrace overlooking The Mall. ⑦.

Lodges

Brakendene Lodge, Ext 10, Plot 15113, Loruo Road (☎312886, fax 306246). Friendly establishment only a three-minute walk from The Mall, near the Princess Marina Hospital. Price includes breakfast. Family lodges (up to 4 children) also available. ③.

Cresta Lodge, Private Bag 00126, Samora Machel Drive (☎375375 or 312431). Somewhat more expensive than the other lodges, but with the facilities to make it worthwhile. ⑥.

Lolwapa Lodge, Ext 12, Plot 3412, Maakakgang Close (☎301200). Homely place reached by taking a second left after the circle just past the polytechnic going towards the university. ④.

Mokolodi Nature Reserve, 15km from Gaborone on the Lobatse road (main office PO Box 170, 183 Queen's Road, The Mall, Gaborone; ☎353959, fax 313973; see p.275). Scenic, clean 3-bed and 6-bed chalets with well-equipped kitchens, in a peaceful haven by a waterhole, excellent for game watching; higher prices at weekends. They also offer dormitory accommodation for P30 per night, including bedding, showers and light breakfast. They will pick you up from the airport for P10 per person (minimum P30). ②–③.

Pabelelo Way Lodge, Plot 838, Pabelelo Way, near the African Mall (☎ 351682). ③.

Camping and hostels

Camping is not permitted around Gaborone. However, if you keep a low profile, it's possible to go outside the city and sleep somewhere in the bush – the most promising direction is to head out on the Molepolole road for at least half an hour. Particularly if you make for the rocky hilltops, you should be able to find a fairly secluded spot. If your nerve fails, the *Mogotel* on the Molepolole road (see above) allows camping in an unappetizing gravelly courtyard in the middle of the hotel (P10 per night); you must call in advance to get permission. Minibuses to Molepolole leave from the station or you can wait on the Molepolole road, near the station off Nelson Mandela Drive, for a combi or lift. Slightly cheaper is the *St Clare Lion Park* (P5 adult, P2 child; ☎/fax 372711), 17km south of Gaborone.

Unfortunately, the *YWCA* in Gaborone no longer accepts passing backpackers. However, there is the new, attractive option of staying in **dormitories** at the Mokolodi Nature Reserve (see "Lodges" above). Finally, if you're desperate, consider taking the overnight sleeper train to Francistown.

The City

Life in Gaborone centres very much around its various shopping malls. **The Mall**, the most central, is a large, relaxed pedestrian precinct where you'll find everything from banks and embassies to chemists and bookshops. People stroll about the walkways, which are dotted with acacias and lined with bricked flowerbeds. Built on a ceremonial axis, the top end of The Mall leads to government ministries, the National Assembly and the President's Office. At the other end is the library and Town Hall, opposite the **National Museum** and **Art Gallery**.

The **African Mall**, about ten minutes' walk along the dirt road behind the Botswana Road combi stop (opposite the *President Hotel*), has a wide selection of slightly more downmarket shops and eating places. This is where much of Gaborone's nightlife in centred. Everything north of Nyerere Drive is known as **Broadhurst**. Nearly 4km north of The Mall, the **Broadhurst Mall** (combi routes 1 and 2), comprising the **Kagiso Centre**, **BBS Mall** and **Roshini Centre**, is more upmarket and has just about everything you could need from a shopping centre. The **No Mathata Centre**, closer in opposite Maru-a-Pula School (combi route 2), contains some good restaurants and night spots. **The Village** at Tlokweng, 3km east of the railway station (combi route 4), boasts a health centre and cinema as well as a live music venue.

Immediately around the station, you'll find the closest thing the city has to a **market** – if you want to escape the new town ambience of Gaborone, this is the best place to wander. Although Botswana's desert climate means that little fresh produce is grown, the market is a good place to get your hair cut, buy low-quality African music cassettes and savour such local delicacies as mopane worms, pickled spinach, goat and *bojalwa* (sorghum beer).

Situated about 1km east of Broadhurst, from Limpopo Drive, the small **Gaborone Game Reserve** (daily 6.30am–6.30pm; P10 per person, P6 per vehicle) was opened to give the Gaborone public an opportunity to see wildlife in its natural habitat, though it's not as impressive as Mokolodi (see p.275). It's mainly inhabited by antelope; there's also a white rhino in a separate enclosure.

The National Museum

Tues-Fri 9am-6pm, at & Sun 9am-5pm. Free

Botswana's **National Museum** provides a good opportunity to size up this vast country and get a grip on its different people, environments and wildlife. Specializing in fauna and ethnographic material, the museum includes some fine examples of craftwork.

Near the entrance, the new Swedish-designed exhibition on the **prehistory** of Botswana has proved rather controversial, since many Batswana feel it does not represent their view of the origins of man. Many consider the idea of evolution to be racist and feel that Matsieng Cave (see p.278), from which they believe the first man to have emerged, should have been included.

In the **wildlife** section there are stuffed cats aplenty. Besides the predictable lions, there are examples of two rare and beautiful desert cats: one, the **black-footed cat**, the size of a domestic cat, is an exquisite gingery brown feline about which little is known, beyond the fact that it is confined to the Kalahari. The other is the **caracal** or desert lynx, which leaps high into the air to catch birds. San-speakers call the female caracal "bride of the dawn", the incarnation of the morning star with the same name. Less romantic, at the far end of the museum, is a reconstruction of the **biggest crocodile** ever shot in Botswana. Truly monstrous, it's the subject of innumerable tales surrounding its killing.

Although a permanent hunter-gatherer lifestyle has now largely come to an end in Botswana, the museum should satisfy your curiosity about how **desert dwellers** can survive – including what arrow poisons they use. Larvae of the beige-spotted *Poyclada flexuosa* beetles are the commonest raw material of the poison. These insignificant and deceptively innocuous-looking grubs are gathered from the marula tree. The display of roots eaten by the Kalahari dwellers is also intriguing. These vegetables are surprisingly large, around ten or twenty times as big as the average carrot or parsnip. Various gourds, such as the Tsama melon, supply the only source of moisture during the seven-month dry season, and continue to supplement the diet of San farm workers nowadays.

The best **regional craft collection** is in the display about the Hambukushu of the Okavango region. Notice particularly the beautiful oval grain storage basket – unmatched by any similar article you'll find for sale.

The **museum shop** has the cheapest selection of crafts in town: you'll find some good San crafts, baskets, books and postcards, and they also keep *Pelegano*'s ceramics (see "Crafts" below). You can't buy anything over the weekend or after 4.30pm.

The Octagon

The **Octagon collection** from sub-Saharan Africa ranges from painting and sculpture to crafts and textiles, and is often mistaken for the Art Gallery (see below). The exhibition is meant to be replaced every two years but has remained the same for at least three years with no imminent plans for change. In the centre, there is an impressive display of giant grain-carrying baskets and Hurutshe pots. The array of **children's toys** is charming, with its tin aeroplanes, diggers, bikes and vans – all the more impressive when you realize they're made by the children themselves from old bits of scrap.

Most fascinating are the drawings and paintings by the **first European travellers** to Botswana. Wildebeest seem to have incited great fear – Samuel Daniell's nineteenth-century engraving *The Gnoo* shows a terrifying beast of almost mythical proportions, while Thomas Baines' enormous wildebeest, from the same era, lunges towards a British soldier, who has his gun at the ready.

Of the Botswana offerings, look out for a prominent carved wooden buffalo. Thought to be of Yei origin, the blockish buffalo, with another tiny buffalo on the tip of its tail, gives a sense of the solidity and implacability of the species. Before being drawn to the colourful puppets from Mali, don't miss "The Bovers", a very funny wood sculpture by Zephamia Tshumu of Zimbabwe, and the case of **San artefacts**. Besides intricately beaded bags, the **engraved ostrich eggs** are of particular note. Some shells have only abstract designs while others are of animals. One shell has a group of four stylized giraffes with turtle-shaped backs, and a fifth curving its neck delicately round the shell to reach a plant.

The Art Gallery

The **Art Gallery**, part of the museum complex, hosts a variety of interesting but transitory exhibitions, including photography. Most of the work is by contemporary African artists. Exhibitions usually last only a few weeks so what you see will depend on when you arrive. It's all very modern and chic, with whitewashed walls and a curving stone staircase, and most of the exhibits are for sale.

Craft shops

There are three **craft shops** to browse around in Gaborone itself, besides the museum shop (see above). *Botswanacraft*, in The Mall, has a representative collection of country-wide crafts including some beautiful and well-displayed **baskets** (though the best selection of baskets, and slightly cheaper, is to be found in Maun); expect to pay P60–80. Other worthwhile objects are **San pouches** and **ostrich-egg shell jewellery**, a selection of **woven items** from Mochudi, and some appealingly stylized **wooden animals** from around the Shashi area and Serowe. At first glance they all look alike, but some are more expressively carved than others, so it's worth choosing carefully. Favourite subjects are baboons, leopards and antelope.

Camphill is a spacious warehouse shop on the Old Molepolole Road, just behind the long-distance bus station. Besides a diverse selection of crafts, they sell furniture and some beautiful (though pricy) **clothes**. They also have an especially good range of postcards depicting Gui and San artwork, and a small gallery with original work on sale. All proceeds go to Kuru Art Project, for the benefit of the artists of the Kalahari. *Jewel of Africa*, in the African Mall, has a good selection of slightly more expensive artefacts and curios.

Botswanacraft also keeps a selection of pottery from *Pelegano Crafts*; their hand-painted **animal ceramics** – which have every appearance of being wooden – are particularly nice. If you're in Gaborone for a while it's worth visiting their shop in **Gabane village**, 17km out of the city, just off the new Kanye road. Another worthwhile out-of-town craft excursion is to the *Mokolodi Co-operative*, signposted off the Lobatse road, where women print brightly coloured cloth and make clay jewellery. While you can watch work in progress any time during the week, the shop is only open on Saturdays.

Eating and drinking

Food is a lot cheaper and easier to find in Gaborone than a room, and **drinking** is the country's national pastime. Apart from the hotel dining rooms or grills – which are perfectly adequate – the choices for **eating out** are dispersed among the city's various malls and along out of town roads.

Around The Mall

In the centre of town, **around The Mall**, the most relaxed and enjoyable bar for visitors is undoubtedly the terrace of the *President Hotel*, which faces onto the centre of The Mall, and provides unmatched opportunities for people-watching and contemplation of the passing scene. The grand steps make it an obvious meeting place. The terrace is good for iced drinks, tea and snacks but is closed in the evening and on Sunday. Virtually opposite, *Foodland*, the most popular takeaway in The Mall, does delicious, cheap local food, as well as sandwiches, pies and a vast selection of chilled drinks. The samosas are particularly good; most food is gone by 4pm although the official closing time is 6pm. *King's*, further up The Mall, does similar takeaway food but with slightly more Western influence. Their hamburgers are good and tasty, as is their ice cream.

In the **African Mall,** *Juicy Bites* serves good, cheap local food as well as hamburgers, hot dogs and curries (open 8am–2.30pm). *Bis Milla*, in the centre of the same mall, has a similar selection but stays open until 6pm; there are outdoor tables in the shade, which is rare in Gaborone. At night, *Harley's* is definitely the place to go. It's lively, fun and often crowded. The food is good and reasonably priced, and for once **vegetarians** can do well, with a good selection of savoury crepes and pancakes instead of the usual gigantic steaks and hamburgers. The *Taj*, also in the African Mall, is more expensive but serves reasonable curries. *Dukes*, a more upmarket restaurant, offers an eclectic variety of food ranging from local to Mongolian fare. The waiters are extremely keen to help; on Wednesday, Thursday and Saturday nights it becomes a live jazz venue.

In the backstreets near the African Mall, you can savour high-class French-style cuisine at the Swiss-owned *Le Bougainville* (☎356693). Towards Broadhurst, drinking and snacking at the *Gaborone Sun* pool on Nyerere Drive is a very pleasant way to idle away a few hours.

Broadhurst

With your own transport, or by taking the Broadhurst combi route 1 or 2, *Pam's Place* in the **Kagiso Centre** at Broadhurst is recommended for coffee, snacks and lunches, or try *Spurs* for a Southern African imitation of Tex-Mex and traditional American food. Portuguese-style "peri-peri" chicken is served at *Nando's* on the corner across the car park. If you prefer to stick to familiar American fried chicken, *Chicken Licken* in the cool, shady **Roshini Centre** (opposite the Kagiso Centre) is the place to go. Here you'll also find an excellent bakery with delicious fresh bread and continental-style patisseries, as well as pizza and pies.

In the **Broadhurst North Mall,** near the BBS building, *Kgotla* dishes up good snacks and lunches, with great vegetarian options as well as richer fare for meat-eaters (open daily 9am–9pm). *Alfredo's* is recommended for Italian food. At the **Julius Nyerere (Old Spar) Shopping Centre**, 2km north of The Mall, *The Moghul* serves reasonably priced Indian and Pakistani food, with a very good buffet lunch. In the same centre, *Sugar and Spicy* supplies an alluring selection of gateaux, tarts, cakes and biscuits.

South of the centre

About 3km out on the Tlokweng Road, *The Swiss Chalet* serves Swiss and Italian dishes in a high-class but pleasant ambience. Further on, in **The Village**, the *Orient Express* is a high-quality Chinese restaurant. Their spacious grounds allow for indoor and outdoor seating, and you may well get a chance to tuck into an exotic buffet whist listening to live South African jazz (look out for posters).

Along the Lobatse road on the southwestern outskirts of town, *Mike's Kitchen* at **Kgali View Shopping Centre** offers a variety of food and an American-style bar. It's mostly frequented by a young, white South African crowd and has a smart-casual dress code.

Finally, for a special, though rather expensive, meal out of town, the large, thatched, open-air restaurant at the *Mokolodi Nature Reserve* (☎328692; see p.275) offers a variety of high-quality food in a cool, breezy atmosphere, with a stunning view across the park to the hills. At night you can look up at the stars as you sample your ostrich kebab or tuck into a large portion of death by chocolate. The restaurant is open for lunch and dinner (Tues–Sat), as well as Sunday brunch, and you should book in advance.

Nightlife and entertainment

You'll find several lively drinking places in Gaborone, especially at the weekend when there's always **live music** and somewhere to dance, though it's worth noting that the names and themes of nightclubs and music venues change quite frequently. The end of the month, after payday, brings the most exuberant events. *Maitisong* at Maru-a-Pula School is Botswana's main centre for **performing arts**, hosting local drama as well as some exceptional performances from outside the country.

Look out for posters in town announcing occasional public **picnics**. These are delightful afternoon drinking and dancing affairs at out-of-town venues, usually with a live band. For Sunday afternoon outdoor beer and bopping, try *Bodiba* on the road to Molepolole. **National holidays** bring forth a feast of activities in Gaborone which go on all weekend. If your visit coincides with President's Day or Botswana Day festivities (mid-July and end of Sept) be prepared for soccer matches, traditional dancing and singing, BDF (Botswana Defence Force) displays, exhibitions and church services on a grand scale.

Nightlife
The *Gaborone Travel Inn* at the railway station is the most central of the nightspots, with a rollicking bar and live music every weekend. For serious drinking, *Buddies*, at the **No Mathata Shopping Centre** (just ten minutes' walk from the *Gaborone Sun Hotel*), offers a relaxed garden bar atmosphere; on Sundays you'll be treated to live jazz from 4pm to midnight. *Sinatra's*, also in the No Mathata Centre, has a disco and occasional live bands at the weekend, and takeaways are on the go outside until 3 or 4am. Alternatively, *Rewards* is a popular drinking spot opposite the *Gaborone Sun Hotel*; for a British-style pub, try the *Bull and Bush* on the old Francistown Road.

The best bet for live music is *Blue Note*, an open-air venue in **Mogoditshane** (turn right at the junction just after the *Spar*, the building is on the right-hand side, with "Entertainment Centre" painted on the wall in black). The other possibility for live gigs is *Night Shift* in the **BBS Mall** in Broadhurst. The bar upstairs is a disco turned pool hall, so you can check your technique in one of the many wall mirrors. Downstairs is the club, where things don't get going until after midnight.

Look out also for **Botswana Defence Force band** performances. Military bands may conjure up images of brass and marching, but the two BDF bands play slick African music, derivative of Soweto and Zimbabwean beats.

Movies and performing arts
Botswana's only cultural centre is **Maitisong** (☎371809), the new hall at Maru-a-Pula School, about 500m from the *Gaborone Sun Hotel*. While the school itself is private and highly exclusive, it does have an admirable policy of opening its facilities to the public. At weekends local kids can use the swimming pool, and *Maitisong* is not only the venue for **plays** from neighbouring states, **dance**, **concerts** or simply **films**, but also for functions such as conferences, and classes in dance and music. Performances are varied and average something like every third night throughout the year; newspapers publish details of what's on.

The **theatre group** to watch out for is the newly formed *Baranodi* which specializes in drama by African playwrights. Another interesting company is *Reetsanang*, a commu-

EMBASSIES & OTHER DIPLOMATIC MISSIONS

Denmark 142 Mengwe Close, PO Box 367 (☎353770).

France 761 Robinson Rd, PO Box 1424 (☎353683).

Germany Professional House, BBS Mall, PO Box 315 (☎353143).

Netherlands Haile Selassie Rd, PO Box 10055 (☎351691–2).

Nigeria Nigeria House, The Mall, PO Box 274 (☎313561).

Norway Development House, The Mall, PO Box 879 (☎351501).

Russia 4711 Tawana Close, PO Box 81 (☎353389 or 353739).

UK Queen's Rd, Private Bag 0023 (☎352841).

USA Badiredi House, The Mall, PO Box 90 (☎353982–4).

Zambia Zambia House, The Mall, PO Box 362 (☎351951–2).

Zimbabwe 1st Floor, IGI House, PO Box 1232 (☎314495–7).

nity-based theatre group, which occasionally performs at *Maitisong*. Funded by aid agencies they go into villages to research local social or political problems, which they then dramatize at the *kgotla*, the place where disputes are traditionally heard and settled.

For unchallenging escapism, the programme of **movies** at the *Capitol Cinema* in The Mall is heavy on celluloid action and recent Hollywood releases.

Listings

Airline offices *Air Botswana*, BIC House, Lower Mall (☎305500); also agent for *Air Malawi, Air Mauritius, Air Tanzania, Air Zimbabwe, KLM, Lesotho Airways, Lufthansa, Royal Swazi Airways, SAS* and *Swissair. Air India*, Zambia Close (☎313880). *BA*, upstairs at Hernamo Centre, BBS Mall, Broadhurst (☎372594). *Zambia Airways*, 1st Floor Zambia House, Lower Mall (☎312027).

American Express *Manica Travel Services* in The Mall, Botsalano House, Botswana Rd (☎352021).

Banks Mon–Fri 8.30am–2.30pm, Sat 8.30am–12.30pm. There are several branches of the three commercial banks around the Mall area, but note that the smaller *Barclays* and *Standard Chartered* on the station side of The Mall won't change travellers' cheques; try the bigger ones in the central section.

Books *Botswana Book Centre*, Upper Mall is the best bookshop in this part of Africa, with an excellent selection of African writing, as well as paperback imports and books on Botswana. Imported reading matter is far cheaper here than in Zimbabwe, so this is definitely the place to stock up. *Botsalo Books* at Broadhurst Shopping Centre is also recommended, though not central.

Camping equipment *Gaborones Hardware*, Lower Mall, sells camping gas and tents. Also try *Explosion* in the covered left-hand corner of the African Mall or *Game* on the road to the *Oasis Motel*.

Car rental *Holiday Car Rentals* at *Gaborone Sun Hotel*, Nyerere Drive (☎353970), for 4WD rental. *Avis* (Head Office ☎313093, Central Reservations ☎353745) and *Hertz* (☎353970) both have offices at the airport for 4WD or sedan rental, with similar deals.

Car repairs and parts *Blue Chip Services* at plot 22074, Broadhurst (☎307351 or 300820), is probably the best in town. More centrally there are several places along Haile Selassie Road. *AAA Motors*, Molepolole Road past the *Mogotel*, is good for Land Rover spares.

Chemists – emergency *Botschem*, Nyerere Drive (Mon–Sat 9am–7pm, Sun 9–10am; ☎353108, after hours ☎371385).

Doctors Dr D. B. Dickinson has a surgery on Independence Avenue (☎353424). Other doctors are listed in the first few pages of the pink section at the front of the phone directory.

Fabrics *TimbaTrading* in the African Mall has a good selection of Zambian and Zimbabwean cottons.

Freight agents *DHL*, Red Cross Building, Independence Ave, PO Box 1077 (☎312000).

Groceries *Fairways* near the station and the *Gaborone Co-op* and *Corner Supermarket* in the centre of The Mall are well stocked. The *Spar* chain supermarkets in Nyerere Drive and at Broadhurst Shopping Centre are pretty good, as is *Pay Less* in the Kagiso Centre, Broadhurst.

Hospitals Princess Marina, Hospital Way off Notwane Road (☎353221). If you have private insurance, you'll avoid queues at the *Gaborone Private Hospital*, plot 8448, Mica Way, Broadhurst (☎/fax 301998–9).

Left luggage at the train station (Mon–Fri 8am–1pm & 2–4pm).

Library Gaborone Library, Independence Ave, below The Mall (Mon–Fri 9am–6pm, Sat 9am–noon), has a small range of international periodicals in the reference reading section. Next to the lending library in a separate building, the BNLS Headquarters is a room with publications just on Botswana. The University library's Botswana Room is open for reading and browsing only (off Mobutu Drive). The British Council, Upper Mall, has a good library (with British papers), as does the US Embassy.

Maps The Department of Surveys and Lands, Private Bag 0037 (☎353251), has excellent OS maps at 1:50,000.

Photocopying *Agfa Copy Shop*, opposite the *President Hotel*, or try *Xerox* behind the post office.

Photography *Photolab*, Upper Mall, does one-hour developing and sells film. For quick passport photos, try *Capital Studios* in the African Mall.

Police Central Police Station, Botswana Road (☎352222), opposite the *President Hotel*.

Post office Mall centre (Mon–Fri 8.15am–1pm & 2–4pm, Sat 8.30–11.30am). Slow postal service but generally reliable. If you only require stamps, go to the parcel office around the corner to avoid queuing.

Telephones Efficient phones outside the post office – or try the quieter ones outside the museum and opposite the tourist office. Phone cards have recently been introduced and can be purchased at the post office.

Train information ☎351401–2.

Train tickets bookable at the station (Mon–Fri 7.30am–1pm & 2–7pm, Sat & Sun 4–7.30pm).

Travel agents In the Upper Mall: *Kudu Travel* (☎372224); *Manica Travel* (☎352021); *Pan African Travel*. All do air bookings and safaris and *Kudu* rents out cars. *Phuti Travel*, Nyerere Drive Shopping Centre (☎314166), sometimes does good deals on flights to London, Nairobi, Lilongwe and Dar-es-Salaam. It's worth enquiring about special rates at other travel agents.

Visa extensions Department of Immigration, State Drive, PO Box 942 (☎374545).

South of Gaborone

One reason for heading south from Gaborone, apart from going to South Africa or joining the main route to the southwest Kalahari (see Chapter Ten), is to visit the **Mokolodi Nature Reserve**, only 15km out of town on the Lobatse road. It's also worth taking time out to climb **Kgali Hill** for great views over the city and the surrounding area.

Kgali Hill and around

On the way to Mokolodi, just 8km from Gaborone on the Lobatse road, the trail to **Kgali Hill** begins by a concrete stile. It's an easy climb, well marked by white arrows, but it's worth setting out early to avoid the intense heat of the day. Don't be put off when, just above the quarry, a fence bars your way; simply crawl under it and continue following the arrows to the top. You'll have to scramble up some rocks to get the view from the summit. If you're feeling more adventurous, this boulder-strewn hill is great for off-trail exploring; you may well be rewarded with close-up viewing of baboons, cute furry dassies (or rock hyraxes) and an interesting variety of birdlife.

Kgali Hill also makes a good day trip in conjunction with a visit to **Gaborone Dam**. To get to the ten-kilometre-long dam, take Mobutu Drive towards Lobatse, turn left at the *Sanitas* sign and continue for 5km to the dam wall. Permission to visit the dam wall itself must be obtained from the Water Utilities Corporation, Luthuli Road, near the railway station in Gaborone. *Sanitas* sells a wide range of fresh herbs, vegetables and plants from their garden nursery. The nearby, and signposted, **lion park** features a lot of lions in cages – not the most of inspiring of places. It is, however, also home to a little-known equestrian centre, with a P15 fee to canter through a private game reserve behind the park.

Mokolodi Nature Reserve

Situated in a beautiful area of bushland ringed by hills, just 15km south of Gaborone, **Mokolodi Nature Reserve** (P6 per adult, P6 per small vehicle) offers an opportunity to see game that has long disappeared from this area of Botswana: white rhino, elephants, antelopes, giraffes, zebras, warthogs, hyenas and monkeys; if you're very lucky, you may glimpse a leopard. A wonderful place to visit, Mokolodi's two aims are conservation and education; educational visits for local schoolchildren are only made possible by the support of the visiting public.

If you have your own vehicle, turn right off the Lobatse road at the sign after Mokolodi village. Alternatively, take the **bus** towards Lobatse or Ramotswa, get off at the turn-off and walk the last 1500m to the entrance. You can drive yourself around the reserve, but it's worth taking a **game drive** with one of the friendly and experienced rangers who really know about the animals (P20 per person for a two-hour tour by day, or P25 for a two-hour night drive). If you're feeling more adventurous, guided **game walks** can be organized. The reserve also has **chalets** and **dormitory accommodation** (see p.267), and an excellent **restaurant** (see p.271).

Otse

The village of **OTSE** (pronounced "Oot-see"), 45km south of Gaborone, is home to the **Mannyelanong Hill Vultury** (Mannyelanong means "place where vultures shit"), where you can watch the vultures circling above the dramatic cliffs which house their nests. In the past this was the nesting site of thousands of birds; sadly, the numbers have severely diminished. To get there, turn left into the village at the petrol station, then immediately bear right and follow the rutted road until you reach a track leading to the cliffs.

Not far north of here, on the western side of the hill, you'll find a large fault in the cliff face, known as **Refuge Cave**. Pottery has been found inside it, and it is thought that the cave was used as a hiding place during the Boer invasions of the 1870s.

Lobatse

There's nothing at all to detain you in the road junction town of **LOBATSE**, 65km south of the capital. It was once Botswana's surrogate capital, because the territory's administrative centre was at Mafeking in South Africa and the **High Court** – the most important colonial institution inside the country – sat here, as it does today. But Lobatse never became important because of its lack of water. Its shining moment of glory came with the visit of King George VI in 1947, when 5km of road was tarred from Lobatse station to the High Court. At Independence, this remained the only piece of tarred road in the country. Now Lobatse is best known for having one of the largest abattoirs and meat-processing plants in Africa. In Khama I Avenue, *Botswana Crafts* is worth a look for locally woven goods.

If you do find yourself stranded here en route to Ghanzi and the west, you are limited to the *Cumberland Hotel* (☎330281 or 332106; ⑤), expensive but comfortable. If you're feeling brave, the surrounding hills are good for camping.

West of Gaborone

Forty kilometres west of Gaborone, **Kopong** is still reached by a dust road. Although not justifying a visit in itself, it is a good place to stop on the way to **Arne's Horse**

Safari. Further south, on the road towards Jwaneng and the Kalahari, the scenery around **Kanye**, particularly the **Kanye Gorge**, is well worth exploring.

Thamaga and Kolobeng

THAMAGA is home to the *Thamaga Pottery Workshop*, which merits a browse if you're passing. Folding *kgotla* chairs, ornately carved and strung with woven leather, are on sale at *Botswelelo Handicrafts*. Fifteen kilometres away at **KOLOBENG**, off the road from Gaborone, you'll find the ruin of **David Livingstone's home** and mission. There's not much to see for now except a few graves and the remains of the floor, but a museum is planned for the site.

Kopong: Arne's Horse Safari

For a taste of the wilderness but with fairly easy access from town (about 40km north-west of Gaborone), **Arne's Horse Safari** offers the perfect location for day-trippers or those wishing to stay longer. Arne, a friendly Swedish jack of all trades, offers tailor-made horseback safaris through the bush for all levels of experience, whether for an hour (P30) or a weekend (he'll provide all camping equipment); he's currently building a wagon for those who don't feel brave enough to mount a horse. Even if you don't want to go on safari, his home on the hill offers a **braai** or a drink with stunning views across the plains. He's also building two thatched self-catering chalets, for which he plans to charge P120 per night for two people. If you're **camping**, you can set up your tent near the bore-hole (P10 per night). A couple of minutes down the hill, Kyomoto's shop supplies a few staples as well as some nice leather sun hats and screen-printed T-shirts.

From Gaborone, take a bus to **Kopong**; if this terminates at Metsimotlhabe, take any local vehicle to Kopong. Arne will collect visitors from Kopong (dial 150 and leave a message on pager 10018), or offer a local driver a couple of pula to drive you all the way.

Kanye

Eighty kilometres southwest of Gaborone is the large, sprawling hilltop settlement of **KANYE**. The town itself has little to recommend it but the route from Gaborone to Kanye affords some of the most interesting and beautiful scenery in the region, especially around Mochupa. Large rocky outcrops line the road, with some impressively jagged hills as you draw near to Kanye. With your own vehicle, it's worth exploring these areas; the journey by bus, however, is hot and arduous. The **Kanye Gorge** especially merits a visit. Turn left at the BP junction, at the sign for Seepapisto Secondary School, and follow the road through a police housing estate; the gorge begins where the road ends. It's well hidden – the entire population of the village once hid themselves here during an Ndebele raid. Continuing south about 1500m along the cliff face (sadly defaced in some parts with crude grafitti), you discover the ruins of a stone-walled village built in the early eighteenth century.

On the way to the gorge, stop for a meal at the *Mmakgodamo Restaurant* (Tues–Fri 10am–3pm & 7–10pm, Sat 6pm–midnight) in the **Rural Industries Innovation Centre** (☎ 340392, fax 340642), where, for a reasonable price, you can taste fresh and exotic dishes not found elsewhere in Botswana. The restaurant is part of an interesting experimental village, comprising a bakery, a forge and various alternative energy projects, which is aimed at improving the standard and quality of enterprise in Botswana.

North of Gaborone

If you're spending any time around Gaborone, make the effort to visit two traditional villages just to the north – also worth the short detour if you're travelling the

Gaborone–Francistown road. **Odi**, roughly 25km from Gaborone, is a boulder-strewn settlement, with a weaving co-op that produces outstanding tapestries depicting rural life and folktales. **Mochudi** is a picturesque village about 40km north of the capital, with the added attraction of a fine museum and craft centre.

Odi and the Lentswe-la-Odi Weavers

Getting to **ODI** by **car** is straightforward. Take the Francistown road out of Gaborone and turn right at the Odi sign, 17km further on. From here, follow the co-op signs assiduously, as sandy tracks splay out through groups of huts and rocky outcrops.

Alternatively, any northbound **bus** from Gaborone will get you as far as the turn-off, from where it's a further 8km **on foot** or **hitching**. A couple of buses per day will actually get you all the way, if you can find out exactly when they're leaving. Otherwise, if you get off at the junction, there's a lively bar and bottle store, where you can refresh yourself before tackling the last stretch.

Lentswe-la-Odi Weavers

Lentswe-la-Odi Weavers is a Swedish-initiated **cooperative**, whose profits have been ploughed back into Odi village to start projects like a bakery, brickyard, general store and market garden. The cooperative is open for viewing on Wednesdays (8am–4.30pm) and at weekends (10am–6pm), when you'll be taken on a tour of the workshops with demonstrations of everything from spinning and dyeing to weaving.

The **tapestries** themselves are on informal display in a cool thatched building. One or two of the weavers have shifted from the formula of huts and livestock to bold animal subjects. Ask one of the women there to explain some of the mythological stories depicted in these bright wools. Besides the large hangings, lovely woollen rugs and woven bedspreads are produced, and browsing here is fun even if you can't afford anything. The tapestries, exhibited and sold abroad, aren't cheap, but they're realistically priced given the labour involved.

Mochudi and Pilane

MOCHUDI is a short distance to the east of the main road to Francistown, about 40km north of Gaborone; **buses and combis** shuttle to and from the capital at a rate of at least one per hour.

At the junction of the main road and the Mochudi turn-off is one-street **PILANE**, where the cheap *Sedibelo Motel* is the only place to stay in the area (and easily reached if you want to avoid the Gaborone accommodation crush). You can get snacks, meals and teas, but expect a long wait. For something light try the *Lovers Rock* or *Arrow Restaurant*. There are also stores selling basics and a good sprinkling of bars.

From Pilane onwards, the approach to Mochudi is extremely unpromising, enough to have you wondering just where this supposedly pretty and traditional place can be. For a couple of kilometres after the turn-off you proceed along a tarred road littered with the usual squashed cans and past a rash of general dealers and bottle stores. However, Mochudi does have a **historical core**, dominated by two impressive colonial-style buildings – the **Dutch Reformed Church** and the **Mochudi National School**, which now houses the **Phuthadikobo Museum**. To get there, turn left at the T-junction, after the Pilane main drag; just before the hospital where the road forks, turn right and follow the road until it ends at the *kgotla*, the traditional court and meeting house, set among the hills.

Mochudi is the "capital" of the Bakgatla tribe, who settled here in 1871 when Boer harassment forced them off their lands in the Transvaal. Bakgatla chiefs have always been progressive, and the regent **Isang Pilane**, who was dissatisfied with missionary education, organized the building of the country's first secondary school. Mochudi's one English-language school taught only up to standard 6 (12–13 years old) and was run by the Dutch Reformed Church, whose missionaries refused to teach such "worldly" subjects as arithmetic. However, useful subjects, not religious indoctrination, were exactly what the Bakgatla wanted and in 1920 they decided to build their own schoolhouse, at the top of the hill which overlooks Mochudi. Men and women worked side by side on the project, and it proved to be a real triumph of community action, establishing a precedent that encouraged secondary education elsewhere in the country. Each man either contributed £5, made some of the school's 300,000 bricks or contributed other labour – and all the materials had to be painstakingly carried up the hill.

These days, it's a very pleasant **walk** to the top of the hill – one of the few places in Botswana to have an expansive view, out across the village and surrounding plains. Given the scarcity of high points in this flat land, it's perhaps not surprising that this one was sacred, and associated with rain-making and Kwanyape the **rain snake**.

All activity in Mochudi centres around the **kgotla** (meeting house), at the bottom of the hill. You're welcome to watch a meeting in progress but are discouraged from entering the structure itself. Sadly, the meticulously maintained compounds which once surrounded the *kgotla* have mostly given way to an assortment of ad hoc concrete housing. Some traditional housing still remains but is looking rather battered. To learn more about the village, "A Guide to Mochudi" can be purchased at the museum shop.

Phuthadikobo Museum

The red-roofed former school, complete with shady verandahs, now serves as the **Phuthadikobo Museum** (Mon–Fri 8am–5pm, Sat & Sun 2–5pm; free), which deals simply with the history of the small settlement of Mochudi. That might sound dull, but don't be put off. It's well displayed, with an excellent collection of early photographs. Among a wide range of weapons, tools, household objects and musical instruments is an impressive **drum** brought by the Bakgatla to Mochudi in 1871, of the kind traditionally used during the initiation of girls. A section on rain-making elucidates the hill's spiritual function.

In the hall of the museum (often used for meetings and training sessions of various kinds), two colourful Odi **tapestries** celebrate the achievements of the regent Isang Pilane, bringing alive the history of the Bakgatla migration. A couple of large papiermâché **puppets** include a caricature of the former South African president P. W. Botha reincarnated as a vampire.

A **silkscreen workshop** is housed in the same building, with fabrics sold at the **museum shop**. Everything is reasonably priced and it's a terrific place to buy gifts. The local hut designs are reproduced in calico, cotton hangings, cushion covers, tablecloths and fabrics which can be bought by the metre. Most imaginative of all are the T-shirts, which make fine souvenirs. If something takes your liking, you should buy it here as the stuff isn't distributed countrywide – even the craft shop in nearby Gaborone carries only a meagre selection.

Matsieng rock carvings

Eight kilometres north of Pilane, and three kilometres north of the Lentswelekul turning, a rough track leads to **Matsieng**, about 700m east of the main road, a hole containing footprint rock carvings. The Tswana believe that this is the site of the creation of man, and that the footprints on the walls belonged to the first human beings, who emerged from the hole, followed by wild and domesticated animals.

THE ROAD TO FRANCISTOWN
AND THE TULI BLOCK

In a country with only two main tarred routes, the smooth ride from **Gaborone to Francistown** is not something to be taken for granted, even if you find the journey uninspiring. Botswana's single railway line runs virtually parallel to the north–south highway, with a station at each of the roadside towns, and there are corrugated-iron buildings and railway hotels at one or two of the bigger places like **Mahalapye** and **Palapye**.

The **railway line** was built by the British South Africa Company at the turn of the century as a vital link from land-locked colonies of Central Africa to the South African coast. In 1904, the British government transferred the land for the railway – as well as some blocks of land in Gaborone, Lobatse and Tuli – to the Company. These, together with the Tati District around Francistown, and the Ghanzi district, became the only white-populated areas in Bechuanaland.

In due course, the railway came under Rhodesian administration, with Rhodesia Railways' coaches and trucks doing the run. From 1974 Botswana began gradually to take it over, and prior to Namibian independence this was the only passenger-train link between the frontline states and South Africa.

Branches from the road which fly off towards the mining towns of **Selebi-Phikwe** and **Orapa** are also tarred, as is the route to **Serowe**, 50km from the main road and worth a deviation. Apart from Serowe and the nearby **Khama Rhino Sanctuary**, the only real attraction along the whole route is in the **Tuli Block** itself. This is a "block" in the simple sense that it is a grouping of private farmlands, and can be approached either from Selebi-Phikwe, or more divertingly through the back routes from Gaborone, hugging the South African border. In fact, the easiest way to get to Tuli is via South Africa, where the roads are tarred up to the border posts.

North along the Francistown road

The landscape changes little on the 433-kilometre journey between Gaborone and Francistown; there's just a relentless acacia-specked flatness waving with grass after the rains arrive. The sky is always enormous.

Local people never travel without a clutch of tins – either beer or coke – and you'll find **bars** in obscure places servicing the national thirst along this highway. One favourite is between Gaborone and Mahalapye, right on the **Tropic of Capricorn**. But the bar is no great tourist extravaganza, just a simple room in someone's back yard. There's no electricity here, so the deep freeze is powered by paraffin, but the drinks are always ice-cold. Outside, a dead bus, sunk in the sand to its wheel arches, has become a chicken coop. You'll know when the Tropic is imminent because a sign on either side announces: *Tropic of Capricon* (sic) *275m*.

Another notable bar is at the turn-off to Selebi-Phikwe, close to Serule. The *Kwena Bottle Store*'s murals painted on the verandah walls – including a crocodile about to gobble up a well-dressed woman who's dropped beer into its jaws – are almost worth a special halt.

Mahalapye

En route to Francistown, you pass through a succession of towns with nondescript garages, takeaways and bars straggled alongside the road – indeed the only attractive parts of these places tend to be the oldest areas, away from the main road and near the stations. One place in this mould is **MAHALAPYE**, 200km up the line (and eminently confusable with Palapye, the next town on). Cross the railway line opposite the post office, take the first left and round the bend 2km to the old, mellow and cheap *Mahalapye Hotel* (PO Box 526; ☎410200), which overlooks a dry riverbed with rocky

SIR SERETSE AND RUTH KHAMA

Seretse Khama's marriage in 1948 to Ruth Williams, a white Englishwoman, carries echoes of Romeo and Juliet. Not only was the match opposed by the family of each, there was also the added dimension of murky political interests – both South African and British – cynically playing with individual lives. In this case, however, the couple emerged to become important figures in independent Botswana.

Seretse, the Bangwato heir, was sent to Oxford to read law shortly after World War II by his uncle, the regent Tshekedi Khama. While completing his legal education at the Inner Temple in London, he met Ruth Williams, originally through a mutual interest in jazz. The couple married in 1948 and returned to Bechuanaland.

Their personal affair turned into a constitutional crisis. Tshekedi Khama was furious; according to Bangwato custom the *mohumagadi* (great wife of the king) must be selected by the community and come from a Tswana royal family. Seretse apologized for not marrying according to custom, but insisted that if his people rejected his wife they would lose him too. Four thousand men supported Seretse against a mere forty for his uncle; but the defeated Tshekedi led his followers away to settle among the Bakwena. African leaders as far afield as Lesotho and Swaziland supported him, fearing the erosion of tradition. For entirely different reasons racist whites in southern Africa were horrified, describing the marriage as nauseating. South African prime minister D.F. Malan called on the British to put a stop to it.

The British Labour government bowed to prejudice and, without any legal basis, it rejected the marriage. It was particularly afraid that South Africa would withhold vital supplies of its recently discovered uranium. Seretse was called to London for talks in 1950, with an assurance that he would be allowed to return to Bechuanaland. He was offered £1100 to relinquish the kingship and live in England for the rest of his life; he refused, and also turned down a job in Jamaica. Breaking its word, the government banned him from returning home for five years. Sir Winston Churchill slammed Labour's dealings as "very disreputable," but when his Tories got their turn to govern in 1951 they made the exile indefinite.

A number of British MPs and organizations took up Seretse's cause in a campaign that continued for six years. In Bechuanaland the Bangwato resisted pressure to elect a new king and instead were subjected to a British-imposed "Native authority". Those who refused to obey him were flogged. Tshekedi Khama, seeing the ugly results of his traditionalist line, made a swift U-turn in 1952. He returned to his people, recognized Ruth as the *mohumagadi* and called for Seretse's immediate return. Tshekedi and the Tswana kings rounded on the British, who they believed were planning to use the Seretse affair to hand over Bechuanaland to South Africa.

The whole issue was finally resolved in July 1956, when Tshekedi travelled to London for a secret meeting with his nephew. They successfully mended their relationship and came to an agreement which they presented to the British authorities. Under its terms neither man would claim the kingship for himself or his children. Later that year Seretse and Ruth returned to Serowe, as private citizens.

Seretse's political involvement did not end there. He successfully led Botswana to Independence in 1966, when he was knighted, and he remained in the position of president until his death in 1980. The Bangwato for their part continued to insist on the restoration of their proper royal line. Though Seretse was never to take up his rightful role, in 1979 his eldest son Brigadier Ian Khama was installed as *kgosi* in Serowe. Lady Khama continues to live in Botswana, where she holds an almost regal status as *Mohumagadi Mma Kgosi* – mother of the *kgosi* – equivalent to the British queen mother.

A Marriage of Inconvenience, by Michael Dutman, published by Unwin Hyman in London in 1990 and linked to a BBC TV documentary, tells the whole story (see "Books" in *Contexts*).

banks and a village perched on the other side. The hotel is a good spot for a stopover or a drink at the **bar**. **Camping** is possible in the grounds, though the washing facilities aren't too promising.

Between the hotel and the railway line, Mahalapye itself has a well-worn, established feel, pretty beneath its shady trees and rocky outcrops and quite different from the impression you get of it when you belt down the main road. Before you leave town, go to *Kaytees Restaurant* (☎410795), at the southern end of town towards Gaborone, for the best fat cakes in the country.

Palapye

The traditional mud huts of **PALAPYE** are surrounded by trimmed rubber bush hedges which thrive in the red sand. There's nothing to detain you here but the town has two inexpensive **hotels** if you get stuck. The *Palapye Hotel* (PO Box 1; ☎420277) has more character, hidden behind masses of bougainvillea next to the station. The newish and slightly pricier *Botsalo Travel Inn* (PO Box 35; ☎420245) on the main road has the added attraction of a **swimming pool**.

Serowe and around

SEROWE is in theory a large traditional Batswana village, textured with rocky outcrops – though in fact the word "village" is rather misleading, as modern buildings have been grafted onto older, thatched areas to give it the appearance of a town rather than a rural hamlet. Despite this, there is a charming rural feel to the place not found in the other villages near to the main road. Electricity has been installed and a tarred road built since the town was immortalized in the writing of **Bessie Head**, Botswana's only internationally known writer, who made her home here after leaving South Africa (see "Books" in *Contexts*).

Serowe was also the birthplace of the late **Sir Seretse Khama**, the charismatic leader who took the country through Independence and was its first president until his death in 1980. He came from a strong line of chiefs of the Bangwato, a major Batswana grouping who were centred here. The Khama family graves, a revered site of pilgrimage, are on the rocky outcrop above the *kgotla* and District Council offices. Ask permission at the *kgotla* before venturing up – they may wish to send you with an escort (strictly no photographs allowed). The site affords stunning views of the surrounding landscape with its unusual flat-topped hills. On Khama III's grave (Seretse's grand-father) is a bronze duiker, totem of the Bangwato. It was sculpted, interestingly enough, not by a Motswana, but by the well-known South African artist, Anton van Wouw. If you're interested in the history of the Khamas, the fascinating **Khama III Memorial Museum** lies at the base of the hill in the middle of Serowe. For Bessie Head enthusiasts, this is the place to view all her papers. Viewing them is by appointment only; ring the museum (☎430519) if you're keen.

There's yet a third reason for Serowe's prominence – the **Brigade Movement** begun in the 1960s by South African political refugee Patrick van Rensburg. Conceived as a revival of the kind of Tswana self-help groups so effectively organized at Mochudi earlier in the century, the Brigades were an attempt to solve the major, interrelated problems of unemployment and skills shortages, especially in the rural areas. Few primary school leavers were able to attend secondary school and their options were limited: to work as herders on cattle posts, to find work in towns, or to go to South Africa and work on the mines. Schools offered no practical training and were elite-orientated.

Van Rensburg's first project was the **Swaneng Hill School**, near the Serowe airstrip, which emphasized manual work, and aimed to foster self-reliance and an awareness of development issues in the pupils. Growing out of these ideas, the Brigade

Movement was aimed at equipping primary school leavers with **practical skills**. The first one was the Builders Brigade in 1965 in Serowe, followed by groups in metalwork, carpentry, weaving and leatherwork. The idea of self-help vocational training spread countrywide and students built their own classrooms and dormitories. From their manual work, they earned enough to pay for the running of the school.

Practicalities
Slightly out of town on the road to Palapye, the *Serowe Hotel* (☎430234; ④) is a charming thatched **hotel**, offering single and double rooms with shared facilities, and English or continental breakfast. The *Tshwaragano Hotel* (☎430377; ③), well located on the hillside in the centre of town, has a very local feel. Rooms are clean and pleasant with en-suite bathrooms, and traditional lunch and supper are available. The bar, open till midnight at weekends, is popular with the locals and sometimes hosts live bands.

For a lunchtime snack, *Sham's Tasty Eats*, at the *Caltex* service station, offers a wide variety of local **food**. Try the *Central Supermarket Restaurant* in the Mall for Indian and Chinese, or *The Spar* for delicious, reasonably priced precooked chicken. The *Welcome Bar*, at the combi station, is a much-frequented **drinking** spot.

The Khama Rhino Sanctuary
Situated on the Kalahari Sandveld, 20km north of Serowe on the Orapa road, the **Khama Rhino Sanctuary** is definitely worth a stopover en route to Maun. The sanctuary, which is home to eight white rhino, was established as a community trust in 1992 and is dedicated to the safeguarding and breeding of Botswana's last remaining rhino (*tshukudu*). The beautiful reserve is also home to other diverse wildlife including gemsbok, hartebeest, wildebeest, brown hyena, jackal, zebra and leopard, and there are abundant opportunities for bird-spotting (bring binoculars).

However, the future of the sanctuary hangs in the balance due to lack of funding. Without the support of tourists, the community cannot pay the maintenance of this unique project, and if the reserve closes, Botswana's rhino will once again face extinction; with the support of visitors, the project will be able to expand. At the time of writing, the sanctuary possesses only one vehicle, so organized game drives are not really feasible. For those with vehicles, a 4WD is recommended. If you have no vehicle, try the *Dennis* service station in Serowe.

Camping facilities are available in stands of *manketi* trees. This is a truly secluded wilderness spot, so be sure you have enough food. For more information about the sanctuary, contact Raymond or Norma Watson, PO Box 10, Serowe (☎430232, fax 430992).

The Tuli Block

The **TULI BLOCK** is the least visited of Botswana's main tourist areas, bypassed by most people as they roll on north. Much of it is privately owned but, despite the fences, there are accessible resorts which do not charge anything like the hefty National Parks entrance fees. Not just lodges either; on the banks of "the great grey green greasy Limpopo all set about with fever trees" (where Kipling's "elephant's child" got a good stretching of his trunk by the crocodile in the *Just-So Stories*), there's a lovely campsite, from which walking expeditions are operated.

Before the whites arrived, Tuli was Bangwato tribal land. Sites dating from the seventh or eighth century indicate an even earlier occupation. The area now consists mostly of white-owned **game farms and private reserves**, many with Afrikaans names painted on their gate posts, dating from the time when the land was ceded to the BSAC for the building of the railway line. Rhodes' railway track didn't pass this way in the end, though, because there were too many rivers to cross.

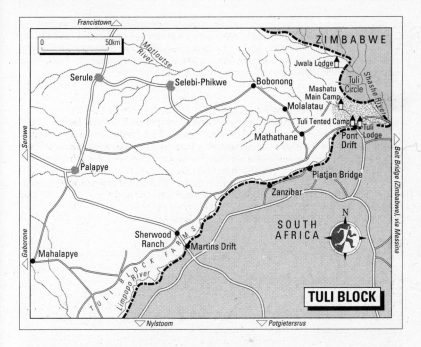

The Tuli Block is several hundred kilometres long, and a narrow 10–20km in width. Outside this strip you'll find traditional villages, some of them very beautiful and worth exploring. The roads are dusty and far from busy. Without a vehicle of some sort Tuli is difficult country to get around, although 4WD isn't essential.

Because Tuli hugs the **South African border**, and road connections there are easier than those within Botswana, many of the Block's white residents cross over to do their shopping and business. There are four border posts along Tuli's 350-kilometre length. All have tarred roads on the South Africa side, making it only six hours to Johannesburg. Messina, in South Africa (though near Zimbabwe's Beit Bridge border), is the nearest reasonably sized place with good shops.

The mining town of **SELEBI-PHIKWE** is Botswana's third largest settlement, a purpose-built place, established in 1967, and complete with shopping malls and an expensive hotel, the *Bosele* (PO Box 177, Selebi-Phikwe; ☎810675; ⑥), part of the upmarket *Marakanelo Group*. If you're **hitching** or going by **truck** through the Tuli Block, Selebi is the place for lifts, but it's not somewhere to visit otherwise.

Back routes through Tuli

The most interesting part of the region is in northern Tuli around the **Motloutse River**. But by car, if you're in no hurry, consider taking a longer, but more interesting route than following the mostly dull Francistown road. Turning off at **Mosomane** (Artesia on some maps), 53km north of Gaborone, this dusty route takes you through some attractive red-earthed villages – with a noticeable lack of the cans which litter most of Botswana's towns.

Twine, criss-crossed over the thatching, produces a braided look while neatly sculpted low adobe walls create wave patterns around courtyards. Villages in Botswana can look deserted. Many Batswana maintain three homes: a family house in the village, a building on cultivated land which women go to from the beginning of the rains in November until the harvest in May or June, and a cattle post, often far away, where mainly boys graze the cattle. Men are also often at the cattle posts and you'll see them on long journeys riding donkeys or horses with a bedroll behind.

Those with money employ others to do the **herding**, often Bakgalakgadi and San. Despite the fact that Botswana has three million cattle and the population is only a million, the national herd is concentrated in the hands of only five percent of the population. The impression you may get of a large rural cattle-owning population is deceptive – nearly half of the people own no cattle at all.

The more direct route through Tuli runs up the Francistown road, as far as possible, then veers east just before Palapye. The road from Palapye to Martin's Drift then hits **SHERWOOD RANCH**, a dilapidated staging post with a handful of shanties made from *chibuku* cartons, one large house, a filling station, post office, general dealer, bar and bottle store. Don't believe the *Shell* road map which indicates a hotel here, another at Zanzibar and a couple of public campsites. They're all long gone. The *Zanzibar Hotel* is a peeling film set of a place, deserted and no longer taking guests. Some miles on, a sign for a hotel and bottle store leads to further derelict scenes. Wire tables and chairs are still outside on the clay-baked terracotta earth. Someone lives in a silver caravan propped up on bricks and the rubbed-out hotel sign now reads "general dealer".

Mashatu Game Reserve and the Pont Drift area

Some of Botswana's most arresting topography is wedged in a triangular salient, around **PONT DRIFT**, between Zimbabwe and South Africa. Strikingly eroded sandstone rock massifs rise out of flat, prickly plains in a landscape resembling the backdrop to a B-movie western. The massifs follow the course of the rivers – principally the Motloutse and the Limpopo – with riverine trees softening the landscape. Semiprecious stones such as agates and crystal quartz litter the beds of the watercourses, which are often dry tracts of sand.

This area has a lot to draw independent travellers, who nonetheless tend to bypass it out of ignorance. A considerable **game** population drifts back and forth across the border in the region adjacent to Zimbabwe's Tuli Circle. There are no national park reserves, only the elephant-browsed Mashatu Game Reserve, privately owned land made doubly attractive by the absence of park fees. But the stock of mammals and avifauna is as good as in the Okavango Delta, and the fascinating landscapes attract enough visitors, even out here, to support a couple of expensive **lodges** and a couple of cheaper **self-catering places**.

Getting there and getting around

Pont Drift is the usual jumping-off point for the lodges of this area. There are no facilities here and it's little more than a border post, with South Africa clearly visible on the other side of the Limpopo. In the rainy season the Motloutse and Limpopo rivers are sometimes impossible to ford, cutting off Pont Drift, bar the **cable car link** across the Limpopo to South Africa. (Few South Africans ford the Limpopo in their own vehicles, preferring to park their vehicles and cross by cableway to the Botswana side, where one of the lodges meets them.)

To get to Pont Drift without a car, **hitch** to Sherwood from Palapye and north up the main Tuli Block road. There isn't much traffic, so expect long waits. Pick-up trucks head that way, especially over the weekend. Another option is to go via Selebi-Phikwe – well connected to both Gaborone and Francistown – to Zanzibar and Pont Drift. Small trucks head, especially at weekends, from Bobonong (on the way from Selebi-Phikwe, and closest town to Pont Drift) for the pretty **villages near Talana Farm** along the Motloutse

River. Talana, a huge commercial and irrigated farming concern is across the Motloutse River from Mashatu Game Reserve. A daily **bus** goes via Bobonong to one of these Talana vicinity villages, Molalatau. On Tuesday and Saturday it continues to Mathathane (about 30km further, to the southeast), returning to Selebi-Phikwe on Wednesday and Sunday. People also use donkey carts to get from one river-bank village to another.

The villages are very traditional and people are friendly, which is just as well as you can't be in any sort of hurry to get anywhere. There are **stores** for basic supplies and you'll have to camp. The villages, which always look freshly swept, are red-walled with boldly painted frescoes and abstract designs. The luxury lodges at Pont Drift are staffed with people from these surrounding villages.

Self-catering accommodation

Tuli Safari Lodge Tented Camp, near Pont Drift (PO Box 32533, Braamfontein 2017, South Africa; ☎Johannesburg 482 2634, fax 482 2635), is set in the middle of Limpopo's riverine forest. It's dominated by a splendid mashatu tree, which is at least a thousand years old, with an immensely thick trunk. Behind the fringing forest alongside the river are sandstone cliffs and rocks which turn orange and red at dawn and dusk. From the top you look onto the forest canopy of slender pale-green fever trees and the giant deep-green mashatus and umbrella trees forming a dense covering. The Limpopo itself is a bright blur, with South Africa beyond. Looking the other way onto stony mopane hillsides, you may spot far-off **elephants**, moving methodically through the landscape. Old bones and bleached cat droppings suggest that leopards come here too. Among the riverside trees you're certain to see antelope coming to drink and shelter in the shade. There's seldom big game in the vicinity so you can walk and scramble around the rocks safely.

Run by the same people as the more expensive *Tuli Lodge* (see below), the camp has four two-bedded tents, with shared and serviced washing and self-catering facilities. The **price** – P130 per day per person for a minimum of four people, or P520 per night for the whole camp if there are less than four of you – includes two game drives and a walk, and transfers from Pont Drift. Camping with your own gear is not allowed.

Sharing the same game as the more expensive Mashatu Game Reserve, **Jwala Game Lodge** (PO Box 781900, Sandton 2146, South Africa; ☎Johannesburg 883 3711) kisses the border, where Zimbabwe's Tuli Circle bulges into Botswana. The landscape around *Jwala* is disturbingly harsh – mopane trees as far as you can see and dry river-beds with coarse black sand. It has a gaunt beauty, nevertheless, and animals thrive here, especially elephants. You're certain to see some action; a couple of waterholes attract terrific concentrations of animals during the dry season.

The camp, set in riverine bush, has five twin-bedded, thatched log cabins on stilts, with an equipped kitchen for self-catering. The only snag is that the camp is available for only one group at a time, at a **rate** of P700, whether there's two or ten of you. The price includes transfers from Pont Drift and game drives in an open land cruiser.

Mashatu Game Reserve and the luxury lodges

The whole Pont Drift area is rich in game and must have been a wildlife paradise before colonial times. Elephant are prominent and you're likely to see the big cats, giraffe, eland and a wide variety of antelope. The only **game park**, Mashatu, is privately run and you're not allowed to camp or picnic on Mashatu property, however tempting. **Mashatu Main Camp** (PO Box 2575, Randburg 2125, South Africa) is expensive, but does provide game drives and value-for-money luxury. They have lodges (P750 per person per day all in) and a bush-chic tented camp (P450) with a more remote feel.

Tuli Lodge (PO Box 32533, Braamfontein 2017, South Africa; ☎Johannesburg 482 2634, fax 482 2635; P450 per person per day all in), close to the Limpopo, is a garden oasis in dry country. Amidst the scorched surroundings, *Tuli*'s clipped lawns, indigenous trees, cool bar and swimming pool, are made all the more delicious. It's thoroughly indulgent, with the big attraction of game drives in Mashatu Game Reserve. Scoring some publicity for the area, the owner of *Tuli* is sponsoring the work of Gareth Patterson, George Adamson's assistant. After Adamson's murder in Kenya in 1989, Patterson took the three young lion cubs he had been rearing from Kenya to Botswana, where he is teaching them to return to the wild. Patterson intends to continue Adamson's *Born Free* work with lions in Botswana.

travel details

Buses

Daily buses and combis **from Gaborone** run north toward **Francistown** and south to **Lobatse**. Some only go as far as intermediate towns – the closer the destination, the more frequent the service. *Greyhound* buses (☎372224) run to **Johannesburg**, leaving from the *Kudu* service station (Mon, Thurs, Fri & Sat at 2.30pm). Combis leave daily, when full, from the bus station.

Trains

A 7-hour, twice-daily service between Gaborone and Francistown, on brand new, air-conditioned trains has been proudly introduced by Botswana Railways. It's the best way to travel along the eastern corridor and is the only air-conditioned train in public timetabled service in Africa. The overnight service continues through to Bulawayo; the sleeper fare includes bedding.

From **Gaborone** to: Bulawayo (daily 9.30pm 14hr); Francistown (Mon–Thurs, Sat & Sun 10am & 9.30pm, Fri 8am & 2.30pm; 7hr); Lobatse (daily 6.50am & 10am).

Flights

Air Botswana runs a limited internal service, with flights every day from Gaborone to Francistown and to Maun, as well as to Johannesburg.

CHAPTER EIGHT

CHOBE AND THE NORTHEAST

The pivotal position of **Francistown** led to its status in colonial times as the "capital of the north". At the end of the line on the Eastern Corridor, it's the last sizeable place you'll go through en route from Bulawayo or southern Botswana to the Makgadikgadi Pans and the teeming game reserves of the north – Chobe National Park and the Okavango Delta.

Making a special trip to traverse the spectacular **Makgadikgadi Pans** is strictly for experienced bush drivers. If you feel up to it, it's worth every penny to shell out and hire a vehicle and equipment for a self-sufficient camping expedition. Easier, and safer, options are to take day trips from Gweta, to splash out on the fly-in *Jack's Camp*, or to join one of the overland trips which stop at the pans en route to Chobe or the Okavango.

There's no big game on the salt flats themselves; their allure lies in the immense freedom of the vast skies and the lonely expanses of landscape. But there is game – huge herds of it – on the grassy plains which sweep away from them, at **Nxai Pan National Park** (best in the rainy season) and directly south, the **Makgadikgadi Pans Game Reserve** (best in the dry). There are further beautiful places – **Baines' Baobabs** and **Kubu Island** – outside the boundaries of the parks, with no entrance fees.

Chobe National Park is renowned for its massive number of elephants, some of which you should see watering along the picturesque Chobe River running past **Kasane**, on the northern side of the park, close to the Zimbabwean border. To explore the park, you'll need your own 4WD and a tent, or a booking in one of the luxury safari camps along the river, or to the south in the wonderful **Savuti**. If you don't have your own transport, it's worth considering one of the **overland expeditions** which travel through the park from Victoria Falls through Kasane to Maun. If you're hitching to Maun, you'll have to go the long way round via Nata (it's on tar, at least), as there is no transport on the direct route through the park.

FRANCISTOWN, NATA AND THE SALT PANS

Although it's Botswana's second biggest town, there's no compelling reason to stay in **Francistown** beyond its sheer convenience as a place where you can get a good night's sleep and stock up with all you'll need for adventuring north. Once you leave Francistown behind, the exhilaration of limitless space unrolls before you – there are no towns for hundreds of kilometres – and some thrilling wildlife experiences await. The first 195km bring you to the junction settlement of **Nata**, from where you can head north to Kasane and the elephant country of Chobe National Park, or west past the vast, eerie **salt pans** toward Maun and the Okavango Delta (see Chapter Nine).

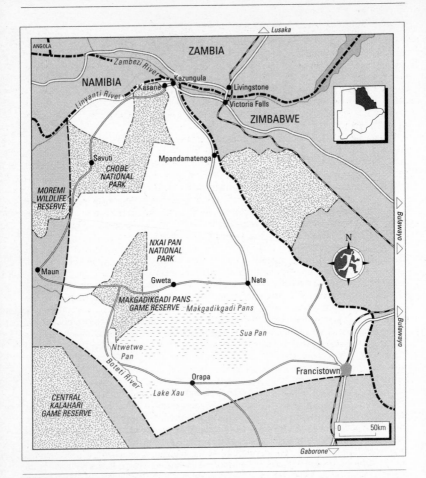

Francistown

As well as being the centre of the region's official and commercial life, **FRANCISTOWN** is at the hub of all Botswana's major transport routes. All tarred roads lead here, midway on the main north–south highway; it's well connected by rail and air to the rest of the country; and Bulawayo in Zimbabwe is just three hours' drive away on a direct road. The relationship to Zimbabwe is concretely visible – Francistown feels, and looks, like orderly, small-town Zimbabwe, with the main difference being that the shops are well stocked, and spare parts are available.

In fact Francistown's connection with Zimbabwe stretches back well before colonial times, when the present artificial boundaries were drawn. **Stone-wall villages** in the Francistown district are of the Khami type, and map the influence of the Rozvi state (see "Zimbabwe: A Historical Framework" in *Contexts*), which by the fifteenth century had risen to power and extended into present Botswana. Unfortunately, the sites are almost all on private land and are difficult to visit.

The pre-colonial name of the settlement, **Nyangabgwe**, meant "approach the rock" in the Kalanga dialect of Shona (which is still spoken in parts of Botswana), referring to a hunter who mistook a rock for an antelope on a hill. Francistown's current name comes from **Daniel Francis**, one of the first white prospectors in the area in the 1860s. Francis was a co-founder of the Northern Light Company, set up to exploit the newly discovered goldfields, and Francistown developed primarily as a company town servicing the mineral extraction industry. Gold, copper and nickel are still mined round about, but are now eclipsed by other deposits in the vicinity – diamonds at **Orapa**, and soda ash at **Sua Pan**.

Francistown today is a compact and neatly planned place, with jacaranda trees lining the streets, a couple of parks and a public swimming pool. The two main roads, **Haskins Street** and **Blue Jacket Street**, run parallel to the railway line, providing everything you're likely to need. However, there are no outstanding attractions to keep you here and most business can be done swiftly before pressing on.

If you do find yourself with the time, it's worth checking out the permanent collection at the **Supa-Ngwao Museum** in the old Francistown Court House. This is the new regional museum for the northeast, and also hosts cultural events. On land adjacent to the north, an open-air museum of traditional Botswana architecture is planned.

Arrival and getting around

Buses and trains arrive in Francistown right in the thick of things; the **railway station** is towards the north end of Haskins Street, and the **bus terminus** at the south. The small **airport** is just outside town, but as few if any independent travellers fly in, there's no public transport. If you've booked into one of the posh hotels, you can arrange in advance to be met. The best way to get around Francistown is by **taxi**; they cost only P1.50 if you're sharing and will take you anywhere you ask.

Accommodation

Francistown offers the chance of a cheap night's stay – rare in Botswana – either in the centre or on the outskirts. There's only one campsite, slightly out of town, but highly recommended.

Grand Lodge Hotel, Haskins St/Selous Ave (☎212300). The former *Grand Hotel* has had a long-overdue refurbishment, but there are still no meals and no bar. ④.

Marang Motel, Old Gaborone Rd (☎213991). By far Francistown's nicest place to stay, on the tree-lined banks of the sandy Tati River, 4km out of town. It has a swimming pool below the terrace and self-contained thatched **chalets** perched on stilts, as well as standard double rooms. The **campsite** (P15 per night) beneath the shady trees along the river bank has washing facilities unparalleled in Botswana. A favourite of the overland expeditions, the campsite is full of people setting off for the wild north, or recently out of the bush having their first taste of such urban comforts as hot water,

---

ACCOMMODATION PRICE CODES IN BOTSWANA

Most accommodation options in our account of Botswana have been given **price codes** to indicate the cost of a single night's lodging. The code for each establishment is based on the cost **per person sharing**; there is usually a supplement for a single person in a room. Prices for establishments that only offer all-inclusive rates (comprising meals, and perhaps guided tours and other services) have not been coded and are given in pula (per person per night).

① under P20	③ P40–60	⑤ P80–100	⑦ P120–140
② P20–40	④ P60–80	⑥ P100–120	⑧ P140–160

mirrors and electric lights. The self-service breakfast here is a great way to set yourself up for a long trek, with mounds of pancakes, corn fritters as well as the customary eggs and bacon. Also highly recommended are Veronica's Irish coffees. Take a taxi, or by car follow Blue Jacket St towards *Thapama Lodge*, take the Matsiloje exit off the big roundabout, keep going straight and the *Marang* is on the right, about a kilometre past the signposted turn-off to Matsiloje. ⑤.

The Satellite Guesthouse (☎214665, fax 202115). Located in the Satellite township, this guest house offers pre-fab accommodation with breakfast. Take a minibus heading for Satellite, or a taxi on the road to Marang. The guest house, in a walled compound, is signposted on the left about 2km from the roundabout, opposite the school for the deaf. ④.

Thapama Lodge, Doc Morgan Ave/Blue Jacket St (☎213872). Francistown's upmarket business hotel, which could just as well be anywhere in the world with its anodyne bars, lounges and bedrooms. ⑦.

YWCA (☎213046). Decent dormitory accommodation for men and women, within walking distance of the town centre. Take the first right off the Marang road after the hospital, at the grocery and *Botsalano* bar. ③.

Eating and shopping

Francistown is one of the very few towns in Botswana with a **fresh-produce market** (corner of Baines and Blue Jacket streets). You can buy cooked maize and groundnuts here, and the bustling courtyard is one of the best places for **fast food**. There are several other fast-food joints and **takeaways** around the bus station and in the Mall Shopping Centre. A good one with vegetarian possibilities is opposite *BGI Crafts* on the other side of the railway line. *Milano's Pizza*, in the Barclay's Plaza, offers decent **pizza**, as does *The House of Pizza*, which has a slightly more interesting atmosphere and also offers **Greek** and local cuisine. More Greek-style meals can be found at *Donna Café* on Selous Avenue. *Kentucky Fried Chicken* has now established itself in the Blue Jacket Plaza.

   Shopping in Francistown is easy and convenient. If you've come straight from Zimbabwe, the selection of goods seems dazzling, with a wide range of foods in the Mall Shopping Centre on Blue Jacket Street/Tainton Avenue. Several new shopping malls have appeared in the last couple of years: the large OK Mall, next to the *Thapama Lodge*, the multistorey Barclay's Plaza Mall and the Blue Jacket Mall. Apart from meat for braaing, *TC's Supermarket* on Haskins Street has a good range of imported foods, including dried noodles, soya chunks and dried curries – all ideal light-weight camping goods. Buy stuff here if you're on your way to Zimbabwe for some hiking, because such goods are unavailable there. For bread, and city luxuries like doughnuts and pastries, head straight for the excellent *Hot'n'Crusty*, also in the Mall. The biggest supermarket is *Score*, in Blue Jacket Street, near the Mall, open during lunchtime. The *Milky Bar* next door does a great waffles and ice-cream breakfast. For cheap booze, the *Grand Bottle Store* in the OK Mall is the best in town.

Nightlife

Francistown's **nightlife** buzzes mostly around hotel **bars**; the *Thapama* pool bar gets very lively on Friday night, and at the end of the month a live band does cover versions of chart hits from the past ten years. For plain beer and billiards, try *Ma Kim's*, the *HO Café* or *Francistown Café*, all found on or near Haskins Street. Boozing, billiards and braai facilities all come together with a lively atmosphere, especially at the weekend, in *Area L* (turn right at the Bulawayo roundabout, then take third left – or take a taxi). There's also one actual **nightclub**, *Bubbles* on Blue Jacket Street, where you can expect a predominance of disco with some African beat. The only **cinema** in town, the *Cine 2000*, is on Blue Jacket Street – don't expect anything out of the ordinary.

Listings

Air Botswana Blue Jacket Plaza (first floor), Blue Jacket St (☎212393).

Banks *Barclays*, Blue Jacket St; *Standard Chartered*, Haskins St.

Bookshops *Botswana Book Centre* in Blue Jacket Mall has a good selection. *Francistown Stationers and Bookshop* on Haskins St has a motley collection of paperbacks and a couple of books about Botswana, as well as a good selection of stationery and magazines.

Camping equipment *Ebrahim Store* on Tainton Ave.

Car rental *Avis* at the airport (☎213901), *Hertz* at the airport or *VIP Travel*, Blue Jacket St (☎215258 or 214524).

Crafts *BGI* across the railway bridge in Francis Ave extension: the enormous elephant head outside leads you to a fine selection of Shashe area baskets, but nothing else is particularly riveting. *Bushman Products*, on New Maun Road (☎213821), sells San crafts and leather products. *Tswana Weaving* (☎214554), in Tswelelo Industrial Complex, sells handwoven woollen tapestries and cotton rugs. *Marothodi*, 5km from the centre off the Gaborone road (☎213646), sells brightly coloured fabrics in beautiful designs, hand-printed clothing, and basketwork.

Dentist Dr Bosman, Baines St, next to *Something Special* (☎212295).

Doctor P. K. Sayana is in the Lobengula St Mall (Mon–Fri 8.30am–noon & 3–6pm, Sat 8.30am–noon; ☎212400, reservations ☎213494). Other doctors are listed in the pink pages at the front of the phone directory.

Emergencies Ambulance ☎997, Police (north end of Haskins St) ☎999.

Hospital *Nyangabgwe Hospital*, situated a few hundred metres east of the roundabout near *Thapama Lodge Hotel.*

Left luggage at the station (Mon–Fri 4.45am–12.30pm & 2–9pm, Sat & Sun 4.45am–10.30am & 5–9pm).

Pharmacy *The Hana Pharmacy*, Blue Jacket Plaza (☎216026), is the best stocked; or try *Phodisong*, the Mall, Blue Jacket St (emergencies ☎213719).

Post office Blue Jacket St.

Public telephones outside *Barclays Bank*, in the Mall, and at *Thapama Lodge Hotel.*

Railway booking office Haskins St (Mon–Fri 8am–1pm & 2–4pm). *Botswana Railways* information on ☎213444.

Records *Meropa Music Salon*, near the top of Blue Jacket St, has tapes and records of Botswana bands, as well as Zimbabwean and South African groups.

Swimming pool *Thapama Lodge Hotel* (plus a gym and squash courts).

Taxis (☎212260), or hail cars with blue number plates.

Travel agents *VIP Travel*, Lobengula Ave/Blue Jacket St (☎213909), can arrange accommodation, transport and car rental.

Visa renewals at the Immigration Department (PO Box 305), in the group of government offices immediately south of the cinema on Blue Jacket St (☎214204 or 212337).

North towards Kasane

The tarred highway north from Francistown divides after 189km at Nata, with north-bound tar continuing to Kasane and westbound newly tarred road to Maun and the Okavango. One possible break in your journey before getting to Nata is the refugee camp at **DUKWE**, 103km from Francistown, just off the main road. Set up during the liberation struggle in Rhodesia, the camp now houses Namibian and Angolan refugees, and some Zimbabweans who have stayed on. There's a tempting variety of craftwork for sale and a thatched public bar. Keep your camera under wraps, however, as photography isn't allowed.

Around 20km south of Nata, the **Nata Sanctuary** is a 230-square-kilometre community project that aims to provide a refuge for wildlife on and around the Sua Pan (daily 7am–7pm; P10 per person, including camping and braai facilities; for further information about the pans, see p.298). To enable the project to work, local people voluntarily relocated their cattle onto adjacent range land. Around 165 varieties of bird have been recorded here, and when the Nata River is flowing the pan attracts water birds from all over Africa – a great opportunity to see flamingoes as well as pelicans, ducks and geese. Mammal species are less abundant; apart from the usual antelopes, you may be lucky enough to see jackals, foxes and monkeys.

Nata

The small village of **NATA** – little more than a crossroads – is totally dependent on through traffic. It centres around the *Sua Pan Bottle Store* and **garage**, which offers the last petrol before Maun, 304km away. Everyone stops here, and it's very much the place to wait for **lifts** to Maun, just before the road swings off west. The **bottle store** has a wide range of drinks, and the fry-ups are very good at the hotel **café**, next door. If you just want a snack, there's first-class biltong to be had in season from the *Wild Beasts Butchery* (complete with paintings of fierce wildebeest on the outside walls). For any **medical needs**, the newish clinic, signposted off the main road, is good. You should however fill your water containers in Francistown rather than relying on the supply at the garage, as Nata suffers from shortages.

The *Sua Pan Lodge* at the garage (☎611220; ④) offers the only **accommodation** in town, conveniently situated on the main road, but it's a bit of a rip-off and not recommended. **Camping** is also available (P10 per person), and there's a pool which can be used by non-residents for P8.

Just 10km south of Nata on the Francistown–Kasane road, the *Nata Lodge* stands in a far nicer setting, among ilala palms and marula and monkey-thorn trees. You can **camp** (P12 per person) or stay in comfortable self-contained three-bed **chalets**, or for a little less, sleep in large four-bed tents (②–③). Book through the *Marang Motel* in Francistown, or write to Private Bag 10, Francistown (☎611210, fax 611260). As well as walking in the surrounding bush, it's possible to take an organized **drive** from the lodge to Sua Pan, for a minimum of four people (P40 per person). If you're only stopping off for a drink – and the bar is a good place to hear bush stories – you can use the swimming pool or have a shower for a couple of pula. If you do spend the night, you can splash out on a candlelit dinner (set menu or *à la carte*) in the thatched dining room – especially good if you've been in the bush for a while. The lodge has a fine selection of **crafts**, which are no more expensive than anywhere else.

North from Nata

Between Nata and Kasane, a long straight stretch where the road borders on Zimbabwe's Hwange National Park, there's a good chance of seeing elephants, ostriches and the odd herd of impala. Along the second half of the 299 monotonous kilometres, the Sibuyu, Kazuma and Kasane **forest reserves** hug the Zimbabwe border in three separate enclaves of teak and *mukwa* woodland and offer some diversion from the endless tar strip. Hitching is difficult because there's little traffic, but there are two buses every morning in each direction between Francistown and Kasane, a five-hour journey via Nata. Enquire at the Nata garage for current times.

This northbound highway traverses the tracks of a nineteenth-century ivory route to the Zambezi. Known as the **Mpandamatenga trail** – the "pick-up-and-carry-road" – its name refers to the reliance of white hunters on black porters. Nowadays, **MPANDAMATENGA**, a former trading post 223km from Nata, signals its existence with a series of grain silos, that rise like mirages from the surrounding maize and sorghum fields. A tamed island in the vast wilderness, it's one of the country's few farming areas, and home to a prosperous agricultural community. There's little more to tempt you to stop, though, than a café, general store and a *Shell* service station.

It's possible to drive **into Zimbabwe** from Mpandamatenga, although there's no official border post. If you decide to take this rarely used exit, you must report to the police at Mpandamatenga before leaving, and, once in Zimbabwe, clear yourself with immigration at Victoria Falls or Bulawayo. Inside Zimbabwe, the road branches north through Matetsi (a major hunting area) to the tarred Bulawayo–Victoria Falls road (65km), and south to Robins Camp in Hwange National Park (48km).

The salt pans

If you take the **road to Maun**, your long journey will carry you through some of Botswana's most remarkable landscapes, second only to the Okavango Delta itself. The road cuts between the enormous complex of the **Makgadikgadi Pans** to the south, and the relatively small – but no less interesting – **Nxai and Kudiakam Pans** to the north. If you're in your own vehicle, there's good reason to make a detour.

The choice of whether to visit Nxai or Makgadikgadi Pans depends on what time of year you're in Botswana, as game migrates from one area to another. In the dry season (April–Nov), Makgadikgadi is best, while during the rains (Nov–March) the animals are attracted northwards to Nxai Pan. It also depends on how bold you are. Nxai Pan has **camping facilities** and it's not too difficult to find your way around, while getting

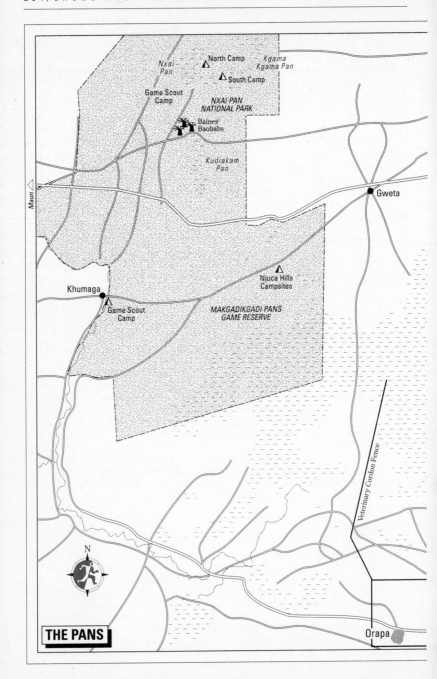

THE PANS

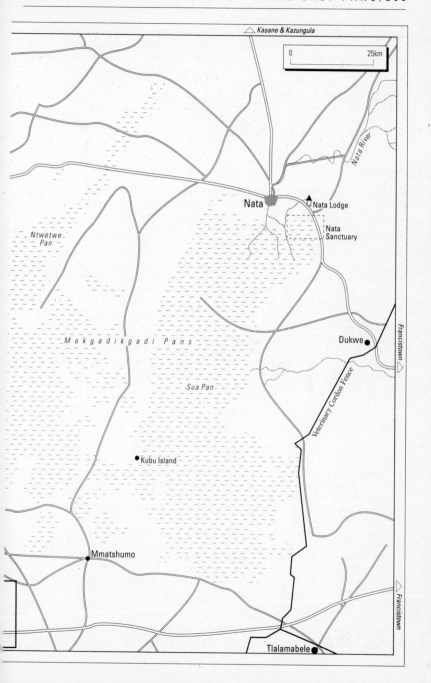

around Makgadikadi, which also has campsites, as well as an upmarket **safari camp**, is a matter of a good sense of direction. Neither compasses nor maps are much help here. Scores of unmapped tracks weave about the vast 4200 square kilometres of game-rich grasslands and bush country that make up the **Makgadikgadi Pans Game Reserve** – the northwest section of Ntwetwe Pan, which is the more westerly of the adjacent depressions of Makgadikgadi. The whole of the pans area demands self-sufficiency in food, water and fuel.

At the southern edge of Nxai Pans National Park, it's well worth making a small detour to the majestic **Baines' Baobabs** at Kudiakam Pan, even if you haven't time to explore Nxai Pan itself.

Gweta

GWETA, around halfway to Maun, is definitely worth a stop, whether you're heading off to the pans or not. It's a thatched village with towering palm trees, grey sand, vagrant donkeys and horses – and a petrol station. Its name is from San and means "where the big frogs meet". In the middle of the settlement, *Gweta Rest Camp*'s modest thatched rondavels blend with the stick- and bush-encircled village huts; **rooms** with or without bathrooms are available, and it's possible to **camp** (Box 124, Gweta; ☎612220; ③–④). A night spent here en route to Maun offers a rare opportunity to stay in a traditional village and experience life going on around you without feeling an intruder. The *Rest Camp* bar and dartboard draw both locals and travellers; or try the bar and restaurant down the road adjoining the shop and bakery – an obvious huddle of buildings on your left as you come into town. The fresh bread, baked in an outside oven, is a welcome surprise in such a small place.

Gweta is a useful **base for exploring the Makgadikgadi Pans**. The *Rest Camp* rents 4x4 bikes, which seat two people and will handle the thick sand, and offers 4WD Landcruiser day trips on the salty expanses for US$75. They also run three-hour game drives to **Nxhasin Pan**, 25km north of Gweta, costing from US$15, and overnight trips there for US$50 per person. If you want to go further, they'll oblige with overland trips around Botswana from US$120 per person.

Makgadikgadi Pans

At 12,000 square kilometres, **MAKGADIKGADI PANS** make an impression through their sheer extent (and the fact that they're almost unpronounceable; the *kg* is pronounced like the *ch* in loch, and the *a* as the *u* in cud: *Muchudichudi*). On maps they look like massive lakes, giving a false impression of the landscape – but a strong clue to its origin. About two million years ago, the Okavango Delta and the pans were part of an enormous lake that flooded across northern Botswana. The deepest parts of the basin became today's Makgadikgadi Pans, comprising **Sua Pan** (sometimes spelled "Sowa") to the east, and **Ntwetwe Pan** to the west, each roughly 100km long by more than 50km wide.

The surfaces of the pans are compact, smooth, grey, blemish-free clay. It sounds bleak, but what's most remarkable about the area is the experience of space. On all horizons, the greys of the pan deepen to blues and blend imperceptibly with the water-colour edges of the sky, creating extraordinary sensations of infinity. They are particularly beautiful after rain, covered by opaque sheets of water meeting sky and cloud. The expansiveness, silence and total isolation are awesome.

On the edges of the pans are **grasslands** – miles and miles of open country which supports cattle in the farmlands around Sua, and migrating herds of game in the reserves.

Life on the pans

The Botswana super-lake is long gone, but its demise can be traced through different **vegetation zones** on the pans, each resulting from varying salt concentrations from place to place. When the super-lake dried out, some two million years ago, the water was concentrated in a shrinking area. The place where the lake was deepest and the water lay longest is now barren because the salinity is strongest. **Grass** grows in abundance right to the edge of these featureless, salty depressions. As the salinity diminishes, **shrubs** are able to grow; furthest away of all come the **trees**, which are least able to cope with the salt.

During a good rainy season, a faint echo of the ancient lake sometimes returns heel- or ankle-deep, in areas near the river mouths, like Nata Delta. But there's nothing faint about the splendid **birdlife** that comes to these waters. The northeast of Sua Pan sometimes swirls with birds, particularly flamingoes and pelicans. Towards the end of the rains and into winter, provided there *is* water, the variety and quantity of water birds at the river mouth is staggering. Ducks and geese nest in reed beds and pelicans on the banks. On the open grasslands close to the water you can see both wattled and crowned cranes in small flocks. But most tantalizing are the elusive flocks of greater and lesser **flamingoes** – here one day, gone the next – which come to feast on algae and the tiny shrimps that, remarkably, lie dormant in the dry sands until the rains return to bring them back to life. At times thousands of flamingoes descend on the pan and you can see them standing delicately in the shallows.

SODA ASH

The **Sua Pan soda ash project** is a mine on Sua Spit, a narrow promontory extending into the pan. Set up jointly by the government of Botswana (with a 48 percent share) and a group of South African companies, it's the most expensive project in Botswana's history, of great significance in the attempt to diversify the country's diamond-based economy.

It aims to provide both South Africa and neighbouring countries with thousands of tonnes of soda ash as well as 700,000 tonnes of salt for regional industrial consumption. (Soda ash, or sodium carbonate, is an alkaline chemical used in a wide variety of manufacturing processes including the making of steel, vanadium, paper, glass and detergents.) Wellheads are dotted over a 200-square-kilometre area, and there are 20 square kilometres of evaporating ponds, with boiler plants. It's all a far cry from the days of San people mining salt, transporting it on donkeys and selling it to the Kalanga.

The major loss caused by the mining operation has been the feeding grounds of the greater and lesser flamingoes. To counter the dismay of environmentalists at the project, the mine has partly financed a new wildlife sanctuary at Sua Pan, the Nata Sanctuary, administered by Nata council, rather than the Department of Wildlife, which means more modest entrance fees. As most of the game was hunted out over the last century by white hunters, the area is being restocked.

Kubu Island

One of the eeriest features of the Makgadikgadi Pans are the fossil-like extrusions of rock – "islands" in a sea of grey sand. Most notable, and magical, is **Kubu Island**, a mound of lumpy rocks, pushing 10m above the pan floor in the southwest corner of Sua Pan. It doesn't sound like much, but in a landscape as flat as a billiard table, it gives you a fantastic view of the surrounding brineland. On the outcrop are the grotesque red-tinged baobabs that inspired Michael Main to write, in his book *Kalahari: Life's Variety in Dune and Delta*:

Gnarled, usually leafless, their dwarfed and twisted forms suggest the agony of ages spent on salted waters beneath a remorseless sun. Some, seen in silhouette against the stark, grey pan, suggest a visit to another world, unutterably remote and lonely.

Most remarkable is the fact that there have been **human settlements** here. On one corner of Kubu Island are the remains of a **dry-stone wall**. There are some stone cairns – not, as you'd expect, burial sites, but some other structure, still unidentified – and a scattering of **stone tools**. Artefacts are often found along the present shoreline – tiny arrowheads, scrapers, crescents and minutely hewn knife blades. Elsewhere on the island are the **ruins** of a village site, the earliest occupation dating as far back as 500 AD and the most recent 1400–1600 AD. Where the inhabitants drew their water remains the biggest mystery. If all this doesn't suffice to fire your imagination, mirages are common. In the early morning, convincing mountains sometimes appear on the horizon, or the pan takes on an oceanic appearance.

Kubu Island can be reached from the track, between the Sua and Ntwetwe pans, beginning 16km west of Nata and heading south; or from the Francistown–Orapa road, setting out from the tiny village of Mmatshumo and climbing over a low escarpment. Kubu isn't terribly easy to find, as there are few landmarks and certainly no signposts. You need to be fully **self-sufficient** and should leave no trace of your stay behind, unlike recent visitors who marked their visit with piles of bottles and graffiti on the baobabs.

Exploring Sua Pan

If you're adventurous and have your own 4WD transport, the *Visitors' Guide to Botswana* by Main, Fowkes and Fowkes (see "Books" in *Contexts*) is useful for its comprehensive directions for **getting around Sua Pan**. There's also a 1:1,000,000 map (obtainable from the Director, Department of Surveys and Lands, Private Bag 0037, Gaborone) of use only to familiarize yourself with the area and not for orientating on Sua. When it's dry and the surfaces firm, it's possible to drive across the pans, but you'll get covered in fine grey dust. If it's wet, creep cautiously around the edges, and wherever possible follow the tracks of any previous vehicle – if they made it, the route is probably safe. If there have been recent heavy rains avoid the pans altogether. And finally, if in any doubt about your driving competence in this unfamiliar territory, don't go.

It is however possible to make short **forays onto the edge of the pan** quite easily, without 4WD. A track that branches westwards off the main Francistown–Nata road will bring you to the fringes of Sua. The turn-off is 15km north of the Dukwe Veterinary Gate – one of the many gates in the network of fences set up across the country to fight foot and mouth disease. There's a sign for "Sua", pointing west to the pan; the road it indicates will lead you to Sua Spit – a "peninsula" which jetties out into the sea of grey dust, and is the site of the soda ash mine (see box above).

Failing that, another track, 20km south of Nata, leads a short way to the edge of the pan. It begins at an unlocked gate, by a big baobab to the left of the road. The management at *Nata Lodge* (see p.293) will be able to advise you on the current situation in the area: which areas are off limits and most importantly, whether flamingoes have been recently sighted and where to spot them.

Finally, a **longer excursion**, but a more rewarding one, is to take the good veterinary track that runs along the cordon fence at Thalamabele, 150km west Francistown on the Orapa road, and travel 97km up the eastern flank of the pan, to arrive at the Dukwe Veterinary Gate on the Francistown–Nata road.

Makgadikgadi Pans Game Reserve

Entrance fee P50 per person per day, payable at one of the Scout Camps, either on the main Nata–Maun road, not far from Gweta (ask in Gweta for directions), or at Khumaga or Nxai Pan. Maps are available at the Scout Camps. Campsites must be prebooked at the Department of Wildlife and National Parks in Maun (☎660376), Francistown (☎212367) or Kasane (☎650235).

MAKGADIKGADI PANS GAME RESERVE is an unfenced area that takes in the northwestern edge of Ntwetwe Pan and reaches the Boteti River in the west, with the Nata–Maun road as its northern boundary. Here it joins up with the Nxai Pan National Park to the north – they're administered as one unit, though still referred to by their separate names. The best time to visit is in the dry season, between April and November, especially from June onwards.

To the north and west of Ntwetwe Pan lie extensive, and magnificently beautiful, grasslands with groves of tall **palm trees** in the north of the area. During the dry season, large herds of **zebras** and **wildebeest** roam between the Boteti River and the pan. The game migrates when there is surface water available, then returns to the Boteti usually from April onwards – so you may see zebra and wildebeest moving from the river to Nxai Pan between February and April. **Gemsboks, springboks, ostriches** and a few **hartebeest** are also found on the plains and there are many **lions**, a few **cheetahs** and occasional **brown hyenas**.

Several unmarked side tracks lead from the main Nata–Maun road to the Makgadikgadi grasslands. One quite major north–south route – unmarked but well worn – begins almost exactly halfway between the two, 150km from Nata. There are two **campsites**, one at **Khumaga** on the Boteti River with a shower, toilet and firewood, and a far more primitive one at **Njuca Hills** with pit latrines only.

For those who can afford it, the only way to explore the desert in absolute comfort is at *Jack's Camp*, a new **safari camp** at the pans 50km south of Gweta (book through *Okavango Tours & Safari*, Box 39, Maun; ☎660220). Guests all fly in and there's a maximum of sixteen people accommodated in luxurious tents. The style is Persian carpets, silver and damask in the desert for US$240 per person per day.

Nxai Pan National Park

Open year-round. Entrance fee P50 per person per day, payable at the Game Scouts Camp. Campsites must be prebooked at the Department of Wildlife and National Parks in Maun (☎660376), Francistown (☎212367) or Kasane (☎650235).

The turn-off to **NXAI PAN NATIONAL PARK** is 170km from Nata. You'll need 4WD, at least for the 35-kilometre sandy track which leads north from the main road to the Game Scouts Camp. Unlike Sua, Nxai Pan is not grey clay, but a fourteen-kilometre stretch of grass with small islands of trees. It's best visited in the rainy season, usually November to March.

Whether or not you see the full array of wildlife depends on the rain and whether numbers have built up after years of drought. Outside the rainy season you may see next to nothing, as the game is migratory. Elephants and buffaloes are rare visitors, only coming if it's very wet. If rains have fallen, the game viewing on the pan can be spectacular, with huge herds of **wildebeest, zebras** and **gemsboks** up to a thousand strong and **giraffes** numbering up to fifty in a herd. **Cheetahs** and **lions** keep their watchful eyes on the bounty. There are small herds of **springboks** and **impalas** (the southernmost point of their range) and occasionally **eland** and **sable antelope**.

The most exciting small mammal to look for is the **bat-eared fox**, present here in large numbers. Scan the ant heaps on which they like to sit and check near clumps of long grass. The size of the fox's **ears** is an indication of their acute sensitivity to sound: they're able to hear insects moving about beneath the ground. As well as being perceptive, bat-eared foxes are incredibly nimble, and supplement their staple diet of termites, beetles and locusts by chasing rodents and reptiles at lightning speed, doubling back on their tracks and continuing the hunt in a single, fluid twist – a delight to watch.

There's a choice of two **campsites** in the park, the better of which is the South Camp, pleasantly situated in a grove of trees a few kilometres from the Game Scout Camp. The North Camp is less appetizing, in a mopane tree clearing, where you may see impala, if nothing else. Both campsites have toilets and erratic cold showers.

Baines' Baobabs

At the southern edge of Nxai Pan park, the trees known as **Baines' Baobabs** are definitely worth taking in. Overlooking **Kudiakam Pan**, the largest of a small salt pan complex, they are named after Thomas Baines, a nineteenth-century explorer, who was also an accomplished artist, particularly well known for his paintings of Victoria Falls. In May 1862, while travelling from Walvis Bay to the Falls with James Chapman, a hunter and trader, he immortalized these impressive baobabs. They look much the same today as when he painted them, 130 years ago – madly majestic in the flat emptiness. Here, outside the park boundaries, you may also see **game** during the rainy season, especially gemsbok and springbok, and perhaps even lion.

The road to Baines' Baobabs is unmarked, but it's not too difficult to find. The easiest route takes the northbound Nxai Pan track, turning right at the crossroads 17km on. This takes you onto the old Nata–Maun road. One kilometre further on, where the road forks, take the right track for 11km until you reach the baobabs. During the rainy season this route can get flooded, in which case you should take the left fork and turn right 13km further on, to reach the trees.

KASANE AND
CHOBE NATIONAL PARK

The small town of **Kasane** is the obvious base if you don't have your own transport and want to get into **Chobe National Park**, Botswana's premier game reserve. It has ample accommodation and camping, and is the only place you'll catch Chobe **game drives** and **river cruises**. With your own transport, Kasane is a pleasant enough place to relax, as well as being the place to stock up with fuel and supplies before going into big game country.

Chobe National Park itself is a far cry from the soft paradise of the Okavango Delta or the watery edges of Moremi Wildlife Reserve (see Chapter Nine); instead, it's a raw and compelling wilderness packed with game. The park was created in 1968, and named after the river that defines its northern boundary. Confusingly, however, this river itself has a number of different names. Where it rises in Angola it's called the **Kuando**; where it first enters Botswana it's the **Linyanti**. It then becomes the **Itenge** and only when it reaches Ngoma back on the Caprivi Strip in Namibia, does it become the **Chobe**. Even its life as the Chobe is short-lived; it soon joins up with the **Zambezi** and together they hit the chasm at Victoria Falls.

Chobe National Park consists of three very distinct main areas – the **riverfront**, the **Ngwezumba region** and the **Mababe Depression** (usually known simply as **Savuti**). The best time to visit the river is during the dry season from June to October, when animals come from the interior to the northern part of the park for water. Savuti and Ngwezumba are good from November to May.

Of the various **National Parks camps** (basic facilities only) scattered across the varying terrain of the park, the closest to Kasane, and the most popular, is **Serondella**, ribboning along the Chobe River. Although the whole park is called Chobe, you'll frequently hear it used to refer just to this river area. Just outside the national park, 55km from Kasane at Ngoma Bridge, is *Buffalo Ridge* campsite; at the other end of the scale in terms of style and cost, the park is served by a handful of **luxury safari lodges**.

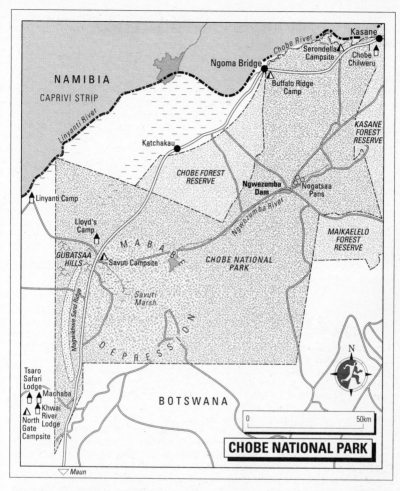

CHOBE NATIONAL PARK

From Serondella two routes bow out southwards, before converging again on Savuti. The first runs west, parallel to the Chobe River, before bearing south into the heart of the national park. The second takes you through Ngwezumba with its mopane forests to **Nogatsaa Pans** and several newly created waterholes. But the ultimate destination, in Chobe, is the **Mababe Depression**, a dead-lake area, comprising the **Savuti Channel and Marsh**. It's renowned for the unusually gentle bull elephants roaming around the campsite, plus the prides of lions that prowl the marsh – a grassy plain formed during the years when this part of Botswana was under the big lake.

Chobe adjoins the Okavango's Moremi Wildlife Reserve in the south, from where it's half a day's journey to Maun. The most direct route between Kasane and Maun entails a tough-going 4WD trip of over 400km through Chobe National Park via Savuti.

THROUGH CHOBE OVERLAND

The least expensive safaris through Chobe – and even they are certainly not cheap – are **overland adventure trips** of 7–16 days. Departures are normally from Maun or Victoria Falls, taking in the highlights of either or both countries. Without your own 4WD, these trips are the best way to get into remote game parks and have the experience of camping in the bush and sitting around camp fires. Trips are also available to Namibia, Malawi, Zaire and South Africa. **Prices** are US$120–240 per day and are mostly all-inclusive. On the cheapest safaris clients usually pitch their own tents and help with some of the chores like cooking, while at the top of the range you just sit pretty, with some of the accommodation in luxury camps or luxury hotels. This price ensures hot showers, sheets on your camp bed and iced drinks.

The companies listed below offer a wide range of departure dates throughout the year. It's best to write off for their brochures to find a trip which suits you. Children under 12 are normally not permitted on safaris.

Afro Ventures Safaris, PO Box 261, Victoria Falls, Zimbabwe (Victoria Falls ☎4588). *Afro Ventures* takes groups no bigger than eight and overnights at the *A'Zambezi River Lodge* at Victoria Falls. They also fly into the Delta to stay at *Xaxaba Camp* on their Okavango package.

Karibu Safari, central reservations PO Box 35196, Northway, Durban 4065, South Africa (☎031/839774, fax 831957). Camping safaris take groups of 8–13 people and are all participatory, with a food fund to cover all meals. One of the culinary delights is freshly baked bread every day. Seven days in the Okavango costs from US$800.

Wilderness Safaris, central reservations PO Box 651171, Benmore 2010, South Africa (☎011/884 1458, fax 011/883 6255). "Participation" 12-day all-inclusive camping safaris to Chobe and the Okavango are 30 percent cheaper than the "first-class" ones – from US$1800 for 12 days fully inclusive, departing from Victoria Falls or Maun. Groups are no bigger than eight.

Besides the larger overland companies, a number of small safari companies will take you around Botswana on exclusive, tailor-made trips. Prices are high, but you can expect excellent photographic opportunities in the game parks, good guides and luxury camping. The best ones to try are based in Maun at *Crocodile Camp* and *Island Safari Lodge*; or check out *Travel Wild* or one of the travel agents in Maun (see p.316).

Together, Chobe and Moremi form a protected range 300km long, providing sanctuary for the great herds of game that follow the ebb and flow of water. There's no public transport through the wilds from Kasane to Maun and hitching is out. If you don't want to see the park, it's better to go by tar via Nata to reach Maun.

The nicest way to see Chobe is in your own vehicle and at your own pace. Vehicles without four-wheel drive can get to Serondella, but no further. You can arrange **4WD hire** in Maun (see p.316) or Kasane, but you definitely need 4WD experience to cope with the heavy sand beyond Serondella, and strong nerves for being in the wild. There are no mechanics, breakdown services, petrol stations or shops, and only very primitive campsites. Without your own 4WD, and if you don't mind being in a group, the best option is to join one of the **mobile safari companies** who traverse the route as part of a Botswana–Victoria Falls trip (see box).

Chobe National Park is open all year, with an **entry fee** of P50 per person per day, reduced to P30 if you're doing a drive or cruise with a registered safari company. The park's northern **gate**, 8km west of Kasane, is where you enter, and pay your fees, if you're camping at Serondella, or driving via Nogatsaa to Savuti and Maun. Serondella Campsite, as well as Savuti and Moremi if you're en route to Maun, must be **prebooked** at the Department of Wildlife and National Parks, Kasane (☎650235).

Kasane and Serondella

Graced by big trees and the beautiful Chobe River, **KASANE** provides a pleasant respite from the dust and dryness of the rest of the country. It was once the imperial centre of the Makololo – eighteenth-century invaders from what is now South Africa, who conquered the local Lozi people – although no evidence of that period now remains. A bunch of dusty administrative buildings, a small mall, a bank, public phone, hospital, a couple of takeaways and some traditional huts are strung out desultorily along the main road. There's a centre of sorts at the western end of the village, the one closest to the park entrance. Here you'll find a small supermarket, a garage, car rental and the *Chobe Safari Lodge*.

Arrival and getting around

Because Kasane is a border town, you're quite likely to hit it as you arrive from one of the neighbouring countries. **From Zimbabwe**, the *UTC* coach from Victoria Falls will let you off at any of the Kasane lodges, or pick you up to go the other way. It's pricy (US$30 one-way) but reliable. **From Zambia** you cross the Zambezi from Livingstone on the Kazungula ferry to the Botswana border post. Try to line up a lift into town while you're on the ferry – it's too far to walk. **From Namibia**, there's a border post at Ngoma Bridge, 55km from Kasane itself, with *Buffalo Ridge Campsite* (☎650430) conveniently adjacent on the western boundary of Chobe – run by a Botswana game veteran, it's invariably less crowded than the Serondella campsite in the national park. 1996 sees the road from Kasane to Ngoma tarred, with plans to take the tar further. From Francistown or Nata **by bus** you'll get dropped near *Chobe Safari Lodge*.

The new Kasane **airport** has further opened up the northeast to international tourists, with direct passenger flights to Maun, Gaborone, Johannesburg and Victoria Falls. There's no public transport to and from the village, but if you're booked into one of the lodges you'll be met. Near the airport at the east end of town, *Northern Air* (☎250234) charter planes.

Avis at *Crest Mowana Safari Lodge* (☎650144) **rents 4WDs** for P255 a day, sedan cars for P140 a day, plus mileage charges; if you're heading to Maun via Savuti, a week's 4WD hire costs around P2527. Charges at *Holiday Car Rental* next to *Chobe Safari Lodge* are slightly lower (☎650226).

Accommodation

At present, the *Chobe Safari Lodge* is the best – and the only central – place to stay in Kasane. The Serondella campsite is described on p.306.

Crest Mowana Safari Lodge, PO Box 335, Kasane (☎650300). A safari hotel with the usual game activities. Service is nothing to write home about. Dullest of the Chobe places to stay. P582 per person all in.

Chobe Chilwero, PO Box 22, Kasane (☎650234). A small, intimate camp with eight thatched bungalows and fantastic views over the river from the hill near the park gate. The camp offers excellent river trips, on which you can see birds and monitor lizards at close quarters, as well as game drives as part of the all-inclusive price of P595 per person per night.

Chobe Game Lodge, PO Box 32, Kasane (☎250340). On the river bank inside the park itself, Botswana's most famous and elegant hotel still trades off the fact that Elizabeth Taylor and Richard Burton had their honeymoon here (after marrying each other for the second time). Of course, the elephants that drink from the river, within sight of the rooms, are a more satisfying reason to spend time in these luxurious surroundings. Even if you can't afford to stay, you're welcome for a drink or meal: their lavish Sunday brunches are worth shelling out for if you're already in the park. P715 per person all in.

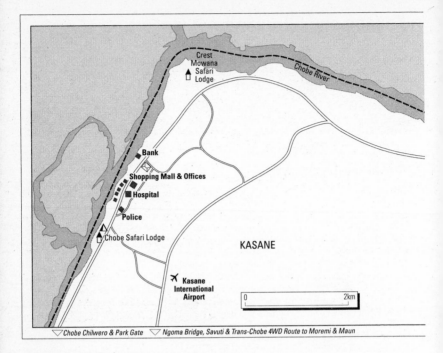

▽ *Chobe Chilwero & Park Gate*   ▽ *Ngoma Bridge, Savuti & Trans-Chobe 4WD Route to Moremi & Maun*

Chobe Safari Lodge, PO Box 10, Kasane (☎250336). The original Chobe hotel – not to be confused with the glamorous *Chobe Game Lodge*. It's a modest and comfortable establishment with a swimming pool on the river bank. There are camping sites (P20) and braaing places along the river, and reasonably priced accommodation in thatched chalets with shared washing facilities, or more expensive en-suite rooms or rondavels. The food's not bad; you can get toasted sandwiches at any time on the terrace, breakfast or a set meal in the hotel dining room. The terrace overlooking the river is a splendid place to watch the sunsets, and listen to the hippos snorting in the dead of night. The lodge is conveniently close to shops and a few minutes' drive from the park gate. From here you can get river cruises and game drives into the park. ④–⑤.

Impalila Island Lodge, Box 70378, Bryanston 2021, South Africa (☎/fax 011/706 7207). Six chalets in riverine forest, right at the meeting of all four neighbouring countries – you'll hear the river flowing by from your bed. Access is by boat from *Crest Mowana Safari Lodge*, though the lodge is technically in Namibia. Recommended. P490 per person all in.

Kubu Lodge, PO Box 43, Kasane (☎650312). Some kilometres east of town on the river, near the Zimbabwean and Zambian borders, smarter than *Safari Lodge* with en-suite rooms and cheaper rondavels, and camping (P20). But the campsite here, next to a crocodile farm, isn't nearly as nice as *Safari Lodge*'s and backpackers aren't made particularly welcome. *Kubu* offers game drives and river cruises into Chobe. ⑤–⑦.

Exploring Chobe's riverfront

Even if you don't have your own transport (see "Arrival and getting around" above for information about vehicle rental), getting into the park is easy enough. **Game drives** leave morning and evening from *Safari Lodge* and *Kubu Lodge*; book at either. The drives aren't cheap (P40–50 per person, plus P30 park entry fee) but you're likely to see a lot of animals in the dry season. The rainy season can be disappointing, especially for elephants.

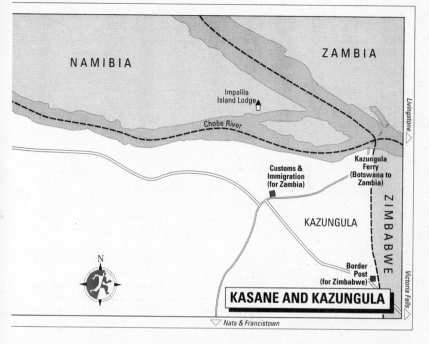

NAMIBIA

ZAMBIA

Impalila
Island Lodge

Chobe River

Livingstone ▷

Customs &
Immigration
(for Zambia)

Kazungula
Ferry
(Botswana to
Zambia)

KAZUNGULA

ZIMBABWE

N

Border
Post
(for Zimbabwe)

Victoria Falls ▷

KASANE AND KAZUNGULA

▽ Nata & Francistown

Afternoons are usually the favoured time for **elephant herds** to make their way to the river, and consequently a wonderful time to see them, en masse, in lovely surroundings. Chobe's 50,000-strong population is legendary. At water they provide excellent slapstick entertainment, as their playfulness comes to the fore in the elephantine equivalent of a booze-up. The best way to see something of the Chobe River is to take the excellent-value **afternoon cruise** from *Chobe Safari Lodge* which goes slowly upriver past the *Chobe Game Lodge.* As you skirt the flood plains you'll see a wealth of animals and birds from the deck of the launch, and you can have a drink at the same time. The *Chobe Fish Eagle* leaves the lodge every day at 3pm for the three-hour cruise and should be booked in advance.

The flood plains, with their different vegetation types – thickets of bush, open grassland and riverine forest – are ideal for **game viewing**. Besides herds of elephant and buffalo, look out for tsessebe, waterbuck, roan and sable antelopes, eland, sable, rhinoceros, giraffe, hyena, kudu and Chobe bushbuck.

Common **water birds** you'll spy on the margins include herons, storks, geese, ducks, jacanas and skimmers. One of the greatest delights is a huge colony of **carmine bee-eaters** that nests in holes in the bank, although not always in the same place each year.

Close to the water, you may spot one of the rarest Botswanan antelope, the **puku**, which bears a passing resemblance to the impala but lacks the latter's distinctive black and white markings. **Red lechwe** are far more commonly sighted antelope in northern Botswana's wetlands – their southernmost range. Although still one of Chobe's common sights, the species faces extinction due to competition with humans for its specialized waterside habitat. Hippos loll in the water and you may spot water monitor lizards or crocodiles basking on the sandy edges of the flood plains.

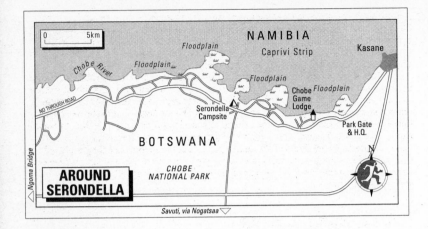

Serondella

Serondella used to be a village and trading station, before the park was created. Forests of teak and mukwa were felled and sent on barges downriver to the Livingstone railway line, and across to Zambia on the Kazungula ferry. The patch of rubble you see on the way to the campsite is a reminder of the villagers who were shifted from here when it was declared parkland, to be resettled at Kasane.

The Serondella **campsite**, 10km west of the park gate, is Chobe's most accessible (even without 4WD) and popular site. There are cold showers, taps and toilets, and no fences. You'll be surrounded by animals, especially elephants, in the dry season; never fall asleep outside your tent or leave it open, however warm the night.

THE CHOBE ELEPHANTS

The big issue at Chobe is **elephants**. The Botswana government prohibited hunting of them and rejected a culling policy for some years, though it now allows hunting of a certain number. The original hunting ban was motivated by the notion that if the elephants have nothing to fear outside reserves, they'll migrate freely beyond the national park boundaries, and thus ease the pressure on parkland itself.

The reason for the policy change is that the land available cannot support the official count of 75,000–80,000 elephants, although this number includes migrating elephants from neighbouring Zimbabwe, Zambia and Namibia; the Chobe Wildlife Trust estimates 50,000. The elephants threaten other species and cause serious environmental damage, especially along Chobe's riverfront where you'll see wrecked mopane trees, ravaged by elephants, which are turning woodland savannah into degraded bushveld. In Botswana there's a passionate anti-culling lobby which argues that elephants cause change, not a simple destruction, of habitat and that the park will establish its own balance, without the stress of slaughtering whole family groups of elephants. In Zimbabwe, most people involved in wildlife management argue for culling. Both countries are in favour of the ivory trade, arguing that their well-managed herds have become so big that regulated trade is in the best interests of the species and the countries' economies. The Southern Africa Centre for Ivory Marketing has agreed a system for marking legally culled tusks: a self-adhesive strip with a hologram, plus a bar code and number. The hope is that illegal traders and poachers will be unable to copy the official hologram on poached ivory.

Renting a car at Kasane for a night or two at Serondella is more rewarding – if you have the cash – than staying in town and doing pricy game drives into the park. Serondella is on the old road from Kasane to Ngoma, the crossing point into Namibia. From this road there are several loops, through varied landscapes – down to the **flood plains**, into areas of **thicket**, or inland into **mopane forest**.

At the western end of Serondella, you can sit on the river bank and watch **elephants** drinking and frolicking a hundred metres away, but be on your guard and never get too close. If you're very lucky and patient, you could see some of the river's beautiful **otters**. For some curious reason, the airstrip near *Chobe Game Lodge* is a preferred spot for **lions** (perhaps because it provides them with a cleared area from which to watch game) and you can usually hear their chilling roars at night. **Baboons**, on the other hand, are the menacing louts of the animal world. They sometimes destroy tents left up during the day – the best tactic is to collapse your tent every morning and take everything with you in the car, if you don't want to return to find it ripped to shreds by these sharp-nailed rogues.

From Kasane to Savuti

From Kasane, there are two routes to choose from for the half-day, 4WD-only **drive to Savuti**. Leave early in the day, be entirely self-sufficient in fuel, water, food and spares, and remember you're in one of the wildest places in the world.

The shorter and more usual, though not especially scenic, route heads west on tar towards **Ngoma Bridge**, the border post with Namibia, with the *Buffalo Ridge* campsite close by (see p.303). There's then good gravel to the village of **Katchakau**, where the route turns south into the Chobe Forest Reserve. Here, the road deteriorates into thick sand ruts for the two-hour journey on to Savuti. Expect the whole journey to take four hours.

The alternative route via Nogatsaa, though it takes around six hours, has several advantages: the road is less sandy, and you'll see more game on the way. Crossing the depression during the rains, however, when the Mababe Depression's "black-cotton" soil is wet, is heavy going, if not impossible. It's another four or five hours to Maun from Savuti.

Nogatsaa, about 70km south of the Chobe River, is part of an extensive complex of pans set in forest which attracts herds of buffalo and elephant, particularly during the rainy season. There is no campsite but you could do it as a day trip from Kasane; it's game all the way on the two-hour stretch to Nogatsaa, and there's a hide overlooking a dam where you can spend a couple of hours.

The Nogatsaa region isn't as spectacular as the riverfront area, but you'll see antelope on the wide-open plains and, in clearings in the mopane woodlands near the pans, you may glimpse **oribi**. This is the only place these compact, dun-coloured antelope occur in Botswana. They live in small parties of two to five, in distinct territories, which the male marks out by rubbing glandular secretions on twigs and grass stems. You're most likely to see them in the early morning, when they're feeding. During the day, and when danger threatens, they lie quietly in tall grass or by a bush or rock.

After Nogatsaa Pans, the route runs parallel to the Ngwezumba River, which flows when rains are good; the Ngwezumba Dam near Tjinga is a fine place to watch elephant and buffalo.

Savuti and the Mababe Depression

Savuti is on the route of every four-wheel-drive expedition to Botswana, though it can be frighteningly dry and harsh, and there's been no water in the Savuti Channel for many years. During the rainy season, there's enough other water around to lure the game, but in drought years animals move off to more permanent water sources. Besides **camping and driving** around the **Mababe area**, you can fly in by light aircraft and stay at a **luxury bush camp**, usually as part of a package to Moremi and the Okavango Delta. And overland trips from Maun to the Chobe River and Victoria Falls invariably spend a night or two at Savuti.

Savuti lies within the **Mababe Depression**, a plain covered with grass and scattered bush, that was once the bed of the primeval lake that covered large parts of the Kalahari. If you've driven south to Savuti via Ngoma Bridge, you'll have crossed the **Magwikhwe Sand Ridge**, which curves across the track and then runs southwards, parallel to it. You'll also see the low sandy bank on your right as you head toward Maun. The ridge is believed to have formed the western shoreline of the former lake. Progress through the deep, soft sand around here is slow and bumpy.

The **Savuti Channel**, part of which runs through the campsite, periodically carries water over 100km from the Linyanti River through a gap in the Magwikhwe Sand Ridge, and spills it onto the floor of the depression, creating the small **Savuti Marsh**. Sometimes it's deep in water, other times cracked dry.

The ebb and flow of the Savuti Channel is something of a mystery. It doesn't flow as a matter of course and has been dry since before 1980. Connected as it is to the Linyanti (Chobe) River, it would seem to stand to reason that when the river's in flood its waters would push through and fill the channel. But as with other waterways in Botswana, nature conspires to confound logic. In some years of exceptional flood the channel has remained dry, and it seems that the flow has more to do with shifts beneath the earth's surface than the state of the waterways themselves. The caprice of the channel leaves its own scarring mark on the landscape. Trees that eagerly took root in the dry bed now stand gnarled and dead – drowned when the waters unexpectedly came flooding down.

The **Gubatsaa Hills** are Savuti's other notable geographical feature, just as intriguing as the channel. These dispersed, rocky outcrops have almost sheer northeastern faces formed by powerful waves crashing into them during the lake days. Sea-smoothed pebbles, rounded by the long-gone tides, can still be found on the lee side. On some of the hills there are rock paintings, not easy to find unless someone who knows directs you – ask one of the game scouts at Savuti camp.

The drama of the ancient lake is now replaced by a dazzling display of **wildlife**. Once the first rains have greened the yellow grass, and allayed the dust, magnificent stretches of grassland fringed with mopane woodland attract elephant, buffalo, wildebeest, impala, giraffe, tsessebe, hartebeest, kudu, warthog, jackal and zebra. When the water disappears on the marsh there is adequate grazing for some time, and when that has gone, many animals move off to the riverfront.

You can spot **prides of lions** on the plain until the grass grows long during the rains, hiding them. A lion research team, and an intrepid Englishwoman who crept around at night studying **hyenas**, are among the scientific groups to have spent time here.

Savuti accommodation

The name Savuti casts an almost mythical spell in the minds of seasoned Botswana veterans. Every one of them has a tale of a close shave with one animal or another and you're assured of some sort of wildlife action at the campsite. It really has the flavour of big-game country, not a place where you'd contemplate stumbling to the loo after dark.

Elephants stroll about the **campsite**, which is no more than a large unfenced area of bush along the Savuti Channel. There are rudimentary toilets and taps, which are regularly destroyed by thirsty elephants, who recently tore off the roof of the washing facilities to get at the water. Fresh fruit, particularly oranges, also bring out the mischievous element in elephant populations, so don't carry them with you and don't feed the elephants, no matter how appealing. A number have had to be shot because their appetite for citrus had them tusking open car boots.

Hyenas also do the rounds at the campsite every night. It's unnerving to hear them sniffing around the tent, inches from where you lie, but they won't bite through tents and they go away if you shout at them. **Baboons** are a more serious menace and, as at Serondella, will lay into tents in search of booty. You'll almost certainly be treated to the roars of lions in the distance too.

The highly recommended **luxury bush camp**, *Lloyd's Camp* (11 Glendower Place, Linksfield Rd, Edenvale, Johannesburg 1610; ☎011/453 7645–6, fax 453 7648; US$250 per person all in), is run by Lloyd Wilmot, one of the sons of Robert Wilmot, a legendary crocodile-hunter. It has a good hide from which you can watch animals coming to drink at very close quarters. Spotlights make for exciting nocturnal viewing as well.

travel details

Buses

Francistown to:

Bulawayo daily at 8.30am (3hr).

Gaborone daily at 7am & 10am (5hr).

Kasane, via Nata, 2 daily, in the mornings (5–6hr).

Lusaka 1 on Fri (16hr), stopping en route at Nata, Kasane, Kazungula (ferry crossing into Zambia), Livingstone, Kalomo, Choma, Monze and Mazabubuka.

Maun, via Nata, 3 daily, 7–9.30am (7hr).

Express minibus from Kasane to Victoria Falls *UTC* usually runs a daily trip between Victoria Falls and Kasane and back, but you need to book ahead to ensure it's running. It costs about US$30 one-way and takes 90min. You can pick it up at any of the Chobe lodges. Ring *UTC* at Victoria Falls (☎4267) to book.

Flights

All the scheduled flights listed below are on *Air Botswana*.

Francistown to:

Gaborone Mon, Wed & Fri (1hr 10min).

Johannesburg Mon, Wed & Fri (2hr).

Maun Mon, Wed & Fri (1hr 15min).

Kasane to:

Gaborone Mon, Thurs, Fri & Sun (2hr 55min).

Johannesburg, via Gaborone and Maun, Mon, Thurs, Fri & Sun (4hr).

Maun Mon, Thurs, Fri & Sun (40min).

Victoria Falls Fri & Sun (20min).

CHAPTER NINE

THE OKAVANGO DELTA

The country was one intricate labyrinth of swamp, with many small streams moving outward from the river into the sandy wastes of the southwest. Where all this water goes to is a mystery.

Aurel Schultz, explorer, 1897

The **Okavango River**, which rises in Angola, flows inland across 1300km of sands and never makes it to the sea. Instead it forms one of the largest inland deltas in the world, trapped between deep fault lines and imperceptibly dammed by rising land in the east. Most of the river's water evaporates on its way downstream, and on the fringes it seeps into the desert. The mighty river dies in a sandy trickle in the Kalahari.

The **Okavango Delta** is a luxuriant oasis in the desert – a place of lagoons, palm islands and secret waterways weaving through papyrus and water lilies. At the bottom of the clear waters are the white sands of the Kalahari Desert. On the edges of the Delta, once riverine trees give over to desert thorn and grass, it's hard to imagine you're so close to so much natural bounty.

The Delta alters its character seasonally – most people visit in the **dry season** (April–Oct) when the flood waters from the Okavango River have pushed through to the southernmost fingers. Up at the Panhandle (between the Caprivi Strip and the main delta) the water arrives two or three months earlier. The channels are at their lowest during the rainy season before the flood waters have come down from Angola.

On the southern edge lies **Maun**, Botswana's tourism capital and a convenient starting point for journeys to most places in the north. With a 4WD you can get to **Moremi Wildlife Reserve** on the eastern margin of the Delta, increasingly the preserve of princes, film stars and the very well-heeled. This is probably the best and wildest animal reserve in Southern Africa, one of the few set within untrammelled wilderness.

Several **onward options** from Maun are covered in this chapter. The northward route leads to the Delta's **Panhandle** and the **Tsodilo Hills**, then around the top through the **Caprivi Strip** to **Chobe**. Returning to Maun from Chobe, you come down through **Savuti** and Moremi, while travelling west takes you to the wild-west cattle ranching town of Ghanzi (see Chapter Ten) on the **road to Namibia**.

ACCOMMODATION PRICE CODES IN BOTSWANA

Most accommodation options in our account of Botswana have been given **price codes** to indicate the cost of a single night's lodging. The code for each establishment is based on the cost **per person sharing**; there is usually a supplement for a single person in a room. Prices for establishments that only offer all-inclusive rates (comprising meals, and perhaps guided tours and other services) have not been coded and are given in pula (per person per night).

① under P20	③ P40–60	⑤ P80–100	⑦ P120–140
② P20–40	④ P60–80	⑥ P100–120	⑧ P140–160

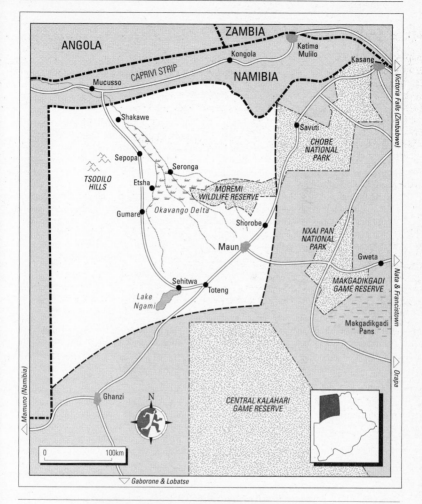

THE EASTERN DELTA

The papyrus-matted **eastern delta** is what most people mean when they talk about "Okavango". This is where most of the lodges are found, in the depths of the exciting island and waterway landscapes that positively teem with wildlife. The way in is through **Maun** – a dusty frontier town of hunters, safari operators and tourists, super-imposed on a sprawling traditional village which was the seat of the king of the Batawana (an offshoot of the main Tswana tribal grouping) for most of this century. It's simply not possible to go it alone in the swamps, but you'll find all the contacts you need for Delta travel in Maun.

The real heart of the Delta is **Moremi Wildlife Reserve**, an exclusive zone (which charges a daily fee of P50 per head) with one foot in the water and the other in savannah. It includes the two high-ground landmasses of **Chief's Island** to its west and the **Moremi Tongue** jutting out of the mainland to the east. Between the two is a changing landscape of both permanent and seasonal wetland that ebbs and flows with the Delta's waters. The contact of extreme drylands with the quenching Okavango gives Moremi the richest variety of habitats in Southern Africa, and access to it is both tightly controlled and bitterly fought over.

The road from Nata to Maun

Short of taking the cross-Chobe route (see Chapter Eight), most trips to Maun by road from Kasane in the north or from Francistown in the south, pass through **Nata** (see Chapter Eight). From here, the once notoriously rough Nata–Maun road, now tarred, hauls through 300km of desert plains and scrubland. The main **landscape** interest on this road is the gentle transition from dense bush and stunted trees to vast, open **grasslands** with tall, stately palms. Gweta (see p.296) is an access point for the **Makgadikgadi Pans** and the grasslands. Keep your eyes peeled for game as you make your way from Gweta to Maun; the road goes right through the gap between the boundaries of the Makgadikgadi Pans Game Reserve and Nxai Pan National Park (also covered in Chapter Eight) and you can regularly spot **giraffes**, **zebras**, **ostriches** and various **antelope** species. You also cross part of the **Pans complex** – a hostile white and grey skin of salty clay stretching to the horizon, where nothing grows.

Maun

MAUN (pronounce to rhyme with "town"), raw and remote, is the sort of place you reach with a sense of achievement. However, although you're finally at the edge of the Okavango Delta, don't be fooled by the maps; you're not in the swamps yet, and access can be expensive. Nevertheless you'll find everything you need here for the final push into the Okavango.

The town is small but sprawling. Straddling the Thamalakane River, it has grown around the traditional capital of the Batawana (a branch of the Batswana) that was first established here in 1915 (see box on p.314). The traditional village is still there and you're bound to see Herero women – relative newcomers from Namibia, who sought refuge among the Batawana – sweep the dust with their colourful bustled Victorian dresses. Superimposed on the original village, unfortunately without any apparent plan, and ever growing, is the main town.

You can't really speak of Maun having a "centre" and there are no street names. There are two shopping malls, with untethered goats and donkeys wandering about, and everything is stretched out along a three-kilometre strip between the malls. The busy airport, close to one mall, the *Ngami Centre*, lays some claim to being the heart of town, with most of the touring industry revolving round it. Four-wheel-drive vehicles roar back and forth, stocking up on supplies for long journeys, collecting tourists from the airport or going about government business. Beyond the airport, continuing east for 14km, you reach **Matlapaneng** on the **Thamalakane River**, effectively a suburb of Maun with the area's only affordable **accommodation** for travellers.

Maun's white residents value the town's **frontier image** – rough, tough, remote and hard-drinking. There was a time when you needed 4WD to drive through the town centre. These days there's a tarred road which allows people to roar in from places like Johannesburg; but 4WDs continue to predominate because once you're off the tar, you're on desert roads.

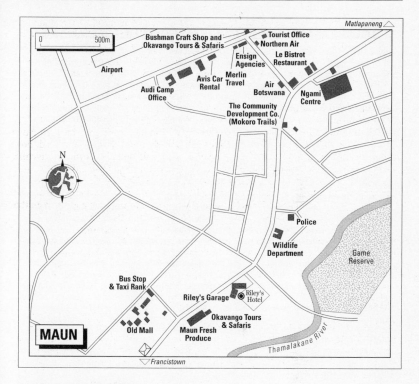

In-town practicalities

Although Maun's **airport** is the busiest in Botswana, it's small enough to bring you instantly into the heart of things. Everything to do with **tourism**, bar a few exceptions, clusters around the airport: **car rental**, **travel agents**, **air charter outfits**, and **curio shops**. You'll find a **bank** and **supermarket** nearby at the *Ngami Centre*. The **buses** from Francistown drop you off at the bus rank at the Old Mall, where you'll find the **post office** and more shops.

There are only two **places to stay** in Maun itself: *Riley's Hotel* and the *Sedia Hotel*. *Riley's*, opposite the Old Mall (PO Box 1, Maun; ☎260204; ⑦), has gone through innumerable changes since its original makeshift construction on the banks of the Thamalakane by the hunter Harry Riley. There's a great outdoor bar, in the garden alongside the swimming pool – an escape from Maun's omnipresent tar and sand – but the hotel is way too luxurious for ordinary travellers and is used mainly by expense-account business people. The *Sedia Hotel* (Private Bag 058, Maun; ☎/fax 660177; ⑤), just out of town on the Matlapaneng Road, is modern and boring, but it is at least cheaper, and allows camping in the garden.

Despite its isolation, Maun's **supermarkets** are well stocked, albeit with South African fruit, vegetables and dry goods. You'll find everything you need for a camping trip. The Mall is the best for meat and biltong, and has a couple of **takeaway** places. In the shopping area near the airport, you'll find *Steers* for steak and hamburgers, and *Le Bistrot*, a good place for lunch, with tables outside and a buzzing bar. The most popular

MAUN – TRADITIONAL CAPITAL OF THE BATAWANA

Since 1915, Maun has been the capital of the Batawana people. The Batawana are now one of the main Batswana groupings, having emerged through strife at the end of the eighteenth century, when they broke away from the Bangwato over a succession dispute.

The disagreement among the Bangwato arose when their king married out of the clan. The bride, who was merely a minor wife, had a son called Tawana. Trouble came when the king declared that Tawana was to be his successor, rather than Khama, the son of his principal wife. The clan split and, following an attack on Tawana by Khama, the king took Tawana away on a migration. After wandering for some years the king took his leave to return home, leaving the breakaway band under his son's leadership and the tribe became known as the Batawana.

During their migrations the Batawana intermarried with other tribes and so managed to swell their numbers. Around 1824 they settled on the banks of Lake Ngami gathering strength and building a powerful state and military force, which dominated the other people of the region: the Bangologa, Bayei and San. In 1830, now under Moremi I, they moved on to escape the marauding Bakololo, who were sweeping north from South Africa. The Bakololo pursued and eventually caught up with the fleeing Batawana on the Linyanti River, surrounding them and taking them as captives to the Chobe River. After a few years the dispossessed Batawana escaped, and eventually managed to re-establish themselves and to rebuild their cattle herds.

Their recovery was impressive. By the mid-nineteenth century the Batawana had forged an effective state that stretched across northern Botswana and extended as far south as Ghanzi. They established their capital at Maun in 1915. The settlement developed along traditional Tswana lines – it became enormous by absorbing foreigners, who were incorporated in geographically distinct wards. You can still pick out the customary organization. In its clearest form, the adobe huts were arranged around courtyards, at the centre of which was the ruling family. Further out were the wards of the Batswana who had split off from other groups and people from other tribes like the Herero and Mbukushu were on the very outskirts. The San were outcasts, not allowed to live in the village unless as servants. Those who chose the settled life had their own separate villages within the orbit of the main settlement.

Patterns are gradually changing. The government is attempting to raise the status of the San and there are some concessions to modern building methods. On mud hut walls in Maun, you can see a kind of "appropriate technology", though, with the shiny ends of beer cans decoratively poking through, where they've been put to good use as infilling.

nightspot, though it also does lunches, is the *Sports Bar and Restaurant*, 6km from Maun on the main road north to Matlapaneng. The food is good and the bar is especially lively at the weekend.

Matlapaneng lodges

All the **affordable accommodation** within reach of Maun is downstream on the Thamalakane River at **MATLAPANENG** – an area which was teeming with game twenty years ago, now long vanished. There's no public transport; but the lodges will collect you from the airport for a reasonable fee.

Some 12km from town, on a tarred road, the lodges and camping sites all have bars and food available. Upstream of Matlapaneng, two lodges and a backpackers' camp cluster along the waterway, paradoxically dry in the rainy season before the flood waters come down. There's little choice pricewise between the lodges; you can expect to pay around P140 for a single room, P165 for a double; *Audi Camp*, the backpackers' place, is the cheapest. Camping costs from P12 per person wherever you go. The lodges, although thoroughly pleasant, are only points of passage, the real destination being the Delta. Some, however, run packages into the Delta that are in fact the cheapest way of penetrating into the exclusive waters.

Audi Camp, Private Bag 28, Maun (☎660599, fax 660581). Camping site with friendly management and clean, beautiful swimming pool. Bar and meals provided. If you don't have your own tent, there are two-person tents and mattresses already erected (P30). The camp organizes the only budget trips into Moremi, the Panhandle and Tsodilo, and like the other lodges does reasonable Delta packages. It's good and cheap, and full of backpackers.

Crocodile Camp, PO Box 46, Maun (☎660265, fax 660793). The camping sites here, which must be booked in advance, are away from the river and inside a fence – safe, but unappealing. The chalets are pleasant and it's generally a relaxing place. Rates do not include meals, though all meals can be catered for. Motorboats or canoes with a poler can be hired. The Camp organizes de luxe mobile safaris into the Delta, using its own tented camp, as well as safaris into other parts of Botswana, Namibia, Zimbabwe and Malawi (from P77.50 per person per night).

Island Safari Lodge, PO Box 116, Maun (☎/fax 660300). Most popular of the lodges with friendly owners, the nicest setting and chalets. Prices are similar to *Crocodile's*, though *Island*'s rate includes an excellent breakfast. Children under 16 stay for free if they're sharing. There's a swimming pool and boat hire. The lodge hires safari vehicles with a driver, does trips into the Delta and also countrywide tours. The campsite is used extensively by overland companies and you should always carry your valuables with you, as the campsite is sometimes vulnerable to local forays.

Entertainment

Entertainment in Maun comes down to **drinking**, which goes on not only in town but at the Matlapaneng lodges, at some of which it is pursued as an acrobatic fine art. One lodge has guests climbing a pole in the middle of the bar and drinking beers whilst doing handstands. Their unmissable speciality is the *upside-down marguerita* (shaken not stirred). The volunteer leans back on the bar, face up, mouth open, while an assortment of hooch, including tequila, is funnelled in at the same time as the barman vibrates the victim's head. They also have relatively normal darts evenings. *The Sports Bar*, between town and the lodges, is the hottest drinking spot on Fridays and Saturdays.

During the day – when there's water – you can rent canoes or pedalos at *Island Safari Lodge* to take a leisurely trip down the still, clear and lily-padded river. Lazing beside the swimming pool is a less energetic option. If you want to cross from one lodge to the other there's an informal ferry . Just wait at the water's edge and someone will be along to ferry you across.

Transport: Landrovers and planes

Remote as it is, Maun is nevertheless the focus for most travel in Botswana. One consequence of its isolation is that modes of transport are strictly limited: four-wheel drive, boat or air.

Self-drive vehicles, notably **Landrovers**, can be rented at *Avis* for adventurous travel into the northern game parks and pans, up to Shakawe or westwards to Ghanzi – all of which are conceivably hitchable but will require some lengthy roadside waits. **Plane charter** isn't as expensive as you'd expect, but can be difficult to arrange in the high season without prior booking. In low season the charter companies are more flexible about taking you to places like Tsodilo and waiting while you look round, as long as they haven't got queues of clients gathering back in Maun. Five-seater planes can be chartered, which is a real option if there's a group of you, for a trip to the Tsodilo Hills. Enquire at *Northern Air* (PO Box 40; ☎660385), *Aer Kavango* (PO Box 169; ☎660393) and *Merlin Services* (see "Travel agents" in the listings below), who have offices around the airport. These companies also run charter flights to Gaborone, Kasane, Victoria Falls and Johannesburg – much cheaper than the regular services but not as frequent.

These air charter companies also arrange **game flights**, offering the chance to see the Delta from above – a memorable vision, but one you'll be rewarded with anyway if you're flying into one of the Delta's camps. From the air, you see the rich patchwork of green and brown ink-blot islands. Spiked with upright palms, their dense green centres bleach out to sandy rings which seep into the water. From the air too, you may see large herds of game scattering away. For **lifts or sharers for a plane charter**, leave messages on the noticeboard at *Maun Fresh Produce*, on the main road next to *Okavango Tours and Safaris*, or the noticeboard at *Le Bistrot*.

Listings

Air Botswana ☎660391. Situated on the airport turn-off, in a stand-alone thatched building on your left.

Banks *Standard Chartered* and *Barclays* are both just southwest of the Mall and are potluck as far as queues go (both open Mon–Fri 8.15am–12.45pm, Sat 8.15–10.45am).

Books *Botswana Book Centre*, in the Mall, has a small selection of books about the country and a few novels.

Camping equipment rental *Kalahari Canvas* parallel to the runway just outside the airport perimeter fence.

Car rental *Avis* are at the end of the left branch just before the airport, next to *Kalahari Canvas* camping shop (Box 130, Maun; ☎660570).

Chemist *Okavango Pharmacy*, Old Mall and on main road near Ngami Centre, can dispense prescriptions and sells the usual chemist's stuff (☎660043).

Curios Best places are *General Trading Company*, opposite the Mall, and *Bushman Craft Shop*, just outside the airport.

Dentist Dr Eric Jorgensen, Top Floor, Roots Tower, the Mall (☎661023).

Doctor Dr Jourdan (☎660482).

Garage *Riley's Garage and Service Station* near the hotel.

Hospital 2km along the main Ghanzi road.

Immigration is in one of the lone buildings on your right as you head toward Matlapaneng, 1km before the airport turn-off.

Newspapers Stationers at the Mall.

Police Located in one of the buildings near Immigration, heading for Matlapaneng on the right just before the airport turn-off.

Post office Along the main road in front of the Mall slightly toward Francistown (Mon–Fri 8.15am–1pm & 2.15–4pm, Sat 8.30–11.30am).

Photographic Available from curio shops (see above).

Travel agents For bookings into the Delta, *Travel Wild* at the airport (PO Box 236, Maun; ☎660493) are probably the most helpful. *Okavango Tours and Safaris* (PO Box 39, Maun; ☎660220 or 660339), opposite the Mall or at the airport, are efficient. *Merlin Travel* (PO Box 13, Maun; ☎660635), opposite the airport, is helpful and can book most things.

Into the Delta

Although the **OKAVANGO DELTA** looks like a large lake on the map, it is in fact the most complex of mazes – channels twisting and turning in on themselves through the thick wetland vegetation, some rejoining main river channels, others coming to a dead end of matted papyrus as far as the eye can tell.

The archetypal Okavango, of islands, lagoons and secret waterways, is the eastern Delta, incorporating the eastern sanctuary of Moremi Wildlife Reserve which straddles both wet and dry terrain (see below). Due to the sizeable **park entrance fees**, however, budget travellers are often forced to satisfy themselves with the region outside Moremi's boundaries. The cheapest deals can get you as far as the borders of

Moremi, north of Maun, which have a very similar geography and vegetation to the reserve itself.

Up in the far north, where the Okavango River enters Botswana as a wide, strong river is the area known as the Panhandle. Here, close to the border with Namibia, are a number of **fishing camps**. These are mostly in the luxury class, but at least two (both of which offer camping) are moderately priced (see below). Along the remote west bank of the Okavango River, you'll still find traditional villages, in an exotic region of palm trees and thick riverine vegetation, reachable from the road (now tarred) to **Shakawe** and Namibia's **Caprivi Strip**. This region also has the welcome addition of a reasonably priced lodge, with camping facilities, near **Etsha.**

Shifting sands: Delta geology

The stillness of the slow-flowing Okavango Delta (a one-in-several-thousand gradient) masks a turbulent character beneath the deep sands over which it drifts. Not only does the Delta change with the seasons, its level varying as the flood waters come down from Angola, but it's also **geologically unstable**, its base shifting, twisting and turning, constantly but imperceptibly.

The region also suffers **earthquakes** – 38 minor ones in one ten-year period – which have brought frequent dramatic changes to the Delta's shape. Channels open and close, one suddenly becoming dry as another bursts forth. One large tremor in Maun in 1952 restored the flow of the bone-dry Boro River. Over the last century these movements have caused the Delta's boundaries to shift over 100km. You can tell this from the distribution of **papyrus** and **palms**. Papyrus is fast-growing and quickly establishes itself where conditions are suitable, whereas the phoenix palm grows much more slowly. Whenever the swamp extends, papyrus marks the new map until the palm catches up. The limits of the two plants are 150km further south than the current perennial swamp on the Thaoge River, while on the Ng-gokha River, the papyrus growth far outstrips that of the palm indicating that the eastern extent of the swamp is recent.

Behind these mysterious shifts and changes lies a deep and ancient past. Long ago, some experts believe, when the Kalahari was wetter and the rocky plate at its base was tilted differently, the Okavango River drained into the Limpopo, which flowed into the Indian Ocean. At this time, much of northern Botswana was flooded by a **super-lake**. As the lake silted up, sedimentation led to the current drainage patterns, and the Delta was left behind as a remnant.

"Wasted waters"

Okavango is now regarded as one of the world's great wildernesses, but it wasn't always so. As recently as 1955 it was described as a useless swamp by one J. H. Wellington, who proposed its wasted waters be turned to transforming it "into one of the richest gardens in Africa". He planned to throw up a mud dyke, the considerable distance from Sepopa to Chief's Island, in order to drain about 12,000 square kilometres to the southeast, which would be farmed.

Before that, **Cecil Rhodes**, too, had his eye on the swamps as a block in his great empire-building schemes. Convinced that Ngamiland was rich in diamonds and minerals – a belief that proved correct after Independence, when diamonds were found at Orapa – Rhodes planned to settle the swamp area with Boer families who would farm it using the plentiful supply of water. But the British government was reluctant to get involved with Okavango, which they saw as a watery wasteland that would be an administrative liability. Placing people in Ghanzi, on the border of Namibia, to nip any German expansion in the bud, seemed a far better investment.

The Delta has remained a contentious issue ever since, with some outlandish proposals to utilize its seemingly **wasted waters**. In a country that suffers badly from low

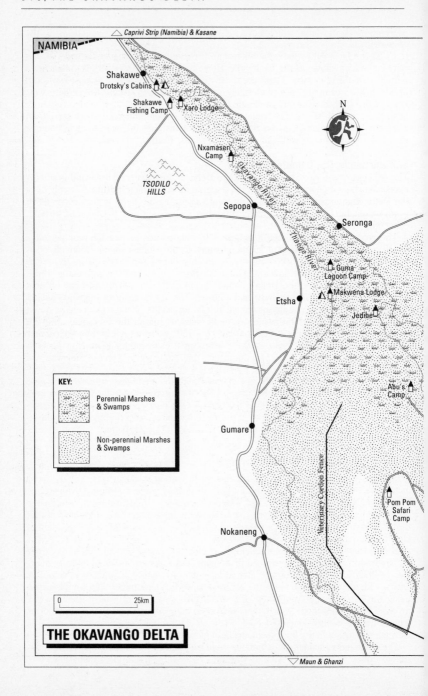

THE OKAVANGO DELTA

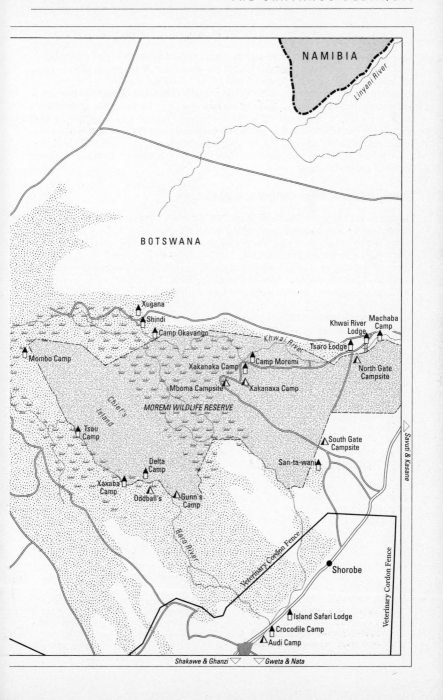

rainfall, the water promises to be a wonderful resource for farming and mining. There are demands for water from nearby Maun, which has no permanent supply – the water runs out in the taps occasionally – and the Orapa diamond mine, a big currency-earner, is looking for more water. Irrigable land in the west could be utilized to provide great self-sufficiency in crops. The Eastern Corridor, too, needs far more water.

But tapping off the waters is liable to create major **ecological changes** in the region and international conservation agencies are lobbying for protection of the wetland habitat. If it goes, they argue, so will some endangered species and thousands of wild animals and birds. Already cattle are encroaching and tsetse fly-spraying has had undesirable effects on the ecology. The veterinary **cordon fence**, passing across the southern edge of the Delta, just north of Maun, marks the present boundary between domestic and wild animals.

Some practicalities: camps and packages

It's easy to get lost in the Okavango Delta. Not just in the mazes of islands and papyrus; negotiating the tour operators, and trying to get what you want without facing bankruptcy can be equally confusing. There's virtually no way of getting onto the waters on your own, so, to set out into the Delta, you'll have to go on some kind of **package**. Although booking well ahead ensures a place, you can usually organize something from Maun, which, together with Matlapaneng, is the hopping-off point for most of Okavango's camps and *mokoro* packages. Beware, however, of local operators making a quick buck out of this. There are reports of unsuspecting or ill-informed travellers being taken into areas outside of Moremi by ill-equipped and largely ignorant guides, where not only are there no controls over littering and general environmental degrada

---

PEOPLE OF THE WATERS

The first people of the waters were the **Banoka** – sometimes called the River Bushmen – of whose origins little is known. The **Mbukushu** and **Bayei**, who arrived in the area in the eighteenth century, appear to be fairly closely related, both being adept wetland farmers and fishermen with the unusual matrilineal system of a chief's succession passing on to his eldest sister's son.

From oral traditions it's reckoned they were living in close proximity around the seventeenth century. Both made similar **migrations** from central Africa and in recent times fled southwards to escape the tyranny of Lozi conquest on the Zambian side of the Zambezi Valley. By 1800 the Bayei appear to have moved into Okavango and to have surrounded the delta. The Mbukushu, too, fled from the expanding borders of the Lozi first to the Kuando River, dividing Botswana from Caprivi, then westwards to Andara on the Okavango River, just south of Angola.

Things in Andara were no better and possibly worse. **Mambari traders** (sons of Portuguese men and African women) arrived on the quest for ivory and Mbukushu leaders began selling their own people as slaves. The subjects got fed up and left their leaders, paddling down the Okavango River until they arrived around the panhandle area of the Delta, where most still live today. **Mekoro** remain the means of getting around on water, poling (like punting) in the shallows, and paddling where the water is deep, in the panhandle area.

The Mbukushu were more reliant on **farming** than the predominantly fishing Bayei, their methods better suited to the deep waters, where they could plant on river banks without the floods rising to spread over the plains. They continue to till the alluvial soils deposited in flood zones, planting, as the waters recede, sorghum, millet, maize and cane in the wet earth. Mbukushu **architecture** is unusual in the use of rectangular rather

tion but where there's little or no game. The **fees** to enter Moremi were raised sharply a few years ago in an attempt to cut down the number of visitors and minimize destruction of the environment. In practice, however, the effect seems to have been that the ecological danger has been shifted out of the parks and into areas where there is no jurisdiction at all.

There are no **bargain deals** into Okavango. You won't get away spending much under P200 for two or three days in a *mokoro*, and even this won't get you deep into the really desirable regions. For this kind of money, you'll be transferred from the lodges in Matlapaneng to the Delta's edge in a 4WD vehicle or a powerboat, and from there be poled around the Delta north of Maun. This gives a good feel of Okavango, although it's not the ideal way to get the most out of your visit; the game viewing is a far cry from the sights inside Moremi Wildlife Reserve, though game in September and October can be very good. You will, however, be spared the stiff fees to enter and camp in the Moremi.

Moremi – the ultimate destination – is geared mainly towards the well-off. It incorporates the large **Chief's Island** and **Moremi Tongue**, which has the advantage of both wetland and dryland habitats, and hence attracts a large variety of game. There are two **low-budget options**: the popular *Oddballs Camp* and *Gunn's Camp*, self-catering outfits geared mainly for campers. The usual scheme of things is to base yourself at the camp (in a tent), whence you hire a *mokoro* to spend several days on the water, camping on islands. *Oddballs* gives you the choice of camping outside the reserve to save paying the Moremi Reserve camping fee, but you will still have to pay the P50 daily Moremi entry fee, on top of your *mokoro* trip. All the other places in Moremi are **luxury camps**, with tariffs that include all meals, all *mokoro* trips and at the dryland camps all game drives. They average P700 per day.

---

than round buildings surrounded by high reed fences. The women are justly renowned for their fine **basketry**.

In the past Mbukushu chiefs were great **rain-makers**. So widespread was their reputation that distant rulers paid handsome tributes for the benefit of their services. Their use of child sacrifice in rain ceremonies and the involvement of the Mbukushu kings in slaving are said – understandably – to have been major factors in precipitating the departure of their subjects. When the migrating Mbukushu arrived in Botswana they brought their fame for opening the skies with them. The custom of sending tribute for rain-making was taken up by the Bayei and continued by the Batawana in the early nineteenth century, once they had penetrated the northern delta.

The **Bayei** are flood-plain farmers who excel at **fishing and hunting** – far more important to their subsistence than for the Mbukushu. Bayei hunters developed elaborate methods for catching fish and game, particularly hippo, the meat of which was a great delicacy. Two methods were used for **hippo hunting**. The more inventive used a spear weighted with rocks and triggered by a tripwire. The more dangerous involved floating down the river into a herd and harpooning the animals, a rope attached to the weapon then being tied to a tree. Once the struggling animal had exhausted itself the hunters would move in for the kill.

When the **Batawana** arrived in the delta, toward the middle of the last century, they conquered the Bayei and forced them into servitude. The vanquished Bayei, who'd previously lived only in small groups, began to adopt the lifestyle of their masters and are now found in large villages, where many raise cattle. The Mbukushu were less affected by contact with the Batawana, but colonialism brought changes to the whole region, probably the most significant being migration to the great economic magnet of Southern Africa: the Johannesburg gold **mines**. The mines had recruitment agencies deep in the bush, flying out new workers. Many men still work on the mines while a number of people are employed in tourism – as polers, bush guides, cooks, cleaners and hunting safari attendants.

OKAVANGO HORSE SAFARIS *Call*

If you ride, one of the most thrilling ways to explore the Delta is on **horseback**. Safaris run between March and September for an average of six days. Rated as one of Africa's top riding safaris, trips are generally booked out well in advance, so plan well ahead. Only proficient riders are accepted. Children are welcome as long as they have passed a pony club riding test. The longest trip lasts ten days and you move to a different camp every three nights. Trips cost US$225 per person per day. Book through *Okavango Horse Safaris*, Private Bag 23, Maun (☎/fax 660493).

The cheapest options: skirting the fringes

Audi Camp, Private Bag 28, Maun (☎660599, fax 660581), behind *Conservation International* opposite the airport. Offers a comprehensive range of no-frills camping trips into Okavango fringes and Moremi. Recommended.

The Community Development Co, Property First Complex, Main Rd, near the airport (☎/fax 661225). Offers basic trips into similar areas as the other budget operations. Each canoe, carrying two people, has a poler who takes you onto the waterways. It is the cheapest of the lot, and what you pay goes directly to the poler, not to a business.

Island Safari Lodge, PO Box 116, Maun (☎/fax 660300). Based just outside Moremi. You are taken by powerboat or land cruiser to the edge of Moremi, where you set off on a canoe with a poler for a few days' camping.

Medium-priced options

Crocodile Camp Expeditions, one of the Matlapaneng lodges (see Maun "Listings"). This place rents out *mekoro*, as well as more upmarket with overland or motorboat mobile safaris in Moremi that provide meals and accommodation. Rates are on a sliding scale depending on number of people – the more clients the cheaper the rate per head.

Gunn's Campsite, on Ntswi Island. Prices comparable to *Oddballs*, with *mokoro* trips, camping in the bush. Transfers are by air. Facilities include a bar, store and the rental of camping equipment, but there's no restaurant. It's much quieter and smaller, without the social scene of *Oddballs*, and just as pretty. Book through *Gunn's* Maun office, opposite the airport (☎660023, fax 660040).

Oddballs, on Noga Island. The other so-called "budget" camp in the Moremi area, and only accessible by air. It has developed a reputation as the trendy young place in the Delta – easy-going, sociable and friendly. It's principally a camping place, though there is a terrific – though dearer – tree house and a reed chalet if you don't fancy camping. A P550 camping package gives you five nights in the Delta, with at least three out of camp in the bush with a guide, plus a return flight from Maun to the Delta, *mokoro* and guide hire, and three nights Park fees. Food and alcohol is not included. Facilities at the camp include home-cooked meals (vegetarians do well), an expensive bar, a small store selling tins and renting out camping equipment (you will probably have to rent stuff unless your own is ultra-lightweight, as there's a 10-kg baggage allowance on the flight). Book through *Okavango Tours and Safaris* in Maun or London.

The luxury camps

If you're after something more luxurious in Moremi, you have to be prepared to pay for it, with minimum inclusive prices upwards of P650 per person per day in the low season (Jan–June), P750 in the high (July–Dec). The **lodges** are comfortable, bush-camp style with a limited number of guests. For the price, you can expect food, drink and activities (game drives, *mokoro* outings or walks) to be included and you'll be hosted and taken good care of. Flights from Maun are usually extra. All have single supplements.

Above all you're unlikely to be disappointed if you do decide to go for this option. Some camps are plusher than others, but all are beautifully set in the Delta. Depending on whether they're land or wetland camps, the emphasis is on game drives or getting onto the water. They offer similar basics: game viewing, birdwatching, boating of some kind and usually fishing. There are several safari operators, usually offering a combination of land or wetland camps, some offering packages that take in several camps with a variety of terrain. A typical minimum stay in the Delta would cost P1900 per person, for three nights, including flights from Maun into the Delta, flights between camps, game park fees, food and accommodation. All are bookable through travel agents in Europe or North America, but you could save yourself a lot by booking directly. None of the camps caters for casual drop-ins and all must be booked in advance. Many are closed during January and February.

Abu Camp Box 40, Maun (☎660211). The Delta's most expensive camp, with activities that centre on riding African elephants – the first place to offer elephant-back safaris in Africa. A five-night package starts at US$4500 per person.

Camp Okavango (*Desert and Delta Safaris*). Silver tea service caps the luxury style, with *mekoro* trips and plenty of birdlife.

Camp Moremi (*Desert and Delta Safaris*). Mozart, waiters in black ties, crystal glasses and stilted conversation. Gorgeous tree-top dining room and big game.

Delta Camp (*Okavango Tours and Safaris*). One of the oldest of the luxury camps, relaxed and beautiful, in the permanent swamp waters. Days centre around guided walks and *mekoro* outings or there's the more adventurous option of going out with a poler on a *mokoro* and camping, with a fair bit of style, in the bush.

Gunn's Camp (*Gunn's* ☎660023, fax 660040)). The only camp at a medium price (P450 per person) in a good area, with walks and *mokoro* trips, but lacking the flair and elegant bush comfort of the others.

Jedibe Island Camp (*Wilderness Safaris*). Tented camp, just east of the Panhandle, in the best fishing area in the Delta. Sitatunga and red lechwe country. There are no motor vehicles on the island which means getting around on foot or *mekoro*.

Khwai River Lodge (*Gametrackers*). Near the North Gate in Moremi, with self-contained brick and thatch chalets. Game – especially elephants and (resident) hippos – can be viewed from the grounds. Accessible by road, maximum 24 guests.

Machaba Camp (*Ker Downey Selby*). A maximum of 12 guests in excellent game-viewing country sited on a 3200-square-kilometre concession adjacent to Moremi.

Mombo Camp (*Wilderness Safaris*). On the border of Moremi in the heart of the Delta, in an area of wide expansive plains with all the big game you could wish for. It's primarily a land camp with 4WD game drives. Maximum 16 guests.

Pom Pom Safari Camp (*Ker Downey Selby*). A tented camp in one of the remotest spots in Okavango, with both game drives and water trips.

DELTA SAFARI OPERATORS

Desert and Delta Safaris, Private Bag 10, Maun (☎66056). Their camps are top of the range, in terms of luxury and price.

Gametrackers, 1st Floor, 137b Sandton Terraces, Eleventh St, Parkmore, Johannesburg 2196, South Africa (☎011/884 2504; fax 011/884 3159). London office: c/o *Orient Express*, 20 Upper Ground, London SE1, UK (☎0171/620 0003). Good all-rounders with several camps.

Hartleys Safaris, Box 69859, Bryanston 2021, Johannesburg, South Africa (☎011/708 1893–5, fax 011/708 1569).

Ker Downey Selby, PO Box 40, Maun (☎260211). London office: 14 Old Bond St, London W1X 3DB, UK (☎0171/629 2044).

Okavango Explorations, Private Bag 48, Maun (☎260528).

Okavango Tours & Safaris, PO Box 39, Maun (☎260220). London office: 28 Bisham Gardens, London N6 6DD, UK (☎0181/341 9442, fax 0181/348 9983). An excellent choice if you are planning a trip from the UK. They sell their own, recommended camps, as well as being a more general agent.

Wilderness Safaris, PO Box 651171, Benmore 2010, South Africa (☎011/8841458, fax 011/883 6255).

GETTING THE MOST FROM THE DELTA

Although the luxury lodges are highly recommended if you can afford them, the best way fully to experience **Okavango** remains the traditional one. That is, to get into the depths of the wilderness by going out on a *mokoro* for several days. You should take the Okavango as slowly as you possibly can. People who fly in for a night and out the next day are usually disappointed – and are wasting their money. We suggest an absolute minimum of two nights **camping** in the Delta. It is a unique and special place and it takes a while to synchronize with its rhythms.

What you get out of your *mokoro* expedition depends firstly on yourself, and secondly on your poler. *Your* effort and enthusiasm are vital. If you know what you want, are enthusiastic and are prepared to make an effort you stand a good chance of having a wonderful time – and one that begins to touch the essence of the Delta.

Do not regard your poler as simply a taxi driver. His familiarity with the waterways, his abilities at manoeuvring the craft and his knowledge of fauna and flora make you completely dependent on him. The greater the rapport you develop the more you'll see and learn. As far as **tasks** go, polers are expected to **pole**, to take you on game-viewing **walks** and to find an island to **camp** on at night. They may well do more, such as cooking, fishing or making coffee in the morning. These are extras and you should reciprocate by sharing your food, or in some such way as tipping.

Some aficionados suggest throwing yourself headlong into the experience by taking the minimum of food – a little maize meal – and relying on the fruits of the Delta. You eat the fish you catch, and gather wild foods with your poler – delicacies like palm nuts, water lilies and honey. But this is strictly for the hardy, must be arranged beforehand and you should offer your poler a decent tip.

San-ta-wani (*Gametrackers*). Moremi, South Gate area. More of a land camp with excellent game viewing on flood plains, palm-covered islands, riparian bush and mopane veld. It takes its name from a Khoi mythical animal. Brick-built African-style huts house a maximum of 16 guests.

Shinde (*Ker Downey Selby*). A camp on an island with fine birdwatching and fishing.

Tsaro Lodge (*Hartleys Safaris*). On the banks of the Khwai River, 160km by road from Maun (or a short flight), just outside the North Gate entrance to Moremi. Game walks and drives are on offer and there's a swimming pool. Thatched bungalows accommodate a maximum of 16 people.

Tsau Camp (*Wilderness Safaris*). Situated in the deep, permanent waters of the Delta. Activities centre on *mokoro* excursions.

Xaxaba Camp (*Gametrackers*). Reed chalets amongst big shady trees on Chief's Island, with walking, boating, fishing and a swimming pool. Maximum 24 guests.

Xakanaxa Camp (*Moremi Safaris*). Tented camp accommodating a maximum of 12 in a large grove of old trees at the beautiful Xakanaxa Lagoon. The Xobega and Godikwe lagoons are a couple of hours by motorboat, with large heronries on the way. There are also game drives through Moremi's ancient forests.

Xugana (*Hartleys Safaris*). On one of the largest lagoons and loveliest settings in Okavango, with a beautiful, natural swimming pool. Angling for tiger fish is one of the attractions and tackle is available. A good bet for photographic tours with chances to see some rare birds and the sitatunga antelope. This was Prince Charles' choice during his 1984 stay in Okavango.

Animal, vegetable and mineral: what to look for in the Delta

When you're in the middle of it, **Okavango** seems an impenetrable jungle of papyrus, rising dense from the waters and reaching fine brush-like ends into the air. In the major channels the flow is fast enough to inhibit the establishment of aquatic plants and it's through these that experienced navigators steer their craft. Getting lost is easy but people have been living in these waters for centuries. Their esoteric knowledge of

SOME PRACTICAL TIPS

• **Don't rush off into the Delta**. Spending a couple of days in Maun, just relaxing and talking to people who have come back from the Delta, is an investment that will pay dividends. Get an idea of what is available, what people did there and what's going to suit you. This will give you an idea of which operator to go for.

• **Find out which polers gave people a good service**, and which camp they work from. Seek them out and ask to go out with them.

• **Fly to your Delta camp**. It's not much more expensive than boating in, and you get a superb overview of Okavango; and you'll have plenty of time on the water once you go out in a *mokoro*. There's a 10-kg baggage allowance, however; leave tents and heavy items in Maun (booking agents will look after it) to make space for food supplies.

• **Buy supplies in Maun**. Prices are inflated inside the Delta. Maize meal, packet soups, rice and tinned foods are convenient. Don't forget matches and a torch.

• **Find out whether your poler is provided with rations** before you leave Maun. If in doubt assume that you'll be feeding him and take enough food for the trip.

• **Spend at least a night at the camp** before launching out into the waters, to give yourself a chance to adjust to the environment.

• **Don't swim without asking**; most places are too risky for swimming. If you want a dip say so, and you can be taken to safe shallow waters.

• **Be prepared to walk to see game**. Most animals are likely to be on the islands and dry areas. It requires some effort to see them, but you'll probably welcome a chance to stretch your legs.

• **Sleep under a mosquito net**. Leave your tent behind, it's bulky and unnecessary out of the rainy season.

routes is something you'll come to appreciate: channels come and go and a few hours floating merges it all into a seamless vision of waterways, weeds and islands. Some channels are so narrow you feel you're heading straight into the weeds as plants spring back to brush past your face, but you finally break through into another channel or a lagoon.

The **lagoons** or *madiba* (singular: *lediba*) are relatively fixed features of Okavango. These large and beautiful expanses of open water, often isolated from the main river routes, are frequently the sites for lodges. It's hard to avoid feeling as though you're in an illustration in a coffee-table book in this stillness and isolation, where the surrounding forests are perfectly reflected on glassy water.

In contrast, many of the **islands** are there only during low water, often raised above the surrounding waters by a fraction of a metre. Sometimes you'll find yourself poled across a lake that a few months previously was savannah grazed by antelope. On the higher islands (those that still hold back the enclosing flood waters) you can hop off for a picnic or camp for the night. Many islands are no more than termite mounds, often only large enough for a single tree.

It's on the **permanent drylands** and islands that you get huge **trees** and an incredible variety of animal species. From your low angle of vision in the *mokoro*, the only indications of the islands dotted about are the towering boughs. **Hyphaene palm savannah** is one of the common land features in the Delta's depths. Often you'll find antelope grazing in open grasslands surrounded by thick forest – the palms dominating. Some of the forests have a deepest-Africa feel and can be slightly unnerving till you break through to more open, sunnier country. A common sight in the damp woods is the serpentine embrace of the strangler fig webbing itself around a host tree. Ninety percent of all trees in Moremi are mopane. You'll also see rain trees which are a mass of pink blossoms in the spring, combretum bush willows (lead wood), African ebony or jackal berry, wild fig, and near North Gate, camel thorn.

Mekoro are hewn from ancient trees in these forests. Large trunked wild ebony is a favourite, specimens between one and five centuries old being used. These craft have been used by the Bayei on the Delta since the middle of the eighteenth century. With their rounded hulls they require quite some skill to balance and manoeuvre. Sitting low in the water the dugouts sway wildly every time you move and it's not a little hair-raising at first. But with experience, you get the hang of being a passenger and take cheer from the rhythmic confidence of the skilled **polers** who have not only to pole, but to balance standing up as well. Be warned, though, that all *mekoro* leak – you will end up sitting in a puddle unless a seat has been provided (standard practice at the luxury lodges).

Although the mirror-still surface is deceptively tranquil, this is still wild Africa. Beneath the delicate waxy **lilies** in all their pale pinks, mauves, blues and whites, are **crocs and hippos**. At one time the swamps were a crocodile hunters' free-for-all and it's reckoned that as many as 20,000 may have been shot in a fifteen-year period. The big two crocodile killers are said to have divided the Delta between them in the late 1950s and 1960s and to have taken every one of the reptiles they came across. One of them, Bobby Wilmot, died from a black mamba bite in the swamps.

Crocodiles notwithstanding, local children wade through the water collecting the rhizome, stems and flowers of **water lilies**. The rhizome and lower stem are roasted (six make a good meal for an adult), while the flower is eaten raw and is used to flavour porridge. During drought, people crack open dry stems of papyrus reeds to chew the sweet pith; it tastes rather like sugar cane.

Keep your eyes open along the water's edge and you may see the leguaans or **water monitors** – large dragon-like lizards whose terrifying looks are all show. They skirt between wet and dry, scavenging for birds' eggs, chicks and anything they can catch.

Delta species

The variety of habitats thrown together produces a wide spectrum of game – 114 species of large mammal. The actual numbers that can be supported by the delicate ecosystem, however, are relatively few. In fact if you're simply after game your visit to Okavango could prove a disappointment – especially if you don't move far from Maun.

As elsewhere, the **dry season** is best for game-viewing and the variations in game from season to season are enormous. Some species, like sable antelope, increase their numbers nearly thirtyfold from their nucleus of only a hundred in the wet season. Nomadic elephants, too, converge here in increased numbers in the dry season. Elephants are mainly seen in the Moremi Tongue between Third Bridge, Xakanaxa and Hippo Pool on the Khwai River. Other species are here more or less permanently – not only water-dwellers like hippos, but also warthog and antelope such as lechwe and sitatunga.

Red lechwe are an endangered water antelope occurring in pockets of Zaire, Zambia and Botswana, with Okavango now being the furthest south they're found. Like sita-tunga, they have become highly adapted to wetland living, following the ebb and flow of the flood waters, sometimes going belly-deep to graze on submerged grasses. Dusk and dawn feeders, they retreat to reed-hidden termite mounds to rest up during the day. Their hooves are long and spread sideways, an adaptation that facilitates rapid passage through mud and enables them to venture onto mats of floating papyrus. **Lions, leop-ards** and **hunting dogs** will pursue lechwe into the wetlands for food. But their real danger has been of slaughter by humans, not for their unappetizing meat, but for their lovely skins which are greatly prized as sleeping mats, aprons and cloaks. In Botswana the Bayei and Basubiya developed their own technique for hunting lechwe using *mekoro*. A team on land would herd the animals into a lake where an awaiting party in dugouts would pole at speed into the animals stabbing in all directions. Nowadays only licensed hunters are allowed to kill lechwe, and a much greater threat is the one to the wetland habitat itself.

The rarest and most fascinating of all the animals you might see is the **sitatunga**, a medium-sized antelope completely adapted to the world of water and papyrus. Shy and rarely seen, this denizen of the reeds has unusually widely splayed hooves that perform well on mud, and when frightened it completely submerges itself leaving only its nostrils protruding for air. One repulsive technique used to hunt them is to set fire to their reedland habitat to flush them out.

If the variety of mammals is broad, the range of **birds** is overwhelming – something around 400 species. With wetland, forest, savannah and desert in such close proximity, the assortment of ecological niches makes this possibly the most concentrated cross-section of birds in the world. Every season in Moremi is unique. Depending on the water level, different waves of animals and birds move through to feed and to breed. Most spectacular of all are the **breeding colonies** in the Xakanaxa and Godikwe lagoons where marabou, open-bill, yellow-bill and saddle-bill **storks**, purple, goliath, grey, black-headed and squacco **herons** as well as egrets and pelicans breed in August and September. Intra-African migrants like **carmine bee-eaters** and various **kingfishers** arrive in the summer when they fill the skies. At *mokoro*-level, African jacanas with stretched-out toes trot over the lily pads as if they're on ballroom floors. The usual waterside **birds of prey** occupy the trees – the fish eagles and the Pel's fishing owl, large and specially adapted with featherless legs for dips in the water and extra-long claws for gripping fish of up to two kilograms.

The best chance you'll get of seeing a **fish eagle** doing its famous downward swoop and liftoff is at the camps, where they toss a fish on the water and whistle for an obliging bird. The **lilac breasted roller** is here too, one of the subcontinent's most beautiful birds and familiar to visitors to drier areas like Hwange National Park in Zimbabwe. It was held in high regard by the Ndebele, whose king Mzilikazi reserved the use of its vivid lilac, blue and green feathers for himself.

After dark, once the people have retired, the wilderness matches urban energy. Night sounds pierce the darkness: distant hyenas whooping or lions roaring far off (sounding far more like wind blowing over an open bottle than the MGM snarl you might expect). But one of the most surprising sounds of all is the quadrophonic chorus of tiny reed **frogs** piping their message into the night – not froggy croaking but like melodic, amplified wind chimes.

Moremi Wildlife Reserve

Vehicle entrance P10 (foreign reg); plus P50 per person daily. Campsites must be pre-booked at the Department of Wildlife and National Parks, Maun (☎660376).

The **MOREMI WILDLIFE RESERVE** is the centrepiece of the Okavango Delta, the most desirable destination for travellers in Botswana – if not all of Southern Africa. In 1963, after extensive depletion of game populations in Botswana, due to hunting and habitat destruction, the **Batawana** declared a reserve on 1800 square kilometres of their tribal land. It was named in honour of their leader, Moremi, as was Chief's Island.

In Moremi, you'll find all the major Okavango **ecotypes**: savannah woodland, mopane forest, riverine woodland, flood plain, reed beds and permanent swamp. The reserve breaks down into **three main areas**, roughly corresponding to broad terrain types: the **dryland peninsula** bounded by the Khwai River to the north, the **seasonal swamp** dominated by Chief's Island, and the **permanent flood lands**, which comprise everything else. This impressive range of habitats means a prodigious variety of **animals**. Large herds of elephant, buffalo, giraffe, zebra, kudu and impala are regularly seen as well as lions, hyenas and hippos; less frequent, but by no means scarce, are magnificent sable antelope, leopard, wild dogs and large crocodiles. As far as **birds** go, Moremi has no equal. Bee-eaters, darters and kingfishers flock among the reeds and dead wood in the channels. Fish eagles are commonly positioned on their "sentry posts" around lagoons and oxbows, and you'll see some very fine heronries at Xakanaxa. The Moremi pans are a sure bet for birdwatchers, always jostling with ducks, waders, storks and as wide a range of waterfowl as you could hope for.

The **prime visiting time** is April to November, out of the rainy season. Many camps close after Christmas until March, though some of them do stay open all year. November and February can sometimes produce soaring temperatures, up to 40° C, and from December to March during the rains, flooding can occur. The roads traced over thick sand may be submerged and the only practical route by car is to go straight from South to North Gate. Midwinter (June & July) can be very chilly in the mornings, although the days are generally bright and sunny. **Mosquitos** are always a problem in the rainy season. And don't let the beauty of the place lull you into a false sense of security. Tourists have been killed here; for example, one who swam in the river and met a large crocodile, and another who slept in the open and was taken by lions.

Moremi by private vehicle

The only independent way into Moremi is to travel across the dry land masses by **4WD** and **camp**, although the substantial entrance and camping fees make even this far from cheap. Moremi is quite beautiful and one of the few places in the region where you can camp out, on your own, and follow small tracks into thick bush, in an open vehicle if you wish. Although driving is an effective way to see animals, it doesn't help you get onto the Delta proper; and while many parts of Moremi are accessible by 4WD, you do need to be fully self-sufficient.

A popular route is **northwards from Maun** through Moremi to Savuti ,and then on to Serondella in northern Chobe (see Chapter Eight), camping all the way. There is no petrol or food on the way, so take everything you need. While you're in Moremi, it's worth spending at least four days and doing a circuit around the four **public campsites** – from South Gate to Mboma, Third Bridge, Xakanaxa and round to North Gate. If you're not going to fly into the Delta, visiting Third Bridge and Xakanaxa at its edge will give you magnificent views of flood plains, open lagoons and reed banks, and the birdlife is stupendous. There are no facilities in Moremi; the private camps will help in emergencies, like minor repairs to broken vehicles, but they're otherwise out of bounds.

At the **campsites** drinking water is available, but facilities are rudimentary (drop toilets). You'll have to get used to the idea of drinking the "swamp" water. It's cool, pure and absolutely free of bugs because it's filtered by extensive areas of reed beds which out-perform any artificial filtering system. Driving after dark is prohibited and camping restricted to official sites, which you must bnook in advance. Unless you've prebooked a site, you will be turned back to Maun. This is part of Botswana's policy to restrict the numbers of people using the parks.

Third Bridge can get fairly full, especially in July. But it has earned its reputation as the best of the campsites with some wonderfully secluded shady spots to dream away a couple of days. It's a lovely place to swim, if you must: but be on the lookout for crocs – a visitor was attacked there in 1989. **Baboons** at the campsite are a real menace – they'll do anything to get at food, including ripping tents apart, opening trunks, turning over trailers, and even confronting humans. You'd best collapse your tent if you're out for a

---

DELTA NAMES

Many of the **names** in the Delta date back to earlier San-speaking inhabitants and are characterized by the large number of "x"s and "c"s, that represent the click sounds released by air escaping when the tongue pulls away from the palate or teeth. Most Europeans find the sounds impossible, and you'll hear places like Xakanaxa pronounced as Ka-cun-icka or Xugana as coo-gunner.

few hours, and leave no food inside. The **bridge** at Third Bridge consists of rough-hewn poles sitting on heavy logs tied together which shudder as you trundle over. **Lions** cross here as well as vehicles – in fact Third Bridge is a regular hangout for them, especially at the end of their hunting season after September. At this time there is no more food in the hunting grounds and more lions return to Moremi, especially males which are too lazy to hunt most of the time. Moremi lions are buffalo-killers which makes for exciting game viewing, but the buffalo themselves, not surprisingly, tend to be skittish.

The **routes** between the campsites are all game drives in themselves. Coming from Maun it's three hours to Third Bridge from the South Gate entrance, and an hour or so from Third Bridge to **Xakanaxa**, making a total of 130km from Maun. At the crescent-shaped lagoon there's a public campsite as well as an exclusive one. Look out for elephants and hippos at night and baboons during the day. At the western extremity of the Moremi peninsula is **Mboma**, about 30km from South Gate and 7km from Third Bridge. Mboma Road from Third Bridge is quite different from Third Bridge/Xakanaxa area, the former more open grass and trees, the latter dense trees and mopane forest.

North Gate, the nicer of the park entrance camps, is 50km from Xakanaxa, taking three or four hours along the Khwai flood plain past large hippo pools. The North Gate camp is well wooded and, on the edge, looks onto a large plain where impala often graze. Leopards slink through the camp at night and there have been extraordinary sightings, like a wild-dog kill, right in camp. Another clattery log bridge crosses the River Khwai with clear, Delta-brown water and water lilies. There are toilets and cold showers. Watch out for the monkeys that help themselves to anything left unattended, and the troops of baboons that breeze through. One of North Gate's disadvantages is noise in the evenings from the Park's employees' village – radios and domestic clatter – but it never goes on too long.

Maun to Savuti

There are two routes **from Maun to Savuti**: the longer runs through Moremi (245km), while the other bypasses the park (197km) and is an hour shorter. Both are a good half day, if not more, on sandy roads; and 4WD is a necessity. From Maun, take the road past the airport to **Matlapaneng Bridge** and on past Okavango River Lodge to **Shorobe** on a good tarred road. At Shorobe you can often buy baskets – there are always a few good ones among the clusters hung at the roadside. Past the tsetse-fly barrier, ignore the next fork in the road and continue 20km to the next junction where you turn left for South Gate. There is a sign – a tiny hand-painted one resting on the road. If you miss this turning, where the two routes divide, you'll find yourself at Savuti, a couple of hours further on, having bypassed Moremi altogether.

WEST: UP THE PANHANDLE OR WESTWARD TO GHANZI

Heading **west** by road from Maun, you can either travel northwest up the Panhandle, skirting the Delta to the border with Namibia at **Shakawe** and taking in **Tsodilo Hills**, or southwest to **Ghanzi** and beyond (see Chapter Ten). There's no big game up the Panhandle, but the rewards are magnificent birdlife and fishing alongside the Okavango River. If you're based at Shakawe, it's a couple of hours drive through thick sand to the awe-inspiring Tsodilo Hills, with their three thousand rock paintings. From Shakawe you can turn east, scoot through the **Caprivi Strip** and end up at **Chobe National Park**. If you want to complete the circle, drive through Chobe to Savuti and take in Moremi before arriving back in Maun. It's a highly recommended 4WD circuit.

Maun to Shakawe

The 370-kilometre Maun to Shakawe road has recently been tarred, and once you're up there it's tar all the way west to Windhoek in Namibia. A daily bus heads for Shakawe via Etsha if you want to explore any of the **fishing camps** on the Panhandle, where the Okavango River is smooth, wide and fast-flowing, edged by huge papyrus beds stretching to a horizon of riverine trees. The only filling station along the way is at **Etsha**, 6, 290km from Maun. The next petrol is at **Bagani** in Namibia, 180km further on, though **Shakawe Fishing Camp**, 14km before Shakawe, usually has petrol and may oblige.

The first stop by road is **TOTENG**, where the track branches north to the Panhandle and south to Ghanzi (see p.337 for details of the route on to Ghanzi). The fork is marked by a simple box-like **general store** stocked with cold drinks and lemon cream biscuits. Near Toteng, Lake Ngami was once recommended for its fabulous birdlife but is now completely dry and dead.

Although the road from Maun looks alluringly close to the Delta on the map, you don't see the swamp at all until after 345km, when you reach **SEPOPA**, a watery settlement with lots of riverine trees. The tar between Sepopa and Shakawe means that the Delta's permanent water is now far more accessible and vehicles sporting canoes have been seen on this road. Mostly though, you'll be treated to less sophisticated scenes – expanses of thorn trees and white sand broken by the occasional village. You'll often pass people going about their business: lone cattle herders on horseback coming or going to distant cattle posts with provisions and a bedroll tied behind saddle; Herero women going shopping or visiting on donkeys; *mekoro* being dragged like sledges by oxen through the sand, with goods or perhaps a passenger inside.

Sehitwa and Gumare

SEHITWA is the next settlement you'll hit – a small traditional place with many Herero inhabitants. From here it's 46km to Tsao, the former capital of this northern district (before Maun), but not remotely worth a stop.

There's nowhere to stay in the unpretentious village of **GUMARE**, but you'll find stores and fresh bread. This is one of the basket-making centres of the northwestern delta, and one recommended stop is the new basketry shop – Gumare's first – next to the bakery, just 700m from the main road. You'll pay less for baskets here than in Maun. A sign indicating *Barclays Bank* points optimistically towards some huts, but don't count on changing money here. It's open on the government monthly payday only, for one and a half hours.

It's worth strolling around Gumare to appreciate the considerable beauty of the simple textures of thatched roofs, mud walls, reed screens and wooden gates that provide privacy to individual **homesteads**. Usually a central courtyard area contains a thatched unwalled shelter – just poles – where the women thresh or stamp grain. Some days you can witness the gory **butcher's tree**, under which a carcass is hacked into marketable pieces. Dripping bloody slabs of meat are hung up to attract an eager crowd, and the flesh is sold by a vague estimate of size – graphic gestures show how much you'll get for a pula.

Etsha

ETSHA, the next stop up from Gumare, is worth a visit, with the modest attractions of a basket shop, cultural centre, shop, petrol and two accommodation possibilities. There are actually thirteen numbered villages all called Etsha along the Etsha Road, which branches off to the right 10km north of Gumare, but when people talk of Etsha they generally mean Etsha 6, which is the only commercial centre. The villages are inhabited by **Mbukushu refugees** who came into Botswana in the late 1960s. A second

THE HEREROS

One of the striking sights of northern Botswana are **Herero** women in Victorian-inspired dress: floor-length bustled skirts, cloaks and elaborate headgear in intense reds, blues and greens. The costume was inherited from nineteenth-century German missionaries in Namibia.

The Herero had originally migrated from east and central Africa to Namibia, where they settled in the sixteenth century. Traditionally they were **nomadic pastoralists**, herding cattle which were at that time absolutely central to their culture; their staple diet was sour milk, and the sale of cattle was taboo in their ancestor-worshipping religion. So important were the **ancestors** that even the supreme being Ndjambi was of little significance next to the first ancestor Mukuru who descended from an omumborombonga tree in Namibia's Etosha Pan. Often as many as two hundred of a man's cattle were killed after his death to please the ancestors.

In 1894 Namibia became a German territory and the colonialists followed the procedures of their European imperialist colleagues elsewhere: the disarming of the Herero, the setting-up of reserves and the imposition of fines and taxes. The Hereros resisted and in 1904 there was an **uprising** in which a large number of German settlers were killed. The whites retaliated with a campaign of extermination that concluded in a crushing Herero defeat. Some Herero managed to flee across the border into Botswana, an event that was to have a profound effect on their culture.

During their wanderings in the desert they lost all their cattle and were forced to throw themselves on the mercy of the Batawana, whose vassals they became. Over time they rebuilt their herds and regained independence, but in the process the cattle lost their religious importance and became financial assets simply to be traded and cashed in. Today the Herero are among northern Botswana's major cattle-owners. Christianity has displaced the old religion, although some Herero still insist on burial in Namibia with the ancestors. It used to be taboo to photograph Herero women, but that has changed as well. Now you will be asked to pay a fee, for what's become a stereotypical posed snap.

wave which followed the route of their nineteenth-century forebears fleeing from the Lozi, these new émigrés were escaping from war-ravaged Angola. While waiting to be resettled, they formed themselves into thirteen parties representing the groups they belonged to in Angola.

About 1000 women around Etsha weave traditional baskets to supplement subsistence farming; their outlet is the *Okavango Basket Shop* at Etsha 6, on the Etsha 1 road. Next door is the **museum** and **cultural centre** "House of the River People" (Mon–Sat 8am–5pm), definitely worth a visit to get a flavour of the traditional material culture of the Bayei, Hambukushu and River Bushmen. This is also where you'll find Etsha's four, simple thatched guesthouses (P30 per person) and camping area (no phone). The best of Etsha's attractions is **Makwena Lodge**, 14km beyond Etsha (see below).

The Panhandle fishing camps

The game has been largely shot out in this area, so the emphasis is on **fishing and birdlife**. The best time for fishing is between April and November, though if you're after the aggressive freshwater **tiger fish**, try August to October. *Mekoro* trips close to the camps can usually be arranged, though the deeper waters are not ideal: one fishing camp's proprietors report hippo attacks and tell of a Japanese tourist who insisted on going it alone and ended up capsized and clinging to papyrus for days. Just south of Shakawe a daily ferry crosses the river to the **eastern side** of the Panhandle, where the biggest settlement is **Seronga** – enquire at the Shakawe Fishing Camp for details.

Drotsky's Cabins, Private Bag 01, Shakawe (☎/fax 661206). Cheaper than its neighbour, the Shakawe Fishing Camp, and a whole lot friendlier. *Drotsky's* has a variety of accommodation options (from P110 per person) set in a garden on the banks of the Okavango, plus camping. There's boat rental too.

Guma Camp (*Ensign Agencies*, Box 66, Maun; ☎660978, fax 660571). Luxury camp in similar vicinity to Makwena Lodge. You can drive to Etsha 13 and get a transfer for the last 11km, negotiable by 4WD only. The all-inclusive rate is P375 per person per night.

Makwena Lodge (*Merlin Travel*, P/Bag 013, Maun; ☎661207, fax 660036). The only budget lodge on the Pandhandle, in an unspoilt and beautiful spot overlooking a large lagoon and shaded by big riverine trees. There's an airstrip, if a group hires a plane from Maun (not as expensive as you'd think), or you can be collected from Etsha 6. Audi Camp also does trips here from Maun (see above). Accommodation is in reed chalets (P75 per person) and there's a fine campsite (P20). Meals are available. It's possible to take *mokoro* trips, and the birdlife is great.

Nxamaseri Camp, Private Bag 23, Maun (☎260493). An intimate and luxurious camp (P485 per person), catering for a maximum of eight people, halfway up the Panhandle – mostly for anglers but good birdwatching too. It's possible to get there by 4WD, but most clients fly in.

Shakawe Fishing Camp (*Travel Wild*, Maun; ☎660822, fax 660493). 14km before Shakawe as you drive up the Panhandle, and a conveniently situated base for the Tsodilo Hills. It's also the only place where you can get fuel between Maun and Shakawe, besides Etsha. Their daily all-inclusive rate is P350. Accommodation is in chalets (P250) or in slightly cheaper tents (P200). Camping is P20 per person. The camp's birdwatching boat trips are worth considering, as the proprietors are knowledgeable ornithologists.

Xaro Lodge (*Okavango Explorations*; address on p.323). Right up the Panhandle, this luxury fishing camp with boating excursions is accessible by 4WD in the dry season. Open March to September. Trips to Tsodilo Hills are also offered.

Shakawe – and into Namibia

SHAKAWE is a one-track town, with several shops all called *Wright's*. You can buy the most basic of basics at *Wright's Trading Store*; over the road in an unpromising looking hut is a home-industry bakery, selling warm bread and buns. However, Shakawe is not simply the dusty roadside village it looks. The tar road is bringing changes and now there's even the odd telephone and generator for electricity. It's also a great transport nexus for local people crossing the river by *mekoro*. Although you don't realize it at first, the river runs just behind the bakery and on a gentle beach you'll come across a *mokoro* terminal, with *mekoro* parked on the bank or in the water, women laden with goods on their heads going to and fro and piles of things waiting to be loaded for the journey back across the water.

The **border** with Namibia is at **MOHEMBO**, 17km to the north. You can change money at *Wright's Trading Store*, and can cross without any problems. Be warned, though, if you are driving from Namibia into Botswana, that your vehicle must be cleared by police in Namibia before you're allowed to leave the country in it.

Into Namibia: the Caprivi Strip

The **CAPRIVI STRIP**, named after a certain Count Caprivi, is a wedge between Botswana and Angola, stretching out from Namibia to touch fingers with Zambia and Zimbabwe. It should properly belong to its northern or southern neighbour; it's one of those arbitrary chunks decided in the negotiating chambers of Europe. The German equivalent to the north–south British Cape to Cairo railway was a projected east–west route, across the Caprivi to the coast. The railway was never built because the Germans never had enough colonies to join the route together. It came to a dead end where it hit the Zambezi, opposite Kasane.

The Caprivi Strip used to be the major flashpoint for battles between SWAPO guerillas and occupying South African troops. Since the South African withdrawal and Namibian independence, it is calm and can be visited easily. A couple of resorts and rest camps on the river punctuate the way to the main town of **Katima Mulilo**. You may still see elephants, although many of those which once walked the roads have been exterminated.

Poppa Falls

The *Namibian Department of National Parks* has provided excellent timber chalets along the Zambezi at **POPPA FALLS** – nothing on the scale of Victoria Falls, but very pretty nevertheless and a recommended stopover. Camping is cheap, and the sites manicured. The place is mainly a retreat for Namibian Afrikaners whose radios cut through the stillness with the fearsome strains of *sakkiesakkie* music – a Southern African equivalent of Cajun on piano accordions. *Suclabo Lodge* (☎067372/6222) is a posher place on the hill overlooking the river, and it offers boat trips and game drives into Khaudum Game Reserve. It's also possible to camp here or rent self-catering bungalows.

From Poppa Falls you could get a ride west and head onto Etosha Pan or the dramatic Atlantic coast. Or you could follow the strip eastwards to Katima Mulilo and move on to either Botswana, Zambia or Zimbabwe.

Katima Mulilo

KATIMA MULILO has an old history, but as a white settlement it's young and raw. Stretched out along the Zambezi, like suburbia in the bush, it's the largest town in Caprivi (nevertheless still pretty small). A virile vein of morbid humour throbs here. The sign on one gate asks *IS THERE LIFE AFTER DEATH?* and answers in the next breath: *TRESPASS AND YOU'LL FIND OUT.*

Katima Mulilo was one of the first big South African bases set up in Namibia after SWAPO began sending fighters in. Apart from the beautiful Zambezi, Katima has only one tourist attraction, the **lavatree**, a hollow old baobab fitted with a public flushing toilet. It's quite surreal, down one of the town's quiet suburban streets, near the *Guinea Fowl Inn*.

The **hotels** and the **campsite** are situated along the river, on the Kasane road. The rather smart *Zambezi Queen Hotel* (☎07351/203) offers cheap camping with excellent showers as well as fairly expensive rooms. Breakfast (or drinks) is a treat on the hotel terrace overlooking the Zambezi. The homelier, prefabricated *Guinea Fowl Inn* is cheaper (☎067352/418). The **commercial centre** is set back about a kilometre away in the opposite direction – a small shopping mall with basics, a bank and a reasonable crafts outlet.

The Tsodilo Hills

Eulogized by Laurens van der Post in his *Lost World of the Kalahari*, the **TSODILO HILLS** have an undeniably magical quality. Although most visitors fly in for a quick visit, the spell of the hills isn't quickly absorbed, and it's well worth spending a few days here exploring the rocks and the three thousand paintings at two hundred different sites. The four hills in the surrounding flatness are a kind of shrine, described by Van der Post as "a great fortress of once living Bushman culture, a Louvre of the desert filled with treasure". Few experiences in Africa can match the excitement of a first glimpse of them – the sand-covered bedrock erupting in four monumental humps which lure you ever closer on the excruciatingly slow journey over gentle sand dunes.

The local !Kung* people call the hills "Male", "Female" and "Child", in descending order of size. The smallest one remains nameless like an infant. In the !Kung tongue they're also known lyrically as the "copper bracelet of the evening" from the way they light up in the dying sun. As hills – offering rocky scrambles over chunky rock levels with crevasses, caves, chimneys and castles – they're fascinating in themselves. It's possible to camp out here, in which case on a windy night you can expect unnerving whisperings as the wind fingers the great boulders and eroded masses. From the hill-tops you get an incredible panorama over the desert – tree-dotted grassland stretching to all four horizons. An island world, Tsodilo is also home to a variety of gecko lizard found nowhere else on earth.

Practicalities

Getting to Tsodilo isn't easy and 4WD is essential. The 40km from Shakawe are likely to be the longest and bumpiest you ever do; it takes between two and four hours. During the rainy season the sand is firmer and the journey easier. The road is extremely narrow, with bushes scraping the sides of the vehicle. There are two routes to the hills: the first turn-off is 13km before Sepopa on the left, with a Botswana museum zebra logo marking the track; the other is close to the **Shakawe Fishing Camp**, 8km before Shakawe. From Maun, it's longer to go via Shakawe but the road is marginally better and Shakawe worth a visit anyway. Astonishingly enough, people have done it **on foot**, but if you follow, take plenty of water and don't go alone. The thick sand will make the journey (two days) hard going. Also, inform the management at Shakawe Fishing Camp. They have a cautionary tale about an intrepid hiker who laughed off their advice to take more than the litre of water he was carrying. The way they tell it, he returned peeling, swollen tongued and in a state of near collapse. Luckily he did return.

Shakawe Fishing Camp has **4WD vehicles** (with five seats) for rent to get you to Tsodilo. Find out if any of their guests intend going to the hills – you may be lucky and find a lift. Also enquire at **Drotsky's Cabins** to see if they're doing any trips. However, neither place is especially keen on taking trips, and you might be better off joining one of **Audi Camp**'s budget expeditions from Maun (see Maun, above). Another option, besides a group of you hiring a five-seater plane in Maun (P1402), is to ask around at the air charter offices in Maun to see whether anyone has booked a **plane** to Tsodilo, who may be willing to sell off one of the seats (again see Maun, above, for details on this).

On arrival at the hills you have to report to the **Mbukushu village** to fill in the visitors' book. There's a basic **campsite**, but as yet no washing facilities, and some useful **caves** for the tentless, including a large, convenient one at the Tsodilo Hills sign. Be sure to take your rubbish and empty bottles away with you – there's no garbage collection. Take sufficient **food**, water and petrol. Although there is a well near the village, it is not to be relied upon. During the rainy season you may well find a spring in the hills; there are a couple on the Female. Ask the guides – but don't count on it.

You can wander around searching for the paintings yourself, or hire a **guide** from the Mbukushu village or the nearer San village. The !Kung-speaking guides are extremely knowledgeable about painting locations and can show you plants used for medicines and poison. They're also exhaustingly energetic and will take you to some of the more inaccessible sites. Assuming you speak no !Kung it can be difficult that the guides speak little or no English. Charges for a day out are very reasonable and the fee is agreed on before you go. The San also have a few curios for sale, such as bows and

---

* The exclamation mark "!" is used in writing a number of African languages to represent one of the several click sounds. See the box on p.348 for more about San clicks.

quivers of arrows and ostrich-shell beads, but if you go to Tsodilo brimming with visionary Van der Post romanticism about the "bushmen", their desultory village near the Male Hill, with its rude shelters, alcohol abuse (some of the guides have serious drinking problems), and people sitting around in the dust, is bound to disappoint.

Paintings and legends

Most of the **paintings** are on exposed rock faces, some high above the ground. They're displayed on all the hills, but the Female has the majority. While on the whole they were painted by San people, here and there you'll come across some by the Bantu-speakers who also lived here. These latter, mostly done in white, differ in style and colour from the reddish San outlines. The pastel colours of the rocks – mauve, pink, honey and ochre – blend strikingly with animals drawn finger thickness in a deep russet. Tiny, spine-tingling hand-prints accompany many of the friezes.

Although thousands of years old, the colours are still ardent. The paintings on the other hand are variable: some animals are breathtaking while others merely indifferent sketches. Besides recognizable animals there are mythological ones, many abstract symbols such as gridded circles and shields containing ladders and depictions of people dancing. Some of the paintings may be as recent as one hundred years, while others could easily be 20,000 years old. Authoritative dates have not been established for the Tsodilo paintings, but similar ones in a cave in Namibia have been verified as 26,000 years old. Nobody knows for sure what was used to paint the pictures and there's no evidence to support the popular idea that blood or eggs were used. It seems most likely that the colouring agents were predominantly earth pigments, plant juices, ash and burnt bone, water and possibly animal or plant oils.

Besides the San, who have many legends about these hills, the Mbukushu have a myth that an omniscient being lowered their first ancestors by rope to the summit of the Male Hill. If you ask Mbukushu, they'll confirm that their origin was on the Zambezi but say spirits live in the hills. These spirits are the ones Van der Post and his party inadvertently angered, which jammed the cameras and prevented all filming, stopped the tape recorders from working and sent bees to attack them at dawn three days in a row. Their party couldn't leave fast enough, but not before they had made a symbolic gesture of contrition – a note buried in a bottle at the base of the paintings now called Van der Post's panel.

travel details

Flights

Maun to: Gaborone (daily; 1hr 30min); Johannesburg (daily; 2hr); Kasane (Mon, Thurs & Sat; 50min); Victoria Falls (Wed, Fri & Sun; 1hr); Windhoek (Wed & Sun; 2hr).

Apart from scheduled flights, you can also often get a seat on one of the many **chartered flights** that leave Maun. For these ask around the travel agents, and the air charter companies.

Buses

Maun to: Francistown (daily at 7.30am & 9am; 5hr); Shakawe (daily at 7am; 7hr).

CHAPTER TEN

THE KALAHARI DESERT

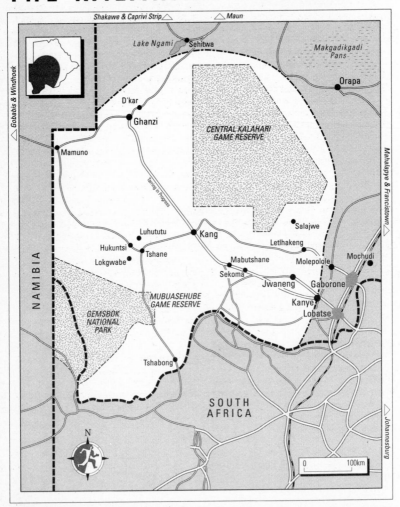

The Okavango Delta aside, the **Kalahari Desert** is for most visitors the defining feature of Botswana. Over two-thirds of the country is covered by the desert and its influence on the life of Botswana is paramount. What distinguishes it as desert is the lack of surface water and scant rain, disguising the underground

ACCOMMODATION PRICE CODES IN BOTSWANA

Most accommodation options in our account of Botswana have been given **price codes** to indicate the cost of a single night's lodging. The code for each establishment is based on the cost **per person sharing**; there is usually a supplement for a single person in a room. Prices for establishments that only offer all-inclusive rates (comprising meals, and perhaps guided tours and other services) have not been coded and are given in pula (per person per night).

① under P20	③ P40–60	⑤ P80–100	⑦ P120–140
② P20–40	④ P60–80	⑥ P100–120	⑧ P140–160

wells which nourish a cover of grass and acacias and support a wide variety of animals and birds. Only in the far southwest will you see archetypal sand dunes.

The Kalahari (or *Kgalakgadi*) is the remaining territory of one of Africa's oldest peoples, the **San** – the "Bushmen" about whom Laurens van der Post wrote with such passion. Over the centuries, they have been pushed by migrating farmers and herders from the easier lands of their ancestors into this harsh environment, where they now barely survive.

Many practical difficulties confront travellers who come in the hope of seeing the Kalahari, but it is feasible. As potential targets, four little-visited **game reserves** lie isolated in the vastness, west and northwest of Gaborone. The closest and most accessible from the capital is **Khutse**, 220km to the northwest. Khutse is an annexe of the **Central Kalahari Game Reserve**, itself off limits to the public, and one of the last preserves of the hunter-gatherer lifestyle.

Mabuasehube Game Reserve, in the southwest corner of the country, abuts the **Gemsbok National Park** which spills over into South Africa. These reserves are far better than Khutse for game viewing, and the landscape of the southwest is archetypal Kalahari – pans, red dunes and scrubby vegetation. But getting to the region takes time and effort (not to mention money) and it's a trip recommended only for experienced desert drivers and campers. There is, in any case, no way into the Gemsbok National Park from Botswana. Access to it is either from South Africa's northern Cape Province, or from Namibia, and all the roads and camping facilities are inside South Africa, beyond the seasonal Nossob River which forms the border. For hardy adventurers, however, the far southwest circuit outlined in this chapter runs southwest of Gaborone through Mabuasehube Reserve and back again along the rough Kalahari cattle trail.

Despite its booming diamond mine, **Jwaneng** on the route from Gaborone and Lobatse is not a recommended stopover. The most compelling Kalahari town, and the de facto capital of the desert is **Ghanzi**, out in the remote west. Ghanzi is about as far out and cut off as you can get. It rests on a vast limestone ridge (despite the deceptive flatness), 300km from its nearest neighbour Maun to the north, and Lobatse more than twice that to the southeast. Both routes follow punishing roads that impact your spine and coat you with dust, though the trans-Kalahari Lobatse–Ghanzi route is now being tarred – at the time of writing, work seems to have been completed as far as Kang. From Ghanzi, with your own transport, it's possible to explore the extremely remote southwest corner of Botswana, with its numerous San settlements.

Khutse Game Reserve

KHUTSE GAME RESERVE is something of a misnomer. It's less a place to see game – you may see very few animals indeed – than a park to experience the unspoilt isolation and immensity of the Kalahari. The night skies are recommendation enough on their own; no light within hundreds of miles interferes with the brilliance of the thick clusters of stars. Yet, in Botswanan terms, the reserve isn't far from Gaborone, and it's a good place to get away from the drabness of the capital for a long weekend.

Khutse doesn't have dunes, but a low cover of herbage and acacias, nourished by underground water and **pans**. The pans are the reserve's dominant feature, remnants of a wetter period some ten to fifteen thousand years ago. Some are wide and grassy, others bare and open, and they offer the best of the park's limited **game viewing**. The severe droughts of the last ten years or so have decimated animal populations as well as food sources but you stand a chance of seeing small herds of **springbok** and **gemsbok**, **hartebeest** and **wildebeest**, and families of **ostriches**. Wildlife is seasonal, passing through in the perpetual search for grazing and water. At any time, however, you may chance on animals licking minerals from the salty pan surfaces.

The **smaller mammals** that you may spot on the pans (often at night) are perhaps the most interesting. Take a good mammal book and sharpen up your eyes to identify mongooses, black-backed jackals, genets, caracals, ratels, porcupines, hedgehogs, ground squirrels, bat-eared foxes, African and beautiful black-footed cats, spring hares, pangolins, aardvarks and aardwolves. If herds of **antelope** are around, there will also be **predators**, including lions.

The number of **bird species** – over 150 – doesn't match what you'd see at Chobe or Okavango, but it's still impressive. One big bird in evidence here and in many parts of Botswana is the **kori bustard**, the world's heaviest flying bird. It weighs an astonishing 40kg and has an immense wingspan. You're more likely to see one on the ground than in the air and you can get quite close before they reluctantly take off. During the mating season, the male makes himself even bigger, puffing out his throat to two or three times its normal size.

Khutse practicalities

Getting to Khutse is a 4WD journey of around five hours from Gaborone. Bring fuel sufficient for at least 600km, and everything you need. You can arrange both **vehicle and camping equipment hire** from *Holiday Car Rentals* (Queen's Road, The Mall, Gaborone; ☎353970).

When to go depends on what you're after, but, as a rule of thumb, August to November is best avoided – it's desperately dry and unbelievably hot and much of the wildlife disappears. The ideal time is in April and May, when the nights, which can get icy in the Kalahari, aren't too bad. Nevertheless, the park is open throughout the year, and other times have their own attractions. After the first rains, at the end of November, the pans are covered with **wild flowers**. December to March has the disadvantage of long grass, with seeds that block the radiator, creating a fire hazard and entailing frequent stops to unclog it. The thick grass also hides many of the animals.

From Gaborone, take the road through Molepolole (last petrol) to Letlhakeng, where the tar ends 110km from the capital. The road deteriorates rapidly thereafter, with deep sandy stretches, making for a bumpy ride with little signposting. Salajwe is the last village before the Khutse gate, 44km further on.

At the gate you can get borehole **water**, but consider bringing your own as it's a bit salty. You can also get a Kgalakgadi or San **guide**, who will camp with you, if you want to be shown around the park and to be initiated into some of the ways plants are used by desert-dwellers. You'll be expected to provide their food and to pay a reasonable daily rate. With formidable powers of observation and eyesight, they also know where best to find animals. If you decide to go it alone, though, you're unlikely to lose your way, as there's only one road in the reserve.

The nicest place to **camp** is at **Moreswe Pan**, two and a half hours beyond the park gate, which you'll almost certainly have to yourself. At Khutse II Pan, 13km from the gate, the road forks. Take the left-hand fork to Moreswe Pan, which is 53km further on. The expansive pan stretches out, in inconceivable vastness, all but filling your field of vision. Where the road peters out, two trees mark the lonely campsite.

Central Kalahari Game Reserve

Adjacent to Khutse's northern border and dominating the centre of the country is the mysterious, boxed-off **Central Kalahari Game Reserve** which has no facilities of any kind, a few boreholes for water and no public access. It's the second largest game reserve in the world, though only a patch in the middle of the Kalahari, whose sands cover about eighty percent of the country.

Until recently, small bands of **San** people, pursuing a traditional hunter-gatherer lifestyle, shared the reserve with a wide variety of game. The droughts of the last ten years or so have effectively ended this traditional life. The drought hasn't stopped **mineral exploration**, though, and geologists are among the few people given permission to traverse the endless grassy scrub.

Mabuasehube Game Reserve and around

In the sand-dune country of the southwest is **MABUASEHUBE GAME RESERVE**, Botswana's most remote and least-visited park. Its name, spelt *Mabuashegube* in the Kgalakgadi language, means "red soil", and applies specifically to its bare, northernmost pan, contrasting it with the others, which are grassy.

Terrible roads serve as a considerable disincentive to casual visitors. This is a destination only for the intrepid. You may not see another vehicle for a week in these parts, so a trip here is not to be undertaken without adequate preparations – lots of water, spares and experience. Naturally enough, it's not a good idea to stray off the main road. At the park itself there are no facilities of any kind, although borehole water is usually available from the game ranger.

Poaching has long been a problem in the southern Kalahari, and this reserve, although unfenced, is a real animal sanctuary. Among the many pans and sand dunes, the rainy season attracts abundant **antelope** and predators – including **lions**, rare **brown hyenas** and **caracals**, though when it's been very dry you may see nothing.

The usual **approach** is from the south through **TSHABONG**, the administrative capital of the Kgalakgadi District. There's precious little here and the road to the Mabuasehube crosses 120km of gentle sand dunes, a solid day of driving on a sandy, corrugated track. Plans for a motel at Tshabong, and to tarmac the road to Gaborone, are likely to increase traffic to the reserve. You may well come across camels wandering around the village. These were originally imported by the police, who used them extensively for patrols in this sandy terrain, but now Tshabong is the last place dromedaries can be seen in Botswana.

Tshabong to Kang through the reserve

The track from Tshabong to Mabuasehube passes northwards through the reserve to **TSHANE**, a tough eight-hour drive, with no settlements or facilities en route. Tshane is one of a cluster of four villages in the Kalahari's heart, along with Lokgwabe, Lehututu and Hukuntsi. Together they're of interest as repositories of Botswana's early history.

Tshane has a notable colonial police station built on high ground overlooking the magnificent **Tshane Pan**, where animals are still watered from hand-dug wells on the pan's edge – a practice unchanged for over 150 years. **LEHUTUTU**, about 10km north of Tshane, features in the accounts of early Kalahari explorers as a thriving commercial centre. Although the place is now all but deserted, the original store is still there and operating. At **LOKGWABE**, 11km southwest of Tshane, you'll find descendants of Simon Cooper who in 1904 led a Khoi anti-colonial rebellion in South West Africa, and was given protection and land here by the British administration. **HUKUNTSI**, 10km west of Tshane, is the administrative centre of the area and here you can get **diesel and petrol**, and **supplies** from the well-stocked store. Although the area is remote, you'll see incongruities like a modern telecommunications tower rising above mud huts.

The main interest of the final stretch, from Tshane to **Kang** is the sprinkling of **San settlements**. But you should only go here if you're doing some serious and informed exploration of the southern Kalahari and are aware that you may not encounter any traffic for a long time. You may be disappointed to find the bushmen you meet wearing jeans and plastic jewellery, not sporting skins or bows and arrows. Once you reach Kang you're back on the relatively important Lobatse–Ghanzi road, which does at least see a reasonable number of vehicles each day.

Approaches to Ghanzi

Lobatse to Ghanzi is an arduous ten-hour journey (4WD only – though there may now be a weekly bus) and a route used, among others, by Ghanzi cattle ranchers (see box), although the **Trans-Kalahari Highway** has got the green light and the route is now tarred between Lobatse and Kang, with Kang to Ghanzi next on the list. It takes five hours, at least, to cover the 280km **from Maun to Ghanzi**, on potholed roads, with very little on the way. While 4WD isn't necessary, you need a high-clearance vehicle. The road has so far been tarred for the first 70km.

Lobatse to Ghanzi

The Trans-Kalahari Highway officially begins at Lobatse, 65km south of Gaborone. **JWANENG**, 127km further on, is the last major place for petrol and supplies, and supports one fairly expensive hotel, the *Mokala* (☎380835; ⑥), with a restaurant and bar. It's modern and takes *Visa*, for those stranded in the Kalahari. For snacks, ice creams and cokes, there are a couple of places in the Mall. Indicative of its move from cattle post to an urban settlement, one of Botswana's best pop groups, Kwanyape, comes from here.

Jwaneng would have remained just another tiny cattle post in the desert, were it not for the discovery of **diamonds**. Opened in 1982, the **Jwaneng mine** is the largest gem mine in the world, producing a staggering 8.9 million carats in 1988. Australia and

---

THE GHANZI-LOBATSE CATTLE ROUTE

Down deep sandy roads, Ghanzi's big cattlemen send their stock on the near-legendary cattle run to the **abattoirs** at Lobatse – apparently the longest in the world and one that confirms your impression that Ghanzi is the capital of Botswana's wild west.

Although most farmers now truck their animals, the practice persists of droving the cattle across the Kalahari plains. Herds many hundred strong kick up dust for the month-long journey, which by all accounts can turn into quite a festive event. Treks leave throughout the cooler dry season. The **cowboys** are invariably skilled San on horseback. Nowadays back-up vehicles take tents and supplies and bring back the horses. The treks move at cattle-pace and night stops are determined by watering points, kraals and bore-holes along the route, about every thirty kilometres. Where there are **lions** (there aren't so many these days) fires are built all around the kraals to ward them off. The cattle can smell predators and without being corralled would stampede, leaving the drovers with days of work to recover them.

Zaire produce greater caratage, but most of their output is industrial grade; Botswana is the world's leading diamond producer in terms of value.

Beyond Jwaneng, the settlements on the way to Ghanzi are all watering points with boreholes established for trekking cattle. Most have a bottle store, a bar and a general dealer; there's a small, cheap hotel at **Mabutshane**, one of the few places to stay in this part of the desert. You'll need to carry petrol, water and food, although you can get petrol (exorbitantly priced) at **Kang**, the biggest village en route which has shops and a school. There's very little sign of habitation on the 280-kilometre stretch between Kang and Ghanzi, although there are some small unsignposted settlements and boreholes set back from the road. A left turn at Kang will bring you via Tshane to the Mabuasehube Game Reserve in the southern Kalahari, described above.

Maun to Ghanzi

On the approach from Maun, the Ghanzi district starts at the **Kuke Gate** – little more than a post in the scrub with huts and a primary school. From its location on a rise you get a rare overview of the Kalahari, stretching endlessly into the blue, and of the infamous **veterinary cordon fence** – an inexorable straight line through the bush.

The gate is attended round the clock, and you'll be asked some routine questions, such as whether you're carrying any animal products; a cursory search may be made, after which you'll be waved on.

D'KAR too is a small place, 35km before you reach Ghanzi, and not devoid of interest. A very active **mission** runs projects to lessen the traumatic transition of a number of San people, settled permanently here, from their ancient self-sufficient way of life into the shock of a global economy. The mission is run by an Afrikaans minister of the traditionally segregated and conservative South African Dutch Reformed Church.

The original mission was set up to bring Christianity to the San living on the Ghanzi farms, but now international aid money is being used to assist **income-generation projects**. The Kuru Development Trust (☎596244), on a 3000-hectare farm, has grown out of this and is owned and run by the N'coahkoe people. They produce traditional crafts and leather goods, notably saddlery, for sale, and collect crafts from all over the region to sell on. There is a **store** in town and the possibility of renting a **room**, **camping** or having a **meal** at the Development Trust – ask at the **craft shop** on your left as you head towards Ghanzi.

THE VETERINARY CORDON FENCE

An extensive system of barriers has been erected around Botswana in an attempt to keep the dreaded **foot-and-mouth disease** under control – an absolutely vital priority in a nation so locked into cattle farming. The fences are an emotive issue; some people, like Mark and Delia Owens, authors of *Cry the Kalahari*, claim that they have been responsible for decimating game populations.

The Owens lived in the Kalahari for seven years between 1974 and 1981, studying predators. Their book contains harrowing accounts of thousands of wildebeest and other animals following their old migration routes across the Central Kalahari Reserve, in search of fresh grazing and water, and dying at the fences, like the one at Kuke, that blocked their way. The Owens assert that no one knows for certain that the wild ungulates are a reservoir of infection, or that foot-and-mouth disease can be held in check by fences. But other scientists question the Owens' allegations, holding up the old theory that disease is transmitted from wild animals to domestic stock. Whoever is right, the Owens' vociferous campaign got them thrown out of the country, and they continue their crusade with lecture tours, mainly in the US.

Ghanzi and the western Kalahari

GHANZI is a historical quirk. Now the centre of an Afrikaner farming district in Southern Africa's oldest independent black republic, it was for millennia the centre of the hunter-gatherers' range. Despite its unpromising appearance, Ghanzi's very remoteness from all other major settlements makes it one of Botswana's more interesting towns for the traveller who manages to penetrate it and gets to meet local inhabitants. The name probably derives from the San word meaning a one-stringed instrument – an unintentional metaphor for its one-horse, dead-end feel. The Batswana imposed their own gloss on the place respelling it *Ghantsi*, which in Setswana means "place of the flies" – an equally apt description.

Some history

It's something of a miracle that Ghanzi exists at all. It progressed fitfully out of the dusty wastes that were the traditional hunting grounds of three San-speaking groups, and, later, cattle-owning Khoi. The first white settler – in the 1870s – was a larger-than-life Afrikaner, **Hendrik van Zyl**, an ex-member of parliament and cabinet minister from the Boer South African Republic (now the Transvaal), who must have had good reasons to leave a prestigious life to gather an existence out of the dust. In fact he seems to have lived well: legend relates he had a two-storey mansion with imported stained-glass windows, and a hundred servants. A notorious hunter and killer, he's said to have shot four hundred elephants in his first year at Ghanzi and was responsible for the death of many San. One story relates how he invited a number of San to a party, accommodating them in a specially built stockade. In retaliation for the murder of a fellow Boer, he shot 33 of them in cold blood. There are several accounts of how he was killed – enough people had good reason. One version claims a revenge killing by San, another that he was murdered by Khoi herders and a third says he was killed by Damara tribesmen for interfering in local affairs. Other Boer trekkers followed in his footsteps, most of them either passing through or staying only briefly.

The real establishment of Ghanzi probably began in the late nineteenth century around one of the largest pans in the district. And at this juncture the even larger figure of **Cecil Rhodes** makes an appearance. Hungry for land, Rhodes had his eye on the western edge of Bechuanaland where it bordered on German territory. Generous historians have said that he recruited settlers to Ghanzi to act as a buffer against German expansionism. Others question how a small group of farmers could do this, contending that Rhodes was more interested in annexing the land in the name of his British South Africa Company, to pave the way for its commercial activities in the hinterland. Rhodes' aim was to occupy the area with bodies, and to do this, a less generous version of history tells how he hijacked a Boer trek that was gathering to go north. Farms and provision of equipment were offered, and the word was put about describing the wonderful climate of Ghanzi. As he had done with such success in Matabeleland, Rhodes sent a delegate to obtain signatures to give him access to lands he had his eye on. A fraudulent title deed was produced in Dutch – a language Sekgoma (the Batawana chief) could not speak, let alone read or write. When the Batawana complained to the British Government, they ordered Rhodes to get a new concession. Sekgoma then refused him access. Rhodes tried to force the government's hand by encouraging the trek to go ahead regardless.

Meanwhile Rhodes finally went too far with the abortive **Jameson Raid** (led by his associate Dr L. S. Jameson), aimed at overthrowing the South African Republic. When the world heard that Botswana had been used as a base for launching the raid, an embarrassed Britain abruptly terminated Rhodes' territorial ambitions. Jameson was

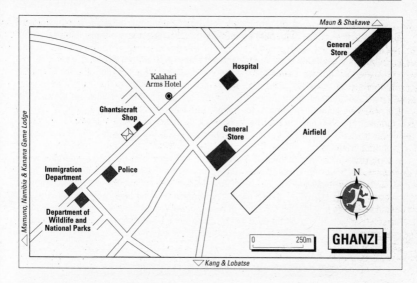

tried and imprisoned, while Rhodes was forced to resign as prime minister of the Cape Colony. However the forces set in motion by Rhodes were released in 1898. The area is unquestionably fine cattle country and the British High Commission was keen on settling the Ghanzi district. It made an ultimatum to Sekgoma: either give up Ghanzi or Britain would take all Ngamiland.

White settlers headed north to Ghanzi, and the Ghanzi farms joined the Tuli Block and Tati District as the only European areas of Bechuanaland. The trekkers were not the salt of the earth that the government had imagined, but fortune-hunters, most of whom deserted their farms within ten years. Things spluttered on for the next half century, until the road was built from Ghanzi to Lobatse, providing more convenient access to the country's big abattoirs. On the new dirt road, Land Rovers replaced the camels of the early colonial police force. The farming community is now extremely prosperous, producing large quantities of Botswana's finest beef. To overcome the isolation, several farmers have their own planes, and landing strips outside their Beverly Hills-style mansions.

Ghanzi practicalities

The main street of Ghanzi – a wide, pink, dusty swathe – heads like a ceremonial axis straight up to the bougainvillea-enclosed **hotel**, around which all activity in Ghanzi seems to revolve. The *Kalahari Arms Hotel* (PO Box 29, Ghanzi; ☎596298; ③–④) is the sole place to stay in Ghanzi itself, but don't count on a room or a more expensive rondavel – it's often full. The **campsite** at the back is pleasant enough, with ablutions, and a place to braai. Get on the right side of the manager who is extremely genial and great fun. If the *Kalahari Arms* is full, the other option is to head 24km west of town to *Kanana Game Lodge* (PO Box 2, Ghanzi; ☎/fax 596166), which has reasonably priced chalets and a campground overlooking a waterhole. In addition Ghanzi has a couple of bottle stores, a general dealer, butcher, shoe shop and a bunch of government offices, all basic concrete sheds. It's a growing town, losing its feeling of isolation with the fairly recent advent of electricity.

Ghantsicraft, between the hotel and post office, shouldn't be missed. It has one of the best collections of San crafts in the country and, as a non-profit organization, costs are kept really low, with ninety percent of the price going to the producer. At the moment **San crafts** must be among the very few, in Southern Africa at least, that are still made to high standards the traditional way, and it's a rare opportunity to get an authentic if not actually used artefact. It won't be possible for long. As the hunter-gathering culture comes to an end (bows and arrows are more or less out of use), the old skills of making hunting sets, beads and bags are disappearing too. It takes a woman weeks of concentrated bouts of work to make one ostrich-egg shell necklace. Besides what *Ghantsicraft* has for sale, it acts as a kind of mini-museum, with cases of beautiful artefacts.

Nightlife in Ghanzi all happens at the hotel, with discos at weekends that have to be seen to be believed. Unintelligible music blares out at a phenomenal wattage from rumbling old speakers. All you hear is a thumping beat but the pace is frantic and people friendly. Outside in the gardens things are sometimes quieter, but no less drunken and in a wild west town the brawling comes as no surprise – it's unlikely to be directed at you if you maintain a bit of discretion. Inside you can get a good **meal** (steak naturally) at the dining room-cum-bar. It's the only place to eat in town. Order

KALAHARI FLORA AND DESERT FOODS

There are about 250 **edible plants** throughout Botswana. Some of the San, such as the /Dau people in the Kalahari, use as many as 180 of them, although only three or four as staples. Knowledge and use of edible plants is on the decrease with the introduction of new crops, imported foods and a cash economy. Coca-cola, canned beer, peanuts and chewing gum are ousting their traditional counterparts and there's a social stigma attached to eating tubers and roots – considered food only for the poorest. During the severe droughts of the 1980s when many plants and animals died, the government provided drought relief in the form of maize meal. For many people, this has now become their staple diet.

Collecting vegetables from the bush is the job of women and girls, a major responsibility given that for traditional hunter-gatherers, this accounts for more than eighty percent of their diet. San working on farms still supplement their diet with wild food, although domestic livestock inevitably tramples and destroys edible plants so they're not so easy to find. From November to May people collect berries, nuts, fruits, roots, tubers, bulbs, shoots, succulents, wild honey and even a species of delicious truffle. Besides plants they also forage for less appealing mopane worms (there are twenty species of edible insect), small mammals, bullfrogs, reptiles, birds and their eggs, and ant eggs.

Before the rains break, from August to November, food is at its scarcest. The sun burns everything up and it becomes very difficult to detect the moisture-bearing plants which are necessary for survival away from any other water sources. Before the advent of boreholes, people obtained all their liquid for eight months of the year from plants. The most remarkable of these, the **morama**, develops a massive, moisture-bearing underground tuber which contains as much as sixty litres of liquid. It betrays its presence by runners above the surface. The runners bear bean-like pods, each containing a couple of *morama* nuts – a great delicacy roasted in the hot sand. Young tubers are chewed for moisture, or roasted and eaten. Also widely eaten are *tsama* melons and wild cucumbers, eaten raw or roasted; their seeds can be dried and pounded into flour. In the northwest, the !Kung-speaking people rely on the *mongongo* nut. The kernel is highly nutritious, while the sweet flesh and skin are eaten raw or boiled.

Botswana has its own intoxicating **palm wine** made from the sap of the palm tree which is left to ferment. Unfortunately, many of the palm trees along the Shashi and Limpopo rivers have died from being over-tapped – the palm juice used to be distilled into a highly toxic and illegal beverage, apparently causing great pain behind the eyes.

before you feel hungry as it takes a while. Meantime, in an outside bar with pack-'em-in pews you can catch an action video of some description.

The Kalahari San

Ghanzi is an area of convergence of all the **San** linguistic groupings – the **!Ko**, **G/wi**, **Gana**, **Tsau**, **/Dau** and **Nharo**. The Nharo are one of the largest San groups in Southern Africa and over half live in the Ghanzi district, in the white farm block where they constitute the ethnic majority.

Most San are employed on farms or are simply squatters; a few are petty entrepreneurs or settled food producers, while many go between life on farms and life in the bush. According to a 1976 government report, the biggest problem facing the San is outright oppression and discrimination by other Ghanzi residents. On numerous occasions they've been asked to leave public meetings or even village Independence celebrations. Tension between Nharo and blacks often leads to fights and brawls, especially at drinking sessions.

The San face a list of chronic **problems** including poverty, massive unemployment, dependency, landlessness, powerlessness and despair, with a standard of living well below that of the average Motswana. Their existential distress has increased so sharply that the healing trance dance, which used to be performed only sporadically, is nowadays conducted very regularly. The word *sheeta* is used to describe the concept of life as a toll of misfortune, sickness and death. The kind of labour they've developed a tradition in – tracking, trekking, riding and unskilled work – has become obsolete on modern ranches where many San have been replaced by black labour. Pay is very low and they're dependent on the farmer for water, food, tobacco and a place to stay.

Poverty and hunger is a certain recipe for stock theft. As the poorest people in Botswana, San have a disproportionate involvement in cattle-rustling and other poverty-related misdemeanours such as hunting without a licence, tax evasion and squatting. At least a third of stock theft is committed by other groups.

What San people want most is a place to be, to combine an agricultural existence with some hunting and gathering. To its credit the government has taken all this on board, approaching the problem by providing water and land as a fundamental means for the San to move into the mainstream of Botswana's development, combined with literacy campaigns and better health facilities to help combat common illnesses like tuberculosis and sexually transmitted diseases.

The San have never had a sense of belonging to a common heritage and consequently few San, if any, campaign for their rights. However outsiders from a variety of perspectives do **campaign** on their behalf, some wishing to maintain what they believe is the ancient lifestyle of these people. The question is a fraught one, with the Botswana government assiduously avoiding any racial recognition – it wants to steer clear of any policy that even vaguely smacks of apartheid. It doesn't want to regard the San as a distinct group with separate rights, but rather as citizens of Botswana in the process of integration.

Romantics, some of them doubtless influenced by the work of Laurens van der Post, say they want the traditional hunter-gatherer lifestyle of the San to be retained. But it's too late for that. A Ghanzi District Council report which came out in 1980 found that something would have to be done fairly urgently about the poverty and the acute hardship of people living in the Central Kalahari Game Reserve, and that their most consistently expressed wish was to be able to live like other Batswana. The report concluded that any development should take place within their home ground, where they had been resident as a group for generations. An important element in the development plans was to be the provision of **waterholes** and self-help agricultural projects.

THE SAN

The San should not be regarded as backward people who failed to progress from hunting and gathering to a "higher" and more sedentary way of life, but as people whose adaptation to the environment was well-nigh total.

David Stephen, *The San of the Kalahari*

The social system of the San embodied everything a searcher for Utopia could want: there were no chiefs, people possessed only one or two items of personal property, a high premium was placed on relationships set up through sharing, decisions were made communally (women participated equally in decision-making), and there was a rich spiritual life which stressed the unity of existence. This "ecological" way of life enabled their continuous survival for longer than any other society. Sadly, though, that's all over – in the 1980s the traditional San way of life finally fizzled to an end.

TERMINOLOGY
The sensitivity of the so-called "bushman problem" is reflected in the linguistic agonizing over what to call them. The most widely used term, with racist and sexist connotations, is **bushmen**, deriving from the early settler *bosmanneken* (men of the bush). It grew out of the belief that they were animals and not people. In the eighteenth and nineteenth centuries, "bushmen" was used for all social outcasts in conflict with the laws of the Cape. The stridently racist "bushies" is also used. Many people, including liberal writers, still use "bushmen", waiting for an acceptable, non-pejorative term to be found.

Several historians have plumped for **San**, but the term refers to a language group and not a culture, and is used derisively by the Khoi (cattle-herding contemporaries of the San) to mean hunter-gatherer. It is currently the respectable term in most academic circles. It's not a term used by the hunter-gatherers themselves, and is rarely used in Botswana outside books. One word they do use to describe themselves is the N'coahkoe, the "red people", but it's not yet in common usage.

The Setswana word **Basarwa**, meaning people from the uninhabited country, is apparently disliked by San themselves because it connotes negative sentiments. The Botswana government, too, has made its own contribution to the debate. In its vigorous attempts to avoid any racial categories associated with apartheid, it has adopted a socially rather than ethnically defined term: **Remote Area Dwellers**. This gets abbreviated to RADs, an unfortunate choice as in Setswana "t" and "d" aren't clearly differentiated, and RADs become "RATs".

THE ORIGINAL SOUTH AFRICANS
As Southern Africa's earliest inhabitants, the San are also the most direct descendants of the late Stone Age. They have hunted and gathered on the subcontinent for a considerable period – paintings in Namibia by their ancestors date back 25,000 years. At one time San-speakers probably spread throughout sub-Saharan Africa, living for most of that period a fairly unaltered existence. But in the last two thousand years, the southward migration of Bantu-speaking farmers forced change upon the San, and the pace has been ever more rapid over the last four hundred years, since the arrival of Europeans.

Archeological evidence suggests that as **Bantu-speaking farmers** progressed south from West Africa they moved into the moister areas avoided by the San and that for a millennium the two groups lived more or less harmoniously side by side. In fact, far from the newcomers simply dominating the incumbents, the modern phonetics of Bantu languages like Xhosa in the Eastern Cape, Zulu in Natal and Swazi in Swaziland show that the blacks from the north were influenced by the people they found. With the arrival of the whites at the Cape in the seventeenth century, a twofold threat eventually brought the San to blows with both Bantu-speakers and Boers.

Over the centuries whites began to annex lands for hunting and farming, hence restricting the hunting grounds of the San and depleting the stocks of huntable game.

San began turning to taking cattle from both Bantu and Boer farmers. The whites in particular came to regard the San as vermin, and early Dutch settlers in the **Cape** felt free to ride out in extermination parties. In the eighteenth century, a full-scale genocidal campaign was under way which resulted in the slaughter of thousands of San and their extinction in the Cape. They were eventually wiped off the South African map and now survive only around the Kalahari Desert – sixty percent in Botswana and the remainder in eastern Namibia and southern Angola.

By the 1850s most of **Botswana** was either claimed by Batswana or other farmers. In these areas the San became absorbed into farming communities and in the more heavily populated areas completely disappeared as a distinct group. They came – and still come – rock bottom of the social order. It was only in remote areas like the Central Kalahari that their traditional way of life continued. By the turn of this century most San had made contact with pastoral people. Many lived semi-traditional lifestyles close to cattle posts – the men became cattle-herders and the women continued to gather wild food. But the fencing of farmland made hunting and gathering more difficult – game became scarce and wild food difficult to find until eventually the San were left with little option but to learn Afrikaans and to work for white farmers.

In 1964, prior to Independence, the British administration became concerned about the plight of the San, who they feared – not without justification – would be badly treated in the new country. In the past San who became attached to Tswana villages were little more than slaves of Batswana families, with no rights under Tswana law. But contrary to British fears, the Botswana government took the problem on board and now regards the San as equal under law, although social prejudice persists.

TRADITIONAL WAYS

Traditional San **bands** consisted of between fifteen and eighty members and had no chief, decisions being made communally. Individuals were free to come and go, and those who failed to get on in one group would simply take themselves elsewhere. Bands were flexible and would vary in size depending on the amount of food locally available – small dispersed groups were better suited to scarce food resources.

San **beliefs** centred around the notion that everything was part of the great web of nature with an equal right to existence. They believed that humans, as mere parts of the cosmos, have no special rights over the animals and birds.

At first sight, **hunting** seems to contradict this idea, but the San were not excessive hunters, rather getting most of their nutrition, often up to ninety percent, from plants collected by women. Hunting was an important social activity stressing the custom of sharing – all the meat from the hunt ended up shared through complex rules. Killing an animal was simultaneously sad (because a fellow creature had died) and joyous (because a spiritual unification had taken place). Wanton killing was totally taboo with the danger of great disaster for overstepping the bounds. In keeping with their cosmology, the San were sensitive to the suffering of other beings and would often go out of their way to spare pain. One researcher reported an incident in which a dung beetle heading for a camp fire was turned around to prevent its injury. And among some groups, even scorpions are spared, unless about to sting.

In San **religion** there was a good god, the giver of life who was also a distant being not much concerned with the mundane dealings of mortals. The evil god on the other hand was a meddlesome trickster, who spent his time stirring trouble. He could change his form, but usually took that of a human. The night-long **trance dance** was the San means to deal with evil and to communicate with the spirit world. It was a healing dance in which a powerful healing force called *n/um* was activated. The men danced while the women sat around the fire, rhythmically clapping and singing. It remains one of the most persistent aspects of their culture, continuing even where San have deserted the traditional ways and lived for generations on white farms.

SAN LANGUAGE

With the end of their traditional culture, language has become the most fundamental factor defining the San. One of the distinctive characteristics of all San languages is the **click sounds**, made by air escaping when the tongue is pulled away from the palate or teeth. All San languages have some common clicks:

/ (dental, tongue pulling from two front top teeth)
// (lateral, tongue pulling from upper right teeth)
! (palatal, tongue pulling from roof of mouth)

Additional clicks are found in some dialects. The above three clicks have been absorbed into the Nguni (southeastern Bantu languages), where they're written as c, x and q respectively.

San languages are extremely difficult for outsiders to pick up, because of their click consonants and the use of high, middle and low tones to distinguish meanings. Most words are monosyllables ending in a vowel or nasal sound. In some languages there's no gender such as "he" and "she", sex being denoted by distinct words like "hen" and "cock". The languages are poor in words referring to abstract concepts but very rich in ones describing everyday actions. There are few terms to distinguish colours, which in the San world-view have no separate existence – colours are simply attributes of plants or objects which already have detailed descriptions.

Many of the San have been attracted out of their traditional lifestyle by permanent water sources of this nature which obviate the need for eternal wandering. Hunting is severely restricted and the old knowledge is disappearing. Alcohol abuse is becoming a growing problem and the transition to life at these borehole villages is a painful one. Packaged government maize meal provides the San with far less nutrition than the array of wild foods that was formerly available to them. Some of the boreholes started off as watering places for game, like the one built in 1963 at Chade, but now there are at least 1300 people living there in very demoralized conditions, dependent on food hand-outs.

On the other hand, the powerful US-backed **wildlife conservation lobby** is keen to see any remaining San out of the Central Kalahari Reserve (it's for animals and safari groups only) while mineral exploration goes on unabated. Recent government policy seems to have shifted towards bringing Remote Area Dwellers (as the government now calls the San) into the mainstream of Botswana's development – removing them from the Central Kalahari to a life of more dependable water sources and food. This is certainly not what all San want. In a 1988 Swedish documentary *When Manna Falls from Heaven*, which looks at Botswana after the diamond revenue, an articulate inhabitant of the Central Kalahari Reserve says his people want to stay exactly where they are. He says he doesn't understand why the government claims it can help them elsewhere and not where they already are.

Onwards from Ghanzi

Ghanzi is a staging post in the Kalahari, dull unless you meet local people and get under the skin of it. Getting there is quite a feat, only matched by the journey away again.

It is possible to **hitch** out of Ghanzi, but be prepared to wait a couple of days. Aid workers, researchers and teachers are a noticeable presence in town and you're bound to bump into them at the hotel. They're a mine of information about local gossip and politics and a grapevine for arranging **lifts**. Locals drive to Maun or Gaborone; ask at the hotel and around for lifts. Monday and Tuesday when cattle trucks go off to Lobatse are said to be good days to try your luck getting to Gaborone. A scheduled **bus** is supposed to leave Ghanzi for Lobatse on Wednesday mornings – ask at the hotel for current information. A much more comfortable alternative if you can afford it is to take one of the twice-weekly **flights** to Gaborone or Maun. Book through the *Kalahari Arms*.

If you're overlanding, the obvious route out of Ghanzi is **west to Windhoek** in Namibia, a journey of 575km which takes around ten hours. Roads are rough but you don't need 4WD. The distance from Ghanzi to the border at Mamuno is 210km; not many vehicles use this route so hitching can be difficult. Note that the Namibian border post closes at 4pm, while Botswana shuts at 5pm. Once at Windhoek, right in the centre of Namibia, there is a camping site, but it's unappealingly floodlit and next to a main road. Nevertheless you're in the heart of one of the most beautiful countries in Africa with the lure of an undeveloped coastline and superb game parks and wilderness areas.

FROM NAMIBIA TO BOTSWANA BY CAR

No vehicle is allowed to leave Namibia without police clearance. Clearance is obtained from any of the main police stations in Namibia. Proof of ownership, the vehicle chassis number, engine number and registration number are required. The rule is strictly enforced and if you haven't got it, you'll be sent back from the border to the nearest town to get it.

PART FOUR

THE

CONTEXTS

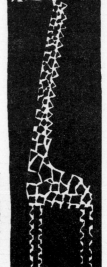

ZIMBABWE:THE HISTORICAL FRAMEWORK

Pre-colonial Zimbabwe enjoyed a political continuity unique in sub-Saharan Africa, being dominated, from the tenth century on, by a succession of Shona states. In successive centuries, the influence of these states stretched east to the coast of Mozambique and west into Botswana's desert lands. It was only in the 1890s, with the arrival of white colonists and the creation of "Rhodesia", that the country's modern boundaries were drawn.

ROCK ARCHIVES

Zimbabwe's **Stone Age** leaps the millennia through the vivid records of its **rock art**. These paintings, often finely realized, most commonly represent religion and ritual – suggesting a long-gone spiritual world that respected all living things as equal in creation. But they also give firm clues about their **hunter-gatherer** artists, depicting the bows and stone-tipped arrows of the male hunter and the digging sticks and bags of the female gatherers. Who exactly were the successors of these, the plateau's first people, remains in some dispute: some theories suggest they were San, like the remaining handful of the region's hunter-gatherers in Botswana; while others favour a people more akin to today's Bantu-speakers.

Farming was the plateau-dwellers' first social revolution – a quantum leap into a vastly different existence that was firmly established by around 200 BC. Although hunter-gatherers had mastered subsistence existence – needing no more than twenty hours a week to forage – farming provided more security and a stable lifestyle, which enabled people to accumulate produce against barren years. It was, though, the slowest of transitions. Hunter-gatherers already possessed the elements of farming, burning grass to bring new shoots to attract animals, and protecting useful plants.

Following the establishment of farming, occasional pictures of sheep appear on cave walls. People still moved about with their herds, but agriculture meant a slower, more static way of life – tilling, seeding and reaping is a lengthy process. Some discovered that ore from certain rocks could be used to make labour-saving tools, and weapons; the first **miners and ironworkers** were farmers. And then came trade, with people who had access to iron (and later gold) bartering their minerals for other goods.

LINEAGES

Hunter-gathering supported only small nomadic bands, but farming culture gradually created more complex societies as people began to map relationships within communities, and to trace back family trees to their first ancestors – the spiritual guardians of each piece of land.

Late **Iron Age** people lived in collections of homesteads, which belonged to **lineages.** Each lineage had its own ancestor, but there was a single major figure – the big daddy of them all. The more direct the relationship to him the more senior the lineage, so daughters from senior lineages began to command a high bride price, as they brought a large number of cattle into the lineage.

In questions of marriage, therefore, the balance of trade favoured the senior lineage every time, and these groups, in consequence, could become quite rich. Around the **tenth century**, the first **towns** emerged in the cattle-lands of Zimbabwe's southwest and in eastern Botswana. The lands here were too dry for horticulture, but great for cattle with plenty of grass and mopane trees – juicy leaves perfect for the dry season when grass dies back.

THE SHONA STATES

It was from the senior lineages that the large herd-owning **ruling classes** came. Their wealth and power catapulted traditional society from subsistence to a patronage system that could muster large armies to build the great public works of the plateau – the **stone-walled towns**. Few other sub-Saharan countries have such imposing evidence left by powerful states over the last millennium.

THE ZIMBABWE STATE

Toward the end of the eleventh century Iron Age Shona-speakers settled at the hilltop site of **Great Zimbabwe**, building a village of pole and dagha huts. Despite large cattle herds, they weren't inordinately wealthy, but by the fourteenth century this had changed. The lineage **herds** had grown to unprecedented numbers and so the power of the rulers had increased. They began to organize their subjects into armies of builders, herders and soldiers.

Although the wealth of Zimbabwe's rulers rested on cattle, the state also developed a **gold trade**, trading on the Mozambique coast. Zimbabwe armies policed the trade and the rulers charged a toll, supplementing their growing riches, which they used to build the famous walls – today's national symbol.

Great Zimbabwe itself became the largest regional centre, with over ten thousand inhabitants. The reason for its eventual **decline** is another disputed issue, but current evidence favours the theory that the area suffered from overpopulation – too many people, too much farming and too many cattle. The land lost its fertility and by the sixteenth century the site of Great Zimbabwe was deserted.

THE MUTAPA STATE – AND THE FIRST PORTUGUESE ENCOUNTERS

The **Mutapa State**, a looser confederation of ruling families, rose as the Zimbabwe State was sliding, to span the fifteenth to twentieth centuries. Better placed for the gold trade, near

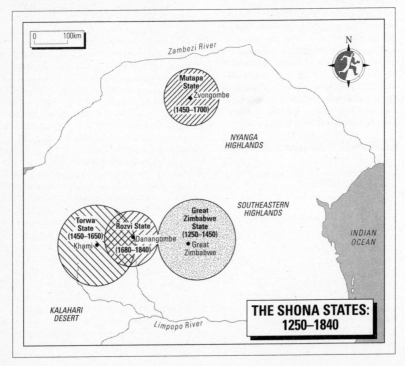

THE SHONA STATES: 1250–1840

the northern gold-fields and the coast, they surrounded their homesteads with stone walls.

Written accounts of the state come from **Portuguese** sailors, who first heard of central African empires, gold and untold riches, from Arab traders. The Portuguese had a tendency to exaggerate, perhaps to encourage backers to give financial support to expeditions – one very apocryphal story had the adventurer Vasco da Gama dubbing the Zambezi "the river of good omens" in 1497, after encountering gold-dust-laden Arab dhows in its Indian Ocean delta.

By 1505 the Portuguese were in control of Sofala on the Mozambique coast, and soon their attention turned to the hinterland, heralding a history of **colonial interference** that was to last over the next four centuries.

In Zimbabwe the Mutapas were the first to taste contact with Europeans; sweet at first, it was soon to sour. The whites were enthralled by tales of Mutapa wealth, the elite garbed in gold and silver embroidered cloths and so overladen with precious bangles that they could hardly move their arms. Their wealth was in fact quite great, stemming from their ability to impose taxes on gold-seekers, ivory-hunters and traders.

Mutually beneficial **barter** between the two powers took place until the Portuguese decided they could no longer brook Swahili competition. In 1569 an army of one thousand led by **Francisco Barreto** set out from Portugal to invade the Mutapa State. Defeated by disease and starvation, the expedition flopped before it arrived, but toward the end of the sixteenth century the Portuguese seized a new opportunity to gain a foothold when they took advantage of successive ruling-class splits in Mutapa. In exchange for military help they eventually gained a free hand in the territory.

In 1629 the Mutapa (or king) became a **vassal of the Portuguese** monarchy, and the Portuguese occupied several towns along the Zambezi, notably Tete and Sena. At its height, their influence extended along the river beyond Kariba and south of Harare to the Kadoma gold-fields. Territory was divided into *prazos* – minifiefdoms controlled by ruling families. Each of these formed private armies and raided the countryside, taking slaves and land, and building markets all over the north.

This first colonial nightmare ended, however, in 1663, when the Mutapa was assassinated and the new ruler rejected Portuguese domination. Forming an alliance with the Rozvi Changamire in the southwest, he drove the Portuguese from Zimbabwe, and they never returned as a credible political force. When they did, it was to Manyika on sufferance of the Manyika rulers, and they had to content themselves with trading through African go-betweens.

For the next 250 years Portuguese influence in the region was very tenuous, with small stretches of coast and a handful of islands coming under their control. It was only after the Berlin Congress of 1884 that they succeeded in getting recognition for the colony of Mozambique and set up an administration to control the entire territory.

TORWA AND THE ROZVI

In its declining years, Great Zimbabwe was eclipsed by a new state – the **Torwa** – in the southwest around present Bulawayo.

As an offshoot of Great Zimbabwe, the Torwa State carried the tradition of **stone construction** to new heights. The ruling dynasty kept apart from the peasantry, intermarrying only within the ruling classes and setting up centres throughout the country. Its *mambos* or rulers wore spun cotton garments and gold, copper and ivory jewellery. They taxed peasants, traders and farmers, and controlled most of the state's cattle. By the seventeenth century, though, the economy was crumbling – mainly through a slow-down in gold exports – and the rulers began to lose their grip. The building of stone walls stagnated, coming to a complete standstill by the end of the century.

There is uncertainty about the origins of the next dynasty, the **Rozvi**. They may have been invaders from the north who conquered the Torwa, or perhaps just a new Torwa dynasty under a different name. Their capital was at **Danangombe** – the walls are still standing – and although the size of the state was relatively small, the extent of their influence was considerable. The state's wealth was based on its powerful army and its capacity to exact tribute even beyond its own borders. This differed from the Mutapa State which was far more dependent on trade.

Rozvi **military power** took it into Mutapa territory where it attacked the ruling dynasty in the 1680s. In the nineteenth century Rozvi might began to weaken from within, and the exaction of tribute became progressively more difficult. The situation was compounded by waves of invading Nguni, and culminated in **Zwangendaba**'s hordes sweeping through on their way north.

THE MFECANE

Through the preceding millennium, Zimbabwe's affairs had been determined largely by the Shona-speakers, who dominated the plateau. At the onset of the nineteenth century, however, an explosion of external events reverberated into the region, bringing the first serious threat from **non-Shona elements**. Over the Drakensberg Mountains, in what is now South Africa's Natal Province, a storm was brewing among the small **Nguni** groups who, as a result of land hunger – aggravated by the encroachment of white settlers – had entered into a virtually constant state of feud with each other.

In 1818, **Shaka**, the illegitimate son of a minor Nguni chief, turned his father's small **Zulu** clan into the most powerful fighting machine in Southern Africa. A shrewd commander and ruthless absolute ruler, he tolerated no opposition and during the 1820s his army swept through the subcontinent, conquering and expanding his power base. Many clans fled, hence the term *mfecane*, meaning "forced migration".

Some of these were the marauding hordes that passed through Shona territory, pillaging but enforcing few lasting changes on the communities they encountered. But two of these raiding armies stayed, exerting very much longer-term effects. In the east, Shoshangane set up the iron-handed **Gaza State**, but it was the **Ndebele State** that made the most lasting impression.

THE NDEBELE STATE

In 1822 an army of the **Khumalo** clan, under their ruler, Mzilikazi, left Natal to escape Shaka's conquests. Wherever they went, however, they were pursued by the unrelenting Zulu *impi*, which moved throughout the region, raiding well into Zimbabwe. Unable to settle and farm, these refugees, who became the Ndebele, were forced to rely on seizing cattle and food as they marched. After years of wandering, which

took them to Botswana and brought them into conflict with the advancing Boers in the Transvaal, they eventually established a capital at **Bulawayo** in the 1840s.

Mzilikazi, who was succeeded by his son, Lobengula, in 1870, had forged a united state from disparate elements. Although at core Zulu, his **Ndebele State** comprised Nguni, Sotho, Tswana and Shona people, picked up on the Khumalo's northward migration. Far from resenting cultural eclipse, Shona youth was eager to be identified with this go-ahead society, to the extent that in 1888 a missionary, Reverend Knothe, commented that:

> They have completely taken over the language, costume and customs of the Ndebele and do not want to know that they are descendants of the Karanga [Shona speakers].

Although Ndebele status was affected by ethnic origins, Mzilikazi wisely ensured that all captives were fully incorporated into the state. Women and children went to live with Ndebele families to learn their language and customs and had the same rights and duties as everyone else. When the boys were ready to marry the king provided them with the necessary bride-wealth cattle.

Most Ndebele were cattle-farmers living in homesteads, others were in the powerful army, which ensured Ndebele control well beyond the farms of its own people. A **tribute system** operated, whereby small states on the periphery signified their dependence on the Ndebele by offering food and cattle. The intention was not to cripple the subject states, which retained most of their wealth, but rather to symbolize their client status. The relationship was symbiotic. The Ndebele wanted peaceful states on their doorstep in which they could graze their cattle, but at the same time their army offered protection against hostile raiders to the smaller states.

THE GAZA INVASIONS

Also in the 1820s, **Shoshangane** fled north with one of the sections of the Zulu-shattered Ndwandwe (Nguni) State, eventually settling amid the **Ndau** (Shona dialect speakers), and completely disrupting their culture. Gaza words passed into the Ndau language, while Ndau men were conscripted into the army and women became Gaza wives.

Unlike the Ndebele, who successfully incorporated their conquered subjects into their state, the **Gaza** were themselves eventually absorbed. They treated the people they conquered as second- and third-class citizens. Subjects such as the Ndau from the southern Eastern Highlands, who accepted Gaza domination, were simply exploited, while others such as Mozambique's Tsonga and Chopi were often sold as slaves to the Portuguese.

A huge area of eastern Zimbabwe and parts of Mozambique were harassed and controlled

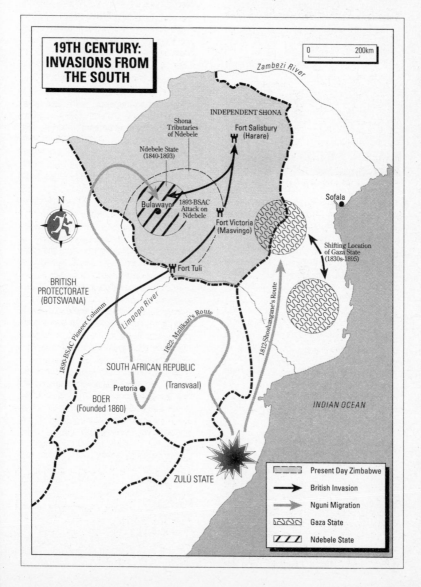

19TH CENTURY:
INVASIONS FROM
THE SOUTH

0   200km

Zambezi River

INDEPENDENT SHONA

Shona
Tributaries
of Ndebele

Fort Salisbury
(Harare)

Ndebele State
(1840-1893)

Bulawayo

1893-BSAC
Attack on
Ndebele

Fort Victoria
(Masvingo)

Sofala

Shifting Location
of Gaza State
(1830s-1895)

N

Fort Tuli

BRITISH
PROTECTORATE
(BOTSWANA)

Limpopo River

1890-BSAC Pioneer Column

1822-Mzilikazi's Route

1812-Shoshangane's Route

SOUTH AFRICAN REPUBLIC

Pretoria

(Transvaal)

INDIAN OCEAN

BOER
(Founded 1860)

ZULU STATE

Present Day Zimbabwe

British Invasion

Nguni Migration

Gaza State

Ndebele State

by the small, permanent **Gaza army**. As in society, the forces were separated according to class. The elite were all born Nguni, while conquered people formed cannon-fodder regiments. In the end the Gaza State was brought down by internal divisions and finally succumbed to **Portuguese** forces in 1895, becoming part of their Mozambique colony.

The Gazas' main mark on the area was the title *Shangaan*, a corruption of Shoshongane's name, which became prized by people of the east. Gaza identity was very attractive to many subjects, especially the youth, some of whom adopted Nguni clan names – which continue today. In military matters Gaza influence was total; the Ndau completely changed their uniform, and adopted the methods of their conquerors.

BRITAIN'S PRIVATIZED INVASIONS

A pair of British hunter-adventurers, Henry Hartley and Frederick Courteney Selous, arrived in Zimbabwe in the 1870s, possibly on the trail of Portuguese stories of gold wealth. They were to find the remains of hundreds of **gold mines**, and wrote home that the country was rich in gold. But, as they were to learn, gold mines didn't necessarily signify the existence of gold – rather its removal; most of the local shallow-cast mines had been exhausted.

Nevertheless, with the discovery of vast gold reefs on South Africa's Witwatersrand, speculators began to believe that something similar was waiting to be discovered in Zimbabwe, and interested parties gathered like flies to get in on the action. In the 1880s **Boer** and **German** agents approached the Ndebele king, Lobengula. Meanwhile, along the Eastern Highlands, the **Portuguese**, too, were surreptitiously muscling in.

THE BRITISH SOUTH AFRICA COMPANY

In the end it was **Cecil John Rhodes** – with the backing of Britain – who gained control of the area north of the Limpopo. Britain was eager to block any expansion by rival powers, while Rhodes, for his part, having made a fortune in the Kimberley diamond mines in South Africa, but losing out on the Witwatersrand, saw rich pickings.

With powerful friends, Rhodes formed the **British South Africa Company**, with the express brief to exploit the lands north of the Limpopo. From the British government's point of view this was a convenient bit of privatized foreign policy, which they naturally endorsed. The BSAC was granted a Royal Charter for the territory north of South Africa and west of Mozambique, to

> make treaties, promulgate laws, maintain a police force, acquire new concessions, make land grants and carry on any lawful trade, commerce or business.

Rhodes's long-term plan was to occupy Zimbabwe, Zambia and Malawi – but his approach was gradual and intent on avoiding immediate confrontation with Lobengula's powerful Ndebele State. In 1890, his private army, the **"Pioneer Column"**, marched north to the site of Harare, skirting lands under Lobengula's control. Immediately the settlers set about looking for gold, which never materialized; many turned to farming instead, taking over traditional Shona lands.

LOBENGULA – AND WAR

Ndebele influence over large parts of Zimbabwe was, at this time, immense. So strong, in fact, that businessmen and politicians in South Africa concluded that it would have to be removed, and by means of war.

A shrewd statesman, **Lobengula** tried to concede as little as possible while keeping his regiments firmly in check. War, he knew, would bring to an end Ndebele pre-eminence in the region. But the forces he faced were insurmountable and Rhodes succeeded in outmanoeuvring him.

Several times Lobengula was deceived. **Moffat**, an agent of Rhodes, presented the king with a treaty which prohibited him from making further agreements with anyone but the British. He refused to sign, but Moffat claimed otherwise and the phoney document was used to keep out the Germans and Portuguese. To tighten the noose further, Lobengula was then lured into agreeing to the **Rudd Concession**, which allowed miners into Matebeleland and provided the means for white entrenchment in Mashonaland. The British made empty verbal promises that the concession would protect the Ndebele from further colonial pressure: only ten miners would prospect and notices would be put in all English and South African papers warning Europeans off. But the BSAC was simply waiting for the right time to invade Matabeleland – an action that began, with a fairly routine event, in 1893.

The first act in the drama was Lobengula's sending of a **Ndebele raiding party** to the Masvingo area, to punish Shona tributaries who had cut a telegraph wire and made mischief between the BSAC and the Ndebele. Similar raids in the past had always been ignored – as was this at first by the local BSAC commander, one Leander Starr Jameson.

But some weeks after, judging the time right for an invasion of Matabeleland, **Jameson** seized on the incident, told the British authorities that the Ndebele were planning to attack white settlers, and mustered an army of pioneers and black mercenaries. Reports were fabricated that this force had been ambushed by Ndebele troops, and the British sent in a powerful battalion from neighbouring Botswana. Jameson, eager to see the destruction of Lobengula's kingdom and concerned that his hands would be tied by less partial forces, hastened to pre-empt their arrival.

Aware of the impending disaster, Lobengula desperately tried to avoid war. Delegates were sent to Cape Town, stressing his **desire for peace** – but they were intercepted and shot. Furious at this, Lobengula, according to one account, appeared before his war-ready troops repeatedly shouting the salute, *Bayete*, before thrusting his assegai to the ground. Its shaft broke – a bad omen.

The **battle**, when it came, was swift. As Ndebele troops approached to meet the advancing enemy they were mercilessly mowed down by machine guns. Their capital, **Bulawayo**, was subsequently razed, and Lobengula fled into the wilderness, where he died the following year.

THE FIRST CHIMURENGA

The Shona had not been conquered by the British in the way that the Ndebele were, and at first welcomed the settlers. **Trade** took place and successful Shona farmers generated sufficient surplus to feed the whites and earn themselves a tidy profit. Only after the gold dream turned to dust did the newcomers start farming seriously, nabbing any fertile land they fancied. For the Shona too, the daydream was short-lived – the happy days of trade and neighbourliness turned into a reality of domination and eviction.

COMPANY LAW

Within years, both Ndebele and Shona found themselves trespassers in their own land, evicted by whites, and subject to British South Africa Company decrees.

Both peoples saw their rights whittled away as they were relegated to dry, infertile and tsetse-infested reserves. The Company, meanwhile, seized the majority of **Ndebele cattle** as spoils of war, claiming it had belonged to Lobengula. In fact the herd had been held in

"LET THEM EAT DOGS"

Speech by Chief Somabulana, rebel leader and spokesman at the 1896 Matopos *indaba* with Rhodes:

We, the Amandabili, the sons of Kumalo, the Izulu, Children of the Stars; we are no dogs! You came, you conquered. The strongest takes the land. We accepted your rule. We lived under you. But not as dogs! If we are to be dogs it is better to be dead.

I myself once visited Bulawayo. I came to pay my respects to the Chief Magistrate. I brought my indunas with me, and my servants. I am a chief. I am expected to travel with attendants and advisers. I came to Bulawayo early in the morning, before the sun had dried the dew, and I sat down before the Court House, sending messages to the Chief Magistrate that I waited to pay my respects

to him. And so I sat until the evening shadows were long.

I sent again to the Chief Magistrate and told him that I did not wish to hurry him in an unmannerly way; I would wait his pleasure; but my people were hungry; and when the white men visited me it was my custom to kill that they might eat. The answer from the Chief Magistrate was that the town was full of dogs; dog to dog; we might kill those and eat them if we could catch them. So I left Bulawayo that night; and when next I tried to visit the Chief Magistrate it was with my impis behind me; no soft words in their mouths; but the assegai in their hands. Who blames me?

(Quoted in Terence Ranger, *The Nineteenth Century in Southern Rhodesia*)

trust by the king on behalf of the whole community. Cattle were more than a treasury, resting at the very core of social relations, and this seizure was an attack on Ndebele culture and society itself. What cattle remained to them were wiped out in the 1895 Rinderpest epidemic, many of them shot by white ranchers eager to stem the spreading disease. The sight of whites randomly potting the dwindling Ndbele herds rankled.

And if that wasn't enough, the colonials sought ways to bring the blacks into the cash economy. Only the payment of pittance wages made it possible for the whites to make the worn-out mines profitable, so a **hut tax** was devised to flush out the "idle natives" from their subsistence existence and into the job market. Blacks saw their traditions under fire and their way of life crumbling.

UPRISING

In 1896, when Rhodes's hatchet man Jameson staged an **abortive coup** against the Boer-controlled South African Republic, a large number of the British South Africa Police (the Company's army) were captured. Spotting their chance, the Ndebele initiated the **First Chimurenga** (liberation war), attacking and killing white farmers and traders.

Much to the surprise of whites, many **Shona** joined forces with the Ndebele, having developed a greater resentment towards the settlers than to their former overlords. The Shona **spirit mediums** of Kaguvi and Nehanda moved around the country inspiring the battle to regain ancestral lands. Whites fled to the forts in the main settlements.

For a while chiefs again controlled their traditional domains, but British reinforcements were sent to crush the Ndebele – a war that proved costly for both sides. Villages and crops were destroyed, while at the same time the conflict was a drain on BSAC coffers. Eventually, both parties came together in the infamous **Matopos indabas** – an agreement made between Rhodes and Ndebele *indunas* (captains). Rhodes made all sorts of promises, including the return of all occupied land; none was kept.

With the Ndebele subdued, the BSAC set about putting down the **Shona rebels**. Unlike the Ndebele, the Shona lacked political unity, and their chiefdoms sometimes sided out of

opportunism with the British, happy to see rivals cut down to size by the settlers. Clinically, systematically and with total ruthlessness the colonial forces moved through Mashonaland, picking off the disunited groups one by one. By 1897 it was all over, though on the scaffold the defiant **medium of Nehanda** prophesied that "my bones will rise". For her, final victory was certain.

RHODESIA – LIMITED COMPANY

Until 1923 the **British South Africa Company** (BSAC) ran **Rhodesia** – as the colonists had dubbed the territories of Mashonaland and Matabeleland – and virtually everything in it.

The Company, and its associated white settlers and immigrants, had hopes that these territories would become a "white country" along the lines of Australia or New Zealand, or even South Africa. Blacks were regarded as somewhat incidental. But in the eighty years following the British takeover Rhodesia's white population reached only 270,000, alongside a black majority that grew from 700,000 in the 1920s to nearly eight million at Independence.

SELL-OFF: THE 1923 CONSTITUTION

The BSAC had anticipated huge profits from their African fiefdom, but by the 1920s these had signally failed to materialize, and they began looking for a way to rid themselves of the albatross. The solution was a referendum offering whites a new constitution. The recommendation of the British High Commission and the Company was to incorporate the territory into the more profitable Union of South Africa, which in 1910 had brought together the two British colonies of the Cape and Natal with the defeated pair of Boer republics.

The idea of being dominated by Afrikaners, however, horrified the Rhodesians, who voted instead for an option of so-called responsible government in a new state that became known as **Southern Rhodesia**. In effect, "responsible government" meant that they were responsible to no one but themselves. Although the British authorities technically reserved the right to veto any legislation that affected African rights, this was never invoked – despite decades of hut taxes, segregation, and land-filching legislation.

The new constitution maintained power in the hands of whites while paying lip service to the idea of a non-racial democracy – a **qualified franchise** based on British citizenship and a minimum annual income that worked to keep most Africans out of the polling booths. With insufficient numbers to maintain control simply through white administrators, the government set about creating a network of sympathetic chiefs by installing puppets and unseating those who didn't go along with official policies.

WEALTH AND INEQUALITY: THE LAND ISSUE

Rhodesia's mineral wealth proved a disappointment to early settlers, and soon after the turn of the century white immigrants looked instead to rewards from **large-scale farming**. The country, in their wake, became one of the most unequal in the world.

A BLACK WORKING CLASS: THE MINES

The Rhodesians' great white myth – developed at the turn of the century and maintained to the present – was that blacks were better off under them because of their modernizing influence. Yet, while it's true that colonialism brought benefits like modern medicine and technology, at the same time it robbed Africans of a way of life that had worked successfully. Poverty was not the natural condition of Africa that the colonials fondly imagined they were improving, and was in fact created by the destruction of the traditional economy.

At the root of these problems lay the land question and the deliberate, forcible creation of a black working class. Cheap black labour was the backbone of white commercial activity, and, through taxes and the restriction of African access to farmlands, blacks were forced out of communal farming into selling their labour as workers. When even that policy failed in the first decade of this century, blacks were simply rounded up and press-ganged into the mines – a system known as *chibaro*.

The **Rhodesian mines** were more notorious than even those in South Africa. Because they were extensively mined out, only very low wages could make them profitable – and working in them was to be avoided at all costs.

Workers gave the mines their own coded names, warning of what could be expected. Celtic Mine was known as Sigebengu (*thugs are in charge*), Old Chum Mine was called Makombera (*you're closed in*) and other names included Maplanki (*planks for punishment*), and Mtshalwana (*you will fight one another*).

THE LAND APPORTIONMENT ACT

The **1930 Land Apportionment Act** set aside half of the country for whites – territory that invariably included the good fertile lands. Enclaves of poor land, meanwhile, became the so-called "**Native Reserves**" (later called the Tribal Trust Lands – many still refer to them as *TTLs*). Land pressure combined with infertile soils gradually forced many more people off the land and into the white economy.

It was from observing the destruction of the reserves through over-cultivation that many whites later drew the conclusion that Africans were bad farmers, forgetting that blacks had farmed these lands effectively for millennia, some accumulating tidy profits by selling off their surplus to white settlers at the turn of the century. For settler farmers, things were pretty rosy, with huge farms and help from the Land Bank to assist commercial agriculture – plus revenue from taxes extracted from Africans.

FEDERATION

Following the 1923 constitution, the influence of the BSAC gradually waned. The mines were bought by the government in 1933 and the railways taken over by South Africa shortly after World War II. Also, despite black opposition, the **Central African Federation** of Southern Rhodesia, Northern Rhodesia (Zambia) and Nyasaland (Malawi) was forged, providing the means for Southern Rhodesia to cream off the mineral riches to the north. The copper wealth of Northern Rhodesia did a lot for Southern Rhodesia, accounting for much of modern Zimbabwe's infrastructure – roads, hospitals and public works such as Lake Kariba.

Through its brief life, the Federation was dogged by black opposition, especially from nationalist movements in Northern Rhodesia and Nyasaland, which brought its collapse in 1963, followed by the independence of the two northernmost members the following year.

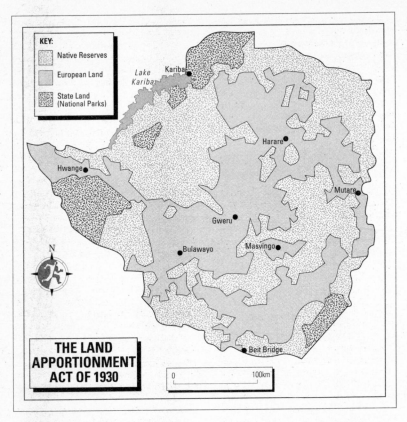

KEY:
  Native Reserves
  European Land
  State Land (National Parks)

THE LAND APPORTIONMENT ACT OF 1930

0   100km

NO LEFT TURN

In 1951, in an attempt to counter the overcrowding caused by the Land Apportionment Act, the **Land Husbandry Act** was passed, causing further resentment. To make space for thousands evicted from white-designated lands, the common grazing areas in the "Native Reserves" were divided into smallholdings of private land. Households were forced to reduce their herds to six head of cattle – most small-scale African farmers ended up worse off than before.

During the 1950s, however, there seemed the possibility of liberalization, as **Garfield Todd**'s ruling United Rhodesia Party discussed the idea of black suffrage. Although Todd saw liberalization essentially as a way to secure a peaceful place for whites, the electorate perceived him as a traitor and booted him out in the 1958 election. While the rest of the country drifted to the right, his sympathies for the nationalists grew and he ended up house-arrested by Ian Smith in the 1960s.

Each government after 1958 was more reactionary than its predecessor, not only putting the brakes on African advancement, but shifting into reverse gear. The crown prince of white domination was **Ian Smith**, whose Rhodesia Front Party led the country down the dead-end road to UDI in 1965. His "thousand-year republic" barely hobbled its way to mid-adolescence.

NATIONALISM: THE GATHERING STORM

In the early years of colonization, black campaigners hoped to use **persuasion** to get the British authorities to give them rights.

Before 1923 there was little activity apart from unsuccessful demands by Lobengula's son, Nyamanda, for the return of his father's cattle. In the 1920s, though, a proliferation of pressure groups were set up to represent middle-class black professionals. The government simply ignored what they had to say. But during the 1940s Benjamin Burombo's **African Voice Association** heralded a more militant phase, spreading resistance among workers and peasants, demanding improved working conditions, higher wages, parliamentary representation and better education.

CONSTITUTIONALISM: THE FIFTIES

It was under the Central African Federation that a **mass nationalist movement** was born, bent on action. The first major challenge was presented by the City Youth League, formed in Harare in 1955 and later expanded into the **African National Youth League**. Its newspaper *Chapupu* was used to galvanize support – which focused on the land question. In 1956 the League organized a bus boycott in Harare against fare increases. The following year it merged with another organization to form the **African National Congress (ANC)** under **Joshua Nkomo**.

Nkomo's ANC attempted a **broad-based approach** covering worker and peasant issues. In the rural areas it organized resistance to unpopular measures like the Land Husbandry Act, while in the urban areas meetings and demonstrations were held. 1959 was a year of expansion and protest against the Federation, prompting Sir Edgar Whitehead's governing United Rhodesia Party to ban the organization, declare a state of emergency, slap nearly 500 members behind bars and introduce a range of legislation to put an end to African demands. Nkomo narrowly escaped arrest because he was in Britain at the time canvassing support.

1960: ZHII, THE NDP AND ZAPU

Far from ending black political activities, this course of repression caused black frustrations to erupt in the resounding explosion of *Zhii*. The term has no direct English translation: it is basically a drastic act against an arch-enemy and signifies total annihilation, complete destruction or reduction to rubble.

A result of the largest uprising since the First Chimurenga, *Zhii* swept the cities when three leaders of the newly formed **National Democratic Party** (NDP) were arrested, and the party responded with the **Salisbury March**. The government banned all meetings, and popular outrage, involving almost 50,000 protesters, spread to Bulawayo, where workers went on strike and symbols of government were attacked. After a week, government bullets put a temporary end to *Zhii*, taking eighteen lives and leaving hundreds injured.

The Federation consequently swung into the 1960s cracking visibly at the edges. Northern Rhodesia and Nyasaland were on target for independence, but the settler government of Southern Rhodesia was intransigent on majority rule. At a conference in Britain a **constitution** was proposed giving blacks 15 seats in a 65-seat parliament. The four NDP representatives accepted the proposal, but on their return were fiercely rebuked by the domestic leadership and party rank and file. The NDP continued to organize against the government until it was banned and its assets seized in 1961.

A week later it re-emerged as the **Zimbabwe African People's Union (ZAPU)**, led by Joshua Nkomo. Sabotage replaced demonstrations, though Nkomo was still convinced that diplomatic pressure could be put on Britain to grant independence to Southern Rhodesia under a majority government. Inside the country, rural dwellers were organized in campaigns of burning the fields of unpopular farmers and destroying equipment, and others squatted white-designated unoccupied lands. In 1962 ZAPU was banned and the leadership exiled to remote rural areas for three months.

SPLITS IN THE RANKS: ZAPU AND ZANU

There was some doubt about where to go from the banning of ZAPU. Nkomo favoured the idea of setting up a government-in-exile to lobby international support, while others urged remaining inside the country and organizing local action.

Under Nkomo's instructions the government-in-exile headed for Dar es Salaam only to receive a lukewarm reception from President Nyerere; they returned home. There were rumblings about Nkomo's leadership on questions of both judgement and the principle of operating from exile. After some arguments Nkomo suspended four members of the ZAPU executive: Robert Mugabe, Ndabaningi Sithole,

Moton Malianga and Leopold Takawira. In 1963 this "dissident" group formed the **Zimbabwe African National Union** (ZANU), with Sithole as president and Mugabe as secretary-general.

An outbreak of fighting between the two organizations provided a convenient excuse for the government to ban them both in 1964 and to declare a state of emergency once again in some urban centres. Various top leaders were arrested, while the organizations set up headquarters in exile in Zambia and Tanzania, and began looking at broadening the struggle to all classes – and to the use of guns.

TALKING TOUGH: UDI

To pacify an increasingly alarmed white electorate, Prime Minister Ian Smith moved swiftly to demonstrate that he was made of stern stuff. Raising two fingers to the nationalists and an increasingly hostile world he issued the **Unilateral Declaration of Independence** (UDI) in 1965, promising White Rhodesians:

We have struck a blow for the preservation of justice, civilization and Christianity and in the spirit of this belief we have this day assumed our sovereign independence. God bless you all.

Alongside this defiance of Britain, Smith refused to speak to the nationalist leaders. Instead, he installed a council of chiefs, paid by his government but which he insisted represented the people.

CHIMURENGA PHASE ONE

UDI was the signal to the nationalist organizations to begin armed action. The **Second Chimurenga** began on April 28, 1966, when seven ZANU guerrillas engaged Rhodesian forces at Chinoyi – and were killed. This episode set the pattern for the next four years of commando hit-and-run actions. The guerrillas were no match for the Rhodesian army and enjoyed virtually no support organization within the country.

The following year, fighters from South Africa's ANC joined forces with ZAPU and operated for some months in Hwange National Park. A number of **ZAPU-ANC camps** were also established inside the country, but once discovered they were fairly easily destroyed by Rhodesian forces – themselves now assisted by South African units. Overall, this first phase of the war remained low-key, and continual

setbacks for the nationalists served to encourage the white belief in their own invincibility.

Britain, meanwhile, despite Rhodesian intransigence, was still eager for some kind of negotiated settlement and Ian Smith and British Prime Minister Harold Wilson met on two occasions on the British warships *HMS Fearless* and *Tiger*. Wilson wanted a few more rights for blacks and moves to majority rule in some far-flung future, but Smith always maintained there would never be a black government in Rhodesia in his lifetime – or those of his children. Both meetings achieved little except to add Wilson to the Rhodesian demonology of degenerate socialist sell-outs.

THE 1969 CONSTITUTION

As the 1960s came to a close, Smith still had everything to play for. The guerrillas were looking pretty impotent and British-imposed **sanctions** were a distinctly half-hearted affair – white Rhodesians could boast the boycott was actually stimulating Rhodesia's internal economy, while the flow of trade remained more or less unchanged in the five years after UDI. South Africa was openly defying sanctions and several multinational companies continued trading: with the knowledge of the British government, Shell and BP were both supplying Rhodesia with oil.

Smith tried to pre-empt any further negotiations by taking matters into his own hands. Yet another constitution was put forward, giving blacks a derisory eight elected seats in a 66-seat parliament. This was Smith's starting point for further discussions with the mother country. But Britain insisted on testing black opinion on the new dispensation prior to any further talks. **Lord Pearce** was despatched to the rebel colony to probe opinion in the cities and the remote rural areas.

Organizing a response was a problem for the nationalist movement, most of whose leaders were either in jail or in exile – but it was also a golden opportunity. ZANU and ZAPU united to form an internal campaigning body under the leadership of **Bishop Muzorewa.** While Rhodesia's government pumped massive resources into cajoling a positive response from blacks, they banned ANC views from the national media. However this small chance to campaign openly was exploited by the nationalists to set up internal networks – the lifeline in the final stage of the liberation struggle.

This was, in fact, the first time in Rhodesia's history that whites heard an authentic voice of black opinion. Having always assumed that they "knew their Africans", they refused to believe the resounding "NO!" that echoed across the country. The Rhodesian Broadcasting Corporation reflected the white prejudice that they alone were in touch with reality:

> The British Government's report revealed very clearly the extreme naivety of the British approach to the test of acceptability, and of the basic assumption that uneducated tribesmen could comprehend a complicated constitutional arrangement.

THE EARLY 1970S: LEARNING THE LESSONS

The early 1970s were a time of rethinking and consolidation. The Pearce Commission findings had shown that contrary to the regime's beliefs, blacks fully comprehended the constitutional arrangement. The bush war of the Sixties had vividly demonstrated the futility of a struggle fought without popular support.

FIGHTING FISH

Early in the 1970s, **Josiah Tongogara**, the commander of ZANU's military wing, **ZANLA**, went to China for training. He came back with Maoist doctrines and strategies, remarkably well suited to Rhodesia. As in China, the Rhodesian revolution was primarily rural, playing on decades-old resentments – the eviction from ancestral lands – and it was in these areas that the liberation movement needed support.

ZANLA adopted the Maoist principle of "guerrillas swimming like fish in the water of the people" – without water they would flounder. Mutual trust and co-operation between farmers and fighters was vital to military success, while at the same time helping to spread political ideas. Young boys were recruited as *mujibas* to spy for the guerrillas and carry messages; girls became *zvimbwidos*, who carried weapons and cooked for them. In the end, so effective were the networks that guerrilla intelligence far outstripped the information the Rhodesian forces were gathering.

ZIPRA – ZAPU's military wing – followed a different strategy that relied less on villagers

and more on infiltrated reception committees. Internal divisions hampered their implementation and their battle plan wasn't fully operational until the war was well advanced in 1977. Some observers put down ZANU's subsequent electoral success to their better wartime organization and integration with the people.

PLAYING FOR TIME

The 1974 **Portuguese coup** and consequent liberation of Mozambique and Angola were catalysts that changed the geopolitics of Southern Africa almost overnight. Suddenly the minority regimes in South Africa and Rhodesia found themselves flanked by independent black governments. The South Africans became concerned about the prospects of radical nationalists coming to power in Rhodesia and began tightening the screws on Smith to force him to the negotiating table.

In a most unlikely bout of co-operation, Kenneth Kaunda of Zambia united with South African Prime Minister John Vorster in persuading Smith to release nationalist leaders like Nkomo and Sithole. **Talks** were held in 1975 on the Victoria Falls railway bridge in the no-man's land between Rhodesia and Zambia. Smith refused to include majority rule on the agenda, and observing that there was a temporary let-up in fighting he saw little reason to pursue the talks, which collapsed like all the previous ones.

THE FINAL PHASE OF WAR

The collapse of the Victoria Falls talks heralded an intensified, no-holds-barred, armed struggle. The Smith regime's complacency about controlling the situation was soon translated into increasingly bitter repression and resistance. In 1975 the ZANU chairman, **Herbert Chitepo**, was blown up in Lusaka by the Rhodesian Central Intelligence Organization. Amid this and other assassinations and disappearances, continued government claims to be fighting for civilization rang extremely hollow.

PEOPLE'S WAR

In white farming areas, **guerrilla attacks on farmers** increased, and a siege existence became the norm, with a whole industry developing around the supply of security equipment, fences, communications networks and an array of "counter-insurgency" devices – tripwire-triggered grenades, mine-proofed vehicles and cars bristling with elaborate "anti-terrorist" weaponry for use on the road. Throughout many areas of the country, whites could travel along main roads only in armed convoys, and even these were frequently ambushed. Guerrillas also hit hotels and tourist centres, while missions and schools could be arbitrarily closed or opened by armed nationalists, who would often demand tithes from teachers in the rural areas.

In the shadowy world of attack and retribution, countless sickening **massacres** occurred – frequently at schools or mission stations – with each side blaming the other. The people who invariably suffered most were ordinary villagers trapped in a nightmare of guerrilla appearances under cover of darkness and armed visits by day from the Rhodesian forces who would brutally beat and torture suspected nationalist sympathizers. The law laid down heavy sentences for people who failed to report the presence of guerrillas – by the end of the war, death was routine punishment for helping armed nationalists. On the other hand the guerrillas were frequently ruthless with informers and government collaborators.

TOTAL WAR

The **Rhodesian army** solution was to hold whole villages responsible for the presence of guerrillas, and army units would storm settlements when nationalists were suspected of being present. In the first half of 1977, Combined Operations HQ reported the killing of 58 "curfew breakers", 53 "running with or assisting terrorists", 13 "failing to halt" and 54 "caught in crossfire".

Official policy, as espoused by the suave right-wing Minister for Information P. K. van der Byl, was:

If villagers harbour terrorists, and terrorists are found running about in villages, naturally they will be bombed and destroyed in any manner which the commander on the spot considers desirable in the suitable prosecution of a successful campaign.

A different approach was the introduction of the dubiously named **protected villages** – intended to isolate the guerrillas from their lifeblood, the peasantry. These "PVs", supposedly to protect villagers from the nationalists, were known by their inhabitants as "the cage" – little more than concentration camps, with guards, curfews, poor sanitation and walks of up to 10km to their livestock and land. Such measures only served to increase their hatred of the government.

By 1976 things were already looking dire for the Smith regime. The war was by now costing over a million dollars a day and the close of 1978 saw over half the country under **Patriotic Front control**. White males were being called up for increasingly lengthy stints, a "Dad's Army" of everyone up to 60-year-olds found themselves involved in the war, while conscription for blacks drove many over the border to join the nationalists. Only by employing a force of 10,000 **mercenaries** – mainly British and South Africans – was Smith able to keep things afloat.

CONTEMPLATING THE IMPOSSIBLE – ELECTIONS

Smith by now admitted that majority rule was inevitable and hoped for a negotiated settlement on his own terms, which would simultaneously bring international recognition. His favoured "moderate" candidate, **Bishop Muzorewa**, seemed a sharp choice at the time – malleable in a way which Nkomo and Mugabe were not, but also with some apparent street credibility through his part in trouncing Smith over the 1969 constitution.

Smith negotiated an internal settlement with Muzorewa and other tame black "leaders". In a 1979 ballot, which excluded ZANU and ZAPU, Muzorewa's **UANC** swept the board. In fact the bishop's campaign was financed by Smith's government, and most of the cleric's speeches and statements were written by an advertising company. Muzorewa, however, became Prime Minister, while Smith continued to control all the instruments of power: the army, police, judiciary and civil service. The now supposedly liberated country was called **Zimbabwe-Rhodesia** – jokingly called Rhobabwe by some.

No one was fooled. The accolades of international recognition failed to materialize, and nor did the expected hordes of demoralized ZANLA and ZIPRA personnel. Instead the **war** rose to an unprecedented ferocity. In May 1979 a relieved and grateful white Rhodesian public joyfully welcomed the election of Margaret Thatcher in Britain, but their elation was short-lived when she proved as unsympathetic as her "socialist" predecessors – the Iron Lady had no intention of recognizing the "Internal Settlement".

LANCASTER HOUSE AGREEMENT

Under siege, the Smith-Muzorewa team found themselves in Britain, and by the end of the year were discussing a new constitution with the Nkomo-Mugabe Patriotic Front at the **Lancaster House conference**. Eager for a rapid settlement in the wake of some Conservative opposition at home, Britain's foreign secretary, Lord Carrington, succeeded in bulldozing through an agreement in just fourteen weeks.

Patriotic Front demands were toned down in the agreement. One man one vote was diluted by allowing the whites, a mere three percent of the population, to hang on to twenty of the one hundred parliamentary seats. The Rhodesian army would form the core of the new defence force and pensions would continue to be paid to civil servants, even if they left the country. Perhaps the biggest concession the PF made was to agree that unoccupied **white farmlands** could not be expropriated without compensation. As the central issue of the liberation struggle, this was – and indeed remains today – a potential post-Independence time bomb.

THE ELECTION

Following the Lancaster House Agreement, the **Patriotic Front split**, and **ZANU** and **ZAPU** launched separate campaigns. The election that followed was crammed with drama, edgy nationalist troops corralled at assembly points, while Rhodesian troops were freely deployed by the interim governor-general. Neatly collected in one place the guerrillas were sitting ducks, but a post-election **coup plan** to massacre them was jettisoned once the extent of the ZANU victory emerged. Several attempts were made on Mugabe's life, while the government and South Africa pumped enormous quantities of cash into Muzorewa's campaign – the slickest razzmatazz ever in central Africa.

Despite a four-day pro-Muzorewa rally, with bands, free food, films, prizes and all, attracting over a million people, the cool cleric failed

to win more than three of the eighty seats. ZAPU took twenty, and whites, for decades accustomed to believing their own propaganda, woke on **March 4, 1980** to the nightmare of a 57-seat **ZANU landslide**.

INDEPENDENCE: THE FIRST DECADE

Independence failed to mark the beginning of the great decline that whites had predicted, as it soon became apparent that **Robert Mugabe** wasn't going to turn the protected villages into re-education camps. In stark contradiction to Bishop Muzorewa's shock-horror predictions, churches were not turned into barracks, concentration camps and dance halls. In fact, for those whites who remained, standards of living remained at much their previous level.

A CAUTIOUS ADVANCE

The government's hands were tied by the Lancaster House Agreement, the fact that seventy percent of investment came from outside the country and by a hostile South Africa breathing over its shoulder. Mozambique's President Samora Machel had advised Mugabe to avoid alienating whites, as had happened in his country, where most of the colonists followed a vindictive scorched-earth tactic of sabotaging infrastructure before leaving for Rhodesia, South Africa or Portugal.

Acknowledging the economic importance of white farmers, reassuring noises were made. Appearing on TV on March 4, Robert Mugabe declared "there is a place for everyone in this country. We want to ensure a sense of security for both the winners and the losers." A year later, once things had settled and it was apparent that no hasty radical reforms were under way, Mugabe, on a visit to Britain, was asked whether he was heading toward a "new Kenya" or a "new Mozambique", to which he replied "a new Zimbabwe", indicating that Zimbabwe would tread a "middle way" between capitalism and socialism.

Minority representatives, from ZAPU and the white community, were brought into the cabinet and the minimum wage for farm workers was rapidly raised by fifty percent, but industrial workers made fewer gains. While moves were made to reassure white farmers and foreign investors, other efforts were made to Africanize Zimbabwe. Segregation was ended, education was enormously extended and free health care was provided to low earners – most of the population.

Zimbabwe raved into the 1980s, with Bob Marley offering his final performance at the **Independence celebrations** on April 17, 1980. The first years were euphoric and the London *Times* reported that the economy had taken off "like a rocket", with GDP advancing at eight percent for two successive years following the nil growth of the final Smith years. But by 1982 growth fell to zero and the precarious national unity began to fracture.

DISSIDENTS

In the ZAPU stronghold of **Matabeleland** there were rumblings of discontent and fighting broke out between ZANU and ZAPU supporters. ZIPRA guerrillas loyal to ZAPU began drifting back to the bush, insisting that they were continuing the struggle for socialism against capitalism and white economic power. When an arms cache was found on Joshua Nkomo's farm, relations between the nationalist parties were severely soured and Nkomo was dropped from the cabinet.

There were renewed attacks on white farmers and, for a couple of years, it looked like the country would again be torn apart by civil war. In sinister moves that looked like a carbon copy of Smith tactics, the government insisted that the dissidents were simply armed gangsters, and refused any negotiations. The ruthless Korean-trained **Fifth Brigade** was sent in to put down the rebels, and thousands of civilians were killed in brutal attempts to flush out the dissidents. Some estimates put the Matabeleland death toll as high as 20,000.

The repression only served to strengthen ZAPU support in Matabeleland, and the government realized the dangers of a tactic that played into the hands of a South Africa eager to export destabilizing wars to its neighbours. Mugabe admitted the error and began talks with Nkomo.

In 1987 the two **parties merged**, although some felt that it was more a case of ZANU swallowing the opposition. Nkomo was given a senior position and Mugabe was upgraded to executive president. By May 1988 the dissidents had given themselves up under an **amnesty**, and all attacks have ceased since

then. Emerging from years in the bush, Mhkwananzi, a dissident spokesman declared:

> Disunity does not pay. We have gone on operations twice, first against the white colonizers and then against the party. We have liberated everybody and now we must forge ahead with our lives.

THE LATE 1980S: UNITY

Any fears that the effective **one-party state** brought about by the merger of the two main parties would close the door on healthy criticism were rapidly dispelled in the late 1980s. There was uproar in parliament over accusations of **corruption** at *Air Zimbabwe*, with some MPs maintaining that money ought to be spent on buses for the people rather than planes. The usually tame press published articles attacking the government for professing socialism while pursuing capitalism for the elite. There were frustrations, too, over the pace of reform with the pre-colonial inequities still remaining firmly in place.

In 1988, the Bulawayo-based *Chronicle* newspaper itself became the centre of the news by breaking a corruption scandal linking senior cabinet ministers with distribution malpractices at the Willowvale car assembly plant. The so-called **Willowgate scandal** created popular outrage, in spite of threats against the *Chronicle* from the Minister of Defence, Enos Nkala. It was in fact Nkala who eventually ended up getting the boot, along with four other ministers.

On the University of Zimbabwe campus, students joined in the protests over government corruption, but were quelled, first by police and then by the removal of grants from student leaders. Believing that the president was on their side, with his "leadership code" aimed at keeping the government clean, they watched him return from a foreign trip to rebuke them for childish behaviour. Only after apologizing for embarrassing him were the grants restored. Meanwhile, support gathered for the rabble-rousing freelance parliamentary opposition led by **Edgar Tekere** – who was expelled from ZANU in 1988.

But the biggest obstacle of all remained **South Africa**, which was constantly making veiled threats against Zimbabwe, and occasionally sending in agents to bomb alleged ANC personnel. Most of Zimbabwe's trade went through its southern neighbour's ports, and South Africa was able to use this fact to apply pressure. At the same time, moves were made to shift trade to the Mozambique port of Beira, Zimbabwe deploying 10,000 troops in Mozambique to defend the **Beira corridor** railroad. As a result, South African-backed **Renamo** (MNR) rebels declared war on Zimbabwe. Although there have been tentative peace moves in Mozambique, at the end of the 1980s MNR activity inside Zimbabwe continued with raids for supplies on peasants in the Eastern Highlands.

INTO THE 1990s

If Zimbabwe kicked off the 1980s in a mood of euphoria and wild optimism, the 1990s began as the decade of disillusion and discontent. In the first ten years of independence the government made remarkable headway in improving conditions for ordinary people. Health care was made more accessible, average life expectancy rose and infant mortality fell, free primary school education was provided and for many people wages increased.

By the end of the 1980s, however, the country faced a series of economic problems. Dissatisfaction with the government found expression in **strikes** and demonstrations by nurses, students and trade unionists. When a "student" anti-corruption meeting was banned in October 1989, **Morgan Tsvangirai**, leader of the Zimbabwe Congress of Trade Unions, spoke out against the "naked use of force to suppress the growing disenchantment of the masses over the rising cost of living, transport problems, unemployment, destitution and other negative socio-economic developments". Tsvangirai was arrested for unspecified reasons, though later released.

The hottest issue, however, was the **land question**, which remains unresolved nearly two decades after liberation. The Lancaster House Agreement failed to make funds available to buy out white farms for redistribution to small-scale farmers, and there were rumblings of dissatisfaction among some landless ex-combatants, who felt betrayed by the revolution. In its first decade in power, Mugabe's government only managed to **resettle** 52,000 families, less than a third of the 162,000 targeted for the first three years following

Independence. In March 1990 Mugabe announced that the government was drafting a plan to provide for the landless, but at the same time he assured nervous white property-owners that the process would be fair. Under the Lancaster House Agreement, Zimbabwe's constitution ensured that for a decade after Independence the government could buy only land that was offered for sale.

Mugabe announced, as a prelude to the March 1990 elections, that the government was planning to amend this restriction to coincide with the tenth anniversary of Independence on April 19, 1990. For Mugabe the heart of the election campaign was to gain a mandate for his cherished ideal of establishing a one-party state, and, aware of the importance of the land issue, he hoped to capture vital rural support.

THE 1990 ELECTION

In the event, the 1990 election campaign was an ugly affair. As Edgar Tekere had promised, his fledgling **ZUM** (Zimbabwe Unity Movement) fought the election, standing on a capitalist and multi-party ticket. Small and poorly funded, it was never a serious threat to ZANU, though, surprisingly, Mugabe seemed to take the opposition threat very seriously. One of the grimmest series of events centred on the Gweru North constituency, where vice-president Simon Muzenda was locked in a tight campaign against ZUM's Patrick Kombayi. On the Saturday before the ballot Kombayi suffered a sharp setback when Mugabe issued a presidential proclamation altering the electoral boundaries to exclude his stronghold. Later that week Kombayi was shot and seriously wounded. Several other ZUM candidates withdrew from contests in other constituencies.

The voting failed to live up to the excitement promised by the campaigning. As was widely expected, ZANU won a massive victory, taking 116 of the 119 contested seats to ZUM's mere two. In the presidential race against Tekere, Mugabe took 78 percent of the votes cast. But the most powerful statement of the poll was apathy, with around half the electorate failing to vote. Mugabe described his victory as a mandate for the establishment of a **one-party state**. When he put the idea to the ZANU Central Committee however, it was roundly defeated.

ESAP – AND DROUGHT

The real issue for Zimbabwe was the problem of **growth** and **job creation**. In conjunction with the IMF and World Bank, the government unveiled the five-year **Economic Structural Adjustment Programme** in October 1991. The plan, known in Zimbabwe by its acronym **Esap**, sought to liberalize the economy and make imports easier, hence rebuilding the country's ageing infrastructure. It marked the Mugabe government's final retreat from socialism.

The most visible effect of the plan has been the appearance of previously unavailable imported goods. The plan appears to be working for business and particularly the tourist industry, which is now able to modernize itself. Less visible is the really serious hardship caused to ordinary people, for whom maize meal and bread, not Kodacolor Gold, is the big issue.

Esap was inspired by a monetarist penchant for slashing government spending. This meant a major reversal of ZANU policies for improving living conditions through public services. Free education ended and the public health care system ceased to deliver affordable care. For example, fees for maternity wards rose by 300 percent in two years. The lifting of price controls saw the cost of staple foods rocket. According to some analysts, living standards fell below those under the Smith regime of the mid-1970s.

The government argued that *Esap* was short-term pain in the interests of long-term gain. But its timing could not have been worse. The launching of the plan coincided with the most severe **drought** for a century. Dams became puddles and the "great, grey, green, greasy Limpopo" was reduced to a dirty, desperate, dry dustbowl. Zimbabwe, once the grain basket of the region, struggled in the grip of a **famine** in which two million lives were at risk.

The seriousness of the situation was as much due to failures of government policy as natural disaster. With the approval of the IMF, Zimbabwe had sold off its contingency maize supplies to pay off the interest on its debt. Maize had to be reimported to feed the starving – at a considerably higher price.

In 1992 after a visit to her homeland, Doris Lessing wrote that "this year may make or break Zimbabwe". In the dry lowveld wildlife began to die off and farmers were forced to shoot starving cattle. The country's tobacco crop (a major forex earner) was devastated, maize (the staple food) withered, and the entire national sugar plantation was wiped out. At the end of the year relief did come. 1993 brought normal rains – and respite.

THE MID-1990S

Economically life in the mid-1990s has become tougher for most people in Zimbabwe. Some blame this on the drought but many economists argue that *Esap* alone is to blame. The economic plan has made virtually anything available – for those who can afford it. But for peasants and many workers at the bottom of the pile bread itself has become an unaffordable luxury. When prices rose in 1993 there was a series of **bread riots** followed by consumer boycotts in some high-density suburbs. Joblessness too continued to grow with the government taking no concrete steps to create employment.

Discontent grew, with the normally loyal *Herald* declaring that "what the government calls cost recovery is seen by the people as total neglect and betrayal of the liberation struggle". Even government minister Didymus Mutasa hit out against Esap which he said had given the country "ten indigenous millionaires against ten million poor workers".

Yet the government went on to enjoy its biggest victory ever in the **1995 general election** – a far more peaceful one than five years earlier. Despite this there was no sense of euphoria in ZANU – rather one of disquiet at the high level of abstentions and the feeling that the government had lost its legitimacy. Some feel that all that holds a delicate consensus together is the authoritative (and authoritarian) figure of Robert Mugabe, now in his seventies. The second half of the 1990s could well see cracks in the ruling party begin to widen as various factions start to position themelves for the post-Mugabe era.

BOTSWANA:THE HISTORICAL FRAMEWORK

The looming presence of South Africa is a recurrent theme in Botswana's history. By the eleventh century, the northern districts of what is now South Africa was firmly in the hands of Sotho people – of whom the Tswana are the western group. Here they lived unchallenged until the eighteenth century. Meanwhile the territory that is today the Republic of Botswana was the undisputed range of San hunter-gatherers and the Kgalagadi people, descendants of very early Batswana immigrants who had mixed freely with them.

The major pre-colonial events in the history of **Tswana-speaking people** – which is very much the same thing as the history of Botswana – were enacted offstage in South Africa. Three hundred years before gold drew whites to establish trade, industry and mines in what became Johannesburg, Tswana people were farming sheep and cattle and cultivating crops in the area. Where skyscrapers now stand, Batswana established the first orderly trading centres, exchanging the livestock of these southern grasslands for iron spears, hoes, tools and ornaments made by the African iron-smelters living in the northern wooded districts – which are today the most luxurious of Johannesburg's suburbs.

For further details on the San, see p.346, and for an idea of the prehistory of the Botswana area, see the opening sections of the Zimbabwe Historical Framework, preceding.

THE FORCED MIGRATIONS

The other main theme of Tswana history has been the constant cycle of fractures and amalgamations within and between **political groups**. When disputes arose, people would split off from the main tribe and migrate under a rival leader.

The most important splits, which formed the modern **Tswana divisions**, again happened in South Africa. Around the mid-eighteenth century some Batswana began to drift **across the Malopo River** into the territory of modern Botswana. Their northwest advance would probably have gone quite slowly had shattering events not disrupted the sedate progress of history.

LAND HUNGER

The fission and fusion that typified Tswana political life in the centuries leading up to the 1800s were small change compared to what was about to follow. As populations grew throughout Southern Africa, **land hunger** arose, caused by movements of people from all directions into the sub-continent.

In the southeast, **Nguni** people occupied the area between the Drakensberg Mountains and the Indian Ocean. The **Sotho-Tswana** group was firmly settled to their north, while

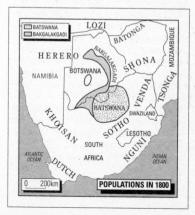

POPULATIONS IN 1800

from Zimbabwe **Shona** people extended well into Botswana's east. North of Botswana, the **Lozi** empire was extending its grasp south and westwards, while from the west **Hereros** were being forced into northern Botswana. From the Cape Colony, the **British** were relentlessly extending their control northwards and eastwards, and **Boers**, resentful of their constant interference, were trekking north to escape.

It was **Zulu amalgamation**, though, that had most dramatic effect. In a very short time during the 1820s the powerful Zulu nation coalesced and sent the shock waves of the *mfecane* – "forced migrations" caused by conquest – throughout Southern Africa. Although the Zulus themselves did not move through the Tswana country, **refugee bands**, fleeing from Zulu terror, did. These groups had in their turn adopted Zulu tactics, and to crushing effect. Two of the fiercest invaders were the band who swept northwards under **Sebitoane** in the mid-1820s, attacking various Batswana groups on their way, and the **Ndebele** who confronted and defeated them, while on their own terrifying campaign of conquest.

The victorious Ndebele, under Mzilikazi, remained in Tswana country, which they planned to settle and make their base. By 1830, they had conquered and absorbed or driven off large numbers of Batswana who were living north of the Vaal River. A network of military *kraals* was set up and the surrounding districts were cleared of any potential enemies.

In the mid-1830s yet another wave of invaders arrived in northern South Africa: **Boers** trekking beyond British control in the Cape. The Boers' advance party had found the land unoccupied and, either unaware of Mzilikazi's *cordon sanitaire* or else simply ignoring it, they began to settle territory that the Batswana still claimed as their traditional lands. A series of battles followed in which Mzilikazi's forces were routed by superior Boer weaponry. The Ndebele retreated into Botswana, where they wandered for a decade before finally coming to rest at Bulawayo in Zimbabwe in the 1840s.

With the Ndebele out of the picture many Tswana returned to the Transvaal, but the apparent respite from conquest was the beginning of the bitter relationship that has marked Tswana relations with the whites to the south ever since.

POLITICAL CHANGES

The forced migrations – *mfecane* – led to major changes in **Tswana political organization**. The harsh realities of conquest meant they had to adapt or die – the old rules ceased to apply. It was no longer feasible for dissenting groups to split off and go it alone, as there was no longer anywhere to go. In such war-ravaged times, small groups were very vulnerable. One vivid lesson of the 1820s and 1830s was to show just how effective centralized states could be against the less organized.

The Batswana probably came out of the chaos better equipped to deal with the colonial onslaught to come. In the aftermath of the forced migrations bigger communities emerged from the wandering fragments. In the 1840s the **Bangwato** heralded the future shape of things, when **King Kgari** reorganized his state, shifting the balance of power away from competing royals and consolidating his own power in a more tightly unified system.

Absorbing the painful lessons brought by the Ndebele, Kgari drove potential competitor tribes out of the surrounding lands and subdued all the weaker local groups, forcing them to pay him tribute. Finally he drew his conquered subjects into an unprecedentedly close political association. He appointed a deputy, to provide a direct link between the centre of power and the subjects on the fringes and to keep an eye on the surrounding districts.

THE BOERS AND THE PROTECTORATE

The peace brought by the **Boer** defeat of Mzilikazi was short-lived, and soon the **Batswana** found themselves under different pressure. Those who streamed back to their traditional lands found they were there on Boer sufferance and many were pressed into forced labour. **Britain** was quite happy to allow this, and in 1852 signed papers acknowledging Boer independence across the Vaal River. Indeed, it went so far as to promise the Boers free access to the gunpowder and weapon markets of the Cape, while agreeing to prevent Africans getting hold of arms and ammunition.

After signing the **agreement with the British**, the Boers called together those Batswana who were still independent and informed them they were now under Boer control. One Tswana ruler who rejected Boer overlordship was **Sechele I** of the **Bakwena**, against whom the whites launched a punitive campaign. Those groups who refused to co-operate against Sechele, like the **Bangwaketse** and **Barolong**, were also punished. Hundreds of women and children were captured by the Boers, crops were destroyed and houses razed. Sechele appealed to Britain for protection but was turned down – Britain had no need for Tswana territory in the 1850s. Right up to the 1870s repeated appeals to the British government for protection were refused. The British attitude only changed in 1884–85, when their own interests became threatened.

In 1885, with unannounced suddenness, Britain told Germany, which occupied neighbouring German South West Africa (now Namibia), that it had declared a **Protectorate** over **Bechuanaland**. Almost as an after-thought, the Batswana states were informed. The annexation was prompted by an attack of British panic that the Germans to the west and the Boers to the east were conspiring to close the gap between them and shut off Britain's route to expansion – the "**Suez Canal to the north**" as arch-colonialist Cecil Rhodes called Tswana country.

THE COUNTDOWN TO PROTECTORATE

During the three years prior to the declaration of the protectorate, British fears took form when Boer mavericks from the Transvaal set up the two small **Republics of Goshen and Stellaland**, just south of the Molopo River in Tswana country and right across the "road to the north". In 1884 British public opinion was aroused by the killing of Christopher Bethell, son of "an important British family" and married to a Morolong. The death had come during a Boer raid on the Barolong capital at Sehuba (just south of modern Botswana). John Mackenzie, a missionary, who had been push-ing for British protection of the Batswana for some time, used this incident to demonstrate why Britain should take control of Tswana terri-tory – to put a stop to Boer bullying.

The British government declared a protecto-rate over Barolong lands with John Mackenzie as Deputy Commissioner. His role, however, was short-lived. The British High Commissioner to South Africa, **Sir Hercules Robinson**, was

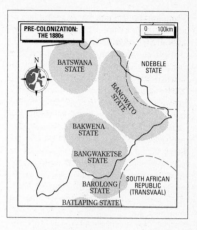

disturbed by Mackenzie's over-sympathetic attitude to the Africans and his failure to deal with the Boers, and he quickly replaced him with **Cecil John Rhodes**.

Rhodes was no more effective at persuading the Boers to jettison their petty republics, which continued to wage war against the Batswana. In 1885 **General Charles Warren** was sent in with a force of 4000 to sort out the troublesome Boers. The Boers took fright at the size of Warren's force and fled back to the Transvaal without firing a shot. Warren extended the Protectorate to 22 degrees south – well into modern Botswana. The territory, designated as the **Bechuanaland Protectorate**, incorpo-rated the lands of three major Tswana king-doms: Ngwato, Ngkwaketse and Kwena.

Following this agreement, though, Sir Hercules Robinson again became unhappy with what he saw as an over-sympathetic attitude to the Africans – this time from Warren, whom he duly dismissed. Suddenly horrified by the new territory on their hands, the British tried to transfer it to the Cape Colony, but the politi-cians there were no more keen to bear the responsibilities of administering a huge chunk of land that offered them no benefit.

In desperation, later in 1885, Britain subse-quently divided Bechuanaland in two. The part south of the Molopo River became a Crown Colony – **British Bechuanaland** – which was annexed to the Cape in 1895 and now forms part of South Africa. The northern section was given the title of **Bechuanaland**

Protectorate, and until Independence had its administrative centre inside South Africa at Mafeking (now Mafikeng).

To many **Batswana**, the declaration of a protectorate came as a surprise. The British justified the move as protection against the Ndebele, the Boers and the Germans. For several decades, pleas for just such protection had been totally ignored, but the British had arrived now that King Khama of the Bangwato had seen off Mzilikazi, and the threat from the Boers had fallen off. As for the Germans, there had never been any trouble from them anyway. Of all the kings, only Khama welcomed British protection. The others spoke out, but eventually resigned themselves to it. All stressed the fact that they wanted no interference in the way they ran their own territories.

The whole issue of Protectorate status remained very vague, no one quite knowing what it meant. The British authorities had no interest in wasting any money trying to govern the territory. They simply wanted to maintain a **military presence** there to secure the road to the north and to protect their regional interests. Even when the Tswana offered men to serve in a territorial police force this was turned down.

Within a few years, discontent became manifest as Tswana leaders complained that British control had failed to stop Boer raids into their territory. In 1889 a conference was called by Rhodes's friend Sydney Shippard, Resident Commissioner for the territory, to discuss the setting-up of an administration. At the meeting all the kings expressed their misgivings about undue British interference.

RHODES SHOWS HIS FACE

During the 1890s the colonial administration encouraged **concession-seekers** to swarm into Bechuanaland – the government stood to collect considerable revenue in taxes if minerals were discovered. However, in 1893 they had a rethink when they realized that a single large company – Rhodes's British South Africa Company (BSAC) – could administer the whole territory to the benefit of British interests, and set up a **Concessions Commission** to cancel as many as possible of the concessions granted by the Tswana rulers.

This was a complete breach of the agreement not to interfere in Tswana domestic affairs, and the kings were outraged, not least at their loss of revenue. The BSAC agreed to pay them an annual allowance.

By 1894 Rhodes and the BSAC were ready to take control of Bechuanaland, having crushed the Ndebele in neighbouring Rhodesia and secured a formal assurance that Britain would transfer the Bechuanaland territory to the Company. To smooth the way, Sir Henry Loch, who opposed the deal, was replaced as High Commissioner by Rhodes's friend Sir Hercules Robinson, who also happened to have shares in the BSAC.

Kings Khama, Bathoen, Sebele and Linchwe, meanwhile, heard of the secret negotiations and petitioned Colonial Secretary Joseph Chamberlain to prevent the proposed transfer. The Tswana leaders had seen the Company's tactics in Rhodesia, and had no intention of following Lobengula's path to disaster (see p.358).

Three of the kings decided to take their campaign to England, with Rhodes trying to waylay the men before they could set sail. First he sent his trusty accomplice Leander Starr Jameson to negotiate a deal with Khama in exchange for all sorts of promises. The shrewd king wasn't taken in. Rhodes himself proved no more successful when he collared the rulers in the Cape, en route to London, and tried to persuade them to cancel the visit. High Commissioner Robinson also tried to abort the trip, but was equally ineffective. The kings finally set sail with their interpreter, the missionary W. C. Willoughby.

In a meeting with Chamberlain they attacked BSAC mismanagement in Rhodesia and insisted on remaining under the Queen's protection. Chamberlain weakly responded that the territory had been promised to the BSAC and he couldn't break his word. He refused to have any further dealings on the matter and, before heading off on a planned holiday, told the kings to deal with Rhodes.

Chamberlain returned from his break to a clutch of letters from church groups and industry, opposing the handover. The kings had wasted no time while Chamberlain was away, campaigning vigorously throughout England and addressing well-attended meetings with the backing of the **London Missionary Society**, which was fully behind Khama – a strong Christian ruler who banned liquor. The

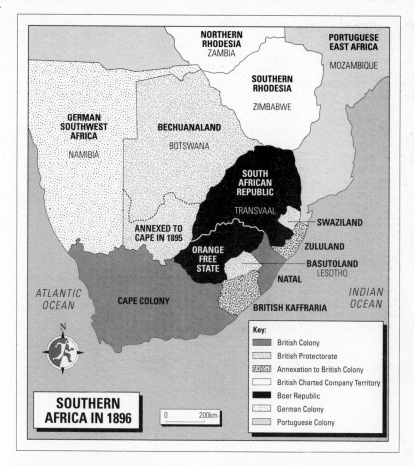

**SOUTHERN
AFRICA IN 1896**

Key:
- British Colony
- British Protectorate
- Annexation to British Colony
- British Charted Company Territory
- Boer Republic
- German Colony
- Portuguese Colony

temperance movement, influential in Britain at the time, gave a lot of support, too, fearing that the BSAC would allow alcohol in Bechuanaland. **Humanitarian** and **anti-slavery groups** lent support as well, outraged by BSAC activity in Rhodesia, and believing that the Crown, not commercial enterprises, should rule the Empire.

Chamberlain backed down. Each king was granted a reserve in which he retained autonomy and the Tswana territories remained a Protectorate under the Queen. Meanwhile, small concessions were made by the Tswana rulers. Land was to be given up for the construction of the BSAC railway and taxes would be introduced to pay for administration. Rhodes was furious at being outwitted but, despite an array of threats against King Khama, was forced to accept the situation.

DEALING WITH THE BOERS

Rhodes and the BSAC didn't give up hope of laying hands on Bechuanaland. While the three kings were in England, BSAC agents had approached some of the minor rulers, such as Ikaneng of the Balete and Montshiwa of the Barolong. Both ceded lands in the east, which the Colonial Office agreed to hand over to the BSAC; but it refused to transfer other territory on the Transvaal border.

Rhodes also despatched his agent, **John Bosman**, to northern Bechuanaland, where he extracted a fraudulent land concession from **Sekgoma**, king of the **Batswana** (the texts of the English and Setswana documents were different). Rhodes planned to settle a group of Boers there, who were preparing to leave for the Ghanzi area. The British government rejected the Bosman Concession at the end of 1894, but Rhodes decided that he would go ahead and encourage the Ghanzi trek with or without permission.

Apart from settling the country, Rhodes had other reasons for wanting territory north of South Africa. British miners in northern South Africa were annoyed by the way the Boer bureaucracy was treating them. Rhodes, himself a mine-owner in the republic, wanted, for economic and political reasons, to see the Transvaal brought into a federation of Southern African states under Britain.

During 1895, Rhodes's friend Jameson trained British South Africa Police from Rhodesia, in preparation for an **attack on the Boer republic** from inside Bechuanaland. Later that year he led his armed band into Afrikaner-controlled territory, expecting the support of British residents. The attack was a fiasco and Jameson's party was rounded up by Boer forces.

Britain became the object of international condemnation, both for using Bechuanaland as a base and for attacking an independent republic. Had the raid succeeded, the British government would probably have been more sanguine, but instead Rhodes was forced to resign as Prime Minister of the Cape, Jameson was imprisoned, and any chances of a Bechuanaland under BSAC control were ended.

Just four years on, however, in 1899, Britain followed in Jameson's tracks and declared war on the Transvaal Republic to further British imperial interests, which leaders like Chamberlain and Milner believed could only be achieved by a unification of Southern Africa. The **Boers** were defeated, but lived to win the peace. In the subsequent union of the two Boer republics and the two British colonies, self-government was granted to the white inhabitants.

The **Afrikaner leadership** of **South Africa** posed a renewed threat to the High Commission territories of Basotholand,

Swaziland and Bechuanaland, now with the clout of a large and powerful state. The **South Africa Act** that established the Union of South Africa in 1910 made provision for these territories and Southern Rhodesia to be added to the Union at a later date.

When the issue of **unification** was raised in 1910, Tswana leaders again put up unanimous opposition. But the pressure was on and in 1924 the South African Prime Minister **General Herzog** began to insist that moves be made for the transfer of the territories. He was eager to extend South Africa's "native policy" throughout Southern Africa, and had considerable support from the white farmers in Bechuanaland. Fearing an uprising in the High Commission territories, Britain refused.

Herzog used **economic pressure** – a tactic that has remained one of South Africa's major levers in its relations with neighbouring states. First he banned the import of cattle from Bechuanaland that fell below a certain weight: an act with potentially devastating effects on a country whose sole export then was beef – though new markets were found in Northern Rhodesia and elsewhere. Further pressure came with the prevention of Tswana migrant labourers from seeking work in South Africa – the main source of wages for Botswana, which had no industry of its own.

The Tswana leadership and British government stood firm against this blackmail. But the question continued to be raised by successive South African governments and General Smuts again threatened to stop beef exports in the 1930s. The question was only laid to rest in 1961, when South Africa became a republic and was expelled from the British Commonwealth.

COLONIAL DEVELOPMENTS – AND UNDERDEVELOPMENT

Once Britain had secured control of Bechuanaland and the road to the north, it more or less forgot about the territory. Already stretched by a huge empire, the government was very reluctant to put any money into the new protectorate. An indication of the half-hearted attitude was the establishment of a tiny **administration** – which was maintained outside the country.

Bechuanaland was different from most other British colonies, where the usual pattern was white occupation to exploit the natural resources of the territory. In such cases there would be mining or farming, and the imposition of taxes to force peasants off the land to seek wages from white employers. Although some areas of the country were set aside for white settlement and did become occupied by white ranchers, Bechuanaland had the rare distinction that the vast majority of its land stayed in the hands of traditional communities.

All this meant that when the colonial administration imposed **taxes**, there weren't sufficient jobs inside the country to support all the employment-seekers. Vast numbers of Bechuanaland's men were forced to seek work in South Africa, cementing in time a long, complex and none-too-happy economic relationship between the Protectorate and its powerful southern neighbour. One of the tragedies of the colonial years is the waste of migrant labour that went into developing South Africa and impoverishing Bechuanaland.

Although Britain ostensibly aimed at minimal intervention in the long-established way of life of the Protectorate, taxation led the way to a breakdown of traditional patterns of life. The kings were responsible for tax collection, from which they received ten percent. Some used the money to develop the community, but others accumulated personal wealth, driving a wedge between themselves and an increasingly impoverished people. With many men away on the South African mines the responsibilities of farming, like ploughing and reaping, increasingly fell to women. Many Tswana rulers were appalled by the damage caused by the migrant labour system – high death rates on the mines, maltreatment, poor wages and the disruption caused to the community – and banned it altogether for a while.

In 1927 the energetic **Sir Charles Rey**, a colourful but somewhat snobbish figure, replaced a succession of time-servers as Resident Commissioner. From then until 1937 he took a very active interest in the territory, attempting to develop the country despite the lack of monetary support. He also tried to reduce the power of the local kings, whom he saw as obstacles to progress.

An incident that sparked action was the trial of a young white called **Phineas McIntosh** by a traditional court in Serowe in 1933. McIntosh had got some Bangwato women pregnant and,

tried by traditional court, was found guilty and sentenced by the Bangwato Regent, Tshekedi Khama, to be flogged (a traditional punishment still meted out). There was outrage from racist whites in South Africa and in the Protectorate itself, and the Regent was deposed by the administration, only to be reinstated two weeks later after protests from whites in Serowe and England.

However, the following year a proclamation was passed to cut the power of the kings. Its most offensive element was that no king could rule without the approval of the British government. This went against traditional law, which held that a leader was born and could only be removed by his own community. **Kings Tshekedi** and **Bathoen II**, with the backing of other leaders, challenged the proclamation on the grounds that it contravened all the agreements made between Britain and the Tswana. They pointed out that Britain had agreed not to interfere with domestic politics, fearing that the erosion of their power was leading toward incorporation into South Africa. They took the administration to court and lost – though the hostility caused thereafter hampered government activity. Eventually the administration softened its stance, in the face of a possible uprising. Rey was sacked and many of the traditional powers restored to the kings.

NATIONALISM AND THE ROAD TO INDEPENDENCE

Throughout the colonial years Bechuanaland remained a rural country, underdeveloped in terms of infrastructure, education and health care. There was hardly any industry to speak of and consequently no urban working class ready to strike for nationalist ideals. **Nationalism** developed almost sedately from the ranks of the African Civil Service Association.

The **African Civil Service Association** had been formed in 1949, mainly to protest the discrimination against black civil servants. It was not until the 1960s that Africans began to be promoted to higher posts than previously. More important perhaps was pressure for a **Legislative Council** along the lines of those which by then existed in other African countries, and which were seen as the first step to independence. In 1961 the first Legislative Council met, with an equal number of blacks and whites. Africans used the body as a forum for criticizing the administration for its neglect of the Protectorate, and to demand independence.

In 1959 came the formation of Botswana's first political party, the **Bechuanaland Protectorate Federal Party**, which opposed the discriminatory racial balance of the Legislative Council. The party, however, never got a real foothold and it folded in 1962.

A more vigorous form of nationalism came via South Africa, following the Sharpeville Massacre in 1960, in which police fired on a crowd of peaceful protesters, killing sixty-nine. In the ensuing repression, 1500 people fled across the border to Bechuanaland, bringing ideas from the developing South African struggle. Many were **ANC** (African National Congress) or **PAC** (Pan-Africanist Congress) members and many were Batswana. Two of these Batswana activists, Motsamai Mpho of the ANC and Philip Matante of the PAC, formed the **Bechuanaland People's Party (BPP)**. The Party demanded immediate independence and organized demonstrations, but failed to get crucial rural support.

It was only with the formation of the **Bechuanaland Democratic Party (BDP)** in 1962 that a truly broad-based force came into existence, under the leadership of the popular **Seretse Khama**. (Seretse had been prevented by Britain from taking over the kingship of the Bangwato, because of his marriage to a white woman — see p280.) The BDP was an authentically local party, with no links to external political organizations, and a base in the conservative rural areas, where it played on the popular support enjoyed by traditional leaders like Khama.

The BDP's policies were also far milder than those of its predecessors, which made it more acceptable to many whites and to the colonial government. In 1965, in line with the new British policy of decolonization and the formation of a Commonwealth of the former colonies, supervised **elections** were held prior to the granting of full independence. The BDP won 28 out of 31 seats, with the other three seats going to the BPP.

INDEPENDENCE AND DIAMONDS

On September 30, 1966 the territory became independent as the **Republic of Botswana** —

one of Africa's poorest nations, with just 11km of tarred road and little visible means of support. There was one consolation — at least the traditional capital at Gaborone was now within the nation's own borders.

In the face of dire forecasts, Botswana saw out its first year unremarkably, though continuing to be little more than a labour pool for the South African mines. However, 1967 saw the beginning of a miraculous transformation, heralded by the discovery of **diamonds** at Orapa.

By the early 1970s the mine was on line and it turned out to be the second largest pipe in the world. This was a real Cinderella story, Botswana turning out to be one of the big three gem diamond producers in the world, alongside South Africa and Russia. Not that this prevented South Africa maintaining its age-old policy of harassment towards the new state, demanding a heavy price for its provision of employment, transport and the supply of raw materials, food and consumer goods.

Botswana's government nonetheless made skilful use of its diamond wealth to negotiate a favourable deal with the huge South African diamond monopoly, **De Beers**, to exploit the new-found mineral wealth. Because the international price of diamonds is maintained by a cartel that finds South Africa and Russia in an unlikely collusion, it would have been easy enough for Botswana to flood the market and ruin this cosy arrangement. Consequently the government managed to secure an agreement that gave it a 50–50 share in diamond mining with De Beers, along with 75 percent of the profits.

OPPOSITION TO APARTHEID

At Independence Botswana found itself hemmed in by Rhodesia to the northeast, South Africa to the south and illegally occupied Namibia wrapping round its west and north, leaving only a tiny gateway of just 100 metres connecting it with sympathetic Zambia.

Sir Seretse Khama, however, was not deterred from expressing his opposition to his neighbours' racist policies. He consistently **condemned apartheid**, criticizing both Rhodesia and South Africa for their racial policies — a bold move considering Botswana's precarious position.

Botswana's anti-apartheid stance wasn't limited to words, either, with Seretse Khama offering asylum to **refugees** from the white minority-run countries. In 1974 – following the coup in Portugal that brought independence to its colonies – Botswana, along with Angola, Mozambique and Tanzania formed a grouping known as the **Front Line States** with the aim of providing diplomatic support to the Rhodesian and Namibian liberation struggles.

Beyond this moral support, Botswana assiduously avoided taking any active part in the Southern African liberation wars and never allowed any external organization to have military bases on its territory. This has failed, however, to prevent **attacks** by its white-ruled neighbours. In 1977 the Rhodesians began a campaign of terror against Botswana, launching several raids across the border on the pretext of pre-emptive strikes against non-existent guerrilla training camps. As a result, unarmed Botswana formed its small professional army, the Botswana Defence Force.

Economically, the Front Line States fought back against South Africa's stranglehold over the region by uniting in 1979 in the **Southern African Development Coordination Conference** (SADCC). Since the preparatory talks in 1977, Botswana has played a leading role in the organization, Botswana's president chairing SADCC since 1980. The other members of the conference were Zimbabwe, Mozambique, Lesotho, Swaziland, Angola, Zambia, Malawi, Tanzania and Namibia is likely to join. Under Mandela's leadership, South Africa has joined the organization, now known as SADC, which aims to co-ordinate trade and development in the region.

THE 1980S

Sir Seretse Khama, Botswana's president from Independence, lived just long enough to see Zimbabwe achieve independence. After his death in 1980, Vice-President **Dr Quett Masire** took over leadership of the BDP and the country. The new president had a narrower support base than his predecessor. Sir Seretse was both a member of the Ngwato royal family – the largest of the Tswana groups – and a genuine populist, who had led his country to independence. Masire lacked the benefit of tribal authority and drew far narrower support from his own small Ngwaketse group, among which he faced considerable opposition from conservative elements.

There were fears that Masire's administration might signal a break with Sir Seretse's social concerns. While Khama was bothered by the prospect of growing inequality in his country, Masire favoured an unapologetically rampant form of capitalism, despite its attendant problems. Questioned on the issue he commented:

I don't think it's a feature we can hope to prevent altogether. Men are born equal, but they are not equal in their intellectual capacities, in their willingness to put their shoulder to the wheel, and their desire to acquire knowledge.

In the **1984 general elections**, Masire's BDP party again won a decisive victory, taking 29 of the 34 elected seats. But local elections, held on the same day, indicated different trends. Disquiet about **growing unemployment** emerged when the BDP lost control of every town council apart from Selebi-Phikwe.

Throughout the 1980s, Botswana's internal problems were compounded by **harassment from outside the country**. Although the collapse of the Smith regime in Rhodesia brought incursions from the northeast to an end, a more frightening onslaught began from the south. **South Africa's strategy** was altogether more coordinated, more comprehensive and more sinister than anything Rhodesia had dreamed up. While using the same pretexts as its Rhodesian allies – attacks on non-existent guerrilla camps – the real reason behind South Africa's web of military, economic and diplomatic pressure was to bring Botswana to heel: to put an end to its anti-apartheid statements, gain formal recognition for the bogus "independent" bantustans, get South African refugees expelled and to sign a phony non-aggression pact – like the Nkomati Accord forced on a desperate Mozambique.

In 1981 South Africa was annoyed when Botswana received Soviet arms supplies for the BDF. The incident was blown up and the Afrikaans pro-apartheid newspaper *Beeld* accused Botswana of being "a Cuba" in South Africa's backyard. President Masire explained that the weapons would enable Botswana to police its own borders more effectively to prevent guerrillas from crossing into South Africa – exactly what South Africa was demanding. The stepping up of border security failed to stem South African destabilization.

SOUTH AFRICAN INTERVENTION IN THE 1980s

1981–82 Almost-monthly incidents take place, involving South African troops in Namibia firing on the Botswana army, fishermen and game rangers, and the kidnap and murder of civilians.

February 1982 Peter Lengene, Soweto student leader and refugee for six years, is kidnapped in Gaborone and hustled over the border.

August 1982 Bomb explodes in alleged SWAPO house in Gaborone.

1983 Border clashes and problems with South African agents persist through the year.

November 1983 Botswana army patrol intercepts two South African vehicles near Dukwe apparently intent on taking dissidents to the border to infiltrate Zimbabwe.

1984 Three meetings are held between South Africa and Botswana. South Africa uses threats, including economic blackmail, to pressurize its neighbour into signing a "peace accord". Botswana refuses to give in.

February 1985 Nat Serache, former journalist in South Africa and BBC correspondent, escapes an explosion at his Gaborone house.

May 1985 Car bomb in Gaborone kills Vernon Nkadimeng, son of the general secretary of the South African Congress of Trade Unions.

June 1985 South African commandos launch mortar and machine gun attack on houses of refugees in Gaborone killing twelve, including several people with no South African links.

May 1986 South African units launch a combined series of attacks on Zambia, Zimbabwe and Botswana. One person in Mogaditsane, near Gaborone, dies.

April 1987 The South African government plays to its domestic audience in the face of an approaching May general election with renewed warnings of attacks on the front line states. A Gaborone bomb blast kills four, just hours after one such threat.

March 1988 South Africa admits involvement in killing four alleged ANC members in a raid on a Gaborone house.

June 1988 Two South African soldiers are arrested south of Gaborone after opening fire on the BDF during an abortive commando raid. A car bomb goes off in Gaborone soon after.

September 1988 An attempt to spring the South Africans from prison in Botswana fails, and they receive ten-year sentences.

December 1988 South African commandos kill two people in a border village. One person dies when a bomb goes off in Gaborone.

Despite South African incursions, bombings and commando raids into Gaborone and unsuccessful political interference aimed at creating a Mozambique-style MNR movement to destabilize from within, Botswana stood its ground and refused to give in on any of these issues. In the face of this, Botswana remains the longest-established democratic country in Southern Africa. It is one of the rare African **multi-party states** with the distinction of having **no political prisoners**. And in 1985, even the Johannesburg *Financial Mail* described Botswana's as "the best managed economy in Africa".

INTO THE 1990s

Remarkable as Botswana's economic and political success has been since Independence, with its status shifting from one of the world's twenty poorest countries to Africa's fastest-growing economy, it is still dogged by **dependency**. Most of its imports continue to come from South Africa and it's easy, with all the

South African products around, to feel that you're simply in a province of that country. In certain vital sectors, however, Botswana has made a determined effort to detach itself from South Africa, opting for independent electricity supplies and satellite telecommunications and its own currency and international airport.

But Botswana faces **internal problems** of its own for the future – most seriously, a rapid **population explosion** that threatens to far outstrip job creation. Urbanization, too, with its attendant problems of housing shortage, high rents and growing inequality, has taken place at a phenomenal rate that far overtakes all planning predictions.

While the traditional and rural-based BDP has maintained control of the country, winning every election since Independence, there are signs that the large urban population may stray towards the new **Botswana National Front**, which calls for far greater state intervention in the economy and accuses the government of allowing an excessive capital outflow.

But **BDP rural support** continues, despite large disparities in wealth distribution in the countryside, with much of the fertile lands in the hands of cattle barons and wealthy farmers while elsewhere there's poverty. The BNF has criticized the government's policies for dealing with these issues as short-sighted tinkering, and has attacked the government for making little attempt to restructure wealth distribution. "All the BDP can do is give away hand-outs as if the people are chickens", BNF representative Paul Rantao said in 1989, referring to food aid provided during droughts.

However, with eighty percent of the population still in the rural areas – traditional BDP country – there's unlikely to be any change in government this century. And the BDP does seem to be taking criticisms on board, initiating **rural projects** to transfer some resources to the poor rural areas. But social changes continue apace and the increasingly young population has rising expectations and declining allegiance to the old guard of tribally based political leaders. A wave of strikes in the late 1980s pointed to new problems for the government, whose future is going to depend on its ability to satisfy the demands of the growing urban populations – and particularly so given whatever changes take place across the border in South Africa.

WRITING FROM ZIMBABWE

Zimbabwe has long possessed a rich oral literature but until the 1890s Shona and Ndebele were not written, and although before Independence there may have been blacks ready to bare their souls about the experience of being colonized, the printing presses were in white hands. Black writers, therefore, had limited possibilities for publication. All manuscripts were vetted by the Rhodesia Literature Bureau, which allowed for more than direct government censorship: through its workshops, pamphlets and advice to authors, it forced the creative production of several decades through particular, restricted channels. Anything political was, naturally, quite out of the question.

During the **liberation struggle**, some fiction and its authors found their way to Britain and acclaim. Writers such as **Dambudzo Marechera** appeared in print outside the country. But at home, throughout the war, non-fiction and music proved more effective voices than literature, for the story that had, with increasing urgency, to be told.

With **Independence** in 1980, however, poets came home from foreign universities and from the guerilla camps. From the offices, factories and classrooms people came together in workshops and a writers' union was formed. The liberation struggle was naturally enough a major concern for most writers, combined with an optimism for the new order. Creative opportunities seemed unlimited.

A decade on, despite the occasional reappearance of government censorship, the result is a stimulating mixture: fine, crafted works from masters such as **Charles Mungoshi** are published alongside fast, bad, township **gangster stories**; **war novels** alongside **love poems**; **love novels** alongside **war poems**; the first stabs at **satire** in a new black state. Perhaps most fascinating are the **autobiographies** out of the silenced past – prison life, existence on farms, on the front line, behind

I scratched around in the rubbish dump with other kids, looking for comics, magazines, books, broken toys, anything that could help us kids pass the time in the ghetto.... You could say my very first books were the books which the rabidly racist Rusape whites were reading at the time.

I took to the English language like a duck takes to water. I was therefore a keen accomplice and student in my own mental colonization.... For a black writer, the language is very racist: you have to have harrowing fights and hair-raising panga duels with it before you can make it do all you want it to do.

Dambudzo Marechera: quoted on the cover of *Dambudzo Marechera 1952–1987* (Baobab Books, Harare 1988).

guns, or simply picking veld flowers – from a society that was divided and remains so. These are still early days in Zimbabwe's search for its voice. Expect everything, especially surprises.

CHARLES MUNGOSHI

Charles Mungoshi is arguably the finest voice of pre-Independence black despair. His characters face each other across a desolate silence that language cannot bridge – a historical or human condition depending on your reading. "Words are handles made to the smith's fancy and are liable to break under stress," he wrote, "They are too much fat on the hard unbreaking sinews of life."

The story below is from the *Coming of the Dry Season* – not overtly political, but nevertheless banned by the Smith regime.

THE LIFT

When they were tired of going round the factories and shops in search of jobs, the boys went to the tall buildings at the heart of the city for their daily ride in the lifts. It was the only fun they had and it made them forget a little their burning bellies and tired feet.

There were lots of clouds flung about the sky like cotton balls in a field. It was rather chilly and the boys felt sharply the pleasant warmth of the sun when it came out of the clouds, and both of them unconsciously looked up irritably when it darted behind another cloud.

At present, their minds, usually the colour of the changing streets and just as desolate, were fixed on the ride in the lifts.

Pearl Assurance Building, one of the tallest buildings in the city, had a guard at the wide entrance.

'Can I help you?' the guard asked.

'We would like to go up.'

'Floor?'

'Tenth.'

'What for?'

The boys looked at each other and hazarded an answer.

'We are doing correspondence courses.'

The guard looked at them suspiciously and then dismissed them with a flick of the hand.

'You are not allowed up there.'

The boys looked at the guard as if they had not heard him. Then their eyes turned to gaze at the wall above the lift where numbers went on and off in amber to show the lift coming down.

'There has been much stealing up there lately,' the guard said.

'We are not thieves.'

The guard's eyes swept over their heads and he dismissed them from his attention.

'Go away, boys.'

The boys turned to go. They passed two European boys of their own age. Looking back, the boys saw the guard take off his cap to the Europeans who did not answer him and quickly entered the lift and disappeared.

'Why did you allow those two to go up?'

'*You* are not allowed up there.'

The boys went out onto the street. It was not yet noon and they had nowhere to go and nothing to do to kill the time until night when they would go home to sleep.

'Wish I had kept that shilling after all,' one of them, thinner than the other, said.

'We had to have something to eat.'

'All the same, we could have used it now. It's so much nicer to have something to eat when you don't have anything to do.'

They were moving toward Salisbury Park. They had not talked of the park yet both of them knew that that was the only place left to go and rest.

'I was a fool to use that shilling,' the thin one said again.

His friend didn't answer because he always felt irritated by his companion's mourning for things that could have been. He felt like shouting at him to stop it but he controlled himself. He didn't care for words when he was tired. They made him even more tired than he really was.

'This is unbearable,' the thin one said once more.

But his friend kept quiet. He was hungry and there was nowhere to get money from. The thin one looked at him, knew that he would be asked why he was looking at him, and kept quiet, knowing that this would only lead to a quarrel. But all the same, it could have been so much better if his friend would talk, then he wouldn't have to think and feel that he was not wanted, so lonely and so hopeless. The park was almost deserted except for two or three people lying on the forbidden grass, asleep or pretending to be asleep.

The thin one said, 'They are going to start trouble with the authorities.'

His friend answered him this time. 'It's silly to forbid people from lying on the grass. What is it there for?'

'It's the rules.'

'To hell with the rules.'

They found a bench under some bamboos and sat down. Immediately they had sat down, the talkative one said, 'They are not allowed to lie on the grass.'

'You have said that already.'

The thin boy looked at his friend and said nothing more. His friend leaned back on the bench and closed his eyes, pretending to go to sleep but the other one knew that this was the cue for him to keep quiet. Both of them were under a strain. They wanted to be somewhere else; the swimming pool, the beer hall — anywhere where there were people and fun and a chance to forget themselves. But there was only the wide empty park and themselves.

The sleepless one looked around the park. He tried to steady his thoughts on the flowers and the trees and the light in the leaves of the trees on the grass and the tall buildings of the city beyond the trees and the immense space of sky above the city, but there was nowhere his thoughts could rest and he was forced to come back to himself.

But he was tired of looking into himself, of asking himself why he was like this and not like that, tired of examining himself, of finding faults with himself, tired of judging and condemning himself. He was tired of the whole circling process of his thoughts, so tired that he wanted movement — any movement, to feel that he was going somewhere and not just stationary. The feeling of doing nothing, of being nothing, oppressed and frightened him. He must talk at least: that gave him a sense of direction, a feeling of really moving towards something. But his friend would not talk.

'That guard was just a nuisance. We wanted nothing except a ride. Only one ride in the lift.'

His friend stirred impatiently and said, 'Perhaps he was right. Lift rides are so short anyway.'

'But sometimes you get off a lift and find the sun has set.'

'Why don't you try to get some sleep? The sun would set faster.'

'I can't sleep during the day.'

'Then shut up please and let me sleep.'

The thin boy watched his friend as he moved towards the further end of the bench after these words. He moved towards the other end and closed his eyes. But he opened them again, worried about the space between them and the empty space that had opened up in him on closing his eyes.

'Can't we do something?' he asked.

Without a word, his friend rose and walked away to another bench and sat down, staring through the trees across the park toward the city. The thin one stayed in his place and struggled to keep himself seated, afraid to stand up and follow his friend, afraid to make even the smallest movement with his body that he knew before he had made it would fall into the pattern of yesterday, today and tomorrow.

So he tried to hurry the night when the darkness would hold his thoughts together and he wouldn't be worried by the distance between their two benches, the space that isolated them; so that looking at the two of them from afar, he saw that they were not friends. Not quite friends.

*Reproduced, with permission, from **Coming of the Dry Season** (Zimbabwe Publishing House, 1981).*

FREEDOM T.V. NYAMUBAYA

Writers published after Independence are invariably involved in the debate as to whether a writer should be primarily concerned with burning political issues, or with "art". The poet Freedom T. V. Nyamubaya fought with ZANLA in the Second Chimurenga. Military comparisons in her work are irresistible: the poems are forceful, direct and bullet-like. Despite her political objectives, her poems remain funny, perceptive and tender.

The poem below is the opening piece of her first collection of poems, *On the Road Again*, which establishes Comrade Freedom's position in the argument for a literature of commitment:

Now that I have put my gun down
For almost obvious reasons
The enemy still is here invisible
My barrel has no definite target
now
Let my hands work —
My mouth sing —
My pencil write —
About the same things my bullet
aimed at.

*Reproduced, with permission, from **On the Road Again** (Zimbabwe Publishing House, Harare 1986).*

CHENJERAI HOVE

Chenjerai Hove, too, calls for engaged, progressive writing; authors who identify with the lives and struggles of the people. The following extract from his Noma Award-winning novel *Bones* (interestingly narrated by a woman), addresses, as do his poems, the issues and experiences of the Independence War.

FROM "BONES"

Do you know Chisaga? He is a good man, but his greed for women is a bit too much. He came to me and pleaded that he will do anything if he can sleep with me. I said that was also my idea for a long time. But since he was the first to mention it, I want him to do something before he can sleep with me. I said he should steal some money for me from Manyepo's safe in the house where he cooks for him every day. Since Manyepo trusts him so much, he will not think it is him. Manyepo will think of other people who have been caught stealing mangoes, but not Chisaga. So Chisaga has stolen the money for me. He expects to sleep with me when he is not working, one of these days. But he will have nobody to sleep with because I knew what I was doing. Do not open your mouth so much, child. The things men will do to satisfy the desire of their things are very surprising. Men will kill their own mothers if they stop them from satisfying the desire of their things. They can dig a hole through a mountain if you tell them you will be waiting the other side of the hill to give them your thing. Men are like children, my mother used to say. They rule everything, like children. Do they not say children are like kings? You let them play with fire, but you always keep looking. You always keep looking at them so that they do not burn their fingers. This is what we do all the time. Look and watch over them. If it were not for men, do you think your grandfather would have died in places where they could not return his body for burial? Did your mother not say that your grandfather died fighting a war started by a man called Hikila who wanted to rule the whole earth? Think of that, a man who does not even know how to cook for himself wants to rule the whole earth. That is what men are like. They look after their things erect in front of them and think they are kings. They do not know that it is just desire shooting out of them, nothing else. So child, you do what you can with the weaknesses of men, but do not let them play with your body. It is your last property, you will die with it. So do not let people waste it like any rubbish they pick up in the village rubbish heap. I know this because my mouth has eaten medicines which even a dog would vomit. My ear has heard things even a witch would faint to hear . . .

*   *   *   *   *

The fighters leave him to go home without making any promises. Then after a few days of walking and seeing with their own eyes the poverty of the people, they decide they cannot wait much longer. The people did not have much to give them. If the fighters do not feed, Marita says, they will stop fighting and go working in the fields. But they had seen so much poverty that it became harsh to their eyes. Let us leave, they said to each other. Let us look for better areas where there are fields that can give something to the farmers. Our

hopes will die if we continue to see children dying every day and the cattle licking the soil as if it contains salt. We have learnt that we must free our people from poverty. Poverty is worse than war, they say. You can stop war through talking. You can't stop poverty through talking. So we must fight with all we have so that our people cannot continue to be buried in this ant-hill of poverty.

*Reproduced with permission, from **Bones** (Baobab Books, Harare 1988).*

DAMBUDZO MARECHERA

Not all Zimbabwe's literary figures share Hove's and Nyamubaya's view of the artist's role. Most flamboyant and controversial among the dissenting was Dambudzo Marechera, well known outside Zimbabwe since his novella and short stories, *House of Hunger*, won the Guardian Fiction Prize.

Before his death in 1987 at the age of 35, Marechera was the *enfant terrible* of Zimbabwean letters. Genius or madman – public opinion remains undecided, although he had become a minor cult figure by the time of his death. Some refuse to label him an "African writer" – and they include Marechera himself: "I would question anyone calling me an African writer. Either you are a writer or you are not. If you are a writer for a specific nation or a specific race, then fuck you."

IDENTIFY THE IDENTITY PARADE

I am the luggage no one will claim;
The out-of-place turd all deny
Responsibility;
The incredulous sneer all tuck away
beneath bland smiles;
The loud fart all silently agree never
happened;
The sheer bad breath you politely confront
with mouthwashed platitudes: 'After all, it's
POETRY.'
I am the rat every cat secretly admires;
The cat every dog secretly fears;
The pervert every honest citizen surprises
in his own mirror: POET.

THE FEAR AND LOATHING OUT OF HARARE

What is it about Harare . . .?
Is it the nightlife, the hotels,
the nightclubs? Or the melancholy
solitary walk back to the flat
when a tawny, almost rubescent dawn
is signalling from within the dark
confines of another pent-up night? For four
years I had not ventured out of the City –
the rest of the country only existed in
news reports about dissidents, co-operatives,
and Blair toilets, not to mention Binga
where it was reported that the main meal
of each drought-stricken day was a
tray of fried grass.

THE TREES OF THE DAY

Trees too tired to carry the burden
Of leaf and bud, of bird and bough
Too harassed by the rigours of unemployment
The drought-glare of high rents
And the spiralling cost of water and mealie-
meal
Trees shrivelled into abortion by the forest fires
Of dumped political policies
Trees whose Kachasu-veined twig-fingers
Can no longer clench into the people's fist
But wearily wipe dripping noses, wearily wave
away
The fly-ridden promises issuing out of the
public Lavatory
Trees under which, hungry and homeless
I emerge from seed to drill a single root into
the
Salt stone soils
The effort a scream of despair.

Reproduced, with permission, from **Dambudzo
Marechera 1952–1987** *(Baobab Books, Harare
1988).*

TSITSI DANGAREMBGA

**Tsitsi Dangarembga is a formidable new
talent from the same generation as
Marechera: her first novel, *Nervous
Conditions*, excerpted below, won the
1989 Commonwealth Literature Prize. The
book is a triumph for women's writing as
well as for Zimbabwean literature. Its
opening sentence, "I was not sorry when
my brother died", signals its defiance of
what is acceptable in a dutiful daughter in
its tale of a young black woman growing
up in Rhodesia. This extract is about the
return of the young narrator's uncle,
Babamukuru, from university in Britain.**

FROM "NERVOUS CONDITIONS"

Babamukuru came home in cavalcade of motor
vehicles, sighted four miles away on the main
road by three jubilant pairs of eyes. Netsai
and I and little Shupikai, whose mother was
one of the relatives gathered to celebrate the
occasion of Babamukuru's return, watched as
the cavalcade progressed, distressingly
slowly, now disappearing behind clumps of
trees, now reappearing hours later, or so it
seemed, no more than a few hundred yards
nearer. The vigil lasted twenty minutes. We
watched from a rock on the hill behind the
homestead until the carts disappeared for the
last time into the home-stretch. Then we went
wild. We slid off our rock, skinning elbows
and knees on the way, scrambled oblivious
through bushes that scratched our legs,
dashed out on to the road and ran on. 'Ba-ba-
mu-ku-ru! Ba-ba-mu-ku-ru!' we chanted,
running and jumping and waving our skinny
arms about all at the same time, skirts swirling, bottoms jutting as we capered. Shupikai,
several yards behind, started to cry, still
tottering along and chanting through her sobs,
because we had left her behind and because
she was excited. Her crisis was so inconvenient. I considered ignoring her, which could
not be done. Dashing back, I snatched her up
to continue the mad welcome with her
perched on my hip.

My aunt Gladys, the one who is my father's
womb-sister, older than him but younger than
Babamukuru, came first, her husband behind
the wheel of a gallant if rickety old Austin.
They hooted long and loud. We waved and
shouted and danced. Then came Babamukuru,
his car large and impressive, all sparkling metal
and polished dark green. It was too much for
me. I could have clambered on to the bonnet
but, with Shupi in my arms, had to be content
with a song: '*Mauya, mauya. Mauya,
Babamukuru!*' Netsai picked up the melody.
Our vocal cords vibrating through wide arcs, we
made an unbelievable racket. Singing and
advancing we ushered Babamukuru on to the
homestead, hardly noticing Babamunini

Thomas, who brought up the rear, not noticing Maini Patience, who was with him, at all.

Slowly the cavalcade progressed towards the yard, which by now was full of rejoicing relatives. My father jumped out of Babamukuru's car and, brandishing a staff like a victory spear, bounded over the bumpy road, leaping into the air and landing on one knee, to get up and leap again and pose like a warrior inflicting a death wound. '*Hezvo!*' he cried 'Do you see him? Our returning prince. Do you see him? Observe him well. He has returned. Our father and benefactor has returned appeased, having devoured English letters with a ferocious appetite! Did you think degrees were indigestible? If so, look at my brother. He has digested them! If you want to see an educated man, look at my brother, big brother to us all!' The spear aimed high and low, thrust to the right, to the left. All was conquered.

The cars rolled to a stop beneath the mango trees. Tete Gladys disembarked with difficulty, with false starts and strenuous breathing; because she was so large, it was not altogether clear how she had managed to insert herself into the car in the first place. But her mass was not frivolous. It had a ponderous presence which rendered any situation, even her attempts to remove herself from her car, weighty and serious. We did not giggle, did not think of it.

On her feet at last, Tete straightened herself, planted herself firmly, feet astride, in the dust. Clenched fists settling on hips, elbows jutting aggressively, she defied any contradiction of my father's eulogy. 'Do you hear?' she demanded, 'what Jeremiah is saying? If you have not heard, listen well. It is the truth he is speaking! Truly our prince has returned today! Full of knowledge. Knowledge that will benefit us all! Pururuuru!' she ululated, shuffling with small gracious jumps to embrace my mother. 'Pururuuru!' They ululated. 'He has returned. Our prince has returned!'

Babamukuru stepped out of his car, paused behind its open door, removed his hat to smile graciously, joyfully, at us all. Indeed, my Babamukuru had returned. I saw him only for a moment. The next minute he was drowned in a sea of bodies belonging to uncles, aunts and nephews; grandmothers, grandfathers and nieces; brothers and sisters of the womb and not of the womb. The clan had gathered to welcome its returning hero. His hand was shaken, his head was rubbed, his legs were embraced. I was there too, wanting to touch Babamukuru, to talk, to tell him I was glad that he had returned. Babamukuru made his fair-sized form as expansive as possible, holding his arms out and bending low so that we all could be embraced, could embrace him. He was happy. He was smiling. 'Yes, yes,' he kept saying. 'It is good, it is good.' We moved, dancing and ululating and kicking up a fine dust-storm from our stamping feet, to the house.

Babamukuru stepped inside, followed by a retinue of grandfathers, uncles and brothers. Various paternal aunts, who could join them by virtue of their patriarchal status and were not too shy to do so, mingled with men. Behind them danced female relatives of the lower strata. Maiguru entered last and alone, except for her two children, smiling quietly and inconspicuously. Dressed in flat brown shoes and a pleated polyester dress very much like the one Babamukuru bought for my mother the Christmas before he left, she did not look as though she had been to England. My cousin Nyasha, pretty bright Nyasha, on the other hand, obviously had. There was no other explanation for the tiny little dress she wore, hardly enough of it to cover her thighs. She was self-conscious though, constantly clasping her hands behind her buttocks to prevent her dress from riding up, and observing everybody through veiled vigilant eyes to see what we were thinking. Catching me examining her, she smiled slightly and shrugged, 'I shouldn't have worn it,' her eyes seemed to say. Unfortunately, she had worn it. I could not condone her lack of decorum. I would not give my approval. I turned away.

Reproduced, with permission, from **Nervous Conditions** *(The Women's Press, London; and Zimbabwe Publishing House, Harare 1988).*

BRUCE MOORE-KING

The work of a new white writer, Bruce Moore-King, *White Man Black War* has had a considerable impact within Zimbabwe and abroad. A former soldier in one of Rhodesia's crack regiments, Moore-King questions the society and the interests he fought for and for which so many died, interspersing military experi-

ences of terrible brutality, recounted in unflinching dead-pan style, with philosophical deliberations.

FROM "WHITE MAN BLACK WAR"

A man hangs spreadeagled, handcuffed to a steel bed-frame. Outside the small, prefabricated rondavel, the land is wet and soaked, a quagmire of mud, farm roads turned into river beds. Half a mile from the rondavel an army truck stands buried to the axles in clay. Twenty yards from the rondavel stands the main ranch house. Over the gate leading into the garden a sign reads "Makorski River Ranch – Manager". In the garden around the rondavel, bedraggled rose bushes, thick clumps of bougainvillea, a group of tattered banana trees.

The bed-frame is standing propped against the interior of the rondavel, almost vertical. The man is naked, handcuffs tight at each hand and each ankle, stretching him. His head is lolling, face gazing blindly down at his feet, but shortly the frame will be rotated and he will hang upside-down.

Around the ranch house a maze of trenches and barbed wire meanders, dotted with green canvas tents and heavily covered ammunition pits. There are numerous mortar craters, the freshest having arrived the night before. The ranch manager and his wife have elected to stay, a show of deliberate defiance, and the man on the bed-frame is their boss boy, they've known him for nine years.

There are three elements of the security forces present on the ranch, a company of territorials on call up, a platoon of special police constabulary – black men in blue overalls – under the command of an eighteen-year-old white policeman, and the troop of Grey's Scouts that have been helicoptered in because of the deteriorating situation on the ranch.

There are two men in the rondavel with the prisoner, an SB officer, and the commander of the Grey's troop. The latter is a short, very powerfully built man in his early forties, a professional soldier, ex-British SAS, ex-Foreign Legion, former Warrant Officer in the Rhodesian

SAS. The two are sitting on camp stools, drinking Cokes.

The special police constables are equipped with old .303s, but their commander has taken their magazines away from them, as they have developed a tendency to fire somewhat erratically when the base comes under mortar attack. The night before the Grey's commander had found himself under fire from two directions, as the enemy fired into the base, and the constables fired out from the centre, with the troops in the middle.

The man on the bed-frame groans, and the troop commander speaks: "Give us a hand". Together they rotate the bed-frame until the man is hanging upside-down. The troop commander, Kelly, picks up a length of thick, high-pressure compressor hose and hits the prisoner across the thighs and testicles with it. The prisoner screams.

"I thought that would wake you up, you sonofabitch!".

A corporal enters, muddy and wet. He glances at the two men, nods to the SB officer, then sits down, propping his rifle beside him. He opens a Coke, picks up a *Playboy*, and begins reading it.

*   *   *   *   *

I do not think my memories of the reality of the society we held before the war are incorrect.

I can understand, now, why our countrymen took up arms against us. And if these actions and attitudes and forms of selective ignorance displayed by my tribe once caused blood and fire to spread across the land called Rhodesia, what will these same actions and attitudes and forms of selective ignorance produce in this land called Zimbabwe?

Must my tribe reinforce their Creed of racial superiority by denying these, the victors of the war, the basic humanness of the ability to Anger?

Reproduced, with permission, from **White Man Black War** *(Baobab Books, Harare 1988).*

• *article by Annie Holmes*

WRITING FROM BOTSWANA

While there is no written literary tradition in Botswana, oral literature has always thrived, as throughout Southern Africa, and has inspired collections from numerous outsiders – most notably Sir Laurens van der Post, who retells various San myths in *The Heart of the Hunter*, the sequel to the *Lost World of the Kalahari*. Extracts that follow include both San tales and the less well-known (at least outside Africa) form of praise poetry.

That there is, as yet, little written literature is perhaps inevitable, given a rural country with such a tiny population. Furthermore, Botswana did not experience a liberation struggle – the impetus or inspiration for so much modern African writing. However, the country's literature has a towering figure in the South African exile Bessie Head, who made her home in Serowe; her novels explore inner states and universal concerns through the particular of rural Botswanan life.

PRAISE POETRY

Poetry praising a chief was traditionally one of the most important forms of literary expression in Southern Africa. Here's a translation of a Tswana praise poem with a difference. In a twentieth-century adaptation of the form, it eulogizes the Bulawayo–Johannesburg train that passes through Botswana.

THE TRAIN

I am the black centipede, with my shining nose, rushing through the peoples' hills, minding none of these.
I drink water from the fountains of the powerful magicians
yet no one could e'er bewitch me, neither sorcerers or witches.
Searing sunshine does not stop me, nor does darkness halt my journey.
I have conquered hills and valleys where the leopard is a-lurking,
where the lions crunch the thighbones of their victims, warm and bloody.
When I race along the sand dunes whirling sandclouds fill the skyline.
People ask me where I come from, but they never heard those place names,
ask what journey-food I carry, but I shall arrive tomorrow!
I am not delayed by hunger, nor do blistering feet delay me.
Distant hamlets hear my warning when I overtake the springbok.
I am like a moving village, full of people, never tiring.

SAN TALES

The innumerable **San myths** vary from region to region, and from clan to clan. The G/wi San of central Botswana, for instance, attribute the fierce rainstorms of the Kalahari to the anger of a mythical giant leopard. Lightning is the light of rage flashing in its eyes and at the same time its thunderous roar rolls round the land. Other stories seek to explain features of the night sky, such as the waxing and waning of the moon and why the stars are in particular formations. The !Kung San reckon the stars of the belt of Orion are three zebra, shot at by the Great God while out hunting.

The piece below is a typical cosmological San myth, translated into poetic form.

THE REBIRTH OF THE OSTRICH

He is an ostrich. He is male.
A hungry man goes out to hunt.
He kills the ostrich at his eggs.
The man's wife plucks the ostrich while the ostrich's feathers are with blood.
She throws the feathers in the bush.
She and her husband eat the flesh.

A whirlwind comes. He blows up high
a little feather dipped in blood.
The whirlwind leaves, the feather falls
into a pool where it gets wet.
The little feather that gets wet
becomes alive because it soaks.
While it drinks water it becomes
a living thing of ostrich flesh.
The living thing gets legs and wings.
It puts on feathers, grows a head.
It lies and grows inside the pool.
It leaves the water. It is soft,

with little feathers that are black,
for he, who from the water comes,
he in an ostrich. He is male.

The little ostrich wants to grow.
He lies upon the water's edge.
He dries his feathers in the sun.
He, stretching, lifts his neck. He moves
his legs. He stands upon his feet.

His feet are weak. He walks. He goes
to make them stronger. He lies down
upon his breast to make it hard;
he makes his breastbone hard.
His bones are strong, his heavy flesh
is full of feathers that are black.
His legs are big, his knees are large.
He roars. He has grown up. He is
a grown-up ostrich. He is male.

The ostrich wants to scratch. His claws
scratch out a place that is a nest.
He roars because his ribs are strong.
His voice is loud. His voice is sweet.

He, strutting, goes to look for wives
on plains where she-ostriches feed.
He calls to them. His voice is sweet.
They come to him. He takes them home,
they lie upon the ground. They make
it soft. They sleep. They flap their wings.
Flapping their wings, they make their eggs.
He lets them go so that they may eat,
while he remains to tend the eggs.
They are his children. Therefore he
takes care of them when the jackals howl.
He kicks the jackal with his feet.
The jackals fear him. He is strong.

He is the one the wind blew up,
the feather that was dipped in blood,
the feather that fell in the pool.
He is the feather that became
once more an ostrich who is male.

THE DAY WE DIE

The day we die
the wind comes down
to take away
our footprints.
The wind makes dust
to cover up

the marks we left
while walking.

For otherwise
the thing would seem
as if we were still living.

Therefore the wind
is he who comes
to blow away
our footprints.

Translated by Arthur Markowitz.

*Reprinted with permission from **The Rebirth of the Ostrich** (National Museum and Art Gallery, Gaborone 1971).*

BESSIE HEAD

Bessie Head's portrayals of village life are unparalleled, and throughout her work she imbues Botswana's flat dry landscape with a lasting beauty. The novels are pretty heavyweight offerings; in her short stories, by contrast, she shows a warm, humorous touch. Until her death in 1988, she was undeniably the country's leading literary figure.

THE SPECIAL ONE

I was a newcomer to the village at that time and teaching at one of the primary schools. Mrs Maleboge was one of my colleagues, a short, stout woman, with a very sad face, who always wore a shawl and a white cotton kerchief wound rather unbecomingly around her head; the kerchief obscured a quarter part of her face so that her sad black eyes stared out from under it. She moved very slowly like the olden-day sailing ships blown by a steady breeze and her speech was as slow and steady as her walk. As soon as one became acquainted with her, she'd start to talk about the great tragedy in her life. Apparently, her husband had left her a small inheritance of cattle at his death, enough to have made her life comfortable in old age. The inheritance had been stolen from her by his brothers and so she was forced to seek employment in her old age when she should have been resting (she was sixty years old). She could stand for about an hour and outline details of the court case she had had with her brothers-in-law, and then stare quietly into the distance and comment: "I lost it because women are just dogs in this society." She did it to me twice, pinned me down and made me listen to this story, so that I developed an anxiety to avoid her. It was impossible to say: "Excuse me, I have to hurry somewhere" — she was too regal and commanded attention once she had started talking.

One day, without any change of expression, she said to me: "You must come to the baptismal party for my grandchild. It's on Sunday." Perhaps she didn't mean it, she was just self-absorbed, but her expression implied that the baptismal party was sad too like everything else. She also gave me directions to her home: "I live near the church. Just get near the church, then ask anyone in the surroundings where I live. They will show you my yard. . ."

So that was what I did, used the church as a guide mark and then stood looking around, confused. Thousands of little footpaths spread out all round it towards thousands of yards, all with the same look. Where did I go from here? Suddenly along the footpath on which I was standing, a woman came walking towards me. She was walking rather rapidly and in a peculiar way with the wide, swaying footsteps of a drunk. She only cared about herself because she was looking at nothing and she would have walked right past me had I not said, with some desperation: "Please, do you know the yard of Mrs Maleboge?"

She stopped abruptly in the midst of her wide, swaying walk, turned around and looked directly at me.

"Why do you want to know where Mrs Maleboge lives?" she asked.

"She invited me to the baptism party of her grandchild," I replied, uneasily. There was something wrong with the woman and she frightened me a little. To my surprise, she gasped and broke into a very friendly smile.

"How can Mrs Maleboge do this!" she exclaimed. "I am her best friend and she never told me that she was having a party! I am going to the party too! Come, I'll take you to her home. It's just around the corner."

That settled me a little and I was enchanted by the way she had had her mind entirely set on going somewhere else, and now had her mind entirely set on going to Mrs Maleboge's party. She had a light chiffon scarf wound

around her head and she suddenly wrenched it off and began swinging it to and fro with the rhythm of her walk, like a young girl. I thought she might be in her late thirties and her mat of closely cropped brown hair clung neatly to her head. She told me later that her name was Gaenametse, which literally translated means there-is-no-water but translated in a figurative way meant that at the time she was born, the marriage between her parents had been very unsatisfactory.

When we entered the yard of Mrs Maleboge, there were quite a number of guests assembled already. The old woman walked straight towards us, looking brighter and brisker than usual and taking me by the arm she said: "Special guests must enter the hut and be served separately. That is our custom."

Gaenametse and I entered the hut and as soon as the door was closed, my companion flung herself at Mrs Maleboge and began teasing and joking about the fact that her best friend had not invited her to the party but she was here all the same. They were really old friends, with a dialogue, and as soon as we were seated, Gaenametse picked up the dialogue at the exact point at which it had been left off when they last met.

"He's gone to her again!" she burst out. "I am at my wit's end, Mma Maleboge. My love for my husband has reached the over-limit stage. I cannot part from him."

So acute was her misery that her whole body was shaken by sobs. And I thought: "That clears up the mystery of her frightening way of walking. She's at the point of breakdown."

I gathered from what they did next, that they had been through this ritual a number of times. Mrs Maleboge sank to her knees, closed her eyes and began earnestly to implore Jesus to come to the aid of her friend. They formed a touching and complete circle of concentration. Gaenametse did not close her eyes. She stared intently at Mrs Maleboge's face as though expecting her at any moment to make contact with Jesus, and she did not want to miss that moment when it arrived. This effort of concentration so sharpened and heightened every feature in her face that I remember wondering why the unknown husband did not love such a beautiful woman. I had the impression of someone glowing with life, charm, and vitality.

Mrs Maleboge's prayer went one for well over fifteen minutes. Then she stood up and calmly carried on with her duties as hostess of a baptismal party. Neither woman was put out that a stranger had been witness to their private affairs. Gaenametse sat back, relaxed and calm, prepared to enjoy the party. She made some friendly conversation asking who I was and where I had come from. We were both handed plates of rice and chicken and salad by Mrs Maleboge. She had gone up in my estimation. I was deeply moved by the kindness she displayed towards her distressed friend and the touching and almost futile way in which the two women tried to cope with this eternal problem. Towards evening, Mrs Maleboge walked me a little way home and her final comment on the event was:

"Gaenametse has a very bad husband. He is off from woman to woman, but we are praying about the matter," and she stared quietly and sadly into the distance. She did not have to add that women are just dogs in this society. I believed her by then.

Six months later Gaenametse walked slowly down the road past my home; at least I saw someone I vaguely recognized. She had exchanged the lovely light chiffon scarf for the white cotton kerchief worn by Mrs Maleboge and wound it unbecomingly around her head so that only her eyes peeped out beneath it. A shawl was about her shoulders and her dress reached to the ankles. She had a piece of white crochet work in her hand and worked the crochet needle up and down as she walked. She looked very old and she recognized me more readily than I recognized her. She turned around with that sudden, impulsive movement and friendly smile.

"Oh," she said. "So this is where you live," and she turned in her path and walked straight up to my door.

I made tea, puzzled all the while. I just could not see the wild and beautiful woman of that Sunday. She soon informed me about this chameleon-like change of personality.

"I am divorced from my husband," she said, with a complacent smile.

"I'm sorry to hear that," I said, thinking that that was expected of me. I could see that she did not care a damn.

"Oh everything is going to be all right," she said airily. "I have need of nothing. My father left me a lot of cattle when he died."

She put her head to one side, still with that complacent smile, and stroked the dead body of her marriage: "No one could have loved my husband as much as I did. I loved him too much."

"It's very sad when such things happen," I said.

"Oh, life isn't so bad," she said. "I can tell you a secret. Even old women like Mrs Maleboge are quite happy. They still make love."

I was so startled by this that I burst out: "You don't say!"

She put on the sweet and secret smile of a woman who knows much about this side of life.

"When you are old," she said, "that's the time you make love, more than when you are young. You make love because you are no longer afraid of making babies. You make love with young boys. They all do it but it is done very secretly. No one suspects, that is why they look so respectable in the day time."

It was a bit beyond my imagination – Mrs Maleboge and a young boy! I shrugged my shoulders, lost. It never occurred to me either that this might also be Gaenametse's preoccupation. After we had drunk tea I walked her a little way down the road, and as I was returning to my own home I was accosted by a woman neighbour.

"What are you doing with that one?" she demanded.

I looked back at her, discomforted. It was the height of insult to refer to someone as that one but I was a bit appalled by that story of old women and young boys getting together.

"Don't you ever know what's going on in the village?" the gossipy neighbour persisted. "No one will talk to her. She's a wash-out! She had a terrible divorce case. She was driving the husband mad. She pestered him day and night for the blankets, and even wanted him to do it during the time when she was having her monthly bleeding. Many women have killed men by sleeping with them during that time. It's a dangerous thing and against our custom. The woman will remain alive and the man will die. She was trying to kill the husband, so the court ruled that he'd better be parted from such a terrible woman."

I stared back at her in petrified horror. She must have thought I understood and approved of some of the insane beliefs of a primitive society, and the society was primitive in certain respects – all primitive societies have their holy fear of a woman's menstrual cycle; during that time she is dirty, and a source of death and danger to the surroundings in general. No, what horrified me was the memory of that Sunday; the wide, drunken swaying walk of extreme emotional distress; the tender appeal two women had made to Jesus for help and a sudden insight into the depth of wickedness of the unknown man. He must have anticipated this social reaction to his wife and deliberately invoked the old tribal taboo to boost his image. How she must have cringed and squirmed, and after the divorce tried to build up an image of respect by dressing up like old Mrs Maleboge! It was quite impossible to convey all this to the snickering village gossip, so I simply told her quite seriously, without knowing anything definite about it, that where I came from the men usually slept with the women when they were menstruating so it was all right for me to talk to Gaenametse.

Shortly afterwards, I saw Gaenametse in the central shopping area of the village. She was dressed like Mrs Maleboge but she was off her beam again. Her walk was her own, wide, drunken, and swaying. Soon I noticed that she was following a young man and a young girl who were strolling casually down the dusty dirt road, hand in hand. She caught up with the couple and with a swift movement planted herself firmly in their path. She looked at the young man with a terrible ugly expression. Since I could read it, he must have read it too. It said plainly: "So, I am only good enough to visit at night. I'd like to stroll casually through the village with you, hand in hand." But no word was exchanged. She turned abruptly and swayed her way off into the distance. She was like that, a wild and wayward learner. She must have decided there and then that Mrs Maleboge's tricks were beyond her. She could not keep her emotions within bounds.

Her last image was the final one I saw. A business matter forced me to take a walk to a remote and far-flung part of the village. While on my way back a voice called out gaily: "Hey, what are you doing here?" I turned around and there was Gaenametse briskly sweeping a yard with a broom. She was still dressed like Mrs Maleboge but she looked happy in a complacent kind of way, like the day she had walked down the road with her crochet work.

"Won't you come in for some tea?" she asked. "I watched you walking right to the end of the village and you must be thirsty."

As we walked towards the single mud hut in the yard, she lowered her voice to a whisper: "I have a husband. We are not quite married yet, but he is the priest of our church. He started the church himself because he can heal people. I went to him when my heart was troubled and so we found love. He is a very good man. He's inside now studying the Bible."

The man was seated on a low wooden stool. He was quite elderly, with greying hair. He stood up as we entered and politely clasped his hands together, exchanged greetings, and quietly went back to his Bible study. We drank tea, talked, and then she walked with me a little of the way home.

"You seem happy now," I said. "I cannot forget how unhappy you were that day at Mrs Maleboge's party."

She smiled, that sweetly secret smile of a woman who knows how to sort out her love life.

"I have all I need now," she said. "I have a good man. I am his mosadi-raa."

"What does that mean?" I asked.

"It means I am the special one," she said.

As I walked on alone I thought that the old days of polygamy are gone and done with, but the men haven't yet accepted that the women want them to be monogamists.

*Reprinted with permission from **The Collector of Treasures** (Heinemann African Writers Series, 1977).*

TAKE COVER! ZIMBABWE'S POP MUSIC

Zimbabwe resounds to music – traditional, reggae, soul, funk, rock. Loudspeakers bounce on the pavements outside the downtown record bars; nighttime city streets echo with the discos of the central hotels; and transistor radios crackle with ZBC's *Radio Two* – even out at Nyaminyami on the remote banks of Kariba.

The music is varied but dominated by one style today, **local jive**. After years of flirtation with Europe and the Americas, pop music has returned to its roots. Zimbabweans have discovered that their traditional rhythms are as danceable as any in the world – and as marketable! That makes life very exciting for musicians and music lovers alike. Many hotels in Harare, Bulawayo and other major centres have a band of sorts performing live six nights a week, while numerous restaurants, bars, beer halls, community halls and stadiums provide venues for nights and days of good live music. There is no shortage of talent. Equipment, however, is not so plentiful.

And that's where the fairy-tale of music falls apart in Zimbabwe. Not many bands can afford to maintain, let alone purchase, the sparse musical equipment that's available. So people with the money buy the gear, then overwork musicians and underpay them. The record companies play it pretty much the same way,

paying some of the lowest royalties in the world. Inevitably some enterprising groups and individuals do manage to escape this web of exploitation, but for the majority it's a hard way to earn a living. But it's also an age-old way of having a good time, telling a story, and quite romantic into the bargain; so the bands plug away, the joints are jumping, records are selling, music videos are being made . . .

TRADITIONAL MUSIC

Zimbabwe's most popular form of **traditional music** is based on the rhythms and melodies of the **mbira** or thumb piano – basically a small sound box, held between the hands, with a row of metal strips of different lengths plucked by the thumbs. *Mbiras* are used in traditional rituals and players are often spirit mediums, communicating with ancestral spirits through music. The music tends therefore to be hypnotic and repetitive, encouraging simple responses from the audience and inviting participation. Its melody lines run through trilling treble patterns while the bass bounces about in spongy steps reminiscent of a reggae bass line. Because *mbiras* are played with the thumbs only, single notes rather than chords carry the songs. Traditional accompaniment consists of voices (lead and response), *hosho* (shakers and gourds filled with dried seeds etc), drums, and other forms of percussion – such as wooden blocks clapped together, or stamping feet.

MBIRA GROUPS

There are hundreds, if not thousands of **mbira groups** in the country, and if you're lucky you may wander into some village and find one jamming at the local meeting place. Traditional music and dance groups take part in all the festivals and celebrations, from Independence Day to the annual agricultural shows.

Few of these musicians make the transition into the world of mass electronic media unadulterated, but some, such as **Ephat Mjuru**, still play and record within a strictly traditional cultural format. Traditionally a man's instrument, there are now many women *mbira* players in Zimbabwe. One of them, **Amai Muchena**, who performs with Muri ko Muchena (the Muchena family) has been playing since she was 5 years old. She views the instrument as a sacred thing "I don't play in beer halls, because the spirit is like a God to go to if there are problems, but I can play in the Sheraton – there are no drunks there."

In contrast, **Beulah Diago**, a quiet but serene woman who believes strongly in the message of her music, plays in beer halls in Chitungwiza: "Some people don't know *mbira*, like youths in bars, so I take *mbira* to them."

Stella Chiweshe is perhaps the best-known *mbira* player outside Zimbabwe – she's based half the time in Germany, and performs more often overseas than at home. She bends the boundaries by occasionally combining pure *mbira* or *marimba* (a wooden xylophone) with electric bass and western drum kit, underpinning her truly regal voice and presence with dreader-than-dread rhythms. She has provoked some criticism for her avant-garde mixture of sacred and commercial music – controversial in a country where music is so close to the spiritual centre of life. She certainly uses the mystique of the instrument in her shows to good effect, sometimes going into a trance on stage.

Electric guitars slot easily into *mbira* music: turn up the treble, cuff the strings lightly, pluck sequences with a plectrum and a reasonable facsimile of the *mbira* sound is created. A lot of local jive revolves around this technique, the best respected exponent of which is **Thomas Mapfumo**.

Probably the finest *mbira*-style guitarist is **Jonah Moyo** – a veteran of Mapfumo's band, who sometimes plays with his own. His over-tracked lead sequences on Mapfumo's *Shumba* album bear repeated listening.

MARIMBA

The **marimba** is another widely used traditional instrument. Visitors to the Victoria Falls are served up endless renditions of *Auld Lang Syne* and *When the Saints Go Marching In* played on *marimbas*, while trying to enjoy a quiet hotel lunch. *Marimbas* are not meant for such martial music – and it shows (painfully). For the real thing, check out Stella Chiweshe's *Ambuya* album, which uses *marimba* extensively and to brilliant effect.

Authentic **marimba groups** are also found throughout the country, often in schools and community centres. The best-known of these is the **St Peter's Kubatana** school band in Harare.

DANCE, DRUM AND CHORAL GROUPS

Dance, drum and choral groups exist all over Zimbabwe, too. The **National Dance Troupe**, based in Harare, performs at festivals and special venues. Many songs and dances were created by guerillas in the 1970s in order to politicize the masses, and can be heard on the **Chimurenga Songs** series of LPs.

Interestingly, one of the former ZANLA choirmasters became the contemporary pop singer **Comrade Chinx**, who combines political lyrics with *mbira* and drum machines (see below).

BEST JIVE ALIVE

Most foreigners think **Jit Jive** is a generic name for contemporary Zimbabwean music – it's not. *Jit Jive* was coined by the internationally successful Bhundu Boys to identify their brand of upbeat jive. Local bands play music influenced by *mbira*, rhumba, zouk, reggae, salsa, kwela, rock, jazz and soul. What emerges is a complex but coherent mix, shot through with occasional pure strains of Hendrix or Charlie Parker. Styles that defy pigeonholing in established categories are collectively labelled **smanjemanje** which translates as "something new". And there's something new every day.

THOMAS MAPFUMO AND THE BLACKS UNLIMITED

Thomas Mapfumo is a musical and political veteran, having been jailed some time before Independence for his protest songs and populist stance. A hypnotic-eyed, dreadlocked vocalist, he is backed by some of the finest musicians around – and was one of the first African musicians to achieve star status overseas. Some of his chimurenga songs were directly political, while others used the Shona tradition of "deep proverbs" to conceal messages of resistance. Mapfumo's earlier LPs are classics: *Hokoyo, Gwindingwi Rine Shumba*, and *Ndangariro* stand out, as do 12" singles like *Kariba* and the recent *Corruption* (which as a consequence of its subject received little airplay). Mapfumo's reggae outings can, by comparison, be a little tedious, but, if you enjoy dread beat, listen to *Mugara Ndega* (12") and the *Chimurenga for Justice* LP. Don't miss a chance to see him live, at the *Queens Garden* or any of the venues advertised along Harare's Robert Mugabe Road.

OLIVER M'TUKUDZI

Sometimes to be seen with the Zigzag Band (good in their own right), or the Black Spirits, **Oliver M'tukudzi** (*Tuku*) is the other major contender for the title of giant of Zimbabwean music, with a deep soul voice and a high-energy well-choreographed stage act. Heavily influenced by Thomas Mapfumo's chimurenga, he has produced dozens of LPs. Other influences include mbaqanga and rhumba beats, and M'tukudzi is a strong traditionalist who remains committed to his roots.

As with all Zimbabwean musicians, M'tukudzi is very conscious of the importance of his lyrics. He is a deeply moral man – he sang the first AIDS song in a (subsequently banned) Zimbabwean film. His lyrics deal with tradition, and place an emphasis on discipline.

THE BHUNDU BOYS

Jive kings who in the Eighties seemed on the verge of conquering half the Western world (starting with London), and catapulted Zimbabwean jive into the big league, the **Bhundu Boys** were for some years great heroes at home (when they *were* home), playing the very biggest venues. The music which brought them their fame was hard, fast and always melodic, rippling guitars on solid bass and drums beneath multiple vocal harmonies. Their full five-piece sound, regrettably overproduced and overdubbed on their British-recorded *Jit Jive* LP, was heard at its best on their first two LPs, *Bhundu Boys* and *Hupenyu Hwepasi* (the best!), as well as singles like *Simbimbimbo*, *Chemedzevana*, *Chimaninmani* – and stacks more.

They have however in the last few years suffered a series of staggering blows, including the deaths of three successive bass guitarists, and an acrimonious break-up with charismatic front man Biggie Tembo, who later tragically died.

THE JAIROS JIRI BAND

The **Jairos Jiri Band** (or JJB) have been around for many years, having originated in a welfare organization founded by Jairos Jiri to assist disabled Zimbabweans in their full integration into the local culture and economy. They too are no longer the force they used to be, following the imprisonment for rape of their former leader, the blind singer-songwriter Paul Matavaire. However, their back catalogue is extensive, and their songs are renowned for their acute social observations: "Our music differs from overseas music. It has moral lessons telling you how to behave. Songs from overseas are only for entertainment" Look out for their 1980 single *Take Cover*, the story of a guerilla group's journey through the war zone, *JJB Style* from the 1987 LP *Amatshakada*, their 12" versions of *Taurai Zvenyu* (remix), *Handirambi*, and 7" singles such as *Muphurisa*.

SOLOMON SKUZA AND THE KWENJANI BAND

In the same vein as Oliver M'tukudzi, both physically and musically, the late **Solomon Skuza** had a classic blues/soul crooner's quality. He and his band came from Bulawayo. Their LP *Zihlangene* is varied and accomplished, and they issued wonderful singles such as *Iquino Aliso*, *Jennifer* and *Sobukhu*.

MUSIC AND FILM

Queens Garden – at the time the epicentre of Harare music – features, albeit emptied of its unrulier elements, in the Zimbabwean music film **Jit**, directed by Michael Raeburn in 1990. The film, a light-hearted look at Shona tradition and how some people abuse it in their greed, was released in the UK in 1992. It includes a long string of performances by the top Zimbabwean bands, unfortunately all playback music rather than real performance, with Oliver M'tukudzi in a leading role. M'tukudzi also wrote the sound-track of **The Winds of Change**, 1992.

Simon Bright's film, **The Spirit of the People** (Zimmedia, 1990), named after Ephat Mjuru and his band, examines the links between traditional *mbira* music and modern electric jit. It demonstrates the transition from Ephat Mjuru playing traditional *mbira* music, with singing and dancing at the fireside in the rural areas, to the electrified stage sound of Thomas Mapfumo in an urban commercial show with lights, electronic instruments and microphones, but still featuring unmistakable *mbira* strains. The sound quality is poor but the film gives a good overview of different music styles in Zimbabwe.

> *For love with love only I walked in my*
> *father's land, in my mother's land, in my*
> *grandmother's land*
> *You can see for yourself love is enough*
> *Mugabe said this and so did the comrades*
> *Only love love is enough*
>
> Comrade Chinx and Mazana Movement

COMRADE CHINX

The ex-ZANLA choirmaster with the foghorn voice, **Comrade Chinx** is a great entertainer, strutting the stage in combat fatigues, beret and sunshades, as well as an incisive social commentator. His early singles *Zvikomborera*, *Nerudo*, *Magamba Ose* and others experimented with sequencers and drum machines mixed into traditional *mbira*/chant.

Chinx also broke into synthesizer pop; his biggest-selling record *Roger Confirm*, about love through a short wave radio, was made with the help of the group Ilanga. Even with six singles and an excellent LP behind him, however, he can't make music pay and works five days a week for the Zimbabwe Broadcasting Corporation. **Ilanga** themselves were a talented bunch of session musicians, responsible in their own right for a number of LPs, of which the first, entitled simply *Ilanga*, is

the best. Shortly after a rather sour split from Chinx, they went their separate ways.

ZEXIE MANATSA AND THE GREEN ARROWS

The **Green Arrows** have been playing roots jive for about twenty years now, but their upbeat mix of groaning lead vocals (**Zexie**), shrill vocal chorus and solid rhythm unit is still entertaining and danceable. In 1988 a car accident killed two band members and injured others, including Zexie. Fortunately Zexie and the band are back, and they're stirring it up with their savage satire, infuriating many sections of Zimbabwean society. They're not resident at any venue but tour a lot and make the best music videos around. Best LPs are *Mudzimu Ndiringe*, *Antonyo* and *Chipo Chiroorwa*. There are lots of singles.

THE RUNN FAMILY

The only Mutare-based band to make it big in the pop charts in recent years, the **Runn Family**'s peak was a single released immediately after the suspicious air crash death of Mozambican president, Samora Machel. *Hatchina Wekutamba Naye* encapsulated a nation's grief over the death of a proven ally and friend. Honey-

WOMEN MUSICIANS

I have been going around looking for girls but when I find one she can't come to the stage and perform because she's scared of what people will say about her.

Oliver M'tukudzi

The conservatism and chauvinism of Zimbabwe society has meant that women musicians have had a difficult time, and some brilliant musicians are unable to make their way. Thandeka Ngono, formerly singer with Southern Freeway, explains that "it's a lot to do with the attitude that women in show business are whores – that they're cheap and loose. Zimbabwe really does not want to cater for women musicians, but since we are there, there's nothing they can do about it."

Thandeka says that in her experience this is a problem unique to Zimbabwe: "I performed a lot in South Africa, and there were no problems about being a woman musician. The stigma is not there that is here. When I tried to inflitrate here, I had problems. In order to get into a group I would first jam with them so that they could hear that I could sing, but that made it worse! Maybe they thought I was going to take their jobs!"

Her comments are frequently echoed by other women musicians – many of whom feel frustrated by their lack of freedom. Few women make decisions within their band, often finding that the band will not release them to perform alone, and they tend to get a poor deal with money and recording rights. Sexual harassment by band managers and even the audience is also a problem.

In 1990 however a Women Musicians' Advisory Group was set up. Amongst its members are the top female Zimbabwean musicians: Stella Chiweshe, Busi Ncube (Ilanga), Doreen Ncube (Mudzimu), Virginia Jangano (Harare Mambos), Amai Muchena, and Beulah Diago. The group aims to educate women about their rights and advise on discrimination. As Stella Chiweshe puts it: "we are slow but we are coming up – you will see us."

sweet vocals keen over a rippling rhumba-ish backtrack, the beat picks up and the sound swells to a remarkably sweet pop crescendo.

The group play a broad spectrum of pop and jive, numerous cover versions included. You'll find them live in the clubs and hotels around Mutare and, occasionally, Harare. *Hatchina* is one of *the* classic songs of Zimbabwe, and singles such as *Moyo Muti* are worth listening out for. They have released two albums, *Ndoita Wekudinko* and a compilation of old songs.

THE FOUR BROTHERS

The Four Brothers are a straightforward fast Shona band, lyrics above rippling guitar riffs, and strongly influenced by Mapfumo (one of them, Marshall Muhumwe, is Thomas' uncle, and learnt the drums and singing from him). Their first hit, *Makoro* (Congratulations), was dedicated to the freedom fighters at Independence, and they continued to become one of the top Zimbabwean bands during the 1980s.

They call themselves the Four Brothers so that they remain equal and no one brother becomes "big" – a fate that has split too many Zimbabwean bands apart in the past. And despite their prolonged exposure in the West, they stick firmly to their traditional roots, claiming to have "learnt from the lesson of the Bhundu Boys". They deliberately choose to record in Harare rather than the technically superior studios of the UK.

OTHER PROPONENTS OF ELECTRIC MBIRA

Ephat Mjuru and the Spirit of The People are one of the best electric *mbira* groups around. Their music borders on the chimurenga beat, as well as a variety of other influences: afro-jazz, soca and reggae. **Pengaudozoke**, a very dancey new band with a fast rhythm borrowing

> She's the girl I was telling you about
> Vimbai is a beautiful girl
> a heart snatcher – God's masterpiece
> it's not only my idea; many praise her
> Her eyes reflect real tenderness
> Vimbai has a warm heart, warm as a winter
>   blanket
> Her neck is as smooth as the King's horse
> She is a nice girl
>   The Four Brothers

from rhumba as well as chanting traditions, is Oliver M'tukudzi's favourite group – "people thought they wouldn't go far but I could sense they had a unique touch in their music. They are different from the others".

Vadzimba adopt a similar approach to Thomas Mapfumo – drawing from traditional songs and treating them with a *mbira*-guitar translated beat – though with less success. At one time Thomas threatened to sue them for infringement of copyright, but as Vadzimba member Farai put it "Our music is not Thomas' music – just as reggae is not only Bob Marley. The traditional tunes belong to everyone."

The powerfully voiced **Robson Banda**, who plays instantly infectious music with **The New Black Eagles**, has also been influenced by Mapfumo's electric *mbira* music, as well as strains of South African mbaqanga and rhumba beats.

RHUMBA

The Zairean-born **Real Sounds** claim to be "the rhumba kings of Zimbabwe" and they certainly have the brass to prove it, bopping till they drop in fine rhumba style, *Ray-Bans* and all. Now resident in Zimbabwe (at the whim of the Ministry of Home Affairs), they blast away with heart-warming good vibes. At the *Children on the Frontline* music festival they backed Manu Dibango with finesse, and that's a fine credit for any group in the world. Their record releases don't always match the live magic, but go to one of their regular weekend sessions with visiting artists at the *7 Miles Motel*, outside Harare, and judge for yourself if they deserve their self-proclaimed crowns.

Among their rivals on the rhumba scene are the up-and-coming **Khiama Boys**.

JOHN CHIBADURA

John Chibadura, backed by the Tembo Brothers, has been one of the biggest-selling artists in recent years. Shy, private, introverted, and posing as an "anti-star", he has had amazing success, winning the following of young Zimbabweans with the result that all records routinely turn gold. His music combines fast-moving Zimbabwean dance music and rhumba. His lyrics are a grim reflection of social conditions, but, with typical Zimbabwean stoicism, are sung over a defiantly happy beat.

DEVERA NGWENA JAZZ BAND

Long-standing local top-sellers, **Devera Ngwena** play under contract to one of Zimbabwe's big mines. Their music is mainly *rhumba* with occasional *smanjemanje* infusions. Since they're based outside the cities it's difficult to catch them live. Like the Bhundus they tend to play larger venues. Their records (all just called *Devera Ngwena Jazz Band*) are numerous but it's easy to find their latest LP as they're numbered.

JAZZ AND THE SOUTH AFRICAN INFLUENCE

Jazz groups are coming up fast in Zimbabwe, particularly in Bulawayo where the close proximity of South Africa can be clearly heard in the music. **Dorothy Masuka** ("Auntie"), the "mama" of jazz from Bulawayo, with a musical career that spans over forty years, sang with Miriam Makeba and Hugh Masekela in South Africa in her early days, later fleeing to London to escape Ian Smith's Rhodesia, and then campaigning for Zimbabwe all over in Southern Africa.

Like many Bulawayan musicians, she draws a lot on South African influences, playing a mixture of jazz swing and local melodies in a style known as **marabi**. A glamorous and dominating personality, she is one of Zimbabwe's strongest female performers – "to tour with me is a serious thing." A great performer, she dresses in vibrant colours and sweeps up Southern African jazz with her amazingly powerful voice linking it to more traditional beats.

Until their recent split, **Mudzimu** were perhaps the best experimental jazz band in Zimbabwe. Now former members, including drummer Jethro Shasha, are achieving notable success in South Africa.

BROADWAY QUARTET/JAZZ SURVIVORS

Broadway started out in the 1960s and made it big all over central Africa. They split up in 1983 to form two groups – **Broadway Quartet** and the **Jazz Survivors**. They all play regularly at the *Hunyani Hills Hotel* outside Harare, the *Rose and Crown* in Hatfield, Harare, and around the clubs and hotels. Who's playing with whom changes frequently, but you can depend on superb drummers, very hot guitarists, and fine brass players combining to produce all imaginable styles of jazz.

If you're a jazz fan you may be pleasantly surprised by the excellence of these groups' repertoires. Unfortunately, no recordings are available.

SOUTHERN FREEWAY

Southern Freeway is a new group with members from Bulawayo, South Africa and Harare – including the talented session guitarist, Louis Mhlanga. They have backed the South African Steve Dyer, a versatile musician who has spent much time in Botswana, and Bulawayan singer Thandeka Ngono. Their music ranges from mbaqanga, jazz to more Shona-influenced guitar playing and a mixture of all kinds of music. They sing in six languages – Zulu, Xhosa, Ndebele, Shona, Tswana and English. Their first album concentrates on the South African penny whistle, but more recent music has acquired a Shona sound.

LOVEMORE MAJAIVANA AND THE ZULUS

Lovemore Majaivana's music has been shaped by so many influences that he sounds either brilliant or vacant. He's been Zimbabwe's Elvis, its Tom Jones, its Little Richard, and even its Engelbert Humperdinck. His music is based on Zulu/Ndebele rhythms fused with Shona/*mbira* melodies.

His current band, **The Zulus**, originate in Bulawayo, and crank out a powerful beat behind Lovemore's rich, strong voice . . . but there are still those mindless moments. In live performances it's always dance time, but the records don't capture energy. His best LP is an old one – *Isitimela* (with Job's Combination) – but even that had a producer with cardboard ears.

BLACK UMFOLOSI

This a cappella group of singers and dancers from Bulawayo are an amazing sight live with their precise and acrobatic singing and dancing to a strong Zulu beat. They even perform the rarely seen South African miners' gumboot dance.

LOCAL IDIOMS AND WESTERN POP

There is a wealth of choice of good Zimbabwean music, each band exploring its own ways of linking local idioms with Western pop.

ESSENTIAL LISTENING: A DISCOGRAPHY

BANDS

The Frontline Kids
Hupenyu ZINLP005

Stella Chiweshe
* *Ambuya ZMC* / ORB029

Thomas Mapfumo
Hokoyo (Thomas Mapfumo and the Acid Band),
  Gramma
Gwindingwi Rine Shumba Gramma
Shumba EWV22 (compilation of early work)
* *Chimurenga Singles (1976–1980)* ELP 2004
Greatest Hits ASLP5001
* *Zimbabwe-Mozambique* TML100
Corruption MLP51059
Chamunorwa M1075

Ephat Mjuru
Ndiani waunoda baba namai – hit single in
  Zimbabwe
The Spirit of the People ZML1003

Oliver M'tukudzi
1980 Afrika ZMC
* *Sugar Pie* CSLP5001
Psss Psss Hallo CSLP5005
Africa TEL2015

Comrade Chinx
Ngorimba (with Ilanga) ZMC

**Paul Matavire and the Jairos Jiri Sunshine
  Band**
Amatshakda Gramma
Take cover! Various Artists AFRILP01

Bhundu Boys
* *Shabini* AFRILP02 – at their best
* *Hupenyu Hwepasi* Gramma
True Jit WX 129 (1987) – a dreadful warning (with-
  out Biggie):
Absolute Jit AFRILP09 (1990)
Live at King Tut's Wah Wah Hut 09 (1991)

Ilanga
Ilanga ILGLP2

The Four Brothers
Bros COOK023
* *Makorokoto* COOKC014
Rudo Chete KSLP124
Rugare KSLP111

The Runn Family
Hachina Wekutamba Naye and * *Moyo Muti* – hit
  singles in Zimbabwe
Ndoita Wekudiniko Gramma (a compilation of old
  songs, Zimbabwe 1991)

John Chibadura and the Tembo Brothers
The Essential CSLP5002
More of the Essential CSLP5004

Pengaudozoke
Kwatakabva Nenhamo RTP

The Real Sounds
Harare ZML 1015
Seven Miles High BIG1
* *Vende Zako* COOK004 (includes songs for foot-
  ball fans!)

Devera Ngwena
(In Zimbabwe they have produced a series of
  numbered LPs, all titled *Devera Ngwena Jazz
  Band*)
* *Taxi Driver* KK01

The Nyami Nyami Sounds
Kwira Mudenga ZML 1030

James Chimombe and the Ocean City Band
Munakandafa ZIL218

Tobias Areketa
Mavambo

Southern Freeway
Southern Freeway RTP (2nd album includes
  compositions from other members)

The Pied Pipers
People of the World Unite WIZ 5000

Lovemore Majaivana
* *Istimela*
Amandla! ZIM003

Black Umfolosi
* *Unity* WCB020
featured on *Boiling Point – musicians from hot
  countries* WCB022

Dorothy Masuka
Pata Pata Mango Island Records

COMPILATIONS

* *Virgin Records Zimbabwe Frontline 88* EWV9.
  Includes Thomas Mapfumo, Four Brothers, Jonah
  Moyo and Devera Ngwena, Zexie Manatsa,
  Oliver M'tukudzi, Susan Mapfumo and Robson
  Banda.

Spirit of the Eagle Zimbabwe Frontline Vol 2 EWV
  18. Includes Robson Banda, Thomas Mapfumo,
  Four Brothers, Nyami Nyami Sounds.

Under African Skies REQ 745 (BBC). Includes
  Bhundu Boys, Comrade Chinx, Ilanga and
  Lovemore Majaivana.

The late **James Chimombe** was a very talented musician, vocalist and songwriter with the Ocean City Band, with a touch of country in his music, and a great influence on younger Zimbabwean groups.

Tobias Areketa, who also died in 1990, initially worked with Mapfumo. The music he made with the Shazi Band is remarkable for its haunting mournful melodies with words packed in over a relentlessly poignant beat. Unfortunately he only recorded two albums before his death.

The Frontline Kids, a fast young teenage band, whip the crowd up into frenzies with their energetic and aerobic dancing with at times catastrophic results – when they were performing at the Chico and Chinamora concert in Harare in 1991 the crowd twice broke down the gates.

Also known as *Mukadota*, a comic with his own TV series, **Safirio Madzikatire** sings and clowns with a large group of musicians/ comedians – collectively known as **The Sea Cottage Sisters with the Brave Sun Band**. He's regarded as the most accurate satirist of local culture and is much beloved across all age groups. Though now into his fifties, his act remains tirelessly energetic, entertaining and slick. He's Zimbabwe's *Mr Showbiz* in the nicest way and his songs are consistently good, even if they do tend to repeat themselves over the decades. Good LPs include *Ndatenga Motor*, while singles like *Katarina* and *KwaHunyani* stand out. Watch TV for the *KwaHunyani* video and the *Mukadota* series.

AND THE OTHERS . . .

Other bands to watch out for in Zimbabwe include the prolific **Pied Pipers**, **Simon Chimbetu and the Dendera Kings**, **Harare Mambos**, **The Marxist Brothers**, **Leonard Dembo**, **Nyami Nymai Sounds**, the **Rusike Brothers**, **OK Success**, **Sabuku**, **Talking Drum** and **Fanyana Dube** (responsible for the *Nhamo Inerushambwa* single and video).

If you're hooked on **Hendrix** there's even **Doctor Footswitch**, featuring Manu *the superstar*, who plays his Fender with his teeth while upside down over an amp . . . and all that. **Seven Seals** from Harare play steady **reggae**. **Murupha** popped up in 1987 with a lovely single (*Zimbabwe Ndeyenyu/Mai Rugare*) then vanished; and anonymous **guitarists** appear with patched boxwood instruments and nasal voices. There's lots more to find out . . .

• *Michael Philips and Judy Kendall*

BOOKS

Reading up on Zimbabwe before you go poses few problems, and there's no need to take everything with you, either – the country has a flourishing high-quality domestic publishing industry producing both fiction and non-fiction. The best-covered topics, not unexpectedly, are colonization and the two *chimurengas* (liberation struggles), but you'll find material on most subjects. Zimbabwe-produced books aren't always easy to get hold of outside the country, but specialist African/Third World bookshops sometimes stock them, and will certainly be able to order them. The biggest publishing concerns are Zimbabwe Publishing House (ZPH), Baobab and Mambo.

Botswana is another story, with no real indigenous book publishing apart from branches of big British companies involved in educational books. Several glossy tomes are, however, published outside the country, covering natural history and landscape.

ZIMBABWE'S HISTORY

A number of good school texts give a quick and easy **overview** of Zimbabwe's history. They include:

In **Britain**, the **Africa Book Centre** (38 King St, London WC2E 8JT; ☎0171/240 6649) stocks many books on Zimbabwe, and also offers a mail-order service. Particular titles published in Zimbabwe may also be ordered via *Leishman and Taussig* (2B Westgate, Southwell, Notts NG25 0JH).

David Beach *Zimbabwe: A New History for Primary Schools* (College Press, Harare 1982). Account by one of the country's leading historians, giving reliable, readable and condensed coverage of 15,000 years of history.

Peter Garlake and Andre Procter *People Making History* (2 volumes; ZPH, Harare 1985). The first volume covers pre-colonial history, and the second the twentieth century. Aimed at secondary schools, they go into more depth than Beach, with considerable emphasis on class analysis.

S. I. G. Mudenege *A Political History of Munhumutapa* (James Currey, London 1988). A picture of life in a stable African state, inter-reacting with the Portuguese on the coast of Mozambique.

PRE-CHIMURENGA

David Beach *The Shona and Zimbabwe 900–1850: An Outline of Shona History* (Mambo Press, 1980). *The* history of the Shona groupings in their heyday and of events on the Zimbabwean plateau before the arrival of the Ndebele and their conquests in the southwest.

David Beach *War and Politics in Zimbabwe 1840–1900* (Mambo, 1986). A kind of sequel to the above, covering the crumbling at the edges of Shona domination of the region with the arrival of Nguni raiders and finally the *coup de grâce* of British colonial conquest.

Stanlake Samkange *On Trial For My Country* (Heinemann African Writers Series, Oxford 1967). Set up as two trials, this classic dramatized account has Rhodes and Lobengula called in the afterlife to account for their conduct in the events leading up to the BSAC's colonization of Matabeleland.

Elizabeth Schmidt *Peasants, Traders and Wives: Shona Women in the History of Zimbabwe, 1870–1939* (James Currey, London 1992). Fascinating documentation of the lives of women in Southern Rhodesia.

Charles van Onselen *Chibaro: African Mine Labour in Southern Rhodesia 1900–1933* (Pluto, London 1976). Don't be put off by the dry, academic-sounding title. *Chibaro* means "forced or slave labour" and in van Onselen's inimitable way this lively book reveals exactly how the colonial system's tentacles reached into workers' everyday lives, and their response.

THE SECOND CHIMURENGA

The Second Chimurenga was a significant formative phase in the birth of independent Zimbabwe, so it's no surprise that there's a lot of material on the war, the nationalist movement and the decade leading up to liberation.

During this period white Rhodesians published a lot from their point of view, with no shortage of bizarre coffee-table books with dramatic pictures of Fireforce units swooping down on "terrs" – always a simplified vision of good versus evil, in which right (white) was winning. Only since Independence has the other side of the story been told, and although sometimes the picture is again reduced to goodies and baddies, the reader now at least has the freedom to choose which view to take.

Julie Frederikse *None But Ourselves: Masses vs Media in the Making of Zimbabwe* (James Currey, London; Ravan Press, Joburg; ZPH, Harare; Viking Penguin, New York: 1982). An amazing quantity of material, collected and collaged into a complex tapestry of interviews, photographs, quotes from contemporary media and commentary. Very highly recommended.

David Lan *Guns & Rain: Guerrillas & Spirit Mediums in Zimbabwe* (James Currey, London; University of California Press, Berkeley & LA: 1985). A fascinating excursion into the world view of the people of Zimbabwe's remote Dande region along the eastern Zambezi River, and the role of spirit mediums in fostering the liberation struggle among the peasantry.

Terence Ranger *Peasant Consciousness and Guerilla War in Zimbabwe* (James Currey, London; University of California Press: 1985). Anything by Ranger (and he's prolific) is worth reading for the entertaining, rolling narrative argument and gripping insights. *Peasant Consciousness* draws comparisons between the anti-colonial struggle in Zimbabwe and those in Kenya and Mozambique.

Irene Staunton (ed) *Mother of the Revolution* (James Currey, London 1990). A vivid portrait of the war experiences of thirty Zimbabwean women, telling their story in their own words.

POST-INDEPENDENCE ZIMBABWE

John Hatchard *Individual Freedoms and State Security* (James Currey, London 1993). An interesting look at the strength of the Zimbabwean state, and its hold over society.

Dr Peter Iliff *Health for Whom?* Easy to read and authoritative account of the effect of AIDS, poverty and the Structural Adjustment Programme on health and health care in Zimbabwe, with some chilling projections for the future. The author, a doctor in the health care service, writes from his own close experience incorporating thorough research.

Ibbo Mandaza and Lloyd Sachikonye (eds) *The One Party State and Democracy* (SAPES, 1991). Outlines the debate that ensued upon the suggestion by ZANU that Zimbabwe should adopt the one-party system so prevalent in the rest of Africa in the 1980s.

Robin Palmer and Isobel Birch *Zimbabwe, A Land Divided* (Oxfam, 1992). A brief, lively and well-illustrated introduction to the country, which looks at culture as well as providing social information.

Colin Stoneman (ed) *Zimbabwe's Prospects* (Macmillan, 1988). An essay collection looking at possible and probable directions for Zimbabwe into the 1990s – not all of it optimistic, although not all gloom and doom either.

Colin Stoneman and Lionel Cliffe *Zimbabwe* (Pinter Publishers, 1989). Part of the Marxist Regime Series and aimed mainly at students, this somewhat dry account still provides a solid and up-to-date summary of available material on the country's politics, economics and society.

BOTSWANA'S HISTORY

There are few up-to-date histories of Botswana. The only easily available general history is the school text: **T. Tlou and A. Campbell** *History of Botswana* (Macmillan Botswana, Gaborone 1984). It gives solid coverage from prehistoric times through to developments in the early 1980s.

Bessie Head *Serowe: Village of the Rain Wind* (Heinemann African Writers Series, 1981). The story of Serowe over the last 100 years, largely collections of testaments by residents. There are also sound pieces on the Swaneng Project and the Brigades Movement.

Fred Morton and Jeff Ramsay (eds) *The Birth of Botswana* (Longman Botswana, 1987). A useful collection of essays on parties, rulers and regions up to 1966.

THE KALAHARI

Michael Main *Kalahari: Life's Variety in Dune and Delta* (Southern Books, Johannesburg 1987). Fascinating and lively melange of personalized history, natural history, geology, sociology and anthropology, with great anecdotes, well-chosen photographs and a lightness of touch that belies its intelligence.

Mark and Delia Owens *Cry of the Kalahari* (Fontana, 1986). A thoroughly readable Botswana version of *Born Free* by two young US naturalists who spent seven years in the Kalahari studying lions and brown hyenas. Much more of a good yarn than straight natural history, the book has become something of a cult, with tours organized to Deception Valley where the authors worked. They tackle the thorny issue of fences in Botswana which protect cattle, but which they believe cause the deaths of countless wild animals.

Karen Ross *Jewel of the Kalahari: Okavango* (BBC Books, London 1987). Similar in scope to Main's text, this book of the BBC television series isn't quite as well written. On the other hand, coverage is very sound and it provides excellent and interesting background.

Marjorie Shostak *Nisa* (Earthscan, 1990). A fascinating book – both bawdy and romantic – based on the life of a !Kung woman living in a hostile Kalahari environment.

Laurens van der Post *The Lost World of the Kalahari* (Penguin, Harmondsworth 1962). The author's almost spiritual quest to find, and film, San people still existing as pure hunter-gatherers. *The Heart of the Hunter* (Penguin, Harmondsworth) is the sequel, although it can be read on its own, dwelling on the San he met and their mythology.

REGIONAL POLITICS

Joseph Hanlon *Beggar Your Neighbours: Apartheid Power in Southern Africa* (CIIR/ James Currey, London; Indiana University Press, Bloomington: 1986). A comprehensive examination of apartheid South Africa's role in the region, its manoeuvres to maintain pre-eminence through military and economic pressures. There's detailed background on its dealings with each of the frontline states.

Carol B. Thompson *Challenge to Imperialism: The Frontline States in the Liberation of Zimbabwe* (ZPH, Harare 1985). A look at the role of the frontline states in supporting Zimbabwe through its liberation birth-trauma, and strategies for aiding attempts for all the countries to disengage from South African neo-imperialist control.

LIVES

D. N. Beach *Mapondera 1840–1904* (Mambo, 1989). More than simply biography, this account of one of Zimbabwe's last independent rulers, who resisted European conquest, also looks at life in the region just south of the eastern Zambezi River at the eve of colonization. Equally absorbing is the way the book is put together – a fascinating example of the art and craft of writing history. The author eschews "established facts", a notion which he says "involves no original thinking", and instead lays bare the contradictory accounts, which are his raw material.

William Plomer *Cecil Rhodes* (David Philip, Cape Town 1984). There are countless books on Rhodes. Most feed the legend, although the distance of time has made some historians readier to regard him as a flawed colossus – but a giant nonetheless. This is a re-publication of one of the most interesting critical accounts, written several decades ago, against the prevailing grain, by a South African poet-novelist, when colonialism was still regarded as a good thing. It pulls no punches in presenting Rhodes as an immature person driven by his weaknesses.

Sir Charles Rey *Monarch of All I Survey: Bechuanaland Diaries 1929–1937* (Botswana Society, Gaborone; Lilian Barber, NY; James Currey, London: 1988). These dashingly colloquial diaries by the energetic parvenu who was governor of Bechuanaland for eight years, reveal as much about his attitudes to his colleagues and associates as about colonial neglect of the territory. And all brought alive by his humour and personal detail.

Frederick Courtenay Selous *Travel and Adventure in South East Africa* (Century, 1984). Reprint of an account by one of Africa's notorious Victorian hunters and adventurers, who spent time in Zimbabwe just prior to colonization and in the early colonial years.

ARCHEOLOGY, CRAFTS, ARTS AND ARCHITECTURE

Peter Garlake *The Painted Caves* (Modus Publications, Harare 1987). A well-illustrated account of San rock art in Zimbabwe – essential reading for anyone with even the slightest interest in the topic, and the first attempt at a coherent analysis with both interpretation and detailed instructions on where to find 38 of the finest painting sites.

Peter Garlake *The Hunter's Vision* (British Museum, 1995). A turning point in the interpretation of Southern African rock art: the author breaks with regional generalizations and begins to develop a unique understanding of Zimbabwean examples, which he believes are richer and more complex than those found in South Africa. Fascinating.

Peter Garlake *Great Zimbabwe Described and Explained* (ZPH, 1982). A useful little booklet by the leading authority on the topic, condensing his research into a guide for visitors and seemingly discussing every bit of stonework. It includes a useful bibliography for enthusiasts.

Garlake has also produced another brief booklet called *Life at Great Zimbabwe*, which is in many ways the most accessible publication about the place, with pen and ink illustrations providing an impression of how it might have been, and discussion that succeeds in bringing the ruins alive.

And if you're very interested in the whole topic of unravelling the meanings of rock art, look at the large body of work by **J. D. Lewis-Williams**, a pioneer in the field and the starting point for Garlake. Although Lewis-Williams' research is based on rock art in South Africa, it's sufficiently related to be enlightening. Two of his books worth reading are *Believing and Seeing* (Academic Press, London 1981) and *The Rock Art of Southern Africa* (University Press, Cambridge 1983).

M. Arnold *Zimbabwean Stone Sculpture* (Books of Zimbabwe, Bulawayo). Altogether the most solid account of the subject, if less lavishly illustrated than Mor's.

H. Ellert *The Material Culture of Zimbabwe* (Longman Zimbabwe/Sam Gozo, Harare 1984). Authoritative coverage of all aspects of Zimbabwe's traditional arts and crafts, including jewellery, vernacular architecture, carving, ceramics, tools and games.

Peter Jackson *Historic Buildings of Harare* (Quest, Harare 1986). The only coherent assessment of colonial architecture in Zimbabwe by one of the country's top architects. Apart from a catalogue of some of the finest examples of historic buildings, there's also a run-through of the development of Zimbabwe's distinct architectural styles.

F. Mor *Shona Sculpture* (Jongwe, Harare 1987). Written in idiosyncratic and at times impenetrable English, by an Italian sculptor, this book is nevertheless good value for the copious outstanding colour photographs of sculptures.

A. B. Plangger *Serima* (Mambo). Subtitled *Towards an African Expression of Christian Belief*, a well-illustrated account of the sculpture movement nurtured at Serima Mission.

COFFEE-TABLE BOOKS

One of the cheapest and most interesting coffee-table books on **Zimbabwe** is the paperback picture book *The Nature of Zimbabwe*, published in 1988 by the International Union for the Conservation of Nature and Natural Resources, which covers the ecology, the environment and development. Similar volumes have also been published on Botswana and Zambia.

De luxe, glossy books about **Botswana** abound, especially of the Okavango Delta, the Kalahari Desert and its hunter-gatherers. None can be recommended above the others. Spend your £20 or so and marvel.

Herman Potgieter and Clive Walker *Above Africa: Aerial Photography from the Okavango Swamplands* (New Holland, London 1989).

Jacques Gillieron *Kalahari* (New Holland, London).

MUSIC

Chris Stapleton and Chris May *Africa All-Stars – the Pop Music of a Continent* (Paladin, London 1989). The best book on popular African music with country-by-country coverage . . . even though the section on Zimbabwean music is disappointingly brief.

Fred Zindi *Roots Rocking in Zimbabwe* (Mambo, Gweru 1985). A quick run-through of Zimbabwe's musicians by one of the country's major promoters.

FIELD GUIDES

The best field guides to Southern Africa's flora and fauna are published in South Africa. In addition to full-size field guides, **Struik** and **Southern** issue convenient pocket guides on seemingly every topic, from mammals to trees.

BIRDS

Gordon Lindsay Maclean *Robert's Birds of Southern Africa* (New Holland, London 1988). The standard reference work on the sub-continent's entire avifauna population: if it's not in *Robert's* it doesn't exist. Alas, the weight of this tome makes it more a book to consult in a library than to take along.

Ian Sinclair *Field Guide to the Birds of Southern Africa* (Collins, London 1985). A reliable and thankfully, portable guide with good illustrations. Probably the most convenient to take along.

Ian Sinclair *Sasol: Birds of Southern Africa* (Struik, Baobab). Many professionals choose this book for the clarity of its illustrations. Compact and easy to carry on the move.

Michael P. Stuart Irwin *The Birds of Zimbabwe* (Quest, Harare 1981). Targeted on Zimbabwe, this is smaller than *Robert's* (although still quite heavy), but it nevertheless gives outstanding coverage for the area.

MAMMALS

Richard D. Estes *Safari Companion* (Tutorial Press, Zimbabwe; Russel Friedman Books, South Africa: 1993). A long-needed guide on how to understand African wildlife, with interesting and readable information on the behaviour and social structures of the major species.

Theodor Haltenorth and Helmut Diller *Field Guide to the Mammals of Africa* (Collins, London 1989); **Jean Dorst and Pierre Dandelot** *Larger Mammals of Africa* (Collins). Less handy, but solidly researched, detailed and well-illustrated volumes.

Chris and Tilde Stuart *Field Guide to the Mammals of Southern Africa* (New Holland, London 1989). Unless you're visiting countries further north, this is the best book – with its local focus – to take along. It gives excellent background and has clear illustrations to help you recognize a species.

TREES AND PLANTS

Keith Coates Palgrave *Trees of Southern Africa* (Struik, Cape Town 1977). The authoritative book on the subject, but a hefty tome.

Eve Palmer *A Field Guide to the Trees of Southern Africa* (Collins, London 1977). Covers South Africa, Botswana and Namibia, but not specifically the trees of Zimbabwe. On the other hand it's smaller and easier to carry than Coates Palgrave.

MAPS AND TRAVEL GUIDES

Maps have become easier to find in Zimbabwe. The small *Minimap of Zimbabwe* (Struik 1992) is useful, as is the Automobile Association's Zimbabwe map, available from shops or the Association's offices in Harare.

Alec Campbell *The Guide to Botswana* (Winchester, Johannesburg & Gaborone 1980). The classic guide to Botswana as far as background information goes. From archeology and system of government to traditional foods and tourist attractions, it's all there, but the guide is short on practical information for travellers and is now rather dated.

Michael Main and John and Sandra Fowkes *Visitors' Guide to Botswana* (Southern Books, Johannesburg 1987). Excellent for off-road driving and camping in Botswana – the lowdown on preparation and driving techniques, detailed route directions, and information on road conditions, journey lengths and bush driving, as well as camping tips. It should be available in Gaborone, Maun and other tourist centres in Botswana, as well as at specialist bookshops overseas.

FICTION: ZIMBABWE

Only a fraction of the writing produced in Zimbabwe finds its way abroad, but if you've a taste for fiction prepare to splurge when you get there. For extracts from some of the best writers, see p.389. Other names to look out for, besides the authors of the titles listed below, are: Samuel Chimsoro, Kristina Rungano, Musa Zimunya and Eddison Zvogbo (poetry); Barbara Makhalisa, Tim Mcloughlin, Cont Mhlanga, Habbakuk Musengezi and Stanley Nyamfukudza (fiction).

Tsitsi Dangarembga *Nervous Conditions* (Women's Press, London; ZPH, 1988). A riveting story of race, class, gender and growing up in colonial Rhodesia, told with wit and great psychological depth. The best novel yet to emerge from Zimbabwe.

Chenjerai Hove *Bones* (Heinemann African Writers Series, 1991). Award-winning experiences of the war, from a politically engaged writer. His *Shadows* (Heinemann African Writers Series, 1991) is a tragic story of lovers who opt for death.

Wilson Katiyo *A Son of the Soil* (Longman African Classics). A compelling story of a young Zimbabwean's struggle against oppression and hardship, remarkable for its lack of bitterness.

Doris Lessing *The Grass is Singing* (Heinemann African Writers Series, 1973). A portrayal of white Rhodesia unmatched by any writer – as are her physical descriptions of the country. Equally powerful, and emotionally intense, are the novels in the later *Children of Violence Masterwork Series: Landlocked, Martha Quest, Proper Marriage* and *Ripple from the Storm* (Plume 1970). In the same vein, her *Collected African Stories*, published in two volumes, *This was the Old Chief's Country* and *Sun Between their Feet* (Panther, 1979), are not to be missed. *Going Home* (Panther, 1968), which chronicles her return to witness the supposed transformation of the colony during the Federation in the 1950s, still rings unnervingly true to the hardcore sections of the white community today. Her latest book, *African Laughter* (Harper Collins, 1992) tells of the changes she observed on four visits between 1982 and 1992.

Nevanji Madanhire *Goatsmell* (Anvil, 1992). A lively love story focusing on the conflicts dividing modern Zimbabwe – between the sexes, between the Shona and the Ndebele, and between the powerful and the powerless.

Dambudzo Marechera *House of Hunger* (Heinemann African Writers Series, 1978); *Black Sunlight* (Heinemann African Writers Series, 1980). Zimbabwe's internationally best-known writer shocks and amazes with his vigorous and often abrasive prose. His exploits and lifestyle attracted as much notoriety as his writing won acclaim. *Dambudzo Marechera 1952–1987* (Baobab, Harare 1988) is a posthumous collection of writing, quotations and tributes.

Bruce Moore-King *White Man Black War* (Baobab, Harare 1988). A courageous, semi-autobiographical work by an ex-soldier who, out of hindsight or guilt, switches sides and exposes the brutality of the liberation struggle and the underpinning ideology of white supremacy.

Charles Mungoshi *Waiting for the Rain* (Heinemann African Writers Series, Oxford 1977); *Setting Sun and The Rolling World* (Heinemann African Writers Series); *Coming of the Dry Season* (Oxford University Press 1972; ZPH 1981). In spare, aching prose, informed by traditional oral forms, Mungoshi explores the dusty, overworked "native reserves", the urban townships and the terrible bond of abandonment and empty hope between them. Masterly.

Among other books worth looking out for in Heinemann's African Writers Series are *The Setting Sun* and *The Rolling World* by Charles Mungoshi, *Stories from Central and Southern Africa* by Paul Scanlon, *Smouldering Charcoal* by Tiyambe Zeleza, and *Harvest of Thorns* by Shimmer Chinodya.

POETRY

It's worth looking out for the following editions.

Chenjerai Hove *Up in Arms* (ZPH, 1982).

Kadhani and Zimunya (eds) *And Now the Poets Speak.*

Freedom T.V. Nyamubaya *On the Road Again* (ZPH, 1986).

Colin and O'Lan Style (eds) *The Mambo Book of Zimbabwean Verses in English.*

CHILDREN'S LITERATURE

Meshack Asare *Chipo and the Bird on the Hill.* Life at Great Zimbabwe through a child's eyes. Recommended by the authoritative Peter Garlake as a "convincing work of the imagination".

Anne Edwards-Tack *Ngoni's Dream and Other Stories.*

Hugh Lewin's *Jafta* series (Baobab) are all beautifully illustrated and written with the poetic simplicity of a child that feels universal.

Tim Matthews *Tales of the Secret Valley* (Baobab, Harare 1988). A collection of Batonga tales, colourfully illustrated by Colleen Cousins, and interesting for coming out in Ndebele,

Shona, Tonga and English, covering the mother tongues of most Zimbabweans.

Jayne Pilossof *The Mana Pools Colouring Book.*

FICTION: BOTSWANA

There's little indigenous fiction in English from Botswana. The paradox is that a number of outsiders have been inspired by Botswana to write novels, while Setswana-speakers in South Africa have made their contribution in English to South African literature.

Bessie Head *When Rain Clouds Gather* (Heinemann, London 1989). Set in the heart of rural Botswana, this outstanding writer's first novel deals with a South African exile who becomes involved in an agricultural project. The book deals with love, friendship, drought and the fierce forces of tradition. Among her other books, *Maru* (Heinemann African Writers Series, London 1987) is on one level about racial prejudice and loneliness, but a beautifully told love story that is also firmly in the mystical realm. *A Question of Power* (Heinemann African Writers Series, London 1986) goes much further into subjective states and suffering, sliding in and out of sanity. By comparison, the short stories in *The Collector of Treasures* (Heinemann African Writers Series, London 1977) are mostly light and amusing, and alongside her first novel are the best introduction to her work and village life.

Norman Rush *Whites* (Paladin, London 1987). Entertaining and well worth reading, these short stories by a US Peace Corps worker give vivid glimpses into the white sections of Botswana society.

SOL T. PLAATJE

"Having access to the writings of Sol T. Plaatje", wrote Bessie Head, "has been one of the richest experiences of my life. Never was there a man richer in spirit than he. *Native Life* is an astonishing book, crowded with information about all aspects of a black man's life."

Native Life in South Africa (Longman African Classics) is one of the finest pieces of campaigning political journalism to emerge from Southern Africa. It was a response to the South African Natives' Land Act of 1913 – the legal foundation stone for the subsequent formalization of apartheid some 35 years later. The Land Act provided for the division of South Africa into distinct African and white areas, with blacks confined to less than ten percent of the country. It was this policy that led the Batswana kings to fight so hard and ultimately successfully to avoid the realization of white objectives to incorporate Bechuanaland into South Africa.

Plaatje's book begins chillingly: "Awaking on Friday morning, June 20, 1913, the South African native found himself, not actually a slave, but a pariah in the land of his birth." *Native Life* is his eloquent account of his travels through South Africa and the misery, tragic dispossession, poverty and homelessness caused by the shattering law.

Despite his Dutch-sounding name, Sol T. Plaatje's Tswana origins are given away by his rarely mentioned middle name – Tshekisho. And although he was born in 1876 in South Africa he was a full member of the Rolong branch of the Tswana. Largely self-educated – he spoke six African languages as well as English, Dutch and German – he transcended tribal boundaries to become one of the pioneering figures of South African writing and politics, co-founding the African National Congress in 1912.

His later novel *Mhudi* examines the significance of tribal custom and the importance of an African historical perspective.

INDEX

HELP US UPDATE

We've gone to a lot of effort to ensure this edition of *The Rough Guide to Zimbabwe and Botswana* is completely up-to-date and accurate. However, things do change – places get "discovered", opening hours are notoriously fickle – and any suggestions, comments or corrections would be much appreciated.

We'll credit all contributions, and send a copy of the next edition (or any other *Rough Guide* if you prefer) for the best letters. Please mark letters "Rough Guide Zimbabwe & Botswana update", and send to:

Rough Guides, 1 Mercer Street, London WC2H 9QJ
or
Rough Guides, 375 Hudson Street, 9th Floor New York NY10014
or
zimbabwebotswana@roughtravl.co.uk

Amsterdam	1-85828-086-9	£7.99	US$13.95	CAN$16.99
Andalucia	1-85828-094-X	8.99	14.95	18.99
Australia	1-85828-141-5	12.99	19.95	25.99
Bali	1-85828-134-2	8.99	14.95	19.99
Barcelona	1-85828-106-7	8.99	13.95	17.99
Berlin	1-85828-129-6	8.99	14.95	19.99
Brazil	1-85828-102-4	9.99	15.95	19.99
Britain	1-85828-208-X	12.99	19.95	25.99
Brittany & Normandy	1-85828-126-1	8.99	14.95	19.99
Bulgaria	1-85828-183-0	9.99	16.95	22.99
California	1-85828-181-4	10.99	16.95	22.99
Canada	1-85828-130-X	10.99	14.95	19.99
Corsica	1-85828-089-3	8.99	14.95	18.99
Costa Rica	1-85828-136-9	9.99	15.95	21.99
Crete	1-85828-132-6	8.99	14.95	18.99
Cyprus	1-85828-182-2	9.99	16.95	22.99
Czech & Slovak Republics	1-85828-121-0	9.99	16.95	22.99
Egypt	1-85828-075-3	10.99	17.95	21.99
Europe	1-85828-159-8	14.99	19.95	25.99
England	1-85828-160-1	10.99	17.95	23.99
First Time Europe	1-85828-210-1	7.99	9.95	12.99
Florida	1-85828-074-5	8.99	14.95	18.99
France	1-85828-124-5	10.99	16.95	21.99
Germany	1-85828-128-8	11.99	17.95	23.99
Goa	1-85828-156-3	8.99	14.95	19.99
Greece	1-85828-131-8	9.99	16.95	20.99
Greek Islands	1-85828-163-6	8.99	14.95	19.99
Guatemala	1-85828-045-1	9.99	14.95	19.99
Hawaii: Big Island	1-85828-158-X	8.99	12.95	16.99
Hawaii	1-85828-206-3	10.99	16.95	22.99
Holland, Belgium & Luxembourg	1-85828-087-7	9.99	15.95	20.99
Hong Kong	1-85828-066-4	8.99	13.95	17.99
Hungary	1-85828-123-7	8.99	14.95	19.99
India	1-85828-104-0	13.99	22.95	28.99
Ireland	1-85828-179-2	10.99	17.95	23.99
Italy	1-85828-167-9	12.99	19.95	25.99
Kenya	1-85828-043-5	9.99	15.95	20.99
London	1-85828-117-2	8.99	12.95	16.99
Mallorca & Menorca	1-85828-165-2	8.99	14.95	19.99
Malaysia, Singapore & Brunel	1-85828-103-2	9.99	16.95	20.99
Mexico	1-85828-044-3	10.99	16.95	22.99
Morocco	1-85828-040-0	9.99	16.95	21.99
Moscow	1-85828-118-0	8.99	14.95	19.99
Nepal	1-85828-190-3	10.99	17.95	23.99

New York	1-85828-171-7	9.99	15.95	21.99
Pacific Northwest	1-85828-092-3	9.99	14.95	19.99
Paris	1-85828-125-3	7.99	13.95	16.99
Poland	1-85828-168-7	10.99	17.95	23.99
Portugal	1-85828-180-6	9.99	16.95	22.99
Prague	1-85828-122-9	8.99	14.95	19.99
Provence	1-85828-127-X	9.99	16.95	22.99
Pyrenees	1-85828-093-1	8.99	15.95	19.99
Rhodes& the Dodecanese	1-85828-120-2	8.99	14.95	19.99
Romania	1-85828-097-4	9.99	15.95	21.99
San Francisco	1-85828-185-7	8.99	14.95	19.99
Scandinavia	1-85828-039-7	10.99	16.99	21.99
Scotland	1-85828-166-0	9.99	16.95	22.99
Sicily	1-85828-178-4	9.99	16.95	22.99
Singapore	1-85828-135-0	8.99	14.95	19.99
Spain	1-85828-081-8	9.99	16.95	20.99
St Petersburg	1-85828-133-4	8.99	14.95	19.99
Thailand	1-85828-140-7	10.99	17.95	24.99
Tunisia	1-85828-139-3	10.99	17.95	24.99
Turkey	1-85828-088-5	9.99	16.95	20.99
Tuscany & Umbria	1-85828-091-5	8.99	15.95	19.99
USA	1-85828-161-X	14.99	19.95	25.99
Venice	1-85828-170-9	8.99	14.95	19.99
Wales	1-85828-096-6	8.99	14.95	18.99
West Africa	1-85828-101-6	15.99	24.95	34.99
More Women Travel	1-85828-098-2	9.99	14.95	19.99
Zimbabwe & Botswana	1-85828-041-9	10.99	16.95	21.99
Phrasebooks				
Czech	1-85828-148-2	3.50	5.00	7.00
French	1-85828-144-X	3.50	5.00	7.00
German	1-85828-146-6	3.50	5.00	7.00
Greek	1-85828-145-8	3.50	5.00	7.00
Italian	1-85828-143-1	3.50	5.00	7.00
Mexican	1-85828-176-8	3.50	5.00	7.00
Portuguese	1-85828-175-X	3.50	5.00	7.00
Polish	1-85828-174-1	3.50	5.00	7.00
Spanish	1-85828-147-4	3.50	5.00	7.00
Thai	1-85828-177-6	3.50	5.00	7.00
Turkish	1-85828-173-3	3.50	5.00	7.00
Vietnamese	1-85828-172-5	3.50	5.00	7.00
Reference				
Classical Music	1-85828-113-X	12.99	19.95	25.99
Internet	1-85828-198-9	5.00	8.00	10.00
World Music	1-85828-017-6	16.99	22.95	29.99
Jazz	1-85828-137-7	16.99	24.95	34.99

SIMPLY THE BEST

Landela Safaris offers you the choice of six delightful lodges.

Each lodge caters for a maximum of twenty guests and provides the
ultimate in personalised service.

Choose from the rustic simplicity of
Chokamella – Hwange
Gache Gache – Kariba
Sanyati – Kariba
Masuwe – Victoria Falls

or opt for the colonial elegance of
Landela – Harare
Sekuti's Drift – Victoria Falls

For further details and colour brochure:
Landela Safaris
Northfach
Pennorth
Brecon
Powys
LD3 7EJ
UK

Tel: 01874 658470
Fax: 01874 658480

or

Landela Safaris
82 Josiah Chinamano Avenue
PO Box 66293
Harare
ZIMBABWE
Tel (263 4) 734043-6
Fax (263 4) 708119

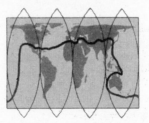